Experimental Use and Bolar Exemptions

AIPPI Law Series

VOLUME 11

Series Editors

AIPPI

Introduction & Contents/Subjects

Books in this series are developed within the framework of the International Association for the Protection of Intellectual Property (AIPPI), a non-affiliated non-profit organization dedicated to the development and improvement of legal regimes for the protection of intellectual property at both national and international levels.

Objective & Readership

The aim is to publish innovative work appealing to practitioners, other users of IP systems and academics.

The titles in this series are listed at the back of this volume.

Experimental Use and Bolar Exemptions

Edited by

David Gilat

Charles A. Boulakia

Daphné Derouane

and

Ralph Nack

Wolters Kluwer

Published by:
Kluwer Law International B.V.
PO Box 316
2400 AH Alphen aan den Rijn
The Netherlands
E-mail: lrs-sales@wolterskluwer.com
Website: www.wolterskluwer.com/en/solutions/kluwerlawinternational

Sold and distributed by:
Wolters Kluwer Legal & Regulatory U.S.
920 Links Avenue
Landisville, PA 17538
United States of America
E-mail: customer.service@wolterskluwer.com

Printed on acid-free paper.

ISBN: 978-94-035-1869-5

e-ISBN: 978-94-035-1879-4
Web PDF ISBN: 978-94-035-1889-3

AIPPI Law Series ISBN 98-888-8020-8

About the Editors

Charles A. Boulakia is a Principal with Smart & Biggar. His practice is primarily directed towards the preparation and prosecution of patent applications in the biotechnology, chemistry, biofuel, oil and gas, and pharmaceutical areas. Charles is Vice-Chair of the AIPPI Standing Committee on Pharma, and the Chair of the AIPPI Canada Patent Committee. He is a member of the selection committee for the Norman Esch Engineering Innovation and Entrepreneurship Award and is a mentor at Toronto Metropolitan University's Law and Business Clinic, iBoost, and the University of Toronto Hatchery. He is also a panelist of the Discipline Committee of the College of Patent and Trademark Agents, where he presides on professional discipline matters.

Daphné Derouane is a European Patent Attorney and holds a Ph.D. in Organic Chemistry from UCLouvain in Belgium. She has over 25 years of experience as in-house patent counsel in industry. Currently, she serves as Associate General Patent Counsel at UCB Biopharma (Belgium), where she leads the IP support for the Research Organization. Her expertise encompasses defining the overall IP strategy of UCB's early-stage assets and technologies, patent drafting & prosecution, providing freedom-to-operate opinions, and the negotiation of a variety of agreements. She also closely monitors external IP developments which are relevant to the pharmaceutical industry to ensure UCB's IP strategies remain fit-for-purpose. Additionally, she is a member of the Board of AIPPI-Belgium and has recently been appointed Vice-Chair of the AIPPI Pharma Standing Committee.

David Gilat is a Senior Partner in the Israeli IP firm Reinhold Cohn Group. His main fields of expertise are Technology (particularly chemistry, pharmaceutics, physics, high technology) and brands. David has been involved in landmark patent, trademark and copyright cases. David is currently teaching at the law faculty of the Reichman University as an adjunct professor, in a course on Law, Technology and Science, and for almost two decades has taught the patent law course at the law faculty of the Tel Aviv University. He served as a research fellow at the Max Planck Institute for Foreign and International Patent, Copyright and Competition Laws, 1992-3, and is the author of "Experimental Use and Patents" IIC Studies (Vol 16 1995). David is an active member of AIPPI's Pharma Committee.

Dr Ralph Nack is a Partner with Noerr in Germany. Ralph is the current Reporter General of AIPPI and has been a member of the AIPPI Bureau since 2014. His practice is directed towards patent litigation and licensing, as well as trade secret litigation. He has particular expertise in litigating standard-essential patent (SEPs) and issues of FRAND licensing. His practice further covers litigious and non-litigious advice in the life science sector, in particular regarding biologics and medical devices. Further, he handles high profile IP transactions and freedom-to-operate projects, in particular in connection with M&A and VC matters. Ralph studied law in Heidelberg, Munich, Washington DC (George Washington University) and Tokyo (Todai University). He is an alumnus of the Max Planck Institute for Intellectual Property and was awarded the Otto Hahn Medal of the Max Planck Society for his scientific work.

About the Contributors

Takanori Abe is an Attorney-at-Law, admitted in both Japan and New York. He is currently a Guest Professor of Osaka University Graduate School of Medicine and formerly a lecturer of The University of Tokyo Graduate School of Medicine and Faculty of Medicine. He is an arbitrator in Japan and sits on various positions in Japanese medical/pharmaceutical societies. Takanori works in wide areas of international and corporate matters with a focus on intellectual property law and international commerce. He has extensive experience on representing and advising multinational and domestic clients in pharmaceutical industry and is currently involved in the drastic battle between brands and also the one between brands and biosimilars/generics.

Enrique Armijo Chávarri, is a Partner with the Spanish IP firm Elzaburu SLP. He has more than 30 years' experience in litigating disputes involving patents, trademarks, designs, copyrights, trade secrets, publicity rights and unfair competition issues (including advertising). He has represented clients, across all market sectors, before the Spanish Patent and Trademark Office (SPTO) and before civil and administrative courts (including the Spanish Supreme Court and the CJEU in Luxembourg). He also advises clients on complex IP transactions. Enrique teaches "European procedural Law" at the Master programs of Universidad Autónoma Madrid, "Patent Litigation" at the Master programs of Universidad de Navarra (Madrid) and "Unfair Competition" at the Master programs of ICADE (Madrid). Enrique is a member of AIPPI Enforcement Committee and AIPPI Spanish Group's Editorial Committee.

Ezgi Baklaci Gulkokar is a Partner at Moroğlu Arseven, focusing her practice on intellectual property litigation and unfair competition disputes. She represents clients whose IP assets are central to their business strategy, crafting multi tiered enforcement approaches to address complex infringement scenarios, including those involving sophisticated infringers and non-practicing entities. Her practice includes representing clients in contentious proceedings involving trademarks, patents, copyrights, and trade secrets. She is also actively involved in domain name dispute resolution as a panelist at the WIPO Arbitration and Mediation Center and Istanbul Arbitration Center.

Martín Bensadon, LL.M. (University of Illinois at Urbana-Champaign), Attorney-at-Law (Argentina) and Partner with the Argentine law firm Marval O'Farrell Mairal. He specializes in industrial property and more particularly in patent law, having advised many national and foreign firms in this area. He has participated in seminars on industrial property and has written various articles on subjects related to his area of specialty in national and international publications as well as a book on Argentine Patent Law. He currently teaches at the Universidad Austral and Universidad de San Andrés. He was a Guest Researcher of the Max Planck Institute for Intellectual Property, Competition and Tax Law and a Visiting Scholar at The George Washington University Law School.

Raúl Bercovitz is a commercial lawyer specialising in IP Law. At present, he is a partner at Santiago Mediano Abogados. He holds a Ph.D. in law from the Complutense University of Madrid, as well as an LL.M from Columbia University. Since 1996 he has worked as a full-time attorney, issuing expert opinions and handling litigation for large companies, the majority Spanish or with subsidiaries in Spain, on diverse issues, mainly on trademarks, patents, industrial designs, unfair competition and copyrights. He has numerous publications on these subjects. Raúl was President of the Spanish group of AIPPI between 2009 and 2013 where he is still today an honorary member. He regularly lectures at different universities and institutions. He also has extensive experience in national and international arbitration proceedings on IP matters.

Anna Bladh Redzic is a Partner with Sandart & Partners. She specializes in intellectual property law, trade secret protection, and dispute resolution. Anna has extensive experience in patent, copyright, and trademark litigation, and regularly acts as counsel in domestic and international arbitrations. She also advises on commercial agreements and IP strategy. Her practice spans key industries including pharmaceuticals, chemistry, IT, media, and industrial sectors. Before joining Sandart, Anna served as Associate Judge, where she adjudicated numerous IP and commercial disputes. She is a member of the AIPPI Pharma Committee, EP Law, a board member of the Swedish Anti-Counterfeit Group (SACG), and a member of the ICC Sweden IP Committee. Anna is a recurring lecturer on topics concerning intellectual property law and is highly ranked by several ranking institutions.

Dr Mariangela Bogni is an Executive Partner at the IP LAW GALLI firm in Italy. She has extensive professional experience in all areas of intellectual property and related fields, including trademarks, designs, unfair competition, PDOs and PGIs, trade secrets, online counterfeiting, advertising and marketing, life sciences, and new plant varieties. She has particular expertise in patent litigation and significant experience in the pharmaceutical sector, including pan-European disputes. She has also advised on design issues and shape trademarks. Dr. Bogni holds a Law Degree from the Università Cattolica del Sacro Cuore di Milano (2000) and a Ph.D. in Intellectual Property Law from the University of Parma (2008). She has been recognized among the leading Italian lawyers in the field of intellectual property and has served as a lecturer in several academic courses.

Thomas Bouvet is an attorney-at-law and certified UPC Representative, partner at Jones Day, in Paris. He obtained his Doctor of Law from Versailles University, France, and holds an LLM from the University of Georgia, USA. Thomas has more than twenty-five years of experience in patent, trade secret, and plant variety rights litigation. His track record in enforcing and defending patents, for start-ups or international groups, is significant. He represented clients before the CJEU in SPC referrals. Thomas is an active member of AIPPI and administrator of Centre Paul Roubier. Thomas is the author of a doctoral thesis on 'The Protection of Vegetal Innovation', co-author of Saisie-contrefaçon (Dalloz, 2013) and of the French chapter of Global Patent Litigation: How and Where to Win (Bloomberg BNA, 2014).

Brigitte Carion-Taravella is a European and French Patent Attorney with over 24 years of expertise in patent prosecution and IP rights management. She holds a Ph.D. in Biochemistry and a Master's in IP Law. Currently, Brigitte leads Sanofi's French and Belgian patent team for Biologics support and oversees European patent policy. She represents Sanofi at EFPIA's IP expert group and INTERPAT. Previously, she managed patent activities at Chanel Parfums Beauté and was global head of patents at Besins Healthcare. Brigitte is actively involved in IP organizations, serving as a full member of the epi council and Secretary of its Biotech committee. She's also vice-president and secretary of AIPPI's French board, former President of ASPI, and a member of EPO's SACEPO for Guidelines and Quality since 2017.

Adam Carr, LLB, PgDip, is an Associate with Mason Hayes & Curran in Dublin, Ireland. Adam is a qualified lawyer in Ireland, and in England and Wales. He advises clients on intellectual property protection and enforcement strategies, and in intellectual property disputes, including copyright, trade mark and patent litigation matters. Adam has been involved in several high-profile IP cases in the Commercial Court including copyright infringement proceedings. He has a specialty in pharmaceutical patent law having spent over six years working for Novartis Pharma AG's patent litigation department enforcing and defending Novartis' product patent portfolio worldwide in patent infringement, revocation and opposition proceedings. Adam has a postgraduate diploma in Intellectual Property Law and Practice from Oxford University and is registered as a Trade Mark Agent in Ireland.

Héctor E. Chagoya-Cortés is a Chemical Engineer and Attorney-at-law, with patents experience since 1997, first holder of the Certified Licensing Professional™ credential in Mexico. He has been consistently recognized as a leading patent professional in several international surveys since 2005. Hector has taught and spoken at numerous college programs, events, courses, seminars and congresses at universities, professional associations and organizations such as WIPO or IMPI. Member of the National College of Chemical and Chemical Engineers (CONIQQ, Mexico) as Engineering Economy expert. He has published a variety of articles and has co-authored book chapters related to licensing, trade secrets, and pharmaceutical law and practice. His leadership has been recognized to preside or serve on the boards of several Mexican and foreign organizations related to intellectual property, technology transfer and chemical engineering.

Eun Jeong Cho is a patent attorney in Kim & Chang's IP group and a registered pharmacist in Korea. She received her B.S. in Pharmacy from Seoul National University,

College of Pharmacy in 2004. Before joining Kim & Chang, she worked as a pharmacist at the Samsung Medical Center in 2004. She also holds a Master of Laws (LL.M.) degree from the University of Washington. With over 15 years of experience, Eun Jeong advises clients on effective strategies for protecting their patent rights. She specializes in patent prosecution, litigation and counseling, with a particular focus on chemistry and life sciences. She has been recognized as a Rising Star (2018-2019) and a Notable Practitioner (2020-2024) in Managing IP STARS.

Soley Çoban is a senior associate with Deris. Ms. Coban joined Deris in 2017. She primarily counsels and assists clients with patent litigation matters. Her key focus of work is complex and multinational patent and unfair competition disputes. She is involved in various pharmaceutical and agrochemical cases as well as employee invention related matters. She also has years of experience in trademark litigation & prosecution matters, and design, copyright and PVR disputes.

Magali Contardi, Ph.D. is an Italian qualified lawyer specialized in Intellectual and Industrial Property, founder of Contardi IP Law, adjunct professor in the LLM in Digital Law at Lyon University, WIPO-Harvard's PatentX on Global Health, and postdoctoral research fellow at Scuola Superiore Sant'Anna in Pisa, Italy. Before founding her firm, Contardi IP Law, she gained experience as an IP attorney in top-tier IP firms in Germany and Italy, served at the International Affairs & Legal Department of the European Patent Office and worked as a legal assistant at the Boards of Appeals of the European Union Intellectual Property Office. She is a member of AIPPI, co-chair of the Young Committee of AIPPI Italy, and a member of the AIPPI Pharma International Committee. She is a member of the Munich and Milan Bar Associations.

Trevor Cook is Of Counsel at Bird & Bird LLP. He is an English solicitor with over 45 years' experience of intellectual property litigation. He was a partner in Bird & Bird LLP in London from 1981 to 2013 and in Wilmer Cutler Pickering Hale & Dorr LLP in New York from 2014 to 2022. He was for several years President of the UK group of AIPPI. In addition to countless articles and book chapters Mr Cook has authored the following books, amongst others: A User's Guide to Patents; Pharmaceuticals Biotechnology and the Law; and A European Perspective as to the Extent to Which Experimental Use, and Certain Other, Defences to Patent Infringement, Apply to Differing Types of Research. He is a general editor of The Modern Law of Patents.

Noel Courage is a Principal with Smart & Biggar LP. His practice is focused on patent prosecution, opinions and agreements in the life sciences area. He has written extensively about IP, with a particular focus on issues pertaining to start up companies. He is a Co-Chair of the McGill University / IP Institute of Canada intensive summer IP course program.

Amy Feng is the Managing Partner and Founding Partner of the law firm Wu, Feng & Zhang (Beijing, China), and is a Chinese Attorney-at-Law, Patent Attorney and Trademark Attorney with 30 years of practice in intellectual property, particularly in the fields of chemistry, pharmaceuticals, and biotech. She is a member of the Pharma Committee of AIPPI. She received Master's and Bachelor's of Science degree from Dalian University of Technology, China in 1995 and 1992, respectively. She also earned an LLM degree in intellectual property law with honours from the John Marshall Law School in Chicago, USA in 2004.

Kevin C.W. Feng is a registered patent attorney with practice emphasis on patent and trademark prosecution and IP-related advisory opinions. He has been particularly familiar with patent infringement and invalidity assessments, as well as trademark registrability and opposition analysis. Kevin has been building IP experiences in fields of, among others, software, artificial intelligence, semiconductor, and pharmaceuticals. Mr. Feng received his M.I.P. degree from the University of New Hampshire School of Law and a B.S. degree in Biochemical Science and Technology from the National Taiwan University. He is the incumbent co-chair for the International Committee of the Taiwan Patent Attorneys Association (TWPAA) as well as the Independent Member Delegate for the AIPPI. He has co-authored AIPPI's Study Questions on behalf of Chinese Taipei annually since 2019.

Carlos Fernández-Dávila Winkler graduated summa cum laude from Pontificia Universidad Catolica del Peru (PUCP), where he also completed his Master's studies in Competition, Regulatory and Intellectual Property Law. His practice areas include Intellectual Property, Competition, Publicity and Consumer Protection, Life Sciences, Corporate Law and Compliance. Carlos is founder of Fernández-Dávila Abogados Law Firm. He participated in the negotiation and implementation of Free Trade Agreements signed with United States of America, the European Free Trade Association and the European Union. He has also served as a professor at the PUCP Postgraduate School and as lecturer of different intellectual property and competition law events. He regularly publishes on IP issues and is considered as a leading lawyer in different publications.

Cláudia Freixinho Serrano is an Attorney-at-Law and a Portuguese Patent and Trademark Attorney at the law firm NLP - Nazaré, Lima, Piriquito Santos & Associados. She has over 20 years of practice in Litigation, having specialized in IP Litigation over the last 14 years. She completed her Law degree from the Faculty of Law of the University of Lisbon in 2003 and has Postgraduate Diplomas in Corporate Law by the University of Coimbra, Intellectual Property Law and Medicinal Products Law by the Faculty of Law of the University of Lisbon and a University Diploma in Patent Litigation in Europe by CEIPI - Center for International Intellectual Property Studies. She was Secretary-General of the Portuguese Group of International Association for the Protection of Intellectual Property (AIPPI), from 2021 to 2025.

Pablo Fuentes is a Partner in the Mexican firm, Breakthrough IP. He holds a BSc degree in Chemistry (UNAM, top 10%) and an LL.M. in Intellectual Property Laws (The University of Edinburgh). His practice is specialized in the preparation, prosecution and litigation of Patent and Trademark cases, especially in the Pharma and Biotec fields. Pablo is one of the two standing members of Mexico in the Pharma committee of AIPPI and co-chair of the SMEs Building Bridges committee at INTA. He teaches IP-Law at UNAM post graduate programs and CENTRO Universities in Mexico, acting also as a mentor for the public programs on IP and Technology Transfer for the government state of Jalisco. He is the author of several articles published both on domestic and international IP-specialized media.

Mariana Gonzalez, partner at Basham, Ringe y Correa, has over 17 years of experience in patent prosecution, IP transactions, and litigation, particularly in the life sciences sector. With degrees in chemistry and law, a master's in top management, and the Certified Licensing Professional® credential, Mariana offers integrated scientific and legal expertise. A recognized authority on Mexico's linkage system and data exclusivity, Mariana also has research experience, including a stay at Ohio State University focusing on DNA base characterization through ultrafast laser spectroscopy. Mariana has acted as an expert witness in significant pharmaceutical litigations, contributing expert opinions in complex cases. Author and co-author of several articles and publications, Mariana has been a frequent speaker in Mexico and abroad at events organized by leading professional associations.

Rana Gosain is a Senior Partner at Daniel Law in Brazil, with more than 30 years of experience in intellectual property. He is an Intellectual Property Agent accredited by the Brazilian PTO and holds a postgraduate degree in Intellectual Property from the Pontifical Catholic University, in collaboration with the Brazilian PTO. Rana specializes in patents and industrial design and has great experience of handling patents, litigation strategies, validity and infringement studies and providing legal advice. Much of his work focuses on the pharmaceuticals and biotechnology area. Rana's current role is to develop the best strategies for protecting and managing IP Portfolios. He also advises clients on a broad range of issues related to Intellectual Property. Rana is an active member of several IP organizations, including ABPI, AIPPI, FICPI, LES and AIPLA.

Dirk Hanekom is Partner with Spoor & Fisher in South Africa. He is a qualified Patent Attorney and admitted as an Attorney of the High Court of South Africa. He specialises in the preparation and prosecution of applications relating to pharmaceutical inventions, including novel compounds, formulations and manufacturing techniques; and other general chemical technologies including petrochemicals, catalysts, polymer chemistry, pesticides and other agricultural remedies, rubber related technologies, and general consumer goods. Dirk also advises clients on regulatory issues relating to these technology areas. He has extensive experience in conducting freedom to operate investigations in South Africa, and the rest of the African continent.

Magnus Hauge Greaker, Cand.jur. (University of Oslo), is a Partner at Thommessen in Oslo. He specializes in patent, trademark, copyright, and trade secrets litigation, with a particular focus on clients in the life sciences, oil and oil services, aquaculture, and technology sectors. Magnus also advises on marketing law, pharmaceutical regulatory law, and administrative law. He has extensive experience from the Norwegian Ministry of Justice, where he contributed to legislative development and served as Acting Deputy Director General. Magnus is admitted to the Supreme Court and is a member of the Norwegian Bar Association. He regularly publishes and lectures on intellectual property law and related topics, and is recognized for his commercial insight and expertise in complex contentious matters.

Simon Holzer is Partner with the Swiss law firm MLL and heads the firm's Technical IP team and its Life Sciences industry group. Simon is specialising in IP disputes in the field of life sciences. He is a member of AIPPI's Pharma Committee. In 2010, the Swiss Parliament appointed Simon as an adjunct judge of the Swiss Federal Patent

Court. Simon is praised by clients and peers as a 'skilled and driven individual', a 'key life sciences expert' and a 'pleasure to work with'.

Dr Eugenio Hoss, LL.M. (MIPLC), Attorney-at-Law (Argentina) and Partner with the Argentine law firm Marval O'Farrell Mairal. He has extensive experience in patent prosecution and litigation in Argentina and other countries in Latin America, having advised many national and foreign clients in this area. He currently teaches at the Universidad de San Andrés. He was a researcher at the Max Planck Institute and obtained a Ph.D. from the University of Munich (Ludwig-Maximilians-Universität) in 2019.

Lucas Huusom is an associate-attorney at LØJE IP, a boutique law firm in Copenhagen, Denmark, specialising in intellectual property and marketing law. His focus areas include designs, trade marks, patents, and EU regulatory protection schemes for medicinal products. Lucas advises a broad range of clients, from solo entrepreneurs to multinational corporations, tailoring solutions to meet diverse legal and commercial needs. He holds a law degree from the University of Copenhagen.

Marta Kawczyńska is a European patent attorney, Polish patent and trademark attorney, professional representative before the UPC, as well as the EU Trademark and Design Attorney. She is a shareholder of POLSERVICE Office in Warsaw, Poland, and chair of its Supervisory Board. Marta specializes in drafting, filing and prosecuting patent applications in the fields of biotechnology, pharma, molecular medicine and diagnostics, both in the national, regional and international procedures, and has vast experience with Supplementary Protection Certificates, as well as in patent ligation proceedings. Marta is Council Member of the European Patent Institute (epi), and VP of the AIPPI Poland. She is a member of the AIPPI's Biotechnology Committee and observer in the AIPPI's Pharma and UPC Committees, and a member of the epi's Committee on Biotechnological Inventions and Pharma.

Gerard Kelly is Co-Head of Dispute Resolution and Head of the Intellectual Property Law team at Mason Hayes and Curran LLP practising in Dublin, Ireland. With a leading reputation in the field, he has acted in many of Ireland's most high-profile and complex IP cases in recent years. He advises domestic and international clients on a broad spectrum of IP issues and disputes, including substantial litigation involving patents, trade marks, passing off, copyright, and design rights. Gerard is also a registered Irish and European trade mark agent and has particular expertise in developing protection and licensing strategies for intellectual property rights.

Dr Khoo Kian Hoe is a registered Singapore patent attorney, and a principal based in the Singapore office of Davies Collison Cave. He specializes in the drafting and prosecution of life sciences patent applications, including molecular biology, protein engineering, immunotherapy, antibody therapeutics, vaccines and medical diagnostics. He is also experienced in providing patent validity and infringement advice. Kian Hoe graduated from the Imperial College London in Biochemistry. He obtained his Ph.D. from the University of Cambridge and served as a research fellow at A*STAR. Kian Hoe is currently a member of the AIPPI Standing Committee for Biotechnology. He is a member of the Examination Committee for the Singapore

Patent Agents Qualifying Examination. He is also an executive committee member of the Association of Singapore Patent Attorneys (ASPA).

Martin Klok is a partner at V.O. Patents & Trademarks, working from the firm's head office in The Hague, the Netherlands. He is qualified to represent clients before the European Patent Office, the Unified Patent Court and the Dutch Patent Office. The major part of Martin's practice focuses on providing technical assistance in litigation cases. He is also active as a representative in EPO opposition cases, as well as in the drafting and prosecution of patent applications. Martin has a Ph.D. degree in chemistry and extensive research experience in the fields of molecular nanotechnology and the relationship food/health. As a patent attorney, Martin specializes in the fields of pharmaceuticals, biomedical technology and food. Martin is also a vice-chair of the AIPPI Standing Committee on Pharmaceuticals.

Takeshi S. Komatani is an IP litigation certified Patent Attorney in Japan and currently a principal attorney at TAKASHIMA International Patent Office and serves as IP counsels for academia, SMEs and big-pharma. Takeshi received his Ph.D. in Pharmaceutical Sciences (University of Tokyo), and qualified as a pharmacist with Kampo/natural medicines certificate. He also received an LL.M (IP Certificate, Keio University) and continues his research in Juridical Science there. He was a researcher at F. Hoffmann-La Roche in Basel, Switzerland. He is a Visiting Professor at Kobe University and Doshisha University. He is a member of AIPPI, serving a number of roles including TRIPS (Vice Chair), IP-GRTK (Head of GR), Pharma, Biotech, PVR, and FTA, and also contributed to the Japan chapter of the AIPPI book Pharmaceutical Test Data Exclusivity.

Matan Kovacs is an attorney-at-law and a partner with Shibolet Law Firm in Israel. Over the years, he has gained significant experience representing leading multinational companies in all manner of intellectual property disputes, with particular focus on patent cases. Matan is regularly involved in complex, high-stakes litigation cases and appears before Israeli courts of all instances, local and international arbitration tribunals, and the Israeli Patent and Trade Mark Office.

Bettina Kövecses, Dr. jur. is Lead Patent Litigation Counsel at Gedeon Richter Plc. She is an IP and life sciences litigator responsible for and dealing with international cross-border patent and SPC litigation and strategy. Before joining Gedeon Richter she spent more than 12 years in private practice at Bird & Bird acting as a key attorney on major Hungarian and international cross-border pharma and medical device litigation cases. Apart from patent enforcement she is experienced in trademark and design law and the regulatory field of foodstuff, medical devices, and pharmaceuticals. She partook in the discussions on the amendments to the Hungarian Patent Act introducing among others the new Bolar provisions. She is board member of the Hungarian Group of AIPPI.

Inchan Andrew Kwon is a U.S.-licensed attorney and patent attorney in Kim & Chang's IP group. His practice at Kim & Chang covers all areas of intellectual property, including patents, trademarks, copyrights, and trade secrets, with a focus on patent litigation and dispute resolution. He has worked on patents in all technical areas, including pharmaceuticals, consumer electronics, semiconductors, and consumer goods. He also has substantial experience handling other related IP matters such as plant variety cases, trade secrets cases, and patent licensing and due diligence matters, as well as relating to general commercial disputes, and fair trade and antitrust. He also has handled numerous international trade and customs matters on behalf of technology and chemical clients, including customs audits, customs criminal investigations, and advance customs valuation cases.

Dr Malathi Lakshmikumaran is Executive Director and Practice Head at Lakshmikumaran & Sridharan, and a registered patent agent in India. With over 30 years of experience in biochemistry and molecular biology, she specializes in plant genomics, biotechnology, and pharmaceutical patents. Formerly Head of the Centre for Bio-resource & Biotechnology at TERI for 17 years, she advises on biodiversity, traditional knowledge, and plant variety protection. She has authored over 100 publications and works closely with start-ups and incubators such as C-CAMP and IIT Delhi. A Ph.D. holder from Pune University, she is a Fellow of the National Academy of Sciences and recipient of several national awards. Dr Lakshmikumaran is active in AIPPI (Biotech Committee), FICPI, and APAA, and has been recognized by IAM Patent 1000 and WIPR as a leading expert in patent prosecution

Miko Leach, LL.B. (King's College London) and Master of Laws (University of Helsinki), is a Senior Associate lawyer working in the Intellectual Property practice at the Helsinki office of Nordic law firm Roschier, Attorneys Ltd. He assists, amongst others, with patent and supplementary protection certificate disputes as well as regulatory advice in the Pharma & Life Sciences industry sector. He is a member of The Finnish Association for Industrial Property Rights.

Wan Chieh (Jenny) Lee is a Parter with Haug Partners LLP in New York. Her practice focuses on strategic counseling, procurement of worldwide patent rights, due diligence, and intellectual property transactions. She routinely advises clients in the pharmaceutical, biotechnology and medical device industries regarding patentability, validity, freedom-to-operate, and regulatory exclusivity. Drawing from her extensive experience across all aspects of patent practice, Ms. Lee develops and executes patent procurement strategies that are aligned with clients' immediate and long-term business goals. She leverages her strong ability to digest complex technical information with her experience in both patent procurement and litigation to provide clients with valuable transactional insights and a unique approach to negotiating intellectual property terms in agreements. She is currently a member of AIPPI's Pharma Committee and is active within the IP community, serving in leadership roles in different organizations and frequently speaking at events.

Monica Leeu is a senior patent attorney managing the Integrated Technology Patent Practice of Kim & Chang. She has practiced all aspects of patent law including patent litigation, patent prosecution and opinion matters. She has extensive experience in patent prosecution and litigation involving various technologies with a focus on pharmaceuticals, chemicals, biotechnology and electronic materials. She has played a leadership role in numerous patent trials and litigations, including some of the leading landmark cases in Korea. Her recent practice involves counseling clients on diverse patent and technology-related issues, including pharmaceutical industry regulations and antitrust laws. She is a member of the Korea Patent Attorneys Association and

AIPPI and participated as a speaker at the World Congress of AIPPI in 2012 and 2022, and AIPPI trilateral meeting in 2014.

Jonas Levernes, Master of Laws (University of Oslo), is an Associate at Thommessen in Oslo. He advises Norwegian and international clients on matters relating to patent law, trademark law, copyright, and marketing law, with a focus on both advisory work and dispute resolution. His legal studies have focused on intellectual property and commercial law. He is a member of the Norwegian Bar Association and contributes to handling a range of legal issues within his areas of practice.

Johanna Lilja is a Partner with Roschier, Attorneys Ltd. She is specialized in intellectual property with a particular focus on patent litigation. Johanna has represented clients in various fields of industry including pharmaceuticals, telecommunications, engineering, energy and shipping industries. In addition, Johanna specializes in various industry-specific regulatory and marketing issues, with a focus on the pharmaceutical, medical device and healthcare sectors. In addition, Johanna works regularly with data protection matters, and advises pharmaceutical, medtech and healthcare companies on questions relating to secondary use of patient data. Her practice also includes advice on clinical study related regulatory and contractual issues. Johanna is Head of Roschier's Data Protection practice, President of the Finnish AIPPI Group and a member of international AIPPI's Standing Committee on Client Attorney Privilege and Standing Committee on Pharma.

Johan Løje is a Partner at LØJE IP, a boutique IP law firm in Copenhagen, Denmark. With over 30 years of experience, he specialises in design, trade marks, and patents, advising on complex IP matters and representing clients before Danish courts and the European Court of Justice. Johan is also an Associate Professor at the University of Copenhagen and serves on the advisory board for the Centre for European Studies in Economic Law (CESEL). He has been appointed as an expert by the European Commission on IP and Unfair Competition, including collaborations with the Republic of China, and by the Danish Design Association.

Juhua Luo is a senior patent attorney and Director at CCPIT Patent and Trademark Law Office, where he leads a dynamic chemical patent department of over 50 attorneys. With more than 20 years of experience, he focuses on patent prosecution, invalidation, infringement, and consulting in biotechnology, pharmaceuticals, and chemistry. He has a proven track record of achieving favourable outcomes for clients and has successfully managed several landmark cases involving cutting-edge biotechnology and blockbuster pharmaceuticals through innovative legal strategies and proactivity.

Nikolaos Lyberis, Dr Jur. (Hamburg) is the Managing Partner of Vayanos Kostopoulos Law Firm (Athens) and of the Lyberis Law Offices (Nicosia). He is Adj. Assistant Professor of Law at the European University Cyprus on IP and Trust Law. He is a patent and trademark litigator representing prestigious companies on IP matters including prosecution and litigation. He is President of the Hellenic Group of AIPPI and member of IP associations in Greece and abroad. He has been a Member of the BoD of the Greek Patent Office (2013-2015) and the BoD of the Hellenic Academy of Industrial Property (2020-2025). He worked 10 years as Legal Advisor at the

Max-Planck Institute of Hamburg for Comparative and International Private Law and participated in Greek legislative committees for the harmonization of trademarks law.

Daisy Machytka is a Hungarian and a European patent attorney with chemical background and a partner with the firm Gödölle, Kékes, Mészáros & Szabó Patent and Trademark Attorneys. She has extensive experience in patent prosecution and litigation. Before entering the field of intellectual property, she was a research fellow of the Hungarian Academy of Sciences, was doing postgraduate studies at the University of Oxford and obtained doctoral degree from the Technical University of Budapest. She was a postdoctoral scholar at the University of Bonn. She is a member of the AIPPI Pharma Committee and the Presidency of the Hungarian Group of AIPPI. She was awarded the Jedlik Ányos Prize by the President of the Hungarian Intellectual Property Office. She has been recognized in IAM Patent 1000 every year since 2012.

Leonor Magalhaes Galvao, Ph.D. is one of the founding partners of magellan IP and the managing partner of the firm. Leonor has over twenty years of experience in the field of intellectual property representing domestic and international clients, ranging from academic institutions to multinational corporations. Leonor regularly presents to audiences worldwide on a variety of topics regarding Brazilian patent law and practice. She has gained much respect in the IP profession as past chair of the Biotechnology Committee of the ABPI and current chair of the IP & Sustainability Standing Committee of AIPPI.

Amira Mangelus is a partner with the Liad Whatstein & Co. leading firm, with more than two decades of extensive experience in litigating patent disputes. She has led major patent oppositions and infringement actions across the life sciences industry, particularly in solid-state chemistry, synthetic organic chemistry, delivery systems, pharmaceutical formulations, dosage regimen and biotech. She manages large patent portfolios and prosecutes applications for leading global pharmaceutical companies. Her strong litigation background enhances her handling of complex prosecution matters, and she works closely with pharmaceutical companies and research institutions to develop global IP strategies. Amira holds a B.Sc.Pharm from The Hebrew University of Jerusalem, and an LL.B. and M.B.A. (2004).

Dr Wojciech Marciniak is a member of the management board of POLSERVICE Patent and Trademark Attorneys Office (Warsaw, Poland), and is Polish Patent and Trademark Attorney as well as a Professional Attorney before the EUIPO. He graduated summa cum laude from Warsaw University of Technology with a Master's degree in chemistry and obtained a Ph.D. from the same University. He worked as a researcher at the University of Technology in Berlin and later as a specialist in a research and development department in the pharmaceutical industry before joining Polservice in 2008. He deals with a broad range of IP issues and specializes in invention protection matters, particularly in the area of chemistry and pharmaceuticals. Dr Marciniak is a member of the AIPPI's Pharma Committee.

Rodrigo Marré Grez is a partner at MICP Abogados with over 30 years of experience advising companies across various industries with a special focus on patent litigation and regulatory matters. He leads the firm's intellectual property/ technology transfer practice. He is highly regarded for his deep expertise in patents and complex patent and trademark litigation, particularly in the life sciences and agrochemical sectors, and is consistently recognized by leading international publications. Rodrigo also advises universities and technology-based companies on technology transfer and related matters. He is a member of several national and international associations, including INTA, ASIPI, AIPPI, ACHIPI, LESI and the Chilean Technology Managers Network (RedGT).

Cyra Nargolwalla is Managing Partner at Plasseraud IP and leads the Healthcare & Life Sciences group. A French & European Patent Attorney and UPC Representative, she specializes in biotechnology and pharmaceuticals (including vaccines, oncology, hormone therapy), with additional expertise in textiles, paper, and food industries. She has significant experience in EPO opposition and appeal proceedings. Cyra serves as Vice-President of the French group of the AIPPI and sits on the International Bureau's Diversity & Inclusion Advisory Committee. She also co-chairs the CNCPI's Diversity & Inclusion Committee and is on the executive committee of APEB. At the IPO, she contributes to both the European Practices and Diversity, Equity & Inclusion Committees. She is consistently ranked among top practitioners in her field.

Carlos R. Olarte is a co-founder of OlarteMoure and is based in Bogota, Colombia. He holds a B.S.E. in both Biomedical and Mechanical Engineering from Duke University (1990) and a J.D. from Chicago-Kent College of Law (1993), later validated at the Pontificia Universidad Javeriana in Bogota (1994). Carlos specializes in patent litigation, licensing strategies, and portfolio development, with a strong focus on the pharmaceutical, life sciences, and telecom sectors. He has represented Global 100 companies and led Colombia's first major SEP enforcement campaigns. His practice also includes counseling local deeptech early-stage projects and funders. He has been an Adjunct Professor of Patent Law at Universidad Externado de Colombia. Carlos is an active member of several IP organizations, including AIPF (President), IPO, ACPI, ASIPI, and AIPPI.

Johnny Petersen is a leading patent litigation with Bech-Bruun law firm in Copenhagen. He has extensive experience advising and litigating across a broad scope of industries, including in particularly pharmaceuticals, biotech, and diagnostics. He is recognized as a leading patent litigator in Denmark with inter alia IAM Patents 1000, and he has for the past 20 years successfully litigated numerous IP cases regarding patents as well as copyrights, designs, and trademarks, before the Danish courts, including high-profile cases before the Danish Supreme Court, and before the CJEU. He also advices on complex licensing agreements.

Julisa Quiliche Chávez is a pharmacist, graduated from the Universidad Nacional de Trujillo, and has completed a Master's program in Intellectual Property with a specialization in Pharmaceutical Law at the Universidad Peruana Cayetano Heredia. She has served as Technical Director for companies importing and distributing pharmaceutical and sanitary products, with experience in implementing and certifying Good Storage Practices, as well as in regulatory processes related to the pharmaceutical sector. She is a Technical Scientific Area Leader at Fernández - Dávila Abogados in Peru. Julisa advises on procedures for obtaining marketing authorizations and making post-approval changes to pharmaceutical, sanitary, and food products and has experience in pharmaceutical and biotechnological patents prosecution and litigation.

Mamta Rani Jha is the Co-Managing Partner at Inttl Advocare, a leading Indian IP law firm, with over 25 years of expertise in Intellectual Property law. She leads the firm's litigation and opposition practice and has represented top global companies in over 500 landmark cases. A Gold Medallist in B.Sc. (Zoology), Mamta specializes in patents, trademarks, emerging technologies, and strategic IP advisory. She is recognized as a Patent Star 2024 by Benchmark Litigation, a Distinguished Practitioner by Asialaw, and she is one of Forbes India's Top 100 Individual Lawyers. An influential voice globally, she has held leadership roles in INTA and APAA. Her work in advocacy, legislative reform, and thought leadership continues to shape IP law at national and international levels.

Markus Rieck LL.M. is a Partner with Fuchs Patentanwälte Partnerschaft mbB in Frankfurt am Main / Germany. He specializes in patent proceedings, with expertise in creative strategic IP advice and contentious patent cases, particularly European Patent Office opposition proceedings. His focus includes the life sciences, pharmaceuticals, in particular antibodies. He holds a pharmacy degree and a Master's degree in European IP law. He is a German and European Patent Attorney, and a representative before the Unified Patent Court. He also serves on the German AIPPI board, the AIPPI Pharma Committee and co-initiated the DABUS Artificial Inventor Project.

Andres Rincon is a Partner and Head Patens & Life Sciences with Cavelier Abogados in Colombia, with 20 + years IP experience, focused on patents, plant breeding rights and life sciences affairs, related to chemical synthesis, biological pharmaceutical and agrochemical products, including test data protection and biosimilars. He holds JD in Law from Pontimcia Universidad Javeriana (Colombia 1998), with specialized studies in IP of Universidad Externado de Colombia (2002), is a scholarship holder from the AlßAN program of the European Commission (2006) and has an LLM IP from the Max Planck Institute and the George Washington University, through the Munich Intellectual Property Law Center, Germany (2007). His main areas of expertise are innovation, drafting, prosecution and litigation of patents and industrial designs. He is an active member of different patent and biotechnology committees before AIPLA, ACPI and AIPPI.

Christophe Ronse is a partner at the Belgian law firm ALTIUS and has over 35 years experience as a litigator. He advises and assists national and international clients in complex litigation and transactions at the Belgian and international level particularly the field of patent law and pharmaceutical law. He is a regular contributor of legal articles in his field and a speaker at conferences, and is co-author of an Overview of Belgian Patent Case Law which is published every 3-4 years in a leading Belgian business law journal. He was president of AIPPI Belgium from 2011 to 2017 and presently serves on the AIPPI Standing Committee on Pharma and the editorial board of ICIP, a Belgian IP law review. He serves as deputy judge at the Court of Appeal of Brussels since 2016.

Nicolas Vincent Ruiz, Ph.D. is Head of Global of Intellectual Property & Brands at ESTEVE PHARMACEUTICALS S.A. and Member of its Scientific and Medical Committee. He is Qualified European and French Patent Attorney with an extensive experience in managing IP Assets and Litigations in Patents and Trademarks at international level. Nicolas is member of the Standing Committees on Pharma and

Biotechnology of the AIPPI, currently member of the Board of the Spanish Group of AIPPI and member of the IP Group of LES Spain & Portugal.

Emma Sandler is an associate at Sandart law firm in Sweden. She is specialized in commercial dispute resolution and in advising within marketing and intellectual property law. She represents clients in various disputes and matters in courts and at regulatory and registration authorities. Emma has got a background in the courts, as she worked as a law clerk at the Stockholm District Court/Patent and Market Court thereafter as a reporting clerk at the Svea Court of Appeal/Patent and Market Court of Appeal. She studied law at Uppsala University and has also studied intellectual property law at St. John's University in New York.

Eliza Jane Saunders is a specialist life science intellectual property lawyer and patent attorney. Eliza has significant experience in IP litigation and advising life science companies and research institutes in relation to collaboration, commercialization, AI, confidential information, regulatory law and IP policy. Eliza's experience is further bolstered by her in-house experience, and molecular biology qualifications. After completing a Master of Law in Intellectual Property (summa cum laude) with WIPO in 2003 and specializing in intellectual property law at Phillips, Ormonde & Fitzpatrick and Griffith Hack in Melbourne, Eliza worked for many years at global firm, DLA Piper Australia, leading the International HealthTech group and litigation teams in a number of significant patent cases. In recent years Eliza has moved towards a more independent IP practice.

Dr Daniel Sieveking, is a Principal with Spruson & Ferguson with over 15 years of experience in Intellectual Property. Daniel has a Ph.D. in Medicine (University of Sydney) and is a registered Australian Patent and Trade Marks attorney and registered New Zealand Patent attorney. He assists a variety of domestic and local and international clients in the preparation and prosecution of patent applications, primarily in the areas of biotechnology, pharmaceuticals and diagnostics. Daniel regularly advises clients in relation to patentability, infringement and validity of patents, obtaining extensions of term for pharmaceutical patents and assists clients in Patent Office proceedings in Australia and New Zealand. Daniel is a member of the AIPPI Standing Committee on Pharma and Biotechnology and is a Fellow of the Institute of Patent and Trade Marks Attorneys of Australia (IPTA).

Jiri Slavik is a Czech & European Patent Attorney, a representative before the UPC, and a European Design Attorney. He is a fully engaged IP professional having vast experience as in-house patent counsel in the pharmaceutical industry, being involved in various IP aspects of the generic & value-added medicines development. He joined the Adalvo IP team in 2021. Before that, he was part of the IP team at Zentiva for more than 6 years. Jiri also concurrently practices as a private practitioner (co-founded IP duo in 2022) and was elected as a full member of the epi Litigation Committee for the term 2023-2026 for the Czech Republic. He has published articles on Kluwer Patent Blog and in other journals and has experience in giving lectures for university students and research scientists.

Dr Richie Tay is a patent scientist in the Singapore office of Davies Collison Cave, where he specialises in the preparation and prosecution of patent applications in the fields of pharmaceuticals, biotechnology, medical technologies, materials, and food and agrotechnology. He also regularly provides advice on patentability and patent strategy in these areas. He obtained his Ph.D. in Engineering Sciences from Harvard University, where his work focused on the use of synthetic biology to generate protein-based materials. He then spent several years at A*STAR's Bioprocessing Technology Institute in Singapore understanding and developing biomanufacturing workflows for recombinant proteins and various therapeutic modalities, including biologics, cell therapies and nucleic acid therapies. He has a Graduate Diploma in IP and Innovation Management from the Singapore University of Social Sciences.

David Tirosh is Legal Counsel at Wix.com, a global SaaS company with a quarter billion users worldwide. He supports a wide range of products and partnerships, with a focus on commercial contracts, product compliance, artificial intelligence, intellectual property, privacy, and data protection. Previously, he was an attorney at S. Horowitz & Co., where he worked extensively with clients in the pharmaceutical sector and handled patents, trademarks, copyright, trade secrets, and IP and commercial litigation. He represented clients before Israeli courts and the Israel Patent Office and was involved in product liability cases and class actions. David holds an LL.B. from The Hebrew University of Jerusalem, where he served on the editorial board of the law review Mishpatim. He has been an AIPPI member since 2023.

John C. Todaro is an Executive Director and Managing Counsel in the Intellectual Property Group of Merck & Co., Inc. John and his team support patent prosecution, due diligence studies and intellectual property counseling worldwide for Merck & Co. products, product candidates and development programs in various therapeutic areas, including immunology, neuroscience, oncology and infectious diseases. John has been a member of the Merck & Co. IP group since 2003. He previously was a senior counsel in the law firm of Darby & Darby P.C., in New York.

Virgilio Topasio Maluk is the Head of the patent department at MICP Abogados and has extensive experience advising clients on all types of patent and technology transfer matters. He advises his clients on protecting their technologies throughout the entire cycle, from patentability reports to patent prosecution, both in Chile and abroad. He also has extensive experience in patent litigation, especially in the pharmaceutical field. He focuses on regulatory matters, particularly related to the pharmaceutical, agrochemical, and food and beverage markets. He has been a visiting professor in various programs related to his areas of expertise and is active in several associations, such as INTA, AIPPI, ACHIPI, and the Network of Technology Managers of Chile (RedGT).

Shohta Ueno, Ph.D. is a Senior Director Assistant General Counsel, Dispute Resolution at Regeneron Pharmaceuticals Inc., based in the UK. Shohta's team provide strategic advice to Regeneron on a broad range of complex, multi-jurisdictional disputes in a wide range of therapeutic areas including ophthalmology, immuno oncology, respiratory, dermatology and genetic medicines. While Shohta deals with all matters relating to disputes, he focuses mostly on non-US IP matters and helps the company navigate through increasingly complex IP landscape. Shohta joined Regeneron in 2018 from a leading IP litigation practice at then Allen & Overy (now A&O Shearman). Shohta initially trained as a scientist before becoming an English solicitor, having obtained an undergraduate degree in Natural Sciences and a Ph.D. in Virology from the University of Cambridge.

Koen Vanhalst, Ph.D. is a Biotechnology expert with a doctorate from the University of Ghent (VIB), Belgium. He previously worked as an Examiner at the European Patent Office, specializing in Biotechnology and Medical Diagnostics. Koen is a certified European and Belgian Patent Attorney and is qualified to act before the Unified Patent Court (UPC). Since 2017, Koen has been a partner at De Clercq & Partners. He also serves on the Belgian Council for Intellectual Property and is active in AIPPI as board member of the Belgian group and as member of the SC Biotech. He was recently also elected as member of the Biotech committee of the European Patent Institute. Koen has been a guest professor at Ghent University since 2015, teaching Intellectual Property to Master students in (Plant) Biotechnology.

Stefan van Kolfschooten, LL.M., is an associate attorney-at-law with Pinsent Masons Netherlands LLP. He holds a bachelor's degree and has hands-on experience in medical imaging, nuclear medicine, radiotherapy. After obtaining a bachelor's degree in law at the University of Utrecht, he specialized in patent law during his master's in Information Law at the University of Amsterdam (cum laude). Stefan now advises in Life Sciences related patent law litigation and regulatory matters.

Mislav Vukina is an attorney-at-law, patent attorney and partner at Law Firm Vukina & Partners ltd in Croatia. His areas of legal expertise include intellectual property law, digital law, data protection law, competition law, and related commercial law contracts. He advises and represents clients across a wide range of regulated and innovation-driven industries, with particular focus on healthcare, life sciences, pharmaceuticals, digital platforms, advertising, and information technology. Mislav is a member of the International Association for the Protection of Intellectual Property (AIPPI), serving on both the Digital Economy Committee and the Information Technology and Internet Committee. He regularly assist clients with legal strategies at the intersection of technology, regulation, and commercialisation.

Sanja Vukina is Attorney at Law and European Patent and Trademark Attorney with over 30 years of experience in intellectual property (IP) law. She is the Founder and Managing Partner of Vukina & Partners, a boutique law firm based in Zagreb, Croatia. For the past four years, Sanja has served as the President of AIPPI Croatia and as Secretary of the Croatian Chamber of Patent and Trademark Attorneys. Throughout her career, she has developed comprehensive expertise in IP across diverse industries, including medical devices and pharmaceuticals. Her legal practice encompasses patent prosecution, invalidation, litigation, and counselling, with a particular focus on chemistry and life sciences. In addition to patents, Sanja provides comprehensive legal services in trademark and industrial design protection, and has significant experience in data protection.

Xinlei (Shirley) Wang is a patent litigator of CCPIT Patent & Trademark Office. She is a committee member of AIPPI Pharma Committee and committee member of LESI Dispute Resolution Committee. She has represented domestic and foreign companies in patent infringement, invalidation, and unfair competition litigations before lots of intermediate people's courts, the Supreme People's Court of China and the

CNIPA. Additionally, she supports clients in patent infringement, IPR and opposition proceedings in Europe and the United States. Shirley received her master's degree in biomedical-engineering from the University of Illinois at Urbana-Champaign, and bachelor's degree in biotechnology from the University of Science and Technology of China.

Milly Wickson is an Associate in the Patent Litigation team at Bristows LLP. Her practice spans the life sciences and technology sectors, and she has experience litigating patents before the UK courts as well as assisting with oppositions and appeals at the European Patent Office. She also advises clients on freedom to operate matters.

Morena Zavaleta is a Partner at Arias and head of the Intellectual Property and Life Sciences practice in Central America. With over 30 years of experience, she leads the IP team across six countries and advises major local and international companies on trademark, copyright, patent, and health regulatory matters. Morena regularly handles IP due diligence for high-profile M&A transactions and represents clients in complex litigation. She is an active member of associations such as ASPI, ASIPI, INTA, MARQUES and IBA, and serves on various IP committees. She also leads pro bono initiatives and champions gender equity in the legal profession. Morena has been recognized as a leading IP lawyer by Chambers Global, Legal 500, WTR, and Managing IP, among others.

Table of Contents

Foreword

Lorenza Ferrari Hofer, President of AIPPI

Dear Reader,

We are pleased to present our AIPPI book on *Experimental Use and Bolar Exemptions*.

As highlighted in the 2023 AIPPI Resolution on Experimental Use and Bolar-type Exemptions (Q288), these exemptions purport to serve distinct purposes and advance different public interests. They exist in several jurisdictions and address the scope of patent protection.

While the public interest in experimental use is a long-term objective of patent protection, aiming to make economic resources available through the introduction of new technologies, the public interest served by the Bolar-type exemption is more short-term, concerning the distribution of medicines based on existing technologies.

Although these exceptions are generally recognized, their scope varies significantly across jurisdictions, leading to differences in how research activities are treated under patent law in different countries.

Against this complex background, global companies with interests worldwide must properly advise their research and development teams.

The purpose of this scientific work is to address these differences and provide sound information in order to understand the reasons and challenges behind them, and eventually establish a basis for harmonizing the laws concerning the scope of these technical exemptions.

We hope this book will be helpful to all interested professionals, global companies, legislators and judges.

We would like to thank all the authors from around the world who contributed to this important work, and we hope you find it interesting.

Lorenza Ferrari Hofer
July 2025

Chapter 1

Introduction

David Gilat

The subject of this book raises questions about the limits of patent protection, encouraging professionals to reflect on the rationale behind patents and the proper scope of the proprietary rights they should confer. It further evokes the question of the balance between the interest in promoting new technologies, which is the bedrock of patent law, and other public interests.

As highlighted in the 2023 AIPPI World Congress Resolution on Experimental Use and Bolar-type Exemptions (Q288), these two exemptions to the patent rights purport to serve distinct purposes and are designed to advance different public interests.

The Experimental Use exemption was traditionally designed to foster technological progress by allowing inventors to conduct experiments on patented subject matter. Patent holders were thus prevented from exercising their rights in a way that could obstruct or hinder innovation, contrary to the fundamental objectives of the patent system. In this sense, the Experimental Use exemption is an inherent part of patent law, as its underlying rationale aligns with that of the patent system itself – namely, the advancement of technology to reduce suffering and enhance public welfare.[1] It is therefore not surprising that the experimental use exception to patents evolved through case law starting from the 19th century in England and in the US.[2]

In contrast, the primary objective of Bolar-type exemptions is to ensure patent rights are not unduly extended due to regulatory hurdles. While this goal also serves to enhance public welfare, it is not intended to promote progress and is aligned with other public policy interests. The so-called Bolar-type exemption emerged as

1. See D. Gilat, *Experimental Use and Patents*, 16 IIC Studies, Wiley-VCH (1995).
2. Justice Joseph Story appellate decision *Whittemore v. Cutter*, 29 Fed. Cas. 1120 (C.C.D. Mass. 1813), *Frearson v. Loe* (1878) 9 Ch. D. 48 (see for example the chapters on Ireland, UK and US). See also comment by Justice N Rajagopala Ayyangar of India (1957) addressing the right of a researcher to use the invention for the purpose of research as opposed to commercial use (India chapter herein).

a compromise between the generic and innovative pharmaceutical industries in the United States following the 1984 US Court of Appeals for the Federal Circuit's ruling in *Roche Products, Inc. v. Bolar Pharmaceutical Co.* In that case, it was held that the obtaining and use of a patented drug (flurazepam hydrochloride) in making dosage form capsules, to obtain data needed for a New Drug Application to the Food and Drug Administration ('FDA'), amounted to patent infringement. It was held that any apparent conflicts between statutes, such as the Food and Drug Act and the Patent Act, should be resolved by Congress rather than the judiciary. Against this background, the Hatch-Waxman Act – formally known as the Drug Price Competition and Patent Term Restoration Act of 1984 – was enacted to establish a balance between the interests of the generic pharmaceutical industry and innovative drug manufacturers. The Act granted patent term extensions to compensate innovators for the loss of effective monopoly caused by lengthy public health regulatory processes, while simultaneously enabling generic manufacturers to prepare for market entry upon patent expiration. This mitigated the so-called 'springboard effect', which had previously extended the patent monopoly of drugs beyond the statutory term because of the time it took for generic manufacturers to be ready and regulatorily compliant.

While the public interest in promoting technological progress is long-term – aiming to expand economic resources through the introduction of new technologies – the public interest served by the Bolar-type exemption is short-term, as it is primarily concerned with the distribution of medicines based on existing technologies. Moreover, the development of innovative drugs requires substantial investment and entails high risks, making the industry heavily patent-oriented to safeguard long-term returns and to allow re-investment in research and innovation. In contrast, investment in generic drug development involves only a fraction of these costs and carries significantly lower risk, meaning the generic industry does not necessarily depend on patents to bring its products to market.

A turning point came with two decisions by the German Federal Court of Justice – *Clinical Trials I* (1995) and *Clinical Trials II* (1997) – which expanded the scope of the Experimental Use exemption, allowing generic manufacturers to conduct clinical trials. However, it was not until 2005 that a Bolar-type exemption was formally introduced into German patent law, implementing European legislation (Directives 2004/27/EG, 2004/28/EG, and 2004/24/EG). The interplay between these landmark decisions and the subsequent legislative developments highlights that while the Experimental Use exemption and Bolar-type exemptions are not fully coextensive, certain activities may fall within the scope of both.

Due to the extremely narrow interpretation of the Experimental Use exemption by US courts, the legal framework for infringement exemptions in the US has evolved in a way that blurs the distinction between the two. In *Merck v. Integra*, the Supreme Court significantly expanded the scope of the Bolar-type exemption to cover even some early-stage experimental activities, 'as long as there is a reasonable basis for believing that the experiments will produce the type of information that are relevant for regulatory approval by the FDA'.[3]

3. See US chapter herein. Interestingly, the US courts felt more bound to the strict 19th century ruling in *Whittemore v. Cutter* than by the language of the legislator in the Hatch Waxman Act. Thus, for example, it was held that applying for marketing approval in agencies other

The blurring of the distinction between the two exemptions is not limited to the US but can also be observed in legislation outside the country. In Japan, for example, the Experiment or Research exemption was directed to the Experimental Use exemption, but as discussed in the Japan chapter herein, the Supreme Court of Japan has interpreted Article 69(i) of the Patent Act to also cover the Bolar-type exemption for obtaining marketing authorization. Similarly, in South Korea, Article 96(1)(i) of the Korean Patent Act as amended in 2010 applies to both exemptions.[4]

As detailed in the UK chapter, in 2014, the UK broadened the scope of the Experimental Use exemption to incorporate a new Bolar-type exemption. Instead of expanding the previously narrow Bolar provision, the UK opted to integrate a much broader Bolar-type exemption within the Experimental Use exemption. This approach aimed to enhance the UK's competitiveness within Europe and align its legislation with the emerging Unified Patent Court (UPC) framework, to which the UK was then a party. As a result, acts performed for the purpose of medicinal product assessments, such as clinical trials, were brought within the scope of the Experimental Use exemption.[5] In contrast, the Irish Patent Act maintains a clear distinction between the two exemptions, reflecting their different underlying rationales. When Ireland introduced a new Bolar-type exemption in 2014, it was incorporated within the framework of the Bolar-type exemption itself, preserving the conceptual separation between the two.[6]

The blurring of the rationale of the exemptions in the various jurisdictions seems to be one of the reasons for divergence between jurisdictions on this issue, which causes uncertainties. The divergence in the scope of the exemptions amongst different jurisdictions may be found even within Europe itself. The divergence is reflected, for example, in the applicability of the Bolar-type exemption to innovators. Although in most European countries, the Bolar-type exemption applies to innovative as well as generic products, this is not the case, for example, in the Netherlands or Greece, or under the Unitary Patent Courts (Article 27(d) UPCA). Another example of divergence is the applicability of the Bolar-type exemption to obtaining marketing authorization in another country (including outside the EU). While in most countries applying for marketing approval outside the EU would fall within the exemption, this does not seem to be the case, for example, in the Netherlands, Greece and Sweden.

The introduction of novel technologies, such as the emergence of biological medical products, also impacted the balance of interests relevant to the exemptions, *inter alia*, due to the high investment and long duration of developing biosimilar drugs. Said developments also have an impact on the scope of the exemptions amongst different jurisdictions.

A point of divergence between jurisdictions arises also in connection with the question as to whether the use of an invention as a research tool would fall under

---

than the FDA does not exclude safe haven under the Bolar-type exemption. Similarly, the US Supreme Court expanded the Bolar-type exemption in the US to encompass, beyond drugs, also medical devices, which are not mentioned in 35 USC 271(e) (1).

4. See South Korea chapter herein.
5. A similar approach was taken, for example, by Belgium with the introduction of a new provision in the law amended on 1 June 2023. See Belgium chapter herein.
6. See Ireland chapter herein.

the Experimental Use exemption. Although in general the exemption does not seem to cover the use of the invention as a research tool, in some jurisdictions it might. This divergence may stem from a conceptual difference regarding the origin and purpose of the Experimental Use exemption. Where the Experimental Use exemption is intended to cover purely academic teaching or research, cf. Argentina, Uruguay and Colombia,[7] the exemption might extend also to use of the invention as a research tool, provided the use is for non-commercial purposes. In other words, where the exemption is strictly limited to private and non-commercial activities, the scope of the exemption might be broader, and cover also use as 'research tool'.[8]

Using the invention as research tool may also cause divergence in another context. For example, according to the 'medicinal product assessment' exemption afforded in the UK, use of a patented invention as a research tool is exempted provided the use is for regulatory purposes (for a so-called 'medicinal product assessment'). In Switzerland, although using a patented research tool falls outside the exemption, the law provides an exception that applies to biotechnical inventions when they are used as research means or tools (e.g. research with a biotechnological process). In such cases, researchers are entitled to a non-exclusive licence to use the biotechnological invention for their research, for an appropriate fee.[9]

The divergence in the applicability of the exemptions, interesting as it may be from the scholar's point of view, creates a challenge for legislators worldwide to harmonize the laws concerning the scope of the exemptions. It also makes it very complex for global companies with interests worldwide to advise their R&D organizations.

We hope this book will be found helpful for the legislators, as well as the innovators, and shall generally provide professionals worldwide with important information on the subject.

I would like to express my sincere gratitude to Charles A. Boulakia and Daphné Derouane for their collaboration throughout the long journey of bringing this book to life – a journey that began with the preparations for the 2023 AIPPI World Congress Resolution (Q288), initiated by the members of the Pharma Committee under the leadership of John C. Todaro, whose inspiration played a key role in enabling us to complete this project.

My thanks also go to all the authors who contributed chapters on the various jurisdictions, to Ralph Nack of AIPPI for overseeing the project, as well as to my assistant Dalia Dil-Iluz and to Steve Lambley of Wolters Kluwer, whose dedication and professionalism were instrumental in ensuring the book's timely completion.

7. See respective chapters herein.
8. It may be argued that such use would not unreasonably prejudice the legitimate interests of the patent owner, taking account of the legitimate interests of third parties – see Art. 30 TRIPS Agreement. See however the Poland chapter distinguishing exempted use for teaching and use as research tools which is not exempted.
9. See Swiss chapter herein.

Chapter 2

Argentina

Martin Bensadon and Eugenio Hoss

1. GENERAL

a. Terminology

There is no distinction between the terms 'exemption' and 'exception' under the applicable law and case law. To maintain consistency, the term 'exemption' will be used as the general term, while the term 'exception' is restricted to issues of evidence and interpretation rules.

The Experimental Use exemption appears in Section 36(a) of the Patent Act. The Bolar-type exemption appears in Section 8 of the Confidentiality Act. In both cases, the legislation refers to situations where the patent has no legal effect and therefore both should be considered as exemptions to infringement.

b. Legal Basis in Argentina

The Experimental Use exemption was enacted in 1996 under Section 36(a) of the new Patent Act.

> 36. The right conferred by a patent shall not have any effect against: (a) a third party who, in the private or academic field and for non-commercial purposes, carries out purely experimental scientific or technological research, testing or teaching activities, and for this purpose manufactures or uses a product or uses a process that is equal to the patented one. ...

The Bolar-type exemption was also enacted in 1996, under Section 8 of the Confidentiality Act.

> 8. In the case of a product or process protected by a patent, any third party may use the invention before the expiration of the patent, for experimental purposes

> and to gather the information required for the approval of a product or process by the competent authority, for its commercialization after the expiration of the patent.

To date, there have not been any cases or regulations discussing the scope or particularities of these exemptions.

2. THE EXPERIMENTAL USE EXEMPTION

a. History and Rationale of Adopting the Experimental Use Exemption

The exemption was included in the original text of the new Patent Act, enacted in 1996 after the approval of the TRIPS Agreement.

The purpose of this provision is clearly to encourage scientific research in the academic and private fields by exempting these activities from the scope of exclusivity rights awarded by patents. The exemption intends to provide a secure research environment for purely academic or private scientific experimentation.

b. The Laws Applicable to the Experimental Use Exemption in Argentina

The Experimental Use exemption was enacted in 1996 under Section 36(a) of the new Patent Act. Section 36 provides as follows:

> 36. The right conferred by a patent shall not have any effect against: (a) a third party who, in the private or academic field and for non-commercial purposes, carries out purely experimental scientific or technological research, testing or teaching activities, and for this purpose manufactures or uses a product or uses a process that is equal to the patented one. ...

There is yet no relevant case law on this issue.

c. Procedural Aspects of Invoking the Experimental Use Exemption

The Experimental Use exemption may be used as a defence in patent litigation proceedings, either in infringement or in declaratory actions.

In Argentina, such proceedings are always under the jurisdiction of the federal courts. Accordingly, the only body that can decide of the legitimacy of an experimental use defence is the federal court.

d. Scope of the Experimental Use Exemption in Argentina

i. Fields of Technology

The Patent Act does not include any field limitations on the Experimental Use exemption. The exemption is thus applicable in all fields of technology.

ii. *Purpose of Experiments/Infringing Activities*

The language of the provision clearly indicates that, in order for the exemption to be applicable, the following requirements should be met: (a) activities limited to purely experimental scientific or technological research, testing or teaching; (b) performed in a private or academic field; and (c) with non-commercial purposes.

Therefore, the exemption does not apply in cases where the research activities have commercial purposes.

The provision does not require that the purpose of the research is to improve an invention. Also, it does not make any distinction between cases where the exemption is invoked for researching on a patented technology ('research on') and cases where the exemption is invoked for using a patented technology ('research with'). There is no relevant case law addressing the exact scope of the exemption, but it is likely that the courts would deem it applicable to both 'research on' and 'research with'.

iii. *Exempted and Prohibited Activities*

Section 36 of the Patent Act provides for a relatively broad defence and does not indicate which specific activities are exempted or prohibited. Although there is no relevant case law, it is likely that manufacture, purchase, use, possession, testing and importation would all be exempt if made in the context of research provided it is for non-commercial purposes.

iv. *Pure Academic vs Commercially Motivated Experimental Use*

The Experimental Use exemption is limited to purely academic or private research. If the person, company or institution carrying out the research activities has any commercial purposes, the exemption is not applicable.

e. Beneficiary Limitations

The Patent Act does not contemplate third party contributions and there is no case law on this issue. However, if a party contracts a third party to perform an activity that, if performed by that third party, would be considered exempt, it is likely that that third party would also be protected by the Experimental Use exemption.

f. Territoriality Issues

As a rule, Argentine courts only enforce and decide on Argentinian patents. Therefore, Argentine courts would probably not address any infringement issue taking place in a territory subject to foreign patents.

g. Burden of Proof and Onus

There is no relevant case law on the burden of proof for experimental use.

However, applying general procedural principles under Argentinian law, the onus would normally lie on the defendant to prove that the exemption applies.

h. Applicability during Patent Term Extension or Supplementary Protection Certificate

This is not applicable as there is no supplementary protection certificate (SPC) in Argentina

3. THE BOLAR-TYPE EXEMPTION

a. History and Rationale of Adopting the Bolar-Type Exemption

The Bolar-type exemption was also enacted in 1996. However, it was not included in the new Patent Act but rather as an additional provision in the Confidentiality Act. It was also enacted after the approval of the TRIPS Agreement.

The Confidentiality Act provides for a general legal framework for the protection of undisclosed information. It also addresses the protection of confidential data submitted for regulatory purposes and its use by third parties under a similar regime. In this context, the legislator also included a Bolar provision, inspired by the Bolar exemption case law developed by US courts.

b. The Laws Applicable to the Bolar-Type Exemption in Argentina

The Bolar-type exemption was enacted in 1996 under Section 8 of the Confidentiality Act. Section 8 reads as follows:

> 8. In the case of a product or process protected by a patent, any third party may use the invention before the expiration of the patent, for experimental purposes and to gather the information required for the approval of a product or process by the competent authority, for its commercialization after the expiration of the patent.

The exemption is drafted in a relatively narrow manner, as it is limited to 'uses' whose purpose is experimental *and* to gather information for the approval of a product or process. Moreover, the exemption is limited to experimental use aimed at gathering information which is *required* by the competent authorities.

c. Procedural Aspects of Invoking the Bolar-Type Exemption

The Bolar-type exemption may be used as a defence in patent litigation proceedings, either in infringement or in declaratory actions.

In Argentina, such proceedings are always under the jurisdiction of the federal courts. Accordingly, the only body that can make a determination of the legitimacy of a Bolar-type exemption defence is the federal court.

d. Scope of the Bolar-Type Exemption in Argentina

i. Fields of Technology

While the Bolar-type exemption provision was originally enacted to address concerns from the pharmaceutical industry, the language of the provision is not limited to pharmaceutical products. The exemption is applicable to any field of technology in which it is necessary to obtain an approval by a competent governmental authority before a product is put on the market.

ii. Purpose of Experiments/Infringing Activities

As indicated above, the Bolar-type exemption is limited to 'uses', the purpose of which is experimental and are aimed at gathering information *required* by the competent authorities and thus necessary for the approval of a product or process.

iii. Exempted and Prohibited Activities

The Bolar-type exemption is limited to uses for experimental purposes and which are aimed at gathering information for the approval of a product or process. The Bolar-type exemption provision only refers to the 'use' of the patented product or process but does not list any specific activities. Therefore, any activity including importation, purchase, manufacture, or storage could be exempted, provided that they have the referred purposes.

Moreover, the language of the provision suggests that the exemption will apply only if the information gathered was required by the competent authorities for the approval of the product or process. Therefore, uses of a patented product or process for the purpose of reimbursement, formulary access or other 'optional' regulatory steps would likely not be deemed covered by the Bolar-type exemption.

Argentinian law does not include any specific provision on stockpiling and there is no relevant case law either. However, courts would likely interpret that stockpiling does not fall within the scope of the Bolar-type exemption, which is limited to acts aimed at obtaining governmental approval. This interpretation would also be supported by the decision issued by the WTO Panel Report in Case DS114.[1]

e. Beneficiary Limitations

There is no limitation as to who can benefit from the Bolar-type exemption. Therefore, in the pharmaceutical field, the exemption would apply both to generic companies and to innovative companies applying for regulatory approval. The exemption would also likely apply to third parties contracted to perform studies on behalf of the party

1. Panel Report, Canada — Patent Protection of Pharmaceutical Products, WTO Doc. WT/DS114/R (adopted April 7, 2000, available at, https://www.wto.org/english/tratop_e/dispu_e/cases_e/ds114_e.htm).

seeking regulatory approval, although there is not yet any relevant case law which has confirmed this.

f. Territoriality Issues

The exemption would likely only apply to activities performed in Argentina, even if the purpose is a regulatory submission in a country other than Argentina. There is however no relevant case law yet.

In the event that activities are carried out by a party and infringe a corresponding patent in another jurisdiction, the infringement issue would not be addressed by Argentinian courts because such courts, as a rule, can only enforce and decide on Argentinian patents.

g. Burden of Proof and Onus

There is no relevant case law on the burden of proof for experimental use. However, applying general procedural principles under Argentinian law, the onus would normally lie on the defendant to prove that the exemption applies.

4. DIFFERENCES BETWEEN THE TWO EXCEPTIONS IN ARGENTINA

The Experimental Use exemption in Argentina has a relatively broad scope in terms of the exempted acts, but is strictly limited to uses with non-commercial purposes. The rationale is clearly aimed at protecting academic and private research activities in universities and other academic institutions.

On the other hand, the Bolar-type exemption is drafted in a relatively narrow manner, as it is limited to 'uses', the purpose of which is experimental and are aimed at gathering information required by the competent authorities for the approval of a product or process. The rationale of this provision clearly differs from the Experimental Use exemption as the Bolar-type exemption is aimed at preventing a regulatory lag between expiry of a patent and generic market entry.

It is clear that the party performing the activities (e.g. academic) and/or the specific purpose (e.g. non-commercial, regulatory approval) will play a decisive role in legitimizing an act under either of the two exemptions and that both exemptions are therefore clearly distinct.

Chapter 3

Australia

Daniel Sieveking and Eliza Jane Saunders

1. GENERAL

a. Terminology

The Experimental Use exemption appears in Section 119C of the Patents Act 1990 (Cth) under the heading 'Infringement exemptions: acts for experimental purposes'.

The Bolar-type exemption appears in Section 119A of the Patents Act 1990 (Cth) under the heading 'Infringement exemptions: acts for obtaining regulatory approval of pharmaceuticals'. A similar exemption for non-pharmaceutical products appears in Section 119B of the Patents Act 1990 (Cth) under the heading 'Infringement exemptions: acts for obtaining regulatory approval (non-pharmaceuticals)'.

These provisions are framed as exemptions to infringement and outline the circumstances under which certain acts will not constitute infringement of a valid patent in Australia.

b. Legal Basis in Australia

The Patents Act 1990 (Cth) was amended in 2012 to codify an Experimental Use exemption to patent infringement. Section 119C provides that:

> (1) A person may, without infringing a patent for an invention, do an act that would infringe the patent apart from this subsection, if the act is done for experimental purposes relating to the subject matter of the invention.
>
> (2) For the purposes of this section, experimental purposes relating to the subject matter of the invention include, but are not limited to, the following:
>
> (a) determining the properties of the invention;
>
> (b) determining the scope of a claim relating to the invention;
>
> (c) improving or modifying the invention;

(d) determining the validity of the patent or of a claim relating to the invention;
(e) determining whether the patent for the invention would be, or has been, infringed by the doing of an act.

In the decade following introduction of the exemption, there has been only one decision relating to Australia's experimental use provisions: *Jusand Nominees Pty Ltd v. Rattlejack Innovations Pty Ltd* [2022] FCA 540.

The Bolar-type exemption is codified in Section 119A of the Patents Act 1990 (Cth):

> (1) The rights of a patentee of a pharmaceutical patent are not infringed by a person exploiting an invention claimed in the patent if the exploitation is solely for:
> (a) purposes connected with obtaining the inclusion in the Australian Register of Therapeutic Goods of goods that:
> (i) are intended for therapeutic use; and
> (ii) are not medical devices as defined in the Therapeutic Goods Act 1989 ; or
> (b) purposes connected with obtaining similar regulatory approval under a law of a foreign country or of a part of a foreign country.
>
> (2) Subsection (1) does not apply to the export from Australia of goods for purposes described in paragraph (1)(b) unless the term of the patent has been extended under Part 3 of Chapter 6 and the goods consist of or contain:
> (a) a pharmaceutical substance per se that is in substance disclosed in the complete specification of the patent and in substance falls within the scope of the claim or claims of that specification; or
> (b) a pharmaceutical substance when produced by a process that involves the use of recombinant DNA technology, that is in substance disclosed in the complete specification of the patent and in substance falls within the scope of the claim or claims of that specification.
>
> (3) In this section:
>
> **'pharmaceutical patent'** means a patent claiming:
> (a) a pharmaceutical substance; or
> (b) a method, use or product relating to a pharmaceutical substance, including any of the following:
> (i) a method for producing a raw material needed to produce the substance;
> (ii) a product that is a raw material needed to produce the substance;
> (iii) a product that is a pro-drug, metabolite or derivative of the substance.

Section 119B of the Patents Act 1990 (Cth) provides for Bolar-type exemptions for non-pharmaceutical patents:

> (1) A person may, without infringing a patent, do an act that would infringe the patent apart from this subsection, if the act is done solely for:
> (a) purposes connected with obtaining an approval required by a law of the Commonwealth or of a State or Territory to exploit a product, method or process; or

(b) purposes connected with obtaining a similar approval under a law of another country or region.

(2) This section does not apply in relation to a pharmaceutical patent within the meaning of subsection 119A(3).

c. Bodies That May Decide on the Legitimacy of Exemptions

Both the Experimental Use exemption and the Bolar-type exemption are used only as a defence in patent infringement proceedings. In Australia, patent proceedings are commonly commenced under the jurisdiction of the Federal Court of Australia. The Supreme Courts of each State and Territory also have jurisdiction to hear patent matters, although they rarely do. The Federal Circuits Court does not have jurisdiction to hear patent matters. Accordingly, the only bodies that can make a determination of the legitimacy of an exemption is the Federal Court of Australia, a Supreme Court of a State or Territory or the High Court of Australia (on appeal from the Full Federal Court of Australia).

2. THE EXPERIMENTAL USE EXEMPTION

a. History and Rationale of Adopting the Experimental Use Exemption

Prior to the introduction of the Experimental Use exemption, the Advisory Council on Intellectual Property (ACIP) and the Australian Law Reform Commission (ALRC) both recognized that there was significant uncertainty as to the existence and scope of any implied experimental use defence to patent infringement in Australia. Both the ALRC and ACIP considered it desirable to remove the uncertainty and recommended the introduction of an Experimental Use exemption into the Act.

The Explanatory Memorandum that accompanied the legislation introducing Section 119C stated that it is intended that the term 'experimental' should be given its ordinary English meaning, and that the exemption should apply to tests, trials and procedures that a researcher or follow-on inventor undertakes as part of discovering new information when testing a principle or supposition.

The Explanatory Memorandum also provided a non-exhaustive list of scenarios in which the provision should apply, so long as the specific acts are undertaken for the predominant purpose of gaining new knowledge, testing a principle or supposition about the invention, or improving an invention, even if the person also had in mind commercializing an improvement to the invention in the future:

- a researcher may be contracted and paid to undertake experiments,
- research may be conducted with a view to ultimately commercializing the end-product of the experimentation, and
- research may be undertaken with, and partially funded by, a commercial partner.

However, the exemption is not intended to apply where the main purpose of the particular alleged experimental act is to commercialize the invention, to manufacture a product for the purpose of sale or use for commercial purposes, or for market research.

b. The Laws Applicable to the Experimental Use Exemption in Australia

Section 119C was introduced into the Act by the Intellectual Property Laws Amendment (Raising the Bar) Act 2012 (Cth) ('Raising the Bar Act').

Section 119C(1) of the Patents Act 1990 (Cth) provides that:

> A person may, without infringing a patent for an invention, do an act that would infringe the patent apart from this subsection, if the act is done for experimental purposes relating to the subject matter of the invention.

As at the date of this publication there has been only one decision relating to Australia's experimental use provisions: *Jusand Nominees Pty Ltd v. Rattlejack Innovations Pty Ltd* [2022] FCA 540.

In *Jusand*, the Court confirmed that the word 'experimental' has its ordinary English meaning and is not limited to work performed in scientific laboratories. However, the Court accepted that it would not be consistent with the object of the Patents Act 1990 (Cth) to apply Section 119C to ordinary commercial activities with minimal or inconsequential experimental purposes.

The Court held that while there may be a commercial aspect or ultimate aim to the experimentation, the experiments should be undertaken for the predominant purposes of gaining new knowledge or testing a principal supposition about the invention. The Court concluded that the reference to 'experimental purposes' connotes at least some application of scientific method to the discovery of new information or testing of a principle or supposition, the testing of a hypothesis, the existence of a protocol or methodology documentation of some kind setting out the purpose of the experiment and the variables to be measured or observed, the recording of results or observations, and the reporting of the results or observations.

The impugned acts in *Jusand* (which were not found on the evidence to involve sufficient scientific method, documentation, formal instructions or detailed monitoring of the product) were characterized by the judge as an ongoing monitoring program, and did not constitute an experiment.

c. Procedural Aspects of Invoking the Experimental Use Exemption

The Experimental Use exemption will be raised in an alleged patent infringer's defence to patent infringement proceedings (a formal pleading responding to the patentee's Statement of Claim alleging patent infringement). Following the close of pleadings, the alleged defendant may be ordered to provide discovery of documents evidencing the activities relating to the alleged experimental conduct. Significant facts, and possibly expert evidence, will then need to be filed evidencing that the alleged infringing acts done relating to the subject matter of the patented invention were for experimental purposes.

d. Scope of the Experimental Use Exemption in Australia

i. Fields of Technology

There are no field-of-technology-based limitations or restrictions on the Experimental Use exemption in Australia. All types of technology may utilize such exemptions.

iii. Purpose of Experiments/Infringing Activities

Section 119C(2) of the Patents Act 1990 (Cth) provides that experimental purposes relating to the subject matter of the invention include, but are not limited to, the following:

(a) determining the properties of the invention;
(b) determining the scope of a claim relating to the invention;
(c) improving or modifying the invention;
(d) determining the validity of the patent or of a claim relating to the invention;
(e) determining whether the patent for the invention would be, or has been, infringed by the doing of an act.

It is possible that experiments could be 'related to' the patented invention, which inherently include the subject matter of a patent, perhaps as part of a larger or more complex experiment. However, experiments are unlikely to 'relate to' the patented invention where, for example, the patented invention is a probe and the experimenter uses the probe to test for a disease rather than investigate the properties of the probe.

In *Jusand*, at [341], it was stated that:

> ...the reference to 'experimental purposes' connotes at least some application of scientific method to the discovering of new information or testing a principle or supposition, the testing of a hypothesis, the existence of a protocol or methodology documentation of some kind setting out the purpose of the experiment and the variables to be measured or observed, the recording of results or observations, and the reporting of the results or observations.

Additionally, the Explanatory Memorandum to the Intellectual Property Laws Amendment (Raising the Bar) Bill 2011 (Cth) states that:

> A 'research tool' is something that is used to facilitate an experiment, rather than something that is the subject of the experiment. For example, a researcher testing the effect of a particular herbicide on different plants might use a patented wetting agent to facilitate uptake of the herbicide. Here use of the wetting agent should not be exempt from infringement. The agent is being used as a tool: the experiments do not relate to it.

Accordingly, the use of patented technology as a 'research tool' is not understood to be exempt from infringement of a patent under the experimental use provisions. This is consistent with the wording of the exemption under Section 119C, which requires the use to be 'relating to the subject matter of the invention'.

iii. Exempted and Prohibited Activities

Section 119C(1) of the Patents Act 1990 (Cth) provides that:

> A person may, without infringing a patent for an invention, do an act that would infringe the patent apart from this subsection, if the act is done for experimental purposes relating to the subject matter of the invention.

Under Australian legislation, 'a patent gives the patentee the exclusive rights, during the term of the patent, to *exploit* the invention and to authorise another person to exploit the invention' (Section 13(1), emphasis added).

The definition of 'exploit' in the Patents Act 1990 (Cth), where the invention is a product, means 'make, hire, sell or otherwise dispose of the product, offer to make, sell, hire or otherwise dispose of it, use or import it, or keep it for the purpose of doing any of those things' and where the invention is a method or process, 'exploit' means 'use the method or process or do any [of the aforementioned acts] in respect of a product resulting from such use'.

Accordingly, all of the above-mentioned activities would fall within the Experimental Use exemption. For example, importation is an act of patent infringement unless the Experimental Use exemption applies. If the importation is for the purpose of taking steps that would fall within the Experimental Use exemption then such importation should not amount to infringement.

iv. Pure Academic vs Commercially Motivated Experimental Use

There is no requirement that experiments be done for 'academic purposes' having 'no commercial value'. The Experimental Use exemption should apply as long as the specific acts are undertaken for the predominant purpose of gaining new knowledge, or testing a principle or supposition about the invention. Therefore, if an activity is conducted primarily for the purpose of improving a patented invention, the activity would be exempt, even if the improvement or development may have commercial value and lead to ultimately commercializing the end-product(s) of the experimentation. However, the exemption will not apply where the predominant purpose of the research is to commercialize a patented invention or to manufacture it for the purpose of sale or use for commercial purposes.

Additionally, 'market research' (e.g., making and using the invention to test the likely commercial demand) on a patented invention is not intended to be exempt.

The boundaries of 'ultimately' commercializing a product and 'predominant' purpose of research have yet to be defined.

e. Beneficiary Limitations

Third party contributions is an uncertain issue – it is not expressly provided for in the legislation and there is no case law on this point.

In circumstances where there is only infringement if a product is used in a particular way, there is an argument that if the purchaser of the product does not infringe (because they can rely on the Section 119C defence), then the supplier would not infringe. This position is based on an interpretation of the indirect infringement section in the Act. Section 117(1) provides that:

> If the use of a product by a person would infringe a patent, the supply of that product by one person to another is an infringement of the patent by the supplier unless the supplier is the patentee or licensee of the patent.

However, other interpretations are possible.

f. Territoriality Issues

Australian courts, in general, will only enforce Australian patents. Therefore, if there were exportation outside of Australia to a jurisdiction where a patent was also held, that jurisdiction's laws would likely also apply. Arguably, supply of a patented invention for experimental use in another jurisdiction would be unlikely to fall within the exemption as the focus would be on the characterization of the relevant acts occurring within Australia.

g. Burden of Proof and Onus

Burden of proof and onus was not expressly dealt with in *Jusand*, which is the only case where experimental use has been considered by the Australian courts to date. Because Section 119C is drafted as an exemption, it is arguable that the patentee has the burden of proving that use by another party was not experimental, rather than requiring the user to establish experimental use. However, it is more likely that experimental use is treated as a defence to infringement, as discussed above, and accordingly the defendant will likely have an obligation to raise the defence of experimental use, as well as an evidentiary onus. As a defence, the burden of proof would likely lie with the defendant.

h. Applicability during Patent Term Extension or Supplementary Protection Certificate

There is no distinguishing between 'regular' patent term and applicability during any patent term extension – accordingly the exemption will be equally applied during any patent term extension. Currently the only form of patent term extension available in Australia is the extension of the term of standard patents claiming pharmaceutical substances.

3. THE BOLAR-TYPE EXEMPTION

a. History and Rationale of Adopting the Bolar-Type Exemption

In order to address *de facto* extensions of patent term caused by regulatory delays for pharmaceuticals, a provision enabling regulatory studies to be undertaken during the life of a patent claiming a pharmaceutical substance *per se* was introduced into the Patents Act 1990 (Cth) with the Intellectual Property Laws Amendment Act 1998.

Under the 1998 provisions, an exemption for so-called 'springboarding' activities only applied to infringement of a pharmaceutical substance patent.

The Intellectual Property Laws Amendment Act 2006 subsequently extended the exemption to cover activities involved in gaining regulatory approval at any time during the life of a pharmaceutical patent. Furthermore, the exemption was extended to encompass other types of 'pharmaceutical patent', not merely patents claiming a pharmaceutical substance *per se*.

b. The Laws Applicable to the Bolar-Type Exemption in Australia

Section 119A of the Australian Patents Act 1990 (Cth) defines the exemption for pharmaceutical patents, which is for activities that need to be undertaken solely in connection with obtaining regulatory approval on the Australian Register of Therapeutic Goods (ARTG) or for obtaining similar foreign regulatory approval, while one or more relevant patents are in force.

Section 119B of the Patents Act 1990 (Cth) provides for Bolar-type exemptions for non-pharmaceutical patents.

c. Procedural Aspects of Invoking the Bolar-Type Exemption

The Bolar-type exemption is used as a defence in litigation proceedings. In Australia, such proceedings are almost always under the jurisdiction of the Federal Court of Australia. However, as with the Experimental Use exemption, the Supreme Courts of Australia's States and Territories also have jurisdiction to hear patent infringement proceedings and responding defences.

d. Scope of the Bolar-Type Exemption in Australia

i. Fields of Technology

Section 119A applies to 'pharmaceutical patents', which encompasses granted patents that claim both pharmaceutical substances and methods, uses or products relating to a pharmaceutical substance.

Under Section 119B, a person does not infringe a non-pharmaceutical patent by exploiting an invention solely for purposes connected with obtaining regulatory approval in Australia or another country to exploit any product, method or process. This defence applies to the exploitation of any product, method or process, including medical devices, therapeutic devices or agricultural chemicals.

ii. Purpose of Experiments/Infringing Activities

The purpose of infringing activities must be connected with obtaining inclusion in the ARTG (or similar foreign regulatory approval) for a registered good or listed good intended for therapeutic use. For example, importation, purchase or manufacturing, solely for the purpose of use in a clinical trial for submission for the purposes of regulatory approval to a regulatory authority, in Australia or elsewhere, would be exempt. See section 3.d.iii. below.

iii. Exempted and Prohibited Activities

Under Section 119A(1)(a), a person does not infringe a pharmaceutical patent by exploiting an invention solely for purposes connected with obtaining inclusion in the ARTG for a registered good or listed good that is intended for therapeutic use. However, the exemption is not available in relation to medical devices or therapeutic devices, or device/medicine 'boundary' goods which have some characteristics of a medical device and some characteristics of a medicine (as set out below, these devices are covered by Section 119B).

Section 119A(1)(b) also exempts from infringement the exploitation of an invention claimed in a pharmaceutical patent for the purpose of obtaining regulatory approval under a law of a foreign country. However, this does not extend to the exportation of goods consisting of or containing a pharmaceutical substance *per se* unless the term of the patent has been extended under the provisions for pharmaceutical patent term extension. Section 119A also does not allow stockpiling of the pharmaceutical product (while the patent is still in force) for later sale.

It is considered that clinical trials (including phases 1, 2 and 3, but not phase 4 if the pharmaceutical is already approved by the Therapeutic Goods Administration) will likely be exempt provided it can be demonstrated that the trial is for the purpose of gaining regulatory approval in the ARTG or a similar approval in another country. However, the exemption would not apply to activities in relation to pricing and reimbursement under the Pharmaceutical Benefits Scheme (PBS).

Case law indicates that seeking a Pharmaceutical Benefits Advisory Committee (PBAC) recommendation providing a guarantee of supply (a necessary precursor to listing on the PBS) *does not* constitute an infringement.[1] However, reliance by a party on Section 119A has been said *in obiter* to be potentially relevant to the question of intention as to steps beyond that point that could potentially amount to patent infringement.[2]

e. Beneficiary Limitations

The exemption applies both to generic companies applying for regulatory approval and to innovative companies, for example, when doing competitive studies.

Section 119A does not appear to link the party exploiting the pharmaceutical good in Australia and the party seeking regulatory approval, and therefore would appear to apply to third parties contracted to perform studies on behalf of the party seeking regulatory approval, although this has not been tested in the courts.

1. *Warner-Lambert Company LLC v. Apotex Pty Ltd* [2017] FCAFC 58.
2. *Juno Pharmaceuticals Pty Ltd v. Celgene Corporation* [2021] FCA 236 as per Beach J.

f. Territoriality Issues

The exemption applies for otherwise infringing activities performed in Australia to satisfy regulatory requirements in other countries. The exemption likely applies to activities in other countries for the purposes of satisfying Australian regulatory requirements, to the extent that Australia would have jurisdiction over those activities. Of course, activities in another country, for the purposes of Australian regulatory submissions, may be subject to another country's laws if there is infringement of a corresponding patent in that country.

g. Burden of Proof and Onus

Because Section 119A and Section 119B are each drafted as an exemption, it is arguable that the patentee has the burden of proving that use by another party was not 'solely for … purposes connected with obtaining [regulatory approval]', rather than requiring the defendant to establish their activities were such. However, it is more likely that the Bolar-type exemption is treated as a defence to infringement, as discussed above, and accordingly the defendant will likely have an obligation to raise the exemption, as well as an evidentiary onus. As a defence, the burden of proof would likely lie with the defendant, at a 'balance of probabilities' level.

h. Applicability during Patent Term Extension or Supplementary Protection Certificate

As noted above in section 3.d.iii., where goods consisting of or containing a pharmaceutical substance *per se* which is subject of the pharmaceutical patent are exported from Australia, then the infringement exemption only applies if the Australian patent has had its term extended under Part 3 of Chapter 6 of the Patents Act 1990 (Cth).

4. DIFFERENCES BETWEEN THE TWO EXEMPTIONS IN AUSTRALIA

In Australia, the three patent infringement exemptions are not co-extensive; they are separate and distinct, and each has its own clearly delineated purpose and use.

Section 119A of the Australian Patents Act 1990 (Cth) relates only to alleged infringement of 'pharmaceutical patents' which are defined in this provision to mean a patent claiming:

(a) a pharmaceutical substance; or
(b) a method, use or product relating to a pharmaceutical substance, including any of the following:
  (i) a method for producing a raw material needed to produce the substance;
  (ii) a product that is a raw material needed to produce the substance;
  (iii) a product that is a pro-drug, metabolite or derivative of the substance.

Section 119A relates to activities that need to be undertaken solely in connection with obtaining regulatory approval on the ARTG or for obtaining similar foreign regulatory approval, while one or more relevant patents are in force.

Section 119B of the Patents Act 1990 (Cth) provides for Bolar-type exemptions for non-pharmaceutical patents only. It relates solely to acts done for: (a) purposes connected with obtaining an approval required by a law of the Commonwealth or of a State or Territory to exploit a product, method or process; or (b) purposes connected with obtaining a similar approval under a law of another country or region. Section 119B(2) specifically states that Section 119B does not apply to a pharmaceutical patent within the meaning of Section 119A

Section 119C of the Patents Act 1990 (Cth) is separate entirely to the bolar exemptions which are limited to regulatory activities, and relates specifically to acts 'done for experimental purposes relating to the subject matter of the invention'. Such subject matter is not limited to any particular field of use.

Chapter 4

Belgium

Koen Vanhalst and Christophe Ronse

1. GENERAL

a. Terminology

The Belgian Code of Economic Law ('CEL') does not use the terms 'exemption' or 'exception' but rather states that the rights of a patent do not apply to certain acts.

In this chapter, the term 'Experimental Use exemption' is used to encompass the general experimental use exemption, available in all technological fields, while the term 'Bolar-type exemption' refers to the specific exemption from patent infringement of acts needed to obtain market approval of medicinal products for human or veterinary use. In Belgium, the term 'Research exemption' is used rather than 'Experimental Use exemption'.

The term 'exemption' refers to activities that fall outside the scope of patent protection and can therefore be conducted without constituting patent infringement.

b. Legal Basis in Belgium

The legal basis for the Experimental Use exemption (Research exemption) can be found in Article XI.34, §1, b) CEL, amended on 1 June 2023 upon entry into force of the Agreement on the Unified Patent Court ('UPCA') to ensure alignment of the CEL with the latter.

The legal basis for the Bolar-type exemption on the other hand stems from Article 6bis, §1 of the Act of 25 March 1964 on medicines for human use ('Medicinal Products Act'),[1] as referred to in Article XI.34, §1, d) CEL.

1. This Act was previously applicable to medicinal products for human as well as veterinary use, but its scope has been limited to human medicinal products following the entry into

As discussed in detail below, there is an additional provision that was more recently introduced in the form of Article XI.34, §1/1 CEL extending the Experimental Use exemption of Article XI.34, §1, b) to 'All acts carried out for the purpose of evaluating medicinal products'.

2. THE EXPERIMENTAL USE EXEMPTION

a. History and Rationale of Adopting the Experimental Use Exemption

Until 2005, Article 28 of the Patents Act of 28 March 1984 provided an exemption for 'experiments which are the object of the patented invention'.

In view of the transposition of Directive 98/44/EC of the European Parliament ('Biotech Directive') into the Belgian Patent Act outlining the conditions of patentability of biotechnological inventions, the Belgian legislator, in order to boost the growing biotech industry in Belgium, decided to broaden the Experimental Use exemption. Through the Law of 28 April 2005 amending the Patents Act of 28 March 1984, the Experimental Use exemption was broadened to exempt 'acts done *on and/or with* the object of the patented invention performed, *for scientific purposes*'.

This amendment broadened the Experimental Use exemption, making it one of the broadest in the European Union.[2] The exemption covered, in addition to acts aimed at further developing the patented inventions ('experiment *on*'), also acts using the patented inventions ('experiment *with*'), provided the use was for scientific purposes.

On the occasion of the parliamentary debate leading to this amendment, the Minister of Economic Affairs explained the wording 'for scientific purposes' to refer, on the one hand, to acts that were performed for purely scientific purposes and, on the other hand, to so-called 'mixed' acts that were performed for both scientific and commercial purposes. Belgian legal doctrine defined these mixed acts as relating to the development of new applications, a new therapeutic effect, a more efficient manufacturing method, a new medical indication, a new method of administration, etc.[3]

In 2013, all laws relating to intellectual property were consolidated in the CEL, more particularly in Book XI.

In 2017 changes were made in the CEL in view of the then presumed 'imminent' entry into force of the Unitary Patent Court Agreement (UPCA) and the text of Article XI.34 §1 b) was amended to be in line with the text of Article 27(b) of the UPCA,[4]

---

force of EU Regulation (EU) 2019/6 of the European Parliament and of the Council of 11 December 2018 on veterinary medicinal products and repealing Directive 2001/82/EC.

2. COOK, T., *A European Perspective as to the Extent to which Experimental Use, and Certain Other, Defences to Patent Infringement, apply to Differing Types of Research* 144 (2006),
3. Verslag namens de commissie, Parl. St. Senaat 2004-2005, nr. 3-1088/3 ; VAN OVERWALLE, G., *Essais avec des médicaments. La situation en Belgique à la lumière de la récente jurisprudence et de la doctrine aux Pays-Bas et en Allemagne* Octrooirecht en geneesmiddelen, Brussels, Bruylant, 65-91 (2000); VAN OVERWALLE, G., *Van groene muizen met rode oortjes: de EUBiotechnologierichtlijn en het Belgisch wetsontwerp van 21 september 2004* Intellectuele Rechten – Droits Intellectuels, Vol. 9; iss. 4, 357 – 386 (2004)
4. Note that the Dutch text of the Law of 19 December 2017 (referring to '*proefnemingen*') was initially different from the French text (referring to '*actes accomplis à titre expérimental*').

now exempting 'acts done for experimental purposes relating to the subject-matter of the patented invention'. This provision finally entered into force on 1 June 2023, together with the UPCA.

The new provision specifically covers acts done for experimental purposes *directly related* to the patented invention itself. It no longer includes acts done *with* the subject matter of the invention for broader scientific purposes, which was previously allowed. The change caused some controversy within the research community since research projects that would have been exempted under the old '*on and with*' provision could cease to be exempted on 1 June 2023.

b. The Laws Applicable to the Experimental Use Exemption in Belgium

As discussed above, the current legal framework governing the Experimental Use exemption in Belgium is outlined in Article XI.34 §1 b) CEL. As of 1 June 2023, the law was amended to align with the UPCA. The updated provision states:

> The rights conferred by a patent shall not extend to acts done for experimental purposes relating to the subject matter of the patented invention.

On the same date, a new provision was introduced as Article XI.34 §1/1 CEL, stipulating:

> All acts carried out for the purpose of evaluating medicinal products shall be considered to be experiments involving the object of the patented invention, within the meaning of paragraph 1(b).

As this additional paragraph deals with the evaluation of medicinal products, we will discuss it more in detail below together with the Bolar-type exemption.

As a sidenote, since amended Article XI.34 § 1 b) CEL and new Article XI.34 § 1/1 CEL were recently introduced, the practical scope of the new exemption remains to be defined through case law.

The revised Article XI.34 § 1 b) CEL now refers to conducting 'acts done for experimental purposes', and no longer to 'acts for scientific purposes'. Based on the *travaux préparatoires* and the linguistic amendment to the Dutch version of this provision adopted in 2024,[5] it is clear that the legislator intended to harmonize Belgian law with the UPCA, suggesting that the scope of the exemption should be interpreted consistently.

However, it remains unclear whether this exemption applies (i) exclusively to purely scientific experiments, (ii) to mixed scientific and commercial experiments, or even (iii) to purely commercial experiments. Additionally, the exemption appears to be narrower than before, as it no longer automatically covers acts performed '*with*' the patented subject matter (e.g., using patented research tools).

Following an amendment by an Act of 19 February 2024, also the Dutch text (now referring to '*handelingen voor experimentele doeleinden*') was fully aligned to the English text of Article 27 *sub* b of the UPCA: 'acts done for experimental purposes relating to the subject-matter of the patented invention'.

5. See the previous footnote.

The latter acts may still be exempted specifically for *medicines*, considering that Article XI.34 § 1/1 CEL exempts '*all acts done for the purpose of evaluating medicines*', discussed below. Depending on the interpretation of the term '*evaluating medicines*', Article XI.34 § 1/1 CEL may in fact broaden the exemption for medicines in other ways as well. The *travaux préparatoires* reflect the legislator's intent to extend the exemption to research on innovative drugs, even for activities that may not have been covered by the general Experimental Use or Bolar-type exemptions (see below).

c. Procedural Aspects of Invoking the Experimental Use Exemption

Since the reform of 2015, only the Brussels Enterprise Court (either French- or Dutch-language) is competent to handle patent disputes in the first instance (Article XI.337 §1 CEL), while the Brussels Court of Appeal has competence for judicial review.

In addition to this, Belgium also hosts a local division of the Unified Patent Court, in Brussels.

As the Experimental Use exemption is an exception to patent infringement, it is to be expected that it will mainly be invoked as a defence against patent infringement.

It should however be noted that case-law on the Experimental Use exemption in Belgium is very rare.

d. Scope of the Experimental Use Exemption in Belgium

i. Fields of Technology

The general Experimental Use exemption of Article XI.34 § 1 b) CEL is not limited to any particular field of technology. However, as already mentioned above, Article XI.34 § 1/1 CEL has introduced an additional exemption for medicinal products.

ii. Purpose of Experiments/Infringing Activities

As indicated above, the changes to the Belgian CEL applicable since June 2023 reduced the scope of the Experimental Use exemption from 'on and/or with' the patented invention, which previously included the further development of research tools and methods as well as their use for experimental purposes, to 'acts done for experimental purposes relating to the subject-matter of the patented invention'.

Although generally seen as a limitation of the scope of the exemption, it is important to note that the term 'for scientific purposes' has been replaced by the term 'for experimental purposes', which is somewhat broader and not only covers scientific research, but also R&D activities performed in an economic context.

Taking into account that it was generally considered that the previously applicable exemption of acts done 'for scientific purposes' included mixed experiments done not only for purely scientific purposes (i.e. the gaining of knowledge) but also for commercial purposes, one can thus expect the presently applicable exemption to be interpreted in a manner which is at least as broad and probably even broader.

iii. Exempted and Prohibited Activities

Any acts which would otherwise qualify as an act of infringement will be exempted, provided they meet the conditions of the exemption. As such, there is no legal limitation on the use of data resulting from exempted activities. Only the nature of the relevant act is relevant to determining infringement.

Prohibited acts are all commercial acts defined in Article XI.28, §§1 and 2 CEL, i.e.:

§1 (a): to manufacture, offer, market, use, import or stock for that purpose;
(b): applying or, if the third party knows or should have known that application of the process covered by the patent is prohibited without the consent of the holder of the patent, offering a process for application in Belgian territory;
(c): to offer, place on the market, use, import or stock a product manufactured directly according to the process covered by the patent;

§2 offering or supplying, on Belgian territory, to a person other than the person entitled to use the patented invention, means relating to an essential element of the invention for the use of that invention, if the third party knows or should have known that those means are suitable and intended for that use.

Consequently, exempted from infringement are all acts listed above when carried out *'for experimental purposes'*. Acts not covered by Article XI.28, §§ 1 and 2 CEL do not constitute infringement regardless of the application of the Experimental Use exemption (e.g. purchase, testing, comparing).

iv. Pure Academic vs Commercially Motivated Experimental Use

The Experimental Use exemption is not limited to acts performed in an academic setting. Moreover, the new Experimental Use exemption no longer contains the criterion of 'scientific purposes' but refers to 'experimental purposes'. As discussed above, one can conclude from this that not only scientific research, but also R&D activities performed in an economic context may fall under this Experimental Use exception.

e. Beneficiary Limitations

Who carries out the R&D activities (a research or knowledge institution, a company or both together) and the nature of the R&D collaboration between the parties involved (mixed or not, service or collaboration, R&D or commercial) are in principle not relevant criteria for whether or not the Experimental Use exemption applies. The Belgian law does not impose any requirement in terms of who can benefit from this exemption.

The provisions defining the Experimental Use exemption focus on the *act* that is exempted, not on the identity of the *party* that is performing it. Therefore, where multiple parties are involved in the exempted acts, they should, in principle, all benefit from the exemption. However, if one of the parties does not actively engage in the exempted acts, and its role is limited to, for instance, the supply of products used in the experiment, such participation should fall outside the scope of the exemption.

This interpretation is supported, *inter alia,* by Article XI.29 § 2 CEL, which explicitly provides that a supplier does not benefit from the Experimental Use exemption in cases of indirect infringement, even if the third parties to whom the supplier supplies are exempted due to their experimental use. There is no reason to conclude differently in cases of direct infringement. The determination of whether a party in a multi-party setting is engaged in experimental activities is likely a factual question, dependent on the specific circumstances of each case.

f. Territoriality Issues

In essence, in accordance with Belgian and EU provisions on conflicts of law, the Experimental Use exemption provided by the laws and regulations of the country where the infringement takes place will apply, unless in case of a joint jurisdiction as, for example, that of the UPC.

The question one needs to ask in this respect is not so much related to the *territory* where the infringement takes place, but whether the *act* itself constitutes an infringement. If the act of infringement is not exempted from infringement in said jurisdiction, for example because it is seen as commercial and not for experimental purposes in said jurisdiction, infringement could be claimed. If data obtained from activities performed with the benefit of the Experimental Use exemption is used for commercial goals in a country that has valid patent protection covering the use of such data, infringement could also be claimed.

g. Burden of Proof and Onus

As a matter of legal principle, the onus of proof rests on the party which alleges something. In other words, it is up to the defendant in an infringement procedure to provide the necessary proof that the acts performed fall under the Experimental Use exemption. The claimant (patentee/exclusive licensee) in this respect can of course contest this and provide proof to the contrary.

h. Applicability during Patent Term Extension or Supplementary Protection Certificate

EU regulation (EC) No. 469/2009 on Supplementary Protection Certificates stipulates in Article 5 that:

> Subject to the provisions of Article 4, the certificate shall confer the same rights as conferred by the basic patent and shall be subject to the same limitations and the same obligations.

For completeness, Article 4 referred to in Article 5, states that:

> the protection conferred by a certificate shall extend only to the product covered by the authorization to place the corresponding medicinal product on the market

> and for any use of the product as a medicinal product that has been authorized before the expiry of the certificate.

Hence there is no difference in the rights conferred by a patent or an SPC implying that there should also not be any difference in the scope of the exemptions applying to said patent rights and SPC.

3. THE BOLAR-TYPE EXEMPTION

a. History and Rationale of Adopting the Bolar-Type Exemption

Article 6*bis*, § 1, Section 12, of the Medicinal Products Act (as amended) provides for a near-literal transposition of Article 10 (6), of EU Directive 2001/83/EC on the Community code relating to medicinal products for human use, i.e. that:

> the necessary studies, tests and trials with a view to the application of the rules and conditions in [the relevant legal provisions relating to the grant of marketing authorisations for generic, hybrid and biosimilar products for human use] and the consequential practical requirements shall not be regarded as contrary to patent rights or to supplementary protection certifications for medicinal products.

Article XI.34 § 1 d), CEL now also explicitly refers to the aforementioned provisions of the Medicinal Products Act (see below).

Under this 'classic' Bolar-type exemption, carrying out the necessary studies, tests and trials with a view to obtaining a marketing authorization for a medicinal product, and any practical requirements arising therefrom, do not constitute infringement of patents or SPCs. This (classic) Bolar-type exemption applies only to generic, hybrid or biosimilar medicines.

Because of political considerations, it was opted in 2017 (at the same time as the above-mentioned amendment introduced to the Experimental Use exemption, which entered into force in 2023) to provide an additional provision in the CEL leading to a broad application of the Experimental Use exemption to *medicines* in Article XI.34 §1/1 CEL (also called the 'Bolar+' exemption). The 'classic' Bolar-type exemption itself in the Medicines Act remains unchanged.

b. The Laws Applicable to the Bolar-Type Exemption in Belgium

As already explained above, the Bolar-type exemption for human generic medicinal products is outlined in Article 34 §1 d) CEL stating that:

> Rights arising from a patent do not apply to: d) acts authorized under Article 6bis, § 1, twelfth paragraph, and § 6, thirteenth paragraph, of the Medicinal Products Act, in relation to a patent for the product within the meaning of these provisions.

For veterinary products, we must now refer to EU Regulation (EU) 2019/6 repealing EU Directive 2001/82/EC. This Regulation stipulates in Article 41 that:

> Conducting the necessary tests, studies and trials with a view to applying for a marketing authorization in accordance with Article 18 shall not be regarded as contrary to patent-related rights or to supplementary-protection certificates for veterinary medicinal products and medicinal products for human use.

As mentioned, in addition to the 'classic' Bolar-type exemption for human generic medicinal products, the new provision under Article XI.34 §1/1 CEL, often referred to as the 'Bolar + ' provision, provides that:

> all acts performed for the purpose of evaluating medicinal products are considered to be experimental acts involving the subject matter of the patented invention concerned, within the meaning of paragraph 1(b).

This additional exemption is in fact broader in scope than the exemption of Article XI.34 §1 d) CEL since it now also covers innovative medicinal products. The latter follows from the wording of the Law, but also from the Explanatory Memorandum to said Law which indicates that:

> The purpose of this addition is to clarify that the so-called 'research exemption' in Article XI.34(1)(b) of the Economic Code also extends to acts that are taken with a view to an approval of a new innovative medicine. The actions taken with a view to an approval of a new innovative medicine are not covered by the existing research exemption, because many of the acts in this context are primarily commercial in nature, nor are they covered by the Bolar exemption since it does cover commercial acts, but only for generic medicines.

In addition, the Council for Intellectual Property[6] observed in its advice of 13 November 2023, that the wider scope of this provision not only concerns innovative medicinal products, but is also situated in two other areas. On the one hand, it refers generally to the evaluation of medicinal products, without distinguishing between medicinal products for human or animal use. On the other hand, the provision also contains no territorial limitation. Where the 'classic' Bolar-type exemption applies to applications for a Belgian or EU market authorization, applicable in Belgium, this 'Bolar + ' exemption (i.e. under Article XI.34 §1/1) appears to be applicable to applications for market authorizations regardless of the territory where these market authorizations will apply.

Henceforth, this general provision will therefore apply as a '*lex generalis*' and apply to acts relating to the regulatory approval of medicinal products for both human and animal use, both within and outside Europe. The 'classic' Bolar-type exemption will continue to apply as a '*lex specialis*' for generic medicines and biosimilars for human use, with a view to obtaining a market authorization in Belgium or applicable in Belgium.[7]

---

6. i.e. an advisory body set up to advise the Belgian authorities on issues of intellectual property.
7. Advice of the Council for Intellectual Property of 13 November 2023 (https://economie.fgov.be/nl/themas/intellectuele-eigendom/instellingen-en-actoren/raad-voor-de-intellectuele/adviezen/advies-van-de-raad-voor-de-1)

c. Procedural Aspects of Invoking the Bolar-Type Exemption

As explained above, only the Brussels Enterprise Court is competent to handle patent disputes in first instance (Article XI.337 §1 CEL), while the Brussels Court of Appeal has competence for judicial review. Belgium also hosts the Brussels local division of the Unified Patent Court.

As the Bolar-type exemption is an exception to patent infringement, it is to be expected that it will mainly be invoked as a defence against patent infringement. We are unaware of any case law relating to this exemption.

d. Scope of the Bolar-Type Exemption in Belgium

i. Fields of Technology

The 'classic' Bolar-type exemption under Article XI.34 §1 d) is limited to the pharmaceutical field, more precisely generic, hybrid or biosimilar medicines for human use.

The additional broader exemption for innovative products ('Bolar + ') is also linked to obtaining marketing authorizations for (human or veterinary) medicinal products and hence is also limited to the pharmaceutical field.

One can question whether or not it is discriminatory to limit this type of exemption to the pharmaceutical field only, since many other fields are also facing regulatory approval requirements (e.g. crop protection products, food products, SEP-regulated products). Whether or not also these fields should be able to benefit from a Bolar-type exemption for the acts needed for obtaining such market approval remains to be answered.

ii. Purpose of Experiments/Infringing Activities

As already indicated above, the Bolar-type exemption in Belgium is two-fold:

The 'classic' Bolar-type exemption is limited to obtaining market approval for generic and biosimilar products and hence will cover for example comparative experimentation with the patented innovator drug in order to prove that the generic or biosimilar product can indeed rely on the data of the innovative drug and obtain market approval. This is a quite narrow scope of exemption.

The 'Bolar + ' exemption introduced on 1 June 2023 is much broader in scope and also includes innovator drugs (and hence also improvements of existing drugs).

With regard to manufacturing, however, one needs to use some caution since such processes can be covered by patents as well and would not automatically fall under the 'classic' Bolar-type exemption since the production can be used for commercial purposes as well. However, manufacturing a medicinal product with the purpose of evaluating this product would likely fall under the 'Bolar + ' exemption.

iii. Exempted and Prohibited Activities

The wording of Article XI.34 §1 d) CEL covers 'Acts authorized under Article 6bis, § 1, twelfth paragraph, and § 6, thirteenth paragraph, of the Law of 25 March 1964 on medicinal products, in relation to a patent for the product within the meaning of these provisions', while Article XI.34 §1/1 CEL provides that 'All acts carried out for the purpose of evaluating medicinal products shall be considered to be experiments involving the subject matter of the patented invention, within the meaning of paragraph 1(b).'

In general, activities of a commercial nature – such as 'offering for sale' – fall outside the scope of the Bolar-type exemption and would constitute patent infringement, as they cannot be classified as experimental acts.

However, considering the language used in the 'Bolar + ' exemption (Article XI.34 § 1/1 CEL) which broadly refers to any acts 'for the evaluation' of medicines, the exemption does not seem to be limited to those trials that have to be followed by an application for regulatory approval.

Also post-approval acts done, for example in the quest for obtaining reimbursement of medicine by the government, will likely be seen as falling within the meaning of 'offering for sale' rather than being part of the 'evaluation' process to obtain market approval. These acts are therefore likely to be deemed commercial and not covered by the exemption.

Stockpiling is generally not permitted under Belgian law, as 'keeping in storage' is considered an infringing act if done with a view to manufacturing, offering, or marketing a patented product. Although recent case law is lacking, deferred sale resulting from stockpiling is unlikely to evade infringement liability.

e. Beneficiary Limitations

The 'classic' Bolar-type exemption under Article XI.34 §1 d) CEL is, as indicated above, limited to generic or biosimilar medicinal products and does not cover innovative medicines. The new 'Bolar + ' exemption under Article XI.34 §1/1 CEL on the contrary was specifically intended to also cover innovative products and hence innovator companies.

In the absence of any relevant case law, it is unclear to what extent the exemption can be invoked by a third party or only by the entity that is applying for regulatory approval and what degree of linkage is needed between both. This will likely be a factual question linked to the circumstance of the case.

f. Territoriality Issues

The 'classic' Bolar-type exemption is as indicated above limited to applications for a market authorization in Belgium or applicable in Belgium, while the new additional exemption under Article XI.34 §1/1 CEL is applicable to applications for market authorizations regardless of the territory where these market authorizations will apply, and even more generally to any acts in view of evaluating medicines.

As explained above with regard to the Experimental Use exemption, the provisions defining the Bolar-type exemptions focus on the *act* that is exempted, not on the identity of the party that is performing them. Therefore, where multiple parties are involved in the exempted acts, they should, in principle, all benefit from the exemption. However, if one of the parties does not actively engage in the exempted acts, and its role is limited to, for instance, the supply of products used in the experiment, such participation should fall outside the scope of the exemption, unless it could somehow qualify as a 'consequential practical requirement' for the purpose of the 'classic' Bolar-type exemption.

g. Burden of Proof and Onus

As a matter of legal principle, the onus of proof rests on the party who alleges something. In other words, it is up to the defendant in an infringement procedure to provide the necessary proof that the acts performed fall under the Bolar-type exemption. The claimant (patentee/licensee) in this respect can of course contest this and provide proof to the contrary.

h. Applicability during Patent Term Extension or Supplementary Protection Certificate

Like the Experimental Use exemption, EU Regulation (EC) No. 469/2009 on Supplementary Protection Certificates stipulates in Article 5 that:

> Subject to the provisions of Article 4, the certificate shall confer the same rights as conferred by the basic patent and shall be subject to the same limitations and the same obligations.

For completeness, Article 4, referred to in Article 5, states that:

> the protection conferred by a certificate shall extend only to the product covered by the authorization to place the corresponding medicinal product on the market and for any use of the product as a medicinal product that has been authorized before the expiry of the certificate.

Hence there is no difference in the rights conferred by a patent or an SPC implying that there should also not be any difference in the scope of the exempted part of said patent rights.

4. DIFFERENCES BETWEEN THE TWO EXCEPTIONS IN BELGIUM

The Bolar-type exemption and the Experimental Use exemption serve different purposes and typically do not directly conflict with each other, although overlaps seem possible.

The Experimental Use exemption is far more general and exonerates acts done for experimental purposes relating to the subject-matter of the patented invention. It aims to foster innovation and scientific progress by allowing researchers to study and experiment with patented technologies. This exemption is spelled out in Article XI.34 §1 a) CEL.

The Bolar-type (and Bolar+) exemptions allow (generic, biosimilar, and now also innovative) drug manufacturers to conduct the necessary tests and trials to obtain regulatory approval before the original patent expires. This ensures that generics or competitors can enter the market immediately after the patent expires, promoting competition and accessibility of drug products. This exemption is spelled out in Article XI.34 §1 d) and Article XI.34 §1/1 CEL.

In practice, these exemptions are designed to coexist harmoniously, each addressing specific needs within the pharmaceutical and research sectors.

The Bolar-type exemption can be seen as granting an exemption for an activity which could otherwise be seen as commercial, i.e. the development of a (generic or biosimilar and now also innovative) drug for commercial use. Such a commercial act would generally not be considered as falling under the standard Experimental Use exemption.

The Bolar-type exemption is thus more focused on facilitating market entry for generics or biosimilars (and now also any other drugs) in the medicinal field, while the Experimental Use exemption supports broader scientific inquiry throughout the full range of technical fields.

There is hence no need to address which one is superior to the other. In some cases, both exemptions will apply to the same act, in other cases only one of the exemptions will apply, but there can never be any conflict between them since cumulative exemption does not cancel out one of the exemptions.

Chapter 5

Brazil

Leonor Magalhaes Galvao and Rana Gosain

1. GENERAL

a. Terminology

The Experimental Use exemption is defined in the Brazilian Industrial Property Law (Law No. 9,279/1996) as 'acts performed by unauthorized third parties, for *experimental purposes*, related to scientific or technological studies or research' (emphasis added).

The Bolar-type exemption is defined in the Brazilian Industrial Property Law as 'acts practiced by unauthorized third parties, with respect to the invention protected by a patent and *exclusively intended for the production of information, data, and test results aiming at obtaining the registration for commercialization in Brazil or in another country*, for the exploitation and commercialization of the patented product' (emphasis added).

b. Legal Basis in Brazil

Article 43, item II of Law No. 9,279/1996 provides the legal basis for the Experimental Use exemption. It states that 'acts performed by unauthorized third parties for experimental purposes, related to scientific or technological studies or research' are not considered patent infringement. This allows researchers to use patented inventions for non-commercial purposes to further scientific knowledge without requiring the patent holder's authorization.

The Bolar-type exemption is grounded in Article 43, item VII of the Industrial Property Law, which was introduced through Law No. 10,196/2001.

This reads as follows:

> Article 43. The provisions of the previous article [patent infringement] do not apply to:
>
> ...
>
> VII. acts practised by unauthorized third parties with respect to the invention protected by a patent and exclusively intended for the production of information, data, and test results aiming at obtaining the registration for commercialization in Brazil or in another country, for the exploitation and commercialization of the patented product after the expiration of the term established in Article 40.

For reference, Article 40 of Law No. 9,279/1996 states that patents of invention are granted a twenty-year term of protection, while utility model patents enjoy a fifteen-year term.

Thus, the provision of Article 43, item VII allows for the use of a patented invention, without the patent holder's consent, in activities considered as mandatory in order to obtain marketing approval for the commercialization of a generic product after the patent expires.

c. Bodies That May Decide on the Legitimacy of Exemptions

Both the Experimental Use exemption and the Bolar-type exemption are used as a defence in enforcement litigation proceedings. In Brazil, such proceedings are always under the jurisdiction of the Lower State Courts and the State Courts of Appeals. Accordingly, the only bodies that can determine the legitimacy of an exemption are these Courts.

It is also important to note that Brazil does not have a common law system, but rather a civil law system. This means there are basically no binding precedents, and lower court judges have significant discretion on how to decide each case. Thus, decisions in Brazil are strongly based on the statutory provisions applicable to the case, and judges are free to give their own interpretation of the law.

2. THE EXPERIMENTAL USE EXEMPTION

a. History and Rationale of Adopting the Experimental Use Exemption

Brazil was one of the early adopters of Intellectual Property Rights legislation. Inventors' privileges were first recognized in 1809, prior to Brazil´s independence from Portugal, and Brazil's first patent law dates back to 1830. This law held that foreign inventions could not be patented in Brazil, a provision that was abolished formally in the revised patent law of 1882, which adopted the Paris Convention's principle of national treatment. Brazil also exploited the freedom provided by the Paris Convention regarding non-patentable subject-matter. Thus, since 1945, inventors of pharmaceutical products, food preparations, and medical procedures were excluded from any patent protection.

These exclusions were modified in order to comply with the TRIPS (Trade-Related Aspects of Intellectual Property Rights) Agreement. The most important modification concerned the patentability of pharmaceutical processes and products, which became possible with the enactment of Law No. 9,279 on 14 May 1996, and which regulates the rights and obligations related to industrial property, among other provisions. The Experimental Use exemption was thus inserted on occasion of the enactment of the Brazilian Industrial Property Law (Law No. 9,279) in 1996.

b. The Laws Applicable to the Experimental Use Exemption in Brazil

Article 42 of Law No. 9,279/1996 defines that 'a patent confers on its titleholder the right to prevent a third party from, without his consent, producing, using, offering for sale, selling or importing' a patented product, a patented process, or a product obtained through a patented process.

In turn, Article 43 establishes the cases (which include both experimental and Bolar-type exemptions) where the provisions of the previous Article do not apply.

The Experimental Use exemption is regulated in Article 43, item II, which states as follows:

> Article 43. The provisions of the previous section do not apply to:
>
> ...
>
> II. acts performed by unauthorized third parties, for experimental purposes, related to scientific or technological studies or research.

c. Procedural Aspects of Invoking the Experimental Use Exemption

The Experimental Use exemption is used as a defence in enforcement litigation proceedings, which, in Brazil, are always under the jurisdiction of the Lower State Courts and the State Courts of Appeals – the only bodies that can determine the legitimacy of an exemption are these Courts.

Additionally, since Brazil does not have a common law system, but rather a civil law system, decisions issued by the Brazilian Courts are strongly based on the statutory provisions applicable to the case, and judges are free to give their own interpretation of the law.

d. Scope of the Experimental Use Exemption in Brazil

i. Fields of Technology

There are no field-of-technology-based limitations or restrictions on the Experimental Use exemption in Brazil. All types of technology may benefit from such exemptions.

ii. Purpose of Experiments/Infringing Activities

'Experimental Use' is defined in the Brazilian Industrial Property Law as an exception to the exclusive rights granted by a patent, and, in view of the TRIPS Agreement's parameters (set forth by Article 30), it should be interpreted in a restrictive manner.

Nevertheless, it is important to stress that the experimental use clause has broad wording (as highlighted in section 2.b. above) and there is a lack of Court decisions construing its limitations. Among the few decisions involving the interpretation of Section 43, item II, one is particularly relevant.

In this non-binding precedent, the First Business Panel of the Sao Paulo Court of Appeals (Appeal No. 0127448-30.2012.8.26.0100) acknowledged the Experimental Use exemption but did not apply it to the concrete case because the defendant failed to present any evidence of the research and experiments it claimed to perform.

In this case, in light of the evidence and documents in the case, the panel of Appellate Judges noted that instead of having the so-called 'Temporary Special Registration – TSR', a certification granted by the Federal Government intended to grant the right to use pesticides and components exclusively for research and experimentation purposes, the defendant had requested a 'Product Registration' certification before the Ministry of Agriculture and Livestock, which should indicate the commercial purpose of importing, exporting and selling the product.

Hence, according to the panel, the research purpose alleged by the defendant had not been demonstrated, in addition to the fact that it did not appear to be in line with the company's corporate objectives, which aimed at the commercial exploitation of chemical products (whether through the sale of goods or by providing consultancy to other companies). As a result, the defendant failed to clarify the objectives, the method, and the partial conclusions obtained with the alleged experimental use, reasons why the exemption could not be applied.

Therefore, the experimental use claim must be backed with sufficient evidence that the use of the patent subject-matter is limited to experimental purposes.

iii. Exempted and Prohibited Activities

Article 43, item II of Law No. 9,279/1996 provides a broad definition of experimental use as it applies to any '*acts* (...) with experimental purposes, related to scientific or technological studies or research' (emphasis added). The exact 'acts' are not specified in wording of this Article, which was probably purposely drafted in a broad manner in order to encompass any use of the patent subject-matter that can be qualified as experimental use. Accordingly, any use of a patented subject-matter – including manufacture, exportation and importation – should be exempt provided that such use is for experimental purposes.

Furthermore, Article 184, item I, further defines that a crime is committed against a patent of invention or a utility model patent by he who 'exports, sells, exhibits or offers for sale, maintains in stock, hides or receives, for *use for economic purposes, a product manufactured in violation of an invention* or utility model patent, or obtained through a patented process' (emphasis added). Thus, the exportation of a patented invention for experimental use, by the same person or someone related thereto, in another jurisdiction does not constitute patent infringement, provided that the product comprising the patented subject-matter was obtained by legitimate means.

In this scenario, the key issue is to understand the role of the exporter, which requires an assessment of the specific circumstances. For instance, if the exporter of the patented subject-matter is acting exclusively for profit, patent infringement would occur in Brazil, even if the exporter's client is solely interested in conducting experimental tests. The rationale of the Brazilian Industrial Property Law is to always prevent any attempt to derive economic gains from an invention without the patentee's authorization.

Similarly, Article 184, item II, forbids the importation of '*...a product that is the subject matter of an invention or utility model patent, or obtained by a means or process patented in the Country*, for the purposes mentioned in the item above [i.e., economic purpose], and *that has not been placed on the foreign market directly by the patent owner or with his consent*' (emphasis added). Thus, the importation of the patented invention for experimental use from another jurisdiction does not lead to infringement, provided that the technology is obtained in accordance with the foreign country's law and that the product has been made available in Brazil under the patentee's consent.

iv. *Pure Academic vs. Commercially Motivated Experimental Use*

The law refers to 'acts performed by unauthorized third parties, with *experimental purposes*, related to scientific or technological studies or research' (emphasis added). Thus, there is no statutory requirement for the exempted acts be done for 'academic purposes' with 'no commercial intent'.

However, the extent of the applicability of the exception to commercial entities or businesses is unclear since there is no clear statutory guidance.

Scholars and intellectual property practitioners argue both in favour and against the application of the experimental use clause in research for profit. Some authors argue that a patent referring to products and processes designed to be used for research and development projects would be useless if Article 43, item II, included research with economic purposes. In this scenario, the patentee would have no one to sell its patented product or process to, because its potential clientele would be free to use the patented object under the referred exception rule.

On the other hand, some scholars and intellectual property practitioners defend an unrestricted application of the Experimental Use exemption. In this scenario, the clause would cover any research and development activity, even if carried out by competitors.

e. Beneficiary Limitations

Third party contributions to Experimental Use have not been directly contemplated by the Brazilian Industrial Property Law or the Courts.

Regarding third party contributions to patent infringement, Article 185 of Law No. 9,279/1996 establishes that 'supplying a component of a patented product, or any material or equipment to execute a patented process, as long as the final application of the component, material or equipment necessarily induces the exploitation of the subject matter of the patent'.

However, if the contributions made by third parties were also made for *bona fide* experimental purposes, they should also be exempted. Similarly to what was outlined in section 2.d.iii. above, determining contributory infringement would also depend on the specifics of the case. If a third party genuinely believes they are assisting someone in performing acts covered by the experimental exemption, contributory infringement would not occur – even if this assistance enables the other person to directly infringe a patent.

f. Territoriality Issues

Article 184, item I, defines as patent infringement the exportation, 'for use for economic purposes, a product manufactured *in violation of an invention or utility model patent*, or obtained through a patented process' (emphasis added).

Thus, the exportation of a patented invention for experimental use in another jurisdiction would not constitute infringement, provided that the product comprising the patented subject-matter was obtained by the same person or someone related thereto by legitimate means. It is important to emphasize that Article 43, item IV, of Law No. 9,279/1996 stipulates that it does not constitute patent infringement if 'a product manufactured according to a process or product patent has been placed on the domestic market directly by the patent holder or with their consent'. This provision, in this specific context, reinforces the idea that the exportation of such patented products would not constitute infringement.

Furthermore, Article 184, item II, forbids the importation of '…a product that is the object of an invention or utility model patent, or obtained by a means or process patented in this country, for the purposes set forth in the preceding item [i.e., economic purpose], *and that has not been placed on the foreign market directly by the patent holder with his consent*' (emphasis added).

Thus, the importation of the patented invention for experimental use from another jurisdiction does not lead to infringement, provided that the technology is obtained in accordance with the foreign country's law and this product has been made available under the patentee's consent.

Lastly, it should of course also be noted that Brazilian courts will only enforce Brazilian law within the Brazilian territory. Therefore, if there was exportation or importation of a good from/to Brazil, to/from a jurisdiction in which such product had patent protection patent, the laws of that jurisdiction would apply.

g. Burden of Proof and Onus

The Brazilian Code of Civil Procedure establishes that the burden of proof lies on the party that claims either a right or a defence. In case a defendant claims the application of the Experimental Use clause, this party will have the burden to prove that such use complies with Article 43, item II, bringing sufficient evidence that demonstrates that the use of the patent subject-matter qualifies as an experimental use.

h. Applicability during Patent Term Extension or Supplementary Protection Certificate

Brazil does not have a formal system for patent term extensions where extensions can be granted to compensate for delays in regulatory approval (e.g. Supplementary Protection Certificates in the EU or Patent Term Extensions in the US). The Brazilian Industrial Property Law does not provide a specific mechanism to extend the term of a patent beyond the standard twenty years from the filing date for invention patents or fifteen years for utility models. Previously, there was a provision in Brazilian law that ensured patents would be valid for at least ten years from the grant date (seven years for utility models), which effectively extended the patent term if there were significant delays in the patent application examination process. However, this provision was declared unconstitutional by the Brazilian Supreme Court in 2021. Currently, the patent term is strictly tied to the filing date, without any minimum period of protection post-grant, even in the case of delayed regulatory approvals.

Thus, since the Brazilian Industrial Property Law does not impose any limitation in terms of time for the application of the Experimental Use exemption, the exemption is applicable at any stage during the regular patent term.

3. THE BOLAR-TYPE EXEMPTION

a. History and Rationale of Adopting the Bolar-Type Exemption

The Bolar-type exemption in Brazil has developed over time, influenced by both domestic and international legal evolution in this matter. The Bolar-type exemption was promulgated to prevent the usual regulatory lag between the expiration of a patent and generic market entry and thus promote the availability of affordable medicines in the country.

The Bolar-type exemption was thus enacted in Law 10,196 of 14 February 2001, which amended and added provisions to the Law No. 9,279/1996, namely item VII of Article 43, and allowed for the first time for generic drug manufacturers to use patented inventions without the patent holder's consent for purposes related to obtaining regulatory approval for a generic version of a patented drug before the patent expires.

Over the years, the Bolar-type exemption has been upheld by Brazilian courts, reinforcing the legality and importance of the provision in promoting public health and Brazil's commitment to balance patent protection with public health needs.

It has since become an essential part of Brazil's strategy to support the local pharmaceutical industry and ensure access to affordable medicines.

b. The Laws Applicable to the Bolar-Type Exemption in Brazil

Article 42 of Law No. 9,279/1996 defines that a 'patent assigns to its owner the right to prevent a third party, without his consent, from producing, using, offering for sale, selling or importing' a patented product, a patented process, or a product obtained through a patented process.

In turn, Article 43 establishes the cases (which include both experimental and Bolar-type type exemptions) where the provisions of the previous Article do not apply.

The Bolar-type exemption is regulated in Brazil by Article 43, item VII, of Law No. 9,279/1996 which states as follows:

> Article 43. The provisions of the previous section [patent infringement] do not apply to:
>
> ...

> VII. acts practised by unauthorized third parties, with respect to the invention protected by a patent and exclusively intended at the production of information, data, and test results aiming at obtaining the registration for commercialization, in Brazil or in another country, for the exploitation and commercialization of the patented product after the expiration of the terms established Article 40 [patent term].

The exemption is drafted in a fairly broad manner, in a sense, in that it relates to *any* act 'aiming exclusively at producing information, data, and test results to seek market approval in Brazil or abroad'. As such, a fairly open and flexible reading of the exemption is warranted in terms of what type of information, data or test results are encompassed by the exemption.

That said, the provision is restrictive when it establishes (i) that it refers to acts aimed *exclusively* at producing information, data, and test results to seek marketing approval in Brazil or abroad and (ii) that the exploitation or commercialization of the referred patented product must only occur *after the expiration of the patent.*

In summary, the language of the statute restricts the Bolar-type exemption to acts carried out to produce information, data, and test results to seek marketing approval, in order to exploit or commercialize the patented and regulated product only after the expiration of the patent. Accordingly, other kinds of objectives or testing would not be encompassed by this exemption.

c. Procedural Aspects of Invoking the Bolar-Type Exemption

The application of the Bolar-type exemption requires evidence that the activities were performed with the intention of obtaining marketing approval, that is, the data produced must be suitable for that end.

However, it is worth mentioning that the statute does not necessarily require that marketing approval is requested or granted or that a regulatory dossier is ultimately submitted before the relevant agencies, nor that specific tests/information are actually presented, but just that the activities are aimed at obtaining information with the objective of potentially seeking marketing approval. In fact, since there is no guarantee that testing will demonstrate the suitability of a product for receiving marketing approval, the exemption naturally covers tests of products that ultimately fail to meet regulatory or business criteria, for which there will be no request for marketing approval.

It is also important to note that Brazil does not have a common law system, but rather a civil law system. This means there are basically no binding precedents, and lower court judges have significant discretion on how to decide each case. Thus, decisions in Brazil are strongly based on the statutory provisions applicable to the case, and judges are free to give their own interpretation of the law.

d. Scope of Bolar-Type Exemption in Brazil

i. Fields of Technology

The Bolar-type exemption was promulgated in Brazil to address concerns from the pharmaceutical industry. However, the Industrial Property Law does not specify the patent subject-matter in terms of technical fields that qualify for the Bolar-type exemption.

Thus, the exemption is not limited to pharmaceutical products and applies to any patented technology area in which it is necessary to submit regulatory information in order to obtain marketing approval for launching a given product in Brazil or abroad.

Hence, this Article may cover pharmaceuticals, biologics, veterinary products, medical devices, diagnostic devices, MedTech devices, or MedTech software, among others.

ii. Purpose of Experiments/Infringing Activities

It seems that any purposes are acceptable, provided they are for producing information, data, and test results to seek marketing approval in Brazil or abroad.

For example, both importation and manufacturing, solely for the purpose of use in a clinical trial for submission for the purposes of regulatory approval to a regulatory authority, in Brazil or abroad, would be exempt.

iii. Exempted and Prohibited Activities

The Bolar-type exemption exclusively covers the use of the patent subject-matter to produce data aiming at obtaining marketing approval, including any preclinical and clinical trials in phase 1 to 4. Any other preparatory act for the exploitation of a third party's invention are, thus, only allowed after the expiration of the patent.

In this sense, at least in theory, preparatory activities such as stockpiling constitute a form of patent infringement and are not covered by the Bolar-type exemption clause.

However, it is important to highlight that, notwithstanding the above, in an infringement lawsuit (*Astrazeneca v. EMS*, 2021) comprising the exploitation of the pharmaceutical active ingredient *dapaglifozin* (aimed at treating type 2 diabetes) by a third-party company in order to obtain a marketing approval before the Brazilian Health Regulatory Agency (ANVISA), the First Business Panel of the Sao Paulo Court of Appeals (Appeal No. 1023176-84.2020.8.26.0100) acknowledged the Bolar-type exemption in the concrete case even in view of the high amounts of the patented product imported by such company.

In this particular dispute, the panel chose to analyse on a broader basis – rather than in a restrictive manner – the Bolar clause and stressed that the total quantity of the imported product does not matter 'provided that it is used solely for legal purposes, which cannot be commercial'.

Additionally, it should be noted that in this case, the importation of the product to be exploited by EMS had been carried out by a smaller company (Gamma Comercio), whose acts were also considered to be covered by the Bolar-type exemption as per the merit decision issued by the Appellate Judges.

Nevertheless, it is worth recalling that this is a non-binding precedent and one of the few decisions rendered so far that analysed the Bolar-type exemption in an excessively broad manner.

In fact, two years later, curiously the same First Business Panel of the Sao Paulo Court of Appeals – whilst analysing the *Bristol v. Zydus* dispute (2023) – had the opportunity to assess, once again, what would be the protection limits covered by the Bolar-type exemption.

This recent infringement dispute involved the analysis of whether the acts of importing/manufacturing/stockpiling carried out by a generic pharmaceutical company (Zydus Nikkho) concerning the active ingredient apixaban (aimed at treating some thrombotic diseases) – which was protected by a patent that was still far from expiring – for the purpose of obtaining marketing approval before ANVISA, would fall within the scope of the Bolar-type exemption.

In this case, due to a sanitary regulatory provision, the Appellate Judges concluded that Zydus's actions exceeded the scope of the Bolar rule. This conclusion was based on the requirement that, once marketing approval is granted, the company holding the registration must launch its generic product within the final two-thirds of the validity period of the expired registration (Article 12, paragraph 8, II, of Law No. 6.360/76). According to the Panel, in this specific case, complying with this requirement would inevitably infringe upon the patent holder's rights, given the patent's validity period.

By emphasizing that the obtaining of a marketing approval from ANVISA served no purpose and was 'without a practical effect', and also that 'a real and effective danger to the exclusivity rights generated by the patent of invention in question was realized', the Panel decided to rule the case in favour of the patentee, in order to prevent any risk of violation of its rights regarding the patent in question.

This case brought to light an interesting discussion regarding the limits of the Bolar-type exemption in Brazil, which is the risk involved in requesting (and obtaining) a marketing approval before ANVISA very early – that is, long before the expiration term of the patent that covers the reference product – given the need for commercial exploitation of the generic product, starting from the twentieth month once the approval is granted, for the purpose of revalidating this registration.

e. Beneficiary Limitations

Third-party contributions to the Bolar-type exemption have not been directly contemplated by the Brazilian Industrial Property Law or the Courts.

However, if the contributions made by third parties (e.g. clinical research organization, hospital, or clinic) involved performing studies on behalf of the party seeking regulatory approval (e.g. generic manufacturer), they should also be exempted.

f. Territoriality Issues

The Bolar-type exemption applies to activities performed in Brazil to satisfy regulatory requirements in other countries. The Bolar-type exemption likely also applies to activities in other countries for the purposes of satisfying Brazilian regulatory requirements, to the extent that Brazil would have jurisdiction over such activities.

Of course, activities in another country, for the purposes of Brazilian regulatory submissions, may be subject to another country's laws if there is infringement of a corresponding patent in that country.

g. Burden of Proof and Onus

The Brazilian Code of Civil Procedure establishes that the burden of proof lies on the party that claims either a right or a defence. In case a defendant claims the application of the Bolar-type exemption clause, this party will have the burden to prove that such act that involves the use of the patent subject-matter complies with Article 43, item VII, bringing sufficient evidence that demonstrates that the acts qualify as a Bolar-type exemption.

h. Applicability during Patent Term Extension or Supplementary Protection Certificate

Brazil does not have a formal system for patent term extensions where extensions can be granted to compensate for delays in regulatory approval (e.g. Supplementary Protection Certificates in the EU or Patent Term Extensions in the US). The Brazilian Industrial Property Law does not provide a specific mechanism to extend the term of a patent beyond the standard twenty years from the filing date for invention patents or fifteen years for utility models. Previously, there was a provision in Brazilian law that ensured patents would be valid for at least ten years from the grant date (seven years for utility models), which effectively extended the patent term if there were significant delays in the patent application examination process. However, this provision was declared unconstitutional by the Brazilian Supreme Court in 2021. Currently, the patent term is strictly tied to the filing date, without any minimum period of protection post-grant, even in the case of delayed regulatory approvals.

Thus, since the Brazilian Industrial Property Law does not impose any limitation in terms of time for the application of the Bolar-type exemption, the exemption is applicable at any stage during the regular patent term.

In this regard, it is noteworthy that the Bolar-type exemption exclusively covers the use of the patented subject-matter for the production of data to obtain market approval. Any other preparatory act for the exploitation of the invention is allowed only after the expiration date.

4. DIFFERENCES BETWEEN THE TWO EXCEPTIONS IN BRAZIL

In Brazil, both the Experimental Use exemption and the Bolar-type exemption are legal provisions that allow certain uses of a patented invention without the patent holder's prior consent.

The Experimental Use exemption allows third parties to use a patented invention for research or experimental purposes. This is typically aimed at scientific research, testing, or educational purposes to advance knowledge or develop new innovations without infringing the patent. This exemption is quite broadly defined and covers activities such as testing the patented invention to understand how it works, conducting experiments to explore potential improvements, or using the invention in academic research.

The Bolar-type exemption is specifically designed to allow the use of a patented invention in the preparation of data required to obtain marketing approval. The main goal is to enable generic manufacturers to bring their products to market as soon as the patent expires, i.e. without unnecessary delays. The Bolar-type exemption is narrowly focused on activities related to obtaining regulatory approval (e.g. conducting bioequivalence studies and submitting data to health authorities). It applies mainly to the pharmaceutical industry but may also be used in other technology fields that require marketing approval.

While more limited, the Bolar-type exemption can include activities that might not be covered under the Experimental Use exemption, which is generally for non-commercial purposes.

The Bolar-type exemption, which was enacted after the Experimental Use exemption, does not preclude, modify, or limit any further rights a person might have under the Experimental Use exemption. These two exemptions are separate and distinct, that when adequately used in isolation or in combination, are powerful tools to balance innovation incentives with the need to address public health concerns and to help foster innovation while ensuring the availability of affordable medicines in the country.

Chapter 6

Canada

Charles A. Boulakia and Noel Courage[1]

1. GENERAL

a. Terminology

The Experimental Use exemption appears in Section 55.2 of the Patent Act under the heading 'Exception – experimentation'. The Bolar-type exemption appears in Section 55.2 of the Patent Act under the heading 'Exception' and is also referred to in this chapter as the 'early working exception'. It is considered just that – an exception to infringement.

b. Legal Basis in Canada

The Experimental Use exemption was enacted in December 2018 under Section 55.3 of the Patent Act. Prior to 2018 Canada had a common law experimental use exemption.

> 55.3(1) An act committed for the purpose of experimentation relating to the subject-matter of a patent is not an infringement of the patent.
>
> (2) The Governor in Council may make regulations respecting:
>
> (a) factors that the court may consider, must consider, or is not permitted to consider in determining whether an act is, or is not, committed for the purpose set out in subsection (1); and
>
> (b) circumstances in which an act is, or is not, committed for the purpose set out in subsection (1).

1. The authors thank Jessica Sudbury and Alan Harris for their valuable contributions to this chapter.

To date there have not been any regulations made defining any factors that must be considered under this new Experimental Use exemption. To date there have not been any cases that consider the metes and bounds of the statutory exception as codified in Section 55.3(1), though there is a fair amount of case law pre-2018 that interprets the common law defence of 'fair dealing' and 'experimental use'.

The Bolar-type exemption is codified in Section 55.2 of the Patent Act:

> 55.2(1) It is not an infringement of a patent for any person to make, construct, use or sell the patented invention solely for uses reasonably related to the development and submission of information required under any law of Canada, a province or a country other than Canada that regulates the manufacture, construction, use or sale of any product.

Section 55.2(6) provides clarification that the Bolar-type exemption provided under Section 55.2(1) does not impact the more general Experimental Use exemption:

> 55.2(6) For greater certainty, subsection (1) does not affect any exception to the exclusive property or privilege granted by a patent that exists at law in respect of acts done privately and on a non-commercial scale or for a non-commercial purpose.

c. Bodies That May Decide on the Legitimacy of Exemptions

Both the Experimental Use exemption and the Bolar-type exemption are used only as defences in litigation proceedings. In Canada, such proceedings are for all practical purposes under the jurisdiction of the Federal Court since that is the only body that can determine the validity of a patent at first instance. Decisions of the Federal Court can be appealed as of right to the Federal Court of Appeal, and appealed with leave to the Supreme Court of Canada.

2. THE EXPERIMENTAL USE EXEMPTION

a. History and Rationale of Adopting the Experimental Use Exemption

Canada has historically had a 'common law' Experimental Use exemption dating back decades. The rationale of the 'Experimental Use exemption' under common law is generally to mitigate situations where enforcement of a patent could undermine the promotion of progress or frustrate the goals or functioning of the patent system. The aim of the statutory exemption was to codify the common law Experimental Use exemption, such codification occurring in December 2018.

Though the general principles of experimental use have been codified, to date there have not been any regulations made defining the factors that should be considered when determining whether a use qualifies under the Experimental Use exemption.

b. The Laws Applicable to the Experimental Use Exemption in Canada

The Experimental Use exemption was codified in December 2018, as Section 55.3 of the Patent Act. Prior to 2018, Canada had a broad Experimental Use exemption under the common law, with case law precedent, but it had not been codified.

Section 55.3 of the Patent Act states:

> 55.3(1) An act committed for the purpose of experimentation relating to the subject-matter of a patent is not an infringement of the patent.
>
> (2) The Governor in Council may make regulations respecting:
>
> (a) factors that the court may consider, must consider, or is not permitted to consider in determining whether an act is, or is not, committed for the purpose set out in subsection (1); and
>
> (b) circumstances in which an act is, or is not, committed for the purpose set out in subsection (1).

To date there have not been any regulations made defining any factors that must be considered under the new Experimental Use exemption. To date there have not been any cases that consider the metes and bounds of the statutory exception as codified in Section 55.3(1), though there is a fair amount of case law pre-2018 that interprets the common law defence of 'fair dealing' and 'experimental use'.

c. Procedural Aspects of Invoking the Experimental Use Exemption

The Experimental Use exemption is used as a defence in litigation proceedings. In Canada, such proceedings are for all practical purposes under the jurisdiction of the Federal Court since that is the only court that can determine the validity of a patent at first instance.

The exemption can be utilized in all patent proceedings, including standard patent infringement proceedings as well as those under the Patented Medicines (Notice of Compliance) Regulations.

d. Scope of the Experimental Use Exemption in Canada

i. Fields of Technology

There are no field-of-technology-based limitations or restrictions on the Experimental Use exemption in Canada. All types of technology may utilize such an exemption.

ii. Purpose of Experiments

Although there has not been any case law interpreting the 2018 statutory framework for experimental use, the 'pre-2018' common law should still be appropriate for determining the scope of the Experimental use exemption in Canada. 'Experimental use' provides broad scope for entirely non-commercial experimentation but is interpreted in a relatively narrow manner with respect to permissible commercial activities. A leading case[2] has stated that 'all that is required is that the infringing product was made merely by way of *bona fide* experiment, and not with the intention of selling and making use of the product in the commercial sense.'

There is no clear case law with respect to conducting research 'with' a patented technology. Section 55.3(1) refers to '[A]n act committed for the purpose of experimentation *relating to* the subject-matter of a patent'. This language seems to exclude use of patented research tools, for experiments relating to inventions unrelated to the research tool. There is no case law on this issue and related issues for example, whether the exemption may be invoked for using a patented method such as a CRISPR methodology or a DNA amplification technology. However, it is likely that such methods would be determined in the same manner as for conducting research 'on' a patented technology – that is, pure non-commercial, experimental use would likely be able to take advantage of the Experimental Use exemption, even if undertaken by a commercial actor, while commercial use, or use in a process for manufacturing something eventually sold, may not be covered – though there is very little if any case law on point.

Similarly, there is no clear case law with respect to making or using a patented product solely for the purpose of improving on it; however, similarly, it is likely that such cases would be determined in the same manner – pure non-commercial use would likely be able to take advantage of the Experimental Use exemption, as would manufacturing or using a compound solely for the purpose of improving on it, though commercial uses (even without sale) likely would not be able to use the exemption.

Manufacturing or using a claimed compound solely for the purpose of testing its properties has been held to not strictly be an infringing activity: the courts have found that testing Is not necessarily infringement.[3]

Factors that have been considered under common law to assess the nature of commercial activity include the amount of product manufactured, whether the product was sold, whether there was any profit directly related to the infringing activities, any actual financial damage suffered by the patentee, and whether the activities were truly *bona fide*.

iii. Exempted and Prohibited Activities

Section 55.3(1) of the Patent Act provides broad defence, in the sense that it applies to any 'act committed for the purpose of experimentation' and does not appear to be limited to manufacture. Though, for example, importation has not been considered by the courts, it is likely exempted. In other words, manufacture, use, importation, would likely all be exempt if made in the context of experiments that are non-commercial in nature. The courts have also found that testing is not necessarily infringing.[4]

That said, the Supreme Court in *Monsanto v. Schmeiser*[5] gives a broad interpretation of 'use' under the Patent Act (as to what 'use' constitutes infringement) – a rebuttable presumption of 'use' exists merely by possessing a product in Canada.

2. *Merck v. Apotex*, 2006 FCA 323, at para. 109.
3. *Dableh v. Ontario Hydro*, 1996 CarswellNat 2592.
4. *Dableh v. Ontario Hydro*, 1996 CarswellNat 2592.
5. *Monsanto v. Schmeiser*, 2004 SCC 34.

The nature of the use can be important to Experimental Use exemptions. The Federal Court in *Laboratories Servier v. Apotex*[6] articulated that 'the purchase or possession of infringing articles in Canada, with a view to sale or trade … constitutes infringement.'

iv. *Pure Academic vs Commercially Motivated Experimental Use*

There is no requirement that experiments be done for 'academic purposes' having 'no commercial value'. However, the extent of the applicability of the exception to commercial entities or businesses is unclear. Though the testing may have some commercial value, it is important that the experimenter does not see commercial gain from the experimentation – in *Smith, Kline & French Inter-American Corp. v. Micro Chemicals*,[7] an important factor in the Supreme Court of Canada's decision was that the experimental compound was kept by Micro Chemicals and never entered into commerce – additionally, another important factor was that no profits were made from the Micro Chemicals activity.

Micro Chemicals was experimenting to establish that they could manufacture a quality product in accordance with a specification – the experimentation was to test their own capabilities, potentially for commercial use. The Supreme Court of Canada found that the testing nevertheless fell under the Experimental Use exemption (strengthening the notion that there will be a broad interpretation of experimental use for testing an invention to see if it can be reproduced).

> …the fact that an applicant puts himself in a position to show that he is possessed of the equipment, skill and know-how by experimentation does not, in my opinion, make him an infringer.

However, the Court noted that if the experimenter took steps to manufacture and sell the product, the exemption would have no longer applied.

Micro Chemicals acknowledges that an Experimental Use exemption applies to a commercial enterprise; that, *in general*, the common law 'Experimental Use' exemption applies if the following factors are present:

(1) the patented product is produced only in small quantities, commensurate with the research activities;
(2) the product remains in the possession of the researcher and does not enter into commerce;
(3) the use of the patented invention causes no loss to the patentee;
(4) the researcher makes no profits from the activities; and
(5) the research and related activities are *bona fide*.

e. Beneficiary Limitations

Third party contributions do not appear to have been contemplated by courts or the law. However, it appears that if contributions by third persons were also made for *bona fide* experimental purposes, they should also be exempted.

6. *Laboratories Servier v. Apotex*, 2008 FC 825.
7. *Smith, Kline & French Inter-American Corp. v. Micro Chemicals*, [1972] S.C.R. 506.

It is noted that in *Micro Chemicals* (supra) it was determined that there was infringement when Micro Chemicals, which was exempt through the Experimental Use exemption for their primary activity, transferred materials to Gryphon, and Gryphon subsequently manufactured tablets and solicited potential customers.

f. Territoriality Issues

Canadian courts, in general, will only enforce Canadian patents. Therefore, if there was exportation outside of Canada to a jurisdiction that also had a patent, that jurisdiction's laws would likely also apply.

g. Burden of Proof and Onus

There have been no cases to date interpreting burden of proof in the context of Section 55.3(1).

Under the interpretation of the common law and Section 55.2(1), which will likely continue to be the interpretation of the courts, the onus lies on the defendant to prove that the exemption applies.[8]

h. Applicability during Patent Term Extension or Supplementary Protection Certificate

There is no distinguishing between 'regular' patent term and applicability during any patent term extension. Currently the only patent term extension available in Canada is a Certificate of Supplementary Protection. Canada is only currently in the process of establishing regulations for Patent Term Adjustment; the regulations as currently drafted do not appear to distinguish between rights (and defences) available during this period and the regular term of the patent.

3. THE BOLAR-TYPE EXEMPTION

a. History and Rationale of Adopting the Bolar-Type Exemption

The Bolar-type exemption was promulgated in order to prevent the usual regulatory lag between expiry of a patent and generic market entry and was created to balance the newly introduced (at the time) patent linking regulatory scheme known as the Patented Medicines (Notice of Compliance) Regulations, which provided an automatic 2 year stay for regulatory approval for certain patented medicines. See *Apotex Inc. v. Merck & Co. Inc.* (FCA) 2009 FCA 187:

> However, having agreed to respect the 20-year monopoly granted by patents, Parliament wished to facilitate the entry of competition immediately thereafter. It acted to eliminate the usual regulatory lag of two years or more after expiry

8. *Merck & Co, supra*, at para. 170: 'The onus is on Apotex to raise these exemptions and to prove them'.

> of a patent for the generic manufacturer to do the work necessary to obtain a NOC [The Canadian pharmaceutical regulatory approval]. Parliament did so by introducing an exemption from the owner's patent rights under which the generic manufacturers could work the patented invention within the 20-year period ('the early working exception') to the extent necessary to obtain a NOC at the time the patent(s) expired (s. 55.2(1)) and to 'stockpile' generic product towards the end of the 20-year period to await lawful market entry (s.55.2(2)). In order to prevent abuse of the 'early working' and 'stockpiling' exceptions to patent protection, the government enacted the NOC Regulations that are at issue in this appeal. [It is noted that the stockpiling exception under Section 55.2(2) was repealed in 2001.]

See also *Bristol-Myers Squibb Co. v. Canada (Attorney General)*, [2005] 1.S.C.R. 533, 2005 SCC 26:

> Under s. 55.2(1), reproduced in the Appendix, the legislator has created an exception, known as the 'early working' exception, by which companies can make use of patents in conducting studies, such as clinical trials to obtain approval for their product from an appropriate government authority as required by a regulatory scheme such as the Food and Drug Regulations. Thus, it permits utilization of the rights under a patent for the benefit of permitting an earlier launch of second entry products after expiry of any relevant patent. When first introduced, s. 55.2 contained a second exception (s. 55.2(2)) which permitted a person to stockpile patented products during the final six months of the term of the patent, provided that such articles were intended for sale after the expiry of the patent. This 'stockpiling' provision was repealed in 2001 following a decision by the World Trade Organization in which it concluded that this exception violated the terms of the Agreement on Trade-Related Aspects of Intellectual Property Rights, 1869 U.N.T.S. 299 (see WTO, Report of the Panel, 'Canada – Patent Protection of Pharmaceutical Products', WTO Doc. WT/DS114/R, March 17, 2000). Section 55.2 sets forth an equilibrium between the protection of patentees' rights and the exemption from infringement for manufacturers that have to make use of patents in conducting studies, such as clinical trials.

b. The Laws Applicable to the Bolar-Type Exemption in Canada

Canada has a Bolar-type exemption, codified in the Patent Act as follows:

> 55.2(1) It is not an infringement of a patent for any person to make, construct, use or sell the patented invention solely for uses reasonably related to the development and submission of information required under any law of Canada, a province or a country other than Canada that regulates the manufacture, construction, use or sale of any product.

The exemption is drafted in a fairly broad manner, in a sense, in that it relates to *any* use '*reasonably related* to the development and submission of information'. As such, a fairly open and flexible reading of the exemption is warranted. It is also broad in that any federal, provincial, or foreign law that regulates the manufacture, construction, use or sale of product is covered – it is not limited to Canadian federal law, nor is it limited to pharmaceutical regulatory compliance ('manufacture, construction, use or sale of *any* product'). However, the exemption only applies to submissions of information '*required*' under the law. Accordingly, it is unclear, from a reading of the Act, whether voluntary submissions, or submissions that are 'reasonably related to the development and submission of information' to a regulatory authority, but not, strictly speaking, *required* by that regulatory authority, would be covered. The case law, discussed below, clarifies this to some extent, in that activities in contemplation of potential future regulatory requirements should be considered exempt.

c. Procedural Aspects of Invoking the Bolar-Type Exemption

The Bolar-type exemption is used as a defence in litigation proceedings. In Canada, such proceedings are for all practical purposes under the jurisdiction of the Federal Court since that is the only court that can determine the validity of a patent at first instance.

d. Scope of Bolar-Type Exemption in Canada

i. Fields of Technology

While codified to address concerns from the pharmaceutical industry, the Bolar-type exemption is not limited to pharmaceutical products, and applies to any technology area in which it is necessary to submit regulatory information. This includes pharmaceuticals, medical devices, and biologics, like the US Bolar provision, but also includes any other making, construction, use, or sales where submission of information is required under any law (in Canada or elsewhere).

ii. Purpose of Experiments/Infringing Activities

It appears any purposes are acceptable, provided they are for experimental activities relating to compiling information for a regulator. For example, importation, purchase, manufacturing, solely for the purpose of use in a clinical trial for submission for the purposes of regulatory approval to a regulatory authority, in Canada or elsewhere, would be exempt. See section 3.d.iii. below.

iii. Exempted and Prohibited Activities

In *Merck v. Apotex*, 2006 FC 524, Section 55.2(1) was interpreted to include any research and development activity related to a regulatory submission for drug approval. For example, in this case, Apotex was retaining samples, and stored 'in the event that they are required for future reference in accordance with regulatory requirements'. The courts have also affirmed that the exception is not limited to pharmaceutical products. In *Merck & Co. v. Apotex Inc.* 2006 FC 524, (affirmed in *Merck & Co., Inc. v. Apotex Inc.* 2006 FCA 323):

> [153] Section 55.2(1) of the Patent Act provides that it is not an infringement of a patent for any person, such as Apotex, to make, construct, use or sell the

patented invention solely for uses reasonably related to the development and submission of information required under any law of Canada, a province, or any other country that regulates the manufacture, construction, use or sale of any product. This exception is clear and unequivocal.

[154] These provisions have been derived from similar provisions found in the United States Drug Pure Competition and Patent Term Restoration Act of 1994, see 202, 98 Stat. 1585 as amended 35 U.S.C. see 271€(1). That United States statute is more restrictive as it speaks only of requirements under United States law and is limited to drugs...

...

[156] The evidence of the Apotex employees clearly shows that Apotex prepared and used lisinopril and materials incorporating lisinopril for the purposes of obtaining permission necessary to sell lisinopril containing drugs in Canada and the United States. While not all such lisinopril and materials may have been ultimately referenced in those submissions, all were directed in one way or another to that purpose. Such use and such materials are exempt from infringement as provided by section 55.2(b).

[157] In addition, further material was routinely taken by Apotex as samples from incoming raw material and of the finished products. These samples are stored in the event that they are required for future reference in accordance with regulatory requirements. These samples never enter the stream of commerce and are ultimately destroyed.

[158] Drug manufacturers are required to retain samples on an ongoing basis by both Canadian and United States federal regulatory authorities. Provisions for doing so are made under the Food and Drug Regulations, C.R.C. c. 870 in Canada and the Food Drug and Cosmetic Act 21 U.S.C. in the United States. The samples taken by Apotex and retained by it were done so incompliance with these provisions. I find that section 55.2(1) is sufficiently broad so as to exempt from infringement such samples taken pursuant to such regulations and needed for submission of information to the relevant government authorities if and when required. I add that, since such material is never sold and is ultimately destroyed, it is difficult to imagine what damage was suffered by any of the Plaintiffs.

The exemption is not limited to pre-market regulatory approval or to samples or information actually submitted to regulatory bodies, extending to 'any samples which are reasonably related to the development and submission of information under legislation or regulations'.[9]

Uses acceptable under Section 55.2(1) include developing suitable formulations and processes, obtaining regulatory approval to sell commercial formulations, demonstrating commercial scale, storage and testing in retained samples in accordance with regulatory compliance:[10]

[162] I accept Apotex's defence of experimental or regulatory use. Mr. Fahner's evidence establishes that Apotex obtained product for the purpose of (i) developing suitable formulations and processes, (ii) obtaining regulatory approval to

9. *Merck & Co., Inc. v. Apotex Inc.*, 2006 FCA 323.
10. *Apotex Inc. v. Shire LLC*, 2018 FC 637.

> sell commercial formulations, (iii) demonstrating that its manufacturing process could be carried out on a commercial scale, and (iv) ensuring that it tested the active pharmaceutical ingredient when it received and retained samples, in accordance with the regulatory requirements for future testing. Moreover, Mr. Fahner's uncontested evidence is that all retained capsules will be used entirely for future research or making demonstration batches. No use will result in a product that will be sold commercially.

Until 2001, 'stockpiling' was codified under Section 55.2(2) of the Patent Act. That Section was repealed in 2001, and as such 'stockpiling', (i.e. the making, constructing, or using of a patented product during the patented period, for the manufacture and storage of articles intended for sale after the date on which the term of the patent expires) is no longer permitted in Canada. See *Teva Canada v. Novartis* AG2013 FC 141:

> It is settled law (and Novartis does not dispute) that Apotex may claim an exemption from liability for certain amounts of the infringing product. However, in order to claim an exemption under either s. 55.2 of the Patent Act or at common law, Apotex bears the burden of demonstrating that the imatinib inventory was used for experimental or regulatory uses and that no portion of the inventory was or will be used commercially.

e. Beneficiary Limitations

The exemption applies both to generic companies applying for regulatory approval and to innovative companies, for example, when doing competitive studies.

The exemption appears to apply to third parties contracted to perform studies on behalf of the party seeking regulatory approval, though this has not been tested in the courts, since, in all cases, litigation has been against the pharmaceutical company (for example, the generic manufacturer) and not the third party clinical research organization, hospital, or clinic.

f. Territoriality Issues

The exemption applies for otherwise infringing activities performed in Canada to satisfy regulatory requirements in other countries. The exemption likely applies to activities in other countries for the purposes of satisfying Canadian regulatory requirements, to the extent that Canada would have jurisdiction over those activities. Of course, activities in another country, for the purposes of Canadian regulatory submissions, may be subject to another country's laws if there is infringement of a corresponding patent in that country.

g. Burden of Proof and Onus

The onus is on the defendant to prove that the exemption applies. See *Merck v. Apotex*, 2006 FC 524:

> [170] I have found that section 55.2(1) of the Patent Act and the common law as to 'fair dealing' afford exemptions as to certain Apotex activity that would

> otherwise infringe the claims at issue. The onus is on Apotex to raise these exemptions and to prove them.

See for example also paragraph 392 of *Teva Canada v. Novartis* AG2013 FC 141:

> It is settled law (and Novartis does not dispute) that Apotex may claim an exemption from liability for certain amounts of the infringing product. However, in order to claim an exemption under either s. 55.2 of the Patent Act or at common law, Apotex bears the burden of demonstrating that the imatinib inventory was used for experimental or regulatory uses and that no portion of the inventory was or will be used commercially.

h. Applicability during Patent Term Extension or Supplementary Protection Certificate

There is no distinguishing between 'regular' patent term and applicability during any patent term extension. Currently the only patent term extension available in Canada is a Certificate of Supplementary Protection. Canada is only currently in the process of establishing regulations for Patent Term Adjustment; the regulations as currently drafted do not appear to distinguish between rights (and defences) available during this period and the regular term of the patent.

4. DIFFERENCES BETWEEN THE TWO EXCEPTIONS IN CANADA

In Canada, the Experimental Use exemption is quite broadly defined. In comparison, the Bolar-type exemption is limited in many ways, in that it is limited to uses reasonably related to the development and submission of information required for regulatory approval and the like. That said, the Bolar-type exemption is also broader in many ways, in that it can include activities that might not be covered under the Experimental Use exemption, which is generally for non-commercial purposes. Interestingly, when enacting the Bolar-type exemption, Canada wanted to make it clear that the Bolar-type exemption did not preclude, modify, or limit any further rights a person might have under the Experimental Use exemption, and enacted a specific provision regarding this:

> 55.2(6) For greater certainty, subsection (1) [the Bolar-type exemption] does not affect any exception to the exclusive property or privilege granted by a patent that exists at law in respect of acts done privately and on a non-commercial scale or for a non-commercial purpose [the Experimental Use exemption].

Thus, the two exemptions are separate and distinct.

Chapter 7

Chile

Rodrigo Marré Grez and Virgilio Topasio Maluk

1. GENERAL

a. Terminology

Both the Bolar-type and Experimental Use exemptions are recognized in Chile under Article 49 of Law 19,039 on Industrial Property, as amended by Law 20,160 of 26 January 2007 and Law 21,355 of 5 July 2021 ('IPL'). These exemptions are defined as limitations to patent rights and may be invoked as a 'defence' by individuals facing patent infringement claims.

b. Legal Basis in Chile

The Experimental Use exemption is legally enacted in letter b) of the new seventh paragraph of Article 49 of the IPL. The wording of the Experimental Use exemption is as follows:

> The right conferred by the patent shall not extend:
>
> ...
>
> b) To the acts performed for exclusively experimental purposes in relation to the object of the patented invention.

The Bolar-type exemption is legally enacted in the new sixth paragraph of Article 49 of the IPL, in the following terms:

> The invention patent does not confer the right to prevent third parties from importing, exporting, manufacturing, producing or using the subject matter protected by a patent with the sole purpose of obtaining health registration or authorization of a pharmaceutical, chemical-agricultural or other product. The

foregoing does not entitle such products to be marketed without the authorization of the patent holder.

2. THE EXPERIMENTAL USE EXEMPTION

a. History and Rationale of Adopting the Experimental Use Exemption

The Experimental Use exemption was included in the IPL through a legal amendment that entered into force in May 2022, specifically, in letter b) of the seventh paragraph of Article 49 of the IPL.

The principle behind said modifications was to update the Chilean law to meet international standards, and to balance the trade-off between protection and access to technology to promote further investigation and innovation.

It has to be noted that, before the entrance into force of the law amendment that enacted the Experimental Use exemption, it was commonly discussed whether noncommercial and experimental use of patented subject matter were allowed. Thus, the legal amendment made possible to establish clearer rules, although, in practice, there are still some ambiguous aspects.

b. The Laws Applicable to the Experimental Use Exemption in Chile

The Experimental Use exemption is legally enacted in letter b) of the seventh paragraph of Article 49 of the IPL. The wording of said provision is as follows:

> The right conferred by the patent shall not extend:
>
> …
>
> b) To the acts performed for exclusively experimental purposes in relation to the object of the patented invention.

c. Procedural Aspects of Invoking the Experimental Use Exemption

The Experimental Use exemption may be used as a defence in litigation proceedings. In Chile, such proceedings are prosecuted before ordinary civil or criminal courts, which are not specialized IP courts.

d. Scope of the Experimental Use Exemption in Chile

i. Fields of Technology

There are no field-of-technology-based limitations or restrictions on the Experimental Use exemption in Chile. All types of technology may utilize such exemption.

ii. Purpose of Experiments/Infringing Activities

Although there has been no case law regarding the Experimental Use exemption in Chile, Article 49 of the IPL would suggest that it only covers 'research on', as it indicates that the exemption only applies to experimentation 'in relation to the object' of the invention. Therefore, it would not allow to use the patented technology, for example, as a tool for other investigations ('research with').

iii. *Exempted and Prohibited Activities*

Letter b) of the seventh paragraph of Article 49 of the IPL provides a broad defence, in the sense that it applies to any '*acts* performed for exclusively experimental purposes' and does not appear to be limited to specific activities, such as manufacture.

Therefore, it is likely that courts would apply the Experimental Use exemption in broad terms to any kind of activity, such as using, manufacturing or importing, as long as it is done exclusively for experimental purposes.

iv. *Pure Academic vs Commercially Motivated Experimental Use*

Article 49 of the IPL states that 'the right conferred by the patent shall not extend to ... acts performed for *exclusively experimental purposes* in relation to the object of the patented invention'.

In this context, the following are possible:

- Non-academic experimentation could be covered by the Experimental Use exemption.
- The Experimental Use exemption would not cover the use of patented tools or processes (when the investigation does not refer to those tools or processes).
- The concept of 'exclusively experimental purposes' is not completely clear and will depend on the interpretation of the judge of the case. To date, there are no relevant regulations or jurisprudence in connection with this aspect.

e. Beneficiary Limitations

The Chilean IPL does not specify whether third parties can take advantage of the Experimental Use exemption, nor has case law addressed said issue.

We consider that there would be arguments for both positions and that the risks for third parties should therefore be analysed on a case-by-case basis.

f. Territoriality Issues

Patent law applies to the entire territory of the Republic of Chile, to the extent that the patent is registered in the country. Therefore, if the patent is not registered in Chile, third parties would be free to use the object of the same.

g. Burden of Proof and Onus

There is no specific provision that regulates the burden of proof in connection with the Experimental Use exemption in Chile.

Consequently, the general rule of the Chilean system established in Article 1698 of the Civil Code should apply. Said provision establishes that 'It is up to the one who alleges the obligations or their extinction to prove them or their extinction'.

Based on the above, the burden of proof would depend on the wording of the claim and its response. In this context, as the Experimental Use exemption is likely to be used as a defence, it is also likely that the court could place the burden of proof of the elements that allow configuration of the exemption on the defendant.

h. Applicability during Patent Term Extension or Supplementary Protection Certificate

There is no distinction between 'regular' patent term and applicability during any patent term extension. Therefore, the Experimental Use exemption in Chile should apply throughout the validity of the patent, including any extensions.

3. THE BOLAR-TYPE EXEMPTION

a. History and Rationale of Adopting the Bolar-Type Exemption

The Bolar-type exemption was introduced in 2007 through Law 20,160, to meet the standards set by the Free Trade Agreements signed with the United States in 2003 and the European Free Trade Association in 2004. Specifically, it was included in the sixth paragraph of Article 49 of the IPL, as follows:

> The invention patent does not confer the right to prevent third parties from importing, exporting, manufacturing or producing the subject matter protected by a patent for the purpose of obtaining health registration or authorization of a pharmaceutical product. This does not entitle such products to be marketed without the authorization of the patent holder.

This article was further amended in 2022 by Law No. 21,355 to explicitly clarify that it applies to the obtaining of chemical-agricultural and other marketing authorizations. The updated wording of the Bolar-type exemption is as follows:

> The invention patent does not confer the right to prevent third parties from importing, exporting, manufacturing, producing or using the subject matter protected by a patent with the sole purpose of obtaining health registration or authorization of a pharmaceutical, *chemical-agricultural or other product*. The foregoing does not entitle such products to be marketed without the authorization of the patent holder. [Emphasis added]

b. The Laws Applicable to the Bolar-Type Exemption in Chile

The Bolar-type exemption is stated in the sixth paragraph of Article 49 of the IPL in the following terms:

> The invention patent does not confer the right to prevent third parties from importing, exporting, manufacturing, producing or using the subject matter

> protected by a patent with the sole purpose of obtaining health registration or authorization of a pharmaceutical, chemical-agricultural or other product. The foregoing does not entitle such products to be marketed without the authorization of the patent holder.

From the wording of the abovementioned provision, it is possible to establish that the Bolar-type exemption is conceived in strict terms, as it is for the 'sole purpose' of obtaining health registration or authorization, but not for other preparatory acts to commercialize the product whose marketing approval is sought, such as importation, offer or promotion.

However, the Bolar-type exemption is broad in the sense that it is not limited to pharmaceuticals, but it can cover any other product requiring health registration or authorization to be commercialized in Chile.

c. Procedural Aspects of Invoking the Bolar-Type Exemption

The Bolar-type exemption may be used as a defence in litigation proceedings. In Chile, such proceedings are prosecuted before ordinary civil or criminal courts, which are not specialized IP courts.

d. Scope of the Bolar-Type Exemption in Chile

i. Fields of Technology

In connection with the fields of technology, the sixth paragraph of Article 49 of the IPL states the Bolar-type exemption is useful for 'health registration or authorization of a pharmaceutical, chemical-agricultural *or other product*'.

Therefore, it would not be limited to pharmaceuticals but would apply to any product that requires health registration or authorization.

ii. Purpose of Experiments/Infringing Activities

According to the sixth paragraph of Article 49 of the IPL, the Bolar-type exemption only allows the import, export, manufacture, production or use of the subject matter protected by a patent with the sole purpose of *obtaining health registration or authorization*.

Therefore, the Bolar-type exemption does not allow the import, export, manufacture, production or use of the subject matter protected by a patent for other purposes, for example, to research and development of new products, and neither to offer nor advertise the product to be registered before the expiration of the patent.

iii. Exempted and Prohibited Activities

The only activities covered by the Bolar-type exemption as stated in the sixth paragraph of Article 49 of the IPL, are the import, export, manufacture, production and use of the subject matter protected by a patent (and with the sole purpose of obtaining health registration or authorization).

Therefore, the following activities are not allowed under the Bolar-type exemption in Chile:

- stockpiling for commercialization;
- offer of the product before the expiration of the patent;
- storage for the purpose of regulatory compliance (unless it is required for obtaining health registration or authorization).

e. Beneficiary Limitations

The Bolar-type exemption applies to any company carrying out the activities mentioned in the sixth paragraph of Article 49 of the IPL, as long as they are for the purpose of obtaining a marketing approval. Therefore, an innovative company could also take advantage of the Bolar-type exemption as long as it is for that purpose.

Regarding third parties, the sixth paragraph of Article 49 of the IPL, which contains the Bolar-type exemption provision, does not expressly mention whether or not the same covers activities carried out by third parties. Furthermore, case law has not ruled on this issue. However, in practice it is common for certain activities to be carried out by third parties. For example, the performance of tests to demonstrate bioequivalence. Therefore, we consider to be unlikely that a court can consider that third-party activity breaches a patent if there is good faith and a direct link between the contracted activity and the registration process of the concerned product.

f. Territoriality Issues

The sixth paragraph of Article 49 of the IPL does not detail whether or not the Bolar-type exemption is applicable in cases where activities are carried out to obtain marketing authorizations abroad. There is also no case law that addresses this issue. Therefore, we consider that this is an open matter for discussion in Chile.

g. Burden of Proof and Onus

There is no specific provision that regulates the burden of proof in connection with Bolar-type exemption in Chile.

Consequently, it should apply the general rule of the Chilean system established in Article 1698 of the Civil Code, which establishes that it is 'up to the one who alleges the obligations or their extinction to prove them or their extinction'.

In this context, as the Bolar-type exemption is likely to be used as a defence, it is also likely that the court could place the burden of proof over the elements that allow configuration of the exemption on the defendant.

h. Applicability during Patent Term Extension or Supplementary Protection Certificate

There is no distinguishing between 'regular' patent term and applicability during any patent term extension. Therefore, Bolar-type exemption in Chile should apply throughout the validity of the patent, including extensions.

4. DIFFERENCES BETWEEN THE TWO EXEMPTIONS IN CHILE

The Bolar-type and Experimental Use exemptions are distinct and independent of each other. While they may overlap in certain aspects, for example, when experimentation is directly carried out to obtain health registration, their rationale, requirements and scope of application is different.

Indeed, the Bolar-type exemption is clearly defined for certain specific activities aimed at obtaining health authorization, while the Experimental Use exemption is defined in a broader manner so that can apply to cases, for example, in which the investigation does not pursue obtaining an authorization. In any case, the Experimental Use exemption has only recently been implemented in Chile and seems to have a wide range of interpretation, which hinders the clear definition of its boundaries.

Chapter 8

China

Juhua Luo, Amy Feng and Xinlei (Shirley) Wang

1. GENERAL

a. Terminology

The Experimental Use exemption and the Bolar-type exemption appear in Article 75, Items (4) and (5), respectively, under the heading 'None of the following shall be deemed as an infringement of patent rights' in Chapter 7, 'Protection of Patent Rights,' of the Patent Law of the People's Republic of China, which took effect on 1 June 2021.

b. Legal Basis in China

The Experimental Use exemption was first codified in Article 62(5) of the first version of the Chinese Patent Law (Chinese Patent Law (1985)). The Experimental Use exemption is provided in Article 75(4) of the current version of the Chinese Patent Law (i.e., Chinese Patent Law (2020)) which entered into force as of 1 June 2021.

Article 75(4) of the Chinese Patent Law (2020) states:

> None of the following shall be deemed as an infringement of patent rights:
>
> ...
>
> (4) Where any person uses the patent concerned specifically for the purposes of scientific research and experimentation.

To date there have not been any regulations made defining any factors that must be considered under the Experimental Use exemption.

The current Bolar-type exemption was first enacted as Article 69(5) of Patent Law of PRC in 2008 and maintained as Article 75(5) of Patent Law revised in 2020, as follows:

> None of the following shall be deemed as an infringement of patent rights:
>
> ...
>
> (5) making, using or importing patented drugs or patented medical devices for the purpose of providing information required for administrative approval, or making or importing patented drugs or patented medical devices especially for the aforementioned activities.

There is no regulation to further clarify any factors of bounds of the Bolar-type exemption.

c. Bodies That May Decide on the Legitimacy of Exemptions

Both the Experimental Use exemption and the Bolar-type exemption are used only as defences in patent infringement proceedings. In China, patent infringement proceedings include administrative proceedings before the administrative authorities for patent affairs and litigation proceedings before the People's Courts. Accordingly, the body that can make a determination of the legitimacy of an exemption is the administrative authorities for patent affairs and the People's Courts.

2. THE EXPERIMENTAL USE EXEMPTION

a. History and Rationale of Adopting the Experimental Use Exemption

The Experimental Use exemption was first codified in Article 62(5) of the first version of the Chinese Patent Law which entered into force as of 1 April 1985. The wording for the Experimental Use exemption has remained the same after the four amendments to the Chinese Patent Law, namely the first amendment (1993), the second amendment (2000), the third amendment (2008) and the fourth amendment (2020).

The rationale behind the Experimental Use exemption under the Chinese Patent Law lies in the principle that scientific innovations are inherently built upon existing technologies. Specifically, if the use of a patented invention for scientific research and experimentation requires authorization from the patent holder, it could hinder third parties' ability to conduct research and development. This, in turn, would impede scientific and technological progress, contradicting the legislative purpose of the patent law.

Though Experimental Use has been codified for almost four decades, to date there have not been any regulations made defining the factors that should be considered when determining whether a use qualifies under the Experimental Use exemption.

b. The Laws Applicable to the Experimental Use Exemption in China

The Experimental Use exemption was first codified in Article 62(5) of the first version of the Chinese Patent Law (Chinese Patent Law (1985)). The Experimental Use exemption is provided in Article 75(4) of the current version of the Chinese Patent Law (i.e., Chinese Patent Law (2020)) which entered into force as of 1 June 2021.

Article 75(4) of the Chinese Patent Law (2020) states:

None of the following shall be deemed as an infringement of patent rights:

...

(4) Where any person uses the patent concerned specifically for the purposes of scientific research and experimentation.

To date there have not been any regulations made defining any factors that must be considered under the Experimental Use exemption.

c. Procedural Aspects of the Experimental Use Exemption

The Experimental Use exemption is used as a defence in administrative proceedings before the administrative authorities for patent affairs and litigation proceedings before the People's Courts.

d. Scope of the Experimental Use Exemption in China

i. Fields of Technology

There are no field-of-technology-based limitations or restrictions on the Experimental Use exemption in China. All types of technology may utilize such an exemption.

ii. Purpose of Experiments

There are no provisions in the Implementing Regulations of the Chinese Patent Law or the Guidelines for Patent Examination providing definitions for 'specifically for the purposes of scientific research and experimentation' in the Experimental Use exemption. In the book *Introduction to the Patent Law of China* authored by Mr. Yin, Xintian (hereinafter 'Yin Book'),[1] Mr. Yin opined that 'scientific research and experimentation' in 'specifically for the purposes of scientific research and experimentation' in the Chinese Patent Law shall refer to the scientific research and experimentation that is conducted on the patented technology per se. The possible purposes of experiments in the Experimental Use exemption include to determine whether the patented technology is feasible from the aspect of technology, to determine the best embodiments to carry out the patented technology and to explore how to improve the patented technology if the experimenter believes that the patented technology is not ideal and wants to look for another better technical solution.[2]

Factors that may be considered to assess whether the activities are conducted specifically for the purposes of scientific research and experimentation include whether the product was actually used for scientific research and experimentation, the amount of product manufactured, whether the scientific research and experimentation was conducted by the implementer per se or the product was provided to the third party for the scientific research and experimentation, and any actual financial damage suffered by the patentee.[3]

1. Intellectual Property Publishing House, 2011.
2. Yin Book, *ibid.*
3. (2022)ZuiGaoFaZhiMinZhong1472, Supreme People's Court in China.

iii. Exempted and Prohibited Activities

The wording 'specifically for the purposes of scientific research and experimentation' in the Chinese Patent Law provides broad defence, in the sense that it applies to any activities 'specifically for the purposes of scientific research and experimentation' and does not appear to be limited to manufacture. In other words, manufacture, use, and importation would likely all be exempted if they are made in the context of scientific research and experimentation that are non-commercial in nature.

The scientific research and experimentation that are conducted on the patented technology per se include the following activities, which are exempted from patent infringement:[4]

(1) Activities of determining by research and experimentation whether the patented technology can achieve the objects of the invention recited in the description and produced the intended technical effects. The purpose of conducting such research and experimentation is to determine whether the patented technology is feasible or not from the technological aspects.
(2) Activities of determining by research and experimentation the best embodiment for carrying out the patented technology. For example, a process patent concerning certain chemical process provides alternative range of parameters, such as that the reaction temperature shall be controlled to the range of 500-700 Celsius. However, the effect at different temperatures within the range of 500-700 Celsius varies, which does not necessarily meet the actual needs of the users. In such eventuality, the conducting of research and experiments to determine the optimal reaction temperature for the patented process is exempted from infringement.
(3) Activities of exploring improvements to the patented technology. For example, after the work in above 1) and 2), the implementer does not believe that the patented technology is ideal, and wants to find a better technical solution by research and experimentation.

The following activities shall *not* be considered as the activities that are conducted on the patented technology per se, and are *not exempted* from patent infringement:[5]

(1) Activities that are not directed to the patented technology per se, but are additional research experimentations by means of the patented technology. For example, for a product patent concerning certain measuring instrument, if the purpose of experimentation by a company or research institute is to determine the property and accuracy of the measuring instrument, the activities conducted by the company or research institute shall be exempted from patent infringement. In contrast, if the measuring instrument is used as a means for developing another technology in a scientific research project, such activities constitute patent infringement.
(2) Activities that are not directed to the patented technology per se, but are research experimentations which are directed to the other aspects of

4. Yin Book, *ibid.*
5. Yin Book, *ibid.*

the patented technology. For example, if the purpose of experimentation conducted by the experimenter on the patented product is to determine how to modify the existing equipment to make it suitable for manufacturing the patented product, or the purpose of experimentation conducted by the experimenter on the patented process is to determine how to modify the existing process to make it suitable for carrying out the patented process, such experimentations constitute patent infringement.

(3) Activities that are not directed to the patented technology per se, but are research experimentations into the commercial aspects of the patented technology. For example, the following activities are infringing activities: the activities of manufacturing the patented products and making a trial sale so as to determine the market demands of the product, and the activities of demonstrating to the customers the patented products manufactured by the experimenter or the status of using the patented process so as to gain the confidence of the customers.

iv. *Pure Academic vs Commercially Motivated Experimental Use*

There is no requirement that experiments be done for 'academic purposes' having 'no commercial value'. However, the extent of the applicability of the exemption to commercial entities or businesses is unclear.

From (2022) ZuiGaoFaZhiMinZhong 1472 delivered by Supreme People's Court in China, it can be concluded that the following factors shall be considered to determine if the Experimental Use exemption applies:

(1) the patented product is produced only in small quantities, commensurate with the research activities;
(2) the product remains in the possession of the researcher and does not enter into commerce;
(3) the use of the patented invention causes no loss to the patentee; and
(4) the research and related activities are *bona fide*.

e. Beneficiary Limitations

Third party contributions do not appear to have been contemplated by courts or law. However, it appears that if contributions by third persons were also made for *bona fide* experimental purposes, they should also be exempted.

f. Territoriality Issues

The administrative authority for patent affairs and the People's Court, in general, will only enforce Chinese patents.

Manufacturing in China for the purpose of export to a country where the product is not patented is considered an infringement.

If there was exportation outside of China to a jurisdiction that also had a patent, that jurisdiction's laws would likely also apply.

g. Burden of Proof and Onus

To date there have not been any regulations interpreting burden of proof in the context of Article 75(4) of the current version of the Chinese Patent Law.

In the author's opinion, the onus lies on the defendant to prove that the exemption applies.

h. Applicability during Patent Term Extension or Supplementary Protection Certificate

Currently the patent term extension available in China is the patent term extension (PTE) and the patent term adjustment, which have been introduced into the Chinese Patent Law (2020) for the first time.

There is no distinguishing between 'regular' patent term and applicability during any patent term adjustment.

During the PTE period, the protection scope of the patent is limited to the new drug approved by National Medical Products Administration (NMPA), and is limited to the technical solutions related to the approved indications of the new drug. Within this protection scope, the rights and obligations of the patentee remain the same as before the PTE. The protection scope of product claims is limited to the new drug product for use in the approved indications. The protection scope of pharmaceutical use claims is limited to the approved indications of the new drug products. The protection scope of preparation method claims is limited to the production process registered in NMPA for the new drug product for use in the approved indications.

3. THE BOLAR-TYPE EXEMPTION

a. History and Rationale of Adopting the Bolar-Type Exemption

Before 2008, the coexistence of the Patent Law and the administrative approval system for drugs and medical devices created a significant limitation. Competitors were only allowed to begin the pre-clinical and clinical research required for administrative approval after the expiration of a patent term. These research processes often required a substantial amount of time, typically spanning several years. As a result, generic or competing drugs and devices could not be made available to customers, even after the relevant patents had expired.

Such collision between patent, drug and medical laws had unreasonably extended the market exclusivity period of patented drug and medical devices, deprived competitors of their legitimate right to develop and improve competitive products and ultimately harmed the interest of the public.

To shorten the gap between patent expiration and market entry of competitor drugs or medical devices, the Bolar-type exemption was introduced into Patent Law of China when amended in 2008 to allow competitors to make, import and use patented drugs/devices in research to collect enough statistics and information required for drug/device administrative approval.

b. The Laws Applicable to the Bolar-Type Exemption in China

The Bolar-type exemption has been codified in the Article 75 of Patent Law of China as below:

> None of the following shall be deemed as an infringement of patent rights:
>
> ...
>
> (5) making, using or importing patented drugs or patented medical devices for the purpose of providing information required for administrative approval, or making or importing patented drugs or patented medical devices especially for the aforementioned activities.

c. Procedural Aspects of Invoking the Bolar-Type Exemption

In China, patent infringement disputes could be resolved either in a civil litigation before an intermediate level or specialized IP court of China, or in an administrative adjudication before the administrative authorities for patent affairs. And as codified in the Patent Law of China under the Chapter 7 'patent right protection', the Bolar-type exemption can be used as a defence against infringement claims in both civil litigations and administrative adjudications. Accordingly, the courts or the administrative authorities for patent affairs will make the judgement as to whether the Bolar-type exemption is applicable in particular dispute.

d. Scope of the Bolar-Type Exemption in China

i. Fields of Technology

As stipulated in Article 75 of Patent Law, the Bolar-type exemption can only be applied to 'patented drugs or patented medical devices', for which a substantial amount of information needs to be submitted to governmental authorities to obtain administrative approval before entry into market. Currently, it is generally understood that the Bolar-type exemption is limited to pharmaceutical products and medical devices, and does not apply to agricultural chemicals and veterinary drugs.

However, there are cases holding that manufacturing and using necessary patented pesticides to obtain data and information required for regulatory approval of pesticide products are not regarded as patent infringement, but these determinations are not based on the Bolar-type exemption provision in patent law; instead, they rely on other ambiguous rationales, such as the absence of conflict with normal patent use and no harm to the patent holder.

ii. Purpose of Experiments/Infringing Activities

The exemption covers activities whose purpose is twofold:

(1) to enable entities requiring administrative approval to generate the necessary information by making, using, or importing patented drugs or medical devices;

(2) to support the activities described in point 1 by making or importing patented drugs or medical devices for the purpose of facilitating them.

For activities under scenario 2 to qualify as part of the Bolar-type exemption, there must be a factual connection to scenario 1—that is, the activities in scenario 2 must demonstrably facilitate those described in scenario 1.

iii. Exempted and Prohibited Activities

In both the verdicts of (2021) Zuigaofazhiminzhong 702 and (2021) Zuigaofazhiminzhong 1158, the Supreme People's Court of China clarified that offering for sale is not qualified as Bolar-type exemption.

In particular, in (2021) Zuigaofazhiminzhong 702:

> Firstly, regarding subject qualification of Bolar exemption. The Bolar exemption includes two types of qualified subjects: one is the entity who implements the patent in order to obtain the information required for administrative approval of generic drugs and medical devices, and the other is the entity who specifically implements the patent for the former entity. The former entity applies for administrative approval for itself, the latter entity assists the former one in applying for administrative approval. Therefore, the existence of former entity is the premise and grounds for the latter entity to use Bolar exemption defence. In this case, [the defendant] has not submitted evidence of the existence of an administrative approval applicant for the production of rivaroxaban drug. [The defendant] objectively expressed its intention to sell the products involved to unspecified targets through its official website and exhibition promotion, and there is no evidence supporting that [the defendant] only advertise to specific enterprises preparing to apply for registration of rivaroxaban products. [The defendant] itself is not the subject of administrative approval for the application of rivaroxaban drugs. Therefore, [the defendant] is not qualified subject to use Bolar exemption.
>
> Secondly, regarding the scope of activities covered by the Bolar exemptions: The activities included under the Bolar exemption are 'manufacturing, use, and import' for the purpose of providing the information required for administrative approval, as well as 'manufacturing and import' specifically to facilitate the former activities, neither of which includes the act of offering to sell activities.

And in (2021) Zuigaofazhiminzhong 1158:

> The Bolar exemption clause adopts closed enumeration for the types of behaviour adjusted, which means that the scope of behaviour adjusted by this exemption clause should not be arbitrarily expanded to 'offering for sale' that are not enumerated in the clause. It should be noted that Article 75, Paragraph 5 of the Patent Law, which provides for administrative approval exemptions for drugs and medical devices, is a legal provision formulated by legislators to reasonably balance the interests of generic drug companies and brand drug companies. When the third amendment to the Patent Law in 2008 introduced the 'Administrative Approval Exemption for Drugs and Medical Devices' clause, the act of offering for sell had already been introduced in the second amendment to the Patent Law in 2000 and was stipulated as an independent form of infringement

alongside manufacturing, sales, and other behaviour. It can be seen that the legislators clearly did not consider including offering for sale behaviour in the scope of Bolar exemption clause, or in other words, the legislators had intended to exclude offering for sale behaviour from the scope of Bolar exemption.

In addition, the legislature or judiciary application of exemption provisions should be very cautious and rigorous. Unless there is sufficient clear basis or reason, the judiciary should not make overly expansive interpretations of exemption provisions. Therefore, it should be considered that sufficient balance of interests has been made in the legislation regarding whether the offering for sale behaviour belongs to the 'Bolar exemption', and hence this issue is no longer within the scope of judicial discretion.

e. Beneficiary Limitations

The Bolar-type exemption includes two types of qualified subjects: one is the entity who implements the patent in order to obtain the information required for administrative approval of generic drugs and medical devices, and the other is the entity who specifically implements the patent for the former entity.

In this sense, it appears that the Bolar-type exemption could be applied to brand drug companies, generic drug companies or even third party companies contracted with the former two to obtain or facilitate others to obtain administrative approval.

f. Territoriality Issues

The *Guidelines for Administrative Decisions on Patent Infringement Disputes* issued by China National Intellectual Property Administration (CNIPA) in 2019 state that the Bolar-type exemption applies to the provision of information to both domestic and foreign drug regulatory authorities.

g. Burden of Proof and Onus

Since the defendant cites the Bolar-type exemption as a defence against an infringing claim, it is the defendant's burden to prove the activities accused is covered by Bolar-type exemption in a particular case.

h. Applicability during Patent Term Extension or Supplementary Protection Certificate

Currently the patent term extension available in China is the PTE and the PTA, which have been introduced into the Chinese Patent Law (2020) for the first time.

It appears that the Bolar-type exemption would be applied equally to patent term extension (including PTA and PTE) as within the regular potent term.

4. DIFFERENCES BETWEEN THE TWO EXEMPTIONS IN CHINA

First, the Experimental Use exemption broadly applies to any field of science and technology, whereas the Bolar-type exemption is limited to a specific area, namely pharmaceuticals and medical devices, making its scope much narrower.

Secondly, the Experimental Use exemption applies to research and experimentation on the patented inventions themselves, aimed at assessing the feasibility of the patented technical solutions, determining the optimal mode of carrying out them, and exploring potential improvements and the like. In contrast, the Bolar-type exemption primarily applies to the conduct of research and testing of patented drugs or patented medical devices with the purpose of providing information required for administrative approval.

As a result, it would be difficult to categorize the research and testing of patented drugs or patented medical devices conducted for the purpose of providing information required for administrative approval as experimental use under the Experimental Use exemption. Therefore, the two exemptions appear to be separate and distinct.

Chapter 9

Colombia

Andres Rincon and Carlos R. Olarte

1. GENERAL

a. Terminology

In the context of patents, 'privilege' refers to the exclusive rights granted to the patent holder, while 'defence' describes legal justifications that limit liability for patent infringement. The term 'exemption' is used to describe specific legal allowances, such as the Bolar-type exemption or Experimental Use exemption, that permit certain activities without constituting patent infringement.

In Colombia, exemptions to patent rights include:

- *Bolar-type exemption*: Allows generics manufacturers to perform necessary tests and trials on patented drugs during the patented period, in order to seek regulatory approval for marketing of the drug after the patent expires.
- *Experimental Use exemption*: Allows the use of a patented invention exclusively for non-commercial research or academic purposes without infringing the patent.

b. Legal Basis in Colombia

Colombia, like other Member States of the Andean Community, applies Andean Decision 486, 2000,[1] which governs the region's Industrial Property Regime. Article

1. Comunidad Andina, Decisión 486 Régimen Común sobre Propiedad Industrial [Common Provision on Industrial Property]. Gaceta Oficial del Acuerdo de Cartagena No. 600 (14 Sept. 2000).

52 of Decision 486 grants patent holders exclusive rights to prevent third parties from manufacturing, selling, or using their patented products.[2]

Article 53(b) provides for the Experimental Use exemption for 'acts realized exclusively with experimental purposes, as regards the object of the patented invention.'[3]

Regarding Bolar-type exemption, Decree No. 729 of 2012 allows third parties to use the claimed subject-matter to generate the information necessary to support an application for the marketing approval of a pharmaceutical or agrochemical product under the condition that it will not be made, used, sold, offered for sale or imported into the territory, other than for the purposes of meeting marketing approval requirements, before the patent expires.[4]

2. THE EXPERIMENTAL USE EXEMPTION

a. History and Rationale of Adopting the Experimental Use Exemption

The Experimental Use exemption found in Article 53 of Andean Decision 486 is directly linked to the provisions of the TRIPS Agreement (1995),[5] particularly Article 30,[6] which allows Member States to implement limited exemption to patent rights. These exemptions, however, must not conflict with the normal exploitation of the patent or unreasonably harm the legitimate interests of the patent owner, while considering the interests of third parties.[7]

b. The Laws Applicable to the Experimental Use Exemption in Colombia

Article 53(b) of Andean Decision 486:

> Article 53. A patent owner may not exercise the right referred to in the previous article with respect to the following acts:
>
> ...
>
> b) acts realized exclusively with experimental purposes, as regards the object of the patented invention;

---

2. *Ibid.*, Art. 52
3. *Ibid.*, Art. 53 (b)
4. Decreto [Decree] 729, Por el cual se reglamentan parcialmente las Decisiones 486 y 689 de la Comisión de la Comunidad Andina [which partially implements Decisions 486 and 689 of the Andean Community Commission] (2012) (COL).
5. Decisión 486, supra n. 1. Art. 53
6. 'Exemption to Rights Conferred. Member may provide limited exemption to the exclusive rights conferred by a patent, provided that such exemption do not unreasonably conflict with a normal exploitation of the patent and do not unreasonably prejudice the legitimate interests of the patent owner, taking account of the legitimate interests of third parties.'
7. Agreement on Trade-Related Aspects of Intellectual Property Rights (Marrakesh, Morocco, 15 April 1994), Marrakesh Agreement Establishing the World Trade Organization, Annex 1C, The Legal Texts: The Results of the Uruguay Round of Multilateral Trade Negotiations 321 (1999), 1869 U.N.T.S. 299, 33 I.L.M. 1197 (1994) [hereinafter TRIPS Agreement].

c. Procedural Aspects of Invoking the Experimental Use Exemption[8]

In Colombia, patent-related disputes, including those involving the Experimental Use exemption, are generally handled within the framework of a patent infringement case. When accused of infringement, the defendant may raise the Experimental Use exemption as an affirmative defence, arguing and proving that their activities fall exclusively under the scope of non-commercial academic or scientific research.

d. Scope of the Experimental Use Exemption in Colombia

i. *Fields of Technology*

There are no specific technology field limitations.

ii. *Purpose of Experiments/Infringing Activities*

The Experimental Use exemption applies exclusively to non-commercial research activities. There is no case law on point. In principle, it allows experimentation with a patented invention for improving upon it, corroborating scientific principles, or conducting academic research. However, equally in principle, the Experimental Use exemption does not extend to cover activities aimed at commercializing the invention or using it as a research tool for profit-oriented purposes.

iii. *Exempted and Prohibited Activities*

Activities that do not qualify for the Experimental Use exemption include the commercial exploitation of the patented product, including importation, sale, or offering for sale. The generation of experimental data for purposes other than academic or scientific research (e.g., for market approval or commercialization) is not covered by the Experimental Use exemption, but rather by the Bolar-type exemption that will be explained below.

iv. *Pure Academic vs Commercially Motivated Experimental Use*

In Colombia, the Experimental Use exemption is strictly limited to academic research, with no room for commercial activities. If the research directly results in a commercial product or involves any financial gain, the Experimental Use exemption would, in principle, not apply. Again, the quintessential characteristic of the activities typically covered by this exemption is their 'non-commercial' nature. Specifically, the exempted activity should not unfairly curtail the patentholder's essential right to prevent the commercial exploitation of the claimed product (stemming from TRIPS Article 28.1).[9] Evidently, evaluating any fairness or reasonableness standard often involves a difficult balancing of competing interests. Again, there is no case law on point.

8. Decisión 486, *supra* n.1. Art. 53
9. TRIPS Agreement, *supra* n. 7, Art. 28.1

e. Beneficiary Limitations

While Article 53 of Andean Decision 486 does not explicitly address whether third parties can invoke the Experimental Use exemption,[10] the focus on non-commercial research suggests that third parties may benefit from the Experimental Use exemption if they are conducting research under contract for a primary party, provided the research itself remains non-commercial in nature.

f. Territoriality Issues

The exemption only applies within the jurisdiction of Colombia. If the results of the experiment are used to infringe a corresponding patent in another jurisdiction, such act would in principle be outside the personal jurisdiction of a Colombian court.

g. Burden of Proof and Onus

The party invoking the Experimental Use exemption bears the burden of proof, and must demonstrate that the allegedly infringing activity was conducted exclusively for non-commercial, scientific, or academic purposes.

In such cases, the following types of evidence are admissible:

- expert opinions and testimony provided by the parties, which can be subject to cross-examination;
- court-appointed expert opinions;
- site inspections; and
- requests for the production of documents.

Colombian procedural law also allows for pre-litigation discovery motions, enabling parties to conduct site inspections, request document production, and take depositions or obtain testimony from witnesses and experts before the trial begins. This process is designed to gather relevant evidence in support of the party's claims or defences.

h. Applicability during Patent Term Extension or Supplementary Protection Certificate

In Colombia, there is no explicit time limitation on the Experimental Use exemption. Given that the purpose of the Experimental Use exemption is to allow non-commercial research and experimentation regardless of the patent's commercial life, this protection should extend through the entire duration of the patent, including any extensions or supplemental protections granted. Therefore, the exemption remains applicable throughout the extended patent term.

10. Decisión 486, *supra* n.1. Art. 53

3. THE BOLAR-TYPE EXEMPTION

a. History and Rationale of Adopting the Bolar-Type Exemption

Colombia, like other Member States of the Andean Community, applies Andean Decision 486, 2000, which governs the region's Industrial Property Regime. Article 52 of Decision 486 grants patent holders exclusive rights to prevent third parties from manufacturing, selling, or using their patented products.[11]

The original text of Andean Decision 486 does not incorporate a Bolar-type exemption. However, due to bilateral commitments acquired by Colombia and Peru in the framework of Free Trade Agreements (FTAs), Member States to the Andean Community were authorized by means of Andean Decision 689, 2008 to provide internal legislation on this issue on the assumption it would not be considered a violation to the Andean IP Regime.[12] In line with this authorization, Colombia implemented a Bolar-type exemption through Decree No. 729 of 2012.[13] It allows third parties to use the claimed subject-matter to generate the information necessary to support an application for the marketing approval of a pharmaceutical or agrochemical product under the condition that it will not be made, used, sold, offered for sale or imported into the territory, other than for the purposes of meeting marketing approval requirements, before the patent expires.

b. The Laws Applicable to the Bolar-Type Exemption in Colombia

Andean Decision 689, 2008 states:

> Article 1.- The Member Countries, through their internal regulations, will be authorized, in the terms expressly indicated in paragraphs a) to j), to develop and deepen only the following provisions of Decision 486:
>
> ...
>
> e) Article 53: Include the possibility to use the subject-matter protected by a patent to generate the information necessary to support the application for marketing approval of a product.[14][15]

Colombian Decree 729, 2012 states:

---

11. *Ibid.*, Art. 52
12. Comunidad Andina, Decisión 689, Adecuación de determinados artículos de la Decisión 486 - Régimen Común sobre Propiedad Industrial, para permitir el desarrollo y profundización de Derechos de Propiedad Industrial a través de la normativa interna de los Países Miembros [Adequacy of Certain Articles of Decision 486 Establishing Common Regime on Industrial Property, Allowing the Development and Deepening of the Industrial Property Rights Across the Internal Regulation of the Members States]. Gaceta Oficial del Acuerdo de Cartagena No. 1646 (15 sep. 2008).
13. Decree 729, *supra* n.4
14. Member Countries understand this possibility as the Bolar-type exemption that facilitates the granting of market approval requests.
15. Decisión 689, *supra* n.12, Art 1 and 53

> Article 3. Exemption to the right conferred by the patent. In addition to the acts provided for in Article 53 of Andean Decision 486, the owner may not exercise the right conferred by the patent, with respect to the acts carried out to generate the information necessary to present an application for required approval for a product to enter the market once the patent expires. In this sense, third parties will be authorized to manufacture, use, sell, offer for sale or import any object of the patented invention exclusively for the aforementioned purpose.
>
> If a product is manufactured, used, sold, offered for sale or imported under the exemption of the previous paragraph, it may only be exported for the purpose of meeting the approval requirements in Colombia.[16]

c. Procedural Aspects of Invoking the Bolar-Type Exemption

In Colombia, patent-related disputes, including those involving the Bolar-type exemption, are generally handled within the framework of a patent infringement case. When accused of infringement, the defendant may raise the Bolar-type exemption as an affirmative defence, arguing and proving that their activities fall exclusively under the scope of meeting the approval requirements in Colombia.

d. Scope of the Bolar-Type Exemption in Colombia

i. Fields of Technology

As opposed to the Experimental Use exemption, where there are no specific technology field limitations, the Bolar-type exemption is limited to technological fields in which a market approval is required, i.e. pharma, biotechnology, medical devices, food and dietary products.

ii. Purpose of Experiments/Infringing Activities

The Bolar-type exemption applies exclusively to market approval activities. Before the exemption existed, requesting a market approval of a product allegedly covered by a granted patent could be understood as an instance of infringement, providing legal standing to sue with the sole evidence of the market approval request. With the Bolar-type exemption in place, it allows third parties to use the claimed subject-matter to generate the information necessary to support an application for the marketing approval of a pharmaceutical or agrochemical product under the condition that it will not be made, used, sold, offered for sale or imported into the territory, other than for the purposes of meeting marketing approval requirements, before the patent expires. The Bolar-type exemption does not extend to cover activities aimed at commercializing the product while the patent remains in force.

16. Decree 729, *supra* n.4, Art. 3

iii. Exempted and Prohibited Activities

The Bolar-type exemption allows third parties to carry out acts strictly necessary to generate the information of a market approval application, including manufacture, use, sell, offer for sale or import any object of the patented invention exclusively for the aforementioned purpose. There are no specific limitations or a specific time frame to legitimately make use of this exemption, nor particular case law on the matter. However, common wisdom would suggest that the third party may manufacture the product only to the extent required to obtain the necessary material to generate regulatory data, but not to prepare enough quantity for an upcoming launch of a product in a commercial scale. The Bolar-type exemption is limited only to activities linked to obtaining samples for filing with the Colombian regulatory authority and obtaining data required by the regulatory authority. The Bolar-type exemption is not established for commercial purposes. Therefore, it is not aimed to allow stockpiling even with the market approval granted by the authority.

e. Beneficiary Limitations

Article 3 does not explicitly address who has legal standing to invoke the Bolar-type exemption and it is certainly not limited to generic companies, meaning even innovative manufacturers may benefit from it, to the extent it is the same entity that is applying for the market approval, or in the framework of a contractual relationship seeking collaboration for the sole purpose of applying and obtaining market approval.[17]

f. Territoriality Issues

The Bolar-type exemption applies only within the jurisdiction of Colombia. If the results of the market approval request are used to infringe a corresponding patent in another jurisdiction, such act would in principle be outside the personal jurisdiction of a Colombian court.

g. Burden of Proof and Onus

The party invoking the Bolar-type exemption bears the burden of proof and must demonstrate that the allegedly infringing activity was conducted exclusively to generate the information necessary to present an application for required approval for a product to enter the market once the patent expires.

h. Applicability during Patent Term Extension or Supplementary Protection Certificate

There is no explicit time limitation on the Bolar-type exemption. Given that the purpose of the Bolar-type exemption is to allow the generation of information

17. *Ibid.*

necessary for obtaining market approval, regardless of the patent's commercial life, this protection should extend through the entire duration of the patent, including any extensions or supplemental protections granted. Therefore, the Bolar-type exemption should remain applicable throughout the extended patent term.

4. DIFFERENCES BETWEEN THE TWO EXEMPTIONS IN COLOMBIA

Although addressed in different statutes, both exemptions are provided within the Colombian legislation and there are no provisions in the law allowing to understand that both limitations cannot coexist. While the Experimental Use exemption may only be brought exclusively to non-commercial research activities, it is possible to assume that a positive result achieved with those activities may trigger a commercial interest and become a regulatory limitation in the framework of a market approval application for all acts carried out to generate the necessary information. Although both exemptions are useful as an active defence against infringement allegations, the Experimental Use exemption is limited to academics while the Bolar-type exemption would add the fulfilment of a preliminary commercial need of obtaining market approval that, once achieved, would not allow that third party for preparatory acts on a commercial scale.

Chapter 10

Croatia

Sanja Vukina and Mislav Vukina

1. GENERAL

a. Terminology

The Experimental Use exemption appears in Article 98 of the Croatian Patent Act under the heading 'Exemption of exclusive rights'. The Bolar-type exemption appears in Article 98 of the current Patent Act under the heading 'Exemption of exclusive rights'. It is considered an exception of patent rights.

b. Legal Basis in Croatia

The Bolar-type and Experimental Use exemptions were first enacted in 1999 in the Croatian Patent Act. Each subsequent Patent Act also contains Experimental Use and Bolar-type exemptions.

2. THE EXPERIMENTAL USE EXEMPTION

a. History and Rationale of Adopting the Experimental Use Exemption

The Experimental Use exemption was first enacted in 1999, with the rationale of mitigating situations where enforcement of a patent could undermine the promotion of progress or frustrate the goals or functioning of the patent system.

Each subsequent Patent Act also contains the Experimental Use exemption. To date there have not been any regulations made defining the factors that should be considered when determining whether a use qualifies under the Experimental Use exemption.

b. The Laws Applicable to the Experimental Use Exemption in Croatia

The Experimental Use exemption appears in Article 98 of the current Patent Act under the heading 'Exemption of exclusive rights', which prescribes:

> The exclusive right of the patent holder to exploit the invention does not apply to:
>
> activities undertaken for research and development, as well as experimental purposes, related to the subject matter of the patent or supplementary protection certificate, including actions necessary for obtaining authorization to place on the market a product that is a medicine for human and/or veterinary use.

To date there have not been any regulations made defining any factors that must be considered under the new Experimental Use exemption.

c. Procedural aspects of invoking the exemption

The Experimental Use exemption is used as a defence in litigation proceedings. In Croatia, such proceedings are always under the jurisdiction of one of the five IP Commercial Courts.

d. Scope of the Experimental Use Exemption in Croatia

i. Fields of Technology

There are no field-of-technology-based limitations or restrictions on the Experimental Use exemption in Croatia. All types of technology may utilize this exemption.

ii. Purpose of Experiments/Infringing Activities

There has not been any case law interpreting the Experimental Use exemption. Accordingly, it is unclear whether the purpose of the experiments or infringing activities are a factor in consideration of whether the exemption applies. However, it appears to apply to any acts committed that are for the purpose of experimentation.

iii. Exempted and Prohibited Activities

There has not been any case law interpreting the Experimental Use exemption. Accordingly, it is unclear what activities are covered under the exemption. That said, the Experimental Use exemption appears in Article 98 of the current Patent Act under the heading 'Exemption of exclusive rights'. Accordingly, it would be reasonable to interpret the exemption to apply to any exclusive rights granted by a patent, so long as they are committed for the purpose of experimentation, including manufacture, sale, and use.

iv. *Pure Academic vs Commercially Motivated Experimental Use*

There has been no case law interpreting the Experimental Use exemption. However, there does not appear to be a requirement that experiments be done for 'academic purposes' having 'no commercial value'. Any activities that are for the purpose of experimentation, including those that are commercially motivated, should be included.

e. Beneficiary Limitations

There has been no case law interpreting the Experimental Use exemption, and the statute does not specify any beneficiary limitations. Accordingly, third party contributions have not been contemplated by courts or law and remain an open question.

f. Territoriality Issues

Croatian courts will only enforce Croatian patents, or EPO validations in Croatia. Therefore, if there were exportation outside of Croatia to a jurisdiction that also had a patent, that jurisdiction's laws and jurisdiction would likely also apply.

g. Burden of Proof and Onus

There have been no cases to date interpreting burden of proof in the context of Article 98.

h. Applicability during Patent Term Extension or Supplementary Protection Certificate

Currently the only patent term extension available in Croatia is a supplementary protection certificate (SPC). There is no distinguishing between the application of the Experimental Use exemption in the 'regular' patent term and during any patent term extension.

3. THE BOLAR-TYPE EXEMPTION

a. History and Rationale of Adopting the Bolar-Type Exemption

The Bolar-type exemption was promulgated in order to prevent the usual regulatory lag between expiry of a patent and pharmaceutical market entry.

b. The Laws Applicable to the Bolar-Type Exemption in Croatia

Croatia's Bolar type exemption is prescribed in Article 98 of the Patent Act as follows:

> The exclusive right of the patent holder to exploit the invention does not apply to:
>
> activities undertaken for research and development, as well as experimental purposes, related to the subject matter of the patent or supplementary protection

certificate, including actions necessary for obtaining authorization to place on the market a product that is a medicine for human and/or veterinary use.

The Croatian Bolar-type exemption is limited to a product that is a medicine for human and/or veterinary use. Furthermore, it has been widely debated whether the Croatian Bolar-type exemption covers only medicine marketing authorizations or if the Bolar-type exemption also covers authorizations before the Croatian Health Insurance Fund. More than 75% of medicines for human consumption sold in Croatia are either fully or partially paid for by the Croatian Health Insurance Fund. The Croatian Health Insurance Fund may fully pay or participate in payment only for the medicines which are put on the Croatian Health Insurance Fund medicine list. Therefore, for a generic product to effectively enter the market, the generic needs to be put on the medicine list of the Croatian Health Insurance Fund.

In its Decision Pž-2513/2024 dated 8 July 2024, the High Commercial Court determined that the Croatian Bolar-type exemption also applies to the actions necessary for preparing a request to put the medicine on the basic list of medicines of the Croatian Health Insurance Fund.

In its Decision Pž-3335/2024 dated 7 October 2024, the High Commercial Court further determined that actions necessary for preparing a request to put the medicine on the basic *and supplementary* list of medicines of the Croatian Health Insurance Fund is covered by the Bolar-type exemption.

c. Procedural Aspects of Invoking the Bolar-Type Exemption

The Bolar-type exemption is used as a defence in pharma litigation proceedings. In Croatia, such proceedings are always under the jurisdiction of one of the five IP Commercial Courts.

d. Scope of Bolar-Type Exemption in Croatia

i. Fields of Technology

The Bolar-type exemption only applies to the pharmaceutical industry, specifically, to infringement of patents covering medicines for human and/or veterinary use.

ii. Purpose of Experiments/Infringing Activities

The Bolar-type exemption may be used for activities required for obtaining a marketing authorization for a medicine, as well as activities required for adding a medicine to the medicine list (either the basic or supplementary lists) of the Croatian Health Insurance Fund.

iii. Exempted and Prohibited Activities

The High Commercial Court has decided in its Decision Pž-2513/2024 dated 8 July 2024 that the Croatian Bolar-type exemption also applies to the request to put the medicine on the basic list of medicines of the Croatian Health Insurance Fund.

In its Decision Pž-3335/2024 dated 7 October 2024, the High Commercial Court further determined that actions necessary for preparing a request to put the medicine on the basic *and supplementary* list of medicines of the Croatian Health Insurance Fund is covered by the Bolar-type exemption.

e. Beneficiary Limitations

The exemption applies to pharmaceutical companies when applying for marketing authorizations and for putting a medicine on the medicine list (either the basic or supplementary lists) of the Croatian Health Insurance Fund.

There are no cases determining whether the exemption applies to the activities of third parties acting on behalf of a pharmaceutical company, but it is believed that such activities should also be exempt.

f. Territoriality Issues

The exemption applies for the territory of Croatia. Activities outside of the territory of Croatia are not contemplated under Croatian law.

g. Burden of Proof and Onus

The onus is on the defendant to prove that the exemption applies.

h. Applicability during Patent Term Extension or Supplementary Protection Certificate

Currently the only patent term extension available in Croatia is an SPC. There is no distinguishing between a 'regular' patent term and applicability during any patent term extension.

4. DIFFERENCES BETWEEN THE TWO EXCEPTIONS IN CROATIA

In Croatia, the Experimental Use exemption is quite broadly defined and may be applied to any Experimental Use. In comparison, the Bolar-type exemption is limited in many ways. The Bolar-type exemption only covers obtaining a marketing authorization to place on the market a product that is a medicine for human and/or veterinary use and to put a medicine on the list of the Croatian Health Insurance Fund.

Thus, although both exemptions are listed in the same section of the law, they are quite separate and distinct from one another.

Chapter 11

Cyprus

Dr Nikolaos Lyberis

1. GENERAL

Cyprus is a common law country having been a British colony until 1960. The case law of the Supreme Court, as well as of the District Courts, often refers to relevant British judicial precedence which, however, is not binding but rather guides the Cypriot Courts in their decision-making procedure.[1]

Cyprus became a full EU Member State on 1 May 2004. Despite the open political question of the invasion of 1974, the international community, including the European Union (EU) and United Nations (UN), acknowledged the Republic of Cyprus as the only sovereign state entity of Public International Law. Consequently, as of the day of accession of Cyprus to the EU, the *acquis communautaire* was adopted by the new Member State and – at least theoretically – it is applicable on the entire territory of the island. This refers to all fields of EU legislation governing IP rights.

a. Patent Law in Cyprus

i. British Privilege (1960-1998)

As from 1960 (year of establishment of the Republic of Cyprus) until 1 April 1998, the date of enactment of the new Patent Law No. 16(I)/1998 ('Patent Law'), patent protection was granted in Cyprus based only on a corresponding UK patent registration (so called re-registration system). The privileges and rights conferred by a patent registered in Cyprus were in force if the British patent was valid, but without paying patent annuities at the Cypriot Registrar.

1. G. Pikis, *English Common Law, the Rules of Equity and their implementation in Cyprus*, Larnaca 1981, p.75 f., 82.

ii. *Cypriot Patent Law – Accession of Cyprus to the European Patent Convention (EPC)*

Patents are regulated by the Cypriot Patent Law, as amended and valid, in conjunction with the Patent Regulations of 1999, as amended to date.

The accession of the Republic of Cyprus to the EPC (December 1997) led to the incorporation in the above law of provisions enabling the validation of European patents in Cyprus.

The competent authority for the grant of patents is the Registrar of Patents, which is a department of the Direction of Intellectual Property as part of the Registrar's Office for Companies and Intellectual Property. The Registrar's Office is a State Service (Public Administration) of the Republic of Cyprus.

The Cypriot Patent Law provided for the grant of national patents, thereby rendering the registration of a patent in Cyprus independent from the registration of the corresponding patent in the UK, but subject to payment of annuities before the Registrar of Patents.

iii. *Accession of Cyprus to the Patent Cooperation Treaty (PCT)*

Cyprus became a Contracting State of the PCT (December 1997), which was an important change of patent law implemented on 1 April 1998. As of that date, nationals and residents of Cyprus are entitled to file international patent applications through the Cypriot Registrar, the European Patent Office or the International Bureau as Receiving Office.

Furthermore, from the same date it is possible for applicants from abroad to file international applications designating and electing Cyprus. Such designation indicates the interest of the applicant to obtain a European patent that will in due course offer protection in Cyprus under the EPC (Article 75 of the Patent Law). The direct national route on the basis of a PCT application is not possible. In other words, PCT applications can enter the national phase in Cyprus only after a European patent application (EURO-PCT) has been first filed and the patent has been granted.

b. Terminology

There is no Cypriot case law to date dealing terminologically with the legal term *exception* v. *exemption* and the difference(s) between them. They have been approached instead to a very limited extent in theory while commenting on the Cypriot Patent Law.

The term *exemption* is understood as indicating behaviour(s) of a third party that would constitute a defence against a patent infringement claim by the patent proprietor, and as such they are exempted from being characterized as illegal (Article 27(3) and (4) of Patent Law).

The term exemption indicates the legislative limitation of the negative powers that would otherwise enable the patent holder to prohibit certain activities by a third party who makes use of the subject of an invention. Such exempted acts are exhaustively enumerated by the Cypriot Patent Law and are the following:

a. an act concerning a product which has been put on the market by the patentee, or with his express consent, insofar as such an act is performed after that product has been put on the market in Cyprus;
b. an act done privately and on a non-commercial scale, provided that it does not significantly prejudice the economic interests of the patentee;
c. an act of making or using the product for purely experimental purposes or for scientific research;
d. extemporaneous preparation for individual cases, in a pharmacy or by a medical doctor, of a medicine in accordance with a medical prescription or acts concerning the medicine so prepared;
e. supply or offer to supply a third person – other than the patentee – with means, relating to an element of that invention, exclusively for carrying out the invention, if such means are commercial products and the circumstances of the supply of such products do not constitute inducement to infringe the patent.

Accordingly, the term exemption would refer to the use of an invention by a third party that is not considered as infringing, although said use takes place *without* the patentee's consent.

The accepted presumption is that the legislator did not aim at reducing, limiting or depriving the right holder (patentee) of his property's rights, unless there are specific and exceptional circumstances.[2] *Purposive construction* of the exemptions should, however, be available at the discretion of courts. For example, a case concerning the invention of an important pharmaceutical preparation might, under circumstances of the specific case, allow consideration of general interest in terms of public health.

Furthermore, the above exemptions provided for in Article 27(3) and (4) of the Patent Law are *jus cogens*. As such, limitation or even abolishment of the exempted cases by virtue of a contract is prohibited.

c. Legal Basis in Cyprus

Exemptions from patent infringement liability are provided for in the Patent Law.

Specifically, regarding Experimental Use exemptions – among other types of exemptions – Article 27(3) of the Patent Law reads:

> (3) Notwithstanding subsections (1) and (2) of this article, the owner of a patent shall have no right to prevent third parties from performing, without his authorization, the acts referred to in subsections (1) and (2) of this article in the following circumstances:
>
> (i) Where the act concerns a product which has been put on the market by the owner of the patent, or with his express consent, insofar as such an act is performed after that product has been put on the market in Cyprus.

2. P. Polyviou, *Interpretation of Cypriot law*, Nicosia 2023, p.79; Satlanis, Chr., *Methodology of Law for the Cypriot Legal Order*, Nicosia 2018, p.137

(ii) Where the act is done privately and on a non-commercial scale, provided that it does not significantly prejudice the economic interests of the proprietor of the patent.
(iii) Where the act consists of making or using for purely experimental purposes or for scientific research.
(iv) Where the act consists of the extemporaneous preparation for individual cases, in a pharmacy or by a medical doctor, of a medicine in accordance with a medical prescription or acts concerning the medicine so prepared.

To date no regulations or interpretational guidelines have been issued by the Registrar of Patents nor could any case law be located specifying the criteria to be borne in mind when using such defence clauses before court.

Reference to the *Bolar-type exemption* is made in Cypriot Law No. 75(I)/2006 entitled 'The Medicines for Human Use (Quality Control, Supply and Prices)' (transposing Directive 2004/27/EC into Cypriot law), as amended several times until issuance of Law No. 103(I)/2023. This law amends the 'Medicines for Human Use (Quality Control, Supply and Prices)' Law No. 70(I)/2001 (transposing Directive 2001/83/EC into Cypriot law). The provision harmonizing Cypriot law according to EU legislation with regard to the Bolar-type exemption is Article 10B(8) of Law No. 75(I)/2006 and reads as follows:

> Conducting the necessary studies and trials with a view to the application of the provisions of article 10A, subsections (1), (3), (4), (5) and (6) of this article and the consequential practical requirements shall not be regarded as contrary to the provisions of the Patent Law.

The Bolar-type exemption is herewith applicable for generic pharmaceuticals which pursue the grant of a Cypriot or EU marketing authorization invoking a so-called reference medicinal product.[3]

d. Bodies that Are Authorized to Decide on the Legitimacy of Exemptions

Patent infringement cases are adjudicated before the District Court of the respective district where there is: 1) the seat of defendant or 2) the place of infringement. There are six District Courts located in Nicosia, Famagusta, Kerynia, Larnaca, Limassol, and Paphos. Their judicial power covers both ordinary lawsuits and preliminary injunctions when urgent legal interest is invoked.

An appeal against a decision issued by a District Court is filed before the Supreme Court of Cyprus in its appellate jurisdiction.

The above courts are authorized to decide whether invoking the discussed exemptions is legitimate or not.

3. Maucher Jenkins (website publication), *Comparison of Bolar Exemptions Across Europe*, 13 February 2015, as updated on 17 October 2017; see also section 3. Below; https://www.maucherjenkins.com/commentary/update-on-bolar-exemptions-in-europe (2017); https://www.maucherjenkins.com/commentary/comparison-of-bolar-exemptions-across-europe (2015).

There are few cases of patent infringement which have already proceeded to full trial but none of them have so far dealt with exemptions from patent infringement.

2. THE EXPERIMENTAL USE EXEMPTION

a. History and Rationale of Adopting the Experimental Use Exemption

The legislative rationale for the introduction of the Experimental Use exemption is to strike a balance between the legitimate interest of the patentee on the one hand, and that of third parties on the other (Article 30 of TRIPS Agreement). In the framework of this attempt the promotion of research and innovation for the benefit of society should be prioritized. As such, no remuneration can be claimed by the patentee for a third party being exempted from patent infringement liability due to experimental use.

b. The Laws Applicable to the Experimental Use Exemption in Cyprus

With respect to exemptions from patent infringement liability, the Article 27(3)(iii) of the Cypriot Patent Law provides for the research purposes of the use of an invention:

> (3) Notwithstanding subsections (1) and (2) of this article, the owner of a patent shall have no right to prevent third parties from performing, without his authorization, the acts referred to in subsections (1) and (2) of this article in the following circumstances:
>
> ...
>
> (iii) Where the act consists of making or using for purely experimental purposes or for scientific research.

According to Article 27(3)(iii), the patentee is deprived of his right to raise claims against a third party for patent infringement when the act of the latter consists of making or using the subject matter of the patent for purely experimental purposes or for reasons of scientific research.

The exemption of the *use of the invention for purely research purposes* constitutes an important rule of patent law aimed at the promotion of innovation or the avoidance of hindering technological progress in the relevant technical field. This exemption is of essence for conducting basic research. It also touches upon aspects of free and undistorted competition in the market. Consequently, the patentee is not allowed to raise cease and desist claims against third parties, who use the invention solely and exclusively for their research purposes.

c. Procedural Aspects of Invoking the Experimental Use Exemption

Substantial evidence must be presented by the defendant to the competent District Court, which will decide whether there is a legitimate exemption or not. Research protocols and/or laboratory reports, expert opinions, eyewitnesses and sworn statements are some of the crucial evidentiary elements for substantiating an exemption counterclaim in a patent infringement case in Cyprus.

d. Scope of the Experimental Use Exemption in Cyprus

i. Fields of Technology

Almost every invention from all technological branches may, under the applicable legal provisions, be subject to the Experimental Use exemption.

ii. Purpose of Experiments/Infringing Activities

With respect to the purpose of the exempted infringing activities, it should be clarified that this exemption is strictly limited to the experimental use of the invention itself (e.g., reverse engineering). This includes experiments aimed at exploring alternative technical solutions to the same problem, developing improvements to the invention, testing the invention, or investigating whether there are additional, previously unknown outcomes of the inventive activity (such as side effects of a medication). However, using the invention as a research tool to achieve purposes beyond the scope of the patent's protection would require the consent of the patent holder. In the absence of such consent, no exemption would apply, and the user would be held liable for patent infringement.

Exempted use of the invention for research purposes can be not only scientific, but also industrial. This is the case for pre-trials or clinical studies conducted by pharmaceutical companies should these trials be carried out for the above-mentioned admissible purposes. The difference with the Bolar-type exemption is that the latter functions not for academic purposes but rather for the generic manufacturer to be ready to enter the market immediately after the lapse of the patent protection term (see section 3. below).

Research purpose exists also in the framework of academic teaching for the benefit of students and researchers. Such purpose could not be eligible for an exemption counterclaim by the defendant if a specific university is also conducting research on behalf of a company, even less so if said research were conducted on the premises of an industrial enterprise. In the latter two cases only explicitly authorized use of the patent would seem permissible.

iii. Exhaustion of Patentee's Rights

According to Article 27(3)(i) of the Cypriot Patent Law,

> (3) Notwithstanding subsections (1) and (2) of this article, the owner of a patent shall have no right to prevent third parties from performing, without his authorization, the acts referred to in subsections (1) and (2) of this article in the following circumstances:
>
> (i) Where the act concerns a product which has been put on the market by the owner of the patent, or with his express consent, insofar as such an act is performed after that product has been put on the market in Cyprus.

This provision establishes the principle of national exhaustion of the patentee's rights, aligning with the territoriality principle of patent rights in the Republic of Cyprus. For this provision to apply – preventing the patentee from claiming infringement against a third party – the product must have been placed on the market in Cyprus either by the patentee or with their explicit consent. Such consent is deemed to exist when an intermediary is involved in a transaction that reflects the patentee's intention to allow the free circulation of the product on the Cypriot market. Accordingly, any experiments conducted with products purchased from the patent holder, on the Cypriot market are exempted from infringement.

iv. Act Done Privately and on a Non-commercial Scale

According to Article 27(3)(ii) of the Cypriot Patent Law,

> (3) Notwithstanding subsections (1) and (2) of this article, the owner of a patent shall have no right to prevent third parties from performing, without his authorization, the acts referred to in subsections (1) and (2) of this article in the following circumstances:
>
> ...
>
> (ii) Where the act is done privately and on a non-commercial scale, provided that it does not significantly prejudice the economic interests of the proprietor of the patent.

A private and non-professional purported use of the invention refers to the private life of the alleged infringer. This is in compliance with one of the patentability requirements i.e., industrial applicability. In other words, the invention is to be used as an active intervention in economic activities and not in private life. Consequently, the use of an invention not connected to professional activities is not prohibited, according to Article 27(3)(ii) of the Patent Law. A private, non-professional use of the invention can be made, for example, in a family circle or within a close personal friendship.

Any scientifically working person, such as a pharmacist, a medical practitioner, a chemical engineer or a businessman, may be meant under the notion of a professional.

v. Act for the Preparation of a Medicinal Product in a Pharmacy or by a Medical Doctor or Acts Concerning the Medicine so Prepared

According to Article 27(3)(iv) of the Patent Law:

> (3) Notwithstanding subsections (1) and (2) of this article, the owner of a patent shall have no right to prevent third parties from performing, without his authorization, the acts referred to in subsections (1) and (2) of this article in the following circumstances:
>
> ...
>
> (iv) Where the act consists of the extemporaneous preparation for individual cases, in a pharmacy or by a medical doctor, of a medicine in accordance with a medical prescription or acts concerning the medicine so prepared.

This exemption is applicable provided that: a) it refers to the extemporaneous preparation of a medicinal product; b) said preparation is carried out on the premises of a pharmacy; c) for a specific person; and d) for whom an *ad hoc* medical prescription was given. Sales and delivery of such medicines are covered by the exemption. No exemption can be claimed, or exempted activities can cease to be exempted, if the medicinal product is delivered without prescription or is offered to more people beyond the one mentioned in the prescription.

vi. Commercial Products and Circumstances which Do Not Induce a Third Party to Infringe upon a Patent Right

According to Article 27(4) of the Patent Law:

> (4)(a) Subject to paragraph (b) of this subsection, a patent shall also confer on its owner the right to prevent third parties from supplying or offering to supply a person, other than a party entitled to exploit the patented invention, with means, relating to an element of that invention, exclusively for carrying out the invention, when the third party knows, or under the circumstances it is obvious, that those means are suitable and intended to be used for carrying out that invention.
>
> This provision shall not apply when the means are commercial products and the circumstances of the supply of such products do not constitute inducement to infringe the patent.
>
> (b) Persons performing the acts referred to in subsection (3), (ii), (iii) and (iv) of this article shall not be considered to be parties entitled to exploit the invention within the meaning of paragraph (a) of this subsection.

This subsection deals with the prohibition in favour of the patentee, from supplying or offering to supply a third person, who is not entitled to exploit the patented invention, with means being element(s) of the invention that are necessary for the implementation of the invention, if it is known or obvious to the third person that said means are appropriate and destined for execution of the invention.

On the contrary, the patentee cannot prohibit a third party from supplying or offering to supply an unauthorized person with said means, if these are commercial products and their supply does not induce to patent infringement.

Acts performed in the sense of Article 27(3), (ii), (iii) and (iv) are not meant to have been performed by persons entitled to exploit the invention according to Article 27(4)(a) of the Patent Law.

e. Territoriality Issues

The question as to whether the exemption would apply if the results of the experiment are used for infringing a corresponding patent in another jurisdiction has not been dealt with in Cypriot case law, nor has it been discussed in theory. Under any circumstances, extra-territorial applicability of patent law would in principle contravene the rule of territoriality governing the intellectual property laws in Cyprus. Private international law aspects, however, must be considered in such cases. One could argue that no exemption could be claimed under said circumstances in view of a purported patent infringement via another jurisdiction. In other words, the patentee would otherwise be irreparably exposed to unlimited possibilities of cross-border infringements through ordering experiments to be carried out by the infringer extra-territorially with respect to the protected territory of the patent, provided that said experiments are indispensable and their results are destined and used by the infringer in the country of patent protection. It is irrelevant if in the third country, where experiments are carried out, there is patent protection that would allow the patentee to sue the infringer for his acts there.

f. Burden of Proof and Onus

It is the defendant sued for patent infringement who bears the burden of proof for substantiating the Experimental Use exemption applicable to the otherwise infringing activities.

This must be done in that phase of the procedure before the District Courts in which the defendant submits written arguments in defence of the lawsuit. Any such claim raised at a later stage of proceedings will not affect the outcome of the case.

g. Applicability during Patent Term Extension or Supplementary Protection Certificate

The Experimental Use exemption also applies during the term of a supplementary protection certificate (SPC) and a pediatric extension of SPC. This is because, under Cypriot law, the rights of the patentee during the twenty-year patent protection period are applied, *mutatis mutandis*, to SPCs and pediatric extensions to SPCs.

3. THE BOLAR-TYPE EXEMPTION

a. History and Rationale of Adopting the Bolar-Type Exemption

The rationale for adopting the Bolar-type exemption was for the generic manufacturers to be ready to enter the market immediately after the lapse of the patent protection term. This could be achieved by saving time not being obligated to repeat clinical studies and trials before launching their generic products.

Lifting said obstacles for generic manufacturers was in principle successful, except for massive production and stockpiling of their products during the patent protection term of the reference medicinal product, the latter being possible only outside the EU and if good manufacturing practices were applied. Thus, to counter this inefficiency, the SPC Waiver was introduced.[4]

b. The Laws Applicable to the Bolar-Type Exemption in Cyprus

The Bolar-type exemption is provided for in Cypriot Law No. 75(I)/2006 entitled 'The Medicines for Human Use (Quality Control, Supply and Prices)' (transposing Directive 2004/27/EC into Cypriot law), as amended several times until issuance of Law No. 103(I)/2023. This law amends the 'Medicines for Human Use (Quality Control, Supply

4. EU Regulation 2019/933 amending Article 4 EU Regulation 469/2009; D. Lempesi, *The sale of pharmaceuticals*, 2024, p. 206-207; see also section 3.i. below.

and Prices)' Law No. 70(I)/2001 (transposing Directive 2001/83/EC into Cypriot law). The provision harmonizing Cypriot law according to EU legislation with regard to the Bolar-type exemption is Article 10B(8) of Law No. 75(I)/2006 and reads as follows:

> Conducting the necessary studies and trials with a view to the application of the provisions of article 10A, subsections (1), (3), (4), (5) and (6) of this article and the consequential practical requirements shall not be regarded as contrary to the provisions of the Patent Law.

Cypriot Law No. 75(I)/2006 sets out acts necessary for obtaining regulatory approval, and a defendant who raises this defence needs to show that its acts did not exceed those set out in the law.

For example, in case where the generic medicinal product contains esters, ethers, isomers, mixtures of isomers, complexes or derivatives of an active substance as these are included in the meaning of 'active substance', then the applicant for issuance of a marketing authorization for a generic medicinal product shall be obliged to submit additional information providing proof of the safety and/or efficacy of the various salts, esters or derivatives of an authorized active substance.[5] Only actions performed for securing this purpose are exempt from patent infringement.

c. Procedural Aspects of Invoking the Bolar-Type Exemption

The Bolar-type exemption may be invoked with respect to a patent or SPC by the District Courts, in the framework of a patent infringement action, in case the defence is raised by the alleged infringer. The District Courts would decide whether an early working exemption, such as the Bolar-type exemption, for a specific generic pharmaceutical can be claimed by a third party.

The Cypriot authorities responsible for granting marketing authorizations (Pharmaceutical Services, Ministry of Health) and regulating pricing (Pricing Department of Pharmaceutical Services, Ministry of Health) do not consider themselves primarily responsible for protecting intellectual property rights, such as patents, SPCs and potential pediatric extensions to SPCs.

Thus, the Ministry of Health may issue a marketing authorization that would be in force during the patent term, and if a product is launched, a patent infringement action may be brought.

d. Scope of Bolar-Type Exemption in Cyprus

i. Fields of Technology

The Bolar-type exemption concerns generic medicines, bioequivalents and biosimilars all for human use, and processes connected thereto.[6]

---

5. Article 10A(1) of the 'The Medicines for Human Use (Quality Control, Supply and Prices)' Law No. 75(I)/2006.
6. Maucher Jenkins (website publication), *Comparison of Bolar Exemptions Across Europe*, 13 February 2015, as updated on 17 October 2017; M. Stief, *The European Research and*

ii. *Purpose of Experiments/Infringing Activities*

The causal link between the experiments, studies and clinical trials undertaken by the third party, on the one hand, and their aiming at obtaining marketing authorization for a generic medicinal product, on the other hand, is usually the key for considering the admissibility of a Bolar-type exemption claim. Mentioning the name and full data of the reference medicinal product in the request for issuance of a marketing authorization for a generic pharmaceutical is an interesting indication which, however, must be accompanied by further substantial evidence as to whether the legal and procedural requirements and the regulatory scheme for such requests were properly observed by the third party. In this context, the purpose of activities should be clearly explained by the applicant for a marketing authorization for a generic product or at least be reasonably and objectively discernible. Thus, experiments by the applicant purporting to manufacturing a new drug going far beyond the patented composition or process of the reference medicinal product should not be accepted as falling within the Bolar-type exemption.

iii. *Exempted and Prohibited Activities*

A Bolar-type exemption covers by law the preparation of studies and conducting clinical trials for medicinal products. Specifying the exempted and prohibited activities is a matter of interpretation of the relevant legislation mentioned above. Importation, exportation, purchase, or possession of relevant goods with a view to sale or trade should, in principle, fall within the scope of patent or SPC infringing activities. Data obtained through the conducting of relevant experiments should be the property of the patentee or SPC holder and not be disclosed or exploited without an ad hoc consent. Stockpiling should not be permitted considering, among other factors, transparency obstacles and the difficulty of the patentee to locate and investigate storage facilities from where infringing products are put in circulation in the Cypriot market during the protection period of the patent or SPC. Similar situations are often faced because of the application of the SPC waiver (see below section 3.i.).

e. Beneficiary Limitations

The Bolar-type exemption can be used by generic companies only. Expanding the circle of the entities benefiting from this exemption would run contrary to the timely limited legal monopoly of the patentee and be against the principle of interpretation unduly narrowing further the scope of intellectual property rights. Intellectual property rights are intangible assets acknowledged and judicially protected human rights on property including, inter alia, patents and SPCs.[7]

Bolar Exemptions – Background, Status Quo and a Look at the Agreement on UPCA and the EU Commission's New Draft Directive for the Reform of Pharmaceutical Legislation, GRUR International, 73(9), 2024, 824-837

7. 'Movable incorporeal components', T.E. Synodinou, *Property and Trust Law in Cyprus*, Wolters Kluwer, 2020, par. 53 and 328.

According to Article 27(4) of the Patent Law:

(a) Subject to paragraph (b) of this subsection, a patent shall also confer on its owner the right to prevent third parties from supplying or offering to supply a person other than a party entitled to exploit the patented invention, with means, relating to an element of that invention exclusively for carrying out the invention, when the third party knows or under the circumstances it is obvious that those means are suitable and intended to be used for carrying out that invention.

This provision shall not apply when the means are commercial products and the circumstances of the supply of such products do not constitute inducement to infringe the patent.

f. Territoriality Issues

Although no judicial precedence on the Bolar-type exemption could be located, it should apply for otherwise infringing activities performed in Cyprus to fulfil regulatory requirements in other EU Member State(s), but not in non-EU countries.

EU Regulation (EU) 536/2014 on clinical trials on medicinal products for human use is noteworthy from the point of view of the European Internal Market. It established, inter alia, a Europe-wide central system for assessment and approval of clinical trials and a user-friendly EU Portal for all relevant information entries (Article 80 of this Regulation). It also secures transparency in the case of more sponsors. Moreover, if the sponsor – usually a pharmaceutical company or other organization – is seated outside the EU, then a central legal representative must be assigned (Article 74(1) of the Regulation) being responsible for the exchange of communications with the European and each of the involved national competent authorities in the name and on behalf of the sponsor.[8]

Using the results of the experiment infringing a corresponding patent in another jurisdiction should be a matter governed by the law of that other country considering its rules of private international law, unless it is a non-EU country, in which case a Bolar-type exemption should not be expected.

g. Burden of Proof and Onus

It is the defendant in a lawsuit for patent infringement who bears the burden of proof for substantiating the Bolar-type exemption applicable to the otherwise infringing activities.

This must be done in that phase of the procedure before the District Courts (civil jurisdiction) in which the defendant and alleged infringer submits written arguments in defence of the lawsuit. Any such claim raised at a later stage of proceedings will not affect the outcome of the case.

8. On sponsors, CRO, researchers and other parties in a clinical trial contract see: A. Skouteli, *Clinical Trials for Pharmaceuticals*, 2021, p. 126-147.

h. Applicability during Patent Term Extension or Supplementary Protection Certificate

The Bolar-type exemption applies during the protection term of an SPC or an SPC pediatric extension term. This is because, according to Cypriot law, the rules governing the rights of the patentee during the twenty-year protection of a patent are applied, *mutatis mutandis*, to SPCs and pediatric extensions to SPCs.

i. SPC Waiver

The Bolar-type exemption has not completely cured the exclusion of generic producers from the market for the duration of the patent, as it only allows research and the production of experimental products and not their mass production or mass storage. Consequently, generic manufacturers could create a generic version of an original drug with their own original studies, but they could not produce it on a large scale until the patent term of the reference medicinal product expired. As for the storage of finished products in large quantities, this could only be done in countries outside the EU as long as they follow European production standards (Good Manufacturing Practice). Given that the Bolar-type exemption was considered insufficient, Article 4 of EU Regulation No. 469/2009 was amended by EU Regulation No. 2019/933 excluding from the SPC protection products which are destined for export in third countries.

The SPC Manufacturing Waiver Regulation (EU) 2019/933 obtained direct effect in Cyprus in 2019. Said Waiver is subject to notification before the Cypriot Registrar and to the SPC owner so that the latter may inspect whether the SPC right(s) and connected formal and substantial requirements were observed by the third (notifying) party/parties. The notification form needs to be filed at the Registrar's Office for Intellectual Property by a local agent accompanied by the necessary authorization form.

4. DIFFERENCES BETWEEN THE TWO EXEMPTIONS IN CYPRUS

A *prima facie* comparison of Experimental Use and Bolar-type exemptions may show differences from each other as to the purpose of the third party's acts. A closer consideration, however, may lead to the conclusion that there seems to exist a common denominator between them: the Experimental Use exemption is broader as far as applicable fields are concerned, whereas the Bolar-type exemption seems to be broader in types of activities.[9]

9. *See* a comparison between the European and the US approach in: Brian Coggio, '*Experimental use defence at the USPTO: too narrow or too wide?*', *cipa journal* Oct. 2024, vol.53, No. 10, p. 9-13.

Chapter 12

Czech Republic

Jiri Slavik

1. GENERAL

a. Terminology

The Experimental Use exemption codified under Section 18, lit. e) is subsumed, along with Section 17 on prior user rights, in the Patent Act[1] under the heading of 'Limitation of the effects of a patent' in part one, chapter one related to 'Patents for inventions'.

Based on the wording of Section 18, lit. e), this provision includes both – the general Experimental Use exemption, as well as the more specific Bolar-type exemption. Given the structure of the chapter, both exemptions will be treated separately and referred to as the Experimental Use exemption and Bolar-type exemption, although they are part of one legal provision under Section 18, lit. e) of the Patent Act.

b. Legal Basis in the Czech Republic

Section 18 of the Patent Act lists several acts of third parties that shall not be considered as an infringement to patent rights under letters a) to e). Section 18, lit. e) of the Patent Act provides for an explicit basis for the Experimental Use as well as the Bolar-type exemption in the Czech Republic.

> Section 18
>
> The rights of the proprietor of the patent shall not be infringed by use of the protected invention: …

1. Act No. 527/1990 Coll. of 27 November 1990, on Inventions and Rationalisation Proposals (the Patent Act) (as amended up to Act No. 261/2021 Coll. of 1 June 2021).

(c) in the individual preparation of a medicament in a pharmacy based on a medical prescription including acts concerning the medicament so prepared;
(d) in act done for non-commercial purposes;
(e) in act relating to the subject-matter of the invention done for experimental purposes, including experiments and tests necessary under special legal regulation[2] prior to the medicinal product being placed on the market.

c. Bodies That May Decide on the Legitimacy of Exemptions

The Experimental Use exemption (as well as the Bolar-type exemption) is provided by the legislation in the Czech Republic as an exclusion from patent infringement, i.e., as a limitation of the effects of a patent granted to the proprietor. Therefore, upon commencement of court proceedings concerning patent infringement with the competent court (the Municipal Court in Prague is the competent court of first instance in matters of industrial property and the High Court in Prague is the appeal instance), the defendant may invoke this exemption, and the competent court has to rule as to whether the conditions for applying this exemption are met or not, and whether there has been an infringement of patent rights or not.

2. THE EXPERIMENTAL USE EXEMPTION

a. History and Rationale of Adopting the Experimental Use Exemption

The Strasbourg Patent Convention[3] and the Community Patent Convention (CPC)[4] are two regional treaties that have played a significant role in '*Europeanification*'[5] of European patent laws, even though neither of them was ever widely implemented across the whole Europe – the Strasbourg Patent Convention, under the Council of Europe, was designed to harmonize the substantive patent law in Europe (only thirteen countries ratified the treaty or acceded to it); the Community Patent Convention (signed only by nine Member States of the European Economic Community) has never entered into force. Nevertheless, a vast majority of European states have incorporated and harmonized their national patent laws in view of the provisions contained in these treaties, including the Czech Republic. The proposed Article 31 of the CPC relating to the limitation of effects of Community patents included,

2. Act No. 378/2007 Coll. of 6 December 2007, on Medicinal Products and on Amendments to Certain Related Acts (Act on Pharmaceuticals) (as amended up to Act No. 241/2024 Coll. of 10 July 2024).
3. Convention on the Unification of Certain Points of Substantive Law on Patents for Invention (ETS No. 47), signed on 27 November 1963 in Strasbourg.
4. 76/76/EEC: Convention for the European Patent for the common market (Community Patent Convention), OJ L 17 26.01.1976 (amended version was then published as 89/695/EEC: Agreement relating to Community patents, OJ L 401, 30.12.1989, in a failed attempt to revive the Community Patent Convention).
5. Jean-Luc Piotraut *European National IP Laws under the EU Umbrella: From National to European Community IP Law*, 2 Loy. U. Chi. Int'l L. Rev. 61 (2004).

inter alia, the exemption for extemporaneous preparation for individual cases in a pharmacy of a medicine in accordance with a medical prescription or acts concerning the medicine so prepared (implemented in Section 18, lit. c) of the Patent Act), acts done for non-commercial purposes (implemented in Section 18, lit. d) of the Patent Act), and acts done for experimental purposes relating to the subject-matter of the patented invention (implemented in Section 18, lit. e) of the Patent Act).

In its initial version adopted in 1990, the Patent Act included exemptions nowadays listed in Section 18, lit. a) to c): exemption under lit. a) and b) are based on the exemptions provided for also by the Paris Convention;[6] the magistral formula exemption under lit. c) was introduced by the initially adopted version of the Patent Act. It was mentioned in the explanatory memorandum to the Patent Act that this exemption is justified with regard to public health and is also consistent with the international harmonization of patent laws (therefore, in accordance with the above-mentioned aim of harmonization envisioned by the CPC). Thereafter and to date, the Patent Act was amended fourteen times in total.

The Experimental Use exemption under Section 18, lit. e) was introduced by Act No. 116/2000 Coll. of 6 April 2000, on 'Amendments to Certain Acts on the Protection of Industrial Property', which was proposed and implemented due to, among other reasons, the Czech Republic being in preparations for becoming a Member State of the European Patent Organization (EPO) as of 1 July 2002, as well as its previous accession to the World Trade Organization (WTO) on 1 January 1995 as one of its founding members, which included the adoption of the TRIPS Agreement[7] and also in view of the prospective membership of the European Union. Act No. 116/2000 Coll. has (amongst other amendments) broadened the then existing magistral formula exemption (lit. c), so that the 'acts' relating to the medicament so prepared are also considered to be within the scope of the exception, and has introduced a general exemption for non-commercial purposes (lit. d), as well as the Experimental Use exemption (lit. e) itself, without, however, the explicit emphasis on the experiments and tests done for medicinal products (i.e., the Bolar-type exemption).

The explanatory memorandum to this Act does not provide any detailed explanations concerning these amendments and only briefly mentions that these amendments concern the permitted acts of third parties that are expressly provided for by the law. It explicitly singles out the magistral formula exemption (including the disposition of and activities relating to the medicament so prepared) and further states that the exempted activities are in general 'carried out for non-commercial purposes', i.e., acts which are not carried out for profit under the (at the time valid) Commercial Code.

6. Paris Convention for the protection of industrial property of 20 March 1883, as revised at Brussels on 14 December 1900, at Washington on 2 June 1911, at The Hague on 6 November 1925, at London on 2 June 1934, at Lisbon on 31 October 1958, and at Stockholm on 14 July 1967, published in the Decree of the Minister of Foreign Affairs No. 64/1975 Coll. (as amended by Decree No. 81/1985 Coll. of 6 August 1985).
7. The TRIPS Agreement (Agreement on Trade-Related Aspects of Intellectual Property Rights) is Annex 1C of the Marrakesh Agreement Establishing the World Trade Organization (WTO, signed in Marrakesh, Morocco on 15 April 1994 and published in the Communication of the Minister of Foreign Affairs No. 191/1995 Coll. on conclusion of Agreement on establishment of the World Trade Organization (WTO).

It would therefore seem that the legislator, while implementing the Experimental Use exemption based on the CPC directly into the Patent Act, has seen similar purposes in both (or even all) exemptions in Section 18 of the Patent Act, such purposes relating to activities that are not carried out in the context of business activities, i.e., activities carried out for non-commercial purposes and not for profit. This is actually later reflected in some of the case law.

b. The Laws Applicable to the Experimental Use Exemption in the Czech Republic

The Experimental Use exemption has been codified in the Czech Republic as of 10 May 2000, when the amendment to the Patent Act, introduced by Act No. 116/2000 Coll. entered into force, under Section 18, lit. e) of the Patent Act as follows:

> The rights of the proprietor of the patent shall not be infringed by use of the protected invention: ...
>
> (e) in act relating to the subject-matter of the invention done for experimental purposes.

The explanatory memorandum to Act No. 116/2000 Coll. further notes that the exemptions under Section 18 of the Patent Act are to be regulated expressly and specifically and that any extensive interpretation of the scope of the permitted activities in this Section should be eliminated.

The full scope of the Experimental Use exemption as we know it now, under Section 18, lit. e) of the Patent Act (thus, including the part relating specifically to the Bolar-type exemption), has been codified in the Czech Republic as of 31 December 2007, with the adoption of the Act on Pharmaceuticals[8] introducing also certain amendments to the Patent Act, as follows:

> The rights of the proprietor of the patent shall not be infringed by use of the protected invention: ...
>
> (e) in act relating to the subject-matter of the invention done for experimental purposes, including experiments and tests necessary under special legal regulation[9] prior to the medicinal product being placed on the market.

According to the available literature, legal commentaries, commercial databases, the information available from competent courts and the judges, any case law specifically interpreting Section 18, lit. e) of the Patent Act is almost non-existent in the Czech Republic. Thus, any sources suitable to further clarify the scope of the Experimental Use exemption are very scarce. It should be also noted that court decisions, especially lower court decisions and decisions relating to IP matters in general, although they

8. Act No. 378/2007 Coll. of 6 December 2007, on Medicinal Products and on Amendments to Certain Related Acts (Act on Pharmaceuticals) (as amended up to Act No. 241/2024 Coll. of 10 July 2024).
9. Act No. 378/2007 Coll. of 6 December 2007, on Medicinal Products and on Amendments to Certain Related Acts (Act on Pharmaceuticals) (as amended up to Act No. 241/2024 Coll. of 10 July 2024).

shall in essence be accessible to the public, are not being automatically published by the courts in the Czech Republic. Therefore, even identification of the relevant case law itself remains difficult.

c. Procedural Aspects of Invoking the Experimental Use Exemption

The Experimental Use exemption under Section 18, lit. e) of the Patent Act is provided as an exclusion from patent infringement. This provision expressly regulates the permitted acts of third parties that are not considered as an infringement of patent rights. The listed acts, which include experimental use, are therefore considered as a limitation of the rights granted by a patent to the proprietor. Thus, when an action concerning patent infringement is commenced in a court of competent jurisdiction (the Municipal Court in Prague is the competent court of first instance in matters of industrial property according to Section 39(2) of the Act on Courts and Judges[10] and Section 6 of the Enforcement of Industrial Property Rights Act[11]), the defendant may in defence invoke the Experimental Use exemption in that no infringement of the patent rights has occurred. As a result, the competent court will have to rule as to whether this exemption is applicable or not and whether there was infringement of patent rights or not.

d. Scope of the Experimental Use Exemption in the Czech Republic

i. Fields of Technology

The Experimental Use exemption does not distinguish between any fields of technology. Since it is a generally accepted principle of patent law that patents may be granted for inventions in any field of technology, applicability of the Experimental Use exemption shall accordingly and without any express limitation provided by the law be open to any types of patents in any field of technology.

ii. Purpose of Experiments/Infringing Activities

Both domestic and foreign literature note that the Experimental Use exemption forms an integral part of the internationally accepted concept of exemptions to patent infringement (which is highly harmonized in Europe – see section 2.a. above) and that its purpose is to encourage further innovation of inventions described in the published patents and patent applications through follow-up research. It was initially adopted to allow academic research and stimulate further innovation. Therefore, the main objective is to provide the possibility for third parties to freely use the

10. Act No. 6/2002 Coll. of 30 November 2011, on Courts, Judges, Judges and the State Administration of Courts and on Amendments to Certain Other Acts (Act on Courts and Judges) (as amended up to Act No. 285/2023 Coll. of 23 August 2023).
11. Act No. 221/2006 Coll. of 25 April 2006, on Enforcement of Industrial Property Rights and on the Amendment of Industrial Property Protection Acts (Enforcement of Industrial Property Rights Act) (as amended up to Act No. 286/2018 Coll. of 15 November 2018).

protected subject-matter of a patent to, for example, gain new knowledge about the invention, further improve it, investigate its potential new applications or even verify its properties and understand its functioning. It is generally accepted that the activities exempted under the Experimental Use exemption should provide at least some advancement of knowledge in some way.

However, compared to the Private Use exemption (codified in a separate provision under Section 18, lit. d) of the Patent Act) and apart from a purely academic research, activities conducted under the Experimental Use exemption may often be closely connected with potential commercial aspects and will often be carried out with a view to a future commercial exploitation. Setting a bar that should not be too low, on the one hand, so as not to discourage investment into innovation and unduly deprive the patent holder of its negative rights granted by a patent, or too high, on the other hand, so as not to jeopardize possible follow-up research activities and not to artificially prolong the term of the patent, is the main question to be answered when setting the Experimental Use exemption. It is therefore not surprising that even in Europe, courts in different countries adopted various approaches to similar wordings of provision in their respective national laws, sometimes even contradicting each other.

The explanatory memorandum to Act No. 116/2000 Coll. introducing the Experimental Use exemption into the Czech Patent law (at that time, without reference to the specific Bolar-type exemption part) refers to the exempted acts as to activities that are not carried out in the context of business activities, i.e., activities carried out within the meaning of the (at that time valid) Commercial Code for the purpose of making a profit. Therefore, in the context of assessing whether certain activity falls within the Experimental Use exemption or is considered an infringement to patent rights, it seems relevant to take into account the nature of these activities (such that they are not carried out in the course of commercial activities), and the purpose of these activities (such that they are not carried out for the purpose of making a profit).

As noted above, the notion of what constitutes such experimental activities has been interpreted differently throughout Europe. Unfortunately, to date, and as far as the author is aware, this specific point has not been a matter of dispute in any court proceedings in the Czech Republic and therefore either a more narrow or broad interpretation is equally possible. The legal provision emphasizes that the purpose of the activity shall be conducted for experimental purposes – it remains to be seen, whether conducting such experimental activity in view of other purposes in mind as well would be relevant in order for such activity to fall within the Experimental Use exemption and what level of possible commercial exploitation in the future is still acceptable, as long as no profit is sought from that activity.

iii. Exempted and Prohibited Activities

The Experimental Use exemption simply refers to 'act', thus presumably any activity, meeting the above conditions for falling within the Experimental Use exemption seems to be exempted without any limitation as to the type of activity conducted. Given that, conversely, the patent prohibits a very broad array of activities – notably any making, offering, using, importing or stockpiling, which is prohibited without the consent of the proprietor of the patent, said similar range of activities shall, without any explicit limitation in the law, be therefore exempted under the Experimental Use exemption as well. Unfortunately, to date, and as far as the author is aware, this specific point has not been a matter of dispute in any court proceedings in the Czech Republic and therefore no further clarification has been provided.

iv. Pure Academic vs Commercially Motivated Experimental Use

Legal commentaries and specialized literature indicate that experimental activities carried out for the purpose of obtaining new knowledge and without a direct connection of such activities to a business fall within the Experimental Use exemption, while on the other hand, experiments directed towards commercial activities, or experiments carried out to order (i.e., for profit), would generally fall outside of the Experimental Use exemption and would therefore constitute patent infringement.

However, and as mentioned above, research activities may be very often closely connected with a possible commercial exploitation in the future and following the subsequent inclusion of the Bolar-type exemption (which contrary to the preceding principle, is normally conducted in the course of business activities and is very closely connected to future profit making, after the relevant patent expiry) directly into the Experimental Use exemption provision, it remains to be seen how much weight should be given to these criteria and whether (even partially) commercially motivated research and experiments could indeed qualify under the Experimental Use exemption. Unfortunately, to date, and as far as the author is aware, the question of what level of possible commercial motivation of the conducted research activities is still acceptable has been left open by the courts and no further guidance has been provided.

e. Beneficiary Limitations

In comparison to the Private Use Exemption (codified as a separate legal provision under Section 18, lit. d) of the Patent Act) and apart from a purely academic research, activities conducted under the Experimental Use exemption may often be closely connected to, and will often be carried out with a view to, future commercial exploitation. This would be all the more so, if a third party is offering to conduct certain activities or is contracted by another entity to perform such activities in a commercial setting. It would also not be uncommon for commercial entities to make use of universities to perform certain experimental work for which they could even be financially compensated. As mentioned above, legal commentaries and specialized literature indicate that, for example, experiments carried out to order, would generally fall outside of the Experimental Use exemption and would therefore constitute patent infringement. Unfortunately, to date, and as far as the author is aware, this specific point has not been a matter of dispute in any court proceedings in the Czech Republic and therefore it cannot be confirmed or excluded as to whether such activities, and under what conditions, would fall under the Experimental Use exemption or not. However, foreign and especially EU Member State court decisions adjudicating this matter, although not considered binding, may be persuasive for the domestic courts.

f. Territoriality Issues

In view of the generally accepted territoriality principle of patent laws, the Experimental Use exemption under Section 18, lit. e) of the Patent Act shall only apply for activities carried out in the Czech Republic and under the competence of the relevant courts in the Czech Republic (see above). Accordingly, if the result of the acts exempted under the Experimental Use exemption in the Czech Republic are exported and used elsewhere, where a corresponding patent protection applies, it would have to be adjudicated under the law of that country whether importing and carrying out any further acts is considered an infringement to patent rights or not.

g. Burden of Proof and Onus

In proceedings concerning patent infringement, the plaintiff bears the burden of proof in providing evidence to the competent court of any alleged patent infringement. Therefore, if infringement is argued and substantiated by the plaintiff and the defendant wishes to invoke the Experimental Use exemption in order to prove that no infringement of patents rights has occurred as alleged by the plaintiff, the defendant bears the burden of proof to raise this defence in the proceedings and provide sufficient evidence to the competent court that the alleged acts fall under the Experimental Use exemption. To date, and as far as the author is aware, this specific point has not been a matter of dispute in any court proceedings in the Czech Republic.

h. Applicability during Patent Term Extension or Supplementary Protection Certificate

The Experimental Use exemption does not distinguish between its applicability during the patent term and the term of the supplementary protection certificate (SPC). The only extension to the patent term available in the Czech Republic, as *sui generis* IP right, are the SPCs implemented in the European Union for medicinal products[12] and plant protection products.[13] According to this legislation, the subject-matter of the SPC protection is, subject to certain further limitations, confined within the limits of the protection conferred by the basic patent on which the SPC is based. Therefore, the same limitations/exemptions applicable to the basic patent, under the relevant provisions, shall apply to the SPCs as well. Act No. 116/2000 Coll., introducing the Experimental Use exemption into the Patent Act, has also, in view of the prospective membership of the European Union, introduced provisions for national SPCs into the Patent Act, which were fully based on the relevant European SPC legislation in force

12. Regulation (EC) No. 469/2009 of the European Parliament and of the Council of 6 May 2009 concerning the supplementary protection certificate for medicinal products, OJ L 152, 16.6.2009, as amended by Regulation (EU) 2019/933 of the European Parliament and of the Council of 20 May 2019 amending Regulation (EC) No 469/2009 concerning the supplementary protection certificate for medicinal products, OJ L 153, 11.6.2019.
13. Regulation (EC) No. 1610/96 of the European Parliament and of the Council of 23 July 1996 concerning the creation of a supplementary protection certificate for plant protection products, OJ L 198, 8.8.1996.

at that time. The explanatory memorandum to this Act notes that the SPC is a certain extension of the patent term for products that are subject to specific authorization procedures before they may be placed on the market and does also not distinguish between exemptions applicable to patents and/or SPCs.

3. THE BOLAR-TYPE EXEMPTION

a. History and Rationale of Adopting the Bolar-Type Exemption

As noted above, Section 18, lit. e) of the Patent Act provides for an explicit basis for the Experimental Use exemption, as well as the Bolar-type exemption in the Czech Republic. After the inclusion of the Experimental Use exemption in 2000 (by Act No. 116/2000 Coll. – see above), Section 18, lit. e) of the Patent Act was later once again amended by the adoption of the Act on Pharmaceuticals[14] in 2007, that has in itself introduced the Bolar-type exemption in the Czech Republic. At this time, the Czech Republic was already a Member State of the European Union and had to implement, among other things, the newly adopted European legislation, including Regulation (EC) No. 726/2004 on Community procedures for the authorization and supervision of medicinal products for human and veterinary use and establishing a European Medicines Agency (EMA) and Directive 2004/27/EC (amending Directive 2001/83/EC) on the Community code relating to medicinal products for human use, which in itself intended to introduce a harmonized Bolar-type exemption into the European legislation in its Article 10, paragraph 6. This amendment has explicitly implemented the inclusion of 'experiments and tests necessary under special legal regulation[15] prior to the medicinal product being placed on the market' into the previously introduced Experimental Use exemption in Section 18, lit. e) of the Patent Act (i.e., it has finally codified the Bolar-type exemption as being part of the more general Experimental Use exemption in the Czech Republic).

The explanatory memorandum to the Act on Pharmaceuticals, in connection with its proposed amendments to the Patent Act, emphasized the positive impact that could have been expected by this amendment in stimulating the development and research of medicines, including the removal of legal uncertainties in the development of generics while the patent protection of the originator product is in force and the possibility of developing generics even during the patent protection of the original product. In terms of the newly proposed Bolar-type exemption itself, it was noted that with this new provision implemented into the Patent Act, it is now specified that carrying out studies and experiments necessary for the purposes of the registration of medicinal products shall not be considered an infringement of the rights of the owner of the patent or supplementary protection certificate.

14. Act No. 378/2007 Coll. of 6 December 2007, on Medicinal Products and on Amendments to Certain Related Acts (Act on Pharmaceuticals) (as amended up to Act No. 241/2024 Coll. of 10 July 2024).
15. Act No. 378/2007 Coll. of 6 December 2007, on Medicinal Products and on Amendments to Certain Related Acts (Act on Pharmaceuticals) (as amended up to Act No. 241/2024 Coll. of 10 July 2024).

b. The Laws Applicable to the Bolar-Type Exemption in the Czech Republic

The Bolar-type exemption has been codified in the Czech Republic as of 31 December 2007, with the adoption of the Act on Pharmaceuticals introducing also certain amendments to the Patent Act, and has been included into the provision of the more general Experimental Use exemption in Section 18, lit. e) of the Patent Act as follows:

> The rights of the proprietor of the patent shall not be infringed by use of the protected invention: …
>
> (e) in act relating to the subject-matter of the invention done for experimental purposes, including experiments and tests necessary under special legal regulation[16] prior to the medicinal product being placed on the market.

According to the available literature, legal commentaries, commercial databases, the information available from competent courts and the judges, any case law specifically interpreting Section 18, lit. e) of the Patent Act is almost non-existent in the Czech Republic. Thus, any sources suitable to further clarify the scope of the Bolar-type exemption are very scarce. It should be also noted that court decisions, especially first instance court decisions and decisions relating to IP matters in general, although they shall in essence be accessible to the public, are not being automatically published by the courts in the Czech Republic. Therefore, even identification of the relevant case law itself remains difficult.

c. Procedural Aspects of Invoking the Bolar-Type Exemption

The Bolar-type exemption under Section 18, lit. e) of the Patent Act is provided as an exclusion from patent infringement and is included under the more general Experimental Use exemption in the Patent Act – this provision expressly regulates the permitted acts of third parties that are not considered as an infringement of patent rights. The listed acts, which include the Bolar-type exemption, are therefore considered as a limitation of the rights granted by a patent to the proprietor. Thus, when an action concerning patent infringement is commenced in a court of competent jurisdiction (the Municipal Court in Prague is the competent court of first instance in matters of industrial property according to Section 39(2) of the Act on Courts and Judges[17] and Section 6 of the Enforcement of Industrial Property Rights Act[18]), the defendant may in defence invoke the Bolar-type exemption in that no infringement of

16. Act No. 378/2007 Coll. of 6 December 2007, on Medicinal Products and on Amendments to Certain Related Acts (Act on Pharmaceuticals) (as amended up to Act No. 241/2024 Coll. of 10 July 2024).
17. Act No. 6/2002 Coll. of 30 November 2011, on Courts, Judges, Judges and the State Administration of Courts and on Amendments to Certain Other Acts (Act on Courts and Judges) (as amended up to Act No. 285/2023 Coll. of 23 August 2023).
18. Act No. 221/2006 Coll. of 25 April 2006, on Enforcement of Industrial Property Rights and on the Amendment of Industrial Property Protection Acts (Enforcement of Industrial Property Rights Act) (as amended up to Act No. 286/2018 Coll. of 15 November 2018).

the patent rights has occurred. As a result, the competent court will have to rule as to whether this exemption is applicable or not and whether there was an infringement of patent rights or not.

d. Scope of the Bolar-Type Exemption in the Czech Republic

i. Fields of Technology

The Bolar-type exemption is codified under the general Experimental Use exemption in Section 18, lit. e) of the Patent Act. If we were to artificially separate the two exemptions, the part of the provision relating specifically to the Bolar-type exemption in Section 18, lit. e), last sentence, refers specifically to 'experiments and tests necessary under special legal regulation[19] prior to the medicinal product being placed on the market' and contains a footnote in the law referring directly to the Act on Pharmaceuticals. Thus, the Bolar-type exemption itself seems to be limited to the field of medicinal products authorized under the provisions of the Act on Pharmaceuticals. Medicinal products are further defined in Section 2 of the Act on Pharmaceuticals and include a broad range of products, including human and veterinary medicinal products. However, not all such products defined therein are subject to the necessary experiments and tests under this law, before being placed on the market. Therefore, under a strict interpretation, only the products that are subject to such necessary experiments and tests before they may be placed on the market would avail of the Bolar-type exemption. For other products in any other field of technology, it would have to be adjudicated as to whether or not at least the more general Experimental Use exemption under the same provision of the Patent Act would apply in a particular case. To date, and as far as the author is aware, this particular point has not been a matter of dispute in any court proceedings in the Czech Republic.

ii. Purpose of Experiments/Infringing Activities

Apart from the potential limitation to the medicinal products that are subject, under the relevant provisions of the Act on Pharmaceuticals, to the necessary experiments and tests before being placed on the market, the actual wording of the Bolar-type exemption does not contain any limitations as to the specific type of the marketing authorizations of the medicinal product for which the necessary acts are being conducted. As opposed to the intended harmonized Bolar-type exemption under Article 10, paragraph 6 of Directive 2004/27/EC, which specifically refers to the generic (under Article 10, paragraph 1), hybrid (under Article 10, paragraph 3) or biosimilar applications (under Article 10, paragraph 4), the Bolar-type exemption under Section 18, lit. e) of the Patent Act is broader and shall cover also acts that are conducted for

19. Act No. 378/2007 Coll. of 6 December 2007, on Medicinal Products and on Amendments to Certain Related Acts (Act on Pharmaceuticals) (as amended up to Act No. 241/2024 Coll. of 10 July 2024).

the purpose of obtaining, for example, full (innovative) marketing authorizations. This broader interpretation is also supported by at least one literature source.[20]

The included footnote reference in the law to the Act on Pharmaceuticals in the Bolar-type exemption provision regarding the necessary experiments and tests does not contradict this interpretation either, since unlike in Article 10, paragraph 6 of Directive 2004/27/EC, there is no direct reference to the particular provisions of the Act on Pharmaceuticals – all necessary experiments and tests for all types of marketing authorizations are conducted under the Act on Pharmaceuticals, be it for example bioequivalence studies for generic products, submitted under the abridged procedures or pre-clinical and clinical trials for innovative products, submitted as stand-alone dossiers. This does not seem to be affected by the fact that the provisions of the Act on Pharmaceuticals further state that the legal protection of industrial property and trade secrets is not affected in relation to applications for marketing authorizations for generic (Section 27, paragraph 1) and well-established use products (Section 27, paragraph 7), where the applicant is not obliged to submit the results of pre-clinical tests and clinical trials. In terms of the Bolar-type exemption itself, the explanatory memorandum of the Act on Pharmaceuticals again simply refers to the registration of medicinal products in general. To date, and as far as the author is aware, this particular point has not been a matter of dispute in any court proceedings in the Czech Republic.

In *Teva v. Synthon,*[21] the acts considered by the court to fall within the Bolar-type exemption were carried out in the Czech Republic for the purpose of obtaining a marketing authorization for a hybrid generic product (thereby falling also under Article 10, paragraph 3 of Directive 2004/27/EC) and there was no dispute as to the qualification of such product and its marketing authorization to fall under the Bolar-type exemption.

iii. Exempted and Prohibited Activities

The Experimental Use exemption simply refers to 'act', whereas the part of that provision referred to as the Bolar-type exemption states, 'including experiments and tests'. Since both exemptions are part of one legal provision in the law and given the overall wording of that single provision, such that the more general Experimental Use exemption *includes* also experiments and tests, it does not appear sensible to consider that, while assuming that any activity meeting the conditions for falling under the Experimental Use exemption is exempted (see above in section 2.d.iii.),

---

20. European Commission: Directorate-General for Internal Market, Industry, Entrepreneurship and SMEs, Romandini, R., Kur, A., Walz, A., Valtere, L. et al., *Study on the legal aspects of supplementary protection certificates in the EU – Final report*, Publications Office of the European Union, 2018.
21. Decision of the Municipal Court in Prague of 14 November 2017 in *Teva v. Synthon* (case no. 1 Cm 8/2015) – an action for a declaratory judgment seeking that 2993 grams of glatiramer acetate held on stock by the defendant as reference samples (and detained by the customs authorities in the Czech Republic, based on a national application by the patent holder requesting to take action under Act No. 355/2014 Coll.), infringes patent no. CZ 292 247 of which the plaintiff was a registered exclusive licensee.

strictly only enumerated *experiments* and *tests* would be exempted under the Bolar-type provision, when trying to interpret them separately. Such interpretation would also appear to be contrary and more restricted compared to the intended harmonized Bolar-type exemption under Article 10, paragraph 6 of Directive 2004/27/EC that, apart from the necessary studies and trials additionally also covers 'consequential practical requirements' of said activities.

Moreover, for example in *Teva v. Synthon*,[22] stockpiling of the reference samples (which is mandatory under the rules governing medicinal products in the EU Member States) from the batches manufactured solely for the purpose of conducting clinical trials and studies for the purpose of obtaining marketing authorization in the EU (of a hybrid generic product in this case), was considered to fall within the activities covered by the Bolar-type exemption (and in general, was considered as a non-commercial activity as well, with reference also to Section 18, lit. d) of the Patent Act). This further supports the view that the exempted activities under the Bolar-type exemption are covered more broadly, as long as they are related to the purpose of registering medicinal products prior to placing them on the market (i.e., obtaining a marketing authorization) and presumably to non-commercial activities without the aim of making profit.

Furthermore, and although not expressly adjudicated to fall under the Bolar-type exemption provision under Section 18, lit. e) of the Patent Act, the courts have considered that at least the filing of the application for the determination of the maximum price or the amount and terms of reimbursement (under the Act No. 48/1997 Coll. on Public Health Insurance) for generic medicinal products does not constitute infringement of patent rights by offering or an act of unfair competition. In *Merck Canada v. Genericon*,[23] a preliminary injunction was denied, and the court has stated that the defendant cannot be criticized for taking all the necessary preliminary steps to enter the market immediately after the expiry of the patent. On the contrary, the court has considered that granting a preliminary injunction would give the applicant an undue competitive advantage which would effectively prolong its patent monopoly and exclude competitors from the market beyond expiry of the patent. This approach generally corresponds to the European Commission's view stated already in 2009 in the Summary of the Pharmaceutical Sector Inquiry Report[24] (see point 1598) in that applications for pricing and reimbursement status shall not constitute a patent violation, following the same logic as when applying for marketing authorizations (also without direct reference to the Bolar-type exemption therein).

---

22. Decision of the Municipal Court in Prague of 14 November 2017 in *Teva v. Synthon* (case no. 1 Cm 8/2015) – an action for a declaratory judgment seeking that 2993 grams of glatiramer acetate held on stock by the defendant as reference samples (and detained by the customs authorities in the Czech Republic, based on a national application by the patent holder requesting to take action under Act No. 355/2014 Coll.), infringes patent no. CZ 292 247 of which the plaintiff was a registered exclusive licensee.
23. Order of the Municipal Court in Prague of 4 August 2011 in *Merck Canada v. Genericon* (case no. 2 Nc 1066/2011) – an application for a preliminary injunction. Dismissal of the application for a preliminary injunction was upheld in appeal by the order of the High Court in Prague of 30 December 2011 (case no. 3 Cmo 308/2011).
24. European Commission, *Pharmaceutical Sector Inquiry – Final Report*, 8 July 2009.

e. Beneficiary Limitations

In comparison to the Private Use exemption (codified as a separate legal provision under Section 18, lit. d) of the Patent Act), the research conducted under the Bolar-type exemption is closely connected to business activities and is conducted with a view to potential future commercial exploitation after expiry of the patent – this is even more true for acts related to the Bolar-type exemption itself, compared to acts purely related to the general Experimental Use exemption, as discussed above. Moreover, the acts solely covered by the Bolar-type exemption may not always relate to the purpose of gaining or generating new knowledge about the subject-matter of the invention. Rather, the Bolar-type exemption sets a legal fiction under which such allowed acts shall not be considered infringement of patent rights and may be carried out even during the period under which the intellectual property rights are in force, in view of the broader public interest of allowing medicinal products to be placed on the market at a later stage, and right after expiry of the relevant patent protection.

The commercial exploitation and different purpose of the acts presumably covered by the Bolar-type exemption could become even more relevant in cases where a third party is offering to conduct certain activities or is contracted by another entity to perform such activities in a commercial setting (*e.g.*, a supplier of the active pharmaceutical ingredient, a contract manufacturing organization for manufacturing of the drug product, or a contract research organization carrying out certain tests and experiments, performing clinical trials or bioequivalence studies) – such approach is not an exception in the pharmaceutical industry, since not all pharmaceutical companies can reasonably be expected to carry out all the necessary steps on their own. On the contrary, it is very common and usually the case that several entities in different countries are part of the development and manufacturing of a medicinal product, which is also utilized in the preparatory steps prior to obtaining a marketing authorization and before placing the medicinal product on the market. It should be noted that neither the Bolar-type exemption provision nor the provisions of the Act on Pharmaceuticals contain any express limitation as to the entity conducting said experiments and tests.

In the context of Article 10, paragraph 6 of Directive 2004/27/EC, the question as to whether this exemption applies also to third parties, and under which conditions, was referred for a preliminary ruling to the Court of Justice of the European Union (Case C-661/13, *Astellas v. Polpharma*[25]), which would have provided a binding interpretation for the courts of the Member States. However, the case was settled, and the referral was withdrawn before any ruling was rendered. Unfortunately, to date, and as far as the author is aware, this specific point has not been a matter of dispute in any court proceedings in the Czech Republic and therefore it cannot be confirmed or excluded, as to whether such activities, and under what conditions, would fall under the Bolar-type exemption. However, foreign and especially decisions of the other Member States courts on this matter, although not considered binding, may be persuasive for the domestic courts.

25. Request for a preliminary ruling from the Oberlandesgericht Düsseldorf (Germany) lodged on 13 December 2013 – Case C-661/13, *Astellas Pharma Inc. v. Polpharma SA Pharmaceutical Works*, 07.05.2014, ECLI:EU:C:2014:588.

f. Territoriality Issues

In view of the generally accepted territoriality principle of patent laws, the Bolar-type exemption under Section 18, lit. e) of the Patent Act shall only apply to activities carried out in the Czech Republic and under the competence of the relevant courts in the Czech Republic (see above). Accordingly, if the result of the acts exempted under the Bolar-type exemption in the Czech Republic are exported and used elsewhere, where a corresponding patent protection applies, it would have to be adjudicated under the law of that country whether importing and carrying out any further acts is considered an infringement to patent rights or not.

The actual wording of the Bolar-type exemption (and the general Experimental Use exemption) does not expressly contain any limitations as to whether the acts carried out under that exemption are limited only for the purpose of obtaining a marketing authorization of medicinal products in the Czech Republic. According to at least one source,[26] this implies that the Bolar-type exemption in the Czech Republic encompasses also studies directed to generate data for obtaining a marketing authorization in third countries, thereby also outside the EU Member States.

On the other hand, the Bolar-type exemption refers to 'experiments and tests necessary under special legal regulation',[27] with a footnote in the law that said special legal regulation is the Act on Pharmaceuticals. Another reasonable interpretation could equally be that this reference in the law implies certain limitation, in that only experiments and tests necessary to apply for a marketing authorization according to the Act on Pharmaceuticals may be exempted under that provision. As the Act on Pharmaceuticals (that has in its initially adopted version amended the Patent Act to include the Bolar-type exemption, see section 3.a. above) was adopted in view of the new EU legislation and relates not only to purely national procedures, but also to the decentralized and mutual recognition procedures, as well as centralized procedures, it would seem appropriate that the provision covers at least activities necessary for obtaining marketing authorization in the EU, following any of these procedures. Moreover, the relevant activities carried out for the purpose of obtaining marketing authorization of a medicinal product often overlap within commercial environments and cannot be easily *separated (e.g., distinguishing* between activities carried out for the purpose of obtaining marketing authorization in the EU vs. for third countries). It therefore seems sensible not to limit the Bolar-type exemption solely to the activities necessary for obtaining marketing authorization in the EU, but to include those conducted for marketing authorizations abroad as well. The same conclusion follows from the AIPPI Resolution in this matter (see point 10 of the Resolution[28]).

---

26. European Commission: Directorate-General for Internal Market, Industry, Entrepreneurship and SMEs, Romandini, R., Kur, A., Walz, A., Valtere, L. et al., *Study on the legal aspects of supplementary protection certificates in the EU – Final report*, Publications Office of the European Union, 2018.
27. Act No. 378/2007 Coll. of 6 December 2007, on Medicinal Products and on Amendments to Certain Related Acts (Act on Pharmaceuticals) (as amended up to Act No. 241/2024 Coll. of 10 July 2024).
28. AIPPI Adopted Resolution on Experimental Use and Bolar-type Exemptions (Q288), 2023 AIPPI World Congress – Istanbul, 25 October 2023.

In *Teva v. Synthon*,[29] the acts considered by the court to fall within the Bolar-type exemption were carried out in the Czech Republic for the purpose of obtaining a marketing authorization in the EU via the mutual recognition procedure, with the Reference Member State being the Netherlands, and the Czech Republic among the several Concerned Member States in that procedure. Furthermore, it was disclosed that at least part of the earlier manufactured batches were shipped by the defendant to Spain for filling into syringes, which were then used in testing and clinical trials for the purpose of obtaining the marketing authorization. To date, and as far as the author is aware, this particular question as to whether acts carried out in the Czech Republic for the purpose of obtaining a marketing authorization elsewhere in the EU (but not in the Czech Republic) or for obtaining a marketing authorization solely in third countries outside the EU, has not been a matter of dispute in any court proceedings in the Czech Republic.

g. Burden of Proof and Onus

In proceedings concerning patent infringement, the plaintiff bears the burden of proof in providing evidence to the competent court of any alleged patent infringement. Therefore, if infringement is argued and substantiated by the plaintiff and the defendant wishes to invoke the Bolar-type exemption in order to prove that no infringement of patents rights has occurred as alleged by the plaintiff, the defendant bears the burden of proof to raise this defence in the proceedings and provide sufficient evidence to the competent court that the alleged acts fall under the Bolar-type exemption. To date, and as far as the author is aware, this specific point has not been a matter of dispute in any court proceedings in the Czech Republic.

h. Applicability during Patent Term Extension or Supplementary Protection Certificate

The Bolar-type exemption (as part of the general Experimental Use exemption provision) does not distinguish between its applicability during the patent term and the term of the supplementary protection certificate (SPC). The only extension to the patent term available in the Czech Republic, as *sui generis* IP right, is the SPC implemented in the European Union for medicinal products[30] and plant protection

29. Decision of the Municipal Court in Prague of 14 November 2017 in *Teva v. Synthon* (case no. 1 Cm 8/2015) – an action for a declaratory judgment seeking that 2993 grams of glatiramer acetate held on stock by the defendant as reference samples (and detained by the customs authorities in the Czech Republic, based on a national application by the patent holder requesting to take action under Act No. 355/2014 Coll.), infringes patent no. CZ 292 247 of which the plaintiff was a registered exclusive licensee.
30. Regulation (EC) No. 469/2009 of the European Parliament and of the Council of 6 May 2009 concerning the supplementary protection certificate for medicinal products, OJ L 152, 16.6.2009, as amended by Regulation (EU) 2019/933 of the European Parliament and of the Council of 20 May 2019 amending Regulation (EC) No 469/2009 concerning the supplementary protection certificate for medicinal products, OJ L 153, 11.6.2019.

products.[31] According to this legislation, the subject-matter of the SPC protection is (subject to certain limitations), confined within the limits of the protection conferred by the basic patent on which the SPC is based. Therefore, the same limitations/ exemptions as applicable to the basic patent under the relevant provisions should apply to the SPC as well as any protection offered by the SPC shall be limited by the limits of the protection conferred by the basic patent. Thereby, by analogy, since any patent does not offer protection against the acts allowed under the Bolar-type exemption, the SPC is limited in the same manner.

The fact that the Bolar-type exemption should apply to the *sui generis* SPC rights as well was also explicitly mentioned in the explanatory memorandum to the Act on Pharmaceuticals, which implemented the Bolar-type exemption into the Patent Act, in that carrying out studies and experiments necessary for the purposes of the registration of medicinal products shall not be considered an infringement of the rights of the owner of the patent or supplementary protection certificate. Furthermore, the applicability of the Bolar-type exemption also during the SPC term stems from the intended harmonized Bolar-type exemption under Article 10, paragraph 6 of Directive 2004/27/EC which also covers, that the exempted acts 'shall not be regarded as contrary to patent rights or to supplementary protection certificates for medicinal products'.

4. DIFFERENCES BETWEEN THE TWO EXCEPTIONS IN THE CZECH REPUBLIC

It is generally understood that both exemptions aim to cover acts that have a different purpose. While the Experimental Use exemption is intrinsic to patent law, the Bolar-type exemption is extrinsic as it serves the public interest in facilitating early access to medicinal products.[32] However, the way in which both exemptions have been implemented in the Czech Republic means that they are based on the same statutory provision under Section 18, lit. e) of the Patent Act. This provision states that the acts considered to fall within the Bolar-type exemption are essentially a sub-group of and actually form a part of the acts falling within the more general Experimental Use exemption, thereby forming one legal provision. The language of that provision would also seem to imply a similar scope for both exemptions.

The Experimental Use exemption, which at that time did not yet include the Bolar-type exemption, was originally introduced into the Patent Act in accordance with the provisions of the CPC, as part of the international harmonization of patent laws in Europe (see section 2.a. above). When the time then came to introduce also the Bolar-type exemption (in accordance with Article 10, paragraph 6 of Directive 2004/27/EC, see section 3.a. above) as a separate exclusion from patent infringement, it was simply added as part of the broader Experimental Use exemption under the same legal provision. It should be noted that not all the EU Member States adopted

31. Regulation (EC) No. 1610/96 of the European Parliament and of the Council of 23 July 1996 concerning the creation of a supplementary protection certificate for plant protection products, OJ L 198, 8.8.1996.
32. AIPPI Adopted Resolution on Experimental Use and Bolar-type Exemptions (Q288), 2023 AIPPI World Congress – Istanbul, 25 October 2023.

this approach of merely clarifying the scope of the Experimental Use exemption by including the Bolar-type exemption within it.

The inclusion of both exemptions in a single legal provision seems to cause some difficulties when trying to interpret them separately, based on the different concepts and nature of the exempted activities under both exemptions. Moreover, the legislator has indicated that presumably all the exempted activities are overall related to non-commercial activities without any profit making, thereby blurring the boundaries not only between the mixed Bolar-type/Experimental Use exemption, but also even with the Private Use exemption under a separate legal provision. This has also been reflected in the very limited case law available in the Czech Republic on this matter. Overall, the non-commercial character of the exempted activities, especially at the time when these are carried out, seems to be the primary focus and the main reason as to why such activities should fall under the mixed Bolar-type/Experimental Use exemption. Although similar activities carried out solely for commercial reasons and the purpose of making profit would presumably not be exempted, it remains to be clarified by future case law as to what level of commercial involvement is still deemed acceptable.

Chapter 13

Denmark

Johnny Petersen, Johan Løje and Lucas Huusom

1. GENERAL

a. Terminology

The Experimental Use exemption is codified in Section 3(3)(iii) of the Danish Patents Act (*'Patentloven'*), and the Bolar-type exemption is found in Section 3(3)(iv) of that Act. According to the statute, these are instances where the exclusive right of the patent does not apply. This would definitionally make them exemptions. Danish legal tradition is, however, such that the distinction between exemptions (*'Indskrænkninger'*) and exceptions (*'Undtagelser'*) in patent law is mostly theoretical and in practice does not play a large role.

b. Legal Basis in Denmark

Section 3(1) of the Danish Patents Act initially provides the exclusive rights granted by a patent. Then, Section 3(3) lists the exemption to the exclusive right. This list includes the exemption for Experimental Use and the Bolar-type exemption.

> 3(1) The exclusive right obtained through the patent means that others than the patent holder may not exploit the invention without authorization by …
>
> …
>
> (3) The exclusive right does not include
>
> …
>
> (iii) actions carried out for experimental purposes in relation to the subject matter of the patented invention,
>
> (iv) actions limited to the subject matter of the patented invention that are necessary to obtain marketing authorization for a medicinal product

for humans or animals in the EU, in an EU member state, or in other countries, or

(v) ...

The Danish Patents Act is applicable in instances of exploitation in Denmark of either a Danish national patent or a patent with effect in Denmark (for example a patent granted by the European Patent Office (EPO) with Denmark designated as a country of effect, cf. Article 64(1) of the European Patent Convention (EPC)).

c. Bodies That May Decide on the Legitimacy of Exemptions

The Experimental Use and Bolar-type exemptions serve as defences against claims of unlawful patent exploitation. These exemptions are utilised during litigation proceedings, which fall under the jurisdiction of the Danish courts, specifically the Maritime and Commercial High Court.

However, if the patent in question is a 'unitary patent' – a patent granted by the EPO according to the EPC to a 'group of Contracting States, which has provided by a special agreement that a European patent granted for those States has a unitary character throughout their territories' cf. 142(1) of the EPC – the Unified Patent Court (UPC) holds exclusive jurisdiction over actions related to patent infringements and declarations of non-infringement.

2. THE EXPERIMENTAL USE EXEMPTION

a. History and Rationale of Adopting the Experimental Use Exemption

The Experimental Use exemption was implemented in Danish Law with a substantial revision to the Danish Patents Act of 1978 (LFF 1977-12-02 No. 119). The implementation of the Experimental Use exemption into Danish patent law was done in preparation of the [European] Community Patent based on Convention 76/76/EEC relating to the European patent for the common market (Community Patent Convention (CPC)). This Convention included in its Article 31(b) that the 'rights conferred by a Community patent shall not extend to acts done for experimental purposes relating to the subject-matter of the patented invention'.

The CPC was never ratified and thus never entered into force, but its contents have shaped European – and hence Danish – patent law. The reason for the inclusion of the Experimental Use exemption is, however, not explained in the preparatory documents of the CPC, and the Danish preparatory documents simply explain the implementation of the Experimental Use exemption in the Danish Act as being due to the inclusion of the exemption in the CPC.

b. The Laws Applicable to the Experimental Use Exemption in Denmark

The Experimental Use exemption is codified in Section 3(3)(iii) of the Danish Patents Act. The structure of Section 3 of the Act is designed such that Section 3(1) grants the patent proprietor exclusive rights to exploit the patent. Following this, Section 3(3) enumerates specific exploitations of the patent that are excluded from the exclusive rights conferred by Section 3(1).

> 3(1) The exclusive right obtained through the patent means that others than the patent holder may not exploit the invention without authorization by …
>
> …
>
> (3) The exclusive right does not include
>
> …
>
> (iii) actions carried out for experimental purposes in relation to the subject matter of the patented invention,
>
> (iv) …

The Experimental Use exemption allows for testing of the applicability of the invention and potential further development, regardless of whether such activities are done for commercial purposes. Moreover, if the activities are carried out for experimental purposes, the exemption permits reverse engineering and other analyses.

Traditionally, the international legal interpretation of the Experimental Use exemption mandates that it is construed narrowly, meaning that it does not extend to the use of, for example, equipment, methods and substances specifically manufactured for conducting experiments.

Though the Experimental Use exemption has been codified in Danish law for more than forty-five years, there does not – to the knowledge of the present authors – exist any Danish jurisprudence on its use and/or interpretation. Similarly, no regulations have been passed that aid in the interpretation of the rule. Therefore, there are still uncertainties related to its interpretation and use in legal proceedings.

c. Procedural Aspects of Invoking the Experimental Use Exemption

The Experimental Use exemption is a defence that may be employed in infringement cases. Thus, the exemption is used in litigation. In Denmark, litigation where patents play a substantial role falls under the jurisdiction of the Danish Maritime and Commercial High Court (in the first instance).

Since the opening of the UPC on 1 June 2023, the UPC has, according to Article 32 of the UPC Agreement, had exclusive jurisdiction over inter alia (a) actions for actual or threatened infringements of patents with unitary effect, and (b) actions for declarations of non-infringement of patents with unitary effect. This means that litigation relating to infringements of such patents must be brought before the UPC. For patents with unitary effect, the Experimental Use exemption is codified in Article 27(b) of the UPC Agreement.

d. Scope of the Experimental Use Exemption in Denmark

i. Fields of Technology

The Experimental Use exemption is universally applicable across all fields of industry and types of technology. There are no specific limitations or exclusions that restrict the invocation of this exemption to particular sectors, such as pharmaceuticals. This means that the exemption can be employed regardless of the technological domain in question.

ii. Purpose of Experiments/Infringing Activities

There is no Danish jurisprudence addressing the applicability of the exemption based on the purpose of the infringing activity. However, the legal literature suggests that the Experimental Use exemption does not extend to patented inventions intended for use in research and experimentation, i.e. research tools, etc.

Furthermore, the literature assumes that the exemption is applicable only in instances of experimentation 'on' the patented invention and not experimentation 'with' the invention. This means that one may not use the patented invention for research on a different matter. Instead, research may relate to how the patented invention itself functions. This includes researching the applicability of the invention as well as the possibilities for its further development.

In a Norwegian Supreme Court decision of 22 December 2009, regarding the Norwegian version of the Experimental Use exemption – which is practically identical to the Danish version – the majority of the Norwegian Supreme Court found that the exemption must be interpreted strictly/narrowly, and only exempts research that has as its purpose to 'produce new knowledge'. The Danish exemption must likely be interpreted in the same way.

For example, if there exists a thermometer that is the best in the world, one may conduct research on that thermometer in order to research whether the patented technology in the thermometer may be exploited in a different field of technology. One may also research whether the technology in the thermometer may be developed to make an even better thermometer. An experimenter may however not unlawfully obtain or create a patented thermometer with the intention of using it to measure temperatures in different experiments where the researcher needs the best thermometer. Of course, if the experimenter legally purchases the best thermometer, they may use it to measure temperatures according to the principle of exhaustion.

There exists no jurisprudence on the applicability of the Experimental Use exemption in relation to the commercial intention of the experimenter, though it is assumed that the Experimental Use exemption applies to research carried out by industry with commercial intentions. Whether the experimenter is entitled to exploit the generated knowledge is determined through the well-established laws regulating patent infringement; see section 2.d.iii. below.

iii. Exempted and Prohibited Activities

Within Danish law, it is uncertain whether one party (that is not the proprietor of the concerned patent) may take actions that would prima facie fall within the exclusive rights conferred by the patent (for example make, import, or possess the subject matter of the patent) in order to conduct research that would be legal under the Experimental Use exemption. No case law exists to illuminate the issue.

On the one hand, one could argue that the nature of an exemption is such that it does not grant a positive right to the person acting pursuant to the exemption; an exemption only outlines an action that does not fall within the exclusive right of the patent holder, i.e. an action that the patent holder cannot legally hinder. Therefore, an exemption should not be able to grant the experimenter the right to take an action that is (prima facie at least) a non-exempted, patent-infringing action and justify these actions as being for the legal purpose of conducting experiments – the non-infringing end does not justify the infringing means.

Conversely, one could argue that such a restrictive interpretation of the Experimental Use exemption would make the exemption seem redundant. The principle of exhaustion is codified in Danish law in Section 3(3)(ii) of the Danish Patents Act, and if the Experimental Use exemption only allowed the experimenter to conduct experiments on patented technology that the experimenter had lawfully obtained, it would seem that the Experimental Use exemption had no practical effects apart from what follows from the principle of exhaustion. One could therefore argue that the mere fact that both provisions are codified in the Danish Patents Act must entail that they have different applications. One could further argue that if the Experimental Use exemption does not grant an experimenter the right to obtain the technology on which to experiment, the Experimental Use exemption would in practice become illusory, as the patent holder would be able to prevent experiments by not making the technology available for lawful acquisition.

On the above basis, the authors conclude that for the Experimental Use exemption to not become redundant and illusory, the Experimental Use exemption must be presumed to grant experimenters the right to carry out those acts that are necessary (similarly to jurisprudence relating to the Bolar-type exemption; see section 3. below) to be able to conduct experiments under the Experimental Use exemption. Depending on the patented technology, this will include making, importing and storing (a product containing) the patented technology.

If new knowledge is generated through the conducted experimentation, this new knowledge as a point of departure 'belongs' to the experimenter (or the one on whose behalf the experiments are conducted), and the experimenter will in most cases be allowed to exploit the generated knowledge – the experimenter may even be able to patent the knowledge generated. There may, however, be instances where the knowledge generated and/or the nature of the existing patent is such that the knowledge generated falls within the scope of the patent, and in those instances, the experimenter may only exploit the new knowledge (and a potential patent exploiting this generated knowledge) with the consent of the holder of the existing patent. In such cases, the Experimental Use exemption does not grant the experimenter a positive right to infringe or exploit the new knowledge in a patent-infringing manner. Whether the specific exploitation would constitute an infringing exploitation on the patent experimented on is determined based on the established rules governing patent infringement, i.e. primarily an interpretation of the patent claims.

For example, person A patents a tool for skin biopsy, patent X. Patent X is a product patent protecting the tool per se. Person B through experimentation discovers that with minor modifications the patented tool is also suited for performing brain biopsies. Person B patents the modified tool for performing brain biopsies, patent Y. The modifications to the tool and the instructions relating specifically to performing brain biopsies allow its use for brain biopsies to be patented. However, the exploitation of patent Y may fall within the claims of the product patent X, and B is thus not entitled to exploit patent Y without a licence to do so from A as long a patent X is valid and in force.

iv. Pure Academic vs Commercially Motivated Experimental Use

There exists no jurisprudence that specifies whether commercial experimentation is within the scope of the exemption. Purely academic research 'on' the invention is undoubtedly allowed under the Experimental Use exemption.

In the literature, it is assumed that experimentation conducted by the industry for commercial purposes is allowed within the scope of the exemption. Such industrial examination, for example, to discover new areas of applicability or potential developments of the invention, are assumed to be legal despite their potential commercial value. Whether the generated knowledge may be exploited commercially is determined by the rules regulating patent infringement; see section 2.d.iii. above.

e. Beneficiary Limitations

A question that arises is who may invoke the Experimental Use exemption: in a situation where A may, under the Experimental Use exemption, lawfully conduct research on a patented invention, may A contract B to conduct that research on A's behalf? This question is not explicitly answered by the Danish Patents Act, nor is it answered by Danish jurisprudence. As such, a definitive answer cannot be given as to whether research may be contracted to a third party, and whether the Experimental Use exemption is applicable to the situation as a whole.

The present authors are, however, of the strongly held belief that in those instances where A may legally conduct research on a patented invention, A would be allowed to contract B to carry out the experimentation on A's behalf. In practice, contracting experimenters to carry out research is not an uncommon practice. Similarly, as the Experimental Use exemption applies to experimentation conducted for commercial purposes, one must assume that the contracted consultant, B, will legally be allowed to conduct research on an invention that falls within the scope of a patent.

f. Territoriality Issues

The Danish Patents Act only applies, as a point of departure, to patents registered in Denmark, or that have effect in Denmark through designation, where the infringement takes place in Denmark. Accordingly, the Experimental Use exemption in the Danish Patents Act will apply to any patent with effect in Denmark.

According to Section 3(1) of the Danish Patents Act, only the patent holder may make, offer, or place on the market a product which is the subject matter of the patent. This exclusive right extends to offering for sale of products intended to be exported or licensed outside of Denmark. The wording of the provision does, however, not extend to include instances of infringing exploitation of a Danish patent outside of Denmark. As such, exploitation of research results outside of Denmark would not constitute a direct infringement of the Danish patent.

Similarly, the passing on of research results (that are subsequently exploited in a patent-infringing manner outside of Denmark) likely will not constitute contributory infringement: Section 3(2) of the Danish Patents Act specifically states that in order to be liable for contributory patent infringement, a person must either supply or offer for sale means to a third party so that the third party can illegally exploit the patent in *Denmark*. This seems explicitly to rule out that one can be responsible for contributory patent infringement in Denmark for activity carried out outside of Denmark.

It may, of course, however, be an infringement under the patent laws of the territory where the research knowledge is used in an infringing manner. This would depend on the interpretation of the claims of the patent experimented on; see section 2.d.iii. above.

For patents with unitary effect, contributory patent infringement is the subject of Article 26 of the UPC Agreement (where it is referred to as indirect patent infringement). According to Article 26, indirect infringement of a patent subsists where a person supplies or offers to supply, 'within the territory of the Contracting Member *States* in which that patent has effect' with means to illegally exploit the patent. [Emphasis added]

A 'European patent with unitary effect' is simply a European patent granted by the EPO that is not implemented in a single Contracting Member State, but that is instead granted to a 'group of Contracting States, which has provided by a special agreement that a European patent granted for those States has a unitary character throughout their territories' as allowed for by Article 142(1) of the EPC.

As such, the territory for such patents, i.e. the territory where knowledge is gained through experimentation conducted legally in Denmark may be restricted, is thus extended to all Contracting States to the UPC.

g. Burden of Proof and Onus

There has been no jurisprudence on the burden of proof in relation to the applicability of the Experimental Use exemption in Section 3(3)(iii) of the Danish Patents Act.

In theory, the nature of an exemption means that it is for the party alleging infringement to prove that the researcher's actions fall within the scope of the exclusive rights conferred by the patent. If the presiding court is convinced of this, the burden of proof would then shift to the experimenter meaning that the experimenter would have to prove that their actions were exempted from the scope of the exclusive rights of the patent.

This theoretically clear distinction is, however, not as clear in practice. In Danish litigation, a principle of free evaluation of evidence applies. This means that both parties will present all evidence supporting their respective claims, and the court will subsequently examine all presented evidence as it sees fit; very rarely do the Danish courts expressly state that their decisions are based on a rigid application of the principles of burden of proof and one party's failure to lift this burden.

h. Applicability during Patent Term Extension or Supplementary Protection Certificate

Supplementary protection certificates (SPCs) are granted pursuant to an EU regulation, Regulation (EC) No. 469/2009 (the 'SPC Regulation'). The Danish Patents Act simply states that the relevant minister passes the necessary executive orders for the SPC Regulation to be effective in Denmark.

Article 5 of the SPC Regulation has the following wording:

> Subject to the provisions of Article 4, the certificate shall confer the same rights as conferred by the basic patent and shall be subject to the same limitations and the same obligations.

Accordingly, the protection offered by the SPC is the same as that provided by a patent. Thus, the exemptions from the exclusive rights conferred by a patent also apply to the right conferred/extended by an SPC, as an SPC simply extends the right conferred for a patent, meaning that the exceptions and exemptions that apply to a patent also apply to the corresponding SPC.

For patents with unitary effect, the above also applies. Article 30 of the UPC Agreement on the effects of SPCs for patents that fall within the exclusive jurisdiction of the UPC states the following:

> A supplementary protection certificate shall confer the same rights as conferred by the patent and shall be subject to the same limitations and the same obligations.

As the wording is very close to the wording of the SPC Regulation, and as the members of the UPC are, to a large extent, the EU Member States, one would expect the rules to be the same.

3. THE BOLAR-TYPE EXEMPTION

a. History and Rationale of Adopting the Bolar-Type Exemption

The Bolar-type exemption was implemented into Danish law as part of broader European Union reforms. Directive 2001/83, as amended by Directive 2004/27, was designed by the European Commission to facilitate the marketing authorization procedures for generic medicinal products within the European Economic Area (EEA). The primary aim was to allow these procedures to occur during the term of a patent, enabling generic medicinal products to enter the market immediately after the patent expires by demonstrating bioequivalence to an existing authorized medicinal product. This prevents the de facto extension of the protection conferred by a patent, by allowing generics to enter the market immediately after the patent expires.

Article 10(6) of Directive 2001/83/EC, as amended, establishes the minimum scope of the Bolar-type exemption. This provision mandates that EU Member States must exempt all studies and trials necessary for obtaining marketing authorization for generic medicinal products from patent infringement.

EU Member States adopted various approaches when implementing Article 10(6).

In Denmark, the Bolar-type exemption was initially interpreted to be implicitly included in Danish legislation, which led the Minister for Economic and Business Affairs to delay its explicit implementation until the next revision of the Danish Patents Act.

This was because it was assessed that the Bolar-type exemption could be accommodated within the wording of the Danish Patents Act at the time. Therefore, a purely linguistic clarification of the Patents Act was put on hold until a new legislative amendment was carried out.

The Danish Association of the Pharmaceutical Industry and the intellectual property advisory sector subsequently expressed a need for clarification of the exemption provision to highlight the specific rules applicable to the pharmaceutical industry. Because of this, the Minister for Economic and Business Affairs deemed it appropriate to clarify the legal rules in this area.

On 24 January 2007, the Minister for Economic and Business Affairs introduced a bill, LFF 120/24.01.2007, to the Danish Parliament proposing various amendments to the Danish Patents Act. Among these amendments was the formal introduction of rules governing permissible actions related to obtaining market authorization for medicinal products. This bill proposed a new addition to Section 3(3) of the Danish Patents Act, which enumerates actions that do not fall within the scope of the exclusive rights conferred by a patent. This addition explicitly implemented the Bolar-type exemption into Danish law.

The Bolar-type exemption was thus codified as Section 3(3)(iv) of the revised Danish Patents Act.

b. The Laws Applicable to the Bolar-Type Exemption in Denmark

In Denmark the Bolar-type exemption is codified in the Patents Act Section 3(3)(iv) as follows:

> The exclusive rights of a patent do not extend to ... acts limited to the subject-matter of the patented invention which are necessary for obtaining a marketing authorization for a medicinal product for humans or animals in the EU, in an EU member state, or in other countries.

The Danish Patents Act comprises a broader scope for the Bolar-type exemption than required by the EU Directive. Unlike the Directive, the Danish exemption is not limited to actions aimed solely at obtaining marketing authorization for generic products. According to LFF 120/24.01.2007, the exemption applies both to innovative manufacturers as well as generic manufacturers.

In addition to the requirement that actions must be taken to obtain marketing authorization for a medicinal product for humans or animals, it is a further condition that the actions are limited to the subject matter of the patented invention. The provision does not permit the disregard of other existing patent rights. For example, if the activities conducted under the exemption necessitate the use of patented research tools, these tools can only be utilized with the explicit consent of the patent owner.

The actions must be necessary to obtain marketing authorization for a medicinal product for humans or animals. Such actions may include clinical studies, investigations, or other related procedures. The 'necessity' criterion is linked to the requirements in any country where the company wishes to obtain marketing authorization.

The rule enables generic companies to start the time-consuming work of building the necessary documentation for obtaining marketing authorization before the patent expires, thereby allowing generic competition to enter the market earlier than previously.

c. Procedural Aspects of Invoking the Bolar-Type Exemption

In Denmark, the enforcement of intellectual property rights is subject to international harmonization. Consequently, international initiatives such as TRIPS Part III, Article 8 of the Infosoc Directive, and the Enforcement Directive, among others, influence the enforcement of intellectual property rights in Denmark. This influence extends to the interpretation of all rules and laws that implement such harmonization in Danish law, including rules of procedure and sanctions.

The Bolar-type exemption can be invoked in an ordinary civil case and preliminary injunction proceedings. In Denmark, the general rule is that ordinary civil cases as well as preliminary injunction proceedings fall under the jurisdiction of the District Courts in the first instance, cf. Sections 224 and 412 of the Danish Administration of Justice Act ('*Retsplejeloven*'). However, the Maritime and Commercial High Court has subject matter jurisdiction to hear civil cases as well as preliminary injunction proceedings where certain intellectual property acts, including the Danish Patents Act, are of significant importance, cf. Sections 225(2)(4) and 412(1) of the Danish Administration of Justice Act.

In practice, most civil cases concerning intellectual property rights are heard by the Maritime and Commercial High Court in the first instance.

The Danish legal system operates with a two-instance principle, ensuring that a case can at least be heard by two different courts. Therefore, a court decision about the legality of an application of the Bolar-type exemption rendered by the Maritime and Commercial High Court in the first instance is subject to appeal to a higher court. The appeal can either be made to the High Court or exceptionally directly to the Supreme Court.

Since the opening of the UPC on 1 June 2023, the UPC has, according to Article 32 of the UPC Agreement, had exclusive jurisdiction over inter alia (a) actions for actual or threatened infringements of patents with unitary effect, and (b) actions for declarations of non-infringement of patents with unitary effect. This means that litigation relating to infringements of such patents must be brought before the UPC. For patents with unitary effect, the Bolar-type exemption is codified in Article 27(d) of the UPC Agreement.

Therefore, the body most likely to decide on the legitimacy of an application of the Bolar-type exemption in Denmark for a Danish national patent is the Maritime and Commercial High Court in the first instance. If the Bolar-type exemption is pled in relation to a patent with unitary effect, the UPC has jurisdiction.

d. Scope of the Bolar-Type Exemption in Denmark

i. *Fields of Technology*

The Bolar-type exemption only applies to medicinal products for humans and animals in Denmark. The exemption is made because of the specific requirements in the pharmaceutical legislation that must be met before a marketing authorization is issued. Accordingly, due to the purpose of the exemption, the scope of the Bolar-type exemption does not affect other technical fields.

ii. *Purpose of Experiments/Infringing Activities*

Under Danish law, the Bolar-type exemption allows generic manufacturers and others to perform activities such as clinical trials, investigations, and other procedures that are necessary for compiling the documentation required for obtaining marketing authorization for a pharmaceutical product.

It is a requirement that the performed activities are *necessary* to obtain marketing authorization for a medicinal product. Consequently, actions which are not necessary to obtain marketing authorization are not covered by the provision. However, since there are no common global rules for obtaining marketing authorization for medicinal products, the scope of the provision is broad. The actions referred to may be necessary for obtaining marketing authorization in any country. Consequently, the applicability of the provision is not limited to meeting the requirements of a specific country or region for issuing marketing authorization.

iii. *Exempted and Prohibited Activities*

The Danish Bolar-type exemption allows generic manufacturers to prepare for the production and distribution of a generic medicinal product. This includes complying with the necessary statutory procedures under pharmaceutical legislation before the patent expires, so that the generic medicinal product can be ready for sale the day after the patent expires. However, during the period when the patent (and the SPC) is still valid, it is not permitted to produce more of the pharmaceutical product than is necessary for clinical trials of the medicinal product. Actual commercial production of a generic medicinal product can only begin after the expiration of the patent (and the SPC).

Since there are no global regulations specifying the requirements a medicinal product must meet to obtain marketing authorization, the exemption does not have an unambiguous, defined scope, and it applies to all relevant actions necessary to obtain marketing authorization in any country.

e. Beneficiary Limitations

The *travaux préparatoires* to the Danish Patents Act clarify that, beyond enabling the necessary actions to secure marketing authorization for generic medicinal products, the exemption also permits activities involving medicinal products protected by patents or SPCs for the purpose of obtaining marketing authorization for new medicinal products. This means that trials conducted to secure marketing authorization for both generic and innovative products are allowed. Therefore, both the generic and innovative pharmaceutical industries can utilise the exemption. As a result, the scope of the exemption also includes actions by innovative manufacturers involving patent-protected medicinal products to obtain marketing authorization for new products.

f. Territoriality Issues

It follows from the wording of Section 3(3)(iv) of the Patents Act that the exemption also applies when the purpose is a regulatory submission in countries other than Denmark, including other EU Member States as well as third countries.

It is not material whether the person acting under the exemption is the applicant for regulatory approval or otherwise related to it, including but not limited to a contracting party, since the wording of Section 3(3)(iv) of the Patents Act does not specify a particular subject.

Naturally, activities performed in countries other than Denmark, for the purposes of Danish regulatory submissions, must be assessed under the patent laws of such other countries.

g. Burden of Proof and Onus

There has been no jurisprudence specifically on the burden of proof in relation to the applicability of the Experimental Use exemption in Section 3(3)(iv) of the Danish Patents Act.

In theory, the nature of an exemption means that it is for the party alleging infringement to prove that the researcher's actions fall within the scope of the exclusive rights conferred by the patent. If the presiding court is convinced of this, the burden of proof would then shift to the experimenter meaning that the experimenter would have to prove that their actions were exempted from the scope of the exclusive rights of the patent.

Under Danish procedural law, the principle of free evaluation of evidence applies. In cases where an alleged patent infringer seeks to invoke an exemption, the default position is that the burden of proof as a starting point rests with the party asserting the exemption.

h. Applicability during Patent Term Extension or Supplementary Protection Certificate

SPCs are granted pursuant to an EU regulation, Regulation (EC) No. 469/2009. The Danish Patents Act simply states that the relevant minister passes the necessary executive orders for the SPC Regulation to be effective in Denmark.

Article 5 of the SPC Regulation has the following wording:

> Subject to the provisions of Article 4, the certificate shall confer the same rights as conferred by the basic patent and shall be subject to the same limitations and the same obligations.

Accordingly, the protection offered by the SPC is the same as that provided by a patent. Thus, the exemptions from the exclusive rights conferred by a patent also apply to the right conferred/extended by an SPC, as an SPC simply extends the right conferred for a patent, meaning that the exceptions and exemptions that apply to a patent also apply to the corresponding SPC.

For patents with unitary effect, the above also applies. Article 30 of the UPC agreement on the effects of SPCs for patents that fall within the exclusive jurisdiction of the UPC states the following:

> A supplementary protection certificate shall confer the same rights as conferred by the patent and shall be subject to the same limitations and the same obligations.

As the wording is very close to the wording of the SPC Regulation, and as the members of the UPC are, to a large extent, the EU member states, one should expect the rules to be the same.

4. DIFFERENCES BETWEEN THE TWO EXCEPTIONS IN DENMARK

As described above, the Danish Patents Act expressly includes the principle of exhaustion, the Experimental Use exemption as well as the Bolar-type exemption. What this means for the scope of each provision remains unclear as this question has never been before a court.

It would seem that since the Danish Patents Act has codified all three exemptions separately, they must have a different scope.

The Bolar-type exemption has been used in notable litigation cases in practice, but the more general Experimental Use exemption has never been used in litigation. This likewise implies that the scopes of the exemptions are different.

Chapter 14

Ecuador

Eugenio Hoss and Martin Bensadon

1. GENERAL

a. Terminology

There is no distinction between the terms 'exemption' and 'exception' under the applicable law and case law. To maintain consistency, the term 'exemption' will be used as the general term, while the term 'exception' is restricted to issues of evidence and interpretation rules.

The Experimental Use exemption appears in Section 294 of the Organic Code of the Social Economy of Knowledge, Creativity and Innovation ('Ingenios Code') under the heading 'Limitations to the Patent holder's right'. Such a limitation also appears in Section 53 of Andean Community's Decision 486.

The Andean Community is a free trade area comprising Bolivia, Colombia, Ecuador and Peru, and the decisions issued by the Andean Community, such as Decision 486, are supranational regulations which are legally binding for the Member States.

Furthermore, in 2008, an additional provision of Andean Community Decision 689 clarified that Member States can include an additional Bolar-type exemption as part of the existing Experimental Use exemption. The Ingenios Code, which was enacted later, also includes a specific Bolar-type exemption under Section 294.

In both cases, the legislation refers to situations where the patent has no legal effect and should thus be considered as exemptions to infringement.

b. Legal Basis in Ecuador

The Experimental Use exemption was enacted in 2016 under Section 294 of the new Ingenios Code.

> Section 294. Limitations on the Patent Holder's Rights – The owner of a patent may not exercise the right prescribed in the foregoing provision in any of the following cases:
>
> 1. acts carried out in the private sphere and on a non-commercial scale;
> 2. acts carried out for the purpose of experimentation, with respect to the object of the patented invention;
> 3. acts carried out for teaching or scientific or academic research purposes;
>
> ...

The same text also appears in Section 53 of Andean Community's Decision 486.

> Section 53. The owner of a patent may not exercise the right referred to in the preceding provision with respect to the following acts:
>
> (a) acts performed privately and for non-commercial purposes;
> (b) acts carried out exclusively for purposes of experimentation, with respect to the object of the patented invention;
> (c) acts performed exclusively for teaching or scientific or academic research purposes;
>
> ...

Although the Bolar-type exemption was not originally acknowledged as a separate exemption under Ecuadorian law, it was subsequently included under Section 294 of the Ingenios Code, which reads as follows:

> Section 294. Limitations on the Patent Holder's Rights – The owner of a patent may not exercise the right prescribed in the foregoing provision in any of the following cases:
>
> ...
>
> 6. acts related to testing, use, manufacture or sale of a patented invention for the sole purpose of generating and submitting information required for the approval of the manufacture, use or sale of any product, including pharmaceutical and agricultural chemical products, in Ecuador or in another country, as well as for the manufacture of products intended for sale after the expiration date of the patent.

This is supported, *inter alia,* by Section 1 of Andean Community's Decision 689 which provides the following:

> Section 1. The Member States shall be authorized, through their internal regulations, under the terms expressly indicated in paragraphs a) to j), to implement and further elaborate only the following provisions of Decision 486:
>
> ...
>
> (e) Section 53: Include the power to use the subject matter protected by a patent in order to generate the necessary information to support the application for marketing approval of a product.
>
> ...

This Section 1 provides that Section 53 of the Andean Community's Decision 689, related to experimental uses, may extend to uses which would typically be covered under Bolar-type exemptions.

To date, there has not been any case law discussing the scope or particularities of the above-mentioned exemptions.

2. THE EXPERIMENTAL USE EXEMPTION

a. History and Rationale of Adopting the Experimental Use Exemption

The objective of this provision is clearly to encourage scientific research in both the academic and private fields by exempting these activities from the scope of exclusivity rights awarded by patents. The exemption generally intends to provide a secure research environment for private research and purely academic or scientific experimentation.

b. The Laws Applicable to the Experimental Use Exemption in Ecuador

The Experimental Use exemption was enacted in 2016 under Section 294 of the new Ingenios Code.

> Section 294. Limitations on the Patent Holder's Rights – The owner of a patent may not exercise the right prescribed in the foregoing provision in any of the following cases:
>
> 1. acts carried out in the private sphere and on a non-commercial scale;
> 2. acts carried out for the purpose of experimentation, with respect to the object of the patented invention;
> 3. acts carried out for teaching or scientific or academic research purposes;
>
> ...

The same text also appears in Section 53 of Andean Community's Decision 486.

> Section 53. The owner of a patent may not exercise the right referred to in the preceding provision with respect to the following acts:
>
> (a) acts performed privately and for non-commercial purposes;
> (b) acts carried out exclusively for purposes of experimentation, with respect to the object of the patented invention;
> (c) acts performed exclusively for teaching or scientific or academic research purposes;
>
> ...

There is as yet no relevant case law on this issue to provide for further interpretation of the Law. The language of the provision, however, clearly indicates that the exemption is intended to be limited to cases where research is performed in the private sphere with no commercial scale, or where research is purely for experimentation, teaching or academic purposes.

c. Procedural Aspects of Invoking the Experimental Use Exemption

The Experimental Use exemption may be used as a defence in patent litigation proceedings, either in infringement or in declaratory actions.

d. Scope of the Experimental Use Exemption in Ecuador

i. Fields of Technology

The Ingenios Code does not include any field limitations on the Experimental Use exemption. The exemption is thus applicable in all fields of technology.

ii. Purpose of Experiments/Infringing Activities

As indicated above, the exemption is only applicable in cases where research is performed in the private sphere and on a non-commercial scale, or in cases where research is purely for experimentation, teaching or academic purposes.

The provision does not require that the purpose of the research is to improve an invention. Also, it does not make any distinction between cases where the exemption is invoked for researching on a patented technology ('research on') and cases where the exemption is invoked for using a patented technology ('research with'). There is no relevant case law as to the exact scope of the exemption, but it is likely that it would be deemed applicable to both these situations.

Although the limitation regarding non-commercial scale/purpose only applies to acts performed in the private sphere, given the original intent of the Law, it is unlikely that any of the other activities performed for experimentation or academic research would extend to activities with a commercial intent. This being said, there is no relevant case law on this matter which confirms this.

iii. Exempted and Prohibited Activities

Section 294 of the Ingenios Code and Section 53 of the Andean Community's Decision 486, provide for a relatively broad defence and do not provide a specific list of exempted or prohibited activities. Although there is no relevant case law, it is likely that manufacture, purchase, use, possession, testing, importation, would all be exempt if made in the private sphere (with no commercial scale) or purely for experimentation, teaching or academic purposes.

iv. Pure Academic vs Commercially Motivated Experimental Use

Paragraphs 1 and 3 of the Section 294 of the Ingenios Code and a) and c) of Section 53 of the Andean Community's Decision 486 include limitations respectively on non-commercial scale or academic activities. Whilst paragraphs 2 and b) of respectively Section 294 of the Ingenios Code and Section 53 of the Andean Community's Decision 486 refer more broadly to 'experimentation' without any of these limitations, given the original intent of the Law, if a person, company or institution carrying out the research activities has any commercial purposes, the exemption would likely not be applicable.

e. Beneficiary Limitations

The Ingenios Code did not contemplate third party contributions and there is no case law on this issue either. However, if a party contracts a third party to perform an activity that, if performed by that party, would normally be considered exempt, it is likely that that the third party would also be protected by the Experimental Use exemption.

f. Territoriality Issues

As a rule, Ecuadorian courts only enforce and decide on Ecuadorian patents. Therefore, Ecuadorian courts would probably not address any infringement issue relating to activities which would infringe foreign patents.

g. Burden of Proof and Onus

There is no relevant case law on the burden of proof for experimental uses. According to general procedural principles, however, the onus lies on the defendant to prove that the exemption applies.

h. Applicability during Patent Term Extension or Supplementary Protection Certificate

This is not applicable as there is no SPC in Ecuador.

3. THE BOLAR-TYPE EXEMPTION

a. History and Rationale of Adopting the Bolar-Type Exemption

As indicated above, Andean Community Decision 689 clarifies that Member States can include an additional Bolar-type exemption as part of the existing Experimental Use exemption. Additionally, the Ingenios Code includes a specific Bolar-type exemption under Section 294.

b. The Laws Applicable to the Bolar-Type Exemption in Ecuador

The Bolar-type exemption was enacted in 2016 under Section 294 of the new Ingenios Code.

> Section 294. Limitations on the Patent Holder's Rights – The owner of a patent may not exercise the right prescribed in the foregoing provision in any of the following cases:
>
> ...
>
> 6. acts related to testing, use, manufacture or sale of a patented invention for the sole purpose of generating and submitting information required for the approval of the manufacture, use or sale of any product, including

> pharmaceutical and agricultural chemical products, in Ecuador or in another country, as well as for the manufacture of products intended for sale after the expiration date of the patent.

Moreover, Section 1 of Andean Community's Decision 689 provides the following:

> Section 1. The Member States shall be authorized, through their internal regulations, under the terms expressly indicated in paragraphs a) to j), to implement and further elaborate only the following provisions of Decision 486:
>
> ...
>
> (e) Section 53: Include the power to use the subject matter protected by a patent in order to generate the necessary information to support the application for marketing approval of a product.
>
> ...

This Section clarifies that Member States are entitled to extend the Experimental Use exemption under Section 53 of the same Andean Community Decision 689 to include a Bolar-type exemption.

c. Procedural Aspects of Invoking the Bolar-Type Exemption

The Bolar-type exemption may be used as a defence in patent litigation proceedings, either in infringement or in declaratory actions.

d. Scope of the Bolar-Type Exemption in Ecuador

i. Fields of Technology

According to Section 294 of the Ingenios Code, the exemption is applicable to any field of technology in which it is necessary to obtain a market approval from a competent governmental authority. The provision expressly clarifies that pharmaceutical and agricultural chemical products are included in the exemption.

ii. Purpose of Experiments/Infringing Activities

As indicated above, the Bolar-type exemption is limited to acts related to testing, use, manufacture or sale whose sole purpose is generating or submitting information required for the approval from the competent governmental authority.

iii. Exempted and Prohibited Activities

As indicated above, the exemption is limited to acts related to testing, use, manufacture or sale and whose sole purpose is to gather information for the approval of a product.

The last part of Section 294, para. 6 of the Ingenios Code additionally refers to the 'manufacture of products intended for sale after the expiration date of the patent'. The language of the provision is not entirely clear as to whether this last part may be interpreted as a separate and independent exemption allowing stockpiling.

However, there would be strong arguments against said interpretation, as it would contradict Andean Community's Decisions 486 and 689 and the decision issued by the WTO Panel Report in Case DS114,[1] where it concluded that stockpiling violates Article 30 of the TRIPS Agreement. Unfortunately, there is no relevant case law, either at national or regional level.

e. Beneficiary Limitations

There is no mention of limitations for the beneficiary. For pharmaceuticals, the exemption would therefore apply to both generic and innovative companies applying for regulatory approval. The exemption would also seem to apply to third parties contracted to perform studies on behalf of the party seeking regulatory approval, as the relevant provision expressly refers to the sale for the purpose of generating or submitting information required for approval. However, there is no relevant case law on this issue.

f. Territoriality Issues

The exemption applies for activities performed in Ecuador, even if the purpose is a regulatory submission in a country other than Ecuador. There is no relevant case law yet.

If the acts carried out by a party to support such regulatory submission outside Ecuador would infringe a corresponding patent in another jurisdiction, it should be noted that, as a rule, Ecuadorian courts only enforce and decide on Ecuadorian patents. Therefore, Ecuadorian courts would probably not address any infringement issue relating to activities which would infringe foreign patents.

g. Burden of Proof and Onus

We are not aware of any case law on the burden of proof for the Bolar-type exemption. However, applying general procedural principles under Ecuadorian law, the onus would be on the defendant to prove that the exemption applies.

4. DIFFERENCES BETWEEN THE TWO EXCEPTIONS IN ECUADOR

The Experimental Use exemption in Ecuador has a relatively broad scope in terms of the exempted acts. The exemption applies both to cases where research is performed in the private sphere with no commercial scale, and where research is purely for experimentation, teaching or academic purposes.

On the other hand, the Bolar-type exemption is drafted in a relatively narrow manner, although the language of the provision is not entirely clear as to its scope and leaves some room for interpretation. In either case, the rationale of this provision

1. Panel Report, Canada — Patent Protection of Pharmaceutical Products, WTO Doc. WT/DS114/R (adopted April 7, 2000, available at, https://www.wto.org/english/tratop_e/dispu_e/cases_e/ds114_e.htm).

clearly differs from the Experimental Use exemption as it is aimed at preventing a regulatory lag between expiry of a patent and generic market entry.

Chapter 15

El Salvador

Morena Zavaleta

1. GENERAL

a. Terminology

The Salvadoran Intellectual Property Law, which entered into force on 15 February 2025, includes a definition for Bolar-type exemption in Article 3, definition No. 60 as follows:

> It is a limitation of the exclusivity rights granted by a patent, according to which, permits a third party to use the information of the patent without authorization of its owner, for experimental, study and essay purposes, to generate information that is necessary to apply for the corresponding health registration,

and further provides how it is applied in Article 209:

> The rights granted by a patent which is in force, cannot be enforced against the use of a third party of the protected matter to generate the necessary information, to base a health registration application of a pharmaceutical product before the Health Regulation Superintendency, or whoever takes its place or in case of an agricultural chemical before the Agriculture and Cattle Ministry, application that may be authorized once the term of protection of the patent ends; and in case the product is exported outside of the national territory such exportation may be permitted only to satisfy the requirements of approval of sale in El Salvador.

The Experimental Use exemption appears in Article 208 letter b) as follows: 'Acts performed exclusively with experimental purposes over the patented invention that do not prejudice in an unjustifiable manner the normal exploitation of the invention that the title owner may perform or is performing.'

In the former law, the Experimental Use exemption appears in Article 116 letter c), and the Bolar-type exemption appears in Article 116 letter e).

b. Legal Basis in El Salvador

The new Intellectual Property Law, which entered into force on 15 February 2025, includes both the Experimental Use and Bolar-type exemptions.

Previously, the Experimental Use exemption and the Bolar-type exemption were regulated by the former Intellectual Property Law, which entered into force on 16 October 1993.

2. THE EXPERIMENTAL USE EXEMPTION

a. History and Rationale of Adopting the Experimental Use Exemption

The first Salvadoran patent laws enacted in 1901 and 1913 did not include the exemption of experimental use.

Later, the Intellectual Property Law, enacted in 1993, included exemptions of the effects of the patent, in the following activities:

- A third party, that in a private scope and in a non-commercial scale, or for a non-commercial purpose, performs activities related to the patented inventions.
- A third party, that with no commercial purpose, performs manufacturing activities or uses of the invention, with experimental purpose, relative to the object of the patented invention, or with purpose of scientific investigation, academic or learning.

El Salvador, alongside other Central American countries and the Dominican Republic, negotiated a Free Trade Agreement (CAFTA-DR) with the United States between January 2003 and January 2004. This treaty included provisions related to intellectual property. Chapter 15 of the CAFTA-DR Agreement, specifically Article 15.9, provides exemption to the effects of a patent but does not explicitly reference experimental activities. However, it allows for exemption provided that they do not unjustifiably interfere with the normal exploitation of the patent or cause unjustified harm to the legitimate interests of the patent owner, while also taking into account the legitimate interests of third parties. To include the CAFTA-DR provisions in the Salvadoran Intellectual Property Law, amendments were made to the law in 2005, in which a new wording was included with respect to the experimental use exemption, and which is the currently in force wording, as follows:

> Article 116. The effects of the patent do not extend to:
>
> ...
>
> (c) A third party that, without commercial purpose, performs acts of manufacturing or using the invention with experimental purpose related to the object of the patented invention, or with scientific investigation, academic or learning purpose, if does not prejudice in an unjustified manner the normal exploitation of the invention that the title owner is performing or may perform.

However, in the new Intellectual Property Law which entered into force on 15 February 2025, the wording of the Experimental Use exemption has changed as follows:

Article 208. The patent does not provide the right to prevent:

...

(b) Acts performed exclusively with experimental purpose over the patented invention that do not prejudice in an unjustifiable manner the normal exploitation of the invention that the title owner may perform or is performing.

b. The Laws Applicable to the Experimental Use Exemption in El Salvador

The Experimental Use exemption is included in Article 116(c) of the previous Intellectual Property Law as follows:

The effects of the patent do not extend to:

...

(c) A third party that, without commercial purpose, performs acts of manufacturing or using the invention with experimental purpose related to the object of the patented invention, or with scientific investigation, academic or learning purpose, if this does not prejudice in an unjustified manner the normal exploitation of the invention that the title owner is performing or may perform.

This is provided in the new Intellectual Property law, in Article 208, as follows:

The patent does not provide the right to prevent:

...

(b) Acts performed exclusively with experimental purpose over the patented invention that do not prejudice in an unjustifiable manner the normal exploitation of the invention that the title owner may perform or is performing.

c. Procedural Aspects of the Experimental Use Exemption

The Experimental Use exemption may be used as a defence in litigation proceedings.

d. Scope of the Experimental Use Exemption in El Salvador

i. Fields of Technology

There are no field-of-technology-based limitations or restrictions on the Experimental Use exemption.

ii. Purpose of Experiments/Infringing activities

The purpose of the experiments/infringing activities needs to be for scientific investigation, academic or learning purposes.

iii. Exempted and Prohibited Activities

Salvadoran laws do not include any specific exempted or prohibited activities on the Experimental Use exemption, besides that the act does not attempt in an unjustified manner against the normal exploitation of the invention that the owner performs or may perform.

iv. Pure Academic vs Commercially Motivated Experimental Use

The purpose of the experiments/infringing activities needs to be for scientific investigation, academic or learning purposes, thus, not be commercially motivated.

e. Beneficiary Limitations

Third-party participation is not explicitly provided for by law or recognized in any known court decision. However, it is likely that if the actions of third parties were carried out pursuant to a contract, they should also be protected under the Experimental Use exemption.

f. Territoriality Issues

The Salvadoran law does not specify territoriality, nor there are known precedents on how this provision is applied, however it is likely to be interpreted that the use of the experiments/infringing activities shall be applied in El Salvador, and not abroad.

g. Burden of Proof and Onus

The burden of proof for the Experimental Use exemption is on the defendant in a litigation (the person or company that is carrying out the experiments).

h. Applicability during Patent Term Extension or Supplementary Protection Certificate

The law does not make any difference between a 'regular' patent term and applicability during any patent term extension, so the exemption should apply during such patent term extension.

3. THE BOLAR-TYPE EXEMPTION

a. History and Rationale of Adopting the Bolar-Type Exemption

The first Salvadoran patent laws from 1901, and from 1913 did not include the Bolar-type exemption, neither did the Intellectual Property Law enacted in 1993.

El Salvador, along with other Central American countries, negotiated the CAFTA-DR treaty with the United States in January 2003 and January 2004, which included provisions related to Intellectual Property.

CAFTA-DR Intellectual Property Chapter 15, specifically Article 15.9, introduces the Bolar-type exemption in paragraph 5) as follows:

> Consistent with paragraph 3. If a Party (the ratifying countries) permits a third party to use matter of a patent in force to generate information necessary to base a petition for approval of sale of a pharmaceutical or agricultural chemical, this Party shall guarantee that any product manufactured under such authority shall not be manufactured, used or sold in the territory of such Party, for purposes different to those related to the generation of information to satisfy the requirements for the approval for sale of the product once that the patent has expired, and if the Party authorizes the exportation, that the product shall be exported out of the territory of that Party only with the purpose to satisfy the requirements of approval of sale of that Party.

To include the CAFTA-DR provisions in the Salvadoran Intellectual Property Law, in 2005 amendments were made to the law, whereby new wording was introduced with respect to the Bolar-type exemption.

According to Article 166, the effects of the patent do not extend to:

> (e) The use by a third party of the matter subject of protection which patent is in force, to generate the necessary information to base a health registration application of a pharmaceutical product or an agriculture chemical before the Superior Public Health Council or the Ministry of Agriculture and Cattle, application that may be filed once the term of protection of a patent expires; and in case the product is exported outside the national territory, such exportation will be permitted only to satisfy the requirements of approval of such sale in El Salvador.

However, Article 209 of the new Intellectual Property Law, which entered into force on 15 February 2025, has slightly changed the wording of the Bolar-type exemption as follows:

> The rights granted by a patent which is in force, cannot be enforced against the use of a third party of the protected matter to generate the necessary information, to base a health registration application of a pharmaceutical product before the Health Regulation Superintendency, or whoever takes its place or in case of an agricultural chemical before the Agriculture and Cattle Ministry, application that may be authorized once the term of protection of the patent ends; and in case the product is exported outside of the national territory such exportation may be permitted only to satisfy the requirements of approval of sale in El Salvador.

In terms of procedures, in case an application for a health permit/registration was filed, but authorization was not granted due to the existence of a patent in force, once the patent expires, the applicant of the health permit files a writ stating such expiration, so the authorities can conclude the health registration procedures and issue the sale authorization.

b. The Laws Applicable to the Bolar-Type Exemption in El Salvador

The previous Intellectual Property Law provides in Article 116 (e) that the effects of the patent do not extend to:

> 'The use by a third party of the matter subject of protection which patent is in force, to generate the necessary information to base a health registration application of a pharmaceutical product or an agriculture chemical before the Superior Public Health Council or the Ministry of Agriculture and Cattle, application that may be filed once the term of protection of a patent expires; and in case the product is exported outside the national territory, such exportation will be permitted only to satisfy the requirements of approval of such sale in El Salvador.'

However, the current Intellectual Property Law, which entered into force on 15 February 2025, in which a definition for Bolar-type exemption is included, alongside the exemption which differs slightly from the current law.

Article 60 of the new Intellectual Property, defines the Bolar-type exemption as:

> It is the limitation of exclusivity rights granted to a patent, according to which, it is permitted to a third party to use information of the patent, without authorization of the title owner, for experimental, study and essay purposes, to generate information necessary to file a health permit application.

The new law further provides in Article 209 as follows:

> The rights granted by a patent which is in force, cannot be enforced against the use of a third party of the protected matter to generate the necessary information, to base a health registration application of a pharmaceutical product before the Health Regulation Superintendency, or whoever takes its place or in case of an agricultural chemical before the Agriculture and Cattle Ministry, application that may be authorized once the term of protection of the patent ends; and in case the product is exported outside of the national territory such exportation may be permitted only to satisfy the requirements of approval of sale in El Salvador.

c. Procedural Aspects of Invoking the Bolar-Type Exemption

The Bolar-type exemption is used as a defence in litigation proceedings.

d. Scope of the Bolar-Type Exemption in El Salvador

i. Fields of Technology

The Bolar-type exemption is limited to pharmaceuticals and chemical products (human or agricultural/animal).

ii. Purpose of Experiments/Infringing Activities

The purpose of the Bolar-type exemption needs to be to generate the necessary information for basing a health registration application of a pharmaceutical product before the Health Regulation Superintendency or an agricultural chemical product before the Agriculture and Cattle Ministry.

iii. Exempted and Prohibited Activities

The export of the product shall be permitted only to satisfy the requirements of approval of sale in El Salvador.

Also, due to its nature, its importation and/or offering for sale would be prohibited.

e. Beneficiary Limitations

The Bolar-type exemption applies both to generic companies applying for regulatory approval and for innovative companies, for example, when doing competitive studies.

The Bolar-type exemption can be used by the entity that is applying for regulatory approval. It is not specifically provided by law, but it is likely that it may apply to third parties contracted by the company who seek regulatory approval, to perform studies on behalf of the party seeking regulatory approval.

f. Territoriality Issues

The regulatory submission would need to be made in El Salvador. If the regulatory submission is in another country, the exemption would not apply.

g. Burden of Proof and Onus

The burden of proof to establish that the Bolar-type exemption applies to the infringing activities is on the defendant in a litigation, thus, the entity that is using the patent to obtain information to submit a regulatory application.

h. Applicability during Patent Term Extension or Supplementary Protection Certificate

Salvadoran law does not make any difference between 'regular' patent term and applicability during any patent term extension; thus, the Bolar-type exemption also applies during patent term extension.

4. DIFFERENCES BETWEEN THE TWO EXEMPTIONS IN EL SALVADOR

The Experimental Use exemption is broader to the Bolar-type exemption, in respect of the field of technology, as the former applies to any field, and the latter only to the pharmaceutical/chemical field (for humans, agriculture or animals). However, in respect of the commercial or non-commercial purpose, in the case of the Experimental Use exemption may not be commercial, but the Bolar-type exemption is used to apply for regulatory approval, which is always for a commercial end.

Chapter 16
Finland

Johanna Lilja and Miko Leach

1. GENERAL

a. Terminology

The Experimental Use exemption is provided under Section 3(3)(3) of the Patents Act (550/1967, as amended). The exclusive rights conferred by a patent do not extend to the use of the patented invention in experiments concerning the subject-matter of the patented invention.

The Bolar-type exemption is provided under Section 3(3)(4) of the Patents Act. The exclusive rights conferred by a patent do not extend to studies, trials or activities arising out of practical requirements, which concern a patented invention relating to the medicinal product and which are necessary for the purposes of a marketing authorization application.

Both are considered *exceptions* to the scope of the exclusive rights conferred by the patent, and, where applicable, may exempt an infringement of said exclusive rights. In accordance with Section 70d of the Patents Act, the rights and obligations conferred by the patent on which a supplementary protection certificate ('SPC') is granted equally apply to the SPC, which also draws its legal character from Regulation (EC) No. 469/2009 ('SPC Regulation') as directly applicable Union law.

b. Legal Basis in Finland

The Experimental Use exemption was enacted under Section 3(3)(3) of the Patents Act in 1980 and provides: 'The exclusive right shall not apply to: ... (3) use in experiments relating to the invention as such.' (Unofficial translation of the Patents Act.)

There is no leading case law on the Experimental Use exemption from the Supreme Court of Finland – although it should be noted that the Supreme Court has not given many precedents on patent law in general either.

However, in its judgment no. 2629 of 3 September 2007 in case docket no. S 05/667, the Helsinki Court of Appeal (which used to have jurisdiction in patent disputes as an instance of appeal for judgments of the District Court of Helsinki prior to 2013) examined whether an infringer could effectively excuse itself by invoking the Experimental Use exemption under Section 3(3)(3) of the Patents Act.[1] Under the facts at hand, the Helsinki Court of Appeal found that the infringer could not avail itself of the exemption given that the infringing acts had taken place publicly for a commercial use and for a duration of several years. Otherwise, there is little case law on the Experimental Use exemption.

The Bolar-type exemption was implemented under Section 3(3)(4) of the Patents Act in 2006, by virtue of Directive 2004/27 amending Directive 2001/83/EC (Human Medicines Directive), and provides:

> The exclusive right shall not apply to: ... (4) examinations or experiments or measures arising from practical demands which are needed for an application to obtain a marketing authorization for a medicinal product and which relate to the invention concerning that medicinal product. [Unofficial translation of the Patents Act.]

There is no leading case law on the Bolar-type exemption.

c. Bodies That May Decide on the Legitimacy of Exemptions

Both the Experimental Use exemption and the Bolar-type exemption are used only as defences in patent litigation. In Finland, such proceedings fall under the exclusive jurisdiction of the Market Court. Judgments of the Market Court may be appealed to the Supreme Court, subject to leave to appeal. Accordingly, the Market Court and the Supreme Court have jurisdiction to determine the legitimacy of the exemptions.

In addition, as the Bolar-type exemption is based upon an EU Directive, it is possible that certain questions on the Bolar-type exemption could be referred to the Court of Justice of the European Union ('CJEU') for a preliminary ruling. Both the Market Court and Supreme Court can refer to the CJEU for a preliminary ruling.

It should be further noted that European patents, which have not been opted out of the unitary patent system, as well as SPCs granted on such patents, fall also under the parallel jurisdiction of the Unified Patent Court – at least during the transitory period. However, the Unified Patent Court has exclusive jurisdiction for European patents for which unitary effect has been requested ('unitary patents'). Thus, the Unified Patent Court and the Court of Appeal could also decide on the legitimacy of the exemption for patents that fall under the jurisdiction of the Unified Patent Court. A local division of the Unified Patent Court is located in Helsinki. More details can be found in the Chapter dedicated to the Unitary Patent System and the Unified Patent Court.

1. Helsinki Court of Appeal: *Fuuga Controls Oy v. Electrolux Professional Oy* and others, judgment no. 2629 in case docket no. S 05/667 (3 September 2007.

2. THE EXPERIMENTAL USE EXEMPTION

a. History and Rationale of Adopting the Experimental Use Exemption

Section 3(3)(3) of the Patents Act providing for the Experimental Use exemption mirrors Article 27(b) of the Community Patent Convention (which never entered into force). A key function of patent law is to incentivize industrial activity. Thus, it has been considered, in legal literature, that a rationale for the Experimental Use exemption would be to allow experiments aiming at generating new knowledge or improving upon known (also patented) solutions.[2]

b. The Laws Applicable to the Experimental Use Exemption in Finland

As noted, Section 3(3)(3) of the Patents Act provides for the Experimental Use exemption and provides: 'The exclusive right shall not apply to: … (3) use in experiments relating to the invention as such.' (Unofficial translation of the Patents Act.)

The exclusive rights conferred by a patent do not extend to the use of the patented invention in experiments concerning the subject-matter of the patented invention. The wording of the provision provides that, in order to benefit from the exemption, the following two conditions need to be fulfilled: (i) experimental use and (ii) concerning the patented invention. The statutory language does not provide that only experimental use by private persons or in a non-professional capacity would be exempted, as noted in legal literature.[3]

The provisions of the Patents Act are to be interpreted in light of the TRIPS Agreement, which provides, under Article 30, a three-step test for restricting the exclusive rights conferred by the patent. Thus, any restrictions to said exclusive rights shall be, amongst other things, interpreted narrowly so as not to compromise the interests of the patentee. In judgment no. 2629 of 3 September 2007 in case docket no. S 05/667, the Helsinki Court of Appeal did not accept the Experimental Use exemption invoked by the infringer, based upon the facts that were at hand in that case given that the infringing acts had taken place publicly for a commercial use and for a duration of several years.[4]

c. Procedural Aspects of Invoking the Experimental Use Exemption

In accordance with the Patents Act and the SPC Regulation, the Market Court has exclusive jurisdiction in patent and SPC disputes when the dispute is based upon the material provisions of the Patents Act. Thus, purely contractual disputes do not fall within the exclusive jurisdiction of the Market Court. Decisions and judgments of the Market Court may only be appealed directly to the Supreme Court, subject

2. Marcus Norrgård, *Patentin loukkaus* 96 – 97 (Alma Talent Oy 2008).
3. Marcus Norrgård, *Patentin loukkaus* 96 (Alma Talent Oy 2008).
4. Helsinki Court of Appeal: *Fuuga Controls Oy v. Electrolux Professional Oy* and others, judgment no. 2629 in case docket no. S 05/667 (3 September 2007.

to leave to appeal. Thus, the Market Court and Supreme Court have jurisdiction to determine the legitimacy of the exemption.

Given that the Experimental Use exemption may exempt an infringement of the exclusive rights conferred by the patent or SPC, the exemption would primarily be invoked by an alleged infringer in response to, for example, an application for a preliminary injunction or a (main) infringement action (which may comprise declaratory and/or injunctive claims as well as claims for compensation) based on a patent or SPC.

d. Scope of the Experimental Use Exemption in Finland

i. Fields of Technology

Section 3(3)(3) of the Patents Act provides that the exclusive rights conferred by a patent do not extend to the use of the patented invention in experiments concerning the subject-matter of the patented invention. Thus, the Experimental Use exemption would not be limited to any particular field of technology by statutory wording.

ii. Purpose of Experiments/Infringing Activities

According to views expressed in legal literature, the Experimental Use exemption presents a fine line between, on the one hand, infringing activities, which are not exempted and, on the other hand, experimental use, which may be exempted.[5] As the Experimental Use exemption requires *experimental use*, the exemption applies to testing or improving the claimed invention but not to any commercial use thereof. It is permissible to obtain information on how the invention works or does not work, even for assessments of the validity of the patent. Financial interests, as such, do not render experimental use impermissible. However, as discussed above, there is case from the Helsinki Court of Appeal in which a public commercial use was not exempted.[6]

Moreover, it is impermissible to carry out experiments *with* the claimed invention. Only experiments *on* the claimed invention are permissible.[7] The permissibility of experiments *on* the claimed invention thus allow the fulfilment of the purposes of the exemption, namely improvements to the claimed invention or developing a better alternative. However, the use of the claimed invention as a means for subject-matter that does not relate to claimed invention is impermissible.

iii. Exempted and Prohibited Activities

Experiments *with* the claimed invention are prohibited under the Experimental Use exemption, whereas experiments *on* the claimed invention may be exempted thereunder.

---

5. Marcus Norrgård, *Patentin loukkaus* 97 (Alma Talent Oy 2008).
6. Helsinki Court of Appeal: *Fuuga Controls Oy v. Electrolux Professional Oy* and others, judgment no. 2629 in case docket no. S 05/667 (3 September 2007).
7. Marcus Norrgård, *Patentin loukkaus* 97 (Alma Talent Oy 2008).

This dichotomy between experiments *with* and *on* the claimed invention does not address, *per se*, which of the exclusive rights provided under Section 3(1) – (2) of the Patents Act, for example offering, placing on the market, using, importing or possessing, would be exempted or prohibited. Any prohibited or exempted activities would need to be considered on a case-by-case assessment.

iv. *Pure Academic vs Commercially Motivated Experimental Use*

The Experimental Use exemption is not limited to purely academic research; also commercially motivated experimental research may qualify.[8] However, the experimental use must be *on* the claimed invention (not *with* the claimed invention). In addition, the experimental use, in of itself, may not be commercial as was the case in the judgment of the Helsinki Court of Appeal.[9] However, there seems to be no other case law on this matter.

e. Beneficiary Limitations

This issue does not seem to have been addressed in the legislation or case law, whereas it is established that the Experimental Use exemption would not apply if the experimental use is, amongst others, commercial.

f. Territoriality Issues

This does not seem to have been addressed in the legislation or case law. While the exemption could be applicable for any Finnish part of the patent, it is uncertain how the court would interpret the exemption in the described circumstance.

g. Burden of Proof and Onus

The party invoking the Experimental Use exemption as a defence bears the burden of proof. In accordance with Finnish civil procedure, the required standard is one of credible proof.

h. Applicability during Patent Term Extension or Supplementary Protection Certificate

The Experimental Use exemption, if the requirements for reliance on the exemption are fulfilled, would apply for as long as the exclusive rights conferred by the patent or SPC are in force.

8. Marcus Norrgård, *Patentin loukkaus* 96 (Alma Talent Oy 2008).
9. Helsinki Court of Appeal: *Fuuga Controls Oy v. Electrolux Professional Oy* and others, judgment no. 2629 in case docket no. S 05/667 (3 September 2007).

3. THE BOLAR-TYPE EXEMPTION

a. History and Rationale of Adopting the Bolar-Type Exemption

In Finland, the Bolar-type exemption is derived from EU Directives: the provision on the Bolar-type exemption in Finland implements provisions restricting the scope of patent protection added in Article 10(6) of Directive 2001/83/EC on the Community code relating to medicinal products for human use and Article 13(6) of Directive 2001/82/EC on the Community code relating to veterinary medicinal products. These additions are regulated in Directive 2004/27/EC amending Directive 2001/83/EC on the Community code relating to medicinal products for human use and in Directive 2004/28/EC amending Directive 2001/82/EC on the Community code relating to veterinary medicinal products. Each EU Member State has enacted national legislation to implement the exemption formulated in the said EU Directives and thus, the harmonization of the exemption may vary between the Member States.

For example, in Finland, in addition to the situations described in the Directives, the scope of the Bolar-type exemption was extended to also cover studies necessary for obtaining a marketing authorization for an innovative medicinal product, including a combination product.[10]

The aim of the additions to the Directives is to facilitate the entry of generic products into the market. In the *travaux préparatoires* of the Patents Act[11] it was stated that in the previous state of legislation, manufacturers of the competitive medicinal products had to wait for the expiry of the patent or SPC before starting preparations for the marketing authorization application, as some of the actions necessary for a marketing authorization application may infringe the patent or SPC and such activities do not fall under the Experimental Use exemption. It was considered that the Bolar-type exemption enables the preparations for a marketing authorization application to be started during the period of validity of the patent or SPC so that the market entry of competing products would not be delayed by the time required for the marketing authorization procedure. In practice, this would speed up the market entry for generic products by at least the time required for the marketing authorization procedure, i.e. by about one year. Furthermore, according to the *travaux préparatoires* of the Patents Act, the aim of the provision was to help maintain equal operating conditions for the pharmaceutical industry in comparison with several countries outside the European Economic Area ('EEA'), where studies necessary for a marketing authorization application were conducted before the Bolar-type exemption was implemented to the Patents Act.

The Bolar-type exemption was considered necessary for public health reasons and a proportional limitation to the exclusive right of the patent or SPC holder, as the economic implications of the exemption appear only after the expiry of a patent or SPC.

10. Government Bill: HE 255/2005 vp, p. 3 (22 December 2005).
11. Government Bill: HE 255/2005 vp, pp. 2–3 (22 December 2005).

b. The Laws Applicable to the Bolar-Type Exemption in Finland

Finland has a Bolar-type exemption, codified in Section 3(3)(4) Patents Act, which provides:

> The exclusive right shall not apply to: ...
>
> (4) examinations or experiments or measures arising from practical demands which are needed for an application to obtain a marketing authorization for a medicinal product and which relate to the invention concerning that medicinal product.

The Bolar-type exemption (as all exemptions to patent protection) is to be interpreted narrowly. The strict interpretation of the provision is evident also from the *travaux préparatoires* of the Patents Act which provide that studies, trials and measures arising from practical demands must be *necessary* for obtaining a marketing authorization for the medicinal product.[12]

Although the *travaux préparatoires* of the Patents Act[13] provide insight on how the provision should be interpreted in practice, the interpretation is ultimately decided by the court and the *travaux préparatoires* may inform the court in its decision-making.

To date, there has been no case law regarding the Bolar-type exemption, nor is there much legal literature or research on the Bolar-type exemption in Finland. Thus, the guidance for interpretation is currently mainly based on the *travaux préparatoires* of the Patents Act.

c. Procedural Aspects of Invoking the Bolar-Type Exemption

The Bolar-type exemption may be invoked as a defence in patent or SPC infringement proceedings. The applicant usually seeks a preliminary injunction in addition to filing a (main) infringement action. The exemption may be relied upon as a defence in both proceedings.

Applications for a preliminary injunction and infringement actions are filed with the Market Court. As explained above, judgments of the Market Court may be appealed to the Supreme Court, subject to leave to appeal. Therefore, the Market Court and the Supreme Court have jurisdiction to determine the legitimacy of the exemption.

d. Scope of the Bolar-Type Exemption in Finland

i. *Fields of Technology*

The Bolar-type exemption in Finland is specifically targeted at and limited to studies, trials and measures necessary for obtaining a marketing authorization for a *medicinal product*, and hence, the applicability of the exemption is limited to pharmaceutical sector (including veterinary medicinal products and biosimilars).

12. Government Bill: HE 225/2005 vp, p. 2 (22 December 2005).
13. Government Bill: HE 225/2005 vp (22 December 2005).

ii. *Purpose of Experiments/Infringing Activities*

According to the *travaux préparatoires* of the Patents Act, an essential element of the exemption is that the studies, trials and measures arising from practical demands must be *necessary* for obtaining a marketing authorization for the medicinal product. Thus, the purpose of the experiments must be necessary for a marketing authorization application.[14] See also section 3.d.iii. below.

The exemption covers the studies and trials necessary for obtaining a marketing authorization for a generic medicinal product or similar biological product (biosimilar). In addition, the exemption applies to research for obtaining a marketing authorization for a medicinal product which benefits from the marketing authorization of a reference product but does not meet the criteria of a generic medicinal product, for example due to differences in therapeutic indications, strength, pharmaceutical form or route of administration, vis-à-vis the reference medicinal product.[15]

The Government Bill[16] also provides that the exemption may extend beyond the situations covered by Directives 2001/83/EC and 2001/82/EC to cover other kinds of products, including innovative products (including combination products), but the scope of applicability of the exemption to 'innovative medicinal products' is somewhat unclear due to lack of any precedents.

iii. *Exempted and Prohibited Activities*

The exemption applies only to patents protecting the reference product used in an application for a marketing authorization. This includes patents covering the processes of making the reference product.

As stated above in section 3.d.ii., the studies, trials and measures must be *necessary* for obtaining a marketing authorization for the medicinal product. This means that the exemption covers, for example, test manufacturing for authorization of a manufacturing method if that is needed for the marketing authorization and the production scale does not exceed the demands of that purpose. Measures arising from practical demands may be, for example, manufacture or import of raw materials required for the test manufacturing.[17]

However, it is specifically mentioned in the *travaux préparatoires* of the Patents Act[18] that the exemption does not cover actions taken in preparation for patent (or SPC) expiry, such as production of the medicinal product for storage while the exclusive rights pertaining to the patent (or SPC) remain in force. Thus, the experiments and tests must be necessary for obtaining a marketing authorization.

Furthermore, conducting clinical trials for the purpose of obtaining a marketing authorization for a medicinal product is not a general ground for authorizing the use of inventions unrelated to the medicinal product, such as the use of another party's patented intermediates, experimental methods, laboratory equipment or the like.

14. Government Bill: HE 225/2005 vp, p. 2 (22 December 2005).
15. Government Bill: HE 225/2005 vp, pp. 2–3 (22 December 2005).
16. Government Bill: HE 225/2005 vp, p. 3 (22 December 2005).
17. Government Bill: HE 225/2005 vp, p. 2 (22 December 2005).
18. Government Bill: HE 225/2005 vp, p. 2 (22 December 2005).

The scope of the exempted and prohibited activities is, however, somewhat unclear due to the lack of case law regarding the Bolar-type exemption set out in Section 3(3)(4) of the Patents Act.

e. Beneficiary Limitations

The exemption is directed to both generic companies and innovative companies applying for a marketing authorization for their medicinal products.

Neither Section 3(3)(4) of the Patents Act nor the *travaux préparatoires* of the Patents Act differentiate between the party conducting the clinical trials and the applicant for the marketing authorization. Thus, the exemption seems to apply to third parties as well and the decisive factor seems to be whether the actions themselves are *necessary* for obtaining a marketing authorization for the medicinal product, but there is no case law on this question.

f. Territoriality Issues

The application for a marketing authorization sought by the party relying on the Bolar-type exemption may be submitted in Finland or abroad (an EU-wide (centralized) or a foreign marketing authorization), in cases where the infringing activities take place in Finland.

Regarding activities in other countries for the purposes of obtaining a marketing authorization in Finland (as well as in other countries), it is to be decided whether the Market Court has jurisdiction in the matter. It seems that this issue has not been addressed in Finland. Under Section 64 of the Patents Act, the Market Court handles civil matters under the provisions of the Patents Act i.e. mainly related to national patents granted by the Finnish Patent Office, European patents validated in Finland and SPCs.

g. Burden of Proof and Onus

The party invoking the Bolar-type exemption as a defence to infringement claims bears the burden of proof. In accordance with Finnish civil procedure, the required standard is one of credible proof.

h. Applicability during Patent Term Extension or Supplementary Protection Certificate

An SPC provides its holder with the same rights as the basic patent and is subject to the same restrictions and obligations. The Bolar-type exemption may be applicable for as long as the exclusive rights conferred by the (basic) patent or SPC are in force.

4. DIFFERENCES BETWEEN THE TWO EXEMPTIONS IN FINLAND

Both exemptions are provided by Section 3(3) of the Patents Act. However, the Bolar-type exemption derives from Directive 2004/27/EC amending Directive

2001/83/EC on the Community code relating to medicinal products for human use and has been implemented into Finnish legislation, whereas the Experimental Use exemption derives from Article 27(b) of the Community Patent Convention and has been implemented in the Patents Act already before the implementation of the Bolar-type exemption.

The main difference between the two exemptions is that the studies and trials conducted under the Bolar-type exemption must be necessary for obtaining a marketing authorization whereas the studies and trials conducted under the Experimental Use exemption may be of a more general nature, provided that the actions have an experimental purpose, the experiments concern the invention itself and the use is non-commercial.

Furthermore, the Bolar-type exemption only applies to medicinal products, whereas the applicability of the Experimental Use exemption would not be limited to a certain field of technology by statutory wording.

According to the language of the provisions, the two exemptions may, in theory, overlap as infringement may be exempted if either of the exemptions (or both simultaneously) apply in the given circumstances. However, it is envisaged in the *travaux préparatoires* of the Patents Act[19] that many activities falling under the Bolar-type exemption are not in the scope of the Experimental Use exemption as the studies, trials and measures for a marketing authorization application serve mainly commercial objectives. The Experimental Use exemption does not apply to commercial use *per se*.

19. Government Bill: HE 225/2005 vp, p. 2 (22 December 2005).

Chapter 17

France

Brigitte Carion-Taravella, Cyra Nargolwalla and Thomas Bouvet

1. GENERAL

a. Legal Basis

In France, Articles L. 613-3 and L. 614 of the Intellectual Property Code ('IPC') lists the acts that are reserved to the patent owner.

Article L. 613-3 reads as follows:

> The following are prohibited, in the absence of the consent of the owner of the patent:
> (a) the manufacture, offering, placing on the market, use, import, export, transshipment, or possession for the aforesaid purposes of the product that is the subject of the patent;
> (b) the use of a process that is the subject of the patent or, when the third party knows or when the circumstances make it obvious that the use of the process is prohibited without the consent of the owner of the patent, the offer of its use on French territory;
> (c) offering, marketing, using, importing, exporting, transshipping or holding for the aforementioned purposes the product obtained directly by the process that is the subject of the patent.

Article L. 613-4 of the IPC also provides that:

> (1) In the absence of the consent of the patent owner, the delivery or offer of delivery, on French territory, to a person other than those entitled to work the patented invention, of the means of carrying out, on such territory, of the invention relating to an essential element thereof, shall also be forbidden, where the third party knows or where the circumstances make it obvious that these means are suitable and intended for such performance. …

> (3) Those who perform the acts referred to in Article L. 613-5... (b) shall not be considered persons entitled to exploit the invention within the meaning of Section 1.

Article L. 613-5 b) of the IPC contains exceptions and exemptions, which provides for the Experimental Use exemption, reads as follows:

> The rights conferred by the patent do not extend to: ...
> (b) Acts performed on an experimental basis relating to the subject-matter of the patented invention

Article L. 613-5 b) of the IPC provides for an Experimental Use exemption enabling the performance of acts that would, in the absence of this exemption, be considered as acts of infringement in accordance with Article L. 613-3 IPC.

Finally, regarding Bolar-type exemption, the IPC states that:

> The rights conferred by the patent do not extend to ...
> (d) Studies and tests required for obtaining a marketing authorization for a medicinal product, as well as the acts necessary for carrying out such studies and tests and for obtaining the authorization.

b. Bodies That May Decide on the Legitimacy of Exemptions

In France, the Tribunal Judiciaire (TJ, formerly Tribunal de Grande Instance (TGI)) of Paris is the Court responsible for handling patent cases related to the Bolar-type exemption and experimental use. That Court is the only one handling patent related disputes.

Cases concerning these exemptions may also involve the Cour d'Appel (Court of Appeal) if an appeal is made regarding a TJ decision.

A further appeal is also possible in the Cour de Cassation, the French supreme court for civil matters.

2. THE EXPERIMENTAL USE EXEMPTION

a. History and Rationale of Adopting the Experimental Use Exemption

In France, the Experimental Use exemption in patent law is rooted in both national and European law.

The concept of experimental use can be traced back to the IPC, which has undergone several revisions since its inception. The principle aligns with the goal of promoting innovation and research, allowing researchers to test and explore patented inventions without infringing patent rights. This exemption stems from a concern not to impede technical progress[1] and innovation.

The specific legal framework regarding the Experimental Use exemption has evolved over the time. The Experimental Use exemption was officially recognized in France as early as 1968.

1. Paris Court of Appeal, 3 July 2002, No. 2000/14939.

While the concept of experimental use existed prior to this, the formal legal basis for it was established in the 1992 reforms. The IPC was amended in 1992 to include provisions that allow for the use of patented inventions for experimental purposes, specifically for research and development. This was part of the broader reforms that aimed to align French law with European standards, particularly following the adoption of the European Patent Convention (EPC).

Then, in 1998, new amendments were made in the French law, influenced by the Directive 98/44/EC on the legal protection of biotechnological inventions ('Biotech Directive'). These documents provided a framework that many Member States, including France, have followed. The European Biotech Directive influenced the codification of Experimental Use exemptions in French law in several key aspects:

- *Clarification of Scope*: The Biotech Directive provided clearer definitions and guidelines regarding biotechnological inventions, which helped to delineate the boundaries of what constituted experimental use. This clarification was crucial for researchers in biotechnology, allowing them to understand the extent to which they could use patented inventions for research without infringing on patent rights.
- *Promotion of Research and Innovation*: The Biotech Directive emphasized the importance of research and innovation in biotechnology. By reinforcing the Experimental Use exemption, it aimed to encourage scientific exploration and development, ensuring that researchers could build upon existing patented inventions to advance knowledge and technology.
- *Balancing Rights*: The Biotech Directive sought to balance the rights of patent holders with the need for access to scientific knowledge. This balance is reflected in the French law, which allows for experimental use without compensation to the patent holder, provided the use is non-commercial.
- *Harmonization with EU Standards*: The Biotech Directive contributed to harmonizing patent laws across EU Member States, including France. This harmonization ensured that the Experimental Use exemption was consistent with broader European patent law principles, facilitating cross-border research collaborations and reducing legal uncertainties for researchers.

Overall, while the Experimental Use exemption was codified in French law in 1992, the 1998 Biotech Directive further shaped its application and interpretation, particularly in the context of biotechnological research.

French courts have played a significant role in interpreting the scope of the Experimental Use exemption. Landmark cases have helped define what constitutes 'experimental use', clarifying the boundaries between permissible research and infringing activities.

In recent years, there has been an ongoing discussion about the balance between patent protection and the need for scientific freedom. The rise of biotechnology and complex inventions has led to calls for a broader interpretation of the Experimental Use exemption to promote innovation.

Overall, the history of the Experimental Use exemption in France reflects a balance between protecting patent rights and fostering an environment conducive to research and innovation.

b. The Laws Applicable to the Experimental Use Exemption in France

As of now, the Experimental Use exemption in France is defined under Article L. 613-5 of the French IPC:

> The rights conferred by the patent do not extend to: ...
> (b) Acts performed on an experimental basis relating to the subject-matter of the patented invention

There has been case law which *inter alia* has provided guidance on what constitutes 'experimental use'.

c. Procedural Aspects of the Experimental Use Exemption

The Experimental Use exemption is considered, in France, as a defence in the context of an infringement action[2] and is invoked by defendants in patent infringement cases as a defence to argue that their activities fall within the exemption.

The Experimental Use exemption will thus only apply in the presence of alleged acts of infringement[3] and French case law will not examine it if the conditions of infringement are not met.[4]

The Experimental Use exemption could possibly also be used in support to claims for declaration of non-infringement.

d. Scope of the Experimental Use Exemption in France

i. Fields of Technology

There are no field-of-technology-based limitations or restrictions on the Experimental Use exemption in France. All types of technology may utilize such exemptions.

ii. Purpose of Experiments

The law allows for the use of a patented invention without the patent holder's authorization for experimental purposes, including research and development activities.

As a matter of principle, legal exceptions must be interpreted narrowly under French law. Accordingly, like all exceptions to infringement, the Experimental Use exemption is to be interpreted narrowly; the need for a narrow interpretation is frequently recalled by French case law.[5]

The Experimental Use exemption is not *per se* limited to acts performed for 'academic purposes' having 'no commercial value'. The experimental purpose will

2. F. Pollaud-Dulian, *La propriété industrielle*, Economica, 2011; P. Véron & N. Bouche, '*Agir en contrefaçon de brevet invention*', Lexis, 2022.
3. Paris Court of First Instance, 24 November 2009, No. 07/03839.
4. Paris Judicial Court, 11 February 2022, No. 21/06388.
5. Paris Court of Appeal, 3 July 2002, PIBD 2003, No. 758, III, 93; Paris Court of First Instance, 7 October 2005, No. 2002/3956; Paris Court of First Instance, 11 February 2022, No. 21/6388.

of course be satisfied when the acts are performed for academic purposes, provided they relate to the subject-matter of the patented invention. But the experimental purpose also covers tests carried out to evaluate the subject-matter of the invention.

French courts seem to consider that the Experimental Use exemption covers acts of exploitation of products or implementation of processes aimed at verifying the technical interest of the invention that do not lead directly or in the short term to an offer to a potential customer.[6]

Thus, for instance, the presentation of a system, largely commented by national press, will go beyond the Experimental Use exemption, even though such system has remained at the level of a mere project since the purpose of the presentation had 'commercial purposes'.[7]

The Experimental Use exemption is subject to two conditions: the act must (1) be performed on an experimental basis and (2) relate to the subject-matter of the patented invention:

- the experimental basis covers acts performed for research purposes, to assess the teachings of the patent and its validity, or for development, the limit being the commercial purpose.[8] French doctrine and case law agree that only the immediate commercial purpose is excluded. This means experimental acts that do not lead directly or in the short term to commercial exploitation benefit from the exception provided for in Article L. 613-5 b) and such a commercial purpose may be envisaged in the longer term;[9]
- the relation to the subject-matter of the patented invention means that the purpose of the research must be to gain knowledge on the subject-matter of the invention. Such is not the case if the researcher uses a patented invention to gain knowledge on a subject which is not related to the invention, for example to use the patented invention as a research tool or to achieve the development of products[10] unrelated to the invention.

iii. Exempted and Prohibited Activities

The Experimental Use exemption has been admitted in relation to a limited number of acts.[11] For instance, the following activities were considered to benefit from the Experimental Use exemption:

6. Paris Judicial Court, 11 February 2022, No. 21/06388.
7. Paris Court of Appeal, 3 July 2002, No. 2000/14939.
8. Paris Court of Appeal, 3 July 2002, PIBD 2003, No. 758, III, 93; Paris Court of First Instance, 7 October 2005, No. 2002/3956; Paris Court of First Instance, 22 March 2006, No. 03/03518; Paris Court of First Instance, 11 February 2022, No. 21/6388.
9. Passa, *Traité de droit de la propriété industrielle*, LGDJ, 2013, at 566-567; Le Stand, 'Acte de contrefaçon – Elément légal', JurisClasseur Brevets, Lexis, 2018; Paris Court of First Instance, 11 February 2022, No. 21/6388.
10. Véron, 'Contrefaçon de brevet d'invention – Usage expérimental et essais cliniques', *Revue du Droit de la Propriété Intellectuelle* No. 107, January 2000; P. Véron, '*L'exception d'usage expérimental et l'exception "Bolar"*', *Propriétés Intellectuelles* No. 59, April 2016.
11. J. Azéma & J.-C. Galloux, *Droit de la propriété industrielle*, Dalloz, 2017, at 587.

- delivery of products under temporary authorizations;[12]
- acts performed in the context of a research program with the ultimate aim of developing products submitted in support of applications for funding or seeking partnerships which are not in themselves infringing and where it is agreed that the commercial aim is still remote.[13]

Until 2001, and prior to the implementation of a Bolar-type exemption in France, French case law applied the Experimental Use exemption with a broader scope than the wording of the legal provision; for example, it has been used to exempt the following acts:

- acts of exploitation of the invention in the context of bioequivalence tests required to obtain a marketing authorization (MA) as well as necessary tests for the application for an MA, without being followed by the manufacture of additional tablets beyond the pilot batches ordered;[14]
- phase 3 clinical trials carried out to assess a new technique to encapsulate a drug, as their purpose was to acquire new knowledge;[15]
- phase 3 clinical trials carried out to assess the bioequivalence of the drugs, but also to test whether the association of the active ingredient with the litigious technology improved the dosing conditions, while remaining equivalent in terms of treatment efficacy.[16]

Following the implementation of a Bolar-type exemption in French law, the above-mentioned bioequivalence tests are now rather exempted under the Bolar-type exemption.

The Experimental Use exemption has not been admitted in the following cases:

- delivery of products under temporary authorizations when their scope and duration could not characterize acts performed on an experimental basis, especially when the presentation leaflet for temporary authorizations specified that it was not a clinical trial and that it had no investigative objectives;[17]
- a project that remained at the experimental stage but was presented to the public at professional meetings and was the subject of a press release and several articles in major newspapers;[18]
- manufacture of prototypes bearing information that could be regarded as evidence of preparatory acts for actual commercialization;[19]
- canvassing of the target audience and adjustments made to a product in order to satisfy customers;[20]

---

12. Paris Court of First Instance, 11 December 2002, PIBD 2003, No. 767, III, 338.
13. Paris Court of First Instance, 11 February 2022, No. 21/6388.
14. Paris Court of First Instance, 25 January 2002, No. 00-11702.
15. Paris Court of Appeal, 27 January 1999, *Wellcome Foundation v. Parexel International and Flamel*
16. Paris Court of First Instance, 20 February 2001, *Wellcome Fundation v. Parexel International and Flamel*
17. Paris Court of Appeal, 5 September 2003, No. 2003/08407.
18. Paris Court of Appeal, 3 July 2002, PIBD 2003, No. 758, III, 93.
19. Paris Court of First Instance, 30 May 2005, No. 02/03385.
20. Paris Court of Appeal, 7 October 2005, No.02/03956.

- organization of a visit of an experimental site for a company interested in the process and formulation and which offers to acquire a unit incorporating the process in question;[21]
- presentation at trade shows without carrying out experiments,[22] the presentation of a prototype at a trade show being non-experimental in nature when no scientific test has been carried out at the said show.[23]

e. Beneficiary Limitations

There is little case law on this specific situation in France, perhaps because the legal exception provided by Article L. 613-5 IPC applies to acts rather than to the persons conducting those acts.

A third party performing any of the acts reserved to the patent owner as listed in Article L. 613-3 of the IPC risks being liable for patent infringement, unless it can rely on one of the exemptions.

It seems that the commercial supply by a third party of the patented invention to another party for the latter's experimental use would not be covered by the Experimental Use exemption.

A distinction must be made between direct and contributory infringement notably as Article L. 613-4 of the IPC provides that:

> (1) In the absence of the consent of the patent owner, the delivery or offer of delivery, on French territory, to a person other than those entitled to work the patented invention, of the means of carrying out, on such territory, of the invention relating to an essential element thereof, shall also be forbidden, where the third party knows or where the circumstances make it obvious that these means are suitable and intended for such performance....
>
> (3) Those who perform the acts referred to in Article L. 613-5... (b) shall not be considered persons entitled to exploit the invention within the meaning of Section 1.

It can thus be inferred from this Article that, in the context of contributory infringement, third parties performing the acts mentioned in Article L. 613-4 (i.e. supplying essential means) will not benefit from the Experimental Use exemption, even if they supply the essential means to a person benefiting from the exemption.

Similar provisions exist in Article 26(3) of the UPCA.

Regarding contributory infringement, French case law interestingly ruled that:

> In the present case, the fact that in the patient's body, the zinc salt of rosuvastatin, after ingestion, would dissociate from the rosuvastatin in neutral acid form cannot characterize a contributory infringement by BIOGARAN when, on the one hand, the third party referred to in Article L. 613-4 of the IPC, in this case the patient, does not know the mechanism of decomposition of the drug inside

21. Paris Court of First Instance, 22 March 2006, No. 03/03518.
22. Cass. Com., 5 May 2017, No. 15-20.554, Paris Court of First Instance, 22 December 2006, No. 06/08499.
23. Paris Court of Appeal, 20 March 2015, No. 13/00552.

> his body, so that he does not know within the meaning of the aforementioned article that the ingestion of the incriminated drug is intended to implement the claimed invention, and on the other hand, that this ingestion of the drug by the patient being accomplished in a private setting for a non-commercial therapeutic purpose, the rights of the patentee do not extend to these acts.[24]

Regarding direct infringement, it was held that clinical trials conducted by a company on behalf of another seeking to obtain an MA fell within the scope of Article L. 613-5 b).[25] However, these decisions were rendered under Article L. 613-5 b) IPC before the implementation of a Bolar-type exemption in Article L. 613-5 d) IPC by the Act of 26 February 2007.

As of today, there is no clear guidance under French law or case law in relation to this issue and the extent to which third parties could benefit from the Experimental Use exemption is thus unclear.

In any event, the Experimental Use exemption shall be rejected where the technology at issue is the subject of a royalty-bearing collaborative technology transfer and licensing agreement.[26] In such circumstances, case law ruled that the delivery of the means necessary to implement the invention, the offer and use of the patented process, as well as the offer and use of the product directly obtained by the patented process were made for commercial purposes.

The French *Cour de Cassation* also noted that transferring the patented know-how for the sole purpose of producing and marketing the product, in return for a payment, constitutes an unauthorized exploitation of the patented know-how.[27]

f. Territoriality Issues

The French law as codified in Article L.613-5 of the IPC, only provides an exception for acts performed on an experimental basis in France.

If experiments are conducted in another country, it is important to comply with the patent laws in that jurisdiction.

Guidance provided by case law suggests that the Experimental Use exemption does not extend to commercial activities, and therefore a commercial supply of the patented invention for experimental use would not be exempt from patent infringement. However, if the supply is not a commercial supply, in principle the Experimental Use exemption should apply to any acts performed in France which might otherwise amount to patent infringement.

It has been also ruled that the manufacture and intra-group supply of a patented invention from France to Italy have been considered as revealing preparatory acts for an effective marketing insofar as the supply's documentation showed that it did not consist of a mere study aiming at manufacturing prototypes.[28]

24. Paris Court of First Instance, 9 February 2018, *AstraZeneca v. Biogaran*, No. 16/13292.
25. Paris Court of First Instance, 12 October 2001, No. 00/11698; Paris Court of First Instance, 25 January 2002, No. 00/11702.
26. Paris Court of First Instance, 22 November 1996, No. 15088/94.
27. Cass. Com., 19 November 2002, No. 00-15.203.
28. Paris Court of First Instance, 30 May 2003, No. 02.03385.

g. Burden of Proof and Onus

The burden of proof of an Experimental Use exemption lies on the defendant who raises this defence in the context of patent infringement proceedings.[29]When a researcher or entity seeks to rely on the Experimental Use exemption, they must demonstrate that their use of a patented invention qualifies for this exemption. This includes proving that the use is strictly for experimental purposes and not for commercial exploitation. The party claiming the exemption may need to provide evidence such as:

- documentation showing the nature and purpose of the experimental activities;
- details on how the research aligns with scientific inquiry or experimentation;
- evidence that the use does not aim to derive commercial benefits from the patented invention.

The party must prove that the activities conducted were purely experimental and intended for research purposes. This may involve:

- clarifying that the experiments are not aimed at developing a commercial product or service that could compete with the patented invention;
- demonstrating that the research contributes to scientific knowledge or is necessary for further development in the field.

h. Applicability during Patent Term Extension or Supplementary Protection Certificate

There is no distinguishing between 'regular' patent term and applicability during any patent term extension of supplementary protection certificate (SPC) under the French patent law. The Experimental Use exemption, including the period covered by the SPC continues to apply during patent term extension.

3. THE BOLAR-TYPE EXEMPTION

a. History and Rationale of Adopting the Bolar-Type Exemption

French legislation regarding the Bolar-type exemption is strongly influenced by EU legislation, in particular, by Directives 2001/82/EC and 2004/27/EC.

In an attempt to harmonize the position between the different Member States, to speed up the entry of generic products onto the market after patent or SPC expiry and to avoid trials being performed outside the European Union, the so-called Bolar-type exemption was introduced within the European Union to exempt from patent infringement the tests and trials necessary to use the abridged procedure for obtaining an MA.

29. J. Azéma & J.-C. Galloux, *Droit de la propriété industrielle*, Dalloz, 2017, at 588.

The Bolar-type exemption is governed by European Directive 2001/83/EC on the Community Code relating to medicinal products for human use, as amended by European Directive 2004/27/EC, particularly Article 10 thereof.

Article 10(6) of Directive 2001/83/EC, after its amendments by Directive 2004/27 contains a Bolar-type provision,[30] in accordance with the exception provided for in Article 30 of the International Agreement on the Protection of Intellectual Property Rights (TRIPS).[31]

The scope of Article 10(6) of Directive 2001/83/EC is limited by:

- the scope of Directive 2001/83/EC itself, which relates only to medicinal products intended to be placed on the market in Member States, as indicated in Article 2 of the Directive;
- the purpose of Article 10 which, by way of derogation from Article 8, provides for the list of documents and particulars that must accompany an application for an MA in the EU for generic and biosimilar medicinal products.

Before the introduction of the Bolar-type exemption, French case law exempted acts necessary to obtain an MA on the basis of a broad application of the Experimental Use exemption. For example, Phase 3 clinical trials, necessary to obtain an MA, did not fall within the acts prohibited by the patent; the same was true for temporary use authorizations.

Before 2001, it was considered that

- the Experimental Use exemption only applied to acts intended to experiment with new processes or new applications;
- the exemption did not cover bioequivalence tests conducted to demonstrate that a generic drug has the same properties as the patented drug.

In 2001, the Paris Court of First Instance ruled that tests carried out with a view to obtaining an MA do not constitute an infringement:

- 12 October 2001, *Science Union and Laboratoires Servier v. AJC Pharma*:[32] the manufacture of semi-industrial batches carried out within the framework of an application for MA does not constitute an act of infringement;
- 25 January 2002, *Science Union and Laboratoires Servier v. Laboratoires Biophelia*:[33] the manufacture of two pilot batches within the framework of an MA application does not constitute an act of infringement.

---

30. Article 10 (6) of Directive 2004/27/EC: 'Conducting the necessary studies and trials with a view to the application of paragraphs 1, 2, 3 and 4 and the consequential practical requirements shall not be regarded as contrary to patent rights or to supplementary protection certificates for medicinal products'.
31. Article 30 of the TRIPS Agreement: 'Members may provide limited exceptions to the exclusive rights conferred by a patent, provided that such exceptions do not unreasonably conflict with a normal exploitation of the patent and do not unreasonably prejudice the legitimate interests of the patent owner, taking account of the legitimate interests of third parties.'
32. Paris Court of First Instance, 3rd chamber, 2nd section, 12 October 2001, (RG 98/25622)
33. Paris Court of First Instance, 3rd chamber, 2nd section, 25 January 2002, (RG 00/11702)

In 2007, the EU Directives were implemented at the French national level through Law No. 2007-248 of 26 February 2007 containing various provisions for adapting to Community law in the field of medicines. The French Bolar-type exemption is now provided for in Article L. 613-5 (d) of the IPC and has been implemented broadly.

b. The Laws Applicable to the Bolar-Type Exemption in France

The Bolar-type exemption in France is covered by the Article L. 613-5 d) IPC which provides that:

> The rights conferred by the patent do not extend to …
>
> (d) Studies and tests required for obtaining a marketing authorization for a medicinal product, as well as the acts necessary for carrying out such studies and tests and for obtaining the authorization.

This includes (clinical) studies, tests and trials, for example to demonstrate that a product is bioequivalent to a reference medicinal product, so that the shortened procedure for applying for an MA will suffice.

c. Procedural Aspects of Invoking the Bolar-Type Exemption

Similar to the Experimental Use exemption, the Bolar-type exemption is used as a defence in litigation proceedings.

It could also possibly be used in actions for declaration of non-infringement. Regarding those non-infringement actions, the Bolar-type exemption does not generally extend to uses outside of the regulatory approval context.

d. Scope of Bolar-Type Exemption in France

i. Fields of Technology

While codified to address concerns from the pharmaceutical industry, the Bolar-type exemption is not limited to pharmaceutical products. It is important to keep in mind that the 'regulatory approval' is to be understood, regarding the French Bolar-type exemption, only for medicinal products for human and veterinary use, and not, for instance, for plant protection products which are also subject to MAs.

It also does not seem to apply to medical and diagnostic devices.

ii. Purpose of Experiments/Infringing Activities

The primary purpose of the Bolar-type exemption is to permit the use of a patented invention for activities necessary to obtain regulatory approval for generic drugs.

The French Bolar-type exemption contains no limitation as to:

- the type of medicinal product, which can be a reference medicinal product, a generic medicinal product or a biosimilar. It means that the French Bolar-type exemption is not restricted to excepting studies for generic MAs;

- the type of exempted acts, which are those required for obtaining an MA and those necessary for carrying out these required acts;
- the country for which an MA is sought, which can be any country inside or outside the EU.

French case law supports this broad interpretation: in two orders dated 7 October 2014 and 15 December 2014,[34] the Paris Court of first instance expressly recognized that the Bolar-type exemption may apply when trials aim at obtaining MAs outside the EU.[35]

In addition, French case law expressly recognized that the exception benefits not only the applicant to the MA but also companies from the same group and applies to centralized MAs.[36]

It has also been ruled, in Preliminary Injunction proceedings, that compassionate use (*i.e.* access to the medicinal product for specific patents under temporary MA) should fall within the scope of the Bolar-type exemption.[37]

Such exemption can be raised before the judge of summary proceedings, such as in defence to a request for preliminary injunction, and before the judge who will rule on the merits. However, case law ruled that it is for the judge on the merits to determine whether the conditions for the Bolar-type exemption are met.[38]

Regarding the application of the Bolar-type exemption to a third party who assists the MA Holder (MAH) in carrying out the activities, this question is not settled by French case law.[39]

This being said, it seems that the Bolar-type exemption should apply to subcontractors who carry out studies and tests on the MAH's behalf and a few French Court decisions, issued before the implementation of the Bolar-type exemption, have rejected infringement claims made against a third party who assisted the MAH.

34. Paris First Court of Instance, *Sanofi- Aventis Deutschland v. Lilly France*, RG 14/12276 and RG 14/58023.
35. Paris First Court of Instance, 7 October 2014, *Lilly France v. SANOFI AVENTIS Deutschland GmBH*, RG 14/12274; Azéma & Galloux, *Droit de la Propriété Industrielle*, Dalloz, 2017, chap. 2, par. 854.
36. *Ibid.*
37. Paris First Court of Instance, 15 March 2016, *Ono Pharmaceutical, Mr. Honjo, BMS v. MSD France, Schering Plough*, RG 16/51152.
38. Paris First Court of Instance, 15 December 2014, *SANOFI AVENTIS Deutschland v. Lilly France*, RG 14/58023.
39. The Düsseldorf Appeal Court in the *case Astellas Pharma Inc v Polpharma S.A. Pharmaceutical Works* referred several questions relating to the question of the application of the Bolar-type exemption to a third party who assists the MAH in carrying out the activities to the Court of Justice (CJEU, case C-661/13). The German court asked whether it was necessary that the infringing product was actually used solely for the purpose of conducting studies and trials or whether it was sufficient that the third party could have considered, at the time of supplying the infringing product, that the product was going to be used for studies and trials with a view to obtaining an MA. However, these questions were withdrawn prior to being answered by the CJEU (https://curia.europa.eu/juris/document/document.jsf?docid=150355&mode=lst&pageIndex=1&dir=&occ=first&part=1&text=Astellas%2BPharma%2BInc.%2B&doclang=EN&cid=444657#ctx1).

There could be indirect support to such position in the wording of the Article L 613-4 (3) which does not exclude from the definition of 'persons entitled to use the invention', to which an essential means can be legally supplied, those which benefit from the Bolar-type exemption.

iii. Exempted and Prohibited Activities

Under French law, the Bolar-type exemption allows certain activities related to patented inventions, particularly in the pharmaceutical sector, to facilitate the entry of generic drugs into the market.

For instance, exempted activities might be:

- *Regulatory approval preparations*: conducting studies and trials to demonstrate bioequivalence to the patented product and preparing and submitting applications for an MA.
- *Research and development*: activities that are directly related to the research and development of a generic version of a drug may be conducted under the Bolar-type exemption. This includes conducting preclinical and clinical trials necessary for regulatory submissions and performing laboratory tests and analyses related to the safety and efficacy of the generic or biosimilar product.

The exemption applies if the activities are aimed specifically at obtaining regulatory approval and do not involve commercial exploitation of the patented invention during the patent term.

For instance, prohibited activities might be:

- *Commercial exploitation*: any activities that go beyond the preparatory work for regulatory approval and involve commercial exploitation of the patented invention are prohibited. For example, selling or marketing the generic or biosimilar product before the expiration of the patent or SPC; or using the patented invention for purposes not related to obtaining regulatory approval.
- conducting research that is not intended for regulatory submissions;
- using the patented invention for unrelated commercial research or development purposes.

Clinical Trials

Clinical trials are exempted according to Article L. 613.5 d) of the IPC. One of the objectives of the Bolar-type exemption is to facilitate the performance of clinical trials and avoid a large proportion of these trials being carried out outside the EU.

The explanatory memorandum of the proposal for a Directive amending Directive 2001/83/EC makes this clear:[40]

40. https://eur-lex.europa.eu/legal-content/FR/TXT/HTML/?uri=CELEX:52001PC0404(02)&from=EL.

> 4. The applicant for a marketing authorization for a generic medicinal product will be able to carry out the tests necessary for the submission of the dossier before the end of the exclusivity period without infringing the rules on the protection of industrial and commercial property (Article 10(4)). The purpose of this provision is to avoid a large proportion of the required tests being carried out outside the Community, as is currently the case, without affecting the date of arrival of the generics on the market. (III.B). 4).

French law is silent regarding the question of whether there is a difference between the different phases of clinical trials, and no specific case law has been identified on this subject. Due to the broad scope of the Bolar-type exemption in France, combined with the fact that one of the purposes of Phase 1, 2 and 3 trials is to assess whether an MA should be applied for, such trials fall within the exception of Article L. 613-5 d).

Finally, regarding post-MA trials, there is limited case law on whether activities undertaken for regulatory purposes but after the grant of an MA fall within the scope of the French Bolar-type exemption. In this regard, the decision *Lilly v. Sanofi* mentioned hereabove, has considered that the Bolar-type exemption extended to post-MA trials required by the European Medicines Agency (EMA):[41]

> It should also be noted that the [requirement to conduct] tests and clinical trials do not end with the grant of a marketing authorization and that Lilly France still has to carry out clinical trials, stability studies and process validation tests.
>
> It [Eli Lilly] can therefore, and Sanofi-Aventis GmbH finally admitted this both in its pleadings and at the hearing, import, manufacture, use, export and hold any insulin glargine product falling within the scope of the EP 187 patent and the CCP FR C003, in order to: ...
>
> – carry out trials that it may have undertaken to provide to the EMA ...

Pricing and Reimbursement

Seeking pricing and reimbursement listing does not, as such, constitute an infringing act[42] in France[43] and therefore does not need to be exempted under the Bolar-type exemption.

However, certain activities related to pricing and reimbursement may require additional studies and trials to be conducted which could potentially qualify as an infringing making, use or possession of the invention if not exempted. Such additional studies and trials may for instance be required by the Transparency Committee of the '*Haute Autorité de Santé*' ('HAS') in the context of a Health Technology Assessment taking place after an MA is granted and for the purposes of (i) setting a public price

41. Paris Court of First Instance Paris, 15 December, 2014, *Sanofi-Aventis Deutschland v. Lilly France*, RG 14/58023.
42. Infringing acts are defined at Article L. 613-3 of the IP Code as including the making, offering, placing on the market, use, import, export, transshipment or possession for the aforementioned purposes.
43. Paris Court of Appeal, 21 March 2012, *Novartis v. Mylan*, RG 11/12942; Paris Court of Appeal, 15 March 2011, *Mylan v. Du Pont de Nemours*, RG 10/56889; Paris First Court of Instance, 19 August 2010, *Aventis, Sanofi v. Teva*, RG 10/56889.

by the French pricing authority ('CEPS') and (ii) granting reimbursement and setting the reimbursement rate by the National Social Health Insurance Fund ('UCNAM').

Although these studies and trials are performed after the grant of an MA, French case law tends to interpret the scope of the Bolar-type exemption broadly as extending to additional studies and trials to generate data required by regulatory authorities even after the grant of an MA.[44] Therefore, according to such case law, any additional studies and trials required by regulatory authorities in the context of seeking pricing and reimbursement in France would be exempted under the Bolar-type exemption.

Stockpiling

The acts of manufacturing and detaining the patented products pertain to the exclusive rights of the patentee and stockpiling is therefore prohibited in France, while the patent is in force. The French Bolar-type exemption covers clinical studies and trials but not stockpiling for commercial purposes.

For completeness, it should be noted that an isolated decision has been issued by the first instance court of Paris,[45] which ruled that when it is necessary to produce commercial quantities for the purpose of validation and release, this still falls within the scope of the Bolar-type exemption:

> The Bolar exception does not only concern the clinical studies and trials necessary to obtain the MA but also *acts demonstrating the capacity to produce industrially and thus in quantities greater than those sufficient for simple trials.*

With regard to SPCs, it should be remembered that Regulation EU 2019/933 of 20 May 2019 replaced Article 5 of Regulation EC 469/2009 (i.e., the SPC Regulation) to include the so-called SPC manufacturing and stock-piling waiver.

e. Beneficiary Limitations

While the scope of the Directive was limited to trials involving generic or biosimilar medicines, the European Bolar-type exemption as provided for by Article 10(6) was broadly transposed in France. As a result, Article L. 613.5 d) IPC not only covers clinical trials related to an MA applied for generic medicinal products, or biosimilars, but also for innovative drugs (*princeps*).

This has been expressly mentioned in a decision issued by the first instance court of Paris:[46]

> Article L. 613-5 d) of the IP Code has included in French legislation the so-called 'Bolar' exception, which covers both applications for generic marketing

44. See for example Paris First Court of Instance, 15 December, 2014, *Sanofi-Aventis Deutschland v. Lilly France*, RG 14/58023.
45. Paris Court of First Instance Paris, 3rd ch., 1st sect. 7 October 2014, *Lilly France v. Sanofi*, in a Preliminary Injunction situation.
46. Paris Court of First Instance Paris, 15 March 2016, *Ono Pharmaceutical, Mr. Honjo, BMS v. MSD France, Schering Plough*, RG 16/51152.

> authorizations and innovative medicines, in compliance with Article 10(6) of Directive 2001/83/EC ...

In addition, clinical trials performed for obtaining an MA outside the EU are also covered by the exemption provided by Article L. 613.5 d) IPC (see point 8 hereabove). This broad interpretation is supported by French case law.[47] In the first instance decision *Lilly v. Sanofi*, the judge expressly recognized that Lilly was entitled to perform acts towards the obtaining of MAs worldwide:[48]

> It should also be noted that the tests and clinical trials have not been completed with the granting of marketing authorization and that Lilly France still has to carry out clinical trials, stability studies and process validation tests.
>
> It [Eli Lilly] can therefore, and Sanofi-Aventis GmbH finally admitted this both in its pleadings and at the hearing, import, manufacture, use, export and hold any insulin glargine product falling within the scope of the EP 187 patent and the CCP FR C003, in order to:
>
> - send them to the English company Catalent for the preparation of samples used for possible clinical trials
> - to carry out the work necessary to obtain the MA,
> - manufacture and export the cartridges necessary for the conduct of clinical trials in India,
> - to carry out trials that it may have undertaken to provide to the EMA,
> - to provide samples requested by the authorities of various countries in which MA applications are being examined,
> - to conduct temperature, stability and light impact tests (combined with maintenance at room temperature), as well as studies relating to the transport of BIV products between France and Brazil, in order to complete the MA application in Brazil,
> - to keep them as clinical trial controls, when specifically requested.

However, Article 27 of the UPCA appears to confer a narrower scope to the Bolar-type exemption, by referring to the acts defined in Directive 2001/83/CE: only clinical trials for obtaining an MA in the EU, for generic or biosimilar product medicines, appear to be covered by the exemption.

It remains to be seen how the differences between French law and the UPCA will be resolved by judges in the event of dual jurisdiction for a patent.

f. Territoriality Issues

Both the Experimental Use exemption and the Bolar-type exemption are subject to the same territorial limitations.

The Bolar-type exemption applies only if the activities are conducted within the territories where the patent (or SPC) is valid.

47. Paris Court of First Instance Paris, 7 October 2014, *Sanofi-Aventis Deutschland v. Lilly France*, RG 14/12276; Paris Court of First Instance Paris, 15 December 2014, *Sanofi-Aventis Deutschland v. Lilly France*, RG 14/58023.
48. Paris Court of First Instance Paris, 15 December 2014, *Sanofi-Aventis Deutschland v. Lilly France*, RG 14/58023.

If a manufacturer conducts activities related to the Bolar-type exemption outside of France, those activities may not be protected under French law. This means that if the manufacturer seeks to obtain regulatory approval in another country, they must comply with the patent laws of that jurisdiction.

Furthermore, the Bolar-type exemption as implemented in Article L. 613-5 d) of the IPC is not limited to EU MAs but also encompasses acts and assays necessary to obtain an MA abroad.

The Bolar-type exemption is recognized in various forms across EU Member States due to harmonization efforts. However, each country may have specific rules governing its application. Therefore, a manufacturer must ensure that they understand the Bolar-type exemption's scope and applicability in each territory where they operate and any cross-border activities must be examined in light of the patent laws of the respective jurisdictions.

g. Burden of Proof and Onus

Under French law, the burden of proof regarding the Bolar-type exemption typically lies with the party claiming the exemption.

When a manufacturer of generic drugs or a researcher wishes to invoke the Bolar-type exemption, they must demonstrate that their activities fall within the scope of this exemption. This includes showing that the activities are aimed at obtaining regulatory approval for a generic or a biosimilar version of a patented pharmaceutical product.

The party must prove that their use of the patented invention is strictly for experimental purposes related to regulatory submissions and not for commercial exploitation during the patent term. This means that any studies conducted must be necessary for obtaining an MA and should not be aimed at profiting from the patented invention before the expiration of the patent or SPC.

In cases of disputes, French courts will assess the evidence presented by the party invoking the Bolar-type exemption. Courts may consider various factors, including: the nature of the activities conducted (e.g., whether they are for regulatory purposes); the timing of the activities in relation to the patent or SPC; and evidence of intent regarding commercial exploitation versus research or development.

h. Applicability during Patent Term Extension or Supplementary Protection Certificate

The French law and case law do not provide for any time limit applicable to the Bolar-type exemption with respect to the life of the patent and the SPC.

It thus appears possible to rely on this exemption during the entire lifetime of the patent and/or the SPC as long as the acts fall within the exemption (i.e., for obtaining an MA). However, a generic or biosimilar applicant cannot refer to the originator's data to obtain an MA, as long as the data exclusivity period has not expired.

Furthermore, with regard to SPCs, it should be noted that Regulation EU 2019/933 of 20 May 2019 replaced Article 5 of Regulation EC 469/2009 (i.e., the SPC Regulation) to include the so-called SPC manufacturing and stock-piling waiver. The waiver allows manufacturers of generics and biosimilars to manufacture SPC-protected products within the EU (i) for export to non-EU countries where the products are not protected, or (ii) for stockpiling the product in preparation for early market entry immediately after SPC expiry. The manufacturing of an SPC-protected product for stock-piling purposes is limited to a period of six months before the expiry of the SPC.

The purpose of this waiver is to strengthen European competitivity as these acts would otherwise be performed outside the EU.[49]

4. DIFFERENCES BETWEEN THE TWO EXCEPTIONS IN FRANCE

In France, the Experimental Use exemption and the Bolar-type exemption are related concepts, but they serve different purposes and have distinct legal implications.

While the Experimental Use exemption allows individuals or organizations to use a patented invention without the patent holder's authorization for experimental purposes, such as research, testing, or educational activities, the Bolar-type exemption specifically allows for the use of a patented invention in the context of obtaining regulatory approval for generic or biosimilar drugs. It enables manufacturers to conduct the necessary studies and trials to demonstrate that their generic or biosimilar version of a drug is equivalent to the patented one.

In fact, the Experimental Use exemption is broader and supports general research, while the Bolar-type exemption is specifically aimed at facilitating the entry of generic or biosimilar drugs into the market.

Consequently, the Experimental Use exemption applies to various research contexts, whereas the Bolar-type exemption is limited to regulatory activities related to pharmaceuticals or veterinary products. Furthermore, the Experimental Use exemption prohibits any commercial exploitation, while the Bolar-type exemption permits certain research and development activities that are necessary for obtaining regulatory approval, even if they may lead to commercialization later.

In summary, while both exemptions aim to balance patent rights with the need for research and innovation, they operate in different contexts and have distinct legal frameworks in France. Thus, the two exemptions are legally separate and distinct.

49. Whereas no. 7 says 'Regulation (EC) No 469/2009 should, therefore, be amended so as to allow the making of generics and biosimilars for export and storing, while bearing in mind that intellectual property rights remain one of the cornerstones of innovation, competitiveness and growth in the internal market.'

Chapter 18

Germany

Markus Rieck

1. GENERAL

a. Terminology

The Experimental Use exemption as well as the Bolar-type exemption are codified in §11 of the German Patent Act ('*Patentgesetz*', PatG) directly after §§9 and 10 that relate to the effects of a patent. The exemptions define exceptions to the effects of the patent. They apply to situations where an act would constitute an infringing activity but for the exemption. Both exemptions (as well as a third exemption, related to plant breeders) are independent, though their scope may overlap.

b. Legal Basis in Germany

The Experimental Use exemption is codified in §11 No. 2 PatG. It is also referred to as the 'research privilege' ('*Versuchsprivileg*'). §11 PatG also includes the so-called 'Breeder's privilege' in No. 2a and a Bolar-type exemption in No. 2b. These rules are drafted as exceptions to the acts of patent infringement codified in the preceding §9 and §10 PatG.

> §11 (limits to the effects of a patent)
>
> The effects of a patent do not extend to
>
> ...
>
> 2. Acts performed for research purposes that relate to the subject-matter of the patented invention;
>
> 2a. Use of biological material for purposes of breeding, discovery or development of a new plant variety;

2b. Trials and experiments including the practical requirements resulting therefrom which are necessary for obtaining a marketing authorization of a medicinal product in the European Union or a marketing authorization of a medicinal product in the member states of the European Union or in third countries;

...

§12 of the German Utility Model Act ('*Gebrauchsmustergesetz*') has the same Experimental Use exemption as §11 No. 2 PatG. However, there is no Bolar-type exemption or Breeder's privilege for the utility model.

By virtue of Article 64 EPC, the same rules as for German patents also apply for national parts of European patents.

c. Bodies That May Decide on the Legitimacy of Exemptions

All mentioned exemptions from patent infringement are examined by the competent courts in infringement proceedings. These are the Regional Courts ('*Landgericht*') in the first instance, the Higher Regional Courts ('*Oberlandesgericht*') in the second instance, and the Federal Court of Justice ('*Bundesgerichtshof*') in the third instance.

If certain fundamental rights are concerned and all regular court instances are exhausted, the Federal Constitutional Court may accept a case to decide whether these fundamental rights have been violated.

Further, as with all European legislation, questions concerning the interpretation of EU law may be referred to the Court of Justice of the European Union ('CJEU'). This is particularly relevant for the Bolar-type exemption which is based on an EU Directive.

2. THE EXPERIMENTAL USE EXEMPTION

a. History and Rationale of Adopting the Experimental Use Exemption

According to Article 13 of the EU Charter of Fundamental Rights, scientific research shall be free of constraint, whereas according to Article 17 intellectual property shall be protected. Corresponding provisions are in force in Germany's Basic Law ('*Grundgesetz*', Articles 5 (3) and 14). The purpose of the Experimental Use exemption is to balance these fundamental rights, and to foster innovation which is one of the basic purposes of patent law. Patents should not keep companies or scientists from contributing to further technological progress.

Experimental Use exemptions have a long history in Germany. In its current form, the exemption has been in place since 1 January 1981. It was implemented in the German Patent Act after ratification of the Community Patent Convention of 1975 with the purpose of harmonizing patent laws in Europe. Many European countries have very similar rules, which, according to the Federal Court of Justice, must be taken into account when interpreting the German provision; therefore, jurisprudence of other European countries must be considered when interpreting the Experimental Use exemption in Germany.

Before 1981, German patent law also had an Experimental Use exemption. It was implicitly codified in the old Patent Act of 1968 by stating that only the patent proprietor was allowed to use the subject-matter of the invention *in commerce*. Thus, experimental use of patented subject-matter was allowed if it did not constitute use in commerce. This indirect Experimental Use exemption was narrower than today's law which qualifies all acts performed with the goal of gaining knowledge about the patented subject-matter irrespective of whether these acts are ultimately performed for commercial purposes.

b. The Laws Applicable to the Experimental Use Exemption in Germany

The German Patent Act stipulates in §11 No. 2 that 'the effect of a patent does not extend to acts done for experimental purposes relating to the subject matter of the patented invention'.

The structure of the law clarifies that the Experimental Use exemption comes into play when acts are concerned that would be covered by the effects of the patent but for the fact that the acts are done for experimental purposes. Thus, the exemption is relevant in infringement proceedings as a defence against a claim that a certain act is covered by the effects of the patent. The defendant can use the exemption by arguing that the acts performed were done (a) for experimental purposes and (b) relating to the subject-matter of the invention, or in other words for gaining knowledge about the patented subject-matter. From these considerations it is clear that the defendant in a patent infringement trial bears the burden of proof for the requirements of the exemption.

The exemption relates to acts, irrespective of who performs these acts. The acting entity is not limited to universities, research or non-profit institutions. However, the limitation to specific purposes – 'experimental' – clarifies that the person performing the act is still relevant in that the person determines the purpose of the acts. For example, the act of making a patent protected product by a manufacturer for the sole purpose of selling it to a researcher may under certain circumstances not be a qualified act if the manufacturer has no interest in the research results.

The acts must fulfil two requirements: they must be done for experimental purposes and they must relate to the subject-matter of the patented invention.[1] 'Experimental purpose' means that the act is performed to obtain information or knowledge. This 'information or knowledge' is given a broad interpretation by the German courts. The second requirement limits the qualified acts to those performed on the patented subject-matter, meaning that the patented subject-matter is not used as a tool, rather, as the object of the experiment.

There are two landmark Federal Court of Justice decisions relating to the Experimental Use exemption: '*Clinical Trials I*'[2] and '*Clinical Trials II*'.[3] Although from 1995 and 1997 (respectively), the cases are still relevant today, and are still the main guidance for interpretation of the Experimental Use exemption in German patent law. Note that, at the time of these decisions, there was no Bolar-type exemption in Germany.

1. Federal Court of Justice, 11.7.1995, X ZR 99/92 – '*Klinische Versuche I*', section III. 4. a).
2. '*Klinische Versuche I*', supra n.1.
3. Federal Court of Justice, 17.4.1997, X ZR 68/94 – '*Klinische Versuche II*'.

In *Clinical Trials I* the Federal Court of Justice endorsed a liberal approach to experimental use, defining it broadly as 'any (planned) procedure for gaining knowledge, irrespective of the purpose for which the knowledge gained is ultimately intended'. As to the relationship of the experiment to the subject-matter of the invention, the Federal Court of Justice held that the patent protected subject-matter must be the object of the experimental act for the purpose of obtaining knowledge. This is, for example, the case in clinical trials done for the purpose of finding new medical uses for the protected product. Using the patented invention as a tool however is not covered by the exemption.

In *Clinical Trials II* the Federal Court of Justice had to decide on clinical trials performed with the purpose of evaluating efficacy and safety within a *known* medical indication. The Court held that a commercial purpose, such as gathering data for a marketing authorization, does not *per se* conflict with the definition of experimental use. However, if the acts do not relate to the technical teaching underlying the invention, if the extent of the use exceeds that justified by the experimental purpose, or if the acts are carried out with the intention to disturb or hinder sale of the patentee's products, the exemption does not apply.

Thus, even a clinical trial with the purpose of evaluating the efficacy and safety of a pharmaceutical formulation comprising the protected active substance was found to fall under the Experimental Use exemption. The Court emphasized that the Experimental Use exemption is not a 'non-commercial use exemption' and that commercial experiments may be covered by the privilege.

These two decisions suggest the German courts take a very open approach to the Experimental Use exemption. It is not relevant if the ultimate end of the performed acts is commercial as long as the acts are objectively done with the intention to obtain information about the protected invention. This covers, for example, experiments for the purpose of improving a protected product as well as finding new uses or the best way of using the protected product.

c. Procedural Aspects of Invoking the Experimental Use Exemption

Because the Experimental Use exemption is an exception to the effects of the patent, they become relevant in the forums where infringement is discussed. Therefore, they are examined by the competent courts in patent infringement proceedings. These are the Regional Courts in the first instance, the Higher Regional Courts in the second instance, and the Federal Court of Justice in the third instance. The parties may file a constitutional complaint to the Federal Constitutional Court, which the Court will accept in exceptional circumstances relating to violations of constitutionally guaranteed rights.

The Experimental Use exemption has been subject to a constitutional complaint to the Federal Constitutional Court.[4] The complaint was not accepted by the Court, which held that the complaint had no chance of success. In its reasoning, the Constitutional Court confirmed that the Experimental Use exemption is in line with the constitutional protection of property. The German Basic Law protects property but also safeguards the freedom of science and the social responsibility of property

4. Federal Constitutional Court, 10. 5.2000, 1 BvR 1864/95.

('*Sozialbindung des Eigentums*'). According to the Court, the law strikes a fair balance between the interests of the patent proprietor who wants to exploit its monopoly, and the public who benefits from technological progress facilitated by experiments.

d. Scope of the Experimental Use Exemption in Germany

i. Fields of Technology

The Experimental Use exemption is not limited to specific fields of technology. While it has been invoked in the pharmaceutical field most prominently, it applies to all technologies. The purpose of the exemption is to limit the potential negative effects of a patent on the advancement of science. This is relevant to all technical fields.

ii. Purpose of Experiments/Infringing Activities

For an act to be covered by the Experimental Use exemption, it must be performed with the purpose of gaining knowledge on the patented subject-matter, i.e. the patented subject-matter must be the object of the experiment. If the experiment has the purpose of gaining knowledge on different subject-matter, using the patented invention as a tool, the experiment is not covered by the exemption.[5]

The type of knowledge to be gained by the experiment is very broad, including knowledge about the functioning of the invention, improvement of the invention, determining the best way of using the invention, or finding new applications for the patented subject-matter.

In principle, the exemption also applies to protected research tools, i.e. if these tools are used in an experiment that is performed with the purpose of gaining knowledge on the protected research tool, the experiment is covered by the exemption. If, however, the research tool is used as such, i.e., with the purpose of facilitating research on another object, this use will not be privileged.

Experiments that do not relate to the technical teaching of the patented invention, and experiments performed to an extent that is not justified by the research purpose, are not covered by the exemption.[6]

Whether the experiment has a commercial character has no bearing on whether it falls under the exemption, unless the experiment exclusively serves commercial purposes without any purpose of gaining information. Examples of exclusively commercial experiments are investigations of demand, pricing or sales.[7] The Federal Court of Justice has clarified that it is not practicable to determine the degree to which a certain act is commercial or scientific.[8] Instead, any act designed to clarify questions or generate new knowledge about the protected subject-matter is covered by the exemption.

5. '*Klinische Versuche I*', supra n. 1, section III. 4. b) cc).
6. '*Klinische Versuche II*', supra n. 3, 2. Headnote.
7. '*Klinische Versuche II*', supra n. 3, section III. 5. a).
8. '*Klinische Versuche II*', supra n. 3, section III. 6. a).

iii. Exempted and Prohibited Activities

There are no types of activities that are by their nature excluded from the Experimental Use exemption. It can apply to all activities that would otherwise be prohibited by the patent, i.e. manufacture, offer for sale, placing on the market, use, import and possession. The ultimate use of the knowledge or data gained from the experiment is also not limited, even if commercial in nature.

Scale-up experiments performed with the purpose of maximizing the output of a patented product may under certain circumstances exceed the allowed extent of experiments. The same applies to experiments performed exclusively for commercial purposes, such as investigation of demand, pricing or sales; or testing and sampling as part of a tender procedure.

There is very little case law on the Experimental Use exemption in Germany, and there has been little guidance by the courts, particularly concerning the question as to if and how far the exemption extends to acts of contributors, for example suppliers of a protected molecule. If a third party contributes to the experiment, such as by supplying material, without having an interest in the results and without actively ensuring that the contribution is used for exempt acts only, it is likely that these contributing acts will not be exempt.[9]

iv. Pure Academic vs Commercially Motivated Experimental Use

Use *in commerce* was a relevant requirement for patent infringement in a previous version of the patent law, which has not been in force since 1981. Under the current law, there is no distinction between pure academic and commercially motivated experimental use with regard to the exemption. Commercially motivated experimental use is treated the same as academic experiments as long as the experiments do not exclusively serve commercial purposes, for example investigation of demand, pricing or sales. The Federal Court of Justice has clarified that it is not practicable to determine the *degree* to which a certain act is commercial or academic. Instead, the Experimental Use exemption applies if an act is designed to clarify questions or generate new knowledge about the protected subject-matter, regardless of whether commercial or purely academic in nature.[10]

e. Beneficiary Limitations

A third party contributing to the experimental use can benefit from the privilege if they have an interest in the results, i.e. they are a co-experimenter. If the third party is not a co-experimenter, the legal situation still needs clarification. While there appears to be consensus that a supplier must ensure that the supplied product is used for acts that fall under the Experimental Use exemption, it remains unclear what is sufficient to ensure this. Since there is no Federal Court of Justice decision on this matter yet, there are various opinions. It appears to be accepted by most

9. Kühnen, *Handbuch der Patentverletzung* (2023), Chapter E 1084.
10. *'Klinische Versuche II'*, supra n. 3, section III. 6. a).

that a party can use a third party, such as a contract researcher, to help with the experiments. Before the Federal Supreme Court clarifies this question, it is advisable for contributing third parties to agree with the experimenter that the contributory acts are performed under the condition that the experimenter uses the contribution exclusively for exempted purposes.[11]

f. Territoriality Issues

The Experimental Use exemption applies to acts that would otherwise be prohibited under the patent, i.e. acts mentioned in §9 and §10 of the Patent Act. Therefore, the exemption can only apply to acts performed with relevance to Germany.

The results of the experiment are knowledge or information about the patented subject-matter. The exemption applies to acts, not to information. Thus, the acts performed are decisive, not the ultimate use of the information gained from the experiment. If the information is used to facilitate patent infringement abroad, this will be a case for the courts in the relevant country, it will not change the assessment of the acts under the Experimental Use exemption of the German Patent Act.

g. Burden of Proof and Onus

The party invoking the exemption bears the burden of proof for the relevant facts. Notably, the party relying on the exemption must show that the allegedly infringing acts were objectively performed for experimental purposes. Witness testimony on the motives for certain acts may play a role in court. However, objective facts will be decisive in most cases.[12] For example, it should be proven that experiments were planned for gaining specific information about the patented subject-matter. Also, the amount of patented product produced, and all other circumstances must correspond to the planned experimental use.

h. Applicability during Patent Term Extension or Supplementary Protection Certificate

The exemption applies during periods of SPC protection. The reason is that an SPC provides – within the limits of the marketing authorization – the same rights to its holder as the underlying patent.

3. THE BOLAR-TYPE EXEMPTION

a. History and Rationale of Adopting the Bolar-Type Exemption

The Bolar-type exemption was introduced into the Patent Act with effect from 6 September 2005, implementing European legislation (Directives 2004/27/EG,

11. Kühnen, supra n.9, Chapter E 1084; U. Scharen, *Benkard Patentgesetz*, PatG § 11 Rn. 10 (2023).
12. Kühnen, supra n.9, Chapter E 1083.

2004/28/EG, 2004/24/EG). The purpose was to allow generics companies to apply for a marketing authorization before expiry of the relevant patents.

Before the Bolar-type exemption was introduced, clinical research with the purpose of obtaining marketing authorization was already exempt to a large extent under the existing Experimental Use exemption.[13]

One might say that Germany had no need for the Bolar-type exemption because the Federal Court of Justice had already qualified clinical trials as falling under the general Experimental Use exemption. However, some uncertainty remained as to whether the Experimental Use exemption would cover pure bioequivalence trials. It can be argued that bioequivalence trials do not have the purpose of obtaining new information about the patented product, but just *confirming* a suspected similarity between two products.[14]

b. The Laws Applicable to the Bolar-Type Exemption in Germany

The German Bolar-type exemption according to §11 No. 2b of the Patent Act applies to:

> trials and experiments including the practical requirements resulting therefrom which are necessary for obtaining a marketing authorization of a medicinal product in the European Union or a marketing authorization of a medicinal product in the member states of the European Union or in third countries.

Although the Bolar-type exemption was implemented into German law due to a European Community Directive, the implementations differ between European countries. Germany's implementation and interpretation of the exemption can be considered broad both in terms of the covered acts as well as territory.

The Bolar-type exemption is not limited to acts performed on the patented invention. The exemption applies to trials, experiments and the practical requirements that are necessary for obtaining a marketing authorization in any country: Germany, the EU or abroad. The law includes the phrase 'the practical requirements', which allows a very broad interpretation of the exempt acts.

The Bolar-type exemption is not limited to manufacturers of generics and biosimilars but applies equally to originators.[15]

c. Procedural Aspects of Invoking the Bolar-Type Exemption

Because the Bolar-type exemption is an exception to the effects of the patent, it may become relevant in the forums where infringement is discussed – the competent courts in patent infringement proceedings. These are the Regional Courts in the first instance, the Higher Regional Courts in the second instance, and the Federal Court of Justice in the third instance. In exceptional circumstances, the parties may file a constitutional complaint to the Federal Constitutional Court.

---

13. '*Klinische Versuche II*', supra n. 3, 1. Headnote.
14. Higher Regional Court Duesseldorf, 05.12.2013, I-2 U 68/12, section 2. b) aa).
15. Kühnen, supra n.9, Chapter E 1085.

Further, as with all European legislation, questions concerning the interpretation of EU law may be referred to the CJEU.

d. Scope of Bolar-Type Exemption in Germany

i. Fields of Technology

The Bolar-type provision in the German law applies to experiments and trials as well as corresponding practical requirements that are necessary for obtaining a marketing authorization for a medicinal product. This includes pharmaceuticals for humans and animals. It does not include medical devices because those do not underly an approval process. Therefore, the privileged acts are limited to pharmaceutical products.

It has been discussed whether plant protection products should be covered by the Bolar-type exemption. However, the clear wording of the law speaks against extending this exemption to plant protection products.[16]

ii. Purpose of Experiments/Infringing Activities

The Bolar-type exemption applies only to acts that are necessary for obtaining a marketing authorization in Germany, the EU or any other country. Thus, the objective necessity of the acts for obtaining a marketing authorization qualifies them under the Bolar-type exemption. Acts that are not necessary for this purpose are not qualified. Manufacturing a drug for use in a clinical trial is qualified as a 'practical requirement' if the trial is necessary for the marketing authorization.[17]

Research related to improving an old invention is exempted under the general Experimental Use exemption. It may also qualify as an exempted act under the Bolar-type provisions if it is necessary for obtaining a marketing authorization. Other research that is only remotely connected to drug development will likely not be exempted under the Bolar-type exemption but will often be covered by the Experimental Use exemption.

iii. Exempt and Prohibited Activities

There are no types of activities that are by their nature excluded from the Bolar-type exemption. It covers all activities that would otherwise be prohibited by the patent if necessary for regulatory approval. Generally, acts that are not necessary for obtaining regulatory approval are not exempt. For example, early experiments that are not required for approval would not be exempt under the Bolar-type provisions. Acts performed after having obtained a marketing authorization, such as offering for sale or bidding, are also not exempt.

16. M. Stief: *The European Research and Bolar Exemptions – Background, Status Quo and a Look at the Agreement on a Unified Patent Court (UPCA) and the EU Commission's New Draft Directive for the Reform of Pharmaceutical Legislation*, GRUR Int. 824 (2024).
17. U. Scharen, *Benkard Patentgesetz*, PatG § 11 Rn. 10 (2023)

The actual use of the data obtained in a clinical trial within the Bolar-type exemption is not relevant to the application of the exemption. It is decisive whether the clinical trial is necessary for obtaining a marketing authorization in any country.

The Bolar-type exemption was introduced into the law to allow manufacturers of generic drugs to enter the market quickly after expiry of a patent. It was not intended to allow generics manufacturers to fill their stocks with patent infringing products to be put on the market once the patent has expired. Therefore, the type and amount of product must not exceed what is necessary for obtaining regulatory approval.

Stockpiling is not permitted during the life of the patent under the Bolar-type exemption. It may, however, be allowed during the period of SPC protection, subject to further conditions. Regulation EU 2019/933 of 20 May 2019 amended Regulation EC 469/2009 (i.e. the SPC Regulation) to include what is often called the SPC manufacturing and stockpiling waiver. The waiver allows manufacturers of generics and biosimilars to make SPC protected products within the EU for export to non-EU countries where the products are not protected, or for stockpiling the product in preparation for early market entry after SPC expiry. The purpose is to strengthen the European economy as these acts would otherwise be done outside the EU.

To benefit from the SPC manufacturing and stockpiling waiver, the maker of a protected product must notify the German Patent and Trademark Office (or competent authority in other Member State) and the holder of the SPC before starting the exempt acts. The notification will be published by the patent office. No such notification is required in case of the Experimental Use, Breeder's or Bolar-type exemptions. Moreover, making an SPC-protected product for stockpiling is limited to a period of sixth months before expiry of the SPC.

e. Beneficiary Limitations

The exemption can be used by generics manufacturers and originators alike. The German legislator chose to implement a broad Bolar-type exemption in the Patent Act.

There is very little case law on the Bolar-type exemption in Germany. A question remains regarding if and how far the Bolar-type exemption extends to acts of contributors, for example suppliers of a protected molecule. The dominating opinion in the literature, expressed in one Higher Regional Court decision,[18] is that third party supply is exempt if the supplier ensures the supplied product's use is only for acts falling under the exemption. The Court requested the CJEU to decide on this issue. Unfortunately, the underlying dispute was settled so that the CJEU could not comment on these important questions.

There is active debate as to what is sufficient to ensure that a supplied product is used only for exempt acts.[19] It is advisable for the supplier to impose a contractual obligation on the purchaser to use the supplied product for privileged acts only. Since there is as yet no Federal Court of Justice or CJEU decision on this matter, there are also minority opinions, such as that contributor's acts are only covered

18. Higher Regional Court Duesseldorf, 05.12.2013, I-2 U 68/12.
19. M. Stief & T.Matschke, *Das Versuchs- und Bolar-Privileg im Bereich der mittelbaren Patentverletzung*, GRUR 1241 (2021).

by the exemption if the contributor has an interest in the experimental results itself (i.e. it is a 'co-experimenter').

Application for marketing authorization is not necessary for invoking the Bolar-type exemption. The exemption applies to everyone who performs the relevant acts if they are objectively necessary for regulatory approval.

f. Territoriality Issues

The Bolar-type exemption applies even if the purpose is a regulatory submission in another country. This is expressly stated in the law. Whether the performed acts are necessary for obtaining marketing authorization is determined under the law of the country of authorization.

The exemption applies to acts, not to information. Thus, the acts performed are decisive, not the ultimate use of the information gained from the experiment. If the information is used to facilitate patent infringement abroad, this will be a case for the courts in the relevant country, it will not change the assessment of the acts under the Bolar-type exemption in Germany.

g. Burden of Proof and Onus

The party invoking the exemption bears the burden of proof for the relevant facts. Notably, the party relying on the exemption must show that the allegedly infringing acts are objectively necessary for obtaining a marketing authorization in at least one jurisdiction.

h. Applicability during Patent Term Extension or Supplementary Protection Certificate

The exemption still applies during periods of SPC protection. The reason is that an SPC provides – within the limits of the marketing authorization – the same rights to its holder as the underlying patent. Further, stockpiling and manufacturing of a protected product may be allowed at the end of the period of SPC protection – see section 3.d.iii. above.

4. DIFFERENCES BETWEEN THE TWO EXEMPTIONS IN GERMANY

Many of the acts that fall under the Bolar-type exemption are also experiments under the Experimental Use exemption. However, the scope and conditions of the two exemptions are different. For example, the Bolar-type exemption is not limited to experiments performed with the purpose of gaining knowledge about the invention, i.e. performing experiments 'on' the invention. Moreover, it allows acts relating to the 'practical requirements' of experiments and trials necessary for obtaining marketing authorization.

The main difference between the exemptions is in the purposes of the privileged acts: gaining knowledge, or obtaining a marketing authorization. These differences reflect the different legislative intents of the exemptions which will inherently impact the interpretation of these provisions.

Chapter 19

Greece

Dr Nikolaos Lyberis

1. GENERAL

Greece is party to the EPC and PCT agreements on patents. The Greek Industrial Property Office (OBI) applies the so-called formal examination system in terms of limited substantive examination of national patent applications with respect to novelty, inventiveness and industrial applicability. Thus, review of fulfilment of said conditions lies within the competence of civil courts, who may declare a patent null and void *ab initio*.[1]

a. Terminology

There is no Greek case law to date dealing terminologically with the legal term exception v. exemption and the difference(s) between them. They have been approached instead in theory while commenting on the Greek Patent Law No. 1733/1987 ('Patent Law').

The term *exemption* is understood as indicating behaviour(s) of a third party that would constitute a defence against a patent infringement claim by the patent proprietor, and as such they are exempted from being characterized as illegal (Article 10(2) and (3) of the Patent Law).

The term exemption indicates the legislative limitation of the negative powers that would otherwise enable the patent holder to prohibit certain activities by a third party who makes use of the subject of an invention. Such exemptions are exhaustively enumerated by the Greek Patent Law and are the following:

1. Athens Multi-Member Court of First Instance (MMCFI), 729/2009, DEE 2009, 1194; Court of Appeal (CA) of Athens 3676/2010 DEE 2011, 39; Athanassiou in: Kallinikou/Athanassiou/Chrissanthis, *Intellectual Property Law in Greece*, 100-103 (Wolters Kluwer 2nd ed. 2019).

a. use of an invention for non-professional or for research purposes;
b. use of an invention incorporated in a vehicle, railway, vessel or airplane temporarily entering the Greek territory;
c. preparation of a medicinal product in a pharmacy to be delivered to a specific person upon a doctor's prescription, as well as the sale and application of such medicinal product;
d. continued prior use of an invention by a third person – other than the patentee – who, at the filing date respectively priority date, had used the invention in Greece or made necessary preparatory acts for the exploitation thereof;
e. exhaustion of patent rights when the patentee has put patented products on the market or has authorized third parties to do so for use, sale or importation of such products within the EU internal market (Articles 34 and 36 TFEU and relevant CJEU case-law); and
f. compulsory licensing (Articles 13, 14, and 14A of the Patent Law).

Furthermore, it is noteworthy that Article 5(8)(a) of the Patent Law introduces the general legal principles of *bonos mores* and *ordre publique* (Article 281 GCC) into Greek patent law, which may be applied not only as an exception to patentability but also as a limitation to the exempted activities by a third party experimenting on a patented product in a manner contravening said principles.[2] According to Marinos,[3] such research or experimental activity may not be considered per se as prohibited, it may rather be a reflection of the non-patentability or the abuse of a patented invention itself (environmental policy, use of a photocopying machine for reproduction of fake banknotes).

This contribution focuses on experimental use and Bolar-type exemptions only.

Accordingly, the term exemption would refer to the use of an invention by a third party that is not considered as infringing, although said use takes place *without* the patentee's consent.

Furthermore, the above exemptions, provided for in Article 10(2) and (3) of the Patent Law, are *jus cogens*. As such, limitation or even abolishment of the exempted cases by virtue of a contract is prohibited.

b. Legal Basis in Greece

Exemptions from patent infringement liability are provided for in the Patent Law 'about technology transfer, inventions and technological innovation'.

Specifically, regarding *Experimental Use exemptions* – among other types of exemptions – Article 10(2) of the Patent Law provides for the following:

> 2. The owner of the patent may not forbid, in the meaning of the preceding paragraph, the following activities:
>   a. The use of the invention for non-professional or research purposes.
>   ...

2. K. Liberopoulos, *The Law of Inventions*, 2010 (in Greek) p. 151-152.
3. Marinos, *Patent Law*, 2013 (in Greek) p.102-104.

c. The preparation of a pharmaceutical product in a pharmacy for a specific individual, following medical prescription as well as the dispensing and use of said pharmaceutical product under the reservation of Article 25 paragraph 3 of the present Law.

To date, no regulations or interpretational guidelines have been issued by the Greek Patent Office (OBI), nor could any case law be located specifying the criteria to be borne in mind when using such defence clauses before court.

The *Bolar-type exemption* is provided for in the Joint Ministerial Decision (JMD) DYG3a/G.P.32221/2013 which was codified and published in the Government's Official Gazette 1049/B/29.04.2013. Said JMD is entitled 'Harmonization of Greek legislation with the corresponding EU legislation on the production and circulation of medicinal products for human use, in compliance with Directive 2001/83/EC concerning the Community Code relating to medicinal products for human use (L311/28.11.2001), as amended by Directive 2011/62/EU relating to the prevention of the entry into the legal supply chain of falsified medicinal products'.

The Greek patent law provision transposing EU legislation into national law is contained in Article 11(6) of JMD and reads as follows:

> Conducting the necessary studies and trials with a view to the application of paragraphs 1, 2, 3 and 4 and the consequential practical requirements shall not be regarded as contrary to rights protected by patents or supplementary protection certificates for medicinal products.

The Bolar-type exemption is herewith applicable for generic pharmaceuticals for which the grant of a Greek market authorization invoking a so-called reference medicinal product is pursued (see section 3. below).

c. Bodies that Are Authorized to Decide on the Legitimacy of Exemptions

Patent infringement cases are adjudicated before the civil courts of First and Second Instance (Court of Appeal), as well as the Supreme Civil Court (*Areios Pagos*) for revision only concerning legal faults of decisions issued by the aforementioned First and Second Instance Courts. Their judicial power covers both ordinary lawsuits and preliminary injunctions when urgent legal interest is invoked. Said courts are authorized to decide whether exemptions are legitimate or not.

2. THE EXPERIMENTAL USE EXEMPTION

a. History and Rationale of Adopting the Experimental Use Exemption

The legislative rationale for the introduction of the Experimental Use exemption was to strike a balance between legitimate patent protection (negative powers of the patentee) and activities of third parties not affecting the proprietary right of patent exploitation (positive powers of the patentee) (Article 30 of the TRIPS Agreement).

b. The Laws Applicable to the Experimental Use Exemption in Greece

With respect to exemptions from patent infringement liability, Article 10 of the Greek Patent Law makes a distinction between non-professional and research purposes of the use of an invention:

> 2. The owner of the patent may not forbid, in the meaning of the preceding paragraph, the following activities:
>   a. The use of the invention for non-professional or research purposes.

Non-professional use of the invention refers to the private activities of the patentee. This is in compliance with the patentability requirement of industrial applicability. In other words, the invention is to be used as an active intervention in economic activities and not in private and family activities.[4] A private, non-professional use of the invention can be made in a family circle or in the frame of a close personal friendship or even in a broader circle, such as in a private party at home. Consequently, the use of an invention not connected to profit-oriented professional activities is not prohibited, according to Article 10(2) of the Patent Law.

The exemption of the use of the invention for research purposes constitutes an important rule of patent law aimed at the promotion of innovation, or the avoidance of hindering technological progress in the relevant technical field. This exemption is necessary for conducting basic research.[5] It also touches upon aspects of free and undistorted competition in the market. Consequently, the patentee is not allowed to impose cease and desist claims on third parties who use the invention solely for their research purposes.

c. Procedural Aspects of Invoking the Experimental Use Exemption

Substantial evidence must be presented to the competent civil court of First or Second Instance that will decide whether there is a legitimate exemption or not (see also section 1.c. above). Research protocols, laboratory reports, eyewitnesses and sworn statements are some of the crucial evidentiary elements for the defendant raising an exemption claim in a patent infringement case.

d. Scope of the Experimental Use Exemption in Greece

i. Fields of Technology

Almost any invention from every technological branch may, under the applicable legal provisions, be subject to experimental use exemption.

---

4. *Ibid.*, p. 162.
5. *Ibid.*

ii. *Purpose of Experiments/Infringing Activities*

In this context, it should be clarified that this exemption is limited to the experimental use of the invention *per se* (e.g. reverse engineering). This is meant to refer to experimenting on alternative technical solutions to the same technical problem, or to develop improvements of the invention, or to put the invention to the test, or to examine whether there are additional unknown results of the inventive activity, e.g. side effects of medication.[6] However, using the invention as *a supporting research tool* to achieve other purposes going beyond the scope of protection of the patent itself would require the consent of the patent holder, in the absence of which no exemption would be available to the user.[7] It is irrelevant where and by whom such research is conducted.[8]

Exempted use of the invention for research purposes can be not only scientific, but also industrial. This is the case for pre-trials or clinical studies conducted by pharmaceutical companies, provided that such trials are carried out for the above permissible purposes. The difference of the Bolar-type exemption is that experimental use does not serve academic purposes but rather the interest of generic manufacturers to accelerate their entry to the relevant market immediately after the patent or supplementary protection certificate (SPC) expiration.[9]

Research purpose also exists in the framework of academic teaching for the benefit of students and researchers. Such purpose would not be eligible for an exemption claim if a specific university is also conducting research on behalf of a company, even less so if said research were conducted on the premises of an industrial enterprise. In the latter two cases it is obvious that only explicitly authorized use of the patent is permissible.

iii. *Use of the Invention for the Preparation of a Medicinal Product in a Pharmacy*

According to Article 10(2)(c) of the Patent Law:

> 2. The owner of the patent may not forbid, in the meaning of the preceding paragraph, the following activities:
>
> ...
>
> c. The preparation of a pharmaceutical product in a pharmacy for a specific individual, following medical prescription as well as the dispensing and use of said pharmaceutical product under the reservation of Article 25 paragraph 3 of the present Law.

This exemption refers to the preparation of a medicinal product in the premises of a pharmacy for a specific person for whom an ad hoc medical prescription was given. Sales and delivery of such medicines are covered by the exemption. No exemption

6. K. Liberopoulos, *The Law of Inventions*, 2010 (in Greek) p. 150; Marinos, *Patent Law*, 2013 (In Greek) p. 163.
7. Marinos, *Patent Law*, 2013 (in Greek).
8. K. Liberopoulos, *The Law of Inventions*, 2010 (in Greek).
9. N. Rokas, *Industrial Property and Unfair Competition*, 4th ed., 2022, p. 64.

can be claimed or exempted activities can cease to be exempted if the medicinal product is delivered without prescription or is offered to more people beyond the one mentioned in the prescription.

e. Territoriality Issues

The question as to whether the exemption would apply if the results of the experiment(s) are used for infringing upon a corresponding patent in another jurisdiction has not been subject of Greek case law, nor has it been discussed in theory. Extra-territorial applicability of patent law would in principle contravene the rule of territoriality governing the intellectual property laws in Greece. Private international law aspects would also have to be considered in such cases. The problem is due to the low degree of harmonization of patent law in many jurisdictions. One could argue, however, that no exemption could be claimed under said circumstances in view of the purported patent infringement in another jurisdiction. In other words, the patentee would otherwise be exposed to unlimited possibilities of cross-border infringements through ordering experiments by the infringer extra-territorially with respect to the protected territory of the patent, provided that said experiments are indispensable and their results are destined for and are used by the infringer in the country of patent protection.

Specifically, with respect to clinical trial contracts the law of the country where the trials are conducted is usually applicable, although it may also be agreed that any relevant conflict is to be taken to arbitration. The Greek contract template for clinical trials provides for Greek applicable law and Greek jurisdiction.[10]

f. Burden of Proof and Onus

It is the defendant against a lawsuit for patent infringement who bears the burden of proof for substantiating the Experimental Use exemption applicable to the otherwise infringing activities (Marinos, supra, p. 250-251).

This must be done in that phase of the First Instance civil procedure in which the defendant submits written arguments in defence of the lawsuit. Any such claim raised at a later stage of proceedings is not expected to affect the outcome of the case.

g. Applicability during Patent Term Extension or Supplementary Protection Certificate

The Experimental Use exemption applies during the protection term of an SPC or an SPC pediatric extension term. This because according to Greek law, the rules governing the rights of the patentee during the twenty-year protection of a patent are applied, *mutatis mutandis*, on SPCs and pediatric extensions to SPCs.

10. Joint Ministerial Decision 36809/2019; A. Skouteli, *Clinical trials for pharmaceuticals* (in Greek), 2021, p. 125 and 455 f.

3. THE BOLAR-TYPE EXEMPTION

a. History and Rationale of Adopting the Bolar-Type Exemption

The rationale for Greece adopting the Bolar-type exemption was for the generic manufacturers to be ready to enter the market immediately after the lapse of the patent protection term. This could be achieved by saving time not being obligated to repeat clinical studies and trials before launching their generic products.

Lifting said obstacles for generic manufacturers was in principle successful except for massive production and stockpiling of their products during the patent protection term of the reference medicinal product, the latter being possible only outside the EU and if good manufacturing practices were applied. Thus, to counter this inefficiency, the SPC Waiver was introduced.[11]

b. The Laws Applicable to the Bolar-Type Exemption in Greece

The Bolar-type exemption is provided for in the JMD DYG3a/G.P.32221/2013, which was codified and published in the Government's Official Gazette 1049/B/29.04.2013. Said JMD is entitled 'Harmonization of Greek legislation with the corresponding EU legislation on the production and circulation of medicinal products for human use, in compliance with Directive 2001/83/EC concerning the Community Code relating to medicinal products for human use (L311/28.11.2001), as amended by Directive 2011/62/EU relating to the prevention of the entry into the legal supply chain of falsified medicinal products'.

Article 11(6) of JMD reads as follows:

> Conducting the necessary studies and trials with a view to the application of paragraphs 1, 2, 3 and 4 and the consequential practical requirements shall not be regarded as contrary to rights protected by patents or supplementary protection certificates for medicinal products.

For reasons of clarity, it should be mentioned that paragraphs 1, 2, 3 and 4 of Article 11 of JMD contain provisions relating to the legal and formality requirements for generic pharmaceuticals and the necessary petition for them to obtain market authorization (para. 1). They also contain provisions relating to definitions of the terms 'reference of medicinal product' and 'generic medicinal product' (para. 2), and the necessity to present to the market authorization authority the results of appropriate pre-clinical tests or clinical trials, where the medicinal product does not fall within the definition of a generic medicinal product, or where the bioequivalence cannot be demonstrated through bioavailability studies, or in case of changes in the active substance(s) therapeutic indications, strength, pharmaceutical form or route of administration, vis-à-vis the reference medicinal product (para. 3). In para. 4 the requirements for biological medicinal products similar to a reference biological product but not fulfilling the definition of generic medicinal products are regulated.

11. EU Regulation 2019/933 amending Article 4 EU Regulation 469/2009; D. Lempesi, *The sale of pharmaceuticals*, 2024, p. 206-207; see also section 3.i. below.

c. Procedural Aspects of Invoking the Bolar-Type Exemption

The alleged infringer of a patent or SPC may invoke the Bolar-type exemption before the civil courts, in the framework of a patent infringement civil action, to have said action dismissed. The District Courts will decide whether the circumstances of the case would allow, or not, an early working exemption such as the Bolar-type exemption for a specific generic pharmaceutical.

The Greek authorities responsible for the grant of a market authorization (EOF – National Organization for Medicines) and for pricing regulation [Pricing Department of EOF according to Ministerial Decision D3(α) 6295/9-2-2024 (Government's Official Gazette B1100/15.02.2024) about pricing rules and procedure for both compensated and non-compensated pharmaceuticals] do not consider themselves as mainly competent for protecting intellectual property rights, such as patents and SPCs. Thus, the EOF may issue a marketing authorization for a generic product during a patent term, and a pricing decision may also be granted; however, should this product be launched, or even shortly before its imminent market launch, a patent infringement action can be brought.

d. Scope of the Bolar-Type Exemption in Greece

i. Fields of Technology

The Bolar-type exemption concerns generic medicines, bioequivalents and biosimilars all for human use, and processes connected thereto.[12]

ii. Purpose of Experiments/Infringing Activities

The causal link between the experiments, studies and clinical trials undertaken by the third party, on the one hand, and their aiming at obtaining market authorization for a generic medicinal product, on the other hand, is usually the key for considering the admissibility of a Bolar-type exemption claim. Mentioning the name and full data of the reference medicinal product in the request for issuance of a market authorization for a generic pharmaceutical is an interesting indication which, however, must be accompanied by further substantial evidence as to whether the legal and procedural requirements and the regulatory scheme for such requests were properly observed by the third party.

iii. Exempted and Prohibited Activities

A Bolar-type exemption covers by law the preparation of studies and conducting clinical trials for medicinal products. Specifying the exempted and prohibited activities

---

12. Maucher Jenkins (website publication), *Comparison of Bolar Exemptions Across Europe*, 13 February 2015, as updated on 17 October 2017; https://www.maucherjenkins.com/commentary/update-on-bolar-exemptions-in-europe (2017); https://www.maucherjenkins.com/commentary/comparison-of-bolar-exemptions-across-europe (2015).

is a matter of interpretation of the relevant legislation mentioned above. Importation, exportation, purchase, or possession of relevant goods with a view to sale or trade should, in principle, fall within the scope of patent or SPC infringing activities. Data obtained through the conducting of relevant experiments should be considered the property of the patentee or SPC holder and not be disclosed or exploited without an ad hoc consent. Stockpiling should not be permitted considering, among other factors, transparency obstacles and the difficulty of the patentee to locate and investigate storage facilities from where infringing products are put in circulation in the Greek market during the protection period of the patent or SPC. Similar situations are often faced because of the application of the SPC waiver.

e. Beneficiary Limitations

The Bolar-type exemption can be used by generic manufacturers only. They enjoy the exemption vis-à-vis the absolute and exclusive right of exploitation of a patent. Expanding the circle of the entities that may benefit from this exemption would run contrary to the timely limited legal monopoly of the patentee and would render its absolute and exclusive right to patent exploitation uncontrollably weak. IPRs being intangible assets are acknowledged and constitutionally protected as human rights.[13] Consequently, any interpretation broadening the persons or entities e.g. assisting the generic manufacturer would be unconstitutional and prohibited.

f. Territoriality Issues

There is no judicial precedence or discussion in theory concerning territoriality issues in Greece. It might be argued that the Bolar-type exemption could apply outside the country, provided that the purpose is a regulatory submission in another EU Member State, but not in a non-EU country. This by way of analogy with a view to a) the established mutual recognition of national market authorizations between EU Member States, b) the fundamental EU principle of freedom of transborder rendering of services within the European Internal Market and c) the European legal framework for clinical trials.[14] However, the Bolar-type exemption should not apply if the results of the experiment are used for infringing a corresponding patent in another jurisdiction (principles of *bonos mores* and *ordre publique*).

It is material that the person acting under the exemption is the applicant for regulatory approval or, in case of a group of companies, a member thereof, operating under the control of said applicant for applying the Bolar-type exemption. The same applies if the patented invention is used in the same jurisdiction of the relevant regulatory body, i.e. outside Greece, where the experiment was carried out.

13. Article 17(1) and (2) of the Greek Constitution; Article 1 of the First Additional Protocol to ECHR; Supreme Administrative Court (StE) 1116/2014, 4747/2014; Areopag (Supreme Civil Court) 1056/2020; European Court of Human Rights Decision of 21 July 2016, 91, in: *Mamatas et al v Greece*; N. Rokas, *Industrial Property and Unfair Competition*, 4th ed., 2022, p. 9-10; Tsironas, 'The protection of private property and assets', in: Sp. Vlachopoulos, *Fundamental Rights*, p.391 f., 409
14. Regulations 536/2014, 2017/556 and 2017/1569.

The question of data protection remains open with respect to information gained during or as a result of the experiment in Greece, when the regulatory submission takes place in another country. In this respect, the stance of national data protection authorities is crucial and may prove to be a hindering or at least delaying factor, unless there is explicit consent by the involved persons or entities for using said data in another EU jurisdiction.

g. Burden of Proof and Onus

It is the defendant in a lawsuit for patent infringement who bears the burden of proof for substantiating the Bolar-type exemption applicable to the otherwise infringing activities.

This must be done in that phase of the I. Instance civil procedure in which the defendant submits written arguments in defence of the lawsuit. Any such claim raised at a later stage of proceedings is not expected to affect the outcome of the case.

h. Applicability during Patent Term Extension or Supplementary Protection Certificate

The Bolar-type exemption applies during the protection term of an SPC or an SPC pediatric extension term. This is because, according to Greek law, the rules governing the rights of the patentee during the twenty-year protection of a patent are applied, *mutatis mutandis*, to SPCs and pediatric extensions to SPCs.

4. DIFFERENCES BETWEEN THE TWO EXEMPTIONS IN GREECE

A *prima facie* comparison of Experimental Use and Bolar-type exemptions may show differences from each other as to the purpose of the third party's acts. A closer consideration, however, may lead to the conclusion that there seems to exist a common denominator between them: the Experimental Use exemption is broader as far as applicable fields are concerned, whereas the Bolar-type exemption seems to be broader in types of activities.[15]

15. *See* a comparison between the European and the US approach in: Brian Coggio, 'Experimental use defence at the USPTO: too narrow or too wide?', *cipa journal* Oct. 2024, vol.53, no. 10, p. 9-13

Chapter 20

Hungary

Dr Daisy Machytka-Frank and Dr Bettina Kövecses

1. GENERAL

a. Terminology

In Hungary, the Experimental Use exemption appears in Article 19(6)(b) of the Patent Act (see below), while Bolar-type exemption appears in Article 19(6)(c) of the Patent Act. They are considered just that – exemptions/exceptions to infringement, without creating a specific right for use.

In respect of the Experimental Use exemption the relevant Hungarian provision refers to "acts done for experimental purposes connected to the subject matter of the invention" in a general form.

Currently in Hungary, the Bolar-type exemption is limited to medicinal products, so it is a Bolar exemption, but because earlier this exemption was broader (part of the more general Experimental Use exemption and not limited to medicinal products), we use here the term "Bolar-type exemption".

The Bolar-type exemption is not a specific subcategory of the general Experimental Use exemption, but applicable specifically for acts necessary for obtaining a marketing authorization of medicinal product that is the subject matter of the invention.

b. Legal Basis in Hungary

According to Article 19 of Act No. XXXIII of 1995 on the Protection of Inventions by Patents ("Patent Act") effective as of 1 January 2022:

> (1) Patent protection shall afford the holder of the patent (patentee) the exclusive right to exploit the invention.

(2) On the basis of the exclusive right of exploitation, the patentee shall be entitled to prevent any person not having his consent

(a) from making, using, putting on the market or offering for sale a product which is the subject matter of the invention, or stocking or importing the product for such purposes;

...

(6) The exclusive right of exploitation shall not extend to:

...

(b) acts done for experimental purposes connected to the subject matter of the invention;

(c) tests, trials, and any consequential acts necessary to obtain marketing authorization for placing medicinal product on the market in the European Economic Area or in a third country, including especially manufacturing, use, placing on the market, offering for sale, keeping in stock, importing into or exporting from the country, whether or not these acts are carried out directly by the marketing authorization applicant or by any person having economic links with the applicant for that purpose; ...".

Thus, according to the current Patent Act, the Experimental Use exemption and the Bolar-type exemption are distinct.

c. Bodies That May Decide on the Legitimacy of Exemptions

Both the Experimental Use exemption and the Bolar-type exemption are used only as a defence in litigation proceedings. In Hungary, such proceedings are under the exclusive jurisdiction of the Metropolitan Court as first instance and the Metropolitan Appeal Court as second instance courts. The decision of the second instance court may be subject to a petition for judicial review with the Curia (Supreme Court), if certain conditions are met.

2. THE EXPERIMENTAL USE EXEMPTION

a. History and Rationale of Adopting the Experimental Use Exemption

In Hungary, the Experimental Use exemption first appeared in the Patent Act of 1995, i.e. the earlier Patent Acts did not contain any such exemption. The first version of the above cited Article 19(6) of the Patent Act of 1995 was in force until 31 December 2001 with the following relevant wording:

(6) The exclusive right of exploitation shall not extend to:

...

(b) acts done for experimental purposes connected to the subject matter of the invention, including tests and trials necessary for the marketing authorisation of medicinal product; ...

Thus, in the first version of Article 19(6) of the Patent Act, the Experimental Use exemption and Bolar-type exemption were not separated, but the Experimental Use exemption included the Bolar-type exemption as a specific case of the Experimental Use exemption (where the Bolar-type exemption was limited to medicinal products, see also section 3.).

Between 1 January 2002 and 31 December 2021, i.e. for a further twenty years, the Experimental Use exemption and the Bolar-type exemption remained as one exemption under the Experimental Use exemption, but the Bolar-type exemption appeared as a specific case that was no longer limited to medicinal products (see also section 3.).

The initial Explanatory Memorandum for the Patent Act of 1995 introducing the Experimental Use exemption does not explain the rationale for introducing the "Experimental Use exemption".

The Explanatory Memorandum for the current Patent Act (2022 amendments) explains that the exclusive right provided by patent protection is not unlimited and that patent law provides narrow exemptions to this exclusive right. As rationale for having the general Experimental Use exemption and the Bolar-type exemption previously contained together in one provision, the Explanatory Memorandum states that the two exemptions partially overlap. It is added that the separation of the two exemptions appears to be justified both in terms of content and codification. Furthermore, the introduction of a separate Bolar-type exemption is required to harmonize Hungarian law with Directive 2004/27/EC of the European Parliament and of the Council of 31 March 2004 amending Directive 2001/83/EC on the Community code relating to medicinal products for human use (Medicines Directive), because the Experimental Use exemption is regulated in a completely technology-neutral manner. The Explanatory Memorandum also clarifies the scope of the separate Bolar-type exemption. Lack of more detailed rationale for the Experimental Use exemption in the Explanatory Memorandum makes its interpretation uncertain.

b. The Laws Applicable to the Experimental Use Exemption in Hungary

As mentioned already in section 1.b. above, according to the current legislation the Experimental Use exemption is laid down in Article 19(6)(b) of the Patent Act as follows:

> (1) Patent protection shall afford the holder of the patent (patentee) the exclusive right to exploit the invention.
>
> (2) On the basis of the exclusive right of exploitation, the patentee shall be entitled to prevent any person not having his consent
>
> (a) from making, using, putting on the market or offering for sale a product which is the subject matter of the invention, or stocking or importing the product for such purposes;
>
> ...
>
> (6) The exclusive right of exploitation shall not extend to:
>
> ...
>
> (b) acts done for experimental purposes connected to the subject matter of the invention; ...

The case law in Hungary with respect to the Experimental Use exemption is scarce and the few cases known predate the 2022 amendments to the Patent Act. Details of the relevant decisions will be provided below in section 2.d.iii.

c. Procedural Aspects of Invoking the Experimental Use Exemption

In Hungary, the Experimental Use exemption is used as a defence in litigation proceedings and only if the alleged infringer specifically invokes such a defence. The courts cannot invoke and apply this exemption *ex officio*. Such proceedings are under the exclusive jurisdiction of the Metropolitan Court as first instance and the Metropolitan Appeal Court as second instance court. The decision of the second instance court may be subject to a petition for judicial review with the Curia (Supreme Court), if certain conditions are met.

d. Scope of the Experimental Use Exemption in Hungary

i. Fields of Technology

There are no field-of-technology-based limitations or restrictions on the Experimental Use exemption in Hungary. All types of technology may utilize such an exemption.

ii. Purpose of Experiments

Regarding the purpose of the experiments that are exempted based on the Experimental Use exemption, there is no available case law in Hungary.

As cited above, the relevant provision specifies that "acts done for experimental purposes connected to the subject matter of the invention" are exempted, without any restrictions in general as to the purpose of experiments. In fact, the text of the Patent Act states "acts done for experimental purposes", which may not strictly be understood as experiments *per se*, but 'acts' for experimental purposes. The definition of 'acts' should be understood as acts otherwise infringing, namely the closed list of acts listed mentioned by the Patent Act (see in more detail in section 2.d.iii.).

Because before 2022, the Experimental Use and Bolar-type exemptions were regulated together, it can be argued that experiments necessary for obtaining marketing authorization for products other than medicinal products may still be exempted (e.g. for plant protection or animal products) under the Experimental Use exemption. To strengthen such a position, certain product-specific regulatory provisions, such as on "experimental use authorization", could potentially prove to be useful. However, there is no recent – post-2022 – case law confirming this interpretation.

Although the language "connected to the subject matter of the invention" is formally broad, no guidance is provided by the case law as to whether in addition to experiments "on", experiments "with" are also exempted. According to professional views, which has also not been confirmed by case law, the Experimental Use exemption does not generally allow exploitations of patented inventions as research tools.

iii. *Exempted and Prohibited Activities*

The types of acts covered by the Experimental Use exemption are not specified in the Patent Act.

The Patent Act has a closed list of acts that are deemed to be infringing. Namely, the patentee shall be entitled to prevent any person not having his consent from making, using, putting on the market or offering for sale a product which is the subject matter of the invention, or stocking or importing the product for the purposes of putting the product on the market. It seems reasonable to assume that putting on the market or offering for sale a product which is the subject matter of the invention would not generally be covered by the exemption while stocking or importing the product for experimental purposes can be covered by this exemption, depending on the individual circumstances of the case.

There are certain aspects that the courts considered in their former (pre-2022), albeit scarce case law under the Experimental Use exemption already mentioned above and could still be relevant when relying on the current Experimental Use exemption.

a) One of these aspects is the extent of the acts. This means that the extent of the acts should be interpreted as the extent necessary to achieve the scientific purpose of the experiments.

Based on older (pre-2022) case-law, the amount and the source of the substance subject to the experiment could have relevance, i.e.,

- if the amount is considered to be more than as reasonably required for experimental purposes, then the exemption is unlikely to apply;
- if the substance is sourced from a country from where import/shipping/ transport would seem unreasonable for solely testing (e.g. from a more remote country) compared to available alternatives in closer proximity (e.g. for European entities within Europe), then it is a factor the court looks at and considers.

b) Another aspect is that the acts to be exempted should be pursued for experimental purposes, such as academic, scientific or research purposes. Based on an older case where the court assessed the party invoking exemption, it can be concluded that if the party is not engaged in experimental, research and development (R&D) activities in general (e.g., such activity is not listed in the company registry), then the court may consider this as a factor advising against applying the exemption.

Further, if the product remains in the possession of the researcher and does not enter into commerce and/or the experimenter makes no profit from the acts, then these could be additional factors that are believed to support a defence on the basis of the Experimental Use exemption.

iv. *Pure Academic vs Commercially Motivated Experimental Use*

As mentioned above, in the earlier version of Article 19(6) of the Patent Act, the Experimental Use exemption and Bolar-type exemption were not separated. After the above detailed amendment of said Article of the Patent Act, the above cited current Experimental Use exemption is understood to apply in respect to scientific experiments, experimental tests, research, academic research work, and so on. Said relevant provision does not specify that the Experimental Use exemption would be limited exclusively for acts done for academic purposes having no commercial value. However, the case law known to date does not suggest that the Experimental Use exemption could be used for any internal acts that have no experimental purposes, irrespective of whether or not such internal acts do not directly result in "sale" or "profit".

e. Beneficiary Limitations

When considering the Experimental Use exemption, it should be noted that third party contributions usually do not serve experimental purposes from said third party's perspective, but are typically provided for remuneration, which is highly likely to be regarded as pure commercial interest. The above cited Article 19(6)(b) of the Patent Act and the lack of relevant case law do not encourage the view that in the case of economic, for example commercial, interest, a third party's acts would be exempted.

f. Territoriality Issues

Hungarian courts will only enforce Hungarian patents. In case the results of the experiment are used in another jurisdiction, where a relevant patent protection exists, then that jurisdiction's law would also apply when infringement or the Experimental Use exemption is judged.

g. Burden of Proof and Onus

The burden of proof of an Experimental Use exemption lies on the party alleged of patent infringement and raising such a defence.

h. Applicability during Patent Term Extension or Supplementary Protection Certificate

The Experimental Use exemption also applies during patent term extensions, i.e. during the lifetimes of supplementary protection certificates (SPCs).

3. THE BOLAR-TYPE EXEMPTION

a. History and Rationale of Adopting the Bolar-Type Exemption

In Hungary, the Bolar-Type exemption first appeared in the Patent Act of 1995, not as a stand-alone exemption but rather a specific case of the broader Experimental Use exemption. The earlier Patent Acts did not contain any such exemption. The first version of the above cited Article 19(6) of the Patent Act of 1995 was in force until 31 December 2001 with the following wording:

> (6) The exclusive right of exploitation shall not extend to:
>
> …
>
> (b) acts done for experimental purposes connected to the subject matter of the invention, including tests and trials necessary for the marketing authorisation of medicinal product; …

Thus, in the first version of Article 19(6) of the Patent Act, the Bolar-type exemption was included in the Experimental Use exemption and was limited to medicinal products.

Between 1 January 2002 and 31 December 2021, i.e. for a further twenty years, the above cited Article 19(6)(b) was effective with amended text, according to which the Bolar-type exemption was still a specific case of the broader Experimental Use exemption, but no longer limited to medicinal products:

> (6) The exclusive right of exploitation shall not extend to:
>
> …
>
> (b) acts done for experimental purposes connected to the subject matter of the invention, including tests and trials necessary for the marketing authorization of the product constituting the subject matter of the invention or the product obtained by the process constituting the subject matter of the invention; …

The Explanatory Memorandum for the Patent Act of 1995 introducing the Experimental Use exemption including the Bolar-type exemption does not explain the rationale for these exemptions.

According to the Explanatory Memorandum for the amended provision effective between 1 January 2002 and 31 December 2021:

> the amendment of Article 19(6)(b) of the Act is also related to the TRIPS Agreement. The decision in the dispute settlement proceedings initiated by the EC against Canada in the World Trade Organization confirmed that this provision of our current law is in principle in compliance with the TRIPS Agreement (in particular, Article 30 of the TRIPS Agreement), but becomes unambiguous only, if, in accordance with Article 27(1) of the TRIPS Agreement, it is drafted in a technologically neutral manner (i.e. not focusing solely on pharmaceuticals).

Accordingly, earlier, the legislator was of the view that only a technology-neutral exemption is in conformity with the TRIPS requirements.

The Explanatory Memorandum for the latest 2022 amendment of the relevant provision explains the Bolar-type exemption as follows:

> this exclusive right [i.e. provided by patent protection] is not unlimited, patent law provides narrow exemptions to this exclusive right. Such an exemption is the Bolar exemption, which primarily affects the area of the pharmaceutical industry, the purpose of which is that generic pharmaceutical companies can actually enter the market the day after the expiration of patent protection (so-called day-one market entry), which requires carrying out experiments and tests necessary for marketing authorization during the existence of patent protection, which experiments and tests typically take longer.

Further, the Explanatory Memorandum for the 2022 amendment says that the introduction of a separate Bolar-type exemption is required to harmonize Hungarian law with Directive 2004/27/EC of the European Parliament and of the Council of 31 March 2004 amending Directive 2001/83/EC on the Community code relating to medicinal products for human use (Medicines Directive), because the Experimental Use exemption is regulated in a completely technology-neutral manner. The Explanatory Memorandum also clarifies the scope of the separate Bolar-type exemption. Namely, it clarifies, within the framework of EU law, that the experimental use linked to the obtention of a marketing authorization for a medicinal product under the Bolar-type exemption can be applied not only in the national context but also in the case of a registration in another EEA Member State or in a third country.

It further clarifies that for the purposes of Article 19(6)(c) of the Patent Act, the scope of the persons exempted from the exclusive right to exploit and carry out acts linked to the purpose of obtaining a marketing authorization is deemed to include not only an applicant or marketing authorization holder, but also third persons who cooperate with the marketing authorization holder or applicant for the purpose of obtaining a marketing authorization, either within a group of companies or other intermediaries having economic links for that purpose. The acts covered by the Bolar-type exemption shall not exceed the extent necessary to obtain a marketing authorization for a medicinal product.

b. The Laws Applicable to Bolar-Type Exemption in Hungary

As mentioned already above, since 2022 Hungary has had a Bolar-type exemption that is separated from the Experimental Use exemption and codified in Article 19(6)(c) of the Patent Act as follows:

> (1) Patent protection shall afford the holder of the patent (patentee) the exclusive right to exploit the invention.
>
> (2) On the basis of the exclusive right of exploitation, the patentee shall be entitled to prevent any person not having his consent
>
> (a) from making, using, putting on the market or offering for sale a product which is the subject matter of the invention, or stocking or importing the product for such purposes;
>
> ...
>
> (6) The exclusive right of exploitation shall not extend to:
>
> ...
>
> (c) tests, trials, and any consequential acts necessary to obtain marketing authorization for placing medicinal product on the market in the European Economic Area or in a third country, including especially manufacturing, use, placing on the market, offering for sale, keeping in stock, importing into or exporting from the country, whether or not these acts are carried out directly by the marketing authorization applicant or by any person having economic links with the applicant for that purpose; ...

As is apparent from the citation, apart from the field-of-technology-based limitation (i.e. limitation to medicinal products), the Bolar-type exemption is drafted in a broad manner. Since the amendments in 2022, no case law has been known with respect to new Bolar-type exemption in Hungary.

c. Procedural Aspects of Invoking the Bolar-Type Exemption

In Hungary, such proceedings are always under the exclusive jurisdiction of the Metropolitan Court as first instance and the Metropolitan Appeal Court as second instance court. The decision of the second instance court may be subject to a petition for judicial review with the Curia (Supreme Court), if certain conditions are met.

d. Scope of Bolar-Type Exemption in Hungary

i. *Fields of Technology*

As of 1 January 2022, in Hungary the Bolar-type exemption is limited to medicinal products.

ii. *Purpose of Experiments/Infringing Activities*

The wording of the provision relating to the Bolar-type exemption cited above clearly specifies that acts are exempted if their purpose is to obtain marketing authorization for placing medicinal product on the market in the European Economic Area or in a third country. The acts covered by the Bolar-type exemption shall not exceed the extent necessary to obtain a marketing authorization for a medicinal product.

iii. *Exempted and Prohibited Activities*

The wording of the relevant provision cited above provides the acts that are exempted by the Bolar-type exemption as follows: "tests, trials, and any consequential acts necessary to obtain marketing authorization for placing medicinal product on the market in the European Economic Area or in a third country, including especially production, use, selling or other marketing, offering for sale, stocking, importing or exporting". The listed exempted acts mirror the infringing acts listed in the Patent Act while adding exporting as well. It is noted that this list of exempted acts is not exhaustive. No case law is known in Hungary with respect to the Bolar-type exemption post-2022.

e. Beneficiary Limitations

The exemption applies both to generic companies and innovative companies applying for marketing authorization, as well as to third parties contracted to perform acts on behalf of the party seeking marketing authorization either within a group of companies or other intermediaries having economic links for that purpose.

f. Territoriality Issues

The exemption applies for otherwise infringing acts performed in Hungary to satisfy regulatory requirements in the European Economic Area or in a third country.

g. Burden of Proof and Onus

The onus is on the defendant to prove that the exemption applies.

h. Applicability during Patent Term Extension or Supplementary Protection Certificate

The Bolar-type exemption also applies during patent term extensions, i.e. during the lifetimes of SPCs.

4. DIFFERENCES BETWEEN THE TWO EXEMPTIONS IN HUNGARY

The Experimental Use exemption appears in Article 19(6)(b) of the Patent Act, while the Bolar-type exemption appears in Article 19(6)(c) of the Patent Act (see both above). Thus, since 2022 the two exemptions are separate, although they may overlap in some aspects.

As can be seen from the above citations from the Patent Act, with respect to Bolar-type exemption, the Patent Act provides much more detailed guidance than with respect to Experimental Use exemption.

The Bolar-type exemption is linked to the defined administrative purpose of the experiments, the purpose of which is to obtain a marketing authorization for a medicinal product, and, thus, contrary to the Experimental Use exemption, it is independent of the scientific content of the experiment.

Regarding the fields of technology affected, the Experimental Use exemption is technology-neutral and seemingly much broader than the Bolar-type exemption, which is limited to medicinal products only. Yet the lack of case law and uncertainty about its scope makes it application less favourable and unpredictable.

While the post-2022 Bolar-type exemption clearly exempts the acts of third parties – either within a group of companies or other intermediaries having economic links for that purpose – there is some uncertainty as to whether this would also apply for the Experimental Use exemption.

Due to the short wording of the provision for the Experimental Use exemption and the scarcity of relevant case law it is not possible to draw further conclusions regarding differences between the two exemptions.

Chapter 21

India

Mamta Rani Jha and Dr Malathi Lakshmikumaran

---

1. GENERAL

a. Terminology

India's Experimental Use and research exemption is provided in Section 47(3) of the Patents Act, 1970 ('Act') under the heading 'Grant of patents to be subject to certain conditions' and reads as follows:

> 47. Grant of patents to be subject to certain conditions –
>
> ...
>
> (3) any machine, apparatus or other article in respect of which the patent is granted or any article made by the use of the process in respect of which the patent is granted, may be made or used, and any process in respect of which the patent is granted may be used, by any person, for the purpose merely of *experiment or research including the imparting of instructions to pupils*; (emphasis added)

On the other hand, the Bolar-type exemption is given in Section 107A(a) of the Act under the heading 'Certain acts not to be considered as infringement' and reads as follows:

> 107A. Certain acts not to be considered as infringement. – For the purposes of this Act,
>
> – any act of making, constructing, using, selling or importing a patented invention solely for uses reasonably *related to the development and submissions of information required under any law* for the time being in force, in India, or in a country other than India, that regulates the manufacture, construction, use, sale or import of any product; (emphasis added)

Both are considered as a defence to patent infringement under the Indian patent regime.

b. Legal Basis in India

The Experimental Use and research exemption under Section 47(3) was originally introduced in the Act, and since then it has remained untouched, albeit with indirect and faint considerations made by the courts in some cases (as shall be seen below). Notwithstanding this, the complete scope and ambit of the purpose of experimentation or research mentioned under Section 47(3) is yet to be tested in any court of law in India.

On the other hand, the Bolar-type exemption under Section 107A(a) was introduced by way of amendment in 2002 as part of India's compliance with the Trade-Related Aspects of Intellectual Property Rights Agreement ('TRIPS'). According to the Report of the Joint Committee on the Patents (Second Amendment) Bill, 1999, the Bolar-type exemption was proposed to be inserted to facilitate availability of products, particularly generic drugs, immediately after the expiry of the term of the patent.[1] Thereafter, it was amended in 2005 to insert the expression 'import' and the provision has since remained untouched.

2. THE EXPERIMENTAL USE EXEMPTION

a. History and Rationale of Adopting the Experimental Use Exemption

In India, the first legislation relating to patents dates back to 1856.[2] Since then, the Indian patents law has substantially developed and evolved. In this line of development, the first major step was undertaken post independence when it was felt that the Indian Patents and Designs Act, 1911 (the then governing legislation) was not fulfilling its objective[3] and patent law in India was developing at a slow pace.[4] Consequently, in 1957, the Government of India appointed Justice N. Rajagopala Ayyangar to examine the question of revision of patent law to suit India's needs at the time.[5] After extensive deliberation, a slew of recommendations proffered by Justice Ayyangar were accepted and formed basis for the introduction of the Patents Act, 1970, which has not been replaced since.[6]

In the context of experimental use, Justice Ayyangar, at the outset, noted two things: first, the need to identify the right of a researcher to use the invention for the purpose of *research* as opposed to *commercial use;* and, secondly, the uncertainty of the law on this topic by considering a passage from Blanco White's treatise on

1. https://spicyip.com/wp-content/uploads/2020/02/Patents-Act-REPORT-OF-THE-JOINT-COMMITTEE-19-Dec-2001.pdf at page 10.
2. https://ipindia.gov.in/history-of-indian-patent system.htm#: ~ :text = The%20first%20 legislation%20in%20India,disclose%20secret%20of%20their%20inventions.
3. https://www.ipindia.gov.in/history-of-indian-patent-system.htm
4. Pratibha M. Singh on Patent Law, Vol 1, page 2.
5. *Ibid.*
6. https://www.ipindia.gov.in/history-of-indian-patent-system.htm

Patents.[7] Thus, from the foundations of 'necessity of a right for experimental use' and 'uncertainty which surrounds said right', Justice Ayyangar expressed the view that:

> I consider it desirable that the law should specifically exempt use of the patented articles or processes or the use of articles or products made by the use of the patented process or patented machine or apparatus for experimental purposes from being actionable as an infringement.[8]

Moreover, in this discussion, he also considered the case of *United Telephone Co. v. Sharples* (2 RPC 28) where the use of magneto telephones and transmitters for the purpose of instructing pupils was considered infringement and not put under the category of experimental usage.[9] Disagreeing with the *dictum* of this case, he was of the view that it was a case of experimental use and that the construction of the patentee's rights adopted in that decision *unduly hampered technical education*.[10] Therefore, based on his judgement of the *dictum* in *Sharples*, he recommended the insertion of the words 'including the use of the patented article or process for the purpose of imparting instruction to pupils' into Section 27, which finally read:

> 27. Rights of a patentee. – (1) Subject to the provisions of this Act, a patent granted either before or after the commencement of this Act, shall confer upon the patentee:
>
> ...
>
> (2) Notwithstanding anything in this Act, the making or using of a patented machine or apparatus or other article, or the use of a patented process or the use of an article made by the use of the patented process, machine or apparatus for the purposes merely of experiment or research including the imparting of instruction to pupils and not by way of commercial use, shall not be deemed to constitute an infringement of the rights conferred on a patentee by this Act.[11]

Before proceeding further, it is crucial to note that language of Section 27 was inclusive of the aspect of statutory rights granted by a patent and the exception to these right by way of experimental use. However, in 1965 when the Government of India introduced the Patents Bill, 1965[12] the draft language of the provision was modified, and two crucial changes were introduced. First, the rights of patentee and the conditions imposed on those rights were distinguished. In other words, the language was modified to have two different sections wherein the statutory rights of the patentee (Section 47 of the 1965 Bill) were distinguished from the Experimental Use exemption (Section 48(d) of the 1965 Bill). The Experimental Use exemption as per the Patents Bill, 1965 is as follows:

7. Justice N Rajagopala Ayyangar, 'Report on the Revision of Patent Law', September 1959, para. 488.
8. *Ibid.*
9. *Ibid.*, para. 489.
10. *Ibid.*, para. 489.
11. *Ibid.*, para. 492.
12. https://eparlib.nic.in/bitstream/123456789/755572/1/jcb_03_1966_patents_bill.pdf

Section 48. Patent rights not infringed when used for certain purposes

Notwithstanding anything contained in this Act:

...

(d) the making or use of a patented machine or apparatus or other article or the use of a patented process or the use of an article made by the use of the patented process, machine or apparatus for the purpose merely of experiment or research, including the imparting of instructions to pupils,

shall not be deemed to constitute an infringement of the rights conferred on the patentee by this Act in respect of a patent granted, whether before or after the commencement of this Act.

The second development was that despite recommendation by Ayyangar Committee (*supra*) to exclude cases where experimentation had a commercial purpose, this recommendation was not undertaken by the legislature in the final draft. Thus, the final Section at the time of enactment of the Patents Act, 1970 read:

47. Grant of patents to be subject to certain conditions. – The grant of a patent under this Act shall be subject to the condition that –

(3) *any machine, apparatus or other article in respect of which the patent is granted or any article made by the use of the process in respect of which the patent is granted, may be made or used, and any process in respect of which the patent is granted may be used, by any person, for the purpose merely of experiment or research including the imparting of instructions to pupils*; (emphasis added)

The tenor of these changes is discussed below.

b. The Laws Applicable to the Experimental Use Exemption in India

An examination of the literal text in Section 47(3) illustrates two things: first, under its scope, it includes three types of patents: products, processes and products obtained by a process; and second, the right of an individual under this clause is qualified via the phrase: 'for the purpose merely of experiment or research including the imparting of instructions to pupils.' Thus, the exemption of Section 47(3) seems operable only when the 'use' of a patented invention fulfils this condition. Having said that, the text of Sub-section (3) remains unamended and has also not seen any instance where courts could directly assess the scope and contours of its application. Therefore, the applicability of the condition and confines of Section 47(3) are yet to be examined.[13]

Having said that, there are only few instances where indirect references to Section 47(3) have been made by Indian courts. For instance, a single bench of the Kerala High Court in *Low Heat Driers Pvt. Ltd. v. Biju George* [2010 (2) KHC 566] ('*Heat Driers*') at para. 37 observed that:

It is true that Ext. A17 patent is granted subject to the conditions specified under Section 47 of the Act *which are really the superior right of user of the*

13. https://www.mondaq.com/india/patent/654062/experimentation-research-exemption-in-indian-patent-law-scope-and-ambit-of-section-473-remains-uncertain

> *Government or the user for experiment or research or for imparting of instructions to pupils and the like and not for the commercial exploitation by any private individual.* (emphasis added)

This was a significant observation since the aspect of 'commercial exploitation' in cases of experimental usage is evidently missing from Section 47(3). Thereafter, a Division Bench of the Delhi High Court in *Bayer v. Union of India* 2019 (78) PTC 521 [Del][DB] (hereinafter '*Bayer*') reaffirmed the above findings. At para. 68 of the judgement, in context of the Experimental Use exemption, the court observed:

> the course of the experimental exception- both before and after the TRIPS has shown the adoption, generally of a broad approach, to permit use of all kinds. *Broadly, the courts' approach has been not to enjoin or prohibit purely experimental or scientific activity, as long as it does not have any primary commercial undertones.* (emphasis added)

The conclusion of this discussion indicates the permissibility of the Experimental Use exemption in India, inasmuch the 'use' is not commercial in nature. Having said that, we must not lose sight of the fact that these judgements do not establish the *dictum* for Section 47(3) since the provision was addressed in passing. Moreover (as we shall see below), the aspect of 'commercial undertones' in context of the Experimental Use exemption also requires thorough and in-depth reconsideration.

c. Procedural Aspects of Invoking the Experimental Use Exemption

In India, the Experimental Use exemption could be used as a defence in cases of patent infringement. The relevant provision in this regard is Section 107 of the Act and reads as follows:

> 107. Defences, etc., in suits for infringement. – (1) In any suit for infringement of a patent every ground on which it may be revoked under section 64 shall be available as a ground for defence.
>
> (2) In any suit for infringement of a patent by the making, using or importation of any machine, apparatus of other article or by the using of any process or by the importation, use or distribution or any medicine or drug, *it shall be a ground for defence that such making, using, importation or distribution is in accordance with any one or more of the conditions specified in section 47.* (emphasis added)

Thus, so far as the Experimental Use exemption is shown to be fulfilled, it could be used as a valid defence in cases of patent infringement. Keeping this in mind, as per Section 104 of the Act, in India, patent infringement proceedings can be initiated by the plaintiff in all courts including and above the District Court. Accordingly, if a suit for infringement is instituted in any court including and above the District Court, such court can make a determination on the legitimacy of the Experimental Use exemption. However, it is apposite to mention that if the relief sought in these cases exceeds the pecuniary jurisdiction of the District Court, then the case shall be transferred to an Indian High Court pursuant to Section 7 of the Commercial Courts Act, 2015.

d. Scope of the Experimental Use Exemption in India

i. Fields of Technology

Section 47(3) opens with:

> any machine, apparatus or other article in respect of which the patent is granted or any other article made by the use of the process in respect of which the patent is granted, may be made or used, and any process in respect of which the patent is granted may be used ...

While the shortage of judgments does not fully bring to light the ambit of Section 47(3), a textual interpretation of the text indicates that the expression seeks to include a product, a process, and a product obtained by a process. Thus, from a basic perusal of the provision there appears to be no field of technology that has been restricted under this Section.

ii. Purpose of Experiments/Infringing Activities

As previously noted, a shortage of court analysis on Section 47(3) leaves its scope to be ambiguous; and, as a result, two challenges emanate from this position: first, to determine whether Section 47(3) is an 'experiment *on*' or 'experiment *with*' exception; and secondly, to determine the facet of the 'commercial undertones' in cases of experimental use. Let us examine both.

An 'experiment *on*' exemption incorporates two circumstances: first, when someone uses an invention to study and confirm that it is worked in the manner so described; and secondly, (which is a broader interpretation) when someone uses the invention to *improve upon* or *invent around* the invention.[14]

On the other hand, an 'experiment *with*' exemption entails use of an invention *as it is*, not necessarily to study or appreciate or improve upon it. For instance, an invention whose predominant utility is to assist in research itself (also known as research tools) constitutes as an example of 'experiment with' exemption.[15]

Before proceeding further, it is apposite to mention that discerning whether a patented invention has been 'experimented on' rather than 'experimented with' may be viewed as an exercise in semantics where distinction between the two is hard to ascertain.[16] Notwithstanding this caveat, it has been pointed out in academia that a distinction between the two ought to be struck by the courts.[17] This is particularly the case in view of the broad nature of the 'experiment with' exemption,[18] which might impede the realization of the statutory rights of the patentee. Let us analyse this aspect in some detail.

---

14. https://www.ipmall.info/sites/default/files/hosted_resources/IDEA/idea-vol50-no4-basheer-reddy.pdf, at page 853
15. *Ibid.*
16. https://core.ac.uk/download/pdf/267979901.pdf at page 40 (footnote 202)
17. Basheer, at page 854.
18. https://core.ac.uk/download/pdf/267979901.pdf at page 40

Section 47(3) has a qualifier wherein the rights of an individual to 'use' a patent is qualified via the phrase: 'for the *purpose merely* of experiment or research including the imparting of instructions to pupils' (emphasis added). In context of this qualifier, it has been pointed out that the term 'merely' appearing after the word 'purpose' and before the qualifying phrase logically limits the application of Section 47(3) to cases of experiments, research or educational purposes.[19] Therefore, if 'use' under Section 47(3) is qualified for experiments, research or educational purposes, Section 47(3) must be in the nature of an 'experiment on' exemption for two reasons:

- first, use of an invention to 'experiment with' a patent would *presumably* not qualify as a use 'merely for the purpose of experiment or research' (on account of its broad nature);[20] and
- secondly, permitting such use would likely affect the statutory rights granted to the patentee under Section 48 of the Act and possibly affect the desired legislative scheme.

Put differently, if someone uses an invention by claiming an 'experiment with' exemption, they need not license this use from the patentee, thereby affecting patentee's statutory rights and escaping potential infringement. Therefore, on the basis of a textual interpretation, it appears that Section 47(3) encapsulates an 'experiment on' exemption. On this footing, let us examine the aspect regarding commercial undertones.

The courts in *Low Heat* and *Bayer* (*supra*) seem to establish the *prima facie* position that the Experimental Use exemption is applicable where 'use', so to speak, is altruistic. In this regard, the Delhi's High Court division bench judgement in *Bayer v. Union of India* 2019 (78) PTC 521 [Del][DB] at para. 68 notes:

> ... the course of the experimental exception- both before and after the TRIPS has shown the adoption, generally of a broad approach, to permit use of all kinds. *Broadly, the courts' approach has been not to enjoin or prohibit purely experimental or scientific activity, as long as it does not have any primary commercial undertones*. (emphasis added)

Herein, it must be examined what the court meant by 'primary commercial undertones' since experiments on a patented invention which *improve* or *invent around* the invention are bound to have some commercial effect. Thus, it becomes pertinent to ask whether such experiments could be allowed? Although there is no conclusive answer to this query, the court in *Bayer* sheds some light on it. For instance, talking in terms of the Bolar-type exemption, at para. 92 the court observed:

> If the purpose of the sale is to ultimately exploit the patented invention and either work upon it or 'work around' or work it through research so as to be prepared to apply for the patent for approval to market it once the patent tenure ends, there can be no impairment of the patentee's rights. The natural consequence of that sale cannot be curtailed by a contrived interpretation to say that it is only information that can be sold or exported, not the patented invention ...

19. Basheer, at page 854.
20. *Ibid.*

Although this observation was made in the context of the Bolar-type exemption, it could be applicable in cases of the Experimental Use exemption for two reasons.

First, at paras 117-119 of *Bayer,* the court highlighted that the Experimental Use exemption in India should be interpreted in light of two crucial paradigms: India's international obligation under TRIPS and other International Human Right Covenants, and the court's constitutional obligations to uphold Article 47 (Duty of the State to raise the level of nutrition and the standard of living and to improve public health) and Article 21 (Right to life) of the Indian Constitution. Keeping this mind, the court held:

> Given these paradigms, an interpretation that furthers the objectives of Section 107A (and the previous research enabling existing in the Patents Act, i.e. Section 47) and Article 30 of TRIPS is to be preferred.[21]

Thus, it appears that since the court in *Bayer* preferred a purposive construction of the Experimental Use exemption (albeit, in the limited context of a Bolar-type exemption), it could be concluded that Section 47(3) is broad enough to incorporate those patents which *improve* or *invent around* the invention. From this point of view, the Court's finding of 'commercial undertones' will mean that *the exemption will include cases of improving or inventing around the invention for research, but would not extend to cases where the primary reason for conducting the experiment is to reap commercial benefits or see commercial gain.*

Secondly, *Bayer* must also be considered in light of the fact that despite the recommendation by the Ayyangar Committee to exclude cases where experimentation had a commercial purpose, *this recommendation was not undertaken by the legislature.* Therefore, this could reasonably indicate the intent of the parliament to expand the scope of Section 47(3) to include experimental use which *improves* or *invents around* an invention.

iii. Exempted and Prohibited Activities

As previously noted, the nature of activities prohibited under the Experimental Use exemption are commercial activities, although they too fall within the ambit of possible interpretation on account of the broad language of Section 47(3). Moreover, Section 107 of the Act provides for defences in suits for infringement. Specifically, Section 47(3) provides that making, using, or importation of any machine, apparatus, article, or process shall be a ground for defence if it is in accordance with conditions specified in Section 47. Therefore, if making, using, or importation is done for the purposes of experiments, it shall be exempted from infringement.

iv. Pure Academic vs Commercially Motivated Experimental Use

There is no clear delineation in Section 47(3) which could compartmentalize the Experimental Use exemption in categories of 'pure academic use' and 'commercially motivated use'. However, as noted above, in view of *Bayer,* the Experimental Use

21. Para. 119

exemption could also be said to include cases of commercially motivated experimental use as long as it does not directly result in a sale or profit for the researcher. For example, if an educational institution has a patent, which a teacher uses for the purpose of research, experiments, or educating their pupils, this use is likely to be outside the scope of infringement.

e. Beneficiary Limitations

At present, case law or Section 47(3) do not appear to contemplate exemption by use of third parties. However, in lieu of the position set out thus far, it is reasonable to conclude that if a third party conducts an experiment within the confines of Section 47(3) – that is to say, *for the purpose merely of experiment or research including the imparting of instructions to pupils* and does not see commercial gain from it – such use should be exempted.

f. Territoriality Issues

Patent law is territorial in nature, therefore any conflict arising on account of infringement or related concerns in a foreign jurisdiction will most likely be subject to the law of *that* jurisdiction.

g. Burden of Proof and Onus

There have been no cases to identify the burden of proof in this context. Therefore, the position which is likely to continue is that as set out by Section 109 of *The Bhartiya Sakshya Adhiniyam, 2023* (The Indian Evidence Act) which states that burden of proof must lie on the party who relies on a fact. Accordingly, since the Experimental Use exemption is a defence against patent infringement, the onus will be on the defendant.

h. Applicability during Patent Term Extension or Supplementary Protection Certificate

At present, India does not have patent term extension or SPC.

3. THE BOLAR-TYPE EXEMPTION

a. History and Rationale of Adopting the Bolar-Type Exemption

Unlike the Experimental Use exemption, the Bolar-type exemption was not originally present in the 1970 Act and was subsequently introduced as an amendment in 2002. Evidently, the need for such a provision was felt when India began to align its patent law in compliance with the TRIPS Agreement. The reason for introducing the Bolar-type exemption was explained by the Report of the Joint Committee on the Patents (Second Amendment) Bill, 1999[22] as follows:

> This clause seeks to insert a new Section 107-A in the principal Act, relating to certain acts which are not to be considered as infringement. *This provision has been made to ensure prompt availability of products, particularly generic drugs, immediately after expiry of the term of the patent.* The amendment in this clause has been made to make a provision in consonance with the Bolar provisions at the global level. The other amendment in this clause is correction of a typographical error.[23] (emphasis added)

More light was shed upon the origin and need for the Bolar-type exemption by the Delhi High Court in *AstraZeneca v. Alkem Laboratories CS* (Comm) No. 410/2020, wherein the court observed:

> Section 107A of the Act was introduced to balance the interest of public in lieu of extension of patent term to 20 years for patents across the board for all inventions. *Section 107A, in this spirit, facilitates timely entry of generic drugs by exempting certain activities such as research and development and obtaining regulatory approvals from the pale of infringement actions. The purpose being that manufacturers of generic drugs should be in a position to commence their activities immediately upon the expiry of the patent in the interest of the public at large.* These statutory safeguards were put in place to balance its international commitment under the Agreement on Trade-Related Aspects of Intellectual Property Rights as against India's obligation to protect the health of its citizens. (emphasis added)

Therefore, against the backdrop of 'international commitment' and 'health', the Bolar-type exemption was contemplated for the first time in the Patents (Second Amendment) Bill, 1999,[24] and eventually found its way in the Patents (Amendment) Act, 2002, wherein it was introduced as Section 107A making it a product of trade negotiations. Thereafter, the Patent (Amendment) Bill, 2003, proposed insertion of the expression 'import' in Section 107A – which was adopted, and the provision has since remained untouched.

b. The Laws Applicable to the Bolar-Type Exemption in India

The Bolar-type exemption is codified in the Patent Act under Section 107A:

> 107A. Certain acts not to be considered as infringement. – For the purposes of this Act,
>
> (a) *any act of making, constructing, using, selling or importing a patented invention solely for uses reasonably related to the development and submission of information required under any law for the time being*

22. https://spicyip.com/wp-content/uploads/2020/02/Patents-Act-REPORT-OF-THE-JOINT-COMMITTEE-19-Dec-2001.pdf at page 10.
23. *Ibid*
24. https://spicyip.com/wp-content/uploads/2020/02/Patents-Act-REPORT-OF-THE-JOINT-COMMITTEE-19-Dec-2001.pdf at page 10.

> *in force, in India, or in a country other than India, that regulates the manufacture*, construction, use, sale or import of any product;
>
> (a) importation of patented products by any person from a person who is duly authorized under the law to produce and sell or distribute the product, shall not be considered as a infringement of patent rights.
>
> *shall not be considered as an infringement of patent rights.* (emphasis added)

A first glance at the basic provision indicates the wide range of acts which could be undertaken *vis-à-vis* a patented invention and the condition which restricts such acts for 'uses reasonably related to the development and submission of information required under any law in India or outside.' However, a quick glance also reveals that Section 107A does not include the expression 'export' and yet allows the exemption to operate 'in a country other than India.' This seemingly apparent contradiction, along with the full purport of the Bolar-type exemption, was addressed by a Division Bench of the Delhi High Court in *Bayer* (*supra*). This case was part of a long-running separate contentious litigation between Bayer (plaintiff) vis-à-vis Natco Pharma and Alembic Chemicals Ltd. (respondent/defendant) over the drugs 'Sorafenib' and 'Rivaroxaban' developed by Bayer and used in the treatment of kidney and liver cancer and as an anticoagulant medication. In this case, one of the principal questions before the court was to determine if exports of a product for performing acts outside India 'solely for uses reasonably *related to the development and submissions of information required under any law*', could be made under the scheme of the Bolar-type exemption. Answering in the affirmative, the court preferred a purposive construction of Section 107A and reasoned that if it could be shown that the 'purpose' of the sale is to carry out experimentation or research, or to develop information, then scope of the expression 'sale' cannot be narrowed to exclude exports.[25] In this context, the court also clarified that the natural consequence of a sale, where the patented invention is worked *around* or worked *upon* to apply for a new invention after the term of a patented invention ends will not amount to infringement.[26] Additionally, the court rejected Bayer's argument that export must only mean sale of information generated by experimenting within India, thereby clarifying the scope of the Bolar-type exemption in India, which the plaintiff otherwise intended to restrict.[27] Crucially, the court also clarified the approach which must be considered at the time of interpreting Section 107A. At para. 117, the court observed:

> TRIPS recognized the need for Bolar like research provisions, enabling research and development in numerous ways which relieve those involved in such activities, of the charge of patent infringement. Therefore, a constricted and narrow textual interpretation of such provisions is not called for.

Therefore, the provision of the Bolar-type exemption, as it stands in the statute book, is wide in its ambit and warrants a purposive interpretation, especially after *Bayer*. It is crucial to note that the *ratio* of *Bayer* has been followed by a single bench of

25. Para. 92
26. *Ibid.*
27. Para. 94.

the Delhi High Court in *Merck Sharp & Dohme Corp. vs. SMS Pharmaceuticals Ltd.*, (2021) 87 PTC 398.

c. Procedural Aspects of Invoking the Bolar-Type Exemption

The Bolar-type exemption could be used as a defence *qua* proceedings of patent infringement. This position is reaffirmed in *Bayer* where the court held that Section 107A is not an exemption to the statutory rights conferred upon a patentee under Section 48. On the contrary, the rights of a patentee are subject to the Bolar-type exemption, therefore, making Section 107A a valid defence.[28] Keeping this in mind, as per Section 104 of the Act, in India, patent infringement proceedings can be initiated by the plaintiff in all courts including and above the District Court. Accordingly, if a suit for infringement is instituted in any court including and above the District Court, such court can make a determination on legitimacy of the Bolar-type exemption. However, it is apposite to mention that if the relief sought exceeds the pecuniary jurisdiction of the District Court, then a case of this nature shall be transferred to an Indian High Court pursuant to Section 7 of the Commercial Courts Act, 2015. In this regard, it is apposite to mention that the court in *Bayer* (*supra*) also observed that since patent infringement proceedings generally do not involve questions of public law, such disputes should not be the subject matter of High Court writ jurisdiction under Article 226 of the Constitution of India (which provides the constitutional mandate for the enforcement of fundamental rights) and must be approached with civil remedies.[29]

d. Scope of the Bolar-Type Exemption in India

i. Fields of Technology

As previously noted, Section 107A was introduced to ensure prompt availability of products and generic drugs upon expiry of a patent. Thus, the purpose for its enactment was broad *ab initio* and does not seem to contemplate a bar on any field of technology. This position is evident from a basic reading of the text of Section 107A, which uses the words ‘patented invention’ and ‘any product’, and therefore, does not seem to *specify* the fields of technology upon which it may be applicable. Additionally, the aforesaid position is also corroborated by the court in *Bayer* (*supra*) where, highlighting need for Bolar-type provisions to enable research and development, the Court held that a *constricted and narrow textual interpretation of such provision is not called for.*[30] Therefore, there appears to be no bar on the fields of technology which can seek this exemption.

28. Para. 89
29. Para. 121
30. Para. 117.

ii. *Purpose of Experiments/Infringing Activities*

The shortage of case law to fully appreciate the scope of activities under the Bolar-type exemption calls for a general outlook. In this context, upon perusal of the basic text and the decision of *Bayer* (*supra*) the only limitation which surfaces for our consideration is that of 'reasonable use'. The basic provision reads that 'any act' could be undertaken under the exemption inasmuch it is 'reasonably related to the development and submission of information required under any law in India or outside of India'. Some assistance could also be drawn from *Bayer* wherein the court acknowledged that the term 'reasonably related' could not be contained with strict interpretation and must depend on facts and circumstances of each case.[31] Nevertheless, the court postulated ten factors to be taken into consideration in such cases, which, *inter alia*, include:[32]

- first, the patent granted;
- secondly, nature of the product sought to be exported;
- thirdly, details of the party importing the product;
- fourthly, particulars regarding end use of the product;
- fifthly, particulars regarding relevant regulations; and,
- sixthly, verification regarding the authentication of third parties through the Indian mission.

What inevitably falls from court's analysis in *Bayer* is that as long as the purpose of the use is to carry out experimentation or research, or to and develop information without commercial exploitation of the patent, it will be exempted.[33] In this regard, it may be clarified that if acts of the defendant result in commercial gain, they shall not constitute infringement as long as such acts are reasonably related to the development and submission of information required under the law. This was clarified by the court in *Bayer* at para. 92:

> *Once it is held that patented inventions can be sold for the purpose of carrying on research which fulfils the regulatory requirements of India, there cannot be any bar or an interpretation narrowing the scope of such sale. What is important is the purpose of the sale, i.e. objective of carrying on experiment, research and developing information (in the form of reports, outcomes etc.).* If the purpose of the sale is to ultimately exploit the patented invention and either work upon it or 'work around' or work it through research so as to be prepared to apply for the patent for approval to market it once the patent tenure ends, there can be no impairment of the patentee's rights. *The natural consequence of that sale cannot be curtailed by a contrived interpretation to say that it is only information that can be sold or exported, not the patented invention.* (emphasis added)

A similar observation was also given by a single bench of Delhi High Court in *Merck Sharp* (supra), where, at para. 59, court observed:

31. Para. 108.
32. Para. 112.
33. Para. 106

> 59. [Plaintiff] submits…that the present defendant is actuated, not by any public spirit of research or development, but by purely commercial interests, to sell the patented drug at a profit. That, in my view, cannot be a guiding consideration, *where Section 107A of the Patents Act is concerned, provided the API is ultimately to be used for research and development. Commercial gain, even if reaped by the defendant in the process, cannot disentitle it to the benefit of Section 107A. Charity is foreign to commerce.* (emphasis added).

Therefore, as long as the acts specified under Section 107A are undertaken to carry on experiment and research and developing information without commercially exploiting a patent, i.e., the scheme of Bolar-type exemption in India, they shall be exempted from infringement.

iii. Exempted and Prohibited Activities

As noted above, the Bolar-type exemption is applicable as long as it could be shown that the 'purpose' behind conducting an activity postulated within the provision was reasonably related to the development and submission of information required under the law. Therefore, if the necessary purpose could be shown then activities such as making, constructing, using, selling, importing, and exporting shall be exempted. Moreover, what inevitably falls from this is that *if a patented invention is worked for purely commercial purposes*, such use shall not be covered by the exemption and will be prohibited and injuncted. The court has summarized this position in no uncertain terms at para. 116 of *Bayer*:

> … neither the quantity used nor the place of research and development or information (i.e. within the country granting patent or on foreign soil) is per se conclusive that the claim to use the Bolar or research exception has to be rejected. *Instead, the conduct or action of the individual or entity making, using, constructing or selling the patented product or invention and the purpose for which it sought to be used (i.e. end use and that it should not be commercial) would be important and decisive whether the exporting or purchasing entity intends to use the patented product for commercial purposes.* (emphasis added)

Thus, the prohibition is clear. In this regard, it is apposite to mention that *Bayer* confirms that this prohibition extends to the aspect of data generated from experiments. Consequently, the outcome of this is that the data generated in these experiments could be used for a variety of purposes such as clinical trials in the creation of and advancement of new health technologies, inasmuch it is not commercially exploited by the user.[34] Furthermore, *Bayer* also confirms the Indian position on regulatory compliance in other countries. The court, in light of its stance regarding 'purpose' of the experiment, clarified that exporting data generated in trials *for the purpose of development of information in compliance with regulations or laws of the importing country is permissible.*[35] Accordingly, what follows is that the storage of data for the purpose of regulatory compliance in a foreign country will also be permissible.

34. Para. 94.
35. Para. 93.

However, the court did not clarify what type of data is exempted under the Bolar-type provision.

Lastly, the Act is silent on the aspect of stockpiling. However, in this regard, it must be noted that the court in *Bayer* analysed the findings given by the WTO in the *Canada Dispute* case [DS 114] regarding stockpiling and observed that the stockpiling exception under Section 55.2(2) of the Canadian Patent Act was held to be illegal by the WTO. Crucially, the court in *Bayer* also noted that the phraseology of the Canadian provision on Bolar-type exemption (Section 55.2.1) is closely similar to Section 107A(a), and therefore the *Canada Dispute* case assumes significance for the purpose of interpretation.[36] Therefore, stockpiling a patented invention, in the context of the Bolar-type exemption, is inevitably bound to affect the statutory right granted to a patentee *vide* Section 48 of the Act and should be 'read out' of the scope of the Bolar-type exemption.

e. Beneficiary Limitations

The court in *Bayer* held that *interpretation that furthers the objectives of Section 107A is to be preferred.*[37] Thus, the wide ambit of exemption in India to further India's commitment towards TRIPS and the courts' commitment towards upholding the crucial tenets of the Indian Constitution, such as the Right to Life (Article 21) indicates a purposive construction on the aspect of beneficiaries and is likely to include innovative manufacturers and third party manufacturers.[38] A degree of linkage between the exempted activity and the person seeking regulatory approval will require determination of facts in each case.

f. Territoriality Issues

The issue of territoriality was a crucial argument in the *Bayer* case. Bayer argued that the regulatory requirements of other countries in the context of the Bolar-type exemption must mean that the overseas requirements are to be met *through experimental use in India*. Moreover, they also contended that reference to other nation's laws with respect to the research requirement means that information developed in India can be exported.[39] The court rejected this line of argument as 'strained and artificial'.[40] The court appreciated that the law of other countries may require experimentation to be carried within their country, and thus observed:

> Likewise, the reference of another country i.e the export for reasonably complying with the laws of another country in relation to the kind of research and experimentation needed is something that cannot be dictated by interpretation of Indian law alone. *It is plausible – even reasonable – that many nations may require experimentation or research to be carried on in their soil nationally so as*

36. Para. 104.
37. Para. 119.
38. Para. 120.
39. Para. 91.
40. Para. 92.

> *to be able to supervise the process and then oversee the outcome*. It is, therefore, not possible to dictate the behaviour and legal requirements of other nations by confining the research exception within the territory of India.[41] (emphasis added)
>
> The natural interpretation of the expression 'use' is in all its senses. In this context, it would be necessary to recognize *that in regard to various products, especially those concerning the pharmaceutical, medicinal preparations, surgical and diagnostic purposes and those relating to the agriculture or bio-chemical sector, it may be critical for a database of populations, drugs and co-relation, with disease and its relationship with characteristics that are predominantly local. National regimes might well insist that such research and experimentation in regard to those aspects be either entirely or at least in part be carried on in their territory*. In this context, therefore, it is held that the expressions, 'making, constructing, using, selling or importing patented articles solely for uses reasonably related to development and submission of information required under any law for the time being in force … or in a country other than India that regulates the manufacturing, construction, use, sale or import of any product', consequently, has to be given a wide import. *It is, therefore, open that the sale of the article or invention for the purpose of development of information in compliance with the reasonable requirements of developing countries, solely for purposes of research or development falls within Section 107A(a)*.[42] (emphasis added)

Thus, the Bolar-type exemption is applicable to fulfil the reasonable requirements of developing countries inasmuch as it is related to research and development of information. On the flipside, the exemption is likely to apply in all such countries where the Indian regulatory requirements are sought to be fulfilled. However, it appears that in the latter case, such activities will be subject to those country's laws. Thus, in cases of infringement arising in foreign jurisdictions, quite evidently, the law of those jurisdictions will apply.

g. Burden of Proof and Onus

As noted above, the court in *Bayer* observed that the Bolar-type exemption is not an exemption to the statutory rights conferred upon a patentee. *Per contra*, the rights of a patentee are subject to the Bolar-type exemption. Explaining its rationale, the court at para. 89 observed:

> *In the present case, this court notices that Section 107A is not made subject to the other provisions of the Act – on the other hand, Section 48, which talks of the rights of a patent holder is subject to other provisions of the Act that includes Section 107A*. Furthermore, Bayer's argument that Section 107A constitutes an exception, cannot be accepted. *It is an independent provision with a specific history behind it and was subject to intensive Parliamentary debate and scrutiny by a Joint Committee report. Furthermore, it was enacted in response to the TRIPS enabling provision to the member countries to evolve national legislation*

41. Para. 92
42. Para. 93.

> *facilitating research and progress in fields covered by the patents* ... (emphasis added)

Thus, under the Indian patent regime, Section 107A is a valid defence in cases of infringement, and consequently, the burden of proof to avail this defence lies on the Defendant. This understanding was corroborated by the Court at para. 112 of the judgment, where it observed:

> 112. The approach of the learned single judge in permitting export, without any inquiry and holding that export of 1000 or 2000 tablets constituted reasonable use, in this case, cannot be countenanced. *In such case, upon the patent proprietor alleging the infringement was to institute legal proceedings to injunct the alleged exporter or seller, it is equally possible for the seller or exporter to seek a declaration or appropriate relief (including in a suit for groundless threat, if such action lies) that its overseas sales are for research and purposes covered by Section 107A.* (emphasis added)

The legal position *qua* burden of proof is also evident from the recent case of *Merck Sharp & Dohme Corp. vs. SMS Pharmaceuticals Ltd.*, (2021) 87 PTC 398, where at para. 12, court observed:

> 12. *The written statement presses into service Section 107-A of the Patents Act, along with the judgment of this Court in Bayer Corpn. v. Union of India* [Bayer Corpn. v. Union of India, *2019 SCC OnLine Del 8209: (2019) 78 PTC 521], to contend that the activities of the defendant were permissible, as the defendant was only engaged in sale and export of Sitagliptin Hydrochloride for the purposes of research and development.* The written statement has also dealt, point-by-point, with the various results, cited by the plaintiff as having been obtained consequent on investigation, to demonstrate that these results do not, in any way, indicate that the defendant was selling Sitagliptin Hydrochloride for commercial purposes or in commercial quantities (emphasis added).

Thus, under the Indian patent regime, the burden of proof to take this line of defence rests on the defendant.

h. Applicability during Patent Term Extension or Supplementary Protection Certificate

At present, India does not have patent term extension or SPC.

4. DIFFERENCES BETWEEN THE TWO EXCEPTIONS IN INDIA

We have already noted the difference in statutory provisions between the Experimental Use exemption and Bolar-type exemption. However, the rationale behind adopting them was also quite different. The origin of the Experimental Use exemption is premised on two aspects: first, the right of a researcher to use the invention – albeit, not commercially – for the purpose of experiment and research; and secondly, to further the purpose of imparting education to pupils. The Bolar-type exemption, on other hand, was promulgated with the rationale to allow certain activities if they are related to research and development in order to facilitate ease in the access of products and generic drugs. Accordingly, the primary point of distinction between the two stems from their purpose of promulgation. Under this distinction, the Experimental Use exemption is limited to experimenting in relation to a patented invention to either check the validity of its claim, or improve and invent around it. *Per contra*, any activity under the Bolar-type exemption is for the purpose of allowing manufacturers of generic drugs (or products) to be in a position to commence their activities immediately upon the expiry of the patent. In addition, the Bolar-type exemption also allows any person to share data generated in experiments outside India in desired cases. Therefore, what inevitably falls from this is the wide scope of the Bolar-type exemption in terms of activities – such as selling, constructing and importing – which could be undertaken to achieve the desired purpose of its promulgation. By the same token, the restricted scope of the Bolar-type exemption also becomes apparent since all said activities could be undertaken only when they are *required* by law. In other words, the Bolar-type exemption cannot be utilized as freely as the Experimental Use exemption.

Hence, it appears that the Indian Bolar-type exemption and the Experimental Use exemption are both wide and narrow in their scope. However, it must be recalled that *the scope of the Bolar-type exemption has been expanded by the court in* Bayer *by a preferring a constructive interpretation, whereas the scope of experimental usage is yet to be tested in the court of law.*

Having said that, both exemptions are similar in four aspects: first, both exemptions provide a wide scope for the field of technology in which they could be applicable; secondly, both exclude commercial undertones in the 'use' of a patented invention; thirdly, both provide experimental use of the patented invention; and fourthly, both act as defence in cases of patent infringement.

Chapter 22

Ireland

Gerard Kelly and Adam Carr

1. GENERAL

a. Terminology

The Experimental Use exemption is contained in Section 42(1)(b) of the Patents Act 1992 under the heading 'Limitation of effect of patent'.

The Bolar-type exemption is contained in Section 42(1)(g) and (h) of the Patents Act 1992 under the heading 'Limitation of effect of patent'.

Both are considered exemptions to infringement, placing limitations on the scope of patent rights and what is therefore considered an infringing act.

b. Legal Basis in Ireland

The Patents Act 1992 (and as amended subsequently by the Patents (Amendment) Act 2006) came into effect on 1 August 1992, ratifying the European Patent Convention ('EPC') and Patent Co-operation Treaty ('PCT'), and repealing the Patents Act 1964 and the Patents (Amendment) Act 1966. The Experimental Use exemption was enacted on the same date under Section 42(1)(b) of the Patents Act 1992:

> 42(1) The rights conferred by a patent shall not extend to –
> (b) acts done for experimental purposes relating to the subject-matter of the relevant patented invention;

To date there have not been any cases in Ireland considering the scope of the statutory Experimental Use exemption under Section 42(1)(b).

The Bolar-type exemption is provided under Section 42(1)(g) and (h) of the Patents Act 1992, as amended in 2006 by the European Communities (Limitation of Effect of Patent) Regulations 2006 (SI 50/2006), and as further amended by the Intellectual Property (Miscellaneous Provisions) Act 2014.

> 42(1) The rights conferred by a patent shall not extend to-
> (g) acts done in relation to the subject matter of the relevant patented invention which consist of:
> (i) acts done in conducting the necessary studies, tests and trials which are conducted with a view to satisfying the application requirements of paragraphs 1, 2, 3 and 4 of Article 10 of Directive 2001/83/EC of the European Parliament and of the Council of 6 November 2001 (at last amended by Directive 2004/27/EC of the European Parliament and of the Council of 31 March 2004) for a marketing authorization in respect of a medicinal product for human use, or
> (ii) acts done in conducting the necessary studies, tests and trials which are conducted with a view to satisfying the application requirements of paragraphs 1 to 5 of Article 13 of Directive 2001/82/EC of the European Parliament and of the Council of 6 November 2001 (as last amended by Directive 2004/28/EC of the European Parliament and of the Council of 31 March 2004) for a marketing authorization in respect of a veterinary medicinal product, or
> (iii) any other act which is required as a consequence of the acts referred to in subparagraph (i) or (ii) for the purposes specified in those subparagraphs, as appropriate.
> (h) insofar as paragraph (g) does not apply, acts done in relation to the subject matter of the relevant patented invention which consist of:
> (i) acts done in conducting studies, tests, experiments and trials (including clinical trials and field trials) with a view to satisfying the application requirements for a marketing authorisation or similar instrument (howsoever described) that is required by the law of the State or of any other state in order to sell or supply or offer to sell or supply:
> (I) a medicinal product for human use, within the meaning of subsection (2), or
> (II) a veterinary medicinal product, within the meaning of subsection (2),
> or
> (ii) any other act done which is required as a consequence of the acts referred to in subparagraph (i) for the purposes specified in that subparagraph, as appropriate.

To date there have not been any cases in Ireland considering the scope of the statutory Bolar-type exemption under Section 42(1)(g) and (h).

c. Bodies That May Decide on the Legitimacy of Exemptions

Both the Experimental Use exemption and the Bolar-type exemption are raised as defences to patent infringement claims in litigation proceedings. In Ireland, typically such cases will be heard before the Commercial Court (a division of the High Court) and will be entered into the IP & Technology List, a sub-division of the Commercial

Court which came into operation on 22 October 2021. An IP & Technology List Judge would therefore determine the legitimacy of a claimed exemption. Short-term patents (those lasting a maximum of ten years) can also be enforced in the Circuit Court. In such instances, a Circuit Court Judge would determine the legitimacy of a claimed exemption.

2. THE EXPERIMENTAL USE EXEMPTION

a. History and Rationale of Adopting the Experimental Use Exemption

There had been no cases in Ireland establishing a common law Experimental Use exemption prior to the enactment of the statutory exemption. However, the Irish courts would typically have looked to the common law Experimental Use exemption established in the UK dating back to 1878 in the case of *Frearson v. Loe.*[1] The rationale for the Experimental Use exemption is that there should be no prohibition on 'the mere making for the purpose of experiment, and not for a fraudulent purpose' so long as there is no use for commercial gain. Further, the underlying rationale for the exemption is to encourage scientific research while protecting the legitimate interests of the patentee.[2]

Although the Experimental Use exemption has now been codified in Irish law following the adoption of the EPC and PCT, there have yet to be any cases in Ireland considering the scope of the Experimental Use exemption.

b. The Laws Applicable to the Experimental Use Exemption in Ireland

The Patents Act 1992 (and as amended subsequently by the Patents (Amendment) Act 2006) came into effect on 1 August 1992, ratifying the EPC and PCT, and repealing the Patents Act 1964 and the Patents (Amendment) Act 1966. The Experimental Use exemption was enacted on the same date under Section 42(1)(b) of the Patents Act 1992:

> 42(1) The rights conferred by a patent shall not extend to-
> (b) acts done for experimental purposes relating to the subject-matter of the relevant patented invention;

There have been no cases in Ireland discussing the Experimental Use exemption in any detail, nor regulations defining any elements of the statute.

c. Procedural Aspects of Invoking the Experimental Use Exemption

The Experimental Use exemption is raised as a defence in patent infringement proceedings. In Ireland, such proceedings are typically heard by the Commercial Court (a division of the High Court), specifically on the IP & Technology List subdivision, and is the relevant body to determine the legitimacy of an Experimental Use exemption.

1. *Frearson v. Loe* (1878) 9 Ch. D. 48.
2. *Corevalve Inc v. Edwards Lifesciences AG* [2009] EWHC 6 (Pat).

Short-term patents (those lasting a maximum of ten years) can also be enforced in the Circuit Court. In such instances, a Circuit Court Judge would determine the legitimacy of an Experimental Use exemption.

d. Scope of the Experimental Use Exemption in Ireland

i. Fields of Technology

There are no restrictions or limitations in Ireland as to which field of technology may claim an Experimental Use exemption.

ii. Purpose of Experiments/Infringing Activities

Although there have been no cases in Ireland discussing the purpose of experiments, precedent in other common law countries expands on what can be regarded as 'experimental purposes'. In the leading case of *Monsanto Co. v. Stauffer Chemical Co.*,[3] the UK Court of Appeal found that 'Trials carried out in order to discover something unknown or to test a hypothesis or even in order to find out whether something which is known to work in specific conditions...will work in different conditions can fairly...be regarded as experiments', so long as the experimental purpose relates to the patented invention. However, 'trials carried out in order to demonstrate to a third party that a product works or, in order to amass information to satisfy a third party, whether a customer or a [regulatory] body...that the product works as its maker claims are not...to be regarded as acts done for experimental purposes'. The exemption therefore has very few limitations other than the experimental purpose needing to relate to the patented invention. There has been no case law discussing the distinction between 'researching on' and 'researching with' the invention in Ireland but, construed in the wording of the statute, if the experimentation relates to the invention covered by the patent that is allegedly infringed whereby the invention is 'researched on' to develop or enhance it without commercial gain, the exemption may be relied upon. However, following the rationale in *Monsanto*[3] 'researching with' the invention for experimental purposes that do not relate to the subject-matter of that patented invention, for example to gain regulatory approval for a product falling within the scope of the patented invention for commercial purposes, is unlikely to fall within the exemption.

One limitation to note is where the purpose of the experiment is seen to go beyond the academic toward commercial purposes. In *Smith Kline & French Laboratories Ltd v. Attorney-General*[4] (a New Zealand Court of Appeal case) the notion of experimental vs commercial purposes was considered.

> Doubtless experimentation will usually have an ultimate commercial objective; where it ends and infringement begins must often be a matter of degree. If the person concerned keeps his activities to himself, and does no more than further his own knowledge or skill, even though commercial advantage may be his final

3. *Monsanto Co. v. Stauffer Chemical Co.* [1985] RPC 515.
4. *Smith Kline & French Laboratories Ltd v. Attorney-General* (1991) 22 IPR 143.

> goal, he does not infringe. But if he goes beyond that, and uses the invention or makes it available to others, in a way that serves to advance in the actual market place, then he infringes.

This point was addressed in *Monsanto*[3] where it was found that 'If the person concerned...does no more than further his own knowledge or skill, even though commercial advantage may be his final goal, he does not infringe'. Whilst generally accepted that experimentation could ultimately have a commercial purpose, it appears that such acts are infringing where they extend to the marketplace at large. The purpose of the alleged infringer in relation to their acts of experimentation will therefore be a key consideration for Irish courts when considering Section 42(1)(b) as a defence and will be decided on a case-by-case basis. *Meter-Tech LLC v. British Gas Trading Ltd*[5] (discussed at section 2.d.iv.) considered the relevant factors in determining whether a purpose is experimental or not and provides guidance on such an assessment.

iii. Exempted and Prohibited Activities

Section 42(1)(b) does not specify any activities as prohibited or exempted, instead referring to *any* acts done for experimental purposes relating to the subject-matter of the relevant patented invention. The Act therefore provides a very broad defence in relation to the acts that may evoke the exemption so long as they are done for experimental, non-commercial purposes.

Although not considered in case law in Ireland, it can be said that any of the infringing acts under Section 40 or Section 41, such as manufacture or importation, would be exempt from infringement so long as it can be shown that they were carried out for experimental, non-commercial purposes.

iv. Pure Academic vs Commercially Motivated Experimental Use

As discussed in section 2.d.ii. above, the purpose of the experimental use, and the ability to avail of the exemption, lies in the degree to which the use is commercially motivated. The principle in *Monsanto*[3] applies; 'pure academic' and 'commercially motivated' experimental use need not be mutually exclusive, and that some furtherance of knowledge or skill may have a commercial end goal. It is the degree to which the balance shifts toward commercial motivations which is key.

Whilst there has been no case law in Ireland considering the issue, in the UK case of *Meter-Tech LLC v. British Gas Trading Ltd*,[5] the court considered a number of factors to determine whether infringing use was for experimental purposes:

(i) whether the acts were properly characterized as trials for scientific or developmental research;
(ii) whether trials were carried out to discover something technically unknown or to test a technical hypothesis (or simply to discover whether the product was commercially acceptable to the market);

5. *Meter-Tech LLC v. British Gas Trading Ltd* [2016] EWHC 2278 (Pat).

(iii) whether trials were intended to find out whether something which was known to work in specific conditions would work in different conditions, such as small v large scale;
(iv) whether the trials were carried out mainly to demonstrate to a third-party customer or regulator that a product worked; or
(v) whether the trial's main purpose was to generate revenue as a result of the invention's use in the trial itself.

British Gas was unsuccessful in its experimental use defence as it failed to show that its use had been genuine research relating to the development of improvements in metering.

Equally, in the earlier UK case of *Corevalve v. Edwards Lifesciences*[2] the court stated that where a defendant has mixed purposes, the exemption only applies where the dominant purpose of the defendant's acts is to 'generate information of scientific or technical value'. As Corevalve also intended to establish confidence in its product in the market and to generate immediate revenue, any research into clinical indications or modifications could not be said to be its preponderant purpose.

e. Beneficiary Limitations

The issue of third-party contributions to experimental use have not been considered by the courts in Ireland. However, it is reasonable to assume, following the case law above, that if such contributions were made by third parties that they would also be exempt so long as they are seen to be for experimental, non-commercial purposes.

f. Territoriality Issues

The statutory exemption does not address territorial scope, but fundamentally Irish courts have jurisdiction over proceedings for Irish patent infringement and have the power to enforce Irish patents.

Irish courts may also preside over proceedings concerning European patents so long as the plaintiff and the defendant either ordinarily reside in Ireland or carry out any profession, business or occupation in Ireland. In practice, this is likely to be cases where Ireland is a designated Member State of the European patent and the infringing act took place in Ireland.

g. Burden of Proof and Onus

There have been no cases concerning the Experimental Use exemption in Ireland to determine where the burden of proof lies for raising such a defence. However, it can reasonably be assumed that the courts will uphold the typical principles of Irish civil proceedings and that it would be for the party raising the defence to prove that it should avail of the exemption.

h. Applicability during Patent Term Extension or Supplementary Protection Certificate

Claims of patent infringement under Section 40 and Section 41 of the Patents Act 1992 apply to 'a patent while it is in force'. No distinction is made between the term of a patent as initially granted or the extended term following grant of an SPC. Therefore, the ability to avail of an experimental use defence would apply where the patent term has been extended by SPC.

3. THE BOLAR TYPE EXEMPTION

a. History and Rationale of Adopting the Bolar-Type Exemption

As discussed previously, the statutory exemption of experimental use, whilst fairly broad in terms of its application, is limited by what use can reasonably be considered experimental. Use for the purposes of conducting clinical trials in the pursuit of marketing authorizations from regulatory authorities for medicinal products (a required step before entering the marketplace) is an activity which is arguably not covered by the Experimental Use exemption. Such activity is particularly salient for generic pharmaceutical manufacturers preparing to launch generic versions of patented pharmaceuticals upon expiry of the patent term.

The adoption of the Bolar-type exemption in Europe and, consequently, Ireland, seeks to address this industry specific gap and provides generic manufacturers with certainty regarding such activity. Amendment of Section 42(1) inserted the Bolar-type exemption to exempt studies, tests, and trials necessary for applying for marketing authorization for a medicinal product for human or veterinary use. The exemption was further expanded in 2014, following a consultation by the Irish Government in 2012, to bring it closer to other EU Member States, such as Germany and the UK, to specify that: clinical and field trials, and consequential acts, are covered by the exemption; that the exemption applies to innovative as well as generic products; and that it applies for the purposes of obtaining marketing authorization in Ireland and any other country (including outside the EU). The rationale behind the expansion was to provide clarity as to what research activities could be carried out in Ireland for the purposes of seeking marketing authorization and to therefore make it a more attractive location for pharmaceutical research.

b. The Laws Applicable to the Bolar-Type Exemption in Ireland

The Bolar-type exemption is provided under Section 42(1)(g) and (h) of the Patents Act 1992, as amended in 2006 by the European Communities (Limitation of Effect of Patent) Regulations 2006 (SI 50/2006) and as further amended by the Intellectual Property (Miscellaneous Provisions) Act 2014:

> 42(1) The rights conferred by a patent shall not extend to-
> (g) acts done in relation to the subject matter of the relevant patented invention which consist of:

- (i) acts done in conducting the necessary studies, tests and trials which are conducted with a view to satisfying the application requirements of paragraphs 1, 2, 3 and 4 of Article 10 of Directive 2001/83/EC of the European Parliament and of the Council of 6 November 2001 (at last amended by Directive 2004/27/EC of the European Parliament and of the Council of 31 March 2004) for a marketing authorization in respect of a medicinal product for human use, or
- (ii) acts done in conducting the necessary studies, tests and trials which are conducted with a view to satisfying the application requirements of paragraphs 1 to 5 of Article 13 of Directive 2001/82/EC of the European Parliament and of the Council of 6 November 2001 (as last amended by Directive 2004/28/EC of the European Parliament and of the Council of 31 March 2004) for a marketing authorization in respect of a veterinary medicinal product, or
- (iii) any other act which is required as a consequence of the acts referred to in subparagraph (i) or (ii) for the purposes specified in those subparagraphs, as appropriate.

(h) insofar as paragraph (g) does not apply, acts done in relation to the subject matter of the relevant patented invention which consist of:

- (i) acts done in conducting studies, tests, experiments and trials (including clinical trials and field trials) with a view to satisfying the application requirements for a marketing authorisation or similar instrument (howsoever described) that is required by the law of the State or of any other state in order to sell or supply or offer to sell or supply:
  - (I) a medicinal product for human use, within the meaning of subsection (2), or
  - (II) a veterinary medicinal product, within the meaning of subsection (2),

  or
- (ii) any other act done which is required as a consequence of the acts referred to in subparagraph (i) for the purposes specified in that subparagraph, as appropriate.

To date there have not been any cases in Ireland considering the scope of the statutory Bolar-type exemption under Section 42(1)(g) and (h).

However, the adoption of the Bolar-type exemption under Subsection (g), and the further amendments to expand the provision under Subsection (h) to include innovative medicines and a worldwide geographical scope, suggests a more flexible interpretation of the provision will be taken by the courts (although still viewed within the specific scope of trials conducted for the purpose of obtaining marketing authorization for a human medicinal or veterinary medicinal product). It is also arguable that the amendment to include Subsection (h) with its more expansive scope effectively means that Subsection (g) is redundant.

c. Procedural Aspects of Invoking the Bolar-Type Exemption

The Bolar-type exemption is raised as a defence in patent infringement proceedings. In Ireland, such proceedings are typically heard by the Commercial Court (a division of the High Court), specifically on the IP & Technology List subdivision, which is the relevant body to determine the legitimacy of a Bolar-type exemption.

Short-term patents (those lasting a maximum of ten years) can also be enforced in the Circuit Court. In such instances, a Circuit Court Judge would determine the legitimacy of a Bolar-type exemption.

d. Scope of the Bolar-Type Exemption in Ireland

i. Fields of Technology

Section 42(1)(g) and (h) state that the exemption applies to trials conducted for the purpose of obtaining marketing authorization for a human medicinal or veterinary medicinal product. Section 42(2) defines medicinal product for human use as any substance or combination of substances for treating or preventing disease, or restoring, correcting or modifying physiological features (similarly for veterinary medicinal products). 'Substance' is that of any of human, animal, vegetable or chemical origin. The exemption is therefore limited to pharmaceuticals and biologics and would not apply to medical devices, for example, nor any other field of technology.

ii. Purpose of Experiments/Infringing Activities

There have been no cases in Ireland considering what purpose is necessary for the experiments/infringing activities so we are guided by the wording of the statute. It appears that the Patents Act 1992 would exempt any acts so long as their purpose is for conducting experiments and trials with a view to satisfying the application requirements for a marketing authorization in order to sell or supply, or offer to sell or supply, human medicinal products or veterinary medicinal products.

A UK case of note is *Merck Sharp Dohme Corp v. Teva Pharma BV.*[6] The court considered the purpose of Section 60(5)(i) Patents Act 1977 (the UK equivalent of Section 42(g)), accepting that there are good reasons why a pharmaceutical would obtain a marketing authorization for its infringing medicinal product some time in advance of patent expiry in order to allow for an orderly launch on patent expiry, and that doing so is not itself an act of infringement. However, the exemption was not to be used to facilitate infringement before expiry, i.e. gaining marketing authorization to launch a competing medicinal product prior to patent expiry.

iii. Exempted and Prohibited Activities

There have been no cases in Ireland considering activities which may fall outside the scope of the Bolar-type exemption. As stated in section 3.d.ii., if a pharmaceutical can show that its purpose is conducting trials to obtain marketing authorization for a medicinal product, then infringing acts under Section 40 and Section 41 such as making, importing or using are likely to be found exempt.

---

6. *Merck Sharp Dohme Corp v. Teva Pharma BV* [2012] EWHC 627 (Pat).

As noted in *Merck*,[7] the exemption cannot be used to facilitate an intent to latterly commit infringing acts. The case considered whether threat could be inferred from obtaining marketing authorization, in a scenario where Teva had gained its marketing authorization just under two years before patent expiry and could theoretically launch a competing product within months of the authorization, and within the patent term. The court found that inference could be drawn from Teva's actions that it intended to infringe Merck's patent, who were subsequently awarded an injunction.

e. Beneficiary Limitations

The issue of third party contributions to the Bolar-type exemption has not been considered by the courts in Ireland. It is reasonable to assume that a pharmaceutical company may engage a third party to either assist with its trials or to conduct them on its behalf. Given the narrow, yet non-prohibitive, nature of the Bolar-type exemption in Ireland, any third-party contributions to experiments or trials are also likely to be found exempt so long as they were provided for the purpose of conducting trials with a view to obtaining marketing authorization for a human medicinal or veterinary medicinal product.

f. Territoriality Issues

Section 42(g) is limited to European marketing authorizations (and by extension, marketing authorization in Ireland). Section 42(h) does not have a territorial limitation and would equally apply to regulatory submissions in any other country.

There have been no cases in Ireland considering whether the exemption would still apply if the results of experiments conducted in Ireland were used to infringe a patent in another jurisdiction, nor whether the person acting under the exemption is the applicant for regulatory approval (or related to it in some capacity).

g. Burden of Proof and Onus

There have been no cases considering the Bolar-type exemption in Ireland, to determine where the burden of proof lies for raising such a defence. However, it can reasonably be assumed that the courts will uphold the typical principles of Irish civil proceedings and that it would be for the party raising the defence to prove that it should avail of the exemption.

h. Applicability during Patent Term Extension or Supplementary Protection Certificate

Claims of patent infringement under Section 40 and Section 41 of the Patents Act 1992 apply to 'a patent while it is in force'. No distinction is made between the term of a patent as initially granted or the extended term following grant of an SPC. Therefore, the ability to avail of the Bolar-type exemption would apply where the patent term

7. *Ibid.*

has been extended by an SPC. In the case of pharmaceutical patents, to which the SPC mechanism applies in most instances due to the longer period of necessary research and regulatory requirements before commercialization, it is highly likely that a patent would be in its SPC term where a pharmaceutical is seeking marketing authorization and would rely on a Bolar-type defence.

4. DIFFERENCES BETWEEN THE TWO EXCEPTIONS IN IRELAND

Although both exemptions derive from Section 42 of the Patents Act 1992, the main difference between the Experimental Use and the Bolar-type exemptions in Ireland lies in their scope and specificity.

The Experimental Use exemption is broadly defined and is not restricted by technological area. As noted in *Monsanto*,[3] the purpose of the Experimental Use exemption is to protect persons who do no more than further their own knowledge or skill, even if a commercial benefit may be their ultimate aim, whilst upholding the rights of the patentee. The degree to which the experimenter's purpose shifts toward the commercial will ultimately dictate whether they may avail of the exemption or not.

The Bolar-type exemption, by comparison, is applicable in very specific circumstances: where a person conducts experiments or trials with a view to obtaining marketing authorization for a human medicinal or veterinary medicinal product. The exemption is therefore restricted to pharmaceuticals and biologics but thereafter, is relatively unrestricted, applying to most, if not all, infringing acts, to innovative and generic products equally, and applies to marketing authorizations sought worldwide.

The exemptions are therefore largely separate and distinct. In the applicable circumstances, a defendant would raise a Bolar-type defence whereas in all other instances, a defendant would claim an Experimental Use exemption.

Chapter 23

Israel

David Gilat, Matan Kovacs, Amira Mangelus and David Tirosh

1. GENERAL

a. Terminology

The Experimental Use exemption appears in Section 1 of the Patents Law 5727-1967('the Patents Law') under the definition of the term 'exploitation of an invention'.

The Bolar-type exemption appears in Section 54A of the Patents Law under the heading 'Experimental act to obtain a license'.

b. Legal Basis in Israel

According to Section 49 of the Patents Law, a patentee is entitled to prevent any other person from exploiting the invention for which the patent has been granted without their permission or unlawfully. The definition of 'exploitation of an invention' appears in Section 1 of the Patents Law. Both the Experimental Use exemption and Bolar-type exemption appear as exceptions to the definition of 'exploitation of an invention' as follows:

(1) an act that is not on a commercial scale and is not commercial in character;

(2) an experimental act in connection with an invention, the objective of which is to improve an invention or to develop another invention;

(3) an act performed under the provisions of section 54A.

Subsection (1) was included in the original language of the Patents Law; Subsections (2) and (3) were introduced in 1998.

The discussion of these exemptions in the case law is relatively scarce. Regarding the first alternative, it was held by the District Court[1] that since, according to the statutory definition, the requirements of 'commercial nature' and 'commercial scope' are cumulative (private non-commercial use), it follows that while exploiting an invention for pure research and promotion of science is permissible, doing so with a view to expanding one's business is not. In another decision[2] issued prior to the enactment of the experimental act and Bolar-type exemptions, it was ruled that an act performed in connection with an invention in order to improve an invention is exempt, even if it is of a commercial nature or scope.[3] Another decision, issued after the amendment to the law, warned that if the experimental act is 'a cover' for carrying out commercial acts, such as acts intended to penetrate markets and preparing marketing channels, it would not be exempt.[4]

The Bolar-type exemption is codified in Section 54A of the Patents Law, which reads as follows:

> An experimental act, which is part of an effort to obtain a license to market the product after the patent has lapsed, does not constitute 'exploitation of an invention' if the following two conditions are met:
>
> (1) the effort to obtain the license was made in order to obtain a license in Israel or in a country in which an experimental act on a patent-protected invention for the purpose of obtaining a license is permitted before the patent lapses;
>
> (2) any product under the terms of this section is not used – both while the patent is in effect or thereafter – for any purpose other than obtaining a license as aforesaid;
>
> for purposes of this section, 'license' – certification, permit, or any other document required under Law to market a product.

To date, there has been only one non-binding court decision that considered the metes and bounds of the Bolar-type exemption, as detailed in section 3.b. below.

c. Bodies That May Decide on the Legitimacy of Exemptions

Both the Experimental Use exemption and the Bolar-type exemption are used as defences in infringement proceedings. In Israel, such proceedings are under the jurisdiction of the District Courts as the first instance or the Supreme Court as the appellate instance.

---

1. D.C.C (T.A.) 1512/93 *The Wellcome Foundation Limited v. Teva Pharmaceutical Industries Ltd.* [Nevo]
2. D.C.M. (T.A.) 19682/05 *Transkaryotic Therapies Inc. v. Genzyme Corporation* [Nevo] (the 'Genzyme Matter')
3. D.C.A (T.A.) 2790/96 *Biogen Inc. v. General Bio-Technology (Israel) Ltd.* [Nevo] (the 'Biogen Matter').
4. D.C.M (Jm.) 814/05 *Orbotech Ltd. v. Camtek Ltd.* [Nevo] (the 'Orbotech Matter')

2. THE EXPERIMENTAL USE EXEMPTION

a. History and Rationale of Adopting the Experimental Use Exemption

Originally, the Patents Law only included a sole exemption in the form of non-commercial use. This was changed in 1998, when another exemption was added, namely, for experimental acts in connection with the invention, the objective of which is to improve an invention or to develop another invention.

The rationale for the original exemption (non-commercial acts) is that such acts do not affect the proprietor's interests and may contribute to the advancement of knowledge.

The rationale for the added exemption (an act carried out in order '*to improve the invention or develop another invention*') is to promote technological progress and thus fulfil the objectives of the patent system.

b. The Laws Applicable to the Experimental Use Exemption in Israel

Section 49 of the Patents Law defines infringement, and states that a patentee is entitled to prevent any other person from *exploiting the invention* for which the patent has been granted without their permission or unlawfully.

Uses that are non-commercial in nature or scope, or experimental acts made in order to improve a patented invention or to develop another invention, fall outside the definition of 'exploitation of an invention' and thus do not amount to patent infringement.

The definition of 'exploitation of an invention' in Section 1 of the Patents Law includes the following exemptions:

(1) an act that is not on a commercial scale and is not commercial in character;

(2) an experimental act in connection with an invention, the objective of which is to improve an invention or to develop another invention;

Subsection (1) was included in the original language of the Patents Law; Subsection (2) was introduced in 1998.

The language of the exemptions raises several questions, which are yet to be dealt with by the case law. For example, it is not clear what would be considered 'improvement upon an invention' or 'another invention' and this will be left to case law. Also, what acts would be regarded as 'in connection with an invention' may be open to interpretation. The Patents Law does not define the term 'invention' but rather defines the term 'patent-eligible invention'.

c. Procedural Aspects of Invoking the Experimental Use Exemption

The question of whether a given act falls within the Experimental Use exemption is likely to arise primarily in the context of an infringement claim, where the defendant will raise the exemption as a defence, or in the framework of an action for declaratory judgment of non-infringement.

The question has also arisen (perhaps unjustifiably) in the context of so-called 'novelty destroying experimental use doctrine', where the claim of experimental prior use was raised by the plaintiff. In such cases it was in the interest of the plaintiff to show that its prior public use was experimental and did not amount to 'exploitation' (according to Section 4(2) of the Patents Law, an invention lacks novelty if published 'by *exploitation* or exhibition, in a manner that enables a skilled person to make it according to the particulars thus made known' (emphasis added)).[5]

d. Scope of the Experimental Use Exemption in Israel

i. *Fields of Technology*

The Experimental Use exemption is not limited to a given field and is applicable to all fields of technology (i.e., to any patented invention).

ii. *Purpose of Experiments/Infringing Activities*

As noted above, acts that do not interfere with the economic interest of the patentee are outside the scope of the negative right afforded by a patent under Section 49. Thus, a given experimental activity that is commercial in nature or scope, would be considered a non-permissible exploitation of the invention, unless done in order to improve the patented invention or to develop another invention. The rationale is that experimental activity that aims at promoting progress is in line with the purpose of the Patents Law, and patents ought not be used to hinder progress.[6]

In addition, the Law does not specifically address the issue of whether the use of patented research tools for improving or developing other inventions is exempt, nor has the case law addressed this issue. The minutes of the Knesset Committee suggest that there was no intention to include research tools as such under the exemption. However, it was held in the Genzyme Matter that where a patented matter is used as a benchmark (i.e. as comparator), such use would be deemed an act for developing another invention, that would fall under the exemption.

iii. *Exempted and Prohibited Activities*

The Patents Law defines 'exploitation of an invention' (i.e., prohibited activities) as follows:

> (1) in respect of an invention that is a product – any act that is one of the following: production, use, offer for sale, sale, or import for purposes of one of the said acts;
>
> (2) in respect of an invention that is a process – use of the process, and in respect of a product directly derived from the process – any act that is one of

5. D.C.C (T.A.) 2624-05 *Kleiman Meteor Ltd. v. Hadar Dror* [Nevo]; D.C.M (T.A.) 1023/97 *CQM v. Bulltech Energy* [Nevo]
6. See in the Biogen Matter discussed above.

the following: production, use, offer for sale, sale, or import for purposes of one of the said acts.

There is no separate list of activities that may be covered by the exemption, and it appears that all of the listed exploiting activities would be exempted if the underlying conditions are met, so long as they are 'experimental'.

iv. Pure Academic vs Commercially Motivated Experimental Use

As noted above, an act of 'pure science' is exempted as long as it is not carried out *on a commercial scale and is not commercial in character*. Still, a commercially motivated experimental act would be nonetheless exempted, provided it is carried out in order to improve an invention or to develop another invention and is not a cover for non-experimental commercial acts.

e. Beneficiary Limitations

There is no statutory provision in the Patents Law discussing the conferring of protection on third parties, nor has the case law addressed this issue. However, it is reasonable to assume that the exemption applies to third parties contracted to assist in conducting the experiments.

f. Territoriality Issues

The Patents Law is applicable only in the territory of the State of Israel.

Yet, in one non-binding decision, the Jerusalem District Court issued a *Mareva* type (*ad personam*) injunction against activities carried out abroad, because they were based on experiments in Israel that were not aimed at improving a patented invention or making another invention, and thus did not fall under the exemption. Said order was issued on the basis of principles of unjust enrichment.[7]

g. Burden of Proof and Onus

The party claiming the applicability of the exemption bears the onus to prove that the terms of the exemption are fulfilled.

h. Applicability during Patent Term Extension or Supplementary Protection Certificate

The extension term of a patent is regarded in the same manner as the initial twenty-year term, and as a result, the same exemptions will apply.

7. See in the Orobtech Matter discussed above.

3. THE BOLAR-TYPE EXEMPTION

a. History and Rationale of Adopting the Bolar-Type Exemption

In the past, courts have ruled that activities conducted during the patent protection period of innovative drugs, and aimed at obtaining marketing authorization for generic drugs, constituted infringement. These rulings were based on the language of the Patents Law, which entitled the patentee to prevent any other person from making any use of the invention, except where the use is both on a non-commercial scale and of a non-commercial nature, as discussed above.

This legal reality placed the Israeli generic industry at a perceived disadvantage compared to generic companies in territories where the law permitted such activities during the patent protection period, in particular the USA. Thus, US companies could secure drug marketing authorization for their generic products during the patent term, whereas Israeli companies could only commence regulatory preparations after the patent expired, delaying their entry to the market and possibly impacting exports from Israel.

To address these competitive disadvantages ostensibly faced by the Israeli generic industry, the Israeli Legislature introduced a Bolar-type exemption on February 17, 1998, as part of Amendment No. 3 to the Patents Law. The Amendment revised the definition of 'exploitation of an invention' in Section 1 of the Patents Law to exclude from exploitation – and thus, from infringement – experimental acts towards obtaining a regulatory licence for use in sales after the patent has expired, in Israel or in a country where a Bolar-type exemption is recognized.

b. The Laws Applicable to the Bolar-Type Exemption in Israel

The Bolar-type exemption is codified in the Patents Law. According to Section 49 of the Patents Law, a patentee is entitled to prevent any other person from *exploiting the invention* for which the patent has been granted without consent or unlawfully. The term 'exploitation of an invention' in Section 1 of the Patents Law excludes any act performed under the provision of Section 54A.

Section 54A reads as follows:

> An experimental act, which is part of an effort to obtain a license to market the product after the patent has lapsed, does not constitute 'exploitation of an invention' if the following two conditions are met:
>
> (1) the effort to obtain the license is made in order to obtain a license in Israel or in a country in which an experimental act on a patent-protected invention for the purpose of obtaining a license is permitted before the patent lapses;
>
> (2) any product produced under the terms of this section is not used – both while the patent is in effect or thereafter – for any purpose other than obtaining a license as aforesaid;
>
> for purposes of this section, 'license' – certification, permit, or any other document required under Law to market a product.

According to a non-binding court judgment, the exemption under Section 54A applies to experimental acts aimed at obtaining a licence to market both generic and innovative products. The subjective intentions of the party performing the experimental acts are irrelevant when determining whether they are covered by the exemption; instead, they must be evaluated based on whether they are reasonably connected to the licensing efforts. Additionally, the experimenting party is bound to act in good faith, but merely performing experimental acts under the exemption does not imply, by itself, bad faith or guarantee of future infringement and does not justify an order for the experimenting party to disclose information related to the invention.[8] Thus, while the judgment addressed many of the key questions regarding the scope of the exemption, it did not address questions such as whether the data obtained through the experiments were used solely for obtaining a regulatory approval in Israel or in a country where a Bolar-type exemption is recognized, or whether they were used for purposes other than obtaining a licence as aforesaid.

c. Procedural Aspects of Invoking the Bolar-Type Exemption

The Bolar-type exemption may be used as a defence in patent infringement proceedings or as a claim for declaratory judgment of non-infringement, where a party seeks a court order affirming their use of the invention is exempt from infringement. Such proceedings are under the jurisdiction of the relevant District Courts as courts of first instance or the Supreme Court as the court of appeal.

d. Scope of the Bolar-Type Exemption in Israel

i. Fields of Technology

While designed to address concerns from the pharmaceutical industry, the Bolar-type exemption is not limited to pharmaceutical products but rather covers any product that requires regulatory approval (including, for example, crop protection products).

ii. Purpose of Experiments/Infringing Activities

It appears that any acts are acceptable, provided that their purpose is to obtain a licence to market the product after the patent has lapsed in Israel or in a country where a Bolar-type exemption is recognized, and provided that any product so produced was not used – both while the patent is in effect or thereafter – for any purpose other than obtaining a licence as aforesaid.

iii. Exempted and Prohibited Activities

The Israeli Bolar-type exemption is purpose-limited; it is specifically restricted to experimental acts aimed at obtaining regulatory approval to market the product after the patent has lapsed, either in Israel or in a country where a Bolar-type exemption is

8. See in the Genzyme Matter discussed above.

recognized. The law specifies that any use of a product made under these conditions for purposes beyond those related to obtaining regulatory approval is not exempt, both during the patent's term and after its expiration. While not explicitly stated in the Law, activities such as stockpiling and production for export are inherently excluded from the exemption.

e. Beneficiary Limitations

According to a non-binding court decision,[9] the exemption applies both to generic companies applying for regulatory approval and to innovative companies. The Patents Law does not address the question of whether the exemption can be utilized by third parties or the required linkage between the exempted activity and the entity seeking regulatory approval. However, it is reasonable to assume that the exemption applies to third parties contracted to conduct studies on behalf of the party seeking regulatory approval.

f. Territoriality Issues

The exemption applies to experimental acts conducted in Israel aimed at obtaining regulatory approval either in Israel or in other countries where a Bolar-type exemption is recognized. It is likely that experimental acts conducted in other countries to obtain regulatory approval in Israel are also exempt if Israel has jurisdiction over those activities. However, these acts may still be subject to the laws of the other country if they involve infringing on a corresponding patent there.

g. Burden of Proof and Onus

In the context of an infringement proceeding or a motion for a declaratory judgment of non-infringement, the onus is on the party claiming an exemption to prove that the Bolar-type exemption applies.

h. Applicability during Patent Term Extension or Supplementary Protection Certificate

The Israeli Bolar-type exemption still applies during patent term extension, which means that the prohibition not to use the invention – both while the patent is in effect or thereafter – for any purpose other than obtaining a licence continues during the patent term extension.

4. DIFFERENCES BETWEEN THE TWO EXEMPTIONS IN ISRAEL

The rationales for each of the exemptions are different. The rationale for the Experimental Use exemption is to not have patents hinder research and development in

9. See in the Genzyme Matter discussed above.

the art, as well as to not disallow acts that are not commercial and are, therefore, unlikely to substantially injure the interests of the patent proprietor.

The rationale behind the Bolar-type exemption reflects the compromise struck in the USA between innovators and generics in the aftermath of *Roche v. Bolar* and is intended to remedy the disadvantage suffered by Israeli generic companies in comparison to their counterparts abroad, particularly in the USA. The purpose was to prevent the so-called 'spring-board effect' – a *de facto* patent term extension – so as to allow generic manufacturers to be ready to launch the products as soon as possible following the patent's lapse.

While the rationales for each of the exemptions are different, there could be an overlap between them, and co-extension is possible; in one case,[10] the District Court held that clinical trials held in order to obtain regulatory approval may also amount to an act carried out to create a new invention or improve an existing one, as the product used in these trials was allegedly more effective than the product claimed in the patent discussed there.

In the event that both exemptions apply, the consequences would be the same, as the scope of the exemption is the same – all exemptions cover 'an act', and one exemption is not superior to the other.

10. See in the Genzyme Matter discussed above.

Chapter 24

Italy

Magali Contardi and Mariangela Bogni

1. GENERAL

a. Terminology

The Experimental Use exemption appears in Article 68(1) (a-*bis*) of the Italian Industrial Property Code ('IPC').

The so-called 'Bolar-type exemption' – equally referred to as the 'Bolar clause', or as the 'Bolar exception' or 'Bolar exemption' in the first Supreme Court decision dealing with it in 2024 – is regulated by Article 68(1)(b) IPC.

Both fall under the 'patent right limitations' provided by Article 68 IPC, which lists all activities related to the lawful use of a patented invention under certain conditions provided by the same regulation.

b. Legal Basis in Italy

The Experimental Use exemption was provided for in the original text of Article 68 IPC, adopted by Legislative Decree No. 30 of 10 February 2005. Prior to the enactment of the IPC, the Experimental Use exemption was regulated under the so-called Invention Law (i.e. by Royal Decree No. 1127 of 29 June 1939, as amended by Presidential Decree No. 338/1979), and was largely recognized by Italian legal doctrine and case law.[1] In Italian case law, the Supreme Court of Cassation, in its

1. *See* Cesare Galli, 'Limitazioni del Diritto di Brevetto – Commento all'articolo 68 del Codice della Proprietà Industriale' Codice Commentato della Proprietà Industriale e Intellettuale 741 et seq(GALLI-GAMBINO, ed, UTET Giuridica 2011).; Luigi Carlo Ubertazzi, 'Limitazioni del Diritto di Brevetto – Commento all'articolo 68 del Codice della Proprietà Industriale' 7th Commentario Breve alle Leggi su Proprietà Intellettuale e Concorrenza 510-511 (ed Luigi Carlo Ubertazzi CEDAM 2019).

Decision No. 640 dated 2 February 1976, had held that the mere manufacture of a patented product for experimental purposes, without subsequent sale, did not constitute patent infringement, as it did not involve the economic exploitation of the invention.

The Bolar-type exemption was expressly encoded for the first time into the Italian legal system in the original text of Article 68 IPC, introduced by the Legislative Decree No. 30 of 10 February 2005. It contained, however, ambiguous wording, as it had incorporated the new regulation of preparatory activities for obtaining a marketing authorization for a medicine into the exception of experimental use. The IPC review introduced by Legislative Decree No. 131 of 13 August 2010, therefore, proceeded with a ''split'' of the two exemptions, thus keeping separate, on the one hand, the Experimental Use exemption (limited to the cases of experiments conducted on the invention), and, on the other hand, preparatory activities in view of obtaining a marketing authorization for medicines for which the rationale of exclusion from the scope of patent protection is different. Before the introduction of the IPC, the Italian courts diverged on whether to recognize the lawfulness of activities carried out by parties other than the patentee in order to obtain, before the exclusivity expired, marketing authorization for a medicine. In some cases, even when such activities did not include exploitation of patented invention. For instance, the Court of Turin, in its decision dated 24 September 1984,[2] had stated that even filing an application for marketing authorization of a generic drug constituted patent infringement. On the contrary, a decision from the Court of Milan[3] had included those activities aimed at obtaining marketing authorization and conducted while the patent was still in force under the Experimental Use exemption.

The amendment to Article 68 IPC introduced by Legislative Decree No. 131 of 13 August 2010, provided a time limit for the 'Bolar-type exemption' to operate, stipulating, in Article 68(1*bis*) IPC that:

> companies intending to produce pharmaceutical specialties outside patent coverage may initiate the registration procedure of the product containing the active ingredient in advance of one year before the expiration of SPC, or failing that, of the patent on the active ingredient, taking into account any extension.

The entire provision was later deleted by Decree Law No. 1 of 24 January 2012, converted with amendments into Law No. 27 of 24 March 2012.

Finally, on 1 July 2019, EU Reg. No. 933/2019 came into effect, which amended the rules governing supplementary protection certificates (SPCs) to introduce the 'SPC Manufacturing Waiver'. This regulation allows the production of active ingredients still covered by an SPC for export to countries where patent or supplementary protection does not exist or has already expired and, to a limited extent, for their storage in preparation for market release immediately after the expiration of the certificate. The rationale of the SPC Manufacturing Waiver is to mitigate the 'competitive

2. In *Giurispurdenza Annotata di diritto ind*ustriale,623, Giuffrè, (1984)
3. 12 June 1995, in *Diritto Industriale, 13 Giuffrè* (1996).

disadvantage' faced by European generic drug manufacturers compared to non-EU countries where supplementary protection is weaker or non-existent.[4]

2. THE EXPERIMENTAL USE EXEMPTION

a. History and Rationale of Adopting the Experimental Use Exemption

The *rationale* of the Experimental Use exemption is to ensure that the patent system, created to incentivize research, does not become an obstacle to research itself.[5] This exemption is also deemed applicable when the experimental implementation of someone else's patented invention takes place in the context of business activity, and thus for profit, and not only in the context of 'pure' research conducted by non-profit scientific institutions.

The doctrine and the (scarce) case law dealing with the subject seem to indicate that the activities covered by the Experimental Use exemption are those directed at acquiring new knowledge and overcoming the patented invention, while experiments directed at proving the concrete feasibility and effectiveness of the patented product or process are outside the scope of the exemption. This is further explained in section 3.d.ii. below.

b. The Laws Applicable to the Experimental Use Exemption in Italy

As mentioned above, the Experimental Use exemption was provided for in the original text of Article 68 IPC related to 'Limitations on Patent rights', adopted by Legislative Decree No. 30 of 10 February 2005, paragraph a-*bis* and reads as follows:

> [Article 68 – Limitations on patent rights]
>
> Whatever the object of the invention may be, the exclusive authority attributed by patent rights does not extend to the following:
>
> (a) actions carried out privately and for non-commercial purposes, or on an experimental basis even if aimed at obtaining, also in foreign countries, a marketing authorisation for a pharmaceutical product and the consequent practical steps including the preparation and use of the pharmacologically active raw materials required for this purpose.

It was further amended by Legislative Decree No. 131 of 13 August 2010, as follows:

> [Article 68 – Limitations on patent rights]
>
> Whatever the object of the invention may be, the exclusive authority attributed by patent rights does not extend to the following:
>
> (a) actions carried out privately and for non-commercial purposes, or on an experimental basis.

4. Cesare Galli, Il Regolamento Europeo sul 'SPC manufacturing waiver' e il suo inquadramento sistematico', 68, 6, Rivista di Diritto Industriale, Giuffrè 398-422 (2019).
5. Cesare Galli., L'uso sperimentale dell'altrui Invenzione brevettata, I, 48:1Rivista di Diritto Industriale, Giuffrè, 17-36,(1998)

The text of the rule currently in force is the one amended by Legislative Decree No. 18 of 2019, article 1, paragraph 1(d), which reads as follows:

> [Article 68 – Limitations on patent rights]
>
> Whatever the object of the invention may be, the exclusive authority attributed by patent rights does not extend to the following:
>
> ...
>
> (a-*bis*) actions carried out as experimentation relate to the object of the patented invention or to the use of biological material with the aim of production, or to the discovery and development of other vegetable.

Italian case law on the Experimental Use exemption is not rich. Therefore, it is difficult to identify a clear and established way of interpretation.

The issues related to the Experimental Use exemption were addressed in the past two decades by the Court of Cassation, 30 April 2003, in *Giur. ann. dir. ind.*, 4621, according to which the Experimental Use exemption includes 'the identification of new molecules, or new compounds within the general formula covered by the patent, or of further and different production processes'; and the Court of Bologna, 12 September 2008, in *Giur. ann. dir. ind*, 5380, whereby 'experimental activity that is aimed at obtaining new knowledge that allows the overcoming of already acquired inventions is lawful'.

Whether or not the Experimental Use exemption applies to the implementation of the invention by a party other than the patent owner has to be established on the basis of an *ex ante*, and not *ex post*, assessment of the suitability of the research to achieve new knowledge and an overcoming of the invention.[6]

The Court of Bologna, 12 September 2008, clarified that:

> unequivocal and unambiguous signs of commercial purposes (such as the inclusion of goods in catalogs or the preparation of equipment for large-scale production) exclude the lawfulness of the experimental activity.

In essence, interpretation of the aforementioned case law suggests that, regardless of the declared purpose of the activity, experimental activity may still be considered an infringement if its execution contradicts the mere intent of experimentation. This could occur, for example, if the quantities produced are on an industrial scale, which may indicate an underlying commercial intent.

c. Procedural Aspects of Invoking the Experimental Use Exemption

In Italy, the Experimental Use exemption is considered a limitation to the exclusive rights granted by a patent. Therefore, it can be raised as a defence against patent infringement claims or to support claims for non-infringement assessment (that can be brought, also as a matter of urgency, on the assumption that the activity of implementing the invention for experimental purposes is challenged, explicitly or implicitly, by the patentee). The burden of proof for the infringement falls on the

6. *See*, among others, Cesare Galli, L'uso sperimentale dell'altrui Invenzione brevettato, Rivista di Diritto Industriale, I, 48:1, Giuffrè, 17-36, (1998).

patent holder, whereas the burden of proof of the applicability of the Experimental Use exemption lies with the defendant.

Jurisdiction over intellectual property litigation in Italy falls under the Enterprise Specialized Division of Italian Courts (*'Sezioni Specializzate in Materia d'Impresa'*). There are twenty-two Specialized Divisions in enterprise matters across the country. However, when one of the parties is a foreign entity, only eleven of these Specialized Divisions have jurisdiction. Appeals from decisions issued by the Specialized Division at the first instance are heard by the Courts of Appeal (*'Corte d'Appello'*). These Courts of Appeal also have Specialized Divisions dedicated to intellectual property that is in the capital of each Region, except for Lombardy, Trentino-Alto Adige, and Sicily (which have two Specialized Divisions), and Valle D'Aosta (where jurisdiction is assigned to the Court of Turin). The final instance for intellectual property cases is typically the Supreme Court of Cassation (*'Corte Suprema di Cassazione'*), specifically the Civil Sections.

With the entry into force of the Agreement on a Unified Patent Court (June 2023), the UPC handles litigation over European patents with unitary effects and over European patents without unitary effect and which have not been 'opted out', in the latter case having concurrent jurisdiction with that of the national courts (see specific chapter dealing with the Unified Patent Court).

d. Scope of the Experimental Use Exemption in Italy

i. Fields of Technology

There are no field-of-technology-based limitations or restrictions on the Experimental Use exemption in Italy. All types of technology may invoke such an exemption.

ii. Purpose of Experiments/Infringing Activities

Article 68(1)(a-*bis*) IPC covers acts performed on an experimental basis relating to the subject matter of the patented invention, the use of biological material for cultivation purposes, or the discovery and development of other plant varieties. As such, the applicability of the Experimental Use exemption depends on the experimental nature of the activities irrespective of whether there are underlying commercial intentions.

The IPC provision does not explicitly address the use of the invention as a research tool, nor does it explicitly limit the applicability of the exception to experimental activities aimed at improving the invention. However, an authoritative doctrine has suggested that because the *rationale* of the exemption is to stimulate progress, a purely applicative experimentation or mere implementation of the patent may not qualify for the exemption.[7] On this basis, a clear distinction has been drawn in doctrine between research '*on*', or 'having as an object' the patented invention (benefiting from the exemption as it aims to surpass or improve it) and

7. *See* Cesare Galli, L'uso sperimentale dell'altrui Invenzione brevettata, Rivista di Diritto Industriale, I, 48:1, Giuffrè, 20-22 (1998).

research *using* or '*with*' the invention (not covered by the exemption, as it merely applies and tests the invention).

Along the same lines, the decisions of the Court of Cassation, 30 April 2003, No. 38183 and Court of Bologna, 12 September 2008, have found lawful those activities that seek to obtain new knowledge or improvements beyond the inventions already covered by existing patents.

There has not been any recent case law establishing that the Experimental Use exemption can only be used if the purpose is to improve on an invention.

iii. Exempted and Prohibited Activities

Article 68 IPC ('Limitation of Patent Rights') provides limitations to the rights conferred to patent holders. The Experimental Use exemption provided in Article 68(1)(a-*bis)* IPC therefore applies to any 'act conducted as experimentation' without limiting the type of act covered.

As mentioned above, some of the activities that would be covered by the exemption, based on case law and doctrine, are:

- identification of new molecules, or new compounds within the general formula covered by the granted patent;
- identification of further and different production processes;
- experimental activity aimed at obtaining new knowledge or improvements beyond the existing inventions covered by the patents.

Activities which, based on case law and doctrine, would appear not to be covered by the exemption are:

- activities which unequivocally and unambiguously have a commercial purpose (such as the inclusion of goods in catalogues or the preparation of equipment for large-scale production);
- experiments directed at proving the concrete feasibility and effectiveness of the patented product or process, or research *using* or '*with*' the invention, because both are not in line with the notion of progress or improvement of the existing invention.

iv. Pure Academic vs Commercially Motivated Experimental Use

Under Italian law, the application of the Experimental Use exemption is not limited to purely academic research. Acts having 'no commercial purpose' are regulated by a different paragraph of the IPC, i.e. Article 68 (1)(a) IPC.

The Experimental Use exemption also applies to experiments conducted within the context of business activities aimed at generating profit and not only to those carried out within the realm of 'pure' research conducted by non-profit scientific institutions.[8] Therefore, the lawfulness of the acts that could abstractly constitute patent infringement is contingent solely on their experimental nature (as outlined

8. Cesare Galli, L'uso sperimentale dell'altrui Invenzione brevettata, Rivista di Diritto Industriale, I, 48:1, Giuffrè 17 (1998).

above in sections 2.d.ii and 2.d.iii). The context in which these acts are performed, as well as any underlying commercial interests, are irrelevant.

However, case law pre-IPC did not clearly recognize that a non-commercial purpose is not a prerequisite for applying the Experimental Use exemption. For instance, in Vincenza Court's decision of 7 February 1996,[9] the court excluded the application of the Experimental Use exemption in the presence of a commercial purpose.

A contrario, the decision of the Court of Bologna 12 September 2008 stated that 'unequivocal and unambiguous signs of commercial purposes (such as the inclusion of goods in catalogues or the preparation of equipment for large-scale production) exclude the lawfulness of the experimental activity', teaching that an activity that is in itself unequivocally commercial is excluded from the application of the Experimental Use exemption.

e. Beneficiary Limitations

In Italy, there is no established interpretative guideline on the subjective scope of the exemption. Still, according to an authoritative doctrine, the lawfulness of the acts that could abstractly constitute patent infringement is subordinate exclusively to their experimental character, regardless of the context in which they are carried out or by whom (whether by a public entity or a private company), without any limitation concerning the specific organizational or production methods in which the research activity takes place. The Experimental Use exemption applies to acts carried out either directly by the party conducting the research or by third parties, such as through a contractual arrangement to perform experimental activities on behalf of another company. Thus, the involvement of third parties in the experimental process does not affect the applicability of the exemption.

This view appears to be in line with the Court of Cassation's recent ruling No. 18372 of 5 July 2024, which delimited the perimeter of the Bolar-type exemption in objective terms, holding that patent rights cannot be enforced against the activities required to obtain a marketing authorization regardless of whether they are carried out directly by the marketing authorization applicant or by third parties commissioned by the applicant.

f. Territoriality Issues

There is no case law addressing this issue.

However, the discriminating factor for the purposes of applying the Experimental Use exemption or not would likely be the objective nature – to be assessed *ex ante* also considering the contractual relations between those carrying out this activity and any third parties – of the experimental activity carried out in Italy.

9. In Giurisprudenza Annotata di Diritto Industriale, Giuffrè, I 96, 658.

g. Burden of Proof and Onus

In Italy, the Experimental Use exemption is considered a limitation on the exclusive rights granted by a patent. Therefore, it can be raised as a defence against patent infringement claims or to support claims for declaration of non-infringement. The burden of proof for the infringement falls on the patent holder, whereas the burden of proof of the applicability of the Experimental Use exemption lies with the defendant.

h. Applicability during Patent Term Extension or Supplementary Protection Certificate

The IPC does not establish temporal limitation to the Experimental Use exemption. Therefore, there is no distinction between its applicability during the 'regular' patent term and any patent term extension.

SPCs were first introduced in Italy by Law No. 349 of 19 October 1991 (which added Article 4-*bis* to Royal Decree No. 1127/1939). However, with the introduction of Regulation (EEC) No. 1768/92 at the EU level on 2 January 1993, Article 4-*bis* was implicitly repealed and replaced by the provisions of the Regulation. Regulation No. 1768/92 was later superseded by Regulation No. 469/2009/EC on 6 May 2009.

3. THE BOLAR-TYPE EXEMPTION

a. History and Rationale of Adopting the Bolar-Type Exemption

As recalled by the Court of Cassation in the recent Decision No. 18372 of 5 July 2024, the *rationale* of the introduction of the Bolar-type exemption in the Italian legal system is to facilitate the timely entry of generic drugs into the market so as not to prolong '*de facto*' the duration of the exclusivity. The provision allows generic/biosimilar drug manufacturers to begin the necessary administrative and experimental activities to obtain marketing authorization when the relevant patent is still in force, thereby introducing limitations to the exclusive rights of the patent holder.

b. The Laws Applicable to Bolar-Type Exemption in Italy

As mentioned above, the Bolar-type exemption was provided for in the original text of Article 68 IPC related to 'Limitations on Patent Rights', adopted by Legislative Decree No. 30 of 10 February 2005, paragraph b).

The text reads as follows:

> [Article 68 – Limitations on patent rights]
>
> 1. Whatever the object of the invention may be, the exclusive authority attributed by patent rights does not extend to the following:
>   (a) actions carried out privately and for non-commercial purposes, or on an experimental basis even if aimed at obtaining, also in foreign countries, a marketing authorisation for a pharmaceutical product and the consequent practical steps including the preparation and use of the pharmacologically active raw materials required for this purpose;

It was further amended by Legislative Decree No. 131 of 13 August 2010, as follows:

> [Article 68 – Limitations on patent rights]
>
> 1. Whatever the object of the invention may be, the exclusive authority attributed by patent rights does not extend to the following:
>
> ...
>
> (b) studies and trials aimed at obtaining a marketing authorization for a drug, including in foreign countries, and the resulting practical requirements including the preparation and utilization of the pharma cologically active raw materials strictly necessary for the same;
>
> ...
>
> 1-*bis*. Notwithstanding the provision of paragraph 1, companies wishing to manufacture outside patent protection may initiate the registration procedure for the product containing the active ingredient one year in advance of the expiry of the supplementary coverage or, failing that, of the patent coverage of the active ingredient, also taking into account any extension.
>
> ...

Paragraph 1-*bis* of the rule was abolished by Law No. 27/2012 of 24 March 2012. The text of Article 68 currently in force therefore reads as follows:

> [Article 68 – Limitations on patent rights]
>
> 1. Whatever the object of the invention may be, the exclusive authority attributed by patent rights does not extend to the following:
>
> ...
>
> (b) studies and trials aimed at obtaining a marketing authorization for a drug, including in foreign countries, and the resulting practical requirements including the preparation and utilization of the pharmacologically active raw materials strictly necessary for the same.
>
> ...

As we will explain below, the Bolar-type exemption is formulated in the Italian legal system in objective terms. Accordingly, the Bolar-type exemption means that patent rights cannot be used to prevent activities necessary for obtaining marketing authorization, whether these are carried out by the applicant of the marketing authorization themselves, or by a third party on their behalf.

The recent Court of Cassation Decision No. 18732 of 5 July 2024, clarified the conditions under which the exemption operates in the latter case (see sections 3.d. and 3.e. below).

In Italy, the Bolar-type exemption, insofar as it does not provide for time limits as to when it is legitimate to begin activities aimed at obtaining marketing authorization, allows obtaining the marketing authorization and negotiating with the Agenzia Italiana del Farmaco (AIFA) on the price of the drug in advance of the patent/SPC expiry. It can therefore happen that 'non originator' drugs are placed on the market despite the fact that the patent/SPC of the originator is still in force but the regulatory exclusivity of the originator drug has expired.

However, Article 18(2) of Law No. 118 of 5 August 2022 (the so-called DDL Concorrenza 2021) provides that:

> Equivalent drugs referred to in Paragraph 2 may be reimbursed at the expense of the National Health Service from the date of expiration of the patent or supplementary protection certificate on the active ingredient, published by the Ministry of Economic Development in accordance with the provisions of the law in force.

Before the expiration of the patent/SPC on the active ingredient, therefore, generic drug manufacturers may find themselves, from the regulatory point of view, in a position to enter the market – subject to the possibility for the patent holder to apply for injunctions, even as an urgency measure, invoking its industrial property rights – but not being able to benefit from reimbursement by the National Health Service, under which citizens pay only part of the price of the medicine.

The non-reimbursability of the generic drug is provided only for medicines whose active ingredient is still protected as such by a patent or SPC, while the same rule is not provided for the case in which there are patents other than active ingredient patents, such as patents of formulation, dosage regimen or new use.

In this sense, DDL Concorrenza 2021 codified the teaching of administrative case law, which interpreted in this sense Article 11(1) of Law No. 189 of 8 November 2012 (the so-called Balduzzi Law), repealed by the same DDL Concorrenza 2021 and which provided that:

> medicines equivalent, in accordance with the law, to medicines whose patent or supplementary protection certificate is expiring cannot be classified as medicines paid for by the National Health Service with effect prior to the date of expiration of the patent or supplementary protection certificate, published by the Ministry of Economic Development pursuant to the provisions of the law in force.

It is uncertain whether the judicial declaration of patent invalidity that has not yet become final is sufficient to disapply the provision of non-reimbursability of the generic drug.

In Italy, the legitimacy of the above-mentioned rules is questioned as possibly infringing the prohibition of patent linkage.

c. Procedural Aspects of Invoking the Bolar-Type Exemption

In Italy, the Bolar-type exemption is considered a limitation to the exclusive rights granted by a patent. Therefore, it can be invoked as a defence in the case of infringement of a patent or to support an action for declaration of non-infringement, which can be brought also as matter of urgency, on the assumption that the activity of implementing the invention for the purpose of obtaining the marketing authorization is contested, explicitly or implicitly, by the patent owner.

Jurisdiction over intellectual property disputes in Italy is up to Enterprise Specialized Divisions of the Civil Courts (‘*Sezioni Specializzate in Materia d’Impresa*’). There are twenty-two Enterprise Specialized Divisions throughout the country. However, when one of the parties is a foreign entity, only eleven of these courts have jurisdiction. Appeals against decisions issued by Enterprise Specialized Divisions in the first instance are heard by the Courts of Appeal (‘*Corti d’Appello*’). These Courts of Appeal also have Specialized Divisions dedicated to intellectual property issues and they are located in the capital of each Region, with the exception of Lombardy,

Trentino-Alto Adige, and Sicily (which have two Specialized Divisions), and Valle d'Aosta (where jurisdiction is assigned to the Turin Court of Appeal Specialized Division). The final instance for intellectual property cases is typically the Court of Cassation.

With the entry into force of the Agreement on a Unified Patent Court (June 2023), the UPC handles disputes over European patents with unitary effect and European patents without unitary effect which have not been 'opted out', in the latter case having concurrent jurisdiction with that of the national court.

d. Scope of the Bolar-Type Exemption in Italy

i. Fields of Technology

The Bolar-type exemption applies exclusively to all activities necessary for obtaining – even in a foreign country, belonging or not to the territory of the European Union – the marketing authorization of a drug, including the manufacture of pharmacologically active materials strictly necessary for this purpose.

It therefore applies exclusively to the pharmaceutical field.

ii. Purpose of Experiments/Infringing Activities

All activities that are not necessary for and directed towards obtaining, even in countries other than Italy, marketing authorization for a drug are excluded from the scope of the Bolar-type exemption. If the conditions are met, the Experimental Use exemption can be invoked for activities falling out the scope of the Bolar-type exemption.

iii. Exempted and Prohibited Activities

The Bolar-type exemption covers all (and only) third-party patent implementation activities necessary to obtain marketing authorization for a drug in Italy or in a foreign country, including a non-EU country.

Article 68(1)(b) IPC stipulates that it also includes the 'preparation and use of pharmacologically active raw materials ... strictly necessary' for carrying out the 'studies and experiments' aimed at obtaining the marketing authorization itself.

Thus, it must be considered lawful to produce and import or export pharmacologically active raw materials covered by a third-party patent, in the quantity strictly justified by the purpose envisaged by the rule, without the possibility of making stocks.

Price and Reimbursement procedures ('P&R') for equivalent or biosimilar medicines are exempted acts, as explicitly confirmed by the recent Article 17 of Law 118/2022 that repealed Article 11 of Law Decree 158/2012 ('Balduzzi Decree'). In fact, such activities should be considered lawful in themselves, since they do not constitute implementation of the third party's patent.

The exemption does not cover commercial activities with no regulatory purpose (e.g., manufacturing, offering patented products and placing them on the market;

see also section 3.e., commenting on Supreme Court of Cassation No. 18372 of 5 July 2024).

There is no case law or doctrine in Italy concerning data obtained from studies and experiments conducted by the use of pharmacologically active raw materials covered by third-party patents. The mere preservation of such data seems to have to be considered lawful, while, as far as their use for purposes other than regulatory purposes is concerned, a problem may arise related to the fact that Article 66 of the IPC reserves to the patent holder the right not only to 'implement the invention', but also to 'profit from it in the territory of the State'.

e. Beneficiary Limitations

The subjective scope of the exemption has been only recently litigated before the Italian courts. There is no case law on this aspect before 2018.[10]

The issue that was recently addressed was whether the production of the active ingredient and subsequent experiments should be considered lawful and fall within the scope of the Bolar-type exemption only if the entity conducting them is the same as the one applying for the marketing authorization, or if, conversely, the exemption also applies to the same activities carried out by a third-party supplier that does not request the marketing authorization. The Court of Cassation Decision No. 18372 of 5 July 2024 (confirming the teachings expressed by the Milan Court of Appeal Decision No. 1785/2021, published on 8 June 2021, and upholding the Court of Milan Decision No. 8273/2018 of 24 July 2018), clarified that:

> The Bolar exemption can also be considered applicable to the activities of third parties producing the active ingredient of the patented drug for registration purposes, not for themselves but for generic third parties who are not equipped to produce on their own but intend to enter the market at the expiration of the patent exclusivity. However, this broad interpretation of the exemption presupposes that, for the Bolar purpose to characterize the activities of the active ingredient producer ab initio and ex ante, in addition to the prior request by the generic manufacturer, such registration purpose must be defined at the contractual level as a limit on use, as a commitment to use the active ingredient in accordance with the Bolar objectives.

Therefore:

- The Bolar-type exemption does not require that the subject applying for marketing authorization directly manufactures the active ingredient or personally conducts the experimentation activities. Third-party suppliers might benefit from the exemption under certain conditions.
- The exemption applies both to generic manufacturers 'with in-house production facilities' and to third-party manufacturers contracted by smaller generic companies 'without their own operational facilities', taking into account that the timelines related to the production of the active ingredient

10. Francesca Morri, Why you can Bolar also with third parties. Riflessioni sulla portata soggettiva dell'art. 68.1 b) CPI, Rivista di Diritto Industriale, LXV, Giuffrè, 195-210 (2016).

(including those required to obtain various regulatory authorizations) are the same in both cases.

- Active ingredient manufacturers may advertise their activities in general terms, allowing interested generic companies to approach them to produce the active ingredient on their behalf (for the purpose of obtaining the drug's marketing authorization).

From an objective standpoint, the production or offering of the product is excluded from the exemption if it is unrelated to the purpose of obtaining a marketing authorization. The provision exempts activities specifically aimed at submitting a marketing authorization application, and this purpose must be unequivocally clear, particularly when the activity is conducted on behalf of third parties for registration of a third-party product rather than for the manufacturer's own registration. If the active ingredient manufacturer is a third party, there must be a clear contractual relationship with the generic company. The Bolar-type exemption purpose must be explicit from the outset, contractually regulated, and in the event of a breach, a penalty must be stipulated.

f. Territoriality Issues

Article 68(1) IPC expressly provides that the Bolar-type exemption also applies to activities necessary for the granting of the marketing authorization even in a country other than Italy. According to the Supreme Court's recent interpretation of the rules, the exemption applies even if such activities are carried out by a third party, upon properly contracted assignment with the person applying for the marketing authorization.

g. Burden of Proof and Onus

The burden of proof for establishing that the carried-out activities are within the scope of the Bolar-type exemption, because they are strictly necessary for obtaining marketing authorization for a drug, rests on the party seeking to rely on this defence.

h. Applicability during Patent Term Extension or Supplementary Protection Certificate

The IPC does not establish temporal limitation to the Bolar-type exemption. Therefore, there is no distinction between its applicability during the 'regular' patent term and any patent term extension.

4. DIFFERENCES BETWEEN THE TWO EXCEPTIONS IN ITALY

The two exemptions are clearly separate and distinct. To emphasize this distinction, the 2010 Reform of the IPC introduced a clear separation between the two categories of exclusions: on the one hand, Experimental Use, (Article 68(1)(a-*bis*) IPC); and on the other, activities that are preparatory to obtaining marketing authorization for pharmaceuticals (Article 68(1)(b) IPC).

There is, however, a partially common *rationale* to the two hypotheses, and that is to prevent patent exclusivity from being used to contain competition beyond what is necessary and acceptable for patent exclusivity to function according to its purpose which is not to perpetuate a patent holder's exclusivity artificially (for example because of regulatory delays) and allow improvements to existing inventions.

Chapter 25

Japan

Takeshi S. Komatani and Takanori Abe

1. GENERAL

A patent grants exclusivity rights to the holder. It is acknowledged that limitations on those exclusivity rights are sometimes needed. Therefore, Article 30 of the Agreement on Trade-Related Aspects of Intellectual Property Rights (TRIPS Agreement) legislated 'Exceptions to Rights Conferred' which stipulates:

> [M]embers may provide limited exceptions to the exclusive rights conferred by a patent, provided that such exceptions do not unreasonably conflict with a normal exploitation of the patent and do not unreasonably prejudice the legitimate interests of the patent owner, taking account of the legitimate interests of third parties.

Japan provides such an exception in Article 69 (Limitations of Patent Right) of the Patent Act, which provides (among others) exemptions for experimental or research purposes.

This exception is interpreted to encompass both the Experimental Use exemption and the Bolar-type exemption.[1] Originally, Article 69(1) was directed only to the Experimental Use exemption, but as discussed below in detail, the Supreme Court of Japan has interpreted that the same statute also covers acts related to the obtaining of a marketing authorization (i.e. a Bolar-type exemption).

Historically, the Experimental Use exemption was introduced in the Patent Act Amendment enacted in 1909, which stipulated that 'application of patented inventions for the purpose of research or experimentation'[2] and 'products made through such

1. In Japan, the term experimental use 'exception' is commonly used, however as the AIPPI Pharma committee uses 'exemption' in the Resolution Q288 (2023) for both Experimental Use type and Bolar-type, in this article we use 'exemption' for the two types for consistency.
2. 1909 Patent Act of Japan, Art 29(i).

research or experimentation'[3] were exempt from the patent right. The subsequent Patent Act of 1921 continued the provisions of the 1909 Act, and stipulated that a patent right would not be effective for 'the working of a patented invention for the purpose of research or experiment'.[4] The current Act is a result of a 1959 amendment of the law which limited the scope of the patent right to 'business',[5] though the Article 69(1) exemption stipulating that test or research is exempted is almost the same as that of the 1921 law.

The Patent Act of Japan has the purpose stipulated as 'to encourage invention and thereby contribute to the development of industry'.[6] Under such a purpose of the act, to give effect to the patent right to testing or research for the purpose of technological progress is considered to actually hinder technological progress and undermine the development of industry. Therefore, in order to realize the legal purpose of the Patent Act, the Experimental Use exemption was stipulated in Article 69(1), thereby legislatively resolving the point of harmony between the patentee and the public interest.

These exemptions are interpreted to balance the interests of patent holders with the public interest in fostering innovation and ensuring access to generic medicines.

2. THE EXPERIMENTAL USE EXEMPTION

a. History and Rationale of Adopting the Experimental Use Exemption

The Experimental Use exemption in Japan allows for the use of a patented invention for 'experimental' and 'research' purposes without constituting an infringement. This includes activities aimed at improving or deriving further inventions from the patented technology. The exemption is crucial for academic and industrial research, facilitating advancements in science and technology without the immediate concern of patent infringement.

b. The Laws Applicable to the Experimental Use Exemption in Japan

The Experimental Use exemption is clearly outlined in Article 69(1) of the Japanese Patent Act. This provision states that the effects of the patent rights do not extend to the use of the patented invention for experimental or research purposes. This legal foundation ensures that activities purely aimed at gaining new knowledge or testing hypotheses are not hindered by patent restrictions. The provision creates a 'defence' to infringement, as stipulated therein.

---

3. 1909 Patent Act of Japan, Art 29(iv).
4. 1921 Patent Act of Japan, Art 36(i).
5. 1959 Patent Act of Japan (current Act), Art. 68.
6. Patent Act, Art. 1.

c. Scope of the Experimental Use Exemption in Japan

The scope of the Experimental Use exemption covers a wide range of activities, from basic scientific research to applied industrial research. Read literally, experiments and research are contemplated, however, its purpose is interpreted to mean academic purpose. Thus, it is interpreted to allow researchers to conduct experiments to verify the technical effects of a patented invention, explore new applications, or improve upon existing technologies. The exemption does not cover commercial exploitation of the research findings.

There is little concrete Supreme Court case law[7] for the Experimental use exemption apart from Bolar-type activities. As such, the scope of 'experimental use' is currently unclear, however, according to academic theory,[8] 'experimentation or research' is interpreted to be limited to experimentation or research of the patented invention itself for the purpose of either (1) patentability search, (2) functional search, or (3) testing for the purpose of improvement or development. Someno theorizes that the Experimental Use exemption would not cover infringement by sale or otherwise providing the market with an infringing product for the 'experimental' purpose of market testing (that has nothing to do with technological progress), which is consistent with the Court's decision in 1988.[9] The theories contemplated in Someno are not related to those for obtaining regulatory approval to be worked after the patent expiry,[10] but only for traditional experimental use.

The three above purposes (patentability search, functional search, and testing for the purpose of improvement or development) are considered to be for the purpose of technological progress. Thus, the exception is not limited to acts done for 'academic purposes' having 'no commercial value'. The exemption is interpreted to include some acts having commercial value, such as testing for commercial use, and testing for obtaining regulatory approval for agrochemical/pharmaceutical purposes. In this regard, the law's exceptions are interpreted to include the exploitation of patented inventions as research tools. Specifically, the Patent Act does not explicitly stipulate such an exploitation of patented inventions as research tools as an exception, however, the Experimental Use exemption is considered to include research tool, when such

7. Manufacturing a mould for a doll's head Case (Judgment of 30 January 1984 Tokyo High Court,1980 (ne) 2956): In this case, the defendant made a manufacturing mould that infringed the patented invention, made prototypes and researched doll heads using the mould, and then started manufacturing and selling them as a business using a manufacturing mould that he had developed himself (which did not infringe the patented invention). The court ruled that this was not an infringement of the patent right as it was 'for test and research purposes'.
8. Keiko Someno, 'Shiken kenkyu ni okeru Tokkyo Hatsumei no Jisshi (I) (Implementing Patented Inventions in Testing and Research (I))', AIPPI, Vol. 33, No. 3 (1988), p. 5.
9. Herbicide Case (Judgment of 10 July 1987, 1986 (wa) 671, 1985 (wa) 7463,1985 (wa) 6428): The Tokyo District Court ruled that a test of the efficacy of an herbicide in order to obtain an agrochemical registration for the purpose of marketing the herbicide did not fall under the exception under Article 69(1) of the Patent Law because the test was not for the purpose of technological progress, but for the sole purpose of marketing the herbicide.
10. Someno, *supra* at 7.

falls within the concept of (1) patentability search, (2) functional search, or (3) testing for the purpose of improvement or development.

The scope of infringing acts is relatively broad. Specifically, importation of the patented invention for experimental use from another jurisdiction would amount to infringement. It depends on whether the act falls within the act of importation/assignment or offer for assignment and also whether the act itself constitutes an Experimental Use exemption. Tokyo District Court[11] has held, for example, that regarding the sale by an Indonesian corporation of a patent-infringing product directly to a Japanese customer, although 'assignment' and 'import' in Japan was denied, it was found that the defendant, a related Japanese corporation, had 'offered for assignment' in Japan, affirming infringement of the patent in Japan. So, if the product in suit is not recognized to fall within the scope of the Experimental Use exemption, it may constitute infringement.

d. Burden of Proof and Onus

The burden of proof of an Experimental Use exemption lies on the party alleged of patent infringement who raises the defence in Japan.

Under Japanese practice, the contribution to experiments by a third person other than the person conducting the experiments may constitute patent infringement. However, it depends on whether the act conducted by the persons conducting the experiments falls within the infringement or not. If so, then the third person's act will constitute (contributory) infringement.

3. THE BOLAR-TYPE EXEMPTION

a. History and Rationale of Adopting the Bolar-Type Exemption

The Bolar-type exemption, named after the US case *Roche Products, Inc. v. Bolar Pharmaceutical Co., Inc.*, permits the use of patented inventions in the process of obtaining regulatory approval for generic drugs before the patent expires.

In Japan, historically speaking, there is no such a concept in the legislation. However, in 1976, Japan introduced the 'product patent protection system' by way of an amendment to Article 32 of the Patent Act, and introduced a patent term extension (PTE) system in 1987. As such, there are a number of pharmaceutical companies which filed a number of product patents and in the 1990s there were many product patents which were close to expiry. At that time, a number of generic companies started to conduct experiments for use in marketing authorization, which resulted in a number of lawsuits filed to enforce patents against such activities. In 1999, the Supreme Court interpreted Article 69(1) to include within its scope a Bolar-type exemption, which is based on the interpretation that this exemption is embedded in

11. Sodium glutamate Case (Judgement of 24 September 2020, the Tokyo District Court, 2016 (Wa) 25436), Takanori Abe, *Japan: DOE and cross-border infringement of a biologics process patent*, http://www.abe-law.com/en/publications/paper/4302/, last visited 22 October 2024.

the Patent Act to support the timely market entry of generic drugs, thereby promoting competition and reducing healthcare costs.[12]

b. The Laws Applicable to Bolar-Type Exemption in Japan

Although the Patent Act does not explicitly stipulate a Bolar-type exemption, experimental use has been interpreted by the courts to include a Bolar-type exemption, in a decision of the Supreme Court in the Case 'Drug for Treatment of Pancreatic Disease' (decided 16 April 1999).[13] Specifically, Article 69(1) of the Japanese Patent Act stipulates 'patent right is not effective against the working of the patented invention for experimental or research purposes'. This was interpreted by the Court to include Bolar-type activities.

The Supreme Court has interpreted the Experimental Use exemption stipulated in Article 69(1) to include the working of a patent right by a third party during the patent term solely for the purpose of obtaining marketing authorization, but not for stockpiling. That is, working by a third party during the patent life for the purpose of obtaining regulatory approval to sell the patented product after patent expiry should be recognized since if it is interpreted that the right test does not constitute a 'experimental or research' purpose under Article 69(1) of the Patent Act, and if the production, etc. cannot be performed during the term of the patent right, third parties will not be able to freely use the invention for a considerable period of time even after the term of the patent right has expired, which is considered an unreasonable extension of the patent right. Such an extension is beyond the Patent Act's expectation.

Clinical trials are exempted, but there is a difference between clinical trials phase 1-3 and 4. According to lower court cases,[14] clinical trials are exempted. In

12. Kazufumi Dohi, 'Hatsumei o jisshi shita iyakuhin o tokkyoken no sonzokikan manryōgo, seizō·hanbai suru tame no rinshō shiken to hatsumei no jisshi de aru jigyō no junbi kōi (tokkyoken shingai saishō shobun meirei shinsō shōshi shinsa ni taisuru sokuji kōkoku jiken) (Preparatory acts of business that are clinical trials and implementation of the invention to manufacture and sell pharmaceutical products that implement the invention after the expiration of the patent right (immediate appeal case against the decision to dismiss the petition for an injunction order for patent infringement))', Hatsumei (Invention) Vol. 94, No. 12 (1997), p. 86.
13. Pancreatic disease drug Case (Judgement of 16 April 1999, the Supreme Court, Min-Shu Vol. 53, No. 4, page 627): In the case of a drug for the treatment of pancreatic disease, the Supreme Court ruled as follows: 'In order for a third party to apply for approval under Article 14 of the Pharmaceutical Affairs Law to manufacture and sell a drug (generic drug) that has the same active ingredient, etc., as the drug pertaining to the patented invention after the expiration of the term of the patent right, the third party is required to produce a chemical substance or drug that falls within the technical scope of the patented invention during the term of the patent right. The same applies to the manufacture and sale of pharmaceutical products (generic drugs), etc., for the purpose of filing an application for approval under Article 14 of the Pharmaceutical Affairs Law with respect to the manufacture of such products, and to conduct tests necessary to obtain materials to be attached to the application under Article 69(1) of the Patent Law.'
14. Judgment of 9 February 1998, the Tokyo District Court, 1996 (wa) 8627, Judgment of 22 July 2020, the Tokyo District Court, 2019 (wa) 1409, and Judgment of 9 February 2021, the IP High Court, 2020 (ne) 10051. Takanori Abe, *Clinical trials for original drugs fall*

these cases, the originator company filed a patent infringement lawsuit while another originator company was conducting a clinical trial. The courts held that the clinical trial falls under the Experimental Use exemption. However, only phases 1, 2 and 3 are exempted. There is a difference in the theoretical and literal sense that phase 1, 2 and 3 are worked before the market approval and phase 4 is worked after the market approval and practised in the market. Clinical trials are generally controlled by the Clinical Trials Act and PMD Act.

As such, Japan does not have any detailed exceptions as stipulated in the US corresponding law such as those defined in 35 U.S. Code §271(e)(1), i.e.:

> other than a new animal drug or veterinary biological product (as those terms are used in the Federal Food, Drug, and Cosmetic Act and the Act of March 4, 1913) which is primarily manufactured using recombinant DNA, recombinant RNA, hybridoma technology, or other processes involving site specific genetic manipulation techniques.

c. Scope of the Bolar-Type Exemption in Japan

The Bolar-type exemption in Japan is interpreted as being limited to the work conducted for approval of pharmaceutical products. Although the case law only dealt with *iyakuhin* (drug, pharmaceutical product), it should be interpreted to cover other products which require regulatory approval, including medical devices and agrochemical products, and even med tech software. In the case of pharmaceutical products, in the case of generics, it covers activities such as conducting bioequivalence studies, stability testing, and other necessary procedures required for regulatory submissions. By allowing these activities, the Bolar-type exemption helps to ensure that generic drugs can enter the market promptly once the original patent expires, thereby increasing competition and lowering drug prices. In the case of a third party as originator, the scope of the exemption should be subject to further discussion, as the scope of acts by the originator could be infinite, however the court has not yet clearly defined which acts can be exempted.

Stockpiling, i.e., manufacturing a drug during the patented period, not for clinical trials, but with the purpose of sale after the patented period, is not permitted. Specifically, a 16 April 1999 Supreme Court judgment held that stockpiling is not permitted if a third party manufactures a drug to sell after the patent expires the amount of which exceeds that necessary for the tests to apply for marketing approval.

4. DIFFERENCES BETWEEN THE TWO EXEMPTIONS IN JAPAN

In Japan, patent infringement is exempted as experimental use when the infringement is the result of experiment(s) practised 'on' the patented invention, for example, to study the claimed invention as part of the process of making an improved invention. The Experimental Use exemption aims to promote technological progress by allowing inventors to experiment on patented technologies/subject-matter. The Experimental

---

under experimental use exception, http://www.abe-law.com/publications/paper/3713/, last visited 22 October 2024.

Use exemption covers experiments on the subject-matter of the invention, irrespective of whether the ultimate aim of the experiments may have some commercial value.

In contrast, the Bolar-type exemption prominently serves other public interests, *inter alia* the acceleration of the entry into the market of generic drugs for patients.[15] While the Experimental Use exemption is applicable to all technical fields, the Bolar-type exemption is prominently focused on the medical field and possibly other fields where regulatory approval is required for entering a new product to the market. Unlike many other countries, Japan has no legislation regarding the Bolar-type exemption, however, Bolar-type exemptions are well understood and the Supreme Court of Japan has extended the interpretation of the Experimental Use exemption to include the Bolar-type exemption.

Consistent and predictable Experimental Use and Bolar-type exemptions are an important factor in advancing research in medicine and public health, providing investors, governments, and other stakeholders with certainty that the actions they take for the benefit of humans do not infringe upon the legitimate rights of patent holders.

In conclusion, Japan has a simple clause directed to exemption of patent rights for experimental purposes, but the interpretation of that clause has developed to include within its scope both traditional Experimental Use and Bolar-type exemptions. Particularly, the Experimental Use exemption is interpreted in practice to the following categories: (1) tests related to patentability, (2) tests related to function, and (3) experiments directed to improvement of the invention. The Experimental Use exemption has also been interpreted to include a Bolar-type exemption, directed solely to the extent to obtain marketing authorization but not for stockpiling purpose. Such a Bolar-type exemption is interpreted to apply not only for generics but also for originators, and not only for pharmaceutical products but rather any products requiring a regulatory review and approval.

From a harmonization point of view, we believe that amendment of the Experimental Use exemption would be helpful to clarify that the scope of the exemption clearly applies to both experimental use and Bolar-type activities. Preferably, there should also be more detailed definition of the scope of the Experimental Use exemption in the legislation to explicitly include activities such as (1) patentability search, (2) functional search, or (3) testing for the purpose of improvement or development, and that the exemption is not necessarily limited thereto but also encompasses other experimental activities.

15. http://www.aippi-sg.org/wp-content/uploads/2023/12/Q288-Adopted-Resolution-SC-Pharma.pdf.

Chapter 26

Mexico

Héctor E. Chagoya-Cortés, Pablo Fuentes and Mariana González Vargas

1. GENERAL

a. Terminology

Within this chapter, the following acronyms have the following definitions:

FLPIP – Federal Law for the Protection of Industrial Property (2020)
IPL – Industrial Property Law (1994)
LIT – Law on Inventions and Trademarks (1976)
HSR – Health Supplies Regulations

An 'exception', in the context of litigation, is understood under Mexican law as an argument used by a defendant in opposition to the allowability of a lawsuit brought by a plaintiff, with the intent of demonstrating the inapplicability of the lawsuit and convince the judge to dismiss it. However, the exact same word in Spanish is also used to describe when an action is excluded from a certain law provision, that is, the law is not applicable to a determined situation. Because in English language this kind of exclusion is more specifically described as an 'exemption', this is why Experimental Use and Bolar are qualified as exemptions in this chapter.

b. Legal Basis in Mexico

The FLPIP, in force as of 5 November 2020, establishes experimental use as an exemption to the rights conferred by a patent.

According to Article 57, part I of the FLPIP, the rights conferred by a patent shall not be effective against a third party that performs activities the nature of which are of technology or scientific research, assay or experimental, in the private or academic fields, with non-commercial purposes. The activities included are the production, importation or use of the patented invention.

This is the classic Experimental Use exemption that was present in the former law (IPL).

The Bolar-type exemption is established under different regulations.

For small molecules, the Bolar-type exemption is established in Article 167*bis* of the HSR, as a regulatory exception. Article 167*bis* states:

> Without prejudice to the provisions of the previous two paragraphs, it is possible to request the registration of a generic drug concerning a medication whose active substance or ingredient is protected by a patent, in order to conduct the corresponding studies, tests, and experimental production within the three years prior to the patent expiration. In this case, the health registration will only be granted upon the expiration of the patent.

For biologics, the Bolar-type exemption is established in Article 177*bis*2 of the HSR, which states:

> Without prejudice to the provisions of the previous paragraphs, it is possible to request the registration of a biocomparable drug concerning a biotechnological medication protected by a patent, in order to conduct the corresponding studies, tests, and experimental production, within the eight years prior to the patent expiration. In this case, the health registration will only be granted upon the expiration of the patent.

The 2020 FLPIP includes a broader Bolar-type exemption which removes temporal limitations. Article 57 FLPIP states:

> The right conferred by a patent shall not produce any effects against:
>
> ...
>
> II. A third party that uses, manufactures, offers for sale or imports a product covered by a patent in force, exclusively for generating tests, information and experimental production that are necessary for obtaining health registers for drugs for human health.

Nevertheless, the HSR provisions remain, with their temporal limitations, so in theory HSR currently prevails, so exemptions available under the Bolar principle are to be understood by the Federal Commission for Protection against Health Risks (COFEPRIS) to be applicable only within those time frames.

2. THE EXPERIMENTAL USE EXEMPTION

a. History and Rationale of Adopting the Experimental Use Exemption

A patent is expressly characterized as a privilege, granted in the first constitution as a federation in 1824, and expressly characterized as a privilege in the constitutions that followed in 1857 and 1927. The privilege is defined as right for *exclusively exploiting* an invention or creation and is so characterized in the laws that have regulated the grant of patents as the tool for materializing such constitutional privilege since then.

The patent, the instrument of such constitutional privilege, is intended to be a social pact, subject to certain restrictions. An inventor makes a claim that an invention was made, and the patent is granted with certain restrictions. A key condition for granting such privilege is disclosure.

Disclosure is not only a tool for reproducing the invention once the patent expires, but it meant to foster innovation by allowing other people to study and improve a published invention during the existence of the privilege granted – even to create more inventions. Disclosure is, therefore, one of the core features of the patent system for this reason.

Since 1991, patents are published eighteen months after the filing date. But even prior to 1991, when patents were only published upon grant, the IPL already provided a (limited) Experimental Use exemption, as follows:

> Article 39. The rights conferred by a patent shall not produce any effect:
>
> Against a third party that, with study, scientific or technological research, experimental or recreational purposes, *manufactures* a product *or uses a procedure* that is the same or substantially the same than that patented. (Emphasis added)

The Experimental Use exemption was established only for the manufacture of patented products, because the IPL also had similar restrictions on patent protection itself: the concept of exploitation was also defined as the mandatory manufacture of the patented products in Mexico or the permanent use of the patented products in Mexico (Article 43, LIT).

In 1991, largely as a result of international treaties, patent law changed significantly and from 1991 until 2020, the Experimental Use exemption reads as follows:

> Article 22. The rights conferred by a patent shall not produce any effect against:
>
> A third party who, in the private or academic fields, and with *non-commercial* purposes, performs scientific or technological research activities, *merely experimental, assay or teaching in nature*, and to that end, *manufactures or uses* a product, or uses a process, that is the same than that patented. (Emphasis added)

It is notable that the Experimental Use exemption was kept limited to manufacturing and using if performed with non-commercial purpose, despite that the rights conferred by a patent were broadened under the same law (IPL, 1994). The IPL included as part of the privilege of holding a patent, in addition to the right to prevent others from manufacturing or using the patented product, the right to prevent others from selling, offering for sale, or importing the patented product.

The Experimental Use exemption was interpreted for many years to include a Bolar-type exemption, because of the lack of a Bolar-type exemption in the law (see the corresponding discussion below). Thus, this exemption was alleged to cover activities performed with a patented product for the sake of obtaining a generic drug approval. This was of course a poor interpretation of the exemption, that gave place to controversial decisions that shaped the system back then.

On one hand, the courts (Thesis 2005814[1]) determined:

1. Digital Register: 2005814; Instance: Supreme Court of Justice of the Nation (Mexico); Tenth Epoch; Matter(s): Administrative; Thesis: 1a.XCVI/2014(10a.); Source: Federal Judiciary

> A health registration intends to satisfy one of the greater objectives of the national pharmaceutical policy, *in the sense of guaranteeing the safety and quality of medicaments* with the aim to protect the people from health risks. (Emphasis added)

This decision did not discuss the commercial nature of the register, but it established that an innovative medicament health approval does not grant *per se* any exclusivity rights (independent of data exclusivity). The decision did not establish that a generic drug application is a research activity, nor did it establish a non-commercial nature.

In a complementary decision (Thesis 2005815[2]), a court established that the health register is not the *only* requirement for commercializing a product as follows:

> Thus, the medicament health registration constitutes the administrative act through which the *health authorities endorse that a drug or medicine is effective and safe, and of proper quality*, which does not imply an authorization for free commercialization, as *their commerce and distribution has to be subject to other regulatory rules* related to the commercialization of medicaments. (Emphasis added)

This decision provides further guidance regarding the nature of the health register, by clarifying that it is not the only authorization required for commercialization of medicines, but it did not address the applicability of the then-in-force Experimental Use exemption and whether activities related to application to the health register constituted a research activity exempt by the Experimental Use exemption.

Both decisions lacked a broader analysis regarding the intent of the infringer. Under Article 368 of the General Law on Health (GLH), still current:

> The health authorization is the administrative act through which the competent health authority allows a public or private person the performance of activities related to human health, in the cases and with the requirements and modalities determined by this Law and other applicable general rules. Health authorizations *may take the form of health* licenses, permits, *registrations*, or control cards. (Emphasis added)

Article 376 of the GLH mandates that medicaments (drug products) require health registration.

The key issue is then: what are the activities related to human health that are performed with registered medicaments? For that matter, Article 204 of the same GLH establishes the following provisions.

> Those medicines, medical devices and other health supplies, the narcotics, psicotropic substances and products containing thereof, as well as plaguicides, vegetable nutritiments and dangerous or toxic substances, shall have health authorization under the terms of this law and other regulations for its commercialization or supply.

Weekly Gazette, Book 4, March 2014, Volume 1, page 557.

2. Digital Register: 2005815; Instance: Supreme Court of Justice of the Nation (Mexico); Tenth Epoch; Matter(s): Administrative; Thesis: 1a.XCV/2014(10a.); Source: Federal Judiciary Weekly Gazette, Book 4, March 2014, Volume 1, page 558.

No other activities in the law require a health register for a medicine, which means that the health registration is a necessary but not sufficient condition for commercializing a medicine, under Article 204 as related to Article 376 of the GLH.

Accordingly, there is no other reason for a person to obtain a health registration but to commercialize or supply the medicament, and therefore, a research purpose is not proven. Furthermore, human health research activities do not comprise selling or commercializing of drugs, and no human health research activity requires a health registration, but instead, clinical research protocols require to be authorized even for non-registered drugs. In fact, it would be absurd to ask for a health registration for a drug that was not previously used in humans and which performance is needed to obtain a health registration or approval.

Accordingly, the only purpose of a health register is commercialization or supply of the product. Thus obtaining a health register is not a commercialization as such nor is it the only requirement, but clearly there is no possible intent other than commercialization or supply of the product, both activities that were not exempt under the Experimental Use exemption.

The debate on the interpretation of the Experimental Use exemption applied to drug products is currently irrelevant, since the FLPIP addresses the issue directly.

Further, the FLPIP (2020) broadened the language by using the word 'invention' instead of product or process, perhaps to make it clear that the exemption applies to any kind of invention (i.e. second medical Swiss style). The FLPIP also included consideration for importation:

> Article 57. The rights conferred by a patent shall not produce effect against:
>
> A third party who performs activities of scientific or technological research, merely experimental, assay or teaching in nature, in the private or academic fields and with non-commercial purposes, and to that end, manufactures, imports or uses the patented invention.

b. The Laws Applicable to the Experimental Use Exemption in Mexico

Article 55 of the FLPIP provides the privilege granted by a patent:

> Article 55. The temporary exclusive rights for the exploitation of a patented invention confers to its holder the prerogative of *preventing other persons from manufacturing, using, selling, offering for sale or importing* the patented *invention*, without his consent.
>
> If the subject matter of the patent is a product, the patent confers the right to prevent other persons from manufacturing, using, selling, offering for sale or importing the patented product, without his consent.
>
> If the subject matter of the patent is a process, the patent confers the right to prevent other persons from using the process and from manufacturing, using, selling, offering for sale or importing the product directly obtained from the patented process, without his consent.
>
> The scope of the rights conferred by a patent shall not be interpreted beyond the protected subject matter and the provisions of this law. (Emphasis added)

Article 57 of the FLPIP provides the Experimental Use exemption, as follows:

> Article 57. The rights conferred by a patent shall not produce effect against:
>
> A third party who performs activities of scientific or technological research, merely experimental, assay or teaching in nature, in the private or academic fields and with non-commercial purposes, and to that end, manufactures, imports or uses the patented invention.

The wording of Article 57 was generalized as compared to former laws to broaden the scope of the exemption to any invention, perhaps to cover any patents, as opposed to specific claim categories, but unlike Article 55, lawmakers omitted the distinction made regarding processes in particular.

The generalization is, in our opinion, unfortunate, although other Articles in the law were updated under the same basis to refer to inventions instead of products or processes. For the Experimental Use exemption though, there now seems to be a problem with products obtained by patented processes, as processes cannot be manufactured or imported. In fact, Article 55 of the FLPIP establishes clearly that the activities reserved to the patent holder include manufacture, use, sale, offer for sale and importation of the invention, but unlike the Experimental Use exemption in Article 57, Article 55 further clarifies that such activities are specifically applicable to patented products, and also applicable to the products obtained by a patented process.

That distinction for the purposes of determining the scope of protection of patents, and the absence of such distinction in Article 57, has not yet been interpreted by the courts, but may pose a challenge that failing to distinguish between process and product patents in Article 57 might not be considered 'incidental' despite the fact that the distinction was present in the equivalent Articles of the exemption in previous laws. The intent of Article 57 was to generalize language to broaden the exemption, but in doing so, products of patented processes were (perhaps inadvertently) left out from the exemption.

The practical implications of the lack of distinction between product and process patents in the Experimental Use exemption may not have great impact. Because experimental use is a defence in infringement actions, if a process is not used in Mexico, the possibility of proving that the product was obtained 'directly' from the process abroad becomes more difficult and the appetite to sue for infringement for activities that seem experimental or academic in nature may be lowered significantly under such circumstances.

c. Procedural Aspects of Invoking the Experimental Use Exemption

The Experimental Use exemption is established under Mexican law as a condition by virtue of which a patent does not produce effects against a person performing certain actions. That is, a patent is unenforceable against a person who performs the activities of Article 57 of the FLPIP. This means that, in order to invoke the exemption, a person must first be sued for infringement by the patent owner, who may file the infringement action without the knowledge of the actual objective of certain activities performed with a patented invention, or simply neglect it.

The Mexican litigation system has changed under the FLPIP in that there are now two venues to bring the suit, unlike the former IPL that had only one venue for patent litigation.

In the first of these venues, an infringement action may be brought before the Mexican Institute of Industrial Property (IMPI) by filing a request for an Infringement Administrative Declaration. Such a request must contain, under Article 330 of the FLPIP:

- the applicant's name;
- the address to hear and receive notifications and an e-mail address;
- the name and address of the alleged infringer or his legal representative;
- the purpose of the brief in clear and precise terms;
- a description of the facts;
- the offered proofs;
- the law basis related to the object of the brief.

These requirements imply that the plaintiff must establish clearly an infringement and prove that a determined product, process or activity encroaches on the granted claims of the patent.

Upon filing, IMPI will verify compliance with the requirements of the brief, and if accepted, the suit will be notified to the alleged infringer, who will have ten working days to reply. A reply under Mexican law must deny the accusation, confess, or oppose by utilizing 'exceptions' against the infringement action. Legal proceedings exceptions are, under the Mexican law system, any legal reasons to oppose to the action taken by the plaintiff, including lack of court jurisdiction, payment, prescription, or any other that shows the judge that the proceedings must not continue, either temporarily or definitively.

The Experimental Use exemption is used as such an exception when responding to an infringement action by the defendant. The Experimental Use exemption is applicable to any patent, regardless of its scope of protection or claims, and therefore, it should not matter whether a specific invention was used, but rather the non-commercial purpose of any supposedly infringing activities and the academic, scientific or experimental objective of the same. This means, in turn, that whether the claims are infringed or not is irrelevant to the determination of the applicability of the Experimental Use exemption.

If IMPI (in our opinion incorrectly) proceeds with the infringement action without evaluating the applicability of the Experimental Use exemption, when analysing the causes for infringement, the Experimental Use exemption would then have to be evaluated in the same manner as it should have been studied at the beginning of the proceeding, that is, in spite of the result of the infringement analysis.

There are no express decisions by the court related to the Experimental Use exemption; perhaps because truly non-commercial activities are typically not relevant for patent holders.

The second venue was introduced by the FLPIP, which now includes the option of starting a damages action before civil courts, without the need for a declaration of infringement by IMPI. This new procedure does not yet have enough cases to evaluate its effectiveness. A defendant wishing to use the Experimental Use exemption should oppose the action in their first response to the damages action accordingly.

d. Scope of the Experimental Use Exemption in Mexico

i. Fields of Technology

The Experimental Use exemption can be utilized in all fields of technology. Rather than the field of technology, the intent of the activities is of the essence for its application.

ii. Purpose of Experiments/Infringing Activities

The purpose of the activity is of the essence for determining the applicability of the Experimental Use exemption in Mexico.

The exemption requires demonstrating that the activities that are performed by an alleged infringer are actually 'scientific or technological research'.

The common definition in Spanish of the term 'research' in the closest meaning translates to: 'Perform intellectual and experimental activities systematically with the purpose of increasing the knowledge of a determined matter'.

Whether the activities are systematic or not may be a further issue, and as long as the scientific method is applied or there is a protocol for the experimental activities, one could consider that the activities are systematic, but the purpose of 'increasing the knowledge of a determined matter' implies that the objective is to know something that is not known, which in fact relates to the main meaning of the term research: 'to try to uncover something'.

Accordingly, a research activity must embody somehow the purpose of understanding or knowing something unknown when the activities are performed, and although the repetition of something already performed by a third party may be part of the research activity, the mere objective of repeating what is known may not be considered research.

The Experimental Use exemption in Mexico needs the research to be performed with a non-commercial purpose. In our opinion, a commercial purpose is not proved merely because a company is performing or funding the research activities, but rather the activity itself must have a commercial purpose. Clearly if a patented product is sold, offered for sale or somehow involved in a transaction for which the person performing the activity will have a benefit, it must be considered a commercial purpose.

Under these concepts, there are activities that are more in a grey area that are discussed in the following section.

The importation of a product may or may not have a commercial purpose, because the importation itself is not commercial *per se*.

In Mexico, the manner in which the importation is performed for taxation purposes has relevance the declaration of the commercial or non-commercial nature of the importation itself, and the importation documentation should be considered to determine the commercial nature of the importation as such or otherwise there would also be a violation of tax and imports rules.

The non-commercial nature of the use of a patented research tool is more difficult to determine because the purpose of the tool is specifically for research. A patented research tool might be instrumental in providing certain research services, which in turn might be considered a commercial activity. Particularly if the core of the service is the availability of the research tool to the person who offers the research service, the non-commercial nature of the research could be questionable. If the research tool is a product, and the product is acquired from the patent owner, the concept of exhaustion of rights (rather than the Experimental Use exemption) would operate, but if the product is produced for providing the service (for instance a patented antibody, a patented cell line, which may be produced independently of the patent holder) such activity might not be considered research or might not be considered non-commercial.

Experiments or clinical studies related to the obtention of a health registration of any drug (generic or innovative) is considered a commercial activity, and accordingly does not qualify for opposition using the Experimental Use exemption.

Beyond the non-commercial research purposes requirements of the exemption, other requirements include that the activities are merely of experimental, assay or teaching nature. The term 'teaching' poses a problem of interpretation. Sale and offer for sale, as commercial activities, are not included in the exemption. But manufacture, use and importation are included in the exemption, in the case of the importation, with the considerations of commercial and non-commercial imports discussed above. The broadening of the language to 'patented invention' makes it difficult to establish if importation and use of the products of patented processes is also exempt.

iii. Exempted and Prohibited Activities

The importation of a product may or may not have a commercial purpose, because the importation itself is not commercial *per se*.

The manner in which the importation is performed for taxation purposes is relevant to the commercial or non-commercial nature of the importation, and importation documentation should be considered to determine the commercial nature of the importation as such or otherwise there would also be a violation of tax and imports rules.

The non-commercial nature of the use of a patented research tool is more difficult to determine because the purpose of the tool is specifically for research. A patented research tool might be instrumental in providing certain research services, which in turn might be considered a commercial activity. Particularly if the core of the service is the fact that the research tool is available to the person who offers the research service, the non-commercial nature of the research could be questionable. If the research tool is a product, and the product is acquired from the patent owner, the exhaustion of rights rather than the Experimental Use exemption would be applicable, but if the product is produced for providing the service (for instance a patented antibody, a patented cell line, which may be produced independently of the patent holder) such activity might not be considered research or might not be considered non-commercial.

Any activity directed at obtaining registration on a health register has inherently a commercial purpose, and is therefore not exempt under the Experimental Use exemption.

Teaching is not necessarily research, and may be deemed commercial in purpose. There are no court decisions interpreting teaching activity in the context of a patent infringement, but it seems that if a patented product is obtained, for example, in a laboratory exercise at a school, the courts must decide how to interpret the non-commercial research requirement in an academic environment. For instance, if the school promoted an experiment to obtain a patented product as a key feature of the educational offer, the general non-commercial purpose requirement might not be complied with, and even if the experiment is performed only as an example of a scientific/technical context, the applicability of the Experimental Use exemption might not be straightforward, although conceptually it appears that the intent of including teaching activities as part of the exemption is clear.

Finally, another common situation of interest is whether a company can use the patented product of a competitor. As in the other cases, the research objective and the non-commercial purpose is what will define the applicability of the Experimental Use exemption. The manufacture and use of the product *per se* would not be an infringement if the objective is non-commercial, that is, if the product is not going to be sold, offered for sale or otherwise used as a tool for obtaining directly a commercial benefit from the product itself. If the patented competitor's product is used to develop a new, different product, this would be considered non-commercial research, merely of assay nature, performed in the private ambit, which is exempt from infringement, even though of course the company will want to sell the product resulting from the research.

Moreover, if the patented product is purchased from the patent holder, the exhaustion of rights will allow any further use of the patented product as a different exemption to patent rights.

Finally, data obtained from the experiments is not regulated by Mexican law, and therefore the data as obtained should be considered the property of the person who generated such data. However, if the patented invention is used to continually generate data that is, in turn, commercialized, the non-commercial purpose of the use of the patented invention would not be necessarily complied with and, therefore, the exemption might not be applicable to the commercialization of data that would not be otherwise obtained unless the patented invention was purchased from the patent holder for that purpose.

iv. Pure Academic vs Commercially Motivated Experimental Use

Commercially motivated experimental use of patented inventions, understood as a rationale behind the research, but not as a direct use of a patented invention for a commercial activity, should be assessed just like any other activity for the purposes of the applicability of the Experimental Use exemption.

The exemption is applicable to both academic and private ambits, which means that any person (including a corporation) can use a patented invention for research purposes if and only if the research does not have a commercial purpose.

This means, for instance, that a patented invention may be used in the private context to improve its performance and obtain an improved product. Such activity is subject to the Experimental Use exemption, but the commercialization of the improved product is not if the commercialization of the improved product still infringes the patent. However, if the research is made for the purposes of developing a new and different commercial product, the new product may be commercialized freely because the patent would not be infringed in spite of the fact that the patented invention was used to obtain it.

e. Beneficiary Limitations

The concept of contributory infringement is not applicable in Mexico for patent infringement. In addition, there is nothing in the law implying a difference if the person who performs the activities is performing the same under contract or directly. Therefore, the exemption must be evaluated based on the research and non-commercial purpose principles as applicable to the person conducting the research activities directly.

This means that experimentation by contract, that is, the performance of an experiment in exchange for a payment, is a commercial purpose that might not be included under the Experimental Use exemption. For instance, if a person is hired to produce a patented product in exchange for a payment, conceptually it could be considered that the product was sold by that party, which is a commercial activity, even if the party that contracted the production of the patented product will use it for a non-commercial purpose.

In the case of a pharmaceutical product, the Bolar-type exemption will apply (as discussed below), but from the Experimental Use exemption perspective the product is sold and therefore the patent would be infringed because sale and offer for sale are not included within the Experimental Use exemption.

However, if the experimentation is characterized as a research collaboration where one party will provide a patented product (at cost or not) and the other party will perform certain experiments, both parties may be protected from infringement through the Experimental Use exemption because it might be understood that whoever is funding the production is not purchasing a product but (rather) covering the cost. Of course, this will be determined on the facts. The wording in the contracts between the parties are critical to determine the applicability or not of the exemption in these cases.

Significantly, if the product is acquired from a foreign supplier, under the current law the importer would not be infringing the patent if the quantity and the import permit is expressly issued for a non-commercial/research activity, but the supplier might face an infringement action for the offer for sale and/or the sale in Mexico.

f. Territoriality Issues

The effects of the grant of a Mexican patent are strictly local. Therefore, the purpose of the results or the activities that are performed outside the Mexican territory are not relevant for the applicability of the exemption but rather the activities actually performed within Mexican territory.

As explained above, if a third party sells a product that is patented in Mexico, even from a jurisdiction where the same patent was not filed, such a sale to a party that will perform activities in Mexico that are exempt from infringement under the Experimental Use exemption will be considered an infringement of the Mexican patent, because that would constitute a sale in Mexican territory.

Conversely, where a third party sells a patented product from a jurisdiction where a patent covering the product is in force, the party selling the product would still be infringing the Mexican patent and also the patent in the country of origin, but the use by the person who imported the product for activities performed in Mexico will be allowed if they are for research and non-commercial purposes.

g. Burden of Proof and Onus

The Experimental Use exemption is a defence used against infringement accusations. Therefore, the patent owner must prove that the patent is infringed in order to bring the infringement suit. The patent owner does not need to prove the commercial purpose but only the cause of infringement. In replying to the infringement action, the alleged infringer must reply demonstrating an exception to whatever scope is covered by the patent based on the Experimental Use exemption.

h. Applicability during Patent Term Extension or Supplementary Protection Certificate

SPCs were introduced to Mexico in 2020, for undue delays during patent prosecution, and to compensate delays by one day of protection per two days of delay. Under Article 135 of the FLPIP, 'the Supplementary Certificate of Protection shall confer the same rights tan the patent from which it derives and *shall be subject to the same limitations* and obligations' (emphasis added).

Thus the Experimental Use exemption is applicable during the period of an SPC.

There have been recently a number of court decisions adjusting the term of patents. The Experimental Use exemption is equally applicable in any such patent term adjustments.

3. THE BOLAR-TYPE EXEMPTION

a. History and Rationale of Adopting the Bolar-Type Exemption

The Bolar-type exemption in Mexico was first introduced in 2003, as part of the legal reforms related to the Mexican linkage system. The Mexican linkage system aimed to connect the approval process of pharmaceutical drugs with the patent status covering those drugs, preventing the approval of generic drugs that infringe on existing patents, thus protecting the intellectual property rights of the original patent holders while also facilitating the timely entry of generics into the market once the patents expire.

This initial provision allowed generic drug manufacturers to use patented inventions three years prior to the expiration of a patent without the patent holder's authorization solely for the purpose of obtaining regulatory approval, thus being able to prepare for the commercialization of the generic drug immediately after the relevant patent's expiration.

In 2009, the General Health Law (GHL) was amended to include biotechnological drugs into the regulatory framework and corresponding amendments were made to the HSR to provide more detail about the approval conditions of this drugs.

This led to the provision of an eight-year period of the Bolar-type exemption for biotechnological drugs.

Biotechnological drugs, often referred to as biologics, are typically more complex to develop and manufacture compared to synthetic drugs. The regulatory approval process for biocomparables (the term used in Mexico to denote the equivalent of generics for biologics) also tends to be more intricate, requiring comprehensive clinical trials and detailed comparisons to the original biologic drug. By extending the Bolar-type exemption to these products, Mexico sought to ensure that biocomparables could be developed and approved in a timely manner.

In 2020, the Federal Law for the Protection of Industrial Property (FLPIP) entered into force, abrogating the Industrial Property Law of 1991 and its subsequent reforms and additions. The FLPIP included important changes that modernize the protection and defence of industrial property rights in Mexico, in order to harmonize and adjust Mexican law in this area to the commitments assumed with the signing of the United States-Mexico-Canada Agreement (USMCA) that entered into force on 1 July of that same year.

The law covering the Bolar-type exemption included in the FLPIP intentionally removed temporal limitations (in contrast to the health regulations) and is now a general exception. The new FLPIP includes the Bolar Clause, whereby the right conferred by a patent shall not produce any effects against a third party that uses, manufactures, offers for sale or imports a product covered by a patent in force, exclusively for generating tests, information and experimental production that are necessary for obtaining health registers for drugs.

b. The Laws Applicable to Bolar-Type Exemption in Mexico

The Bolar-type exemption in Mexico was first introduced in 2003. A decree published in the Official Gazette of the Federation on 19 September 2003, added Section IV of Article 167 and Article 167*bis* of the HSR, also Article 47*bis* of the IPL (1994) was added. These norms established the procedures for patent linkage, which links the granting of health registrations for pharmaceutical products to their relevant patents and aims to prevent the granting of health registrations to unauthorized third parties.

The third paragraph of Article 167*bis* of the HSR refers to the so-called Bolar clause, as a regulatory exception, and states:

> Without prejudice to the provisions of the previous two paragraphs, it is possible to request the registration of a generic drug concerning a medication whose active substance or ingredient is protected by a patent, in order to conduct the corresponding studies, tests, and experimental production within the three years prior to the patent expiration. In this case, the health registration will only be granted upon the expiration of the patent.

The language used shows an intention to only consider active ingredient patents, because at the beginning the linkage system was intended only for this kind of patents. Nonetheless, despite this language, in practice, the activities exempted by the Bolar clause are applicable regardless of the claim type covered by the relevant patents.

On 11 June 2009, Article 222*bis* was added to the GHL explicitly incorporating biotechnological drugs into the regulatory framework, which were not previously covered. Following this, further amendments were made to the HSR to establish the special authorization conditions for this specific type of drugs, including the extension of the Bolar-type exemption to biotechnological drugs. Article 177*bis*2 was added, providing a period of eight years before the expiration of a patent covering the biotechnological drug to allow manufacturers to use patented inventions without the patent holder's authorization for the purpose of conducting necessary studies, tests, and experimental production to obtain regulatory approval.

The fourth paragraph of Article 177*bis*2 HSR states:

> Without prejudice to the provisions of the previous paragraphs, it is possible to request the registration of a biocomparable drug concerning a biotechnological medication protected by a patent, in order to conduct the corresponding studies, tests, and experimental production, within the eight years prior to the patent expiration. In this case, the health registration will only be granted upon the expiration of the patent.

In this case the language is broader, and it is even more clear that any kind of patent covering the biologic could be considered for Bolar-type exemption purposes. As of the enactment of this provision, it was understood that a three-year period of Bolar-type exemption was applicable for chemical synthesized drugs and an eight-year period of Bolar-type exemption was applicable for biologics.

Since 5 November 2020, the new Article 57 of the FLPIP included the Bolar-type exemption at a law level. In this sense, Article 57 of the FLPIP states:

> The right conferred by a patent shall not produce any effects against:
>
> ...
>
> II. A third party that uses, manufactures, offers for sale or imports a product covered by a patent in force, exclusively for generating tests, information and experimental production that are necessary for obtaining health registers for drugs for human health.

Accordingly, the Bolar-type exemption included in the FLPIP was not given any timeframe and is now set as a general exception without any temporality. This clearly contrasts with the Bolar-type exemption provided for in Articles 167*bis* and 177*bis*2 of the HSR, which establish the right of interested parties to provide health authorities with information related to their authorization, within three and eight years (for chemical synthesis drugs and biologics, respectively) prior to the expiration of the patent.

The HSR has not been modified and in theory it prevails therefore, exemptions available under a Bolar principle are to be understood by COFEPRIS to be applicable only within those time frames.

On the other hand, it is important to point out that Article 57 of the FLPIP seems to apply only to the use, manufacturing, offer for sale or imports that are '*exclusively* for generating tests, information and experimental production that are *necessary* to obtain health registers for drugs for human health'. It is unclear if this is a restriction to what is strictly necessary by law or by a regulatory authority to obtain a health registration, or if this is also applicable to activities reasonably related to the development and submission of voluntary information to obtain a health registration.

Nevertheless, it is important also to note that there are no court decisions or precedents regarding this topic in Mexico. Accordingly, the outcome in actual litigation is uncertain.

c. Procedural Aspects of Invoking the Bolar-Type Exemption

In Mexico, the Bolar-type exemption is commonly discussed during the procedure of obtaining a health registration before the regulatory body of the Mexican government (COFEPRIS) as part of the linkage system. It also could be used as a defence in patent infringement proceedings.

The linkage system aims to ensure that COFEPRIS, responsible for approving the commercialization of pharmaceutical products, checks with IMPI, the agency in charge of granting and managing patents, before authorizing the sale of a new generic or biocomparable drug. This system is intended to prevent the approval of a generic or biocomparable drug that might infringe on existing patents. In this sense, as part of the linkage system a relevant patent to a pharmaceutical product may be identify by COFEPRIS using the *Gazette for Medicines*, which is published by IMPI in February and August, or by a direct consultation with IMPI which performs a patent search in its database based on the information provided by COFEPRIS about the specific pharmaceutical product. If a relevant patent is identified, and the health registration applicant is not the patent holder or a licensee on record, COFEPRIS will not grant the health registration before the patent expires. However, according to the Bolar-type exemption, COFEPRIS should continue the health registration procedure in order to assess the fulfilment of all the other requirements. If COFEPRIS stops or discards the procedure due to the identification of a relevant patent, the Bolar-type exemption could be invoked by the health registration applicant and eventually it would be IMPI who decides in a first instance whether it is applicable or not.

In case a health registration is granted, the patent holder could file a patent infringement lawsuit against the drug manufacturer before IMPI as a first administrative instance. The patent holder files a complaint, and IMPI investigates and issues a resolution. If either party disagrees with IMPI's decision, they can appeal to the Federal Court of Administrative Justice (TFJA), which reviews the case and can uphold, modify, or overturn IMPI's ruling. If still dissatisfied, the party can further appeal to the Collegiate Circuit Courts (TCC) through an '*amparo*' action, where the TCC reviews the legal aspects of the TFJA's decision. The TCC's decision is generally final.

The patent holder can also take administrative action against the approval granted by COFEPRIS by filing a nullity claim before the TFJA and later before the TCC.

d. Scope of Bolar-Type Exemption in Mexico

i. Fields of Technology

The Bolar-type exemption in Mexico is limited to pharmaceutical products. The exemption is relevant for clinical trials and other activities necessary to obtain regulatory approval for generic and biocomparable drugs.

ii. Purpose of Experiments/Infringing Activities

The Bolar-type exemption is used for activities directly related to obtaining regulatory approval and that are considered 'necessary', such as comparing a new generic drug to a patented drug and conducting clinical trials. It does not extend to research for improving existing inventions unless such improvements are necessary for regulatory compliance.

According to Article 57 of the FLPIP, it is possible to use, manufacture, offer for sale and import a patented product exclusively or generating tests, information and experimental production that are necessary for obtaining health registers for drugs for human health.

iii. Exempted and Prohibited Activities

The Bolar-type exemption covers activities necessary for regulatory submission for drugs for human health, including testing, manufacturing samples, and compiling data for health authorities.

However, it does not cover activities with a commercial intent, such as stockpiling or selling the patented invention before the patent expires. The data generated is purpose-limited, and its use is confined to regulatory approval processes. Activities such as importation or possession for future commercial use do not qualify for the exemption.

e. Beneficiary Limitations

The Bolar-type exemption can be utilized by both generic companies and innovative manufacturers, as long as the activities are necessary for regulatory submission with no immediate commercial purpose.

Third parties involved in the regulatory approval process, such as contract research organizations, could also invoke the exemption. However, there must be a clear linkage between the exempted activity and the regulatory submission by the party seeking approval. This has not, however, been tested in the courts.

f. Territoriality Issues

The Bolar-type exemption applies to activities that would otherwise be infringing, performed in Mexico to meet regulatory requirements in other countries. It likely also applies to activities conducted in other countries to fulfil Mexican regulatory requirements, as far as Mexico has jurisdiction over those activities. However, activities conducted in another country for Mexican regulatory submissions may still be subject to that country's laws if they infringe on a corresponding patent there.

g. Burden of Proof and Onus

The burden of proof lies with the entity invoking the Bolar-type exemption, whether it is during the procedure for obtaining a health registration or during litigation. It should be demonstrated that the activities fall within the scope of the exemption. In theory, this could include detailed documentation of the experimental use and its direct connection to obtaining regulatory approval.

h. Applicability during Patent Term Extension or Supplementary Protection Certificate

The Bolar-type exemption remains applicable during the SPC period according to Article 135 of the FLPIP.

In Mexico, right now there is a window of patent extensions that are possible for some patents that were granted during the period of validity of the old Mexico-USA-Canada free trade agreement, based on a decision issued by the Mexican Supreme Court of Justice in which a seventeen-year period of validity should be guaranteed to any patent granted in such period of validity of the old Mexico-USA-Canada free trade agreement.

Based on this Supreme Court decision, a fair number of extension requests have been granted recently. These Patent extension decisions, which extend the validity of patents on average from one-and-a-half to three years, have been granted in some cases during with the Bolar-type exemption period already available for generic companies; affecting the interests of some generic companies that had started their authorization process with the expectation of a certain launch date.

The time frame to request extensions in Mexico based on this judicial decision will still be available in Mexico for a few more years. We are not aware of any infringement action brought based on a term-extended patent nor any generic company attempting to contest this type of patent extension based on previously acquired Bolar-type exemption rights. However, regardless of the new term, the Bolar-type exemption should still be applicable.

4. DIFFERENCES BETWEEN THE TWO EXCEPTIONS IN MEXICO

In Mexico, the Experimental Use exemption is broadly defined, and it applies to any field of technology. It explicitly excludes Bolar-type activities, considering these commercial in nature.

In contrast, the Bolar-type exemption is limited, and it only applies to activities related to the obtention of a health registration.

The Experimental Use exemption is only considered into the Mexican FLPIP (2020), while the Bolar-type exemption is considered both in the FLPIP and in the GHL and its regulations.

This is relevant because different regulations contain different manners of interpreting the Bolar-type exemption in Mexico. More specifically, health-related laws establish different provisions for the Bolar-type exemption than the FLPIP. The definition and scope of the Bolar-type exemption in each set of laws is different.

It can be concluded therefore that in Mexico, the two exemptions are separate and distinct, and do not overlap.

Chapter 27

The Netherlands

Martin Klok and Stefan van Kolfschooten

1. GENERAL

a. Terminology

The Experimental Use exemption – also referred to as the Research exemption – and the Bolar-type exemption are both considered exceptions to the right of the patentee. Both exemptions can as such be raised as defences to exempt certain acts from being considered patent infringing acts.

b. Legal Basis in the Netherlands

The Experimental Use exemption is codified in Article 54c (b) of the Dutch Patent Act of 1995, as amended on 1 June 2023 ('DPA1995'):

> The rights conferred by a patent shall not extend to:
>
> ...
>
> (b) acts done for experimental purposes relating to the subject-matter of the patented invention;

The Bolar-type exemption is codified in Article 54c (d) DPA1995:

> The rights conferred by a patent shall not extend to:
>
> ...
>
> (d) the acts authorized under Article 13(6) of Directive 2001/82/EC of the European Parliament and of the Council of 6 November 2001 on the Community code relating to veterinary medicinal products (OJ 2001, L 311) or Article 10(6) of Directive 2001/83/EC of the European Parliament and of the Council of 6 November 2001 on the Community code relating to medicinal products for human use (OJ 2001, L 311),

> in relation to a patent for the product within the meaning of either of these directives;

As the original language of the (different versions of the) Patent Act are in Dutch, the translations in this document are unofficial as they are made by the authors and should be treated as such.

2. THE EXPERIMENTAL USE EXEMPTION

a. History and Rationale of Adopting the Experimental Use Exemption

In the Netherlands, the Experimental Use exemption has been intended to exclude from patent protection 'both experiments with a scientific purpose and experiments that take place in a commercial context'. This follows from the explanatory notes to the amendment of the Dutch Patent Act of 29 May 1987.

The Dutch Supreme Court has interpreted the exemption restrictively. The Dutch Supreme Court ruled in 1992 that the exemption of research 'on' the patented invention is warranted in situations where the purpose of the research is of an exclusively scientific nature, or otherwise aims to satisfy goals associated with patent law.[1] This latter criterion can be satisfied if the purpose of research is to 'advance technology'.

Throughout the history of the Experimental Use exemption, the exemption's purpose has been to allow acts that advance science and technology, as this is considered in alignment with the purpose of patent law overall.

b. The Laws Applicable to the Experimental Use Exemption in the Netherlands

The present Dutch Patent Act (DPA1995) was introduced in 1995 as a major amendment of the former Patent Act of 1910 ('DPA1910'). The DPA1910 already contained an Experimental Use exemption as Article 30(3) DPA1910:

> The exclusive rights shall not extend to acts solely serving for research on the patented subject-matter, including the product obtained directly as a result of using the patented process.[2]

With the introduction of the Experimental Use exemption into the DPA1910, the Dutch parliament held the view that not only research for solely scientific purposes was to be excluded from the scope of patent protection, but that the exemption should also extend to research in a business context:

> Doctrine and jurisprudence have always exempted research for solely scientific purposes from the scope of patent protection, but there have been doubts regarding the exemption of research in or for a business. The general view is inclined to also exempt such research, because such research does not affect the essential scope of patent protection, but does contribute to the development

1. Supreme Court, 18 December 1992, ECLI:NL:HR:1992:ZC0801 (*ICI/Medicopharma*).
2. Article 30(3) DPA1910, non-official translation by authors, superseded.

> of technology. In this context, one would allow others than the patent holder to research applications of the patented technology, with the aim of developing said technology further, as well as allowing research with the aim to establish whether application of the patented technology under a license would be profitable. The article thus not only serves the common interest, it can also be in the interest of the patent holder.[3]

In 1987, the DPA1910 was reformulated, among other things, to bring the DPA1910 in line with the Community Patent Convention 76/76/EEC ('CPC'). The CPC contains Article 31(b), which exempts 'acts done for experimental purposes relating to the subject-matter of the patented invention' from the scope of patent protection. Despite the reformulation of the DPA1910 to the DPA1995, the wording of the Experimental Use exemption of Article 30(3) DPA1910 was not changed. From this, it can be inferred that the legislators at the time considered the formulation of the Experimental Use exemption in the DPA1910 to be in line with the Experimental Use exemption in the CPC:

> The exclusive right shall not extend to acts solely serving for research on the patented subject matter, including the product obtained directly as a result of using the patented process.[4]

The discussion in the Dutch parliament on the modifications of the Dutch Patent Act in 1987 clarify that Dutch parliament sought to 'exclude both experiments with a scientific purpose and experiments that take place in a commercial context from the scope of the patent'.[5]

In 2023, the Dutch Patent Act was amended to bring it in line with the Unitary Patent Convention, EU 1257/2012, and the provisions concerning infringement included in the Agreement on a Unified Patent Court ('UPCA', 2013/C 175/01). The UPCA comprises a Experimental Use exemption, which is formulated as:

> The rights conferred by a patent shall not extend to any of the following:
>
> ...
>
> (b) acts done for experimental purposes relating to the subject-matter of the patented invention;[6]

The Experimental Use exemption of former Article 53(3) DPA1995 was reformulated in line with Article 27 UPCA:

> The rights conferred by a patent shall not extend to:
>
> ...
>
> (b) acts done for experimental purposes relating to the subject-matter of the patented invention;[7]

---

3. Explanatory notes to the amendment of the Dutch Patent Act of 12 January 1977, 1974-1975, 13 209, R 967, pages 49-50, non-official translation by authors.
4. Article 53(3) DPA1995, non-official translation by authors, superseded.
5. Explanatory notes to the amendment of the Dutch Patent Act of 29 May 1987, 1984-1985, 19 131, R 1295, page 26, non-official translation by authors.
6. Article 27(b) UPCA.
7. Article 54c (b) DPA1995, non-official translation by authors, currently in force.

The explanatory notes on the reformulation of the Experimental Use exemption to bring it in line with the UPCA clarify that it is not the intention of the legislator the alter the scope of the Experimental Use exemption, despite the difference in wording. The reasoning is based on the CPC cited above and the interpretation of the Experimental Use exemption by the courts:

> Article 27, under b, of the Agreement on a Unified Patent Court corresponds to Article 53 under 3 of the Dutch Patent Act 1995. A comparison between the two articles shows that they differ in wording. The Dutch Patent Act 1995 specifies acts serving for research on the patented subject matter, including the product obtained directly as a result of using the patented process. *However, there is no difference in meaning between the two articles.* Already at the time of the harmonization of the Dutch Patent Act with the Community Patent Convention 1975, in which an identical article is included, the following was noted in the explanatory memorandum:
>
> This paragraph excludes both experiments with a scientific purpose and experiments that take place in a commercial context from the scope of the patent. It corresponds to Article 31, sub b, of the [Community Patent; authors] Convention [current Article 27, section b, of the UPCA].
>
> The Court of Appeal of The Hague also reached the same conclusion, as is evident from HR 23 June 1995, NJ 1996, 463, in which it was considered (paragraph 46):
>
> > 'Considering that the provision on the research exception in the ROW is in accordance with the relevant provision in the Community Patent Convention, and furthermore, that ...'
>
> *In view of the above, the adoption of the text of the Agreement on a Unified Patent Court does not lead to a substantive change in the Patent Act 1995.* However, in addition to the correspondence with the text of the Agreement on a Unified Patent Court and with the text of the Community Patent Convention, it also comes editorially more in line with the patent legislation in the countries surrounding us.[8]

Consequently, although the Experimental Use exemption that is now in force in the Netherlands is worded very differently from its original version, the rationale and intention of the exemption has remained the same: to exclude from the scope of patent protection both experiments with a scientific purpose and experiments that take place in a commercial context.

c. Procedural Aspects of Invoking the Experimental Use Exemption

In the Netherlands, the Experimental Use exemption can be invoked by an alleged infringer as a defence to patent infringement. When a patent holder asserts infringement against a third party, the alleged infringer may invoke present Article 54c (b) DPA1995, and provide reasons why its activities should fall under the Experimental Use exemption. The reasons should be in line with the prevailing case law on the subject.

8. Explanatory notes on the amendment of the Dutch Patent Act, 2018–2019, 35 187 (R2124), No. 3, pages 57-58; emphasis added.

d. Scope of the Experimental Use Exemption in the Netherlands

The present phrasing of the Experimental Use exemption is considerably different from the phrasing of the Experimental Use exemption in the law until 2023 (see above). Although it was clearly the intention of the legislator not to alter the scope of the Experimental Use exemption, all case law on the subject pertains to the former wording, as there have been no decisions considering the issue since 2023.

It remains an open question as to whether the Dutch court agrees with the legislators in that no material difference exists in the scope of the Experimental Use exemption after the 2023 reformulation. The below analysis is with respect to the pre-2023 law, and it is presumed that the intention of the legislator is followed by the court, so that the scope of the present Experimental Use exemption is presumed to be identical to the scope of the Experimental Use exemption in its former wording.

i. Fields of Technology

There is no limitation on the fields of technology that may or may not invoke the Experimental Use exemption. Any field of research may in principle invoke the exemption.

ii. Purpose of Experiments/Infringing Activities

The Experimental Use exemption aims to exclude from infringement acts for solely scientific purposes, as well as acts of an experimental purpose that take place in a commercial context.

As regards the scientific purpose, the Dutch Supreme Court established that experiments 'for a solely scientific purpose' are and were generally considered not to fall within the scope of patent protection.[9] In the same case, it was established that experiments that take place in a commercial context may also be exempt, in so far as they do not materially affect the patent.

The case finds that experiments in a commercial setting may be exempt from patent protection when these experiments aim to achieve a purpose that generally aligns with the purpose of patent law, i.e. the advancement of technology. This may include further development of the patented invention, but also research that aims to establish whether it would be commercially viable to obtain a licence. This, it was ruled, also aligns with the general purpose of patent law, as such research may also benefit the patent holder.

The decision furthermore clarifies that experiments by commercial organizations may also be exempted in so far as they do not 'significantly affect the patent', such as 'verifying that the invention can be applied in practice, or can be developed further'. However, market research or large scale production would not fall under the scope of the Experimental Use exemption.

9. *ICI/Medicopharma*, par. 3.3.2.

In the cases of *Kirin Amgen/Boehringer Mannheim* of 3 February 1994[10] and of 13 March 1996,[11] it was determined that clinical trials with the aim of establishing a further medical use of a patented technology also falls under the Experimental Use exemption.

In the first instance preliminary proceedings of *ARS/Organon* of 14 September 1992,[12] the District Court of The Hague decided that clinical trials organized by Organon and executed in various hospitals are to be considered clinical trials held in the business context of Organon, as the clinical trials were performed under a contract with Organon. These clinical trials were considered to fall under the Experimental Use exemption, even though the results would at some point be used to obtain a marketing authorization.

iii. Exempted and Prohibited Activities

As noted above, market research or large scale production would not fall under the scope of the Experimental Use exemption.[13] Also, research that is aimed 'primarily to provide a basis for international registration and commercial promotion' does not fall under the Experimental Use exemption. A shown unwillingness to license the patented technology is considered indicative of research aimed at marketing, rather than advancing technology.[14]

Research in which a patented invention is recreated with the purpose of establishing a benchmark for newly developed technology also does not fall under the Experimental Use exemption.[15]

iv. Pure Academic vs Commercially Motivated Experimental Use

Purely academic research is generally considered exempt under the Experimental Use exemption, but as outlined, commercially motivated activities may also be exempted. The criterion is whether the commercially motivated research aims to advance technology, and/or aims to achieve a purpose generally associated with patent law.

e. Beneficiary Limitations

The Experimental Use exemption can also be invoked by third parties. In the first instance preliminary proceedings of *ARS/Organon* of 14 September 1992, the District

---

10. Court of Appeal of The Hague in preliminary proceedings, 3 February 1994, docket number 93/960 (*Kirin Amgen/Boehringer Mannheim*).
11. District Court of The Hague in proceedings on the merits, 13 March 1996 (*Boehringer Mannheim/Kirin Amgen*).
12. District Court of The Hague in preliminary proceedings, 14 September 1992, ECLI:NL:RBSGR:1992:AK2093 (*Ares Serono/Organon*) ('ARS/Organon').
13. *ICI/Medicopharma*.
14. *ICI/Medicopharma*, as well as *ARS/Organon*, District Court of The Hague District Court, 3 May 2006, HA ZA 05-2016 (*Angiotech/Sahajanand*) and District Court of The Hague, 17 January 2007, HA ZA 06-261 (*Conor Medsystems/Angiotech*).
15. District Court of The Hague, 17 November 2010, KG ZA 10-1074 (*Tédé/Tetra Laval*).

Court of The Hague decided that clinical trials organized by Organon and executed in various hospitals are to be considered clinical trials held in the business context of Organon, as the clinical trials were performed under a contract with Organon. These clinical trials were considered to fall under the Experimental Use exemption, even though the results would at some point be used to obtain a marketing authorization.

Although this case does not pertain to the situation where the research itself is a commercial activity, the situation serves to show that the contracted party can be exempted under the Experimental Use exemption by the activities of the party who initiated the research.

f. Territoriality Issues

The Dutch court traditionally has taken the view that in cases where there is a Dutch alleged infringer who acts as a central core ('spider in the web') for entities located outside the Netherlands, then in such cases, an injunction can also be given to the entities outside the Netherlands. Although the validity of this doctrine has been under debate recently, it is envisioned that the scope of the Experimental Use exemption could be evaluated along the same lines. That is, research activities of related parties, when executed in other jurisdictions where there also is patent protection, may be exempt if this research complies with the conventional interpretation of research under Dutch patent law.

It is noted that with the amendment of the Dutch Patent Act to bring it in line with the UPCA, territoriality of the Experimental Use exemption within the jurisdictions for which the UPCA is valid, must be considered less of an issue, given that the purpose of the UPCA is to align the Experimental Use exemption for Unitary Patents throughout the UPC jurisdiction.

g. Burden of Proof and Onus

It is well established that the burden of proof that research qualifies as exempt under the Experimental Use exemption lies with the party alleging this is so. This follows from *ICI/Medicopharma*, where the Dutch Supreme Court noted that research by a commercial organization that is exempt on the basis of the purpose of the research, can only be considered exempt if the party responsible for the research 'states, and if necessary proves' that its research aims to establish a purpose commonly associated with the purpose of patent law.

h. Applicability during Patent Term Extension or Supplementary Protection Certificate

The explanatory memorandum to the amendment of the Dutch Patent Act explained that the legislator intended to have the Experimental Use exemption also be applicable to a supplementary protection certificate (SPC). For this reason, research that is exempt from the patent scope will likely also be considered exempt from the scope of the SPC. There is however no case law on the issue.

On the basis of Article 5 of Regulation 1786/92/EC (OJEC L 182), the exceptions to the exclusive rights of the patent holder in Article 53(1) of the 1995 Dutch Patent Act apply equally to supplementary protection certificates. It is therefore not necessary to mention supplementary protection certificates separately.[16]

3. THE BOLAR-TYPE EXEMPTION

a. History and Rationale of Adopting the Bolar-Type Exemption

In the Netherlands, the Bolar-type exemption constitutes a curtailment of the exclusive rights of the patent holder with respect to the performance of necessary studies, tests and trials within the context of obtaining a market authorization for generic or biosimilar medicinal products.

The rationale of the exemption is to remedy an unwanted extension of the patent's protection period. Without the Bolar-type exemption, the manufacturer of a generic drug could only proceed to perform the necessary studies, tests and trials to demonstrate that its product is identical or biosimilar to the patented reference medicine after the patent period has expired, which in practice could lead to delays in the obtainment of marketing authorizations and subsequent market access of generic drugs. This rationale follows from the explanatory notes to the amendment of the Dutch Patent Act of 13 December 2007, implementing Directives 2001/82/EC and 2001/83/EC into the Dutch Patent Act. The introduction of the Bolar-type exemption is a fairly recent development in the Netherlands on which virtually no national case law has been formed to date.

b. The Laws Applicable to the Bolar-Type Exemption in the Netherlands

In 2001, the European Council and Parliament agreed to a comprehensive revision of European pharmaceutical legislation. This revision included the adoption of Directive 2001/83/EC on the Community code relating to medicinal products for human use (OJ L 311) and Directive 2001/82/EC on the Community code relating to veterinary medicinal products (OJ L 311). These Directives were subsequently amended by Directives 2004/28/EC (OJ L 136) and 2004/27/EC (OJ L 136).[17] Newly introduced Articles included the Bolar-type exemption in Article 13(6) in Directive 2001/82/EC and Article 10(6) in Directive 2001/83/EC.

The Articles provided that the performance of necessary studies, tests and trials that serve to demonstrate that a medicinal product is a generic or biosimilar version of a reference medicinal product are not considered to infringe a patent or SPC under specified conditions. The implementation of these directives in the Netherlands led to amendments to DPA1995 in 2007, codifying the Bolar-type exemption in Article 53(4) of the DPA1995:

---

16. Explanatory memorandum to the amendment of the Dutch Patent Act, 13 December 2007, 2005–2006, 30 663 (R 1812), No. 3, p. 3, non-official translation by authors.
17. Directive 2004/28/EC (OJ L 136) amended Directive 2001/82/EC and Directive 2004/27/EC (OJ L 136) amended Directive 2001/83/EC.

> (4) The performance of the necessary studies, tests and trials for the purposes of Article 10, paragraphs 1 to 4, of Directive 2001/83/EC on the Community code relating to medicinal products for human use (OJ L 311) or Article 13, paragraphs 1 to 5, of Directive 2001/82/EC on the Community code relating to veterinary medicinal products (OJ L 311) and the resulting practical requirements are not considered to infringe patents relating to medicinal products for human use and veterinary medicinal products, respectively.[18]

In 2023, as with the amendments to the Experimental Use exemption, the DPA1995 was amended to bring it in line with the Unitary Patent Convention, EU 1257/2012, and the provisions concerning infringement included in the UPCA (2013/C 175/01). The Bolar-type exemption, formerly codified in Article 53(4) DPA1995, was reformulated in line with Article 27(d) UPCA in Article 54c(d) of the current Dutch Patent Act:

> The rights conferred by a patent shall not extend to:
>
> ...
>
> (d) the acts authorized under Article 13(6), of Directive 2001/82/EC of the European Parliament and of the Council of 6 November 2001 on the Community code relating to veterinary medicinal products (OJ 2001, L 311) or Article 10(6), of Directive 2001/83/EC of the European Parliament and of the Council of 6 November 2001 on the Community code relating to medicinal products for human use (OJ 2001, L 311), in relation to a patent for the product within the meaning of either of those directives;[19]

The text in Article 27(d) UPCA refers only to 'acts authorized under Article 13(6) of Directive 2001/82/EC or Article 10(6) of Directive 2001/83/EC' and no longer specifically to conducting the *necessary studies, tests and trials*. The explanatory notes on the reformulation of the Bolar-type exemption in 2023 however clarify that it was not the intention of the legislator the alter the scope of the Bolar-type exemption and the reasoning is still based on the initial implementation of the Articles of Directives 2001/82/EC and 2001/83/EC cited above.[20]

It is undetermined whether the Bolar-type exemption, like the Experimental Use exemption, should be interpreted restrictively. The explanatory memorandum expressly states that it was chosen 'to allow the new Bolar provision to apply alongside the existing experimental use exception ..., because the exemption created by this provision complements (the restrictive interpretation of) the experimental use exception'.[21] There is however no mention of an open or restrictive interpretation for the Bolar-type exemption itself. Nonetheless, such an interpretation may be possible considering that the explanatory memorandum further states that '[a]ll acts other than the performance of necessary studies, tests and experiments (and ensuing practical requirements) within the context of obtaining a market authorization for generic or

18. Article 53(4) DPA1995, non-official translation by authors, superseded.
19. Article 54c(d) DPA1995, non-official translation by authors, presently in force.
20. Explanatory memorandum to the amendment of the Dutch Patent Act, 1 June 2023, 2018–2019, 35 187 (R2124), No. 3, p. 60.
21. Explanatory memorandum to the amendment of the Dutch Patent Act, 13 December 2007, 2005–2006, 30 663 (R 1812), No. 3, p. 3, non-official translation by authors.

biosimilar medicinal products fall outside of the scope of the Bolar exemption'.[22] The wording that the studies, tests and trials must be *necessary* likewise seems to indicate that the provision should indeed be interpreted (somewhat) restrictively alongside the Experimental Use exemption. However, case law has yet to be formed on this topic.

c. Procedural Aspects of Invoking the Bolar-Type Exemption

In the Netherlands, whenever a patent holder asserts its patent against a third party, the alleged infringer may rely on the Bolar-type exemption as a defence to patent infringement. In its defence, the alleged infringer should sufficiently substantiate why the alleged infringing acts would be exempted from infringement under Article 54c(d) DPA1995.

A defence under the Bolar-type exemption may be considered by any court of competent jurisdiction in the Netherlands. The relative jurisdiction with respect to (alleged) patent infringement lies with the (District, Appeal and Supreme) Courts in The Hague.

d. Scope of the Bolar-Type Exemption in the Netherlands

i. Fields of Technology

In the Netherlands, the Bolar-type exemption is limited to carrying out research activities that are necessary to obtain a marketing authorization for a generic, hybrid or biosimilar pharmaceutical. The exemption therefore does not apply for obtaining marketing approval for innovative products. It should moreover be assumed that the exemption cannot be invoked for any other fields of technology such as for the regulatory approval of medical devices, though this remains an open question. For example, in 2007, the District Court saw no need to comment on the question as to whether pre-marketing research for obtaining a CE marking for application of a drug to a stent would fall within the scope of the Bolar-type exemption, as the Directive 2001/83/EC as amended by Directive 2004/27/EC was not yet implemented at the time.[23]

The performance of clinical trials is exempted in the context of the Bolar-type exemption to the extent they are 'necessary'. As long as the statutory conditions are met, the law does not make any distinction between specific phases of clinical trials.

iii. Purpose of Experiments/Infringing Activities

The Bolar-type exemption is limited to the conducting of the necessary studies, tests and trials within the context of obtaining a market authorization for generic or biosimilar medicinal products. Any *improvements* to old, yet still protected inventions would as such not fall under the scope of the Bolar-type exemption but

22. Explanatory memorandum to the amendment of the Dutch Patent Act, 13 December 2007, 2005–2006, 30 663 (R 1812), No. 3, p. 3, non-official translation by authors.
23. District Court of The Hague, 17 January 2007, HA ZA 06-261 (*Conor/Angiotech*), par 4.62.

might be protected via the Experimental Use exemption. The Bolar-type exemption likewise does not exempt the performance of comparisons between new, innovative pharmaceuticals with old but still patented pharmaceutical with the aim of obtaining marketing approval for innovative products. The manufacturing of pharmaceuticals for clinical use is however deemed exempted as long as it is *necessary* for the performance of the studies, tests and trials. What manufacturing quantities should be deemed 'necessary' has yet to be developed in case law.

iii. Exempted and Prohibited Activities

The explanatory memorandum to the introduction of the Bolar-type exemption in the DPA1995 states that '*[a]ll acts other* than the performance of necessary studies, tests and experiments (and ensuing practical requirements) within the context of obtaining a market authorization for generic or biosimilar medicinal products fall outside of the scope of the Bolar exemption'.[24] See also *Pharmachemie/Glaxo Group*, in which the Supreme Court confirmed that including a product in the so-called G-Standard constitutes an offer for sale and hence qualifies as an infringing act:

> The court was right to take as its point of departure that ... offering for one of the acts previously listed in Article 53(1)(b) is to be understood in a broad sense.[25]

As the acts of 'manufacturing' and 'keeping in stock' are included in the acts exclusive to the patentee in Article 53 DPA1995 and the Supreme Court has given a broad interpretation to 'offering' in, for example, *Pharmachemie/Glaxo Group*, stockpiling with the express purpose of sale after the patented period will most likely be considered as patent infringement.

Note that, in Europe, there is the 'SPC manufacturing waiver'. With effect from 1 July 2019, Regulation (EU) 2019/933 amending Regulation (EC) No. 469/2009 on the SPC for medicinal products is in force in the Netherlands. This regulation allows for a company, other than the certificate holder, to – under conditions set out in the Regulation – manufacture and store the protected product during the last six months of the SPC. Thus, this company can market the product into the EU immediately after the end of the SPC (day-one launch stockpiling).

e. Beneficiary Limitations

The Bolar-type exemption is limited to the conducting of the necessary studies, tests and trials within the context of obtaining a market authorization for *generic or biosimilar medicinal products*, and thus not for obtaining marketing approval for innovative products. The law on the exemption however does not consider the *person* seeking regulatory approval, but rather for which purpose the studies, tests and trials are performed. It is as such conceivable that an otherwise innovative manufacturer

24. Explanatory memorandum to the amendment of the Dutch Patent Act, 13 December 2007, 2005–2006, 30 663 (R 1812), No. 3, p. 3, emphasis added.
25. Supreme Court, 22 June 2012, *Pharmachemie/Glaxo Group*, par 3.4.2, non-official translation by authors ('Pharmachemie/Glaxo Group').

may rely on the Bolar-type exemption whenever it performs necessary studies, tests and trials with respect to the regulatory approval for a generic or biosimilar in its product line. There is, however, no case law yet addressing this question.

Likewise, there is not yet any case law addressing the question of whether third parties could benefit from the Bolar-type exemption. In the absence of such guidance, it may be that a Dutch court will take guidance from the case law of foreign courts, such as the German courts.[26]

f. Territoriality Issues

In reference to the amended Directives 2001/82/EC and 2001/83/EC, the text of the Bolar-type exemption refers to marketing authorization procedures in the European Economic Area (and thus not in other territories). As the meaning of the text has not changed with the reformulation of the Dutch Patent Act in 2023, it should be considered that the territorial limitations still apply.

g. Burden of Proof and Onus

In general, the burden of proof is on the defendant who raises a defence against an alleged patent infringement. While concerned with the question of a defence under the Experimental Use exemption, the *Conor Medsystems/Angiotech Pharmaceuticals* judgment seems to confirm that for the Bolar-type exemption, the burden of proof indeed likewise lies with the party alleged of patent infringement who raises the defence.[27]

h. Applicability during Patent Term Extension or Supplementary Protection Certificate

The Dutch implementation of the Bolar-type exemption is not limited in time. It is thus possible to rely on the exemption during the entire lifetime of the patent. The exemption equally applies to SPCs. The legislator however did not deem it necessary to specify this in the text of the Bolar-type exemption:

> On the basis of Article 5 of Regulation 1786/92/EC (OJEC L 182), the exceptions to the exclusive rights of the patent holder in Article 53(1) of the 1995 Dutch Patent Act apply equally to supplementary protection certificates. It is therefore not necessary to mention supplementary protection certificates separately.[28]

---

26. See e.g. Düsseldorf Higher Regional Court, 5 December 2013, docket no. 2 U 68/12 (*Polpharma/Astellas*).
27. District Court of The Hague, 17 January 2007, HA ZA 06-261 (*Conor Medsystems/Angiotech Pharmaceuticals*), par. 4.61.
28. Explanatory memorandum to the amendment of the Dutch Patent Act, 13 December 2007, 2005–2006, 30 663 (R 1812), No. 3, p. 3, non-official translation by authors.

4. DIFFERENCES BETWEEN THE TWO EXEMPTIONS IN THE NETHERLANDS

The Experimental Use exemption and Bolar-type exemption are both implemented in Dutch patent law with a clear view. Both exemptions entail exceptions to the exclusive rights of the patent holder, both can be raised as defences against a claim of infringement and both concern the performance of tests, studies and the like. However, the aim with which the research is performed marks a clear distinction between the two exemptions. Research that is performed to obtain a marketing authorization for a generic (veterinary or human) variant of a medicine would be excluded under the Bolar-type exemption and not under the Experimental Use exemption. Research that is purely academic or otherwise aims to advance technology may be excluded under the Experimental Use exemption.

In this sense, one could say that the Experimental Use exemption and the Bolar-type exemption have been devised with the apparent idea that they be mutually exclusive. It is in any case difficult to envision circumstances where both exemptions could apply. Research that aims to obtain a marketing authorization is prescribed in the relevant Regulations, and research that targets fulfilling these requirements should automatically fall under the Bolar-type exemption. If research falls outside of the scope of the Bolar-type exemption, but aims to advance technology, then it may be excluded under the Experimental Use exemption.

Chapter 28
Norway

Magnus Hauge Greaker and Jonas Levernes

1. GENERAL

a. Terminology

In Norway, the Experimental Use exemption is found in Section 3, third paragraph, no. 3 of the Patents Act, while the Bolar-type exemption is found in Section 3, third paragraph, no. 5. Both are categorized as 'exemptions' to the exclusive right to exploit an invention for commercial purposes. This means that acts that are covered by these exemptions do not constitute patent infringement and can be invoked as a defence in infringement proceedings.

b. Legal Basis in Norway

In Norway, the Experimental Use exemption is codified in Section 3, third paragraph, no. 3 of the Patents Act. According to this provision, the following is exempted from the exclusive rights:

> Exploitation by experiment relating to the subject matter of the invention.

The Bolar-type exemption is found in Section 3, third paragraph, no. 5 of the same Act, which exempts the following from the patentee's exclusive rights:

> Trials, experiments, and similar activities relating to a patented pharmaceutical that are necessary to obtain marketing authorization for a pharmaceutical in a state that is a party to the Agreement of 15 April 1994 establishing the World Trade Organization (WTO Agreement).

The scope of the Experimental Use exemption was clarified in the Norwegian Supreme Court case Rt. 2009 s. 1665 (SINTEF) ('the SINTEF Case'). The Supreme Court found that the exemption only covers activities that can be characterized as experiments relating to the invention, i.e. activities that aim to generate new knowledge, and only covers actions that are necessary for the development of knowledge.

To date, there have been no significant court decisions specifically addressing the scope of the Bolar-type exemption in Norway.

2. THE EXPERIMENTAL USE EXEMPTION

a. History and Rationale of Adopting the Experimental Use Exemption

In Norway, the Experimental Use exemption was enacted in the Patents Act in 1979, but was held to be a part of Norwegian law also before that by way of interpretation of the requirement that only exploitation for commercial purposes constitutes infringement. The rationale is related to the patent bargain, i.e., that anyone should have the opportunity to use a patent as source of knowledge for further research and development also during the duration of the patent protection.

b. The Laws Applicable to the Experimental Use Exemption in Norway

In Norway, the Experimental Use exemption is codified in the Patent Act, Section 3, third paragraph, no. 3. This provision states that the exclusive right shall not include 'Exploitation by experiment relating to the subject matter of the invention'. The exemption not only covers experiments carried out for non-commercial purposes, but also commercial research and development.

However, the experiments must relate to the protected invention and no other subject matters. The scope of this exemption was notably examined in the SINTEF Case, where the Norwegian Supreme Court emphasized that it can only be invoked for activities that can be characterized as 'experiments', i.e. activities that aim to generate new knowledge. This, for example, covers experiments aiming to clarify how the invention works and its effects, finding new applications of the invention, and so on.

c. Procedural Aspects of Invoking the Experimental Use Exemption

The Experimental Use exemption may be used as a defence before the courts in litigation regarding claims of patent infringement both in proceedings on the merits and in preliminary injunctions proceedings. In Norway, matters relating to patent infringement may only be decided by a court. Thus, only a court can make a determination of the legitimacy of the Experimental Use exemption.

d. Scope of the Experimental Use Exemption in Norway

i. Fields of Technology

The Experimental Use exemption applies to all fields of technology.

ii. Purpose of Experiments/Infringing Activities

As a starting point, the invention can be used for any experimental purpose as long as the experiment relates to the protected invention and not other subject matter outside the scope of the invention. The experiment can involve the applicability of the invention or possibilities for improvement or development of new inventions or unpatentable technology that is based on the invention. The exemption also covers commercial research.

However, a limitation is that the exemption can only be invoked for activities that can be characterized as 'experiments', i.e. activities that aim to generate new knowledge, as stated in the SINTEF Case. The Experimental Use exemption only covers actions that are necessary for the development of knowledge. As part of a research and development project, for example, a model of the invention can be manufactured or a computer program can be developed for the purpose of carrying out the invention, and the properties of the invention can be tested.

Experiments pursuant to the Patents Act Section 3, third paragraph, no. 3 will fall under the scope of the exemption regardless of whether the experiment is conducted with commercial intent, as long as the experiment does not diminish the commercial exploitation of the invention available to the patent holder. This being said, a model or computer program, etc., cannot be sold after the project is completed, if this would constitute a direct or indirect infringement of the patent. The SINTEF Case represents an example of such indirect infringement. A computer program was sold after the completion of the project.

Exploitation of substances, tools or methods that are protected by a patent in connection with experiments that are not related to the substances, tools or methods themselves is not covered by the Experimental Use exemption.

iii. Exempted and Prohibited Activities

In Norway, the Experimental Use exemption described in Section 3, third paragraph, no. 3 of the Patent Act is not limited to just manufacturing and possessing a product, etc. The exemption also covers activities such as importation, purchasing, testing, and using the invention to the extent necessary for carrying out experiments, including testing to compare a product to another that is considered a non-infringing competitor. However, the Experimental Use exemption does not allow for activities such as selling a patented product or otherwise putting a patented invention on the market.

Regarding data generated from experiments, Norwegian law does not impose specific restrictions on how this data can be used. However, if use of the data for commercial purposes amounts to patent infringement or indirect patent infringement, such use is not covered by the Experimental Use exemption.

iv. Pure Academic vs Commercially Motivated Experimental Use

In Norway, the Experimental Use exemption is not limited to purely academic research; rather, it also encompasses commercially motivated experimental activities. The Supreme Court's ruling in the SINTEF Case clarified that experiments conducted with commercial intent can still qualify for the exemption, as long as the primary goal is to generate new knowledge about the patented invention. In this case, a computer program could be created for the implementation of the invention. However, the sale of the computer program constituted indirect patent infringement.

e. Beneficiary Limitations

In Norway, the applicability of the Experimental Use exemption to third parties has not been explicitly defined in the law nor in case law. However, it is generally understood that if a third party is contracted to perform activities that would qualify for the exemption if conducted by the original party, the third party will also be protected under the exemption.

f. Territoriality Issues

Whether the Experimental Use exemption applies must be decided based on the activities that have been carried out in Norway. Whether the results from the experiments are used to infringe a corresponding patent outside of Norway will not be relevant for whether there is patent infringement in Norway.

g. Burden of Proof and Onus

In Norwegian law, the party invoking the exemption bears the burden of proof and the obligation to provide evidence.

h. Applicability during Patent Term Extension or Supplementary Protection Certificate

The experiment use exemption applies for the duration of a supplementary protection certificate (SPC). The SPC is the only form of patent extension available in Norway.

3. THE BOLAR-TYPE EXEMPTION

a. History and Rationale of Adopting the Bolar-Type Exemption

The Bolar-type exemption was made a part of Norwegian law in 2009. It is based on Directive 2001/83/EC of the European Parliament and of the Council of 6 November 2001 on the Community code relating to medicinal products for human use, OJ L 311, 28.11.2001, as amended by Directive 2004/27/EC of the European Parliament and of the Council of 31 March 2004, OJ L 136, 30.04.2004, which stipulates that necessary trials related to the application for marketing authorizations for generic medicines can be conducted without being hindered by patent rights. EU Directive 2001/83 Article 10(6) as amended by Directive 2004/27 is a part of the European Economic Area Agreement.

However, the Bolar-type exemption was implemented in Norway with a broader scope than required by EU Directive 2001/83 as amended by Directive 2004/27. While the Bolar-type exemption in the Directive only covers generic products, the

Bolar-type exemption in Norwegian law also covers original products. Further, the Bolar-type exemption in the Directive only covers trials, experiments, and similar activities that are necessary to obtain marketing authorization under the harmonized legislation within the European Economic Area, while the Bolar-type exemption under Norwegian law expands to trials, experiments, and similar activities that are necessary to obtain marketing authorization in any state that is a party to the WTO Agreement.

b. The Laws Applicable to Bolar-Type Exemption in Norway

The Bolar-type exemption is codified in the Patent Act Section 3, third paragraph, no. 5. In accordance with this provision, the following is exempt from the exclusive rights:

> Trials, experiments, and similar activities relating to a patented pharmaceutical that are necessary to obtain marketing authorization for a pharmaceutical in a state that is a party to the Agreement of 15 April 1994 establishing the World Trade Organization (WTO Agreement).

The Norwegian Bolar-type exemption is broad in scope, with no specific definition of 'pharmaceutical' in the Patent Act. It covers substances for treating or preventing diseases in humans and animals, extending beyond generic products to include innovative medicines. The exemption applies to activities necessary for obtaining market approval in any state that is party to the WTO Agreement.

c. Procedural Aspects of Invoking the Bolar-Type Exemption

The Bolar-type exemption is used as a defence against claims of patent infringement in court proceedings. In Norway, the question of patent infringement is brought directly before the regular courts. Thus, only a court can make a determination of the legitimacy of the Bolar-type exemption.

d. Scope of Bolar-Type Exemption in Norway

i. Fields of Technology

Application of the Bolar-type exemption is limited to trials, experiments, and similar activities relating to a *patented pharmaceutical*. The exemption was codified to address concerns from the pharmaceutical industry, and it does not apply to other technological fields.

ii. Purpose of Experiments/Infringing Activities

In accordance with the wording, the purpose of the trials, experiments or similar activities must be to obtain marketing authorization and only activities that are necessary to obtain marketing authorization are covered by the exemption. Activities that go beyond this are not covered by the exemption, such as activities carried out for improving an old invention. Such activities may however be covered by the Experimental Use exemption.

In addition, the exemption applies to both generic and original products. The exemption allows for the manufacturing of such amounts of a patented pharmaceutical that are necessary for conducting such trials etc. that are necessary to obtain marketing authorization. An example would be manufacturing for use in clinical trials, such as for comparing a new drug to an old but patented drug.

iii. Exempted and Prohibited Activities

Certain activities are excluded from the scope of the Bolar-type exemption. The exemption is intended to facilitate trials, experiments and similar activities that are directly related to obtaining regulatory approval for pharmaceuticals.

The exemption does not provide any extended opportunity to, for example, use patented methods, tools, or other aids in trials, etc., of a patented medicine. Also, even though it allows for the production of such quantities of a medicine as necessary to conduct the trials, etc., required to meet the documentation requirements set forth in the application for marketing authorization, it does not permit the establishment of a stockpile of a generic medicine in Norway during the patent period, with the intention of launching the generic medicine on the market as soon as the patent expires.

e. Beneficiary Limitations

The Bolar-type exemption is not limited to generic companies. It also applies to innovative manufacturers. The provision allows innovative companies to conduct necessary studies to demonstrate the safety and efficacy of their products without the risk of infringing patent rights.

The exemption can be used by third parties on behalf of the entity applying for the marketing authorization. Its application is not limited to the applying party.

f. Territoriality Issues

The exemption may apply to activities conducted in Norway that are intended for regulatory submissions in other Member States of the WTO Agreement, allowing companies to perform otherwise infringing activities to meet foreign regulatory requirements. As long as the activities are covered by the Bolar-type exemption, the exemption would be applicable also if results from the activities, such as information, is used to infringe a patent in another jurisdiction. It is not material whether the person acting under the exemption is the applicant for the regulatory approval or otherwise related to it.

g. Burden of Proof and Onus

In Norwegian law, the party invoking the exemption bears the burden of proof and the obligation to provide evidence.

h. Applicability during Patent Term Extension or Supplementary Protection Certificate

The Bolar-type exemption applies for the duration of an SPC. The SPC is the only form of patent extension available in Norway.

There is also an exemption for stockpiling during the last part of the SPC period. Regulation (EC) No. 469/2009 of the European Parliament and of the Council of 6 May 2009 concerning the supplementary protection certificate for medicinal products, OJ L 152, 16.06.2009, was amended by Regulation (EU) 2019/933 of the European Parliament and of the Council of 20 May 2019, OJ L 153, 11.06.2019. In accordance with Regulation 2019/933 Article 1 no. 2, Regulation 469/2009 Article 5 no. 2 a) iii) was amended to the effect that manufacturing and storing of a pharmaceutical product are allowed during the last six months of the SPC protection period. This is to prepare for marketing and sales after the SPC has expired.

4. DIFFERENCES BETWEEN THE TWO EXEMPTIONS IN NORWAY

In Norway, the Experimental Use exemption and the Bolar-type exemption serve distinct purposes, though they may overlap. The Experimental Use exemption is broadly defined for all experiments that relate to the invention, promoting innovation and academic research. In contrast, the Bolar-type exemption is more narrowly focused on activities related to regulatory approval in the pharmaceutical sector, facilitating timely access to pharmaceuticals.

The Experimental Use exemption and the Bolar-type exemption may be overlapping for certain activities, but as both are exemptions to the exclusive rights of the patentee this will not create any conflicts between the two exemptions or issues of supremacy.

Chapter 29

Peru

Carlos Fernández-Dávila Winkler and Julisa Quiliche Chavez

1. GENERAL

a. Terminology

The Experimental Use exemption is provided for in Article 53, subparagraphs b) and c) of Andean Decision 486[1] ('Decision 486'). Article 53 lists the acts in which the patent owner cannot exercise the right conferred by patents, that is, they are considered exemptions[2] to the patent rights.

The Bolar-type exemption is provided for in Article 39 of Legislative Decree 1075[3] ('LD 1075') and should be understood as the power to use the matter protected by a patent to generate the information necessary to support the marketing approval application of a product.

b. Legal Basis in Peru

In Peru, industrial property is regulated by Decision 486 and Legislative Decree 1075 which is a domestic law.

Regarding the Experimental Use exemption, Article 53 of Decision 486 lists the acts exempted from the patent rights, which include acts performed exclusively for experimental purposes (subparagraph b) and those performed for teaching or scientific or academic research purposes (subparagraph c).

1. Andean Decision 486 of 1 December 2020 on Common Regime on Industrial Property.
2. The terms 'exemption' and 'exception' are used indistinctly throughout this chapter.
3. Legislative Decree 1075 of 28 June 2008 on Complementary Provisions to Decision 486 of the Commission of the Andean Community establishing the Common Regime on Industrial Property.

> Article 53. The patentee may not exercise the right referred to in the previous article with respect to the following acts:
>
> ...
>
> (b) acts carried out exclusively for experimental purposes, with respect to the object of the patented invention;
>
> (c) acts carried out exclusively for the purpose of teaching or scientific or academic research;
>
> ...

Nevertheless, Article 39-A of LD 1075 establishes that when the limited exemptions provided for in Article 53 of Decision 486 unjustifiably act against the normal exploitation of the patent or cause unjustified prejudice to the legitimate interests of the patentee, the patentee may exercise his property rights established in Article 52 of said Decision (e.g. to prevent the unauthorized manufacture, offer for sale, sale, use or import of the patented invention).

Regarding the Bolar-type exemption, Andean Decision 689[4] authorized Member Countries of the Andean Community (Peru, Bolivia, Colombia and Ecuador) to include a Bolar-type exemption in their domestic regulations to facilitate the granting of marketing approvals.

As a result, the Bolar-type exemption was included in Peruvian domestic law under Article 39 of DL 1075; this exemption applies to pharmaceutical and agricultural chemical products.

> Article 39. Generation of information by third parties
>
> Without prejudice to the exclusivity rights of the patent owner, a third party may use the material protected by the aforementioned patent only for the purpose of generating the necessary information to support the request for approval to market a pharmaceutical or agricultural chemical product in Peru.
>
> Any product produced by virtue of the previous paragraph may be manufactured, used, sold, offered for sale or imported into the national territory for the generation of information, only in order to comply with the approval requirements to market the product once the expiration of the validity period of the patent. Likewise, the product can be exported only for the purposes of complying with the marketing approval requirements in Peru.

c. Bodies That May Decide on the Legitimacy of Exemptions

The Experimental Use Exemption and the Bolar-type Exemption are likely to be claimed as a means of defence in a patent infringement proceeding. There are two competent authorities involved in this type of proceedings: National Institute for the Defence of Competition and the Protection of Intellectual Property – INDECOPI (administrative authority) and the judiciary.

---

4. Andean Decision 689 of 15 August 2008 on Adaptation of certain articles of Decision 486 – Common Regime on Industrial Property, to allow the development and deepening of Industrial Property Rights through the internal regulations of the Member Countries of 2008 of the Andean Community Commission.

To date there have not been any cases in Peruvian case law where the administrative authority or the judiciary have analysed and/or resolved based on these exemptions.

2. THE EXPERIMENTAL USE EXEMPTION

a. History and Rationale of Adopting the Experimental Use Exemption

The Experimental Use exemption was first regulated by Andean Decision 311.[5] Article 35 of said Decision established that the patent owner may not exercise his rights, among other things, when the use of the patented material takes place for non-profit purposes, at an experimental, academic or scientific level. This provision was maintained in the two subsequent Decisions issued, until 2000.

In 2000, Decision 486 (current regulation) was enacted, and the wording of the Experimental Use exemption was modified. The exemption was divided into two subparagraphs under Article 53: 'b) acts carried out exclusively for experimental purposes, with respect to the object of the patented invention' and 'c) acts carried out exclusively for teaching or scientific or academic research purposes'. These subparagraphs do not include a provision for 'non-profit purposes' or 'non-commercial purpose', that is, currently, this exemption would allow the use of a patented invention for experimental purposes, regardless of whether such use has a commercial purpose or not.

In 2006, the Trade Promotion Agreement between Peru and the United States of America was signed, but only in 2009 did the Peruvian government finish its process of implementing the intellectual property obligations contained in Chapter 16 of the Agreement.[6] In order to comply with the commitments arising from this Agreement, the Peruvian government issued and amended certain domestic regulations on intellectual property, such as DL 1075. Article 39-A of DL 1075 establishes that when the exemptions provided for in Article 53 of Decision 486 unjustifiably act against the normal exploitation of the patent or cause unjustified prejudice to the legitimate interests of the patentee, the patentee may exercise his property rights established in Article 52 of said Decision (e.g. to prevent the unauthorized manufacture, offer for sale, sale, use or import of the patented invention).

b. The Laws Applicable to the Experimental Use Exemption in Peru

The Experimental Use exemption in Peru is regulated by Andean Decision 486 and Legislative Decree 1075.

Article 53 of Decision 486 lists the acts exempted from the rights of the patent owner, which include acts performed exclusively for experimental purposes (subparagraph b) and those performed for teaching or scientific or academic research purposes (subparagraph c).

5. Andean Decision 311 of 12 December 1991 on Common Regime on Industrial Property.
6. Supreme Decree No. 009-2009-MINCETUR of 17 January 2009.

Article 53. The patentee may not exercise the right referred to in the previous article with respect to the following acts:

(a) acts carried out in the private sphere and for non-commercial purposes;
(b) acts carried out exclusively for experimental purposes, with respect to the object of the patented invention;
(c) acts carried out exclusively for the purpose of teaching or scientific or academic research;
(d) acts referred to in Article 5ter of the Paris Convention for the Protection of Industrial Property;
(e) when the patent protects a biological material, except plants, capable of reproducing, use it as an initial basis to obtain a new viable material, unless such obtaining requires the repeated use of the patented entity.

As a result of Trade Promotion Agreement between Peru and the United States of America, Article 39-A was incorporated into LD 1075. This Article establishes that when the exemptions provided for in Article 53 of Decision 486 unjustifiably act against the normal exploitation of the patent or cause unjustified prejudice to the legitimate interests of the patentee, the patentee may exercise his property rights established in Article 52 of said Decision.

Legislative Decree 1075

Article 39-A. Exceptions [sic][7] to the rights conferred

When the limited exceptions [sic][8] provided for in Article 53 of Decision 486 of the Andean Community Commission unjustifiably act against the normal exploitation of the patent or cause unjustified prejudice to the legitimate interests of the patentee, considering the legitimate interests of third parties, the patentee may exercise the rights established in Article 52 of said Decision.

Decision 486

Article 52.- The patent grants its patentee the right to prevent third parties who do not have his consent from performing any of the following acts:

(a) when a product is claimed in the patent:
    (i) manufacturing the product;
    (ii) offer for sale, sell, or use the product; or import it for any of these purposes; and,
(b) when a process is claimed in the patent:
    (i) use the process; or
    (ii) execute any of the acts indicated in literal a) with respect to a product obtained directly through the process.

To date, no additional provisions have been issued to clarify the scope and extent of the Experimental Use exemption.

7. The term 'exception' is the official term used in the Spanish version of Legislative Decree 1075.
8. *Ibid.*

c. Procedural Aspects of Invoking the Experimental Use Exemption

The Experimental Use exemption is likely to be claimed as a means of defence in a patent infringement proceeding. These proceedings can be reviewed by two authorities:

Initially, the exemption would be reviewed at the administrative level by the Patent and Trademark Office (first instance) and the Board of Appeal (second instance) of INDECOPI.

Once the administrative proceeding is over, the case can continue in court at the first, second and third instances of the judiciary.

Additionally, there is the possibility of filing a criminal action directly before the judiciary without the need for a prior adjudication by INDECOPI, as established in Article 222, subparagraph a) of the Criminal Code.[9]

> Article 222.- Whoever, in violation of industrial property rules and rights, stores, manufactures, uses for commercial purposes, offers, distributes, sells, imports or exports, in whole or in part, shall be punished with deprivation of liberty of not less than two nor more than five years, with sixty to three hundred and sixty five days fine and disqualification in accordance with Article 36, paragraph 4) taking into consideration the seriousness of the crime and the value of the damages caused:
>
> (a) A product covered by a patent of invention, or a product manufactured through the use of a process covered by a patent of invention obtained in the country; ...

To date there have not been any cases in Peruvian case law where the Patent Office or the judiciary have analysed the Experimental Use exemption.

d. Scope of the Experimental Use Exemption in Peru

i. *Fields of Technology*

The Experimental Use exemption can be applied in any technological field. Decision 486 does not include any restrictions on the technological fields in which the Experimental Use exemption can be applied.

ii. *Purpose of Experiments/Infringing Activities*

There are no cases in Peruvian case law where the Patent Office or the judiciary have analysed the Experimental Use exemption.

Decision 486 does not list the types of activities covered as experimental use; but lists the activities against which the patentee cannot exercise his industrial property rights and with some limiting provision.

For example, Article 53(b) of Decision 486 expressly limits the scope of acts performed exclusively for experimental purposes to those performed with the object

9. Legislative Decree No. 635 of 8 April 1991.

of the patented invention. In addition, Article 53(b) does not include a provision for 'non-commercial purpose', that is, currently, this exemption would allow the use of an invention for experimental purposes, regardless of whether such use has a commercial purpose or not.

Additionally, Article 53(c) of Decision 486, which regulates acts carried out exclusively for the purpose of teaching or scientific or academic research, does not include a provision for 'non-commercial purposes', that is, currently, this exemption would allow the use of an invention for teaching or scientific or academic purposes, regardless of whether such use has a commercial purpose or not.

iii. Exempted and Prohibited Activities

Decision 486 does not list the types of activities exempted or prohibited by the Experimental Use exemption. In addition, there are no cases in Peruvian case law where the Patent Office or the judiciary have analysed the Experimental Use exemption.

iv. Pure Academic vs Commercially Motivated Experimental Use

'Experimental use' and 'acts done for academic purposes' are regulated as separate exemptions, as observed in subparagraphs b) and c) of Article 53 of Decision 486, respectively. Nevertheless, subparagraph c), referring to 'acts carried out for academic purposes', does not include a provision for 'non-commercial purposes', that is, currently, this exemption would allow the use of an invention for academic purposes, regardless of whether such use has a commercial purpose or not.

e. Beneficiary Limitations

Peruvian laws do not include provisions about third-party contributions. Article 53 of Decision 486 does not specify whether contribution to experiments by third parties other than the persons conducting the experiments is prohibited. In any case, third parties would have to demonstrate that they are also carrying out acts for experimental purposes to be covered by the provisions of Article 53.

f. Territoriality Issues

Peruvian legislation is territorial. Although no case of the Experimental Use exemption has yet been reviewed, the legislation would only apply to cases related to patents granted in Peru.

g. Burden of Proof and Onus

The burden of proof of the Experimental Use exemption lies on the party claiming this exemption. This is based on the provisions of Article 196 of the Code of Civil Procedure,[10] which is applied to all administrative proceedings:

10. Ministerial Resolution No. 010-93-JUS of 22 April 1993.

Article 196.- Burden of proof

Unless law establishes otherwise, the burden of proof corresponds to whoever asserts facts that sustain his claim, or whoever contradicts them alleging new facts.

h. Applicability during Patent Term Extension or Supplementary Protection Certificate

In Peru, the patent term extension or equivalent is not regulated.

LD 1075 only regulates the patent term adjustment when there has been an unjustified delay in the process of granting it; nevertheless, this adjustment does not apply to pharmaceutical patents.

The law does not include provisions that differentiate the scope of patent rights between the original term and an extended term. Accordingly, the Experimental Use exemption would equally apply during any extended term of the patent.

3. THE BOLAR-TYPE EXEMPTION

a. History and Rationale of Adopting the Bolar-Type Exemption

The Bolar-type exemption provisions was adopted in Peru as a result of the Trade Promotion Agreement between Peru and the United States of America (the 'Agreement').

In 2006, the Agreement was signed but the intellectual property obligations contained in Chapter 16 of the Agreement were only implemented in 2009. Since patent-related issues are regulated by the Andean Community regulations, it was necessary to issue an Andean Decision that would allow the inclusion of the Bolar-type exemption in the Peruvian legal system. Thus, Decision 689 was issued: 'Adjustment of certain articles of Decision 486 – Common Regime on Industrial Property, to allow the development and deepening of Industrial Property Rights through the internal regulations of the Member Countries'.

Decision 689 authorized Member Countries of the Andean Community (Peru, Bolivia, Colombia and Ecuador) to include a Bolar-type exemption in their internal regulations to facilitate the granting of marketing approvals. As a result, the Bolar-type exemption was included in Peruvian domestic law under Article 39 of DL 1075 which states that a third party may use the subject-matter protected by a patent only in order to generate the necessary information to support the marketing approval application of a pharmaceutical product or a chemical agricultural product in Peru.

b. The Laws Applicable to the Bolar-Type Exemption in Peru

Andean Decision 689 authorized Member Countries of the Andean Community to include a Bolar-type exemption in their internal regulations.

Article 1.- The Member Countries, through their internal regulations, will be empowered, in the terms expressly indicated in subparagraphs a) to j), to develop and deepen only the following provisions of Decision 486:

...

(e) Article 53: Include the power to use the material protected by a patent in order to generate the necessary information to support the application for marketing approval of a product.[*] ...

* The Member Countries understand this power as the Bolar Exception [sic][11] that facilitates the granting of marketing authorizations.

Peru chose to adopt the powers granted by Decision 689; the Bolar-type exemption was included in Peruvian domestic law under Article 39 of DL 1075.

> Article 39. Generation of information by third parties
>
> Without prejudice to the exclusivity rights of the patent owner, a third party may use the material protected by the aforementioned patent only for the purpose of generating the necessary information to support the request for approval to market a pharmaceutical or agricultural chemical product in Peru.
>
> Any product produced by virtue of the previous paragraph may be manufactured, used, sold, offered for sale or imported into the national territory for the generation of information, only in order to comply with the approval requirements to market the product once the expiration of the validity period of the patent. Likewise, the product can be exported only for the purposes of complying with the marketing approval requirements in Peru.

Article 39 provides a defence mechanism to the generic manufacturer of pharmaceutical or agricultural chemical products in an infringement legal action, and therefore, the burden of proving the conditions for this Bolar-type exemption shall be on the side of such generic manufacturer.

c. Procedural Aspects of Invoking the Bolar-Type Exemption

The Bolar-type exemption can be used as a defence mechanism in patent infringement proceedings. These proceedings can be reviewed by two authorities:

Initially, the exemption would be reviewed at the administrative level by the Patent and Trademark Office (first instance) and the Board of Appeal (second instance) of INDECOPI.

Once the administrative proceeding is over, the case can continue in court at the first, second and third instances of the judiciary.

Additionally, there is the possibility of filing a criminal action directly before the judiciary without the need for a prior adjudication by INDECOPI, as established in Article 222, subparagraph a) of the Criminal Code (Legislative Decree No. 635).

> Article 222. Whoever, in violation of industrial property rules and rights, stores, manufactures, uses for commercial purposes, offers, distributes, sells, imports or exports, in whole or in part, shall be punished with deprivation of liberty of not less than two nor more than five years, with sixty to three hundred and sixty five days fine and disqualification in accordance with Article 36, paragraph 4)

11. The term 'exception' is the official term used in the Spanish version of Andean Decision 689.

taking into consideration the seriousness of the crime and the value of the damages caused:

(a) A product covered by a patent of invention, or a product manufactured through the use of a process covered by a patent of invention obtained in the country; ...

To date there have not been any cases in Peruvian case law where the Patent Office or the judiciary have analysed this exemption.

d. Scope of the Bolar-Type Exemption in Peru

i. Fields of Technology

According to the provisions of Article 39 of DL 1075, the Bolar-type exemption is limited to pharmaceutical and agricultural chemical products.

ii. Purpose of Experiments/Infringing Activities

Although there are no cases where the exemption has been evaluated, the Bolar-type exemption would cover all actions required to generate the necessary information to support the marketing approval of a generic product in Peru, such as quality assays, bioequivalence studies and field pesticides studies.

There is no express provision related to clinical trials. However, they could be exempted if they are only carried out to generate the information to obtain the marketing approval in the country.

Phase 4 clinical trials are usually carried out after obtaining the marketing approval, so, preliminarily, they are likely not be covered by the Bolar-type exemption (which allows generation of the necessary information for the marketing approval application).

iii. Exempted and Prohibited Activities

The manufacture of a product with the express purpose of sale after the patented period is prohibited without the consent of the patent owner. In case of manufacturing the product while the patent is in force, it would be infringing the industrial property rights of the patent owner (Article 52 of Decision 486).

The Bolar-type exemption only allows the use (including manufacture) of the patented invention for the purpose of generating information for the marketing approval application.

e. Beneficiary Limitations

Article 39 of DL 1075 uses broad language, mentioning 'a third party', which would imply that both generic and innovative companies could benefit from the Bolar-type exemption.

It appears that any other party that performs laboratory tests or studies on behalf of the companies conducting the marketing approval, to generate the information necessary to support a product marketing approval application, could also benefit from the Bolar-type exemption.

Third parties would have to prove that the acts they carry out are included in the provisions of Article 39 of DL 1075.

f. Territoriality Issues

Peruvian legislation is territorial. Although no case of Bolar-type exemption has yet been reviewed, the legislation would only apply to cases related to patents granted in Peru.

In addition, Article 39 of DL 1075 only allows the use of the invention (including exports) to generate information to obtain the marketing authorization application *in Peru*. It appears that use of the invention in Peru (for example, conducting clinical studies in Peru) for purposes of marketing authorization in another country, would not be within the scope of the Bolar-type exemption.

g. Burden of Proof and Onus

The burden of proof of the Bolar-type exemption lies on the party claiming this exemption. This is based on the provisions of Article 196 of the Code of Civil Procedure, which is applied to all administrative proceedings:

> Article 196. Burden of proof
>
> Unless law establishes otherwise, the burden of proof corresponds to whoever asserts facts that sustain his claim, or whoever contradicts them alleging new facts.

h. Applicability during Patent Term Extension or Supplementary Protection Certificate

In Peru, the patent term extension or an equivalent is not regulated.

LD 1075 only regulates the patent term adjustment when there has been an unjustified delay in the process of granting it; nevertheless, this adjustment does not apply to pharmaceutical patents.

The law does not include provisions that differentiate the scope of patent rights between the original term and an extended term. Accordingly, the Bolar-type exemption would equally apply during any extended term of the patent.

4. DIFFERENCES BETWEEN THE TWO EXCEPTIONS IN PERU

The Experimental Use exemption and the Bolar-type exemption are regulated separately. In fact, an Andean Decision had to be issued to allow Member Countries of the Andean Community, including Peru, to include the Bolar-type exemption in their regulations, which would denote that these exemptions have a different nature and purpose.

While the Experimental Use exemption is applicable to all technical fields, the Bolar-type exemption is limited to pharmaceutical and agrochemical products and only for the purpose of generating the necessary information to support the marketing authorization application of said products.

To date, there are no cases where the application of these exemptions has been evaluated, so it is not yet known what criteria the authority will apply when a case related to these exemptions arises.

Chapter 30

Poland

Dr Wojciech Marciniak and Marta Kawczyńska

1. GENERAL

a. Terminology

The Experimental Use exemption, in Poland more often referred as research exception or research privilege, is defined in Chapter 5 of Act of 30 June 2000 on Industrial Property Law (IPL), more precisely in Article 69 Section 1 point 3. The Bolar-type exemption or privilege is also laid down in Chapter 5 of IPL, more precisely in Article 69 Section 1 point 4. Both legal instruments are generally regarded as exceptions to the exclusivity granted by a patent.

b. Legal Basis in Poland

Poland is a signatory to most major international treaties, agreements and conventions pertaining to the protection and enforcement of the intellectual property rights. Poland is also a contracting state of the European Patent Organization (EPO) and Member State of the European Union (EU). As Poland is part of the EU, its legal system is bound to a certain extent by the EU judicial system and Polish national law has to be therefore harmonized with the EU law. However, Poland is not a Member State of the Unitary Patent system, which includes the Unified Patent Court.

The statutory provisions pertaining to the Experimental Use exemption in Poland are stipulated in IPL. The current wording of the Experimental Use exemption in Poland has been in place since 2000 under Article 69 Section 1 point 3 of IPL, which defines limitations to patent rights, in particular a fair (or permitted) use of a third party invention protected by a patent.

Article 69, Section 1

The following shall not be considered acts of infringement of a patent:

...

(3) employing of an invention for research and testing purposes, for the evaluation thereof, analysis or teaching;

To date, there are no additional regulations defining the boundaries of the Experimental Use exemption, nor has there been any case law that would clarify the interpretation of the above provision.

The Bolar-type exemption was introduced into IPL in 2000. The present wording is as follows:

Article 69, Section 1

The following shall not be considered acts of infringement of a patent:

...

(4) the exploitation of the invention by making, using, storing, depositing, offering, placing on the market, exporting or importing, in order to carry out acts which, under the law, are required in order to obtain, including by a third party, registration or authorization as a condition for the marketing of certain goods in view of their intended use, in particular, medicinal products in the territory of the European Economic Area or of another State;

To date, there are no other additional regulations defining the boundaries of the Bolar-type exemption in Poland. However, there has been statutory interpretation in the case law, as discussed further, below.

c. Bodies That May Decide on the Legitimacy of Exemptions

Generally, both the Experimental Use exemption and the Bolar-type exemption are used in patent litigation proceedings only. The Polish litigation system is bifurcated, what means that invalidity and infringement cases are examined and decided by different authorities in different proceedings. The IP Court, localized in Warsaw, has the exclusive jurisdiction over intellectual property matters concerning computer programs, inventions, utility models, topographies of integrated circuits, plant varieties and technical secrets of the enterprise. This is the only body that can decide on the applicability of the exemptions.

2. THE EXPERIMENTAL USE EXEMPTION

a. History and Rationale of Adopting the Experimental Use Exemption

The legal framework of the Experimental Use exemption has been largely shaped by the relevant instruments of the international laws, including the TRIPS Agreement.

The Experimental Use exemption was first codified in Polish law in 1993 as an amendment to the Act on Inventive Activity of 1972. At the time, the provision read as follows:

Article 16, Section 8

A patent for an invention is not infringed by using the invention for research purposes.

The Experimental Use exemption took its present form in 2000, with the coming in force of a new law relating to industrial property.

The rationale for the adoption of the Experimental Use exemption in Poland is very similar to that in other jurisdictions, as the shape of regulations adopted by the Polish legislator has largely been determined by the relevant norms of international law. In general, one of the aims of patent system is to promote the development of science and technology, and patent protection shall not limit this development. In other words, the public should be able to benefit from technical knowledge that is contained in patent applications for the purpose of further development in science and technology.

b. The Laws Applicable to the Experimental Use Exemption in Poland

The current wording of the Experimental Use exemption in Poland has been in place since 2000 under Article 69 Section 1 point 3 of IPL. Previously, Poland had a more laconic definition of this exemption.

Article 69, Section 1

The following shall not be considered acts of infringement of a patent:

...

(3) employing of an invention for research and testing purposes, for the evaluation thereof, analysis or teaching;

The exact language of the exemption is drafted slightly differently in Poland as compared to regional and other European legislations, where the exemption is defined as 'use for the purpose of experimentation'. While this leaves some room for interpretation that might lead to the different definitions of the scope of application of the exemption, its spirit shall remain the same.

Until now, no additional regulations have been issued setting the boundaries of the Experimental Use exemption. There is also no case law that would clarify the interpretation of the above provision, therefore all interpretations shall be based on the intellectual property law doctrine related to exceptions to established rules of law.

According to Article 30 of the TRIPS Agreement, patent limitations (and therefore the exceptions to the exclusive rights conferred by a patent such as the Experimental Use and Bolar-type exemptions) are permissible as long as they remain limited, and the following conditions are cumulatively met: the limitations do not unreasonably conflict with a normal exploitation of a patent; they do not unreasonably prejudice the legitimate interests of a patentee; and they take into account the legitimate interests of third parties.[1]

1. Michał du Vall, Paweł du Vall, Piotr Kostański, Justyna Ożegalska-Trybalska, Paweł Podrecki, Elżbieta Traple (scientific ed., *Prawo patentowe* (Wolter Kluwer 2017)

c. Procedural Aspects of Invoking the Experimental Use Exemption

The Experimental Use exemption is generally expected to be invoked only in patent litigation proceedings.

According to Act of 30 June 2000 on Industrial Property Law:

> Article 283
>
> Cases involving civil law claims in the field of industrial property protection, not falling within competence of other authorities shall be decided in civil law procedure in accordance with the general principles of law.

Article 284 of IPL provides examples of case types that shall be decided in civil law procedure. Among many others, infringement of a patent is directly mentioned. In 2020, specialized civil courts that deal with intellectual property matters were established and the Warsaw Regional Court gained exclusive jurisdiction in intellectual property matters concerning inventions.

It may also be possible to raise the exemption as a side argument in other proceedings, such as a patent opposition.

d. Scope of the Experimental Use Exemption in Poland

i. Fields of Technology

All fields of technology appear to qualify for the Experimental Use exemption, though there is no case law on point.

ii. Purpose of Experiments/Infringing Activities

There is no case law related to the Experimental Use exemption, accordingly, interpretation must be made on the basis of legal doctrine. Two possible interpretations exist: in the first, all limitations listed in the regulation, i.e. research and testing purposes, evaluation, analysis or teaching, shall be regarded as independent or autonomous, and therefore employing of the invention for evaluation, analysis or teaching shall not constitute an infringement of the patent even if it is not linked with research or testing purpose.[2]

There is a second, narrower interpretive stream: that all criteria are necessary, i.e. there must be research and testing purposes and done for evaluation, analysis or teaching.[3]

---

2. Andrzej Żakowski & Helena Żakowska-Henzler, *System Prawa Prywatnego, Tom 14A. Prawo własności przemysłowej* 676 (Ryszard Skubisz ed., C.H. Beck, INP PAN 2017); Justyna Ożegalska-Trybalska, *Komentarze Prawa Prywatnego, Tom VIIIA. Prawo Własności Przemysłowej, Komentarz* 647 (Łukasz Żelechowski ed., C.H Beck 2022).
3. Andrzej Żakowski & Helena Żakowska-Henzler, *System Prawa Prywatnego, Tom 14A. Prawo własności przemysłowej* 676 (Ryszard Skubisz ed., C.H. Beck, INP PAN 2017); Tomasz Targosz, *System Prawa Handlowego, Tom 3. Prawo własności przemysłowej*, 402 (C.H. Beck 2015); Justyna Ożegalska-Trybalska, *Ograniczenia ochrony patentowej a naruszenie patentu*, 337-338 (Wolters Kluwer 2019).

Both purposes are implemented when the invention is employed to enhance knowledge on the patented invention, to develop new applications of the invention, to confirm the effect of the invention, to collect specific data as a result of action of the invention, to evaluate and analyse the knowledge and associated phenomena as well as to corroborate scientific principles. And in fact, recalling specific activities (i.e. evaluation and analysis of patented invention or for teaching) shall be regarded as further clarification of the activities that are allowed by the exemption.[4]

One aspect of the Experimental Use exemption seems to be rather uncontroversial, namely employing of an invention for teaching. This aspect could be clearly classified as pure non-commercial activities, in most cases performed in schools, universities and other scientific bodies for the purpose of knowledge transfer in organized manner and based on a teaching program.[5]

Another issue associated with the Experimental Use exemption relates to the research tools. The current wording of the Experimental Use exemption in Poland does not explicitly mention the use of the patented invention as a research tool, which could be understood as laboratory equipment, tools, reagents, tests, cellular receptors, transgenic organisms, enzymes, gene sequences, monoclonal antibodies, etc. Taking into account the fact that in many cases the only purpose of protection of such research tools is their use in research and testing, their commercial use cannot be totally excluded by the Experimental Use exemption. Therefore, in case of research tools, narrow interpretation of the Experimental Use exemption prevails in the doctrine, thus excluding research tools from the exemption.[6]

iii. Exempted and Prohibited Activities

In Polish law, wording of the Experimental Use exemption only defines the purpose of the exempted activities, hence not specifying types of allowed activities. Therefore, it is accepted that, the determination will be made based on the purpose of such activity, namely whether it is purely exploratory or it is undertaken in order to obtain financial or market benefits.[7]

One can quite safely state that activities such as making or using of the patented product or using of the patented method is covered by the Experimental Use exemption, whereas activities storing, depositing offering, placing on the market are not covered by the exemption.[8]

---

4. Andrzej Żakowski & Helena Żakowska-Henzler, *System Prawa Prywatnego, Tom 14A. Prawo własności przemysłowej* 676 (Ryszard Skubisz ed., C.H. Beck, INP PAN 2017).
5. Justyna Ożegalska-Trybalska, *Komentarze Prawa Prywatnego, Tom VIIIA. Prawo Własności Przemysłowej, Komentarz* 647 (Łukasz Żelechowski ed., C.H Beck 2022).
6. Andrzej Żakowski & Helena Żakowska-Henzler, *System Prawa Prywatnego, Tom 14A. Prawo własności przemysłowej* 677 (Ryszard Skubisz ed., C.H. Beck, INP PAN 2017).
7. Justyna Ożegalska-Trybalska, *Komentarze Prawa Prywatnego, Tom VIIIA. Prawo Własności Przemysłowej, Komentarz* 648 (Łukasz Żelechowski ed., C.H Beck 2022).
8. Justyna Ożegalska-Trybalska, *Ograniczenia ochrony patentowej a naruszenie patentu*, 355 (Wolters Kluwer 2019).

iv. Pure Academic vs Commercially Motivated Experimental Use

The IPL does not contemplate whether the exempt activities must be purely academic research, or whether they include activities that are commercially motivated. However, it appears clear that such activities should not be directly associated with obtaining financial or market benefits. Therefore, some research activities performed by a commercial entity, but that do not directly lead to sale or profit, or in other words are not performed for profit or for professional purposes according to Article 63 of IPL, should also be exempted under the Experimental Use exemption.

e. Beneficiary Limitations

The wording of the Experimental Use exemption does not define the beneficiary, but is rather based on the purpose of the allowed activities. That said, unlike the language of the Bolar-type exemption, which explicitly extends to third parties, the language of the Experimental Use exemption does not explicitly extend to third party beneficiaries. Therefore, it is still questionable whether a third party can, for example, produce a patent protected product for another party that is going to use it for research or testing. There are some very cautious opinions that such activities are exempt only if they are performed for the purpose and scope of the party directly involved in the research or testing, and upon request or direct linkage with that party.[9]

f. Territoriality Issues

A Polish court's jurisdiction is the territory of the Republic of Poland, but it seems reasonable that other jurisdiction's laws shall be taken into account when patent is infringed abroad. Note that, although Poland is an EU Member State, it is not however a Member State of the Unitary Patent/Unified Patent Court (UP/UPC) system, therefore infringement cases of exclusive rights in Poland are only dealt by the Polish civil IP Courts.

g. Burden of Proof and Onus

There is currently no legislation or case law considering the burden of proof for the exemption. According to the general rule defined in Article 232 of the Civil Code, the burden of proving a fact shall fall to the person who asserts the legal consequences arising from this fact. Therefore, it is safe to state that a party claiming that its actions are within the scope of the exemption must provide appropriate evidence proving this fact.

9. Justyna Ożegalska-Trybalska, *Komentarze Prawa Prywatnego, Tom VIIIA. Prawo Własności Przemysłowej, Komentarz* 648 (Łukasz Żelechowski ed., C.H Beck 2022).

h. Applicability during Patent Term Extension or Supplementary Protection Certificate

There is no direct information on the applicability of the Experimental Use exemption while an SPC is in force, but since SPC confers the same rights as conferred by the basic patent and shall be subject to the same limitations and the same obligations as stipulated in Regulation (EC) No. 469/2009 of the European Parliament and of the Council of 6 May 2009, it is expected that the Experimental Use exemption would still apply during the term of the SPC.

3. THE BOLAR-TYPE EXEMPTION

a. History and Rationale of Adopting the Bolar-Type Exemption

The history and rationale of the adoption of the Bolar-type exemption in Polish law is essentially the same as in other European countries and goes back to the United States' famous case of 1970s i.e. *Bolar Pharmaceutical Co v. Roche Products*. The introduction of the Bolar-type exemption at the European level was justified by the need to ensure a balance between the position of innovative medicines manufacturers, whose position was strengthened by introduction of SPCs, data exclusivity and market exclusivity, and generic medicines manufacturers. At that time, development and obtaining marketing authorization for generic products in Europe was hampered by the existing law. The European Commission recommended the introduction of mechanisms that would increase the EU generic drugs manufacturers' market share and facilitate access to generic medicines and consequently provided appropriate provisions included in EU Directive 2004/27/EC, which amended the EU Medicinal Products for Human Use Directive (2001/83/EC), and EU Directive 2004/28/EC, which amended EU Directive 2001/82/EC on the Community Code relating to Veterinary Medicinal Products:

> Conducting the necessary studies and trials with a view to the application of paragraphs 1, 2, 3 and 4 [of Article 10] and the consequential practical requirements shall not be regarded as contrary to patent rights or to supplementary protection certificates for medicinal products.

It is important to note that while the EU regulations are binding on all EU Member States and do not require national implementation, the EU Directives need implementation to national laws based on the standard of minimum harmonization, and thus may be implemented into the national laws of the EU Member States in a slightly different manner. As a result, EU Member States such as Poland may introduce the institution of the Bolar-type exemption with a broader scope in order to facilitate the marketing of generic medicinal products as soon as patent protection has ceased. Therefore, there are discrepancies between the various national regulations regarding the Bolar-type exemption.

The original wording of the Bolar-type exemption was introduced in 2000 as follows:

Article 69, Section 1

The following shall not be considered acts of infringement of a patent:

...

(4) the exploitation of the invention to a necessary extent, in order to carry out acts which, under the law, are required in order to obtain registration or authorization as a condition for the marketing of certain goods in view of their intended use, in particular those being medicinal products;

The current wording of the Bolar-type exemption was introduced into the IPL by the amendment in 2019, reportedly as a result of a critical analysis of the case law.

Article 69, Section 1

The following shall not be considered acts of infringement of a patent:

...

(4) the exploitation of the invention by making, using, storing, depositing, offering, placing on the market, exporting or importing, in order to carry out acts which, under the law, are required in order to obtain, including by a third party, registration or authorization as a condition for the marketing of certain goods in view of their intended use, in particular, medicinal products in the territory of the European Economic Area or of another State.

b. The Laws Applicable to Bolar-Type Exemption in Poland

The current wording of the Bolar-type exemption in Poland has been in place since 2000 under Article 69 Section 1 point 4 of IPL.

Article 69, Section 1

The following shall not be considered acts of infringement of a patent:

...

(4) the exploitation of the invention by making, using, storing, depositing, offering, placing on the market, exporting or importing, in order to carry out acts which, under the law, are required in order to obtain, including by a third party, registration or authorization as a condition for the marketing of certain goods in view of their intended use, in particular, medicinal products in the territory of the European Economic Area or of another State.

This provision appears to go beyond pharmaceutical products only, in particular medicinal products or generic medicines, and the regulation might be applicable to other products requiring registration or authorization as a condition for their marketing. The broader application of the exemption to other than medicinal products seems not to be contrary to the regulations, however, seems to require an assessment as to whether the purpose of the exemption is fulfilled.[10]

Further regulation is provided under Article 69 Section 5 of IPL:

10. Oskar Gińko, *Obszary możliwego zastosowania wyjątku Bolara do wyrobów uregulowanych dyrektywami nowego podejścia*, ZNUJ. PPWI 117-125 no. 4 (2023)

Article 69, Section 5

5. Grant of the registration or the authorization referred to in section 1 point 4 shall be without prejudice to civil liability for putting on the market of a product without the patent holder's consent, where such consent is required.

From the language of the legislation, it appears that Poland has adopted a relatively broad implementation of the Bolar-type exemption. However, according to the well-established case law and doctrinal views as stated herein earlier, all legal exceptions shall have rather strict and narrow interpretation.

The current wording of the Bolar-type exemption was shaped by analysis and conclusions from the case law. Controversies related to interpretation of the first wording version of Bolar-type exemption in Poland were revealed in the case *Astellas Pharma INC v. Polpharma.*[11] In this case, defendant Polpharma SA – a leading Polish pharmaceutical provider, and the largest Polish manufacturer of generic medicines and active pharmaceutical ingredients ('APIs') – was accused of patent infringement after it placed an advertisement offering a broad range of APIs, including solifenacin succinate, which was protected by Astellas' substance patent PL182344. A list of APIs offered by Polpharma – including solifenacin succinate – was also published on the company's website, with the following disclaimer:

> Products subject to patent protection are not offered or supplied for commercial purposes in countries where this constitutes an infringement of patent rights. In Poland, patent-protected products are offered solely for experimental purposes or within the confines of the Bolar-type provision, in strict accordance with Polish regulations relating to intellectual property (in this case, solifenacin succinate).

Polpharma claimed that all of its purportedly infringing activities fell within the Bolar-type exemption, because its customers were going to use the APIs only for testing purposes required for registration or marketing approval. Polpharma further argued that numerous generic companies need to get supplies of APIs to perform acts that are legally necessary to obtain registration or authorization from third-party manufacturers, as they cannot manufacture them themselves. Additionally, Polpharma asked the national judge to submit the following preliminary questions to the European Court of Justice (ECJ): 'Is manufacturing of patented substances permissible under Article 10(6) of the Directive 2004/27/EC where the privileged purpose will be conducted by a third party? And if the first question is answered affirmatively, which conditions must be fulfilled by third party so that the supply falls within the requirements of the Directive?' The Gdansk Appeal Court concluded that the preliminary questions were unnecessary, as there is no conflict between a narrow interpretation of the Bolar-type provision and the Treaty on the Functioning of the European Union. The Court held that only the party performing the test itself can take advantage of the Bolar-type exemption, and therefore Polpharma's arguments went too far. For the Court's decision, it was important that Polpharma's only purpose in offering solifenacin succinate was to obtain financial benefits. It was not relevant whether the buyer of the protected substance intended to use it in experiments or for other purposes, such as obtaining marketing authorization.

---

11. *Astellas Pharma INC v. Polpharma,* SA I ACa 320/12 and IX GC 76/11.

At first glance, the decision seems to be consistent with the spirit of the law. However, the legislature's intention was to provide an opportunity to obtain marketing authorization for generic products while the relevant patents are still in force, to enable their sale immediately after the patent expires. Therefore, all activities aimed solely at obtaining registration or marketing authorization should be permitted. It seems unjustified to favour generic manufacturers that are related to the patentee over those which manufacture APIs on their own. Indeed, this may have led to the amendments of 2020, discussed further in section 3.e.

c. Procedural Aspects of Invoking the Bolar-Type Exemption

The Bolar-type exemption is expected generally to be invoked in patent litigation proceedings only. Therefore it can be used in patent litigation cases, which are under jurisdiction of the civil IP court in Warsaw.

It may also be possible to raise the exemption as a side argument in other proceedings, such as a patent opposition.

d. Scope of Bolar-Type Exemption in Poland

i. Fields of Technology

The Bolar-type exemption does not provide any limitations with respect to the field of technology that is covered by the exemption. Therefore, any product that requires registration or authorization to be put on the market is covered by the exemption. There are opinions that it is possible to invoke the Bolar-type exemption with respect to electronic devices for example (not necessarily medical devices) that require certain registration procedures before putting them on the market.[12] Nevertheless, when interpreting the scope of the exemption, one should always bear in mind the purpose for which it was introduced.[13]

ii. Purpose of Experiments/Infringing Activities

The limitation of the patent rights in accordance with the Bolar-type exemption should be interpreted strictly so as not to nullify the principal purpose and function of patent protection. In order to determine whether the entity acted within the exemption, it is necessary to establish whether the entity's conduct pursued the specific purpose set out in Article 69 Section 1 point 4 of IPL – the exempted activities must be carried out in order to obtain registration or authorization required as a condition for the marketing of a good in view of its intended use, in particular, medicinal products, in the territory of the European Economic Area or of another State. Further, a purposive interpretation requires that patent exclusivity should not extend longer than the

12. Oskar Gińko, *Obszary możliwego zastosowania wyjątku Bolara do wyrobów uregulowanych dyrektywami nowego podejścia*, ZNUJ. PPWI 117-125 no. 4 (2023)
13. *For comprehensive study on Bolar exemption in poland see* Agnieszka Sztoldman, *Korzystanie z chronionego wynalazku w celu rejestracji produktu leczniczego* (Wolters Kluwer 2018).

duration of the patent or SPC. As in the case of the Experimental Use exemption, the Bolar-type exemption shall be interpreted in a strict and narrow way, as in case of the interpretation of other exceptions to the rules of law.

iii. Exempted and Prohibited Activities

Under the Bolar-type exemption only specified activities might be recognized as exempted, i.e. making, using, storing, depositing, offering, placing on the market, exporting or importing, in order to carry out acts which, under the law, are required in order to obtain, including by a third party, registration or authorization as a condition for the marketing authorization. This provision does not envisage stockpiling as an exempted activity. Therefore, it seems reasonable to assert that stockpiling is not among activities exempted by the Polish Bolar-type exemption.[14]

e. Beneficiary Limitations

Currently, the Bolar-type exemption in Poland provides a broad exclusion from the patent monopoly, as it is directly stipulated that a patent is not infringed by the manufacturing, using, storing, offering, placing on the market, exporting or importing, of a claimed invention, in order to perform activities which under the provisions of law are required to obtain, either by the party or a third party, registration or authorization, such registration or authorization being a condition for allowing the marketing of certain products in view of their intended use, in particular medicinal products, in the territory of the European Economic Area or of another country. Following the amendment of IPL, as of 27 February 2020, the exclusion is no longer limited to situations in which the entity itself manufactures and handles the registration process.

Before the amendment, the exempted activities had to be performed by the entity applying for the marketing authorization, as confirmed in the judgment of the Polish Supreme Court of 23 October 2013.[15] The exempted activities covered by the Bolar-type exemption could only be performed by the applicant for marketing authorization on its own, without the involvement of third parties, as was the case in this judgement, where the active substance for a Polish generic manufacturer was manufactured under contract by a subcontractor.[16]This judgment most probably has led to the change of the Bolar-type exemption definition in Polish law into the current one, wherein it is clearly stated now that third parties qualify for the exemption. It appears to be permissible to manufacture for a third party, which third party will apply for registration. Note there is to date no case law that would clarify the degree of linkage required between the exempted activity and the person seeking regulatory approval. However, there are some doctrinal views that in determining whether a seller and supplier of a manufactured substance is acting within the Bolar-type

14. Justyna Ożegalska-Trybalska, *Komentarze Prawa Prywatnego, Tom VIIIA. Prawo Własności Przemysłowej, Komentarz* 652 (Łukasz Żelechowski ed., C.H Beck 2022).
15. Astellas Pharma Inc. vs Polpharma IV CSK 92/13
16. Justyna Ożegalska-Trybalska, *Komentarze Prawa Prywatnego, Tom VIIIA. Prawo Własności Przemysłowej, Komentarz* 654 (Łukasz Żelechowski ed., C.H Beck 2022).

exemption the relationship between the two entities – the manufacturer and the purchaser – must be assessed.[17]

Additionally, there is some uncertainty regarding the possibility of application of the Bolar-type exemption in the case of innovative medicines.[18] There is no specific case law in this regard so far.

f. Territoriality Issues

The current wording of the Bolar-type exemption clearly states that a patent is not infringed by activities that are performed in order to obtain registration or authorization, which is the condition for allowing the marketing of certain products in view of their intended use, in particular medicinal products, in the territory of the European Economic Area or of another country.

g. Burden of Proof and Onus

There is currently no legislation or case law considering burden of proof for the exemption. According to general rule defined in Article 232 of the Civil Code, the burden of proving a fact shall fall to the person who asserts legal consequences arising from this fact. Therefore, it is safe to state that a party claiming that its actions are within the scope of the Bolar-type exemption must provide appropriate evidence proving this fact.

h. Applicability during Patent Term Extension or Supplementary Protection Certificate

There is no direct information on the applicability of the Bolar-type exemption while an SPC is in force, but since the SPC confers the same rights as conferred by the basic patent and shall be subject to the same limitations and the same obligations as stipulated in Regulation (EC) No. 469/2009 of the European Parliament and of the Council of 6 May 2009, it is expected that the Bolar-type exemption would still apply during the term of the SPC.

4. DIFFERENCES BETWEEN THE TWO EXCEPTIONS IN POLAND

At first glance, the Experimental Use exemption and Bolar-type exemption appear to be similar legal instruments. They, as well as the whole patent system, should promote the development of science and technology, ensuring benefit for the public from the development of technical knowledge and widening access to innovative products, in particular medicinal products. Despite some similarities, there are however significant differences leading to their different application. First, the

---

17. Sztoldman Agnieszka, *Krąg upoważnionych do działania w ramach wyjątku Bolara*, 2014/2/87-94

18. K. Szczepanowska-Kozłowska, 'Bolar Exemption', in E. Nowińska, U. Promińska, K. Szczepanowska-Kozłowska, *Industrial Property Rights* (Warsaw, 2021).

Experimental Use exemption is only limited to generally non-commercial activities having research or experimental purpose, while the Bolar-type exemption allows certain activities that are required for the purpose of regulatory approval of products, in particular medicinal products. Secondly, it is worth noting that while, in the case of the Experimental Use exemption, the legislator does not enumerate the type of exempted activities, in the case of the Bolar-type exemption the types of exempted activities are specifically listed. Finally, in the Bolar-type exemption the exempted activities may also be performed by a third party, not exclusively by a party applying for the marketing authorization. In view of the above, one may say that these legal instruments complement each other in certain areas of their application, but in general they were designed to be used in different situations. On the one hand, the Experimental Use exemption is designed to be mainly used for the purpose of development of technical knowledge and promoting innovation, thus it seems to be justified to assume that its application and interpretation might be broader than in the case of the Bolar-type exemption. The Bolar-type exemption on the other hand is to be used in highly competitive surrounding, therefore space for various interpretations of the regulation should be as small as possible, as this is the only way for generic manufacturers to prepare for the launch of generic medicines after the expiry of the protection for originator medicines.

Chapter 31

Portugal

Claudia Freixinho Serrano

1. GENERAL

a. Terminology

The Portuguese legislator addressed the issue of the Experimental Use and Bolar-type exemptions by listing the limits of application of the patent right, as set out in the Industrial Property Code (Article 103 §1 (c) of the Industrial Property Code).

Thus, both exemptions are considered exceptions to infringement.

b. Legal Basis in Portugal

In Portugal, this matter is regulated in Article 103 of the Industrial Property Code, which provides, under the heading 'Limitation to the rights conferred by the patent', in its paragraph 1, point (c), that:

> The rights conferred by the patent do not cover … acts carried out exclusively for testing or experimental purposes related to the subject-matter of the patented invention, including experiments for the preparation of the administrative procedures necessary for the approval of products by the competent official bodies, though the industrial or commercial exploitation of those products may not begin before the expiry of the patent that protects them.

c. Bodies That May Decide on the Legitimacy of Exemptions

In Portugal, matters relating to the invocation of industrial property rights, the infringement thereof and exceptions to the rights conferred by patents come under the competence of the Intellectual Property Court, with the High Court of Lisbon being the court of appeal.

The Intellectual Property Court is a court of specialized jurisdiction based in Lisbon, with territorial jurisdiction extending to the national territory. In addition to other matters, such as copyright and related rights, this court is competent, among other things, to hear actions in which the cause of action relates to industrial property, in any of the modalities provided for by law (Article 111 §1 (a) of the Law on the Organization of the Judicial System).

Since 2019, the Lisbon Court of Appeal has had a section specializing in intellectual property and competition, regulation and supervision.

2. THE EXPERIMENTAL USE EXEMPTION

a. History and Rationale of Adopting the Experimental Use Exemption

The Experimental Use exemption is expressly provided for in Portuguese legislation as one of the 'Limitation[s] to the rights conferred by the patent', and makes it possible to conduct otherwise patent infringing acts for experimental purposes in connection with the subject-matter of the patented invention. Although the exemption is broader, the Portuguese courts and doctrine have used this exemption in recent years only when dealing with procedures for obtaining marketing authorizations for generic drugs.

This limitation, despite being expressly established in national law, is a result of the Agreement on Trade-Related Aspects of Intellectual Property Rights (TRIPS Agreement), that is directly applicable by the courts of the Member States, even in disputes between individuals.

Article 30 of the TRIPS Agreement states, under the heading 'Exceptions to the Rights Conferred', that:

> Members may provide limited exceptions to the exclusive rights conferred by a patent, provided that such exceptions do not unreasonably conflict with a normal exploitation of the patent and do not unreasonably prejudice the legitimate interests of the patent owner, taking account of the legitimate interests of third parties.

The Portuguese patent legislation, like that of other EU Member States, defines research and Experimental Use exemptions from patent infringement that allow sufficient room for research activities to promote innovation.

b. The Laws Applicable to the Experimental Use Exemption in Portugal

The Portuguese Industrial Property Code, amended by Decree-Law 110/2018 of 10 December 2018, establishes in Article 103 §1 (c), under the heading 'Limitation to the rights conferred by the patent':

> The rights conferred by the patent do not cover … acts carried out exclusively for testing or experimental purposes related to the subject-matter of the patented invention, including experiments for the preparation of the administrative procedures necessary for the approval of products by the competent official bodies, though the industrial or commercial exploitation of those products may not begin before the expiry of the patent that protects them.

The same provision was included in the previous version of the Industrial Property Code, approved by Decree-Law 36/2003 of 5 March 2003.

c. Procedural Aspects of Invoking the Experimental Use Exemption

Experimental use as a limitation to the rights conferred by a patent can be invoked as a means of defence in an action for infringement of those rights, filed with the competent judicial body – the Intellectual Property Court.

Portuguese legislation also provides that any party wishing to use this exemption can file an action seeking a declaratory judgment, in which such party will have the burden of demonstrating that the acts carried out fall within the Experimental Use exemption. The Intellectual Property Court also has jurisdiction for this action, with the High Court of Lisbon being the court of appeal.

d. Scope of the Experimental Use Exemption in Portugal

i. Fields of Technology

All technological fields can make use of this exemption. However, the main technological fields in which this exemption is mostly applied are the following:

1. *Pharmaceuticals and biotechnology*: Carrying out clinical trials and testing the safety and efficacy of new medicines, and research into new formulations, dosages and methodologies for the composition of drugs.
2. *Chemistry*: Development of new chemical compounds, including the synthesis and characterization of substances, and studies related to the reactivity and properties of chemical materials that have already been patented.
3. *Materials engineering*: Testing new materials that may be used in technological applications, considering physical and mechanical properties.

ii. Purpose of Experiments/Infringing Activities

In accordance with the Portuguese Industrial Property Code, experimental acts are typically not defined exhaustively, but include, for example:

1. *Tests and experiments*: Related to scientific or technical research studying and understanding the patented invention and that is not aimed at commercialization.
2. *Preparatory developments*: activities that seek to assess the safety or efficacy of a patented product or process.

iii. Exempted and Prohibited Activities

Acts carried out not for the purpose of research or development, but for the commercial exploitation of the invention, are prohibited. Although there is no specific case law on this matter to date, doctrine is unanimous in considering that the scope of this exemption does not apply when commercial purposes occur, as the law limits the exemption to 'acts carried out *exclusively* for testing or experimental purposes'.

iv. Pure Academic vs Commercially Motivated Experimental Use

As indicated in the previous point, although there is no specific case law on this matter to date, the law is clear in limiting the exemption to 'acts carried out *exclusively* for testing or experimental purposes', which removes commercially motivated experimental use from the exemption.

e. Beneficiary Limitations

The law does not seem to make a distinction as to which parties can make use of the exemption, preferring to focus on the scope of the activity. If the act carried out exclusively for testing or experimental purposes is contracted out to third parties and carried out by them, this too should be exempted.

f. Territoriality Issues

The Portuguese courts, more specifically the Court of Intellectual Property, are competent to assess the existence of experimental acts, as a limitation of the patent right, in Portuguese territory, only in the case of Portuguese national patents or European patents validated in Portugal.

According to national doctrine, this exception applies regardless of the destination of the results obtained. However, the courts have not yet had the opportunity to rule on this issue.

g. Burden of Proof and Onus

In the context of patent law, the burden of proof that an act is included in the experimental act lies with the party invoking this exemption. In other words, if a person or entity carries out an act that is considered to be experimental in order to support the non-infringement of a patent, it is incumbent on that party to demonstrate that its activity falls within the parameters defined in the legislation for the act to qualify as experimental.

h. Applicability during Patent Term Extension or Supplementary Protection Certificate

The Portuguese legislation indicated above does not provide for any difference in treatment with regard to the limitations of the patent right, whether during the 'regular' term of validity of the patent or during the patent extension or SPC. However, the new wording of Article 5 of Regulation (EC) No. 469/2009 of 6 May 2009, introduced by Regulation (EU) No. 2019/93 of 20 May 2019, allows the manufacture and storage of the manufactured product to take place, in the case of medicinal products, within six months prior to the expiry date of the SPC.

3. THE BOLAR-TYPE EXEMPTION

a. History and Rationale of Adopting the Bolar-Type Exemption

The application in Portugal of the Bolar-type exemption has its origins in Directive 2001/83/EC of the European Parliament and of the Council of 6 November 2001 establishing a Community code relating to medicinal products for human use, the overarching objective of which is to achieve a fair balance between, on the one hand, the rights of patent owners and, on the other hand, the public interest – for example, that of the national health services and users – in obtaining the marketing of generic drugs at more affordable prices than those practised for the sale of reference medicines.

It is in this context that certain acts are authorized during the term of the patent, such as the grant of marketing authorizations for generic drugs and the carrying out of acts exclusively for testing or experimental purposes, as provided for in the scheme laid down in Articles 6 to 12 of Directive 2001/83/EC.

In particular, Article 10(6) of Directive 2001/83/EC enshrined an exception to patent protection (commonly referred to as the 'Bolar' or 'Bolar-type' exemption because it is based on the case law in *Roche Products Inc. v. Bolar Pharmaceutical Co.*, 733 F.2d 858 Fed. Cir. 04/23/1984, United States Court of Appeals for the Federal Circuit), with the aim of allowing certain acts preparatory to the placing on the market of generic drugs, before the expiry of the patents for the reference medicines, to be carried out lawfully, in particular by the holders of marketing authorizations for generic drugs.

b. The Laws Applicable to the Bolar-Type Exemption in Portugal

The Portuguese Industrial Property Code, amended by Decree-Law 110/2018 of 10 December 2018, establishes, as an exception to the rights conferred by a patent:

> acts carried out exclusively for testing or experimental purposes ..., including experiments for the preparation of the administrative procedures necessary for the approval of products by the competent official bodies.[1]

The same provision was included in the previous version of the Industrial Property Code, approved by Decree-Law 36/2003 of 5 March 2003.

The Medicines Statute, approved by Decree-Law 176/2006 of 30 August 2006 (revised by Decree-Law 26/2018 of 24 April 2018), also states in Article 19(8) that:

> The carrying out of the studies and tests necessary for the application of paragraphs 1 to 6 and the practical requirements arising therefrom, including the corresponding grant of authorization provided for in Article 14, are not contrary to the rights relating to patents or supplementary protection certificates for medicinal products.

1. Article 103(1)(c).

c. Procedural Aspects of Invoking the Bolar-Type Exemption

The Bolar-type exemption as a limitation to the rights conferred by a patent can be invoked as a means of defence in an action for infringement of those rights, filed with the competent judicial body – the Intellectual Property Court.

Portuguese legislation also provides that any party wishing to use this exemption can file an action seeking a declaratory judgment, in which such party will have the burden of demonstrating that the acts carried out fall within the Bolar-type exemption. The Intellectual Property Court also has jurisdiction for this action, with the High Court of Lisbon being the court of appeal.

d. Scope of Bolar-Type Exemption in Portugal

i. Fields of Technology

Article 103(1)(c) does not limit the application of the Bolar-type exemption to any technological field, and it has the same application whenever there is a need to prepare administrative procedures for the approval of products by the competent official bodies.

However, in view of the need for the approval of marketing authorizations for medicinal products by INFARMED, Portugal's regulatory agency, it is in the pharmaceutical field that this exemption is mostly applied.

This has led to the existence of a specific provision in the law on medicinal products that specifically regulates this issue, i.e. Article 19(8), which states that:

> The carrying out of the studies and tests necessary for the application of paragraphs 1 to 6 and the practical requirements arising therefrom, including the corresponding grant of authorization provided for in Article 14, are not contrary to the rights relating to patents or supplementary protection certificates for medicinal products.

ii. Purpose of Experiments/Infringing Activities

The application of the Bolar-type exemption includes all acts carried out for the purpose of preparing administrative procedures necessary for the approval of products by the competent official bodies, and all other acts that do not share this purpose constitute infringing activities.

iii. Exempted and Prohibited Activities

The application of the Bolar-type exemption includes all acts carried out for the purpose of preparing administrative procedures necessary for the approval of products by the competent official bodies – studies, tests and trials for the specific purpose of a medical product assessment.

Although the Portuguese courts and doctrine have used this exemption in recent years only when dealing with procedures for obtaining marketing authorizations for generic drugs, the preparation and running of clinical trials on innovative drugs for marketing authorization are also protected from infringement under the provisions of Portuguese legislation.

However, obtaining marketing authorizations under this exemption does not mean that the products in question can be commercially or industrially exploited while the patent is in force. For example, the manufacture and stockpiling of the generic medicinal product which is the subject of this authorization constitute infringing activities.

e. Beneficiary Limitations

It has been accepted by both Portuguese doctrine and case law that the tests and studies carried out by a third party who supplies an active pharmaceutical ingredient fall within the scope of the Bolar-type exemption, and not just those carried out by the beneficiaries of the marketing authorization.

f. Territoriality Issues

The Portuguese courts, more specifically the Intellectual Property Court, are competent to assess whether a given act is covered by the Bolar-type exemption, as a limitation of the patent right, in the Portuguese territory, only in the case of Portuguese national patents or European patents validated in Portugal.

According to national doctrine, the exemption applies regardless of the destination of the results obtained. However, the courts have not yet had the opportunity to rule on this issue.

g. Burden of Proof and Onus

In the context of patent law, the burden of proof for establishing that the Bolar-type exemption applies lies with the party invoking this exemption and seeking to use the exemption to support the non-infringement of a patent.

h. Applicability during Patent Term Extension or Supplementary Protection Certificate

The Portuguese legislation indicated above does not provide for any difference in treatment with regard to the limitations of the patent right, whether during the 'regular' term of validity of the patent or during the patent extension or SPC.

However, the new wording of Article 5 of Regulation (EC) No. 469/2009 of 6 May 2009, introduced by Regulation (EU) No. 2019/93 of 20 May 2019, allows the manufacture and storage of the manufactured product to take place, in the case of medicinal products, within six months prior to the expiry date of the SPC.

4. DIFFERENCES BETWEEN THE TWO EXCEPTIONS IN PORTUGAL

In Portugal, there has been no difference in treatment between the two exemptions, very probably because the legislator chose to regulate them under the same legal provision.

Chapter 32

Singapore

Khoo Kian Hoe and Richie Tay

1. GENERAL

a. Terminology

Singapore has separate statutory provisions for Experimental Use and Bolar-type exemptions. They both appear in Section 66(2) of the Singapore Patents Act and apply to acts done in relation to a Singapore patent.

The Experimental Use exemption appears in Section 66(2)(b) of the Patents Act, which was enacted in 1995. The Bolar-type exemption provision was introduced under Section 66(2)(h) of the Patents Act in 2004.

b. Legal Basis in Singapore

A person infringes a patented product or process if the person does any of the acts that are listed in Section 66(1) of the Patents Act in Singapore without the consent of the patent proprietor. For a product patent, such acts include making, selling, offering to sell, using, importing and stocking the product, and for a process patent, it is prohibited to use or offer for use the process, and to sell, offer to sell, use, import or stock a direct product of the claimed process. A person who does any of these prohibited acts is not liable for infringement if any of the exemptions under Section 66(2) apply.

Section 66(2)(b) provides the Experimental Use exemption. This exemption was present in the first Patents Act enacted in 1995.

Sections 66(2) and (2)(b) state the following:

> 66(2) An act which, apart from this subsection, would constitute an infringement of a patent for an invention is not an infringement of a patent if –
>
> ...

> (b) it is done for experimental purposes relating to the subject matter of the invention;

The Bolar-type exemption was introduced under Section 66(2)(h) of the amended Patents Act in 2004, and states:

> (h) it consists of the doing of anything set out in subsection (1) in relation to the subject matter of the patent to support any application for marketing approval for a pharmaceutical product, provided that any thing produced to support the application is not –
>
> (i) made, used or sold in Singapore; or
>
> (ii) exported outside Singapore,
>
> other than for purposes related to meeting the requirements for marketing approval for that pharmaceutical product;

To date, there has not been any case law that considers how Section 66(2)(b) or Section 66(2)(h) should be interpreted.

c. Bodies That May Decide on the Legitimacy of Exemptions

Both the Experimental Use exemption and the Bolar-type exemption may be used as a defence in an infringement proceeding. Prior to 1 April 2022, matters on patent infringement could be referred to the Intellectual Property Office of Singapore (IPOS) if the parties agreed to refer the matter to IPOS. However, as of 1 April 2022, any patent infringement proceeding has to commence before the High Court. Decisions from the High Court may be appealed before the Court of Appeal. Only the High Court or the Court of Appeal can decide on the legitimacy of the exemptions.

2. THE EXPERIMENTAL USE EXEMPTION

a. History and Rationale of Adopting the Experimental Use Exemption

Singapore's modern patent regime was established with the introduction of the Singapore Patents Act, which came into force on 23 February 1995. The Singapore Patents Act was modelled on the UK Patents Act 1977 and contains an Experimental Use exemption that is codified under Section 66(2)(b).

b. The Laws Applicable to the Experimental Use Exemption in Singapore

The Experimental Use exemption is found under Section 66(2)(b) of the Patents Act, which states:

> 66(2) An act which, apart from this subsection, would constitute an infringement of a patent for an invention is not an infringement of a patent if –
>
> ...
>
> (b) it is done for experimental purposes relating to the subject matter of the invention;

The term 'patent' is defined in Section 2(1) as a patent under the Singapore Patents Act. Thus, the exemption is only applicable to infringing acts performed in relation to a Singapore patent.

c. Procedural Aspects of Invoking the Experimental Use Exemption

The Experimental Use exemption may be used as a defence in a patent infringement proceeding. Prior to 1 April 2022, matters on patent infringement can be referred to the Intellectual Property Office of Singapore (IPOS) if the parties agree to refer the matter to IPOS. However, as of 1 April 2022, any patent infringement proceeding has to commence before the High Court. Decisions from the High Court may be appealed to the Court of Appeal.

d. Scope of the Experimental Use Exemption in Singapore

i. Fields of Technology

There are no technology-specific limitations on the Experimental Use exemption in Singapore. The exemption would appear to apply to all types of technologies.

ii. Purpose of Experiments/Infringing Activities

Section 66(2)(b) exempts activities that would otherwise be infringing which are done for experimental purposes relating to the subject matter of the invention. The Patents Act does not provide a definition for the term 'experimental purposes'. Neither has the scope of this term been clarified by a Singapore court. However, a Singapore court is likely to look to jurisprudence in other Commonwealth jurisdictions (such as the UK) when considering the scope of this term in Singapore. For example, a Singapore court may refer to case law established in the UK case *Monsanto Co. v. Stauffer Chemical Co.* [1985] RPC 515, where it was held that the UK Experimental Use exemption covers activities that seek to generate genuinely new information but not those that seek to verify existing knowledge. A Singapore court may thus construe Section 66(2)(b) to exclude generic or biosimilar drug testing for marketing approval, since such testing generally seeks to verify existing knowledge.

iii. Exempted and Prohibited Activities

Section 66(2)(b) does not expressly limit the scope of the exempted activities that are performed for 'experimental purposes'. As mentioned in section 2.d.ii. above, the breadth of the term 'experimental purposes' has yet to be clarified before a Singapore court. A Singapore court is likely to look to jurisprudence in other Commonwealth jurisdictions (such as the UK) when considering the scope of this term in Singapore.

iv. Pure Academic vs Commercially Motivated Experimental Use

Section 66(2)(b) does not expressly require the infringing activities to be purely academic having no commercial value. However, the breadth of the term 'experimental purposes' has yet to be interpreted before a Singapore court to determine whether it only covers pure academic experimental use as opposed to commercially motivated experimental use. A Singapore court is likely to look to jurisprudence in other Commonwealth jurisdictions (such as the UK) when considering the scope of this term in Singapore.

e. Beneficiary Limitations

There are no statutory provisions relating to contributory infringement in Singapore under the Singapore Patents Act.

A third party may be liable for patent infringement under the common law position on joint tortfeasorship. Joint tortfeasorship may occur when one party conspires with the primary party or induces the infringement, or when two or more persons participate in the common design pursuant to which the infringement acts were carried out.

There is no local guidance as to whether the exemption can be used by third parties. It appears that if contributions by a third party were also made for genuine experimental purposes, they should also be exempted.

f. Territoriality Issues

Section 66(2)(b) relates to an exemption for infringement of a patent under the Singapore Patents Act (see section 2.b. above). Hence, the provision only exempts activities that would otherwise infringe a patent in Singapore.

g. Burden of Proof and Onus

There is no case law interpreting burden of proof in the context of Section 66(2)(b). In infringement proceedings, the onus generally lies on the defendant to prove that an exemption applies.

h. Applicability during Patent Term Extension or Supplementary Protection Certificate

The exemption under Section 66(2)(b) would still apply during a patent term extension.

3. THE BOLAR-TYPE EXEMPTION

a. History and Rationale of Adopting the Bolar-Type Exemption

The Bolar-type exemption provision was introduced into the Patents Act in 2004 under Section 66(2)(h) as a result of the US-Singapore Free Trade Agreement. As explained during the second reading of the Patents (Amendment) Bill in Parliament:[1]

> Section 66(2)(h) allows a generic drug producer to carry out activities covered by a patent without the consent of the patent owner, provided the activities are carried out to support an application to HSA [Health Sciences Authority] for marketing approval for a pharmaceutical product. This will facilitate the manufacture, sale and distribution of generic versions of patented drugs immediately after the patents for those drugs which have expired, something that would benefit consumers.

It was also explained that Section 66(2)(h) serves as a useful counterbalance to the patent term extension provision that was also introduced at that time.

b. The Laws Applicable to the Bolar-Type exemption in Singapore

The Bolar-type exemption is found under Section 66(2)(h) of the Patents Act:

> 66(2) An act which, apart from this subsection, would constitute an infringement of a patent for an invention is not an infringement of a patent if –
>
> ...
>
> (h) it consists of the doing of any thing set out in subsection (1) in relation to the subject matter of the patent to support any application for marketing approval for a pharmaceutical product, provided that any thing produced to support the application is not –
> (i) made, used or sold in Singapore; or
> (ii) exported outside Singapore,
> other than for purposes related to meeting the requirements for marketing approval for that pharmaceutical product;

The term 'patent' is defined in Section 2(1) as a patent under the Singapore Patents Act. Thus, the exemption is only applicable to infringing acts performed in relation to a Singapore patent.

The term 'pharmaceutical product' is defined in Section 2(1) of the Patents Act as:

> 'pharmaceutical product' means a medicinal product which is a substance used wholly or mainly by being administered to a human being for the purpose of treating or preventing disease, but does not include –
> (a) any substance which is used solely –
> (i) for diagnosis or testing; or

1. Second Reading Speech of the Patents (Amendment) Bill 2004 by the Minister of State for Law, *Singapore Parliamentary Debates, Official Report* (15 June 2004), vol. 78 at col. 120.

(ii) as a device or mechanism, or an instrument, apparatus or appliance; or

(b) any substance or class of substances specified in paragraph 2 or 3 of the Schedule.

The substances specified in paragraphs 2 and 3 of the Schedule are traditional medicines, homoeopathic medicines, quasi-medicinal products, raw materials used as an ingredient in the preparation or manufacture of any medicinal product, medicated oils or balms, foods, food additives, food supplements, and any substances occurring naturally in plants, animals or minerals.

The definition of 'marketing approval' is provided in Section 2(1) of the Patents Act, and refers to (a) a product licence under Section 5 of the Medicines Act 1975 granted before 1 November 2016; or (b) a registration under Part 7 of the Health Products Act 2007 granted on or after 1 November 2016. This means that 'marketing approval' is limited to one that is issued by the Health Sciences Authority under the Medicines Act or the Health Products Act.

c. Procedural Aspects of Invoking the Bolar-Type Exemption

The Bolar-type exemption is used as a defence in an infringement proceeding. Prior to 1 April 2022, matters on patent infringement could be referred to the Intellectual Property Office of Singapore (IPOS) if the parties agreed to refer the matter to IPOS. However, as of 1 April 2022, any patent infringement proceeding has to commence before the High Court. Decisions from the High Court may be appealed to the Court of Appeal.

d. Scope of the Bolar-Type Exemption in Singapore

i. Fields of Technology

The Bolar-type exemption is limited to applications for marketing approval for a pharmaceutical product. The term 'pharmaceutical product' is further defined in section 3.b. above.

The Bolar-type exemption also does not apply when seeking marketing approval for medical devices and other substances not considered to be 'pharmaceutical products' according to the Schedule of the Patents Act. The latter includes traditional medicines, homoeopathic medicines, quasi-medicinal products, raw materials used as an ingredient in the preparation or manufacture of any medicinal product, medicated oils or balms, foods, food additives, food supplements, and any substances occurring naturally in plants, animals or minerals.

ii. Purpose of Experiments/Infringing Activities

The exemption applies to any activity that would otherwise be infringing in relation to the subject-matter of a Singapore patent to support an application for marketing approval for a pharmaceutical product before the Health Science Authority. It appears that there is no limitation on the type of exempted activities, provided that they are for the purposes of supporting an application for marketing approval for a pharmaceutical product before the Health Sciences Authority, and provided that the activities do not fall under those mentioned in section 3.d.iii. below. The scope of the Bolar-type exemption provision has not been tested before a Singapore court.

iii. Exempted and Prohibited Activities

Section 66(2)(h) requires that anything produced to support the application for marketing approval should not be (i) made, used or sold in Singapore; or (ii) exported outside Singapore, *other than for purposes* related to meeting the requirements for marketing approval for that pharmaceutical product.

e. Beneficiary Limitations

The exemption is not limited to generic drug companies applying for regulatory approval for generic drugs. It also applies to innovative companies carrying out competitive studies.

As mentioned in section 2.e. above, there are no statutory provisions relating to contributory infringement in Singapore under the Singapore Patents Act. A third party may be liable for patent infringement under the common law position on joint tortfeasorship. The exemption would appear to apply to third parties contracted to perform studies on behalf of the party seeking regulatory approval, although this has not been tested in court.

f. Territoriality Issues

The Bolar-type exemption is limited to clinical testing for obtaining marketing approval before the Health Sciences Authority in Singapore. Hence, the exemption will not apply if the results of the experiment are used for satisfying the regulatory requirements in other countries. Furthermore, a patent is defined in Section 2(1) as a patent under the Singapore Patents Act. Hence, the exemption only applies if the results of the experiment are used for infringing a patent in Singapore.

g. Burden of Proof and Onus

There is no case law interpreting burden of proof in the context of Section 66(2)(h). In infringement proceedings, the onus generally lies on the defendant to prove that the exemption applies.

h. Applicability during Patent Term Extension or Supplementary Protection Certificate

The exemption under Section 66(2)(h) would still apply during a patent term extension.

4. DIFFERENCES BETWEEN THE TWO EXCEPTIONS IN SINGAPORE

The Experimental Use exemption is broadly defined in Singapore and is not limited to any particular field of technology. The exemption has not been tested before a Singapore court but is likely to be construed to exclude generic or biosimilar testing for securing marketing approval. The Bolar-type exemption, on the other hand, exempts clinical testing (e.g. generic or biosimilar clinical testing) for marketing approval in Singapore, and has been important in helping the development of the generics drug industry in Singapore. The Experimental Use exemption and the Bolar-type exemption in Singapore are not co-extensive. However, certain activities such as innovative drug testing for marketing approval may be considered to fall within the scope of both exemptions.

Chapter 33

South Africa

Dirk Hanekom

1. GENERAL

a. Terminology

The South African Patents Act No. 57 of 1978 ('the Patents Act') does not provide for an Experimental Use exemption. The Bolar-type exemption or provision appears under Section 69A of the Patents Act. Section 69A is provided under the heading 'Acts of non-infringement'. Provided that the otherwise infringing acts comply with the requirements of Sections 69A(1) and 69A(2), they will be considered as non-infringing.

b. Legal Basis in South Africa

The Bolar-type exemption was enacted by amendment to the Patents Act through Section 16 of the Patents Amendment Act No. 58 of 2002. The Bolar-type exemption is provided for in Section 69A(1) of the Patents Act:

> 69A(1) It shall not be an act of infringement of a patent to make, use, exercise, offer to dispose of, dispose of or import the patented invention on a non-commercial scale and solely for the purposes reasonably related to the obtaining, development and submission of information required under any law that regulates the manufacture, production, distribution, use or sale of any product.

Section 69A(1) is subject to Section 69A(2), which deals with stockpiling of products:

> 69A(2) It shall not be permitted to possess the patented invention made, used, imported or acquired in terms of subsection (1) for any purpose other than for the obtaining, development or submission of information as contemplated in that subsection.

There are no regulations dealing specifically with Section 69A. Further, to the best of our knowledge, there has not been any court decisions in relation to Section 69A.

2. THE EXPERIMENTAL USE EXEMPTION

a. History and Rationale of Adopting the Experimental Use Exemption

This is not applicable to South Africa.

b. The Laws Applicable to the Experimental Use Exemption in South Africa

This is not applicable to South Africa.

c. Procedural Aspects of Invoking the Experimental Use Exemption

This is not applicable to South Africa.

d. Scope of the Experimental Use Exemption in South Africa

i. Fields of Technology

This is not applicable to South Africa.

ii. Purpose of Experiments/Infringing Activities

This is not applicable to South Africa.

iii. Exempted and Prohibited Activities

This is not applicable to South Africa.

iv. Pure Academic vs Commercially Motivated Experimental Use

This is not applicable to South Africa.

e. Beneficiary Limitations

This is not applicable to South Africa.

f. Territoriality Issues

This is not applicable to South Africa.

g. Burden of Proof and Onus

This is not applicable to South Africa.

h. Applicability during Patent Term Extension or Supplementary Protection Certificate

This is not applicable to South Africa.

3. THE BOLAR-TYPE EXEMPTION

a. History and Rationale of Adopting the Bolar-Type Exemption

South African law does not provide for any form of patent term extension or supplementary protection certificates, and is generally seen to be pro 'access' and 'early entry' of generic competitors. It is believed that Section 69A was introduced to further support the early entry policy or approach.

b. The Laws Applicable to the Bolar-Type Exemption in South Africa

As mentioned in section 1.b. above, the Bolar-type exemption was enacted by amendment to the Patents Act through Section 16 of the Patents Amendment Act No. 58 of 2002. The Bolar-type exemption provides that:

> 69A(1) It shall not be an act of infringement of a patent to make, use, exercise, offer to dispose of, dispose of or import the patented invention on a *non-commercial scale* and solely for the purposes reasonably related to the obtaining, development and submission of information required under any law that regulates the manufacture, production, distribution, use or sale of any product. (Emphasis added)

Section 69A(1) is subject to Section 69A(2), which deals with stockpiling of products.

> 69A(2) It shall not be permitted to possess the patented invention made, used, imported or acquired in terms of subsection (1) for any purpose other than for the obtaining, development or submission of information as contemplated in that subsection.

There are no regulations dealing specifically with Section 69A. Further, to the best of our knowledge, there has not been any Court decisions in relation to Section 69A.

c. Procedural Aspects of Invoking the Bolar-Type Exemption

Section 69A could be raised as a defence in an action for infringement, which matters are heard in the High Court of South Africa sitting as the Court of the Commissioner of Patents.

South African courts have not had an opportunity to consider the scope and application of Section 69A, and we are therefore limited to the wording of the Act.

d. Scope of the Bolar-Type Exemption in South Africa

i. Fields of Technology

The only limitation on Section 69A is that the otherwise infringing acts must be 1) on a non-commercial scale, and 2) solely for the purposes reasonably related to the obtaining, development and submission of information required under any law that regulates the manufacture, production, distribution, use or sale of any product.

It is therefore limited to fields of technology for which a market authorization is delivered.

ii. Purpose of Experiments/Infringing Activities

According to Section 69A, the acts must be performed on a non-commercial scale, but South African Courts have not considered the meaning of non-commercial scale in this context. However, this should be interpreted in the context of the second part of the Section which requires that the acts must be '*solely* for the purposes *reasonably related* to the obtaining, development and submission of information required under any law that regulates the manufacture, production, distribution, use or sale of any product' (emphasis added). Actions outside of the scope required for regulatory approval will therefore not be covered by this Section. For example, it is envisaged that the use of data obtained during the course of such activities for any other purpose, i.e. that which is not required for regulatory approval, would fall outside the scope of the exception.

iii. Exempted and Prohibited Activities

Stockpiling is specifically prohibited as per Section 69A(2).

According to our understanding of the wording of Section 69A, all acts performed *solely* for the purposes reasonably related to obtaining, development and submission of information required by law that regulates a product will qualify for exemption.

It should therefore be irrelevant whether the product is a pharmaceutical or a medical device, for example. Although South African courts have not had an opportunity to interpret the scope of Section 69A, the wording of the Act appears to be broad enough to include medical and diagnostic devices including medtech software.

The intention of the relevant party may be important – activities should be conducted in good faith. Importantly, the actions must be on a 'non-commercial scale' and 'reasonably related' to the regulatory approval sought.

Section 69A could also apply equally to farm feeds and agricultural remedies for example.

e. Beneficiary Limitations

This is not provided for in the wording of the Act, and has not been considered by South African Courts.

f. Territoriality Issues

The South African Courts have not had an opportunity to consider and pronounce on the ambit of Section 69A. However, the words 'any law' in the sentence '... non-commercial scale and solely for the purposes reasonably related to the obtaining, development and submission of information required under any law that regulates the manufacture, production, distribution, use or sale of any product...' certainly raise interesting questions. In our view, the words 'any law' should be restrictively interpreted to mean any South African law, and as such acts conducted in South Africa for regulatory approval elsewhere should, in our view, not qualify for protection under Section 69A.

g. Burden of Proof and Onus

The burden of proof will rest with the party raising the defence.

h. Applicability during Patent Term Extension or Supplementary Protection Certificate

This is not applicable to South Africa.

4. DIFFERENCES BETWEEN THE TWO EXCEPTIONS IN SOUTH AFRICA

This is not applicable to South Africa.

Chapter 34

South Korea

Eun-Jeong Cho, Monica Leeu and Inchan Andrew Kwon

1. GENERAL

a. Terminology

Under Article 96(1)(i) of the Korean Patent Act (KPA), which addresses 'Limitations on Effects of Patents,' exemptions are provided for both experimental use and 'Bolar-type' activities. These exemptions allow for the use of a patented invention for research and testing.

Both the Experimental Use exemption and the Bolar-type exemption are considered 'defences' under Article 96.

b. Legal Basis in Korea

The legal basis for both the Experimental Use exemption and the Bolar-type exemption in Korea is codified in Article 96(1)(i) of the KPA, which states that:

> the effects of a patent shall not extend to the following:
> (i) Practice of a patented invention for purposes of research or testing, (including research or testing to obtain regulatory approval under the Pharmaceutical Affairs Act and for registration of agrochemicals under the Agrochemicals Control Act);

The 2010 amendment to the KPA (27 January 2010) added a parenthetical phrase to Article 96(1) 'including research or testing to obtain regulatory approval under the Pharmaceutical Affairs Act and for registration of agrochemicals under the Agrochemicals Control Act' to clarify that the Article provides for the Bolar-type exemption. This codification responded to earlier case law that already recognized that generic activities relating to bioequivalence tests and comparative dissolution tests were non-infringing under Article 96(1)(i).

2. THE EXPERIMENTAL USE EXEMPTION

a. History and Rationale of Adopting the Experimental Use Exemption

The practice of conducting research and testing on a patented invention, such as to verify the invention's effectiveness or to make improvements, can promote technological advancement and stimulate industrial development, which is consistent with the purpose of the KPA as provided in Article 1. Therefore, Article 96(1)(i) of the Act provides that patent rights do not cover the use of an invention for research and testing purposes, seeking to balance the interests of third parties wishing to use patented inventions with those of patent holders.

In Korea, the Experimental Use exemption was first established in the original KPA (effective 15 October 1946), which stated in Article 97 that activities carried out 'for the purpose of research or experimentation within a suitable scope' do not constitute patent infringement. This provision was then moved to Article 40 during the revision of the KPA on 31 December 1961, which specified that patent rights do not extend to the 'use of a patented invention for research or testing.' While the substance of this provision remained unchanged, its location was moved twice: first, it was moved to Article 46 in the amendment of 8 February 1973, and then to Article 96 in the amendment of 13 January 1990. Further clarification came with the partial amendment on 27 January 2010, which expressly included exemption for research and testing under the Pharmaceutical Affairs Act and the Agrochemicals Control Act (i.e., the Bolar-type exemption).

By providing for the Experimental Use exemption, while a patent holder generally has the right to exclude others from practising the patented invention, the use of inventions for research and testing purposes without the patent holder's permission is recognized as crucial for public policy. This exemption ensures that the KPA's fundamental objectives—to encourage inventions, promote technological progress, and industrial development—are maintained in balance.

b. The Laws Applicable to the Experimental Use Exemption in Korea

The Experimental Use exemption was codified in the original KPA from 1946 under Article 97(3), and is currently provided under Article 96(1)(i) of the current KPA.

> Article 96 (Limitations on Effects of Patents) of the KPA:
>
> (1) The effects of a patent shall not extend to the following:
>
> (i) Practice of a patented invention for the purpose of research or testing (including research or testing to obtain regulatory approval under the Pharmaceutical Affairs Act and for registration of agrochemicals under the Agrochemicals Control Act);

Korean courts look at various factors when determining whether the use of a patented invention falls under the research or testing exemption of Article 96(1)(i). These include whether the use is to investigate the novelty or inventiveness of the patented invention, to research or test the workability of the invention, to verify the effects described in the patent specification, or conversely, to examine marketability or economic feasibility. They also consider whether the use was a tool or means for developing another invention, whether the research or test results were released into the market as prototypes or products, and whether such research or testing harmed or posed a risk of harm to the patent holder's interests. *The Welding Institute v. Wooshin EMC Co.*[1]

c. Procedural Aspects of Invoking the Experimental Use Exemption

The Experimental Use exemption can be used as a defence in litigation or scope confirmation actions. In Korea, litigation falls under the jurisdiction of the District Court, IP High Court, and Supreme Court, while scope confirmation actions are under the jurisdiction of the Intellectual Property Trial and Appeal Board (IPTAB), IP High Court, and Supreme Court.

Therefore, the bodies that can decide on the legitimacy of an Experimental Use exemption include the IPTAB, District Court, IP High Court, and Supreme Court.

d. Scope of the Experimental Use Exemption in Korea

i. Fields of Technology

In Korea, the Experimental Use exemption is not limited or restricted to any specific field of technology, but can apply to all types of technology, regardless of industry.

ii. Purpose of Experiments/Infringing Activities

There have not been many case decisions in Korea regarding the Experimental Use exemption, and courts have not yet provided clear or definitive guidelines on how the exemption should be applied. In determining whether an activity falls within the exemption under Article 96(1)(i), courts generally consider whether practising an invention through such research and testing can be deemed an act that 'encourages inventions, promotes technological progress, and supports industrial development' consistent with the objectives of the KPA. On the other hand, if the research and testing goes beyond the scope necessary for testing the invention, thus excessively limiting the patent holder's rights and opposing the KPA's goal of protecting inventions, then it may fall outside the permissible scope of the exemption.

In view of the ruling in *The Welding Institute v. Wooshin EMC Co.*, in cases where the patented invention is used only as a tool or means for developing other inventions, or where the research or test results are released in the form of a prototype or a product in the market and harms the patentee or the patentee's interests, the exemption under Article 96 is unlikely to be recognized.

1. IP High Court, 16 November 2017 (2016 Na 1455).

iii. Exempted and Prohibited Activities

In *The Welding Institute v. Wooshin EMC Co.* where the defendant, a third party manufacturer, used a machine exclusively used for the patented process to develop a drive shaft using the patented process, the IP High Court determined that the defendant's act was within the Experimental Use exemption outlined in Article 96(1)(i) of the KPA, for the following reasons:

(1) The research and testing conducted by the defendant appeared to be aimed at confirming whether the drive shaft would have the required properties if the patented process was applied to production of the drive shaft. The purpose of the research and testing appeared to be merely to confirm the effect or usefulness of the patented invention and to improve the patented invention, so it was difficult to deem that the patented invention was used only as a tool and means for developing other inventions.
(2) It was difficult to find that the above research and testing harmed the patentee or the patentee's interests, such as by releasing the research and test results in the form of a prototype or product in the market.
(3) To the extent the research and testing concluded that the patented invention could be applied to the production of the drive shaft, it might contribute to the development of technology. In order to commercially use the results of the research and testing, the defendant would need to obtain permission from the patentee, which would be in line with the interests of the patentee.

iv. Pure Academic vs Commercially Motivated Experimental Use

The application of Article 96(1)(i) has not been limited exclusively to research or testing conducted for non-commercial purposes.

For example, in the case of *Binex v. Sanofi-Aventis et al.*,[2] Binex manufactured its generic drug containing the active ingredient of a patented invention, conducted a bioequivalence test and obtained conditional approval for the generic drug from the health authority. Similarly, in the case of *SamChunDang Pharm. v. Sanofi-Aventis et al.*,[3] SamChunDang manufactured its generic drug containing the active ingredient of a patented invention, conducted comparative dissolution tests, and applied for product approval for its generic drug. Furthermore, in *Syngenta Participations AG v. LG CI*,[4] LG CI manufactured its generic pesticide falling within the scope of the patented invention and requested tests necessary to obtain test results for registration of a generic pesticide, in order to sell the generic pesticide after patent expiration. In these cases, courts have interpreted such activities as being covered by the exemption under Article 96(1)(i).

Further, in *The Welding Institute v. Wooshin EMC Co.*, the court decided that the defendant's act of inspecting and demonstrating a machine, which was exclusively

2. IP High Court, 30 December 2008 (2008 Heo 4943).
3. IP High Court, 30 December 2008 (2008 Heo 4936).
4. Seoul Southern District Court, 15 June 2001 (2001 KaHap 1074).

used for the patented process and was manufactured by the defendant as commissioned by the patent licensee, qualified as 'experimental use'.

In light of the above, it can be concluded that the interpretation of Article 96(1)(i) does not outright exclude research and testing that aim at commercial purposes.

e. Beneficiary Limitations

From the few cases on the exemption that have been issued in Korea, it seems likely that courts would conclude that if the experiments themselves are exempt from infringement, then a third party contributing to those experiments would also not be infringing.

f. Territoriality Issues

Based on the principle of territoriality, Korean courts and the IPTAB will only enforce patents that are granted in Korea.

In recent District Court decisions involving a defendant who manufactured and exported generic products for the purpose of seeking approval in a foreign country, regarding the act of manufacturing in Korea, the Court has considered the Experimental Use exemption as a defence against Korean patent infringement, even if the research and testing occurred outside of Korea.

g. Burden of Proof and Onus

The burden of proof of establishing that the Experimental Use exemption applies is on the party accused of patent infringement who asserts this defence.

h. Applicability during Patent Term Extension or Supplementary Protection Certificate

While Korean courts have not specifically addressed this issue, there appears to be little justification for differentiating between the original and extended patent terms when considering exemptions under Article 96(1)(i) of the KPA.

However, it is important to note that under the KPA, the scope of the patent during the patent term extension is generally narrower than the original term, as it is limited to practice of the patent in connection with the underlying approval (e.g. the approved drug indication).

3. THE BOLAR-TYPE EXEMPTION

a. History and Rationale of Adopting the Bolar-Type Exemption

Under KPA Article 96(1)(i), the scope of rights to a patented invention does not extend to 'the use of a patented invention for research or testing purposes'. The Bolar-type exemption has been recognized as a form of 'research or testing' under Article 96(1)(i) in Korea.

In the case of *Binex v. Sanofi-Aventis et al.*, Binex manufactured its generic drug containing the active ingredient of a patented invention, conducted a bioequivalence test and obtained conditional approval for the generic drug from the health authority. Similarly, in the case of *SamChunDang Pharm. v. Sanofi-Aventis et al.*, SamChunDang manufactured its generic drug containing the active ingredient of a patented invention, conducted comparative dissolution tests, and applied for product approval for its generic drug. Furthermore, in the decision of *Syngenta Participations AG v. LG CI*, LG CI manufactured its generic pesticide falling within the scope of the patented invention and requested tests necessary to obtain test results for registration of a generic pesticide, in order to sell the generic pesticide after patent expiration. In these cases, courts have interpreted such activities as being covered by the Bolar-type exemption.

Following these case decisions, the KPA was amended in 2010 to add the parenthetical phrase 'including research or testing to obtain regulatory approval under the Pharmaceutical Affairs Act and for registration of agrochemicals under the Agrochemicals Control Act,' to clarify that research and testing activities that do not fall within the scope of a patent right include research and testing for generic drug approval under the Pharmaceutical Affairs Act and generic pesticide registration under the Agrochemicals Control Act.

b. The Laws Applicable to the Bolar-Type Exemption in Korea

The existence of the Bolar-type exemption is clear from the parenthesis in Article 96(1) of the KPA (i.e. 'including research or testing to obtain regulatory approval under the Pharmaceutical Affairs Act'). This was introduced in 2010 to clarify that 'research or testing' in Article 96 includes research or testing conducted to seek regulatory approval for pharmaceutical products.

In Korea, the Bolar-type exemption is regarded as a type of Experimental Use exemption and is evaluated using the same standards.

That is, Korean courts assess whether the implementation of a patented invention qualifies as 'research or testing' under Article 96(1)(i) of the KPA, based on a comprehensive consideration of several factors, including (i) whether the primary purpose is to investigate the novelty or inventive step of the patented invention, (ii) whether it is aimed at researching or testing the feasibility of the patented invention, (iii) whether the patented invention achieves the effects disclosed in the patent specification, or conversely, (iv) whether the purpose is to evaluate the marketability or economic viability of the patented invention, (v) whether the implementation is utilized as a tool or means for developing another invention, or (vi) whether the research or testing results in prototypes or products being released in the market, which could potentially harm or pose a risk to the interests of the patent holder.[5]

c. Procedural Aspects of Invoking the Bolar-Type Exemption

The Bolar-type exemption can be used as a defence in litigation or scope confirmation actions. In Korea, litigation falls under the jurisdiction of the District Court, IP High

5. *See The Welding Institute v. Wooshin EMC Co., supra.*

Court, and Supreme Court, while scope confirmation actions are under the jurisdiction of the IPTAB, IP High Court, and Supreme Court.

Therefore, the bodies that can determine whether the Bolar-type exemption applies include the IPTAB, District Court, IP High Court, and Supreme Court.

d. Scope of Bolar-Type Exemption in Korea

i. Fields of Technology

Article 96 expressly recites research or testing for the approval of pharmaceuticals under the Pharmaceutical Affairs Act and for the registration of pesticides under the Agrochemicals Control Act as relevant to the Bolar-type exemption. As such, it appears that the Bolar-type exemption is currently limited to pharmaceutical products and pesticide products.

ii. Purpose of Experiments/Infringing Activities

Acts that fall under the Bolar-type exemption include several key activities relating to development and approval of generic/biosimilar products.

Specifically, in *Binex v. Sanofi-Aventis et al.* and *SamChunDang Pharm. v. Sanofi-Aventis et al.*, the generics conducted bioequivalence testing or comparative dissolution testing and applied for generic drug approval, and obtained conditional approval for the generic drug from the health authority, which the IP High Court recognized as being covered by the Bolar-type exemption, as discussed above in section 3.a.

iii. Exempted and Prohibited Activities

Clinical trials for phases 1 to 3 (conducted before approval) would be covered by the Bolar-type exemption. However, the law is not yet clear regarding phase 4 clinical trials, which occur after a generic product has been approved. One District Court has ruled that phase 4 clinical trials also are exempt from infringement.[6]

Regarding stockpiling, while there have not yet been any binding decisions on this issue in Korea, a few lower court cases have suggested that stockpiling as such is prohibited. One District Court has ruled that stockpiling products constitutes patent infringement if the infringer imports active pharmaceutical ingredients in quantities significantly exceeding what is necessary for obtaining regulatory approval, since this would suggest that these products were intended for sale as soon as the patent expired.[7] Conversely, another court has concluded that storing products that were previously manufactured for the purpose of testing in order to secure approval is exempt from infringement, as this practice could be viewed as an extension of the testing process.[8]

---

6. *BMS et al. v. Dong-A ST*, Seoul Central District Court, 10 June 2016 (2014 Ga Hab 560217).
7. *Novartis AG v. SK Chemicals*, Seoul Central District Court, 18 December 2012 (2012 KaHap 2694).
8. *Binex v. Sanofi-Aventis et al., supra.*

e. Beneficiary Limitations

There has not yet been any binding case law on this issue, but nothing in the statute prevents the exemption from applying not only to generic companies seeking regulatory approval, but also to innovator companies conducting comparative studies with competing drugs, or even third parties commissioned to conduct studies on behalf of those applying for regulatory approval, such as clinical research organizations, hospitals, or clinics.

In a recent Supreme Court decision involving a defendant who exported generic products to a third party in Russia for purposes of seeking approval, the Court ruled that Article 96(1)(i) does apply to the defendant's act of manufacturing.[9] In the case, the plaintiff argued that Article 96(1)(i) does not apply since the third party, which conducted clinical studies using the generic products to obtain its own generic approval in Russia, performed the research and testing solely for its own benefit, not for that of the defendant. However, at the intermediate appeal stage, the IP High Court rejected the argument based on the finding that (i) Article 96(1)(i) does not impose any requirement that the person conducting the research and testing must be the same as the one practising the patented invention, and (ii) it would be unreasonable not to apply the exemption considering that many pharmaceutical companies have outsourced manufacturing to Contract Manufacturing Organizations. The Supreme Court affirmed the IP High Court's decision, so the decision has become final and conclusive.

This decision suggests that if a third party conducts research and testing not only on behalf of a person practising a patented invention (e.g., clinical research organizations, hospitals, or clinics) but also for its own benefit (e.g., seeking its own approval), the Bolar-type exemption under Article 96(1)(i) is likely to apply.

f. Territoriality Issues

In recent District Court decisions involving defendants who manufactured and exported generic products for purposes of seeking approval in foreign countries, regarding the act of manufacturing in Korea, the Court has considered the Experimental Use exemption (Bolar-type exemption) to be a defence against Korean patent infringement, even if the clinical studies were conducted outside of Korea for purposes of a foreign regulatory submission.

Those decisions suggest that the Bolar-type exemption may apply even if the purpose is a regulatory submission in a foreign country.

g. Burden of Proof and Onus

The burden of proof of establishing that the Bolar-type exemption applies lies with the party accused of patent infringement.

In a recent case involving a biosimilar company that invoked the Bolar-type exemption in a patent infringement preliminary injunction action, the Seoul Central

9. *Wyeth LLC et al. v. SK Bioscience*, Supreme Court, 15 May 2025 (2025 Da 202970).

District Court determined that the burden of proof of this defence rested with the biosimilar companies and any entities utilizing the patent before expiration. The Court concluded that the biosimilar companies failed to adequately demonstrate that their manufacturing and export activities during the patent's term qualified for the research and testing exemption. While the biosimilar companies presented evidence that their actions were solely for approval-related purposes, the Court ruled in favour of the patent holder. The Court considered the overall quantity of products manufactured and exported, as well as the likelihood that these products could later be sold commercially following research and testing.

h. Applicability during Patent Term Extension or Supplementary Protection Certificate

While Korean courts have not yet addressed this specific issue, the KPA discusses limits to the effect of 'patents' without distinguishing between original and extended patent terms. Thus, there appears to be no compelling reason to differentiate between them for purposes of these exemptions. However, it is important to note that under the Act, the scope of a patent during a patent term extension is generally narrower than during the original term, as it is limited to practices related to the specific approval underlying the patent term extension grant (e.g. the approved drug indication).

4. DIFFERENCES BETWEEN THE TWO EXCEPTIONS IN KOREA

In Korea, the Bolar-type exemption is regarded as a type of Experimental Use exemption and is evaluated using the same standards. Thus, there is no substantial difference between the two exemptions in terms of key legal principles.

The Experimental Use exemption tends to be applied more broadly than in other major patent jurisdictions, particularly the United States. This is likely motivated by the belief that advancing technology throughout the field is a higher priority in Korea than in other countries. However, as Korea's economy has matured and developed, it has become increasingly necessary to modify and clarify these exemptions to align with practices in other developed countries.

Enhanced patent protection plays a crucial role in encouraging inventors to invest in new R&D, especially in fields such as biologics and pharmaceuticals. Therefore, as patent practitioners, we believe that the Bolar-type exemption should be applied more narrowly, and to be limited to activities that are genuinely necessary for obtaining regulatory approval, rather than the current broader interpretations we see in practice. This approach could help streamline the resolution of disputes relating to pharmaceuticals, as the Bolar case law continues to evolve.

Chapter 35

Spain

Nicolas Vincent Ruiz, Raúl Bercovitz and Enrique Armijo Chávarri

1. GENERAL

a. Terminology

The Experimental Use exemption is codified in Article 61.1.b) of the Spanish Patent Act, though, interestingly, the term 'Experimental' is not defined. It should therefore be understood to have the meaning generally admitted in the language.

The wording 'Bolar-type' does not appear in the Patent Act but is commonly used, including in this chapter, to refer to the exemption of infringement provided in Article 61.1.c) of the Patent Act – when activities are studies or trials necessary to obtain regulatory approval for a medicinal product.

'Exemption' in the context of the foregoing is to be understood as an exception to the exclusivity right conferred by a patent and relates to activities that without such exception would be considered as violating and infringing the patent right of the owner.

The terms 'innovative medicinal products' and 'generic medicinal products' are used within this chapter, and are intended to have their generally admitted definitions.

It is noted that SPCs for medicinal products are available in Spain, as under the jurisdiction of the Regulation (EC) No. 469/2009 of the European Parliament and of the Council of 6 May 2009.

b. Legal Basis in Spain

At present, the Spanish Patent Law Act 24/2015 (which derogated and substituted the Patent Act 11/1986) contains an Experimental Use exemption for acts done for experimental purposes, as well as a Bolar-type exemption for use ('studies and trials') necessary for the purpose of obtaining marketing approval for a medicament in Spain or outside of Spain. These are found in Article 61.1.b) and 61.1.c) of the Patent Law Act, as follows:

> Article 61. General limits and exhaustion of patent rights.
>
> 1. The rights conferred by the patent do not extend:
>
> ...
>
> (b) To acts carried out for experimental purposes that refer to the object of the patented invention.
>
> (c) To the realization of the studies and trials necessary to obtain authorisation for the marketing of medicinal products in Spain or outside Spain, and the consequent practical requirements, including the preparation, obtention and use of the active ingredient for these purposes.

c. Bodies That May Decide on the Legitimacy of Exemptions

In Spain, bodies that may decide on the legitimacy of the patent exemptions are the competent Commercial Courts in first instance (only designated commercial courts in the cities of Madrid, Barcelona, Valencia, Granada, A Coruña, Las Palmas and Bilbao), which may be appealed to the corresponding Provincial Court. Finally, the Supreme Court may serve as a third and last instance, when the requisites for filing an appeal in cassation, which are quite restrictive, are met.

2. THE EXPERIMENTAL USE EXEMPTION

a. History and Rationale of Adopting the Experimental Use Exemption

The Experimental Use exemption was enacted for the first time in the former Spanish Patent Act 11/1986, in Article 52.1.b:

> Article 52
>
> 1. The rights contained in the patent do not extend: ...
>
> (b) To acts performed for experimental purposes relating to the object of the patented invention, ...

This provision has been maintained in the new Spanish Patent Act 24/2015 currently in force, with a slightly different wording that does not affect the scope but is aimed to be more precise: 'relating' is replaced by 'that refer to'.

b. The Laws Applicable to the Experimental Use Exemption in Spain

The Spanish Patent Act 24/2015 contemplates the limitation of the rights of the patentee against acts done for experimental purposes in Article 61.1.b):

> Article 61. General limits and exhaustion of patent rights.
>
> 1. The rights conferred by the patent do not extend: ...
>
> (b) To acts carried out for experimental purposes that refer to the object of the patented invention.

c. Procedural Aspects of Invoking the Experimental Use Exemption

The Experimental Use exemption is defined as an exception to the right conferred by the patent and, as such, is used as defence in litigation proceedings, mainly infringement proceedings.

In Spain, such proceedings are under the jurisdiction of some Commercial Courts specifically designated as competent by the General Council of the Judiciary (CGPJ). Only designated Commercial Courts in the cities of Madrid, Barcelona, Valencia, Granada, A Coruña, Las Palmas and Bilbao may be competent, depending on the place of infringement and/or defendant's domicile. Namely:

Andalusia: Commercial Court No. 1 of Granada.
Catalonia: Commercial Courts Nos. 1, 4 and 5 of Barcelona.
Madrid: Commercial Courts Nos. 7, 8, 9, 10 of Madrid.
Valencia: Commercial Court No. 2 of Valencia.
Galicia: Commercial Courts No. 1 and 2 of A Coruña.
Canary Islands: Commercial Courts Nos. 1 and 2 of Las Palmas.
Basque Country: Commercial Court No. 2 of Bilbao.

d. Scope of the Experimental Use Exemption in Spain

i. Fields of Technology

There are no technology field limitations or restrictions on the Experimental Use exemption in Spain. Any type of technology may benefit from the exemption.

ii. Purpose of Experiments/Infringing Activities

The exemption of infringement for experimental use is considered by Spanish Law as a right (although it is frequently used as a defence in other proceedings) and has been interpreted by courts in a narrow manner (see in particular Supreme Court Ruling, Pfizer vs Cinfa, No. 424/2010, Civil Chamber). It is not limited to acts done for academic purposes but includes acts carried out for the purposes of experimentation or trial exclusively of a technical or scientific nature. The purpose of the experiments does constitute a limitation on the exemption.

The exemption is limited to experimental acts *referring to* the object of the patented invention. Consequently, acts carried out *with* the object of the patented invention are not exempt when performed for purposes other than experiments *on* the patented object. In other words, acts performed using the object of a patented invention for any purposes not related to said object will be considered as infringement.

Spanish patent law does not specifically refer to exploitation of patented inventions as research tools. Although the exemption refers to experimental use, without stating any detailed activities, the fact that the Patent Act refers to 'experimental purposes that refer to the object of the patented invention' appears to implicitly exclude the use of the invention as a research tool aiming at experimenting with other objects or matters.

iii. Exempted and Prohibited Activities

Any acts realized *with* the object of the patented invention are excluded from the Experimental Use exemption.

If the patented invention is used for experimental purposes *on* a specimen or sample of the object patented itself, importation of said specimen or sample would not amount to infringement. But importation or commercialization of units of such product on a commercial scale would not be permitted.

The purpose of the activities, whether importation, purchase, or possession with a view to sale or trade, testing, comparing to another product that is contemplated as a non-infringing competitor, cannot qualify for Experimental Use exemption as long as those activities are not realized *on* the object patented itself, but *with* it.

iv. Pure Academic vs Commercially Motivated Experimental Use

There is no requirement that activities should be done for 'academic purposes' having 'no commercial value': although no Spanish court decision has specifically addressed this aspect, it appears that the Experimental Use exemption may be extended to commercial activities. However, they are limited to experiments *on* the object. After activities and/or experiments are conducted on the object of the patented invention, if an innovation based on such activities or experiments is obtained, such innovation should be evaluated for infringement before it is used or offered for sale.

e. Beneficiary Limitations

Spanish law does not relate the acts excluded from the rights conferred by the patent with the author of said acts. Consequently, it may be interpreted that experimental acts are excluded from patent infringement, whether conducted by persons promoting/financing the experiments or by third persons contracted by the former, if said acts constitute experiments *on* the object of the patented invention.

f. Territoriality Issues

The supply of the patented invention for experimental use in another jurisdiction would not amount to patent infringement in Spain, if the purpose of the use is limited to experimental acts *on* the object patented invention. Precaution should be taken when exchanging or shipping the product in order to make clear the purpose of the object/invention supplied.

g. Burden of Proof and Onus

Since there is no specific court decision addressing this aspect, the usual interpretation for patent infringement should be taken into consideration. This means that the defendant should bear the burden of proof to show that the exemption applies.

h. Applicability during Patent Term Extension or Supplementary Protection Certificate

The Experimental Use exemption also applies during any patent term extension, for example, during the life of a supplementary protection certificate (SPC).

3. THE BOLAR-TYPE EXEMPTION

a. History and Rationale of Adopting the Bolar-Type Exemption

The Bolar-type exemption was enacted for the first time in Spain in Article 52.1 b) of the Patent Act 11/1986, of 20 March 1986 after the legislative reform operated by Act 29/2006, of 26 July 2006.

In the former Patent Act 11/1986 (Art. 52.1.b)), the Bolar-type exemption was limited to activities related to the obtention of a marketing authorization for generic medicine only. This limitation disappeared from the wording in the current Spanish Patent Act in order to clarify the necessary use of a patented invention in order to comply with regulatory requirements for any kind of medicinal product (not only for generics). The Bolar-type exemption under current Spanish Act 24/2015 relates to 'studies and trials necessary for the purpose of obtaining Marketing Approval for a medicament'. The drafting does not address the nature of the medicinal product – i.e. whether the product is a generic medicine or an innovative medicine. As such, using the object of a patented invention with the purpose of generating regulatory data requested to obtain a marketing authorization is not considered as patent infringement. The exemption should be broadly interpreted to apply to any medicament or medicinal product.

b. The Laws Applicable to the Bolar-Type Exemption in Spain

Spanish Patent Act 24/2015 contemplates the limitation of the rights of the patentee against use ('studies and trials') for the purpose of obtaining marketing approval for a medicament in Spain or outside of Spain:

> Article 61. General limits and exhaustion of patent rights.
>
> 1. The rights conferred by the patent do not extend:
>
> ...
>
> (c) To the carrying out of the studies and trials necessary to obtain authorisation for the marketing of medicinal products in Spain or outside Spain, and the consequent practical requirements, including the preparation, obtention and use of the active ingredient for these purposes.

c. Procedural Aspects of Invoking the Bolar-Type Exemption

The Bolar-type exemption is defined as an exception to the right conferred by the patent and as such, is used as defence in litigation proceedings, mainly infringement proceedings. In Spain, such proceedings are under the jurisdiction of some

Commercial Courts specifically designated as competent by the CGPJ. Reference is made to section 2.c. above for details.

d. Scope of the Bolar-Type Exemption in Spain

i. Fields of Technology

The Bolar-type exemption in Spain is limited to medicinal products by the current drafting of the Patent Act. Any type of technology and activities may use the exemption as long as it is required or requested by regulatory authorities for the obtention of a marketing authorization of a *medicinal* product.

ii. Purpose of Experiments/Infringing Activities

The scope of the Bolar-type exemption is not limited in time according to Spanish regulation. Any purpose would be accepted to qualify as exempted from infringement as long as the activities are required or requested by regulatory authorities for *medicinal* products. For example, importation, purchase, manufacturing, comparing with an existing drug would be permitted if such acts are carried out solely for the purpose of the invention being used in a clinical trial for submission to a regulatory medicinal agency, in Spain or elsewhere. Likewise, research for improving an old invention may be included in the Bolar-type exemption, but only if necessary to generate regulatory data for marketing approval.

iii. Exempted and Prohibited Activities

Under Spanish law, clinical trials are considered as 'necessary studies and trials' for the purpose of obtaining marketing approval. Consequently, they are exempted from patent infringement. There is no difference between the different Phases 1, 2 or 3. Phase 4 clinical trials are not necessary for the obtention of the marketing authorization and there are serious doubts as to whether they are exempted. Additionally, Phase 4 clinical studies are typically performed after authorization for marketing has been obtained, and as such would represent activities not exempted.

'Stockpiling' generally refers to manufacturing and/or keeping quantities of the product before the lapse of a patent, in order to start marketing (using and selling) said product as quickly as possible after the patent lapse. Consequently, it cannot be considered as an experimental act, or as an act necessary to obtain a marketing authorization. As such it is not permitted under Spanish law. Nevertheless, some authors consider that a conflict of law exists between Patent Act 24/2015 and Act 29/2006 of 26 July 2006, on guarantees and rational use of medicines and health products. The latter states that a pharmaceutical company that holds a marketing authorization is obliged to supply medicaments on the legal conditions established and further that it is obliged to maintain a minimum stock that guarantees adequate continuity of supply. If stockpiling concerns a generic medicine, some opinions consider that a limited stockpiling should be permitted for an authorized generic in order to allow a proper supply quickly after the lapse of the patent. Those arguing in that sense state that it follows that if this were not permitted it would extend *de facto* the duration of the patent, delaying the availability of an authorized medicine to patients.

Activities related to seeking pricing and reimbursement listing are not specifically excluded from rights conferred by the patent under Spanish law. Some case law considered that these activities, and particularly the obtention of price or reimbursement listing, does constitute a patent infringement. During the preparatory discussions of the current Patent Act, the drafting of the new Article 61.1.c) was thought to exempt acts strictly necessary to obtain marketing authorization, as long as they do not consist in acts to prepare access to market. Accordingly, it is not clear under Spanish law whether pricing and reimbursement listing activities would even be considered infringement, though if they were, they would likely not be considered necessary for obtaining marketing approval and they likely would not be exempt under the Bolar-type exemption.

e. Beneficiary Limitations

As indicated above, the Bolar-type exemption in Spain applies both to generic product-related activities and innovative product-related activities. The Spanish Patent Act does not relate the exempted activities with the author. Such exemption should thus apply to third parties performing *studies and trials* on behalf of the party seeking regulatory approval for the medicinal product. Studies and trials are excluded from patent infringement, whether conducted by persons conducting promoting/financing the studies or trials or by third persons contracted by the former, if said acts are aimed at obtaining regulatory approval.

f. Territoriality Issues

From the drafting of the Spanish law, it appears that the Bolar-type exemption applies without territorial limitation where the obtention of a marketing authorization is the purpose of the studies/trials which are being carried out. The activities may relate to either Spanish or foreign marketing authorization. Activities performed in another jurisdiction for the purpose of Spanish regulatory approval should be subject to that specific jurisdiction's practice and law.

g. Burden of Proof and Onus

Spanish patent law is silent on the party bearing the burden of proof that the exemption should apply. Consequently, general practice may apply, and the defendant in a patent infringement litigation should prove that its activities are exempted from infringement under the Bolar exemption.

h. Applicability during Patent Term Extension or Supplementary Protection Certificate

The Bolar-type exemption also applies during any patent term extension, for example, during the life of an SPC.

4. DIFFERENCES BETWEEN THE TWO EXCEPTIONS IN SPAIN

The main difference between the Experimental Use exemption and the Bolar-type exemption lies in the limitation of the latter to activities required for regulatory approval for a medicinal product. The purpose of the experiments, studies or trials is different in both exemptions. The exception of experimental use applies to any technological field whereas the Bolar-type exemption is limited to the medicinal field.

Chapter 36

Sweden

Anna Bladh Redzic and Emma Sandler

1. GENERAL

a. Terminology

Both the Experimental Use exemption and the Bolar-type exemption are considered to be just that, exemptions to infringement as they by their wording are considered to fall outside the scope of protection of the exclusive rights conferred by a patent.

b. Legal Basis in Sweden

The Experimental Use exemption is codified in Chapter 1 Section 3 Paragraph 3 Item 3 of the Patent Act (1967:837). According to said provision the exclusive right granted through a patent does not entail uses of an invention for experiments concerning the invention.

There is also a Bolar-type exemption in Chapter 1 Section 3 Paragraph 3 Item 4 of the Patent Act which states that the exclusive right granted through a patent does not entail studies, tests, examinations and practical measures attributable to a reference pharmaceutical to such extent necessary to obtain a marketing approval for a human or a veterinary medicinal product in the EU or Sweden.

Sweden has also ratified the Agreement on a Unified Patent Court (UPCA) which means that it is a part of the Unified Patent Court (UPC).

The UPCA contains an Experimental Use exemption in Article 27(c) as well as a Bolar-type exemption in Article 27(d), which are dealt with in the UPCA chapter of this book.

The UPC entered into force on 1 June 2023.

2. THE EXPERIMENTAL USE EXEMPTION

a. History and Rationale of Adopting the Experimental Use Exemption

The Experimental Use exemption in the Swedish Patents Act was adopted in 1978 but even before that it was considered part of the case law regarding the scope of the patent protection.[1] According to the *travaux préparatoires*, the basis of the exemption is that patents do not protect use of the invention as a source of knowledge or as a basis for continued research relating to the invention itself (prop. 2003/04:55 s. 124). An important limitation of the exemption is that it applies solely to experimental use relating to the invention, rather than use of the invention (e.g. a measuring tool) for other research fields. The adoption of the exemption in the Patents Act was made to correspond to the exemption in the Convention for the European Patent for the Common Market (Community Patent Convention).

b. The Laws Applicable to the Experimental Use Exemption in Sweden

The Experimental Use exemption is codified in Chapter 1 Section 3 Paragraph 3 Item 3 of the Patent Act and is formulated as an exemption for 'use of an invention for experiments relating to the invention itself'. There is no case law on the scope of the Experimental Use exemption in Sweden. However, exemptions to the protection afforded by intellectual property rights are generally interpreted narrowly in Swedish case law. A Bolar-type exemption was also later adopted, as such use of the invention was considered to fall outside the scope of the Experimental Use exemption.

c. Procedural Aspects of Invoking the Experimental Use Exemption

The Patent and Market Court and Patent and Market Court of Appeal have exclusive jurisdiction in Sweden to try national patent cases. The Experimental Use exemption could be invoked by a defendant in an infringement case, however there is no case law concerning the scope of the Experimental Use exemption in Sweden.

d. Scope of the Experimental Use Exemption in Sweden

i. Fields of Technology

There are no field-of-technology-based limitations or restrictions on the Experimental Use exemption in Sweden. All types of technology may utilize such a exemption.

ii. Purpose of Experiments/Infringing Activities

The Experimental Use exemption can only be relied on for research *on* the invention and not *with* the invention. A classic example is that it does not cover the use of a

1. Government bill prop. 1977/78:1 p. 201.

patented measuring tool for research concerning another invention. According to the *travaux préparatoires*, research on the invention within the meaning of the Experimental Use exemption does cover research with the aim of improving the invention (prop. 2003/2004:55 page 124). Furthermore, the exemption covers some research concerning the collection of data. In Swedish doctrine, the view has been expressed that the exemption is applicable to research which aims to verify data described in the patent, which can be used by competitors to lodge revocation actions.[2]

iii. *Exempted and Prohibited Activities*

It is not clear whether clinical trials conducted to obtain a marketing approval fall within the scope of the Experimental Use exemption (such trials can however fall within the Bolar-type exemption, see more below).

As there is no case law concerning the scope of the Experimental Use exemption, no definite list of allowed activities can be provided. That said, the wording of the provision does not contain any limitation as to which 'use' is encompassed by the exemption. Thus, any use such as manufacture, storage, importation would likely be allowed as long as the use is for the purpose of doing experiments on the invention. In this regard, it is relevant to mention also the principle of exhaustion as this principle would also allow for a right to reverse engineering for patented products that have been put on the market with the consent of the patent holder.

iv. *Pure Academic vs Commercially Motivated Experimental Use*

The Experimental Use exemption in Sweden is not limited to purely academic research but also covers commercial activities. Thus, the research can be made with the aim *inter alia* of obtaining data for a revocation action or to improve the invention. The research does not need to directly result in a sale or profit for the exemption to apply.

e. Beneficiary Limitations

There is no case law or other statement in the *travaux préparatoires* which can provide any guidance on beneficiary limitations. Thus, the legal situation is unclear in this respect.

f. Territoriality Issues

There is no case law or other statement in the *travaux préparatoires* which can provide any guidance on territoriality issues. Thus, the legal situation is unclear in this respect.

g. Burden of Proof and Onus

According to general procedural principles, the burden of proof is likely on the defendant to show the circumstances giving rise to the exemption. The level of proof

2. Domeij, B, Pharmaceutical Patents in Europe, Stockholm 2000, page 296.

required would likely be rather high (shown), unless there are evidentiary difficulties for the defendant which would motivate a lower or reversed burden of proof.

h. Applicability during Patent Term Extension or Supplementary Protection Certificate

The exemption is not limited in time. As a result, the exemption applies during an SPC or similar period.

3. THE BOLAR-TYPE EXEMPTION

a. History and Rationale of Adopting the Bolar-Type Exemption

The Bolar-type exemption in the Patents Act was adopted in 2006 as part of incorporating EU Directives regarding veterinary and human medicinal products into Swedish law. The background to its incorporation is that European case law had held that the studies required by generic companies to obtain marketing authorization for generic medicines were not covered by the Experimental Use exemption. This had resulted in necessary studies being put on hold until the patent, or SPC, had expired, causing delay in the market access. Adopting a Bolar-type exemption would allow for generic drugs to be tested during the patent term and be put on the market upon expiration. The exemption implements the Bolar-type exemption in Article 1.8.6 of the EU Directive 2004/27/EG amending the Human Medicinal Products Directive. Sweden chose to incorporate only the minimum level Bolar-type exemption provided for in the relevant EU Directive. Thus, compared to other EU Member States, Sweden is considered as one of the countries which has a relatively narrow Bolar-type exemption.[3]

b. The Laws Applicable to the Bolar-Type Exemption in Sweden

The Bolar-type exemption is codified in Chapter 1 Section 3 Paragraph 3 Item 4 of the Patent Act and is formulated as follows:

> the following are exempted from infringement:
>
> studies, tests, investigations and practical measures attributable to a reference pharmaceutical to the extent necessary to obtain approval for sale of a pharmaceutical with application of chapter 4, section 13 of the Pharmaceuticals Act (SFS 2015:315) or in other procedures for approval which are based on Article 10.1–4 of Directive 2001/83/EC of the European Parliament and of the Council of 6 November 2001 on the Community code related to medicinal products for human use, worded in accordance with Directive 2004/27/EC of the European Parliament and of the Council, or Article 13.1 of Directive 2001/82/EC of 6 November 2001 on the Community code relating to veterinary medicinal products, worded in accordance with Regulation (EC) No. 596/2009

3. See government bill prop. 2005/06:70 and Hellstadius, Bolarundantaget i förändring, Magna Mater vänskrift till Marianne Levin, 2022, p. 83 ff.

of the European Parliament and of the Council, or Article 13.2–13.5 of Directive 2001/82/EC, worded in accordance with Regulation (EC) No. 2004/28 of the European Parliament and of the Council.

Accordingly, the scope of the Swedish Bolar-type exemption corresponds to the wording of Article 10(6) of the Human Medicinal Products Directive and thus refers to those measures related to a reference medicinal product that are necessary to obtain a marketing authorization for generic products or biosimilars. The exemption also covers activities to obtain a marketing authorization in Sweden or in other EU Member States but not in other countries. However, the Bolar-type exemption has never been tested in Swedish case law and its scope in Swedish law is not fully clarified. It has been discussed, among other things, whether the exemption could also be used for innovative products. However, exemptions to the protection afforded by intellectual property rights are generally interpreted narrowly in Swedish case law.

c. Procedural Aspects of Invoking the Bolar-Type Exemption

The Patent and Market Court and Patent and Market Court of Appeal have exclusive jurisdiction in Sweden to try national patent cases. The Experimental Use exemption could be invoked by a defendant in an infringement case, however there is no case law concerning the scope of the Experimental Use exemption in Sweden.

d. Scope of the Bolar-Type Exemption in Sweden

i. Fields of Technology

The Swedish Bolar-type exemption is limited to pharmaceuticals (for human and veterinary use).

ii. Purpose of Experiments/Infringing Activities

The Bolar-type exemption is limited to research necessary to obtain a marketing approval in accordance with the legislation mentioned above. This usually entails pre-clinical and clinical trials. Research made with the aim of improving an invention but that is not necessary to obtain a marketing approval does not fall under the Bolar-type exemption (but can be exempt under the Experimental Use exemption).

iii. Exempted and Prohibited Activities

The limit is drawn against what is a necessary study, test, investigation and practical measure to obtain a marketing approval. Therefore, it is the regulatory authority's requirements of necessary documentation that set the frame for necessary measures. According to the *travaux préparatoires* the patent holder can likely not object to measures such as import, manufacturing, deposition or making available of the reference pharmaceutical as long as the measures are necessary to obtain a marketing approval. It is also reasonable to assume that some development work regarding manufacturing methods, analysis methods and so on can be carried out under the exemption. The exemption solely applies to the patent pertaining to the reference pharmaceutical and not any other protected method, substance or combination of protected substances (prop. 2005/06:70 pp. 181-183). The exact scope of allowed measures has however not been clarified in any case law.

e. Beneficiary Limitations

The exemption is applicable to generic pharmaceuticals and biosimilars as well as veterinary products. Whether it is applicable to innovative drugs is a debated question and is as yet unclear.[4] Whether the person seeking regulatory approval can contract a third party for performance of any of the necessary measures is unresolved.

f. Territoriality Issues

The exemption applies to applications for regulatory approval in Sweden or other EU Member States.

The exemption likely does not apply if the results of the experiment are used for infringing a corresponding patent in another jurisdiction. This is because the exemption is only applicable to the patent covering the reference pharmaceutical.

Whether the person seeking regulatory approval can contract a third party for performance of any of the necessary measures is unclear under Swedish law.

g. Burden of Proof and Onus

According to general procedural principles, the burden of proof is likely on the defendant to show the circumstances giving rise to the exemption. The level of proof required would likely be rather high (shown), unless there are evidentiary difficulties for the defendant which would motivate a lower or reversed burden of proof.

h. Applicability during Patent Term Extension or Supplementary Protection Certificate

The exemption is not limited in time. As a result, the exemption applies during an SPC or similar period.

4. DIFFERENCES BETWEEN THE TWO EXEMPTIONS IN SWEDEN

In Sweden, the Experimental Use exemption is quite broadly defined. In comparison, the Bolar-type exemption is limited in many ways, in that it is limited to uses necessary to obtain a marketing authorization for generic products or biosimilars. That said, the Bolar-type exemption is also broader in many ways, in that it can include activities that might not be covered under the Experimental Use exemption. Thus, the exemptions are distinct and separate.

4. Hellstadius, Bolarundantaget i förändring, Magna Mater vänskrift till Marianne Levin, 2022.

Chapter 37

Switzerland

Simon Holzer

1. GENERAL

a. Terminology

Article 9(1) of the Swiss Patent Act (PatA) lists exceptions to the right of exclusivity granted by a patent. Article 9(1)(b) and (c) codify the Experimental Use exemption and the Bolar-type exemption, respectively. In the case of these exceptions, the patentee's exclusive rights are limited; the patentee has neither the right to injunctive relief nor the right to assert further claims, such as a claim for financial compensation.

b. Legal Basis in Switzerland

Article 9(1) PatA reads as follows:

> The effects of the patent do not extend to:
>
> ...
>
> b. acts undertaken for research or experimental purposes in order to obtain knowledge about the subject-matter of the invention including its uses; in particular, any scientific research concerning the subject-matter of the invention permitted [Experimental Use exemption];
>
> c. acts necessary for obtaining marketing authorization for a medicinal product in Switzerland or in countries with equivalent medicinal product control [Bolar-type exemption];
>
> ...

Article 9(2) PatA reads as follows:

> Agreements which limit or revoke the powers contained in paragraph 1 are null and void.

Since its entry into force, there have been very few judgments by Swiss courts on Article 9 PatA.[1] In addition, no further regulations have been enacted to define or regulate the exceptions in more detail.

2. THE EXPERIMENTAL USE EXEMPTION

a. History and Rationale of Adopting the Experimental Use Exemption

Before Article 9(1)(b) PatA was introduced, Swiss legal scholars agreed that an experimental use exception existed under Swiss law even without a specific statutory basis. However, there was no consensus on its scope, which led to increasing legal uncertainty. This issue was resolved in 2005 with a major revision of the Swiss Patent Act. Article 9 PatA entered into force on 1 July 2008.

In its message concerning the planned amendment of the Swiss Patent Act of 23 November 2005, the Swiss Federal Council expressed its concern that the legal situation without a clear statutory basis for an Experimental Use exemption could hinder research and investments particularly in the field of biotechnology, and emphasized the importance of the freedom of research and the need for legal certainty due to the progress of the technology.

Legal certainty in the field of patent law is crucial for the innovation process, especially in Switzerland, where the pharma and biotechnology sector has shown growth rates well above the average of other jurisdictions.

b. The Laws Applicable to the Experimental Use Exemption in Switzerland

The Experimental Use exemption is codified in Article 9(1)(b) PatA:

> b. acts undertaken for research or experimental purposes in order to obtain knowledge about the subject-matter of the invention including its uses; in particular, any scientific research concerning the subject-matter of the invention permitted [Experimental Use exemption];

Contractual agreements that limit or revoke this exemption are null and void, which prevents the undermining of the exemption as a result of unequal bargaining positions.

The explanatory notes to the Patent Act published by the Swiss Federal Council made it clear that the Experimental Use exemption and the other exemptions regulated in Article 9 PatA should be understood broadly.

Article 9(1)(b) PatA allows any systematic approach to obtaining knowledge *about* the subject of the patented invention, regardless of the purpose pursued.

The far-reaching Experimental Use exemption is complemented by Article 40b of the Patent Act, which stipulates a licence claim for the use of biotechnological research tools.

1. For one of the rare decisions, *see* e.g. Swiss the judgment of the Swiss Federal Patent Court of 3 January 2023 in the matter S2022_003.

c. Procedural Aspects of Invoking the Experimental Use Exemption

The Swiss Federal Patent Court has exclusive jurisdiction for the assessment of patent infringement issues.[2] Its decisions can be appealed to the Swiss Federal Supreme Court. This means that the Experimental Use exemption is examined by the Swiss Federal Patent Court in civil patent infringement proceedings (in summary proceedings and ordinary proceedings on the merits).

The Swiss Experimental Use exemption, as all the other exceptions set out in Article 9 PatA, arise and exist by virtue of the law, i.e. not only through a judicial act. Acts which are exempted do not infringe the patent rights of the patentee, i.e. these acts are lawful under Swiss law. This means that there is no participation in, contribution to, or instigation of such (exempted) acts under Swiss law. According to Swiss law, contributory infringement or instigation only exists if there is an unlawful (principal) act to which another act contributes. If there is no unlawful principal act, then there is no contributory infringement or instigation either.

The Experimental Use exemption is asserted as a defence argument of the alleged patent infringer in patent infringement proceedings or disputes. If the patentee demonstrates that an act falls under the Swiss Patent Act and realizes all the features of a valid patent claim, the defendant may object that this is an act undertaken for research or experimental purposes in order to obtain knowledge about the subject-matter of the invention including its uses; in particular, any scientific research concerning the subject-matter of the invention.

d. Scope of the Experimental Use Exemption in Switzerland

i. Fields of Technology

The Experimental Use exemption is not limited to a certain field of technology or specific products. It applies to academic research and also to commercial research in all technical areas as long as it is intended to gain additional knowledge about the patented subject-matter.

ii. Purpose of Experiments/Infringing Activities

Article 9(1)(b) PatA allows any systematic approach *to obtaining knowledge about* the subject-matter of the patented invention, regardless of the purpose pursued (i.e., the research can also be commercially oriented). The scope of the Swiss Experimental Use exemption is therefore very broad.

All experiments and studies that are aimed at gaining additional knowledge about the patented invention and/or are intended to further develop the patented technology (e.g., acts for the purpose of verifying the feasibility of the invention or for acquiring knowledge of its nature, effects, uses and possibilities for further development) are covered by the Experimental Use exemption. Experiments that go beyond this purpose require the permission of the patent holder. For example,

2. Article 26(1)(a) Patent Court Act.

gaining insights into commercial aspects such as market demand and price acceptance studies is not considered a valid purpose that is covered by the Swiss Experimental Use exemption.

Moreover, scientific research *with* the patented subject-matter does not fall under the Swiss Experimental Use exemption. The use of patented research tools is not covered by the exemption. However, an exception applies to biotechnical inventions when they are used as research means or tools (e.g. research with a biotechnological process). In such cases, researchers are entitled to a non-exclusive licence to use the biotechnological invention for their research, for an appropriate fee.[3]

iii. Exempted and Prohibited Activities

All testing and research activities that are performed to obtain additional knowledge about the patented invention are exempt from patent protection. As mentioned above, the Swiss Experimental Use exemption has a broad scope.

The exemption extends to all acts according to Article 8 PatA that are necessary for conducting the exempted research activities, such as the manufacturing, storage, importing, and exporting of goods and devices that are the subject of the exempted research.

The application of a patent-protected process and the use of the immediate results of a patented process is also lawful if this is necessary for gaining additional insights into the patented technology.

iv. Pure Academic vs Commercially Motivated Experimental Use

Under Swiss law, it is irrelevant whether the research activities are purely academic or commercially oriented. Contract research carried out with the intention of making a profit also falls under the Experimental Use exemption provided that it is aimed at gaining knowledge about the technical subject-matter of the patented invention.

e. Beneficiary Limitations

Swiss case law has not clarified yet whether third-party manufacturers may produce and offer for sale as well as market patented products subject to the condition that their customers use these products exclusively for experimental and research purposes. However, for the following reasons, this is likely to be the case under Swiss law:

In the light of the broad definition of the Swiss Experimental Use exemption, it is expected that Swiss courts would likely consider that it would frustrate the purpose of the Experimental Use exemption if it did not extend to third parties involved (e.g. as manufacturers or suppliers of the product to be investigated). For instance, in cases where a patented product is not available in a form suitable for research purposes and cannot be easily produced, the purpose of the Experimental

3. *See* Article 40b PatA.

Use exemption would be undermined if contributions of third parties were not covered by the exemption.

In a world based on the division of labour, it would be rather strange to request that an undertaking must carry out all preparatory steps for an experiment itself, namely the production of a device to be examined and its examination. Such a narrow interpretation of the Experimental Use exemption would unduly favour large companies over smaller companies, such as start-ups.

Finally, contributory patent infringement by third parties in Switzerland only arises if neither the contribution of the third party nor the principal act benefit from an exemption under Swiss patent law. Third parties who support an exempted activity in Switzerland without committing direct infringement (e.g. the supply of a machine to be used by another party in a patent-protected process or the supply of an agent for clinical trials if the agent is subject to second medical use patent protection) are not liable for contributory infringement under Swiss law if the principal act is exempted from patent protection.

f. Territoriality Issues

Whether the Swiss Experimental Use exemption applies if, for example, the results of an experiment are used for infringing a patent in another jurisdiction is a matter of private international law. In the area of intellectual property, the territorial scope of patents and exemptions is normally governed by each state. Whether acts with cross-border effects constitute patent infringing acts and what substantive law applies to the assessment of these activities is to be determined by the conflict of law rules of the jurisdiction(s) where protection is sought. If the Swiss conflict of law rules stipulate that certain activities shall be assessed under Swiss law (because they might infringe a patent that is valid in Switzerland), these activities may be exempted from patent protection under the Swiss Experimental Use doctrine.

g. Burden of Proof and Onus

Following general principles of Swiss law, it is the party who relies on the Experimental Use exemption who bears the burden of proof to show that the allegedly patent infringing acts were performed for experimental purposes and that those acts are necessary to improve the knowledge about the subject-matter of the invention.

However, in a decision of 3 January 2023[4] the Swiss Federal Patent Court stated that the patentee must demonstrate that the alleged infringer had performed patent infringing acts that go beyond the activities that are exempted under Swiss patent law.[5]

This statement was made in preliminary injunction proceedings and was not reviewed by a higher instance. The statement does not appear to be consistent with the above-mentioned general principles governing the burden of proof under Swiss law. According to the general principles of Swiss law the party claiming

4. Docket No. S2022_003.
5. *See* para. 23 of the decision S2022_003.

an exemption from patent protection must assert and prove the existence of the relevant facts and it is not up to the patentee to show that the Experimental Use exemption does not apply.

h. Applicability during Patent Term Extension or Supplementary Protection Certificate

The Swiss Experimental Use exemption applies to patents, supplementary protection certificates (SPCs) and any other form of exclusive rights under Swiss patent law (e.g. pediatric SPCs).

3. THE BOLAR-TYPE EXEMPTION

a. History and Rationale of Adopting the Bolar-Type Exemption

Prior to the inclusion of the marketing authorization exception in the Swiss Patent Act in 2008, the legal situation was unclear due to conflicting rulings of Swiss courts. Interestingly, the preliminary draft of the revision of 2008 did not include a statutory exemption for acts related to medicinal product approval procedures, which led to significant criticism. This lack of clarity was addressed with the eventual codification of the Bolar-type exemption in the revision of the Swiss Patent Act of 2008.

The purpose of the Swiss Bolar-type exemption is to facilitate the entry of new drugs into the market right after the expiration of a patent by streamlining the drug approval processes and allowing tests and experiments and other activities that are necessary for obtaining marketing authorizations for new drugs despite existing patent protection. Thus, the patent holder is prevented from de facto extending the patent period, since the Bolar-type exemption allows preparatory actions for the approval of generics to begin before the expiration of the patent protection.

b. The Laws Applicable to the Bolar-Type Exemption in Switzerland

The Swiss Bolar-type exemption is an exemption from patent infringement for activities necessary to obtain regulatory approval for pharmaceutical products for human and veterinary use.

It is a rather broad exemption compared to similar exemptions in other jurisdictions. In particular, it is not limited to generic products. The Swiss Bolar-type exemption extends to all actions that are necessary for obtaining marketing authorization for a medicinal product, meaning they are *conditio sine qua non* for obtaining a marketing authorization.

The Swiss Bolar-type exemption applies to activities for obtaining Swiss marketing authorization and authorization in 'countries with comparable medicinal product control'.

According to a list published by Swissmedic, the Swiss Agency for Therapeutic Products, jurisdictions with a similar control of medicinal products are Australia, the EU and EFTA Member States, Japan, Canada, New Zealand, Singapore and the USA.

c. Procedural Aspects of Invoking the Bolar-Type Exemption

Following general principles of Swiss law, it is the party who relies on the Bolar-type exemption who bears the burden of proof to show that the allegedly patent infringing acts were performed for experimental purposes and that those acts are necessary to improve the knowledge about the subject-matter of the invention.

However, in a decision of 3 January 2023,[6] the Swiss Federal Patent Court stated that the patentee must demonstrate that the alleged infringer had performed patent infringing acts that go beyond the activities that are exempted under Swiss patent law.[7]

This statement was made in preliminary injunction proceedings and was not reviewed by a higher instance. The statement does not appear to be consistent with the above-mentioned general principles governing the burden of proof under Swiss law. According to the general principles of Swiss law the party claiming an exemption from patent protection must assert and prove the existence of the relevant facts and it is not up to the patentee to show that the Bolar-type exemption does not apply.

d. Scope of Bolar-Type Exemption in Switzerland

i. Fields of Technology

The Swiss Bolar-type exemption is not limited to specific fields of technology. The only requirement is that the activities in question are those required for the authorization of a medicinal product. For example, manufacturing a machine that is necessary for the manufacture of drugs that are exclusively used for clinical trials for obtaining a marketing authorization in Switzerland is covered by the Swiss Bolar-type exemption.

ii. Purpose of Experiments/Infringing Activities

The Swiss Bolar-type exemption covers all activities that are necessary for obtaining a marketing authorization, such as pre-clinical and clinical tests, production for clinical trials, import and storage of samples and validation batches, provided that all these activities are undertaken for the purpose of obtaining a marketing authorization. Whether or not an authorization is subsequently granted is irrelevant.

Moreover, the Swiss Bolar-type exemption applies irrespective of whether the medicinal product to be authorized is an innovative medicinal product or a generic medicinal product or a biosimilar. The Swiss Bolar-type exemption also covers activities that are necessary for obtaining a marketing authorization for a new original product.

The Swiss Bolar-type exemption does not extend to medical devices.

---

6. Docket No. S2022_003.
7. *See* para. 23 of the decision S2022_003.

Preclinical or clinical trials that go beyond what is required under the law on medicinal products can still be prohibited by the patent holder, provided that the Experimental Use exemption does not apply.

iii. Exempted and Prohibited Activities

General

All actions that are necessary for obtaining a marketing authorization are exempted from patent protection, i.e. pre-clinical and clinical tests and studies (bioequivalence studies); the manufacturing, importation and storage of the patent-protected product; the submission of samples containing patent protected ingredients to the healthcare authorities as well as the importation or production of samples for this purpose; and the production of batches of the medicinal product for clinical trials.

Whether an act is intended and necessary to obtain a marketing authorization for a medicinal product can only be determined on a case-by-case basis, taking into account all the relevant facts. Since the Swiss legislator wanted to provide a broad interpretation of the marketing authorization privilege, activities that take place early in the development process of a medicinal product should also be covered by the exemption (e.g., the planning and preparation of preclinical studies or the manufacture of the agent for such studies).

Unsuccessful clinical trials

If clinical trials are unsuccessful and no marketing authorization application is filed, the corresponding clinical trials are still exempt from patent protection under the Swiss Bolar-type exemption as long as the trials were originally directed to obtaining a marketing authorization. What matters is the intention at the time the trials are carried out, not whether an application for obtaining a marketing authorization is ultimately submitted.

Phase 4 clinical trials

Phase 4 trials normally take place after the concerned medicinal product is already approved and available on the market. It is therefore questionable whether such trials would also be exempted since they do not seem necessary to obtain regulatory approval. However, to the extent that phase 4 trials were ordered by the competent regulatory body when granting the marketing authorization, such trials should be within the safe harbour.

Stockpiling

The production or storage of protected products as stock for the purpose of marketing them after the patent has expired (so-called stockpiling) is not permitted under the Swiss Bolar-type exemption.

Pricing and reimbursement listing

The activity of seeking pricing and reimbursement with the Swiss Federal Office of Public Health that gives the manufacturer access to the Swiss pricing and reimbursement list is not covered by the exemption of Article 9(1)(c) PatA either.

e. Beneficiary Limitations

The question of whether third parties can also invoke the Bolar-type exemption in addition to the person seeking marketing authorization has not yet been clarified by Swiss case law. Some Swiss scholars, with reference to German authors, are of the opinion that the Swiss Bolar-type exemption also applies if third parties carry out trials on behalf of the applicant who then files the marketing authorization application. This opinion is supported by the fact that the wording of Article 9(1)(c) PatA does not limit the exemption to the *person* of the actual applicant, but only requires that the *acts* in question be necessary for obtaining a marketing authorization.

f. Territoriality Issues

According to the wording of Article 9(1)(c) PatA, the Swiss Bolar-type exemption explicitly applies to activities for obtaining marketing authorizations in countries with equivalent medicinal product control. It follows that the Swiss Bolar-type exemption does not apply to activities for obtaining marketing authorizations in countries other than Australia, the EU and EFTA Member States, Japan, Canada, New Zealand, Singapore and the USA.

Whether the Swiss Bolar-type exemption applies if for example the results of an experiment are used for infringing a patent in another jurisdiction is a matter of private international law. In the area of intellectual property, the territorial scope of patents and exemptions is normally governed by each state. Whether acts with cross-border effects constitute patent infringing acts and what substantive law applies to the assessment of these activities is to be determined by the conflict of law rules of the jurisdiction(s) where protection is sought. If the Swiss conflict of law rules stipulate that certain activities shall be assessed under Swiss law (because they might infringe a patent that is valid in Switzerland), these activities may be exempted from patent protection under the Swiss Experimental Use doctrine.

g. Burden of Proof and Onus

Following general principles of Swiss law, it is the party who relies on the Bolar-type exemption who bears the burden of proof to show that the allegedly patent infringing acts were performed for exemption purposes.

However, in a decision of 3 January 2023,[8] the Swiss Federal Patent Court stated that the patentee must demonstrate that the alleged infringer had performed

8. Docket No. S2022_003.

patent infringing acts that go beyond the activities that are exempted under Swiss patent law.[9]

This statement was made in preliminary injunction proceedings and was not reviewed by a higher instance. The statement does not appear to be consistent with the above-mentioned general principles governing the burden of proof under Swiss law. According to the general principles of Swiss law the party claiming an exemption from patent protection must assert and prove the existence of the relevant facts and it is not up to the patentee to show that the Bolar-type exemption does not apply.

h. Applicability during Patent Term Extension or Supplementary Protection Certificate

Based on the current legislation, existing guidance, and relevant case law, there is no indication that the Swiss Bolar-type exemption would not apply during a patent term extension, i.e., an SPC or any other extension of the patent term (e.g., a pediatric SPC).

4. DIFFERENCES BETWEEN THE TWO EXCEPTIONS IN SWITZERLAND

In Switzerland, both the Experimental Use exemption and the Bolar-type exemption under Article 9 PatA are statutory exceptions to the exclusive rights conferred by a patent, SPC, or pediatric SPC.

While the two exemptions share a common goal of balancing the patentee's rights with broader societal interests, their rationales, scope and implications are different.

The co-existence of the two exemptions and the rather broad interpretation of the exemptions provide a wide degree of flexibility in the fields of research and product development in Switzerland.

The scope of the two exemptions can overlap (for example with respect to biosimilar studies for new generic pharmaceutical products that normally fall under the Experimental Use exemption and the Bolar-type exemption) but there are also situations where only the Experimental Use exemption or the Swiss Bolar-type exemption applies (or neither of the two).

For example, while the Experimental Use exemption allows research aimed at gaining additional knowledge about the patented invention, it does not extend to using the invention as a research tool. However, such use may still be permitted under the Bolar-type exemption if the concerned activities are necessary for regulatory approval.

Neither exemption takes precedence over the other.

9. *See* para. 23 of the decision S2022_003.

Chapter 38
Taiwan

Kevin C.W. Feng

1. GENERAL

a. Terminology

The experimental use is an 'exemption' to the exercise of patent rights. The Taiwan Intellectual Property (IP) Office explained the Experimental Use exemption as a limitation to the enforceability of patents. Similarly, the Bolar-type exemption is also an exemption to the enforceability of patent rights.

b. Legal Basis in Taiwan

The Experimental Use exemption clause was introduced for the first time in May 1944 when the Patent Act was promulgated. Since then, there have been several amendments that have led to the provisions in force today.

The Experimental Use exemption is codified as Article 59(1)(2) of the 2011 Patent Act, which reads that:

> The effects of a patent right shall not extend to ... necessary acts to exploit the invention for research or experimental purpose(s).

In addition to patent rights, Article 120 of the Patent Act provides that the Article 59(1)(2) applies *mutatis mutandis* to utility models.

The Bolar-type exemption (or the exemption for pharmaceuticals research and trials) was enacted to Article 60 of the Patent Act in the 2011 Amendment.

It reads that:

> The effects of the patent right shall not extend to research and trials, including their practical requirements, necessary for obtaining registration and market

> approval of medicaments under the Pharmaceutical Affairs Act or obtaining market approval of pharmaceuticals from a foreign country.

Taiwan is not a common law jurisdiction. The courts adjudicate a case relying on the statutory laws created by legislature. Although the *stare decisis* is not one of the judicial doctrines in Taiwan, the precedent judgements *de facto* serve pivotally referential values to forecast similar cases in the future. There have been several judgements from the IP and Commercial Court peripherally concerning the two exemptions, even if they were not the core issue in a case.

c. Bodies that May Decide on the Legitimacy of Exemptions

Both the Experimental Use exemption and the Bolar-type exemption are infringement defences in a litigation proceeding. In Taiwan, a patent infringement dispute can be resolved at the IP and Commercial Court or at a District Court. Therefore, a defence under the exemptions can be raised in either forum.

2. THE EXPERIMENTAL USE EXEMPTION

a. History and Rationale of Adopting the Experimental Use Exemption

The legislative rationale set forth that the policy goal is to ensure the protection of research and experimental activities on the subject invention to facilitate the improvement or innovation of the invention.

Before 2011, the clause on the research exemption prescribed in Article 57(1)(1) read as follows:

> The effects of an invention patent right shall not extend to … exploitation of the invention for research, educational or experimental purpose(s), without engaging a profit-making activity.

In 2011, the Amendment to the Patent Act removed the requirement of 'without engaging a profit-making activity' and the act of 'educational purpose' from the statute. However, the element of 'necessary' was introduced to foster prioritization of innovation over the existing invention, which innovation would benefit the entire society to a greater extent than the profit that would be gained by a party.

The current law therefore applies regardless of whether or not there is a notion of profit, in accordance with the German Law (German Patent Act, Section 11, Subsection 2) and counterpart laws (e.g. Patents Act 1977 of the UK, Section 60(5)(b)) and the International Union for the Protection of New Varieties of Plants (UPOV, 1991, Article 15(1)(ii)). It was also considered under the current law that the previous stipulation of an act for the purpose of education was redundant since almost all educational practice of a patent involves research and experiments. An educationally purposed act is therefore duplicative and would by default be covered by the acts for research or development. Only a necessary act 'directly' associated with the make, use, sale, and so on, of the invention would not be covered by the exemption, to avoid an excessive expansive scope of the exemption clause.

b. The Laws Applicable to the Experimental Use Exemption in Taiwan

Article 59(1)(2) of the Patent Act reads that: '[t]he effects of an invention patent right shall not extend to ... necessary acts to exploit the invention for research or experimental purpose(s)'.

The scope of the exemption is quite broad as it refers to acts performed for research and experimental purposes.

A court may interpret the experimental use in a narrower manner by limiting the exemption to the experiment itself or the act of exploiting the patent by manufacture, offer for sale, sale, use, or import.

There has been some case law which has clarified the boundaries of the exemption.

c. Procedural Aspects of Invoking the Experimental Use Exemption

The Experimental Use exemption is a defence in a civil litigation proceeding.

When the defence is raised, the court has the discretion to decide at which stage in a proceeding to examine the defence. It can happen either before or after the infringement finding. But if the court has found infringement in the first place, the court would sometimes leave the defence unanswered.[1]

d. Scope of the Experimental Use Exemption in Taiwan

i. Fields of Technology

The Experimental Use exemption is not restrictive of the areas of application. It therefore applies to all fields of technologies. The court opined that an experiment covered in the exemption not only refers to academic research or experiments but also includes the industrial ones.[2]

ii. Purpose of Experiments/Infringing Activities

The purpose of the exemption is defined quite broadly as being for research or experimental purpose.

Whether a research or experiment aims for profit or not is no longer of relevance to exempt such an activity, since the 2011 Amendment to the Patent Act removed the requirement for non-profit-seeking (see section 2.a.).

Furthermore, the Taiwan IP Office explained that eligible research or experimentation is performed 'on' the invention. An example of 'research on' would be to determine whether the patented technology can be reproduced according to the disclosure, to ascertain the best mode provided in the description, or to develop any possible improvements based on the patented technology. On the contrary, if

1. Cases 103-CivilPatentTrial-No. 70 and 110-CivilPatentTrial-No. 85, IP and Commercial Court.
2. Case 108-CivilPatentTrial-No. 38, IP and Commercial Court.

research is conducted 'with' the patented technology serving as a means or a tool, such research is not covered by the exemption.

Considering the above, it will be generally admitted under Taiwan law (and case law) that if the research or experimental results are manufactured, used (e.g. as a tool), assigned or transposed to a different situation than the one that is covered by the patent, it may constitute patent infringement.

iii. Exempted and Prohibited Activities

The exempted activities include experiments *per se* and the directly associated acts of practising the patent, namely the manufacture, offer for sale, sale, use, or import. For example, the profitable sale of a product made of research or experiment that is within a reasonable scale/size may not be subject to the enforceability of a patent. However, export is not a kind of patent practice, so it is not within the scope of exemption.

The use of the data generated from the experiments should be careful and limited, as also discussed above in the context of 'research with'. The legislative rationale stated that the Experimental Use exemption aims at the improvement of inventions. By interpretation, the data should therefore be used in a way conducive to the improvement, advancement, refinement, or the like, of the patent invention which is researched.

The court has determined that the exemption covers series of tests performed on a patented material for the purpose of quality assurance, given that there is no manufacture or sale of the products which can be directly produced according to the patented process of manufacture.[3] Conversely, an accused party may be found infringing if producing or selling the products made by practising the patented process.

The courts have also clarified that an application for marketing approval of a drug itself or an application for the pricing and listing reimbursement of a drug under the national health insurance program is not covered by the exemption as decided in Case 110-CivilPatentTrial-No. 13.

The courts have also clarified that a test run of an electrolyte reactor before the delivery to the customer would not be covered by the current exemption because its testing is not based on the purpose of the research or experiment but is required before the machine is delivered.[4]

iv. Pure Academic vs Commercially Motivated Experimental Use

The exemption does not limit the activities to those done for 'academic purposes' or having 'no commercial value.' However, an exempted act must be reasonably experimental.

3. Case 104-CivilPatentTrial-No. 54, IP and Commercial Court.
4. Case 103-CivilPatentTrial-No. 70, IP and Commercial Court.

e. Beneficiary Limitations

Non-profit-seeking is not a requisite to raise the exemption. If a third party practises the patent technology for the purpose of conducting research contracted by another party in exchange for a financial compensation from that party, the third party should be able to raise the exemption on its own.

f. Territoriality Issues

The Experimental Use exemption applies only to a case where a Taiwanese patent is allegedly infringed. If a patented product is sold in Taiwan for experimental use performed inside Taiwan, it can be covered by the exemption. However, export is not patent practice, suggesting that an exportation of a patented product made in Taiwan to a foreign country would be beyond the Taiwanese courts' jurisdiction.

g. Burden of Proof and Onus

The defendant bears the burden of proof in defence against an infringement accusation. The Code of Civil Procedure is the fundamental rule governing the allocation of evidentiary duty. According to Article 277 of the Code of Civil Procedure, a party bears the burden of proof regarding the facts which he or she alleges in his or her favour. Since raising the Experimental Use exemption is advantageous to the defendant, the defendant bears the burden to demonstrate that in a pending case the elements of the exemption are present.

At least two components need to be established: (1) the use is purposed for research or experiment; and (2) the practice of the patent is necessary, or reasonably correlating to the research or experiment. Before that, the plaintiff shall firstly prove that the defendant practises the patent.

h. Applicability during Patent Term Extension or Supplementary Protection Certificate

The Experimental Use exemption is still applicable during a patent term extension (PTE). However, during a PTE, the enforceable scope of a patent becomes narrower.

Article 56 of the Patent Act reads as follows:

> The scope of a patent, of which a term extension has been granted, shall be limited to only the effective ingredients and use stated in the regulatory approval concerned.

Therefore, in practice, the scope of a patent during a PTE shall be limited to only the active ingredients and use stated in the regulatory approval concerned. That is, the only enforceable scope is limited to the combination of the indication and the active ingredient which is claimed in the patent. Therefore, by interpretation, the Experimental Use exemption should remain applicable when the defendant practises the patent in research or experimentation involving the claimed matters or methods concerning the indication provided in the regulatory approval. Use of the active ingredient beyond the approved indication would not be assessed under the Experimental Use exemption but because of the narrow interpretation of the PTE, would likely not constitute an infringement.

3. THE BOLAR-TYPE EXEMPTION

a. History and Rationale of Adopting the Bolar-Type Exemption

The Bolar-type exemption was introduced in the Patent Act for the first time in the 2011 Amendment. A Bolar-type exemption was previously enacted in the Pharmaceutical Act in 2005. However, much criticism have been raised concerning the appropriateness of instituting a legal defence against a patent assertion in the pharmaceutical statute. In this previous version of the Bolar-type exemption, the 'actor' and the 'timing' of the activity were restrictive elements, i.e. only the practice of an act 'before' the regulatory filing by the 'applicant' was covered. When the Patent Act was overhauled in 2011, the clause was then removed from the Pharmaceutical Act and transposed to the Patent Act with a significant modification. The 'actor' and the 'timing' are no longer the limiting elements and only the 'purpose' of the practice is material to whether the Bolar-type exemption applies to a case.

Taiwan's Bolar-type exemption was inspired by foreign counterpart legislative or judiciary example of the US,[5] the European Union,[6] and Japan.[7] Inspired and motivated by the foreign examples, Taiwan introduced the Bolar-type exemption primarily based on the policy considerations of encouraging the new drug development, incentivizing the industry of generic products, facilitating the launch of the more affordable equivalent drug products, and so forth.

b. The Laws Applicable to the Bolar-Type Exemption in Taiwan

The legal basis for regulatory approvals is in the Pharmaceutical Affairs Act. Article 39 of the Pharmaceutical Affairs Act provides that:

> For the manufacturing and import of drugs, information concerning the ingredients ... shall be filed with the central competent health authority for registration and market approval. No manufacturing or importation of such drugs shall be allowed until a drug permit license is approved and issued.

Similarly, Article 40 of the Pharmaceutical Affairs Act provides that:

> For the manufacturing and import of medical devices, an application ... shall be filed with the central competent health authority for registration and market

5. Drug Price Competition and Patent Term Restoration Act of 1984 (Hatch-Waxman Act), 35 U.S.C. § 271(e)(1) (2020).
6. Directive 2001/83/EC of the European Parliament and of the Council of 6 November 2001 on the Community code relating to medicinal products for human use, Article 10(6).
7. Case No.1998(ju)153, *Ono Pharmaceuticals v. Kyoto Pharmaceuticals Industries*, Supreme Court, Second Petty Bench, 1999.

approval. No manufacturing and importation shall be allowed until a medical device permit license is approved and issued.

Article 60 of the Patent Act reads that:

> [t]he effects of the patent right shall not extend to research and trials, including their practical requirements, necessary for obtaining registration and market approval of medicaments under the Pharmaceutical Affairs Act or obtaining market approval of pharmaceuticals from a foreign country.

The 'medicaments' refers to new drugs and generic drugs, as well as medical devices (Article 4 of the Pharmaceutical Affairs Act).

Compared to the Experimental Use exemption, the field of applicability is narrower since it is limited to an act, the purpose of which is to obtain the regulatory approval of the drug products, including generic and innovator drugs, or medical devices.

c. Procedural Aspects of Invoking the Bolar-Type Exemption

Similar to the Experimental Use exemption, the Bolar-type exemption is a defence in a civil litigation proceeding.

d. Scope of the Bolar-Type Exemption in Taiwan

i. Fields of Technology

The Bolar-type exemption covers research, trials, and their necessary auxiliary activities for generating scientific data prepared to be submitted to the pharmaceutical authority.

ii. Purpose of Experiments/Infringing Activities

The Bolar-type exemption is specific to the activities necessary for obtaining a pharmaceutical regulatory approval. In contrast with the Experimental Use exemption, the Bolar-type exemption does not apply to research and experiments practised on the patented invention for an improvement or a further innovation.

iii. Exempted and Prohibited Activities

The activities exempted under the Bolar clause include pre-clinical activities and clinical trials themselves. Other necessary activities of 'manufacture, offer for sale, sale, use, or import' that are associated with these trials are all covered. As per the legislative rationale, these associated activities of patent practice must be reasonably correlated with the trials and the eligibility of them shall not be extravagantly extended.

Timing of the exemptible activity is of no relevance since the 2011 Amendment. The element of 'before the filing' was removed from the old version of the provision in 2011. It was also confirmed later by the court that to assess whether the practice of patent is covered by the exemption or whether these acts are performed before the filing of an application does not matter. For example, even after a filing, the subsequent trials and the implementation are also exempt from infringement so long as they directly purport to the regulatory approval.[8]

The law does not address the consequence applying when the data generated from the practice of the invention was used for purposes beyond submission for regulatory approval. Theoretically speaking, if the data is used not for its legislative purpose, the practice of the invention may be considered infringement.

For the definition of the 'research and trials', the court opined that if a defendant used a patented method to dissemble and analyse a drug and then attempt a different method to generate another drug possessing the same therapeutic effect, then said disassembly and analysis can be considered an exemptible research and trials.[9]

In terms of the territorial reach, the Bolar-type exemption also applies to acts performed in Taiwan but for seeking an approval from a foreign regulatory authority, as modelled on the German counterpart legislature.

On the other hand, activities performed not for the purpose of obtaining regulatory approval, such as a hospital's listing of trials for an approved drug before entering its inventory and becoming available for its physician's prescriptions, are not exempted.

Furthermore, the manufacture of a patented drug during the life of a patent in order to increase drug inventory ready for a fast launch immediately after the patent's expiry, namely the stockpiling, is not exempted. Stock-piling is not considered a 'necessary' act for seeking regulatory approval.

In addition, the court clarified that an application for a drug's regulatory approval *per se* is not addressed by the Bolar clause.[10]

e. Beneficiary Limitations

As per the legislative rationale, the Bolar-type exemption is eligible for both innovator drugs and generic drugs.

For a third person's liability, it depends on the nature of the necessary activities that the third party engages. The identity of 'actor' does not matter whereas the 'purpose' determines whether the Bolar clause applies. Suppose an accused activity is considered a trial *per se* or a use of patent directly related to the trial, it should be exempt, irrespective of the identity of the actor.

Furthermore, in Taiwan, indirect infringement is contingent on the finding of direct infringement. When an experiment or trial as a directly infringing activity is exempted, a third person who made contribution as an indirect act is not considered infringing. Hence, if the main actor or the regulatory applicant is exempt, directly related activities performed by an auxiliary or aiding third person to the regulatory applicant should be exempt as well.

8. Cases 110-CivilPatentTrial-No. 4 and 110-CivilPatentTrial-No. 9, IP and Commercial Court.
9. Case 94-IPAppeal-No. 26, Taiwan High Court.
10. Cases 110-CivilPatentTrial-No. 13 and 109-CivilPatentTrial-No. 46, IP and Commercial Court.

f. Territoriality Issues

The Bolar-type exemption applies to medical data which are generated in Taiwan and submitted to a foreign pharmaceutical authority from which a foreign regulatory approval is sought. As to whether the Bolar clause is still applicable if the data are purported to another relevant regulatory agency, the answer should be positive because the purpose remains to seek approval for the later sale of a medicament. Nevertheless, in Taiwan, the Taiwan Food and Drug Administration is the only administrative authority to issues regulatory approval to medicaments.

The law does not require that the beneficiary of the exemption be the applicant for the regulatory approval. The nature of the activities weighs more than the actor's identity. The applicant may therefore engage with multiple auxiliary parties and their activities should be covered if also directly related to the application for regulatory approval.

g. Burden of Proof and Onus

The defendant has the onus to prove that in his or her case the engaged trials and necessary activities are exempt under the Bolar-type clause. As per Article 277 of the Code of Civil Procedure, the establishment of the Bolar-type clause is in favour of the defendant so the defendant shall prove it being applicable. Yet, before a defence, the plaintiff shall first demonstrate that the defendant practises the patent.

h. Applicability during Patent Term Extension or Supplementary Protection Certificate

There is no restriction on the applicability of the Bolar clause during the patent term extension as compared to the regular patent term. Notably, the scope of enforceability of the patent is narrower during the patent term extension. It is therefore likely that the Bolar clause will not be necessary when a pharmaceutical patent is practised during the patent term extension in contrast to during the regular term.

4. DIFFERENCES BETWEEN THE TWO EXCEPTIONS IN TAIWAN

The Experimental Use exemption is of broader scope of applicability than the Bolar-type exemption. The former can defend a practice of patent in all fields of research and experiments, whereas the latter is specific to a pharmaceutical purpose.

The legislative histories and policy purposes differentiate. The first version of the Experimental Use exemption was enacted together with the rest of the Patent Act at the time it was promulgated. Several amendments took place over time. On the contrary, the Bolar-type exemption was not introduced until 2005 and only became the current version in 2011. In view of the policy goal, the Experimental Use exemption was designed for others' exploration for inventive improvement or insights whereas the Bolar-type exemption was made for seeking a quicker launch of more affordable medical product equivalent.

When the Bolar-type exemption was made to facilitate the availability of affordable drug equivalent in 2005, it implied a commercial purpose. At that time, the commercial purpose was a negative element in the Experimental Use exemption. Such bifurcation in historical origin and development denoted the parallel legislative initiatives and the distinct scopes of applicability between the two exemptions.

Chapter 39

Türkiye

Ezgi Baklaci Gulkokar and Soley Çoban

1. GENERAL

a. Terminology

Experimental Use and Bolar-type exemptions are legal concepts used as a defence against an infringement allegation in a patent infringement action or a determination of non-infringement action. As patent law is a civil matter, unless an alleged infringer puts forward such defence, the Turkish courts cannot and will not take into account Bolar-type and Experimental Use exemptions, even if the conditions are met.

Throughout the Türkiye chapter, both legal concepts are referred to as 'exemptions', though more accurately they are 'exceptions' of patent infringement in Turkish patent law – meaning that in these special circumstances (Bolar-type and Experimental Use), the general rule that *the use of a patented invention without the consent of the patentee constitutes patent infringement* does not apply.

b. Legal Basis in Türkiye

The Experimental Use and Bolar-type exemptions are codified in Article 85/3-(b) and (c) of the Industrial Property Code (IPC) as follows:

> (3) The following acts shall remain outside the scope of rights conferred by a patent:
>
> ...
>
> (b) Acts involving a patented invention for experimental purposes,
>
> (c) Acts involving a patented invention for experimental purposes including the marketing authorization of pharmaceuticals and the necessary tests and experiments for this.
>
> ...

Article 85 outlines specific exemptions from patent protection, particularly concerning experimental activities. Experimental acts involving the patented invention, and experimental acts involving the marketing authorization of pharmaceuticals, are not subject to the usual restrictions of patent protection, as they are considered to be outside the scope of the rights conferred by a patent.

2. THE EXPERIMENTAL USE EXEMPTION

a. History and Rationale of Adopting the Experimental Use Exemption

The Experimental Use exemption was formally recognized by the addition of subsection (f) to Article 75 of the now-repealed Decree-Law No. 551, via Article 3 of Law No. 5194, dated 22 June 2004. This Article was also included in the IPC, which was published in the Official Gazette No. 29944 on 10 January 2017, and became effective on that date.

The Experimental Use exemption regulated under the IPC is based on Article 30 of the TRIPS Agreement. The IPC's preamble explains that this exemption is provided with an aim to support technological developments.

Article 75 of Decree-Law No. 551 specifies that the use of a patented invention for experimental purposes does not constitute an infringement of patent rights. This Article is designed to encourage research and experimental use of patented inventions. It allows scientific research to benefit from patented technologies without violating patent rights.

The Experimental Use exemption is recognized as a significant tool for creating a competitive environment for the production of technical knowledge. It is considered essential to acknowledge this exemption in order to achieve the informational and incentivizing effects anticipated from the patent system. The Experimental Use exemption was established by regulation to fulfil the objectives expected from the patent system.

b. The Laws Applicable to the Experimental Use Exemption in Türkiye

In Türkiye, the legal framework governing the Experimental Use exemption is primarily outlined in the IPC and the TRIPS Agreement. The IPC specifically addresses the patent rights and includes an Article related to the Experimental Use exemption.

Article 85/3-(b) of the IPC states as follows:

> (3) The following acts shall remain outside the scope of rights conferred by a patent:
>
> ...
>
> (b) Acts involving a patented invention for experimental purposes,

Thus, under Article 85/3-(b) of the IPC, it is explicitly stated that the use of a patented invention for experimental purposes is permitted without infringing the patent rights. This allows researchers and entities to engage in experimentation and research activities aimed at advancing scientific knowledge and technological development without the risk of patent infringement.

Furthermore, the TRIPS Agreement, to which Türkiye is a signatory, also provides a basis for the Experimental Use exemption. Article 30 of the TRIPS Agreement permits members to establish limited exceptions to the exclusive rights conferred by a patent, which can include the use of a patented invention for experimentation.

> TRIPS Article 30: Exceptions to Rights Conferred
>
> Members may provide limited exemptions to the exclusive rights conferred by a patent, provided that such exemptions do not unreasonably conflict with a normal exploitation of the patent and do not unreasonably prejudice the legitimate interests of the patent owner, taking account of the legitimate interests of third parties.

c. Procedural Aspects of Invoking the Experimental Use Exemption

In practice, the Experimental Use exemption is regulated as a defence. It can be argued in patent infringement actions initiated at the courts, and in actions for a determination of non-infringement.

d. Scope of the Experimental Use Exemption in Türkiye

i. Fields of Technology

The IPC does not provide any field of technology limitations to the experimental use. The Experimental Use exemption can be utilized in any technological field.

ii. Purpose of Experiments/Infringing Activities

The reason behind the Experimental Use exemption under Article 85/3-(b) of IPC is as follows: 'Experimental acts comprising the invention subject for a patent are excluded from the scope of patent protection because such acts may improve technological progress.' Thus, the aim of the experimental use is improving technological process.

When applying this exemption, it is necessary and important to determine whether:

- the experiment in question is of a nature that can contribute to technological development; and
- there is a commercial purpose or not.

Even though one should aim to contribute to technology and innovation to qualify for the Experimental Use exemption, the individual or entity does not need to be an academician. A commercial entity exploring new, additional, or alternative aspects of the invention that were previously unknown can also benefit from the exemption. This implies that an action considered as 'experimental use' does not need to be entirely devoid of commercial objectives.

However, the commercial gain obtained from products resulting from the experimental use of a patent should not fall within the scope of the exemption and should be regarded as patent infringement. Similarly, if an individual or entity manufactures and markets the invention without the patent holder's permission, under the guise of 'experimenting' to determine whether the patented invention can achieve commercial success in the market, it should also be considered patent infringement. The quantity of products produced and the overall extent of the 'experimental' activities involving the patented invention can serve as indicators to assess whether the actions were genuinely limited to experimentation.

iii. Exempted and Prohibited Activities

Under the Turkish legal system, the Experimental Use exemption applies within a specific legal framework and certain activities are specifically prohibited or exempted.

The possession of a patented invention for the purpose of sale, import or trade cannot be considered within the scope of the exemption. The importation or purchase of a patented product for the purpose of sale or trade is also not covered by the Experimental Use exemption.

Transactions necessary for the placing on the market or licensing of a patented product are not covered by the exemption. Such procedures must be carried out in accordance with the relevant legislation.

The intended use of data obtained through tests and experiments conducted under the Experimental Use exemption is limited. Such data may only be used for experimental purposes and commercial exploitation of such data violates the patentee's rights.

As a result, in the Turkish legal system, the Experimental Use exemption is limited to only certain tests and experiments and specifically excludes activities for commercial purposes, such as imports, sales and marketing. The use of the data obtained is also restricted by certain limits, and the use of such data for commercial purposes would lead to infringement of patent rights.

iv. Pure Academic vs Commercially Motivated Experimental Use

Article 85/3-(b) of the IPC states that 'experimental acts involving the patented invention' are allowed, which means that a patented invention can be examined for experimental purposes without the need to obtain permission from the patent holder. This Article 85/3-(b) highlights that such acts can be utilized in research and development (R&D) activities. The primary objective of experimental use is to 'acquire new knowledge'. In this context, the commercial intent behind the experiment or the commercial nature of the R&D activities is not of primary importance. As long as no direct commercial benefit is gained from the use and the products developed within the scope of R&D are not introduced to the market, all experimental uses of the patent are permitted.

This interpretation aligns with the intent behind the Bolar-type exemption as well, which seeks to balance the rights of patent holders with the need for innovation and research in various fields.

e. Beneficiary Limitations

They key factors in assessing whether an activity qualifies under the Experimental Use exemption are technological advancement and lack of direct commercial benefit. As long as these criteria met, third parties (e.g., a research organization or laboratory) engaged by a party for experimental purposes, even for profit, will benefit from the exemption.

However, the validity of this situation depends on the nature and purpose of the experiments. That is, the experiments conducted by the third party must not lead to a commercial result.

f. Territoriality Issues

The Experimental Use exemption does not apply if the results of the experiment are used to infringe a related patent in another jurisdiction. The experimental use must be for the sole purpose of acquiring new knowledge and R&D, and in order to benefit from such an exemption, the results obtained must be used solely for experimental purposes, without being associated with other patents. As long as the infringement in other country has commercial purpose, the act would not fall within the scope of experimental use and would instead constitute patent infringement.

g. Burden of Proof and Onus

Experimental use is used as a defence; and any party claiming non-infringement should prove that the acts are within the scope of the Experimental Use exemption.

h. Applicability during Patent Term Extension or Supplementary Protection Certificate

The patent term is twenty years and it is applicable to the acts conducted during this period. The patent term cannot be extended in Türkiye and SPC does not exist in Türkiye.

3. THE BOLAR-TYPE EXEMPTION

a. History and Rationale of Adopting the Bolar-Type Exemption

Türkiye adopted the Bolar-type exemption with the amendment made to the abrogated Decree Law on Patents in 2004 as part of its efforts to align its intellectual property laws with European Union (EU) standards in light of Decision No. 2/97 of the EC-Türkiye Association Council and Article 39/3 of TRIPS.

The Bolar-type exemption Article in the abrogated Decree Law was carried to the Turkish IPC and entered into force on 10 January 2017.

b. The Laws Applicable to Bolar-Type Exemption in Türkiye

Article 85/3-(c) of the IPC reads as follows:

> (3) The following acts shall remain outside the scope of rights conferred by a patent:
>
> ...
>
> (c) Acts involving a patented invention for experimental purposes including the marketing authorization of pharmaceuticals and the necessary tests and experiments for this.
>
> ...

Thus, 'Acts involving a patented invention for experimental purposes including the marketing authorization of pharmaceuticals and the necessary tests and experiments for this' constitutes an exemption to the rights arising from the patent and these acts do not infringe the right protected by the patent.

The justification behind Article 85/3-(c) is to shorten the delay for the launch of generic drugs at the end of the patent protection period, by allowing generic authorization procedures to be performed and concluded during the patent protection period. Further justification is provided by the concept that experimental acts related to the inventions within the scope of this subparagraph may contribute to technological developments.

Precedent decisions of the Regional Appellate Court (second instance) and the Supreme Court (third instance) mention similar justification in their decisions regarding the Bolar-type exemption which state that in order for the generic drug manufacturer to be able to put a drug on the market the day after the expiry of the patent term, it is necessary to conduct tests and experiments before this date.

The wording of Article 85/3-(c) appears to exclude activities related to reimbursement listing, since it mentions marketing authorization. However, this has been treated inconsistently by the courts: it has been observed that in some higher courts' decisions, reimbursement listing has also been found exempt from patent protection under this Article, thus causing an open/flexible reading of the exemption. However, there also exist decisions in the opposite direction, which hold that reimbursement listing would not be exempt but rather be a patent infringement. Both the motivation of the Article and the precedent decisions of higher courts states that the rationale of the Article, i.e. Bolar-type exemption, is to ensure that the generic medicine can be placed on the market as soon as the patent protection expires. Accordingly, only acts related to putting the medicine on the market should be included in the scope of this exemption. Reimbursement listing is not required for marketing authorization (i.e. to be able to put the drug on the market). Additionally, according to the Regulation on Licensing of Medicinal Products for Human Use, marketing authorization is defined as examination and approval procedures carried out by the Turkish Medicines and Medical Devices Agency in order to put a human medicinal product on the market. In contrast, reimbursement listing is an act carried out by the Social Security Institution. This clear divide appears to differentiate the two activities, making it easier to exclude reimbursement listing activities from the legal definition of marketing authorization.

c. Procedural Aspects of Invoking the Bolar-Type Exemption

Bolar-type exemption can be raised as a defence in patent infringement action or in determination of non-infringement action by the alleged infringer.

The judiciary is a three-level system. Patent disputes are first brought before civil courts of intellectual and industrial property rights which are established in Istanbul, Ankara, and Izmir to handle disputes related to intellectual property, including patent litigation. In regions where there is no specialized intellectual property court, the cases are heard by civil courts of general jurisdiction that hear not only intellectual property cases, but all kinds of cases related to property rights and personal assets. The competent first instance court in patent infringement action is the court of the residence of the plaintiff or of the place where the wrongful act was committed, or otherwise where the effects of such act have been observed. If the plaintiff does not have a residence in Türkiye, the competent court shall be the court where the place of work of the registered patent attorney is located on the date of filing of the action. The competent court in determination of non-infringement action is the court of the residence of the defendant (patentee) is located.

Decisions of the first instance courts are appealed before the Regional Appellate Court and its decisions are appealed to the Supreme Court.

All three courts of different levels have jurisdiction to determine the legitimacy of a Bolar-type exemption as well as the procedures and context under which the exemption may be raised.

d. Scope of Bolar-Type Exemption in Türkiye

i. Fields of Technology

The Bolar-type exemption is limited to pharmaceuticals.

ii. Purpose of Experiments/Infringing Activities

As per the precedent decisions of the Supreme Court, acts performed for the purpose of obtaining marketing authorization, whether or not they have a commercial purpose, are within the scope of the Bolar-type exemption. The precedent decisions of the Supreme Court only examine whether experiments conducted for the purpose of obtaining marketing authorization constitute patent infringement. Any other purpose for experiments has not yet been tested in the courts.

The related Article does not provide a further limitation other than that experiments shall be related to obtaining marketing authorization. Meaning that purposes such as improving an old invention, comparing a new drug to a patented drug, or manufacturing a drug for use in clinical trials could be exempted from patent infringement, if the purpose of these acts is related to obtaining marketing authorization. The burden of proving that the purpose of these acts is to obtain a marketing authorization is on the party that asserts such a defence.

There are contradictory decisions of higher courts' as to whether activities for the purpose of obtaining or applying for reimbursement listing constitute patent infringement as mentioned above.

iii. Exempted and Prohibited Activities

The motivation of this Article as stated by the legislator is:

> Subparagraph (c) of the third paragraph stipulates that patented pharmaceutical products may be used in the tests and experiments required for the authorization of generic pharmaceutical products, provided that no mass production other than that required for authorization is made, stored and offered for sale.

On some occasions, the Turkish Medicines and Medical Devices Agency may request samples of the finished product from the authorization applicant in small quantities. Accordingly, the motivation of the Article states that production is permitted only if such production is required for authorization.

Storing/stockpiling and offer for sale are prohibited activities as per the motivation of the Article. It could be expected that storing is permitted only if such storage is due to marketing authorization and if in low amounts.

There are contradictory decisions of higher courts' as to whether activities for the purpose of obtaining or applying for reimbursement listing constitute patent infringement.

e. Beneficiary Limitations

The exemption can be used by any party, including an innovative manufacturer, that uses a patented invention to conduct experiments to obtain marketing authorization.

Though it has not been tested in the courts, a third party that does not seek regulatory approval itself but assists the entity that is applying for the regulatory approval may also benefit from the exemption. If the third party could prove that its act (e.g. importation of patented the active pharmaceutical ingredient (API)) aims at conducting experiments to obtain marketing authorization, the acts of the third party may not amount to infringement. Such a third party has the burden of proof to demonstrate that the purpose of its acts is related to obtaining marketing authorization.

f. Territoriality Issues

The territoriality of the Bolar-type exemption has not been tested in the courts. There are different arguments as to whether the exemption applies if the results of the experiment are used for a regulatory approval in another country. The argument against the exemption of such acts is that the Bolar-type exemption ensures the access of Turkish citizens/residents to affordable drugs and if the experiments are conducted in Türkiye, but marketing authorization is sought elsewhere, such access would be hampered. The argument in favour of the exemption of such acts is that the test and experiments contribute to technological developments and attract investment even if marketing authorization is sought in another country.

If the results of the experiment conducted in Türkiye are used for infringing a patent in another jurisdiction, the acts conducted in Turkey would likely still be exempted from patent infringement either due to Experimental Use exemption or due to Bolar-type exemption – if those results are used for regulatory approval as well.

g. Burden of Proof and Onus

As per the Turkish Procedural Code, the burden of proof rests on the party who derives a right in his/her favour from the legal conclusion attached to the alleged fact. Accordingly, the burden of proof is on the party which asserts Bolar-type exemption as a defence.

h. Applicability during Patent Term Extension or Supplementary Protection Certificate

The patent term is twenty years and it is applicable to the acts conducted during this period. The patent term cannot be extended in Türkiye and SPC does not exist in Türkiye.

4. DIFFERENCES BETWEEN THE TWO EXCEPTIONS IN TÜRKIYE

a. Rationale

The preamble of the Experimental Use exemption states that the rationale behind this exemption is to contribute to technological developments.

The preamble of the Bolar-type exemption states that in addition to contributing to technological developments, the rationale behind this exemption is to shorten the time to market for generic medicines for which authorization procedures have already been concluded at the end of the patent protection period.

b. Commercial Purpose

While the Bolar-type exemption has an explicit commercial character, whether the Experimental Use exemption defence can be used for experimental acts with commercial purpose is unclear from the wording of the related Article. The doctrine states that the experiments should not have a commercial purpose. It is again stated in the doctrine that experiments aimed at *finding and revealing something unknown* are within the scope of the exemption. There is no court decision that evaluates whether the experimental use will constitute an exemption if it includes commercial purposes.

c. Field of Technology

The Experimental Use exemption applies to all fields of technology whereas the Bolar-type exemption is specifically tailored for the pharmaceutical field. Where there is an overlap between the two exemptions (when they both apply to an act), the Bolar-type exemption would be applied due to its specific use in regulatory approvals.

Chapter 40

Unified Patent Court

Anna Bladh Redzic[1]

1. GENERAL

a. Introduction and Terminology

The Unified Patent Court ('UPC') is a Court, common to currently eighteen EU Member States[2] for which the Agreement on a Unified Patent Court ('UPCA') has taken effect.

The UPC entered into force on 1 June 2023 and is a Court set up to decide in particular on the infringement and validity of both European patents with unitary effect ('Unitary Patents') and classic European patents. The UPC comprises judges from different participating Member States of the European Union.

The opening of the UPC has created a new dynamic for European patent litigation: the UPC will have 'exclusive' jurisdiction in respect of Unitary Patents and European patents. However, a during a transitional period of seven years (which can be extended by another seven years), parties will have the choice to bring an infringement or revocation action with regard to a European patent which has not been opted out, either before a national jurisdiction or before the UPC, pursuant to Article 83(1) of the UPCA. The owner of a European patent can also 'opt out' the European patent of the jurisdiction of the UPC altogether, in accordance with Article 83(3) of the UPCA, provided litigation has not been commenced before the UPC.

1. This work has benefited from the valuable comments and intellectual input of Domien Op de Beeck at Bird & Bird, to whom I extend my sincere thanks.
2. The Member States which have ratified the UPCA at the time of writing this chapter per 19 December 2024 were Austria, Belgium, Bulgaria, Denmark, Estonia, Finland, France, Germany, Italy, Latvia, Lithuania, Luxembourg, Malta, Netherlands, Portugal, Romania, Slovenia, Sweden.

Once this 'opt out' option is exercised, the patentee will also be able to withdraw it, provided litigation has not been commenced before a national court.

As a result, two systems will coexist in parallel: the European patents for which the opt-out option has been chosen will be litigated exclusively before the national courts, while the other European patents (that have not been subject to an opting-out) will be litigated before the UPC or before national courts according to the choice of the parties.

The same European patents may thus be subject to different legal provisions within a single UPC Member State, depending on the circumstances. Consequently, also with respect to the Experimental Use exemption and the Bolar-type[3] exemption, different provisions will apply within a UPC Member State.[4]

The UPC is a new court and there has, as the time of writing this chapter, not been any UPC decisions regarding the Experimental Use and Bolar-type exemptions. Thus, until the first binding decisions have been rendered by the UPC in this regard, several uncertainties will remain regarding the exact scope of exemptions.

b. Legal Basis

The UPCA harmonizes in large parts the scope of the exclusive rights conferred by a European patent for which the UPC has jurisdiction as well as for Unitary Patents (which are always subject to the jurisdiction of the UPC). While Articles 25 and 26 UPCA set out the scope of the exclusive rights conferred by a patent, Article 27 UPCA contains a number of specific limitations on the effects of a patent, including an Experimental Use exemption and a Bolar-type exemption.[5] The limitations in Article 27 UPCA are considered to be an exemption to infringement as, by their wording, they fall outside the scope of protection of the exclusive rights conferred by a patent.

Article 27(b) UPCA contains an Experimental Use exemption and has the following wording:

> The rights conferred by a patent shall not extend to any of the following:
>
> ...
>
> (b) acts done for experimental purposes relating to the subject-matter of the patented invention

Thus, to benefit from this exemption, the acts must: (i) be done for experimental purposes; and (ii) relate to the subject-matter of the patented invention.

There is also a Bolar-type exemption in Article 27(d) UPCA which provides that the rights conferred by a patent shall not extend to:

3. The Bolar-type exemption is named after a US decision, *Roche Products, Inc. v. Bolar Pharmaceutical Co.* (U.S. Court of Appeals for the Federal Circuit – 733 F.2d 858 (Fed. Cir. 1984)).
4. The Unitary Patent Package & Unified Patent Court. Problems, Possible Improvements and Alternatives, Desaunettes, Luc ; de Visscher, Fernand ; Strowel, Alain, Chapter 22, Research and bolar exemptions from UPC, Belgian and French perspectives, Olivier Mignolet, François Jonquères, Estelle Thiebaut & Hannelore Daems, p. 497.
5. Articles 28-29 UPCA also contain limitations regarding prior use and the principle of exhaustion.

the acts allowed pursuant to Article 13(6) of Directive 2001/82/EC[6] [the 'Veterinary Medicinal Products Directive'] or Article 10(6) of Directive 2001/83/EC[7] [the 'Human Medicinal Products Directive'] in respect of any patent covering the product within the meaning of either of those Directives.

Thus, the UPCA implements the Bolar-type exemption as it is formulated in the above EU legislative acts (see further in section 3. below).

2. THE EXPERIMENTAL USE EXEMPTION

a. History and Rationale of Adopting the Experimental Use Exemption

The UPCA largely harmonizes the scope of rights, exceptions and limitations for European patents, as well as for Unitary Patents for which the UPC will have jurisdiction.

The wording of the Experimental Use exemption in Article 27(b) UPCA corresponds to the exemption found in the Community Patent Convention of 1975, a convention which can be regarded as a predecessor to the UPC framework but which never entered into force for lack of political compromise.[8]

The rationale for the Experimental Use exemption is not further explained in the UPCA. However, the need to encourage scientific progress by allowing research for improvement has been one of the main reasons for implementing the Experimental Use exemption in most EU Member States which are part of the UPC. Said exemption is also grounded in the principle of the sufficiency of disclosure, as it is crucial for a person skilled in the art to be able to reproduce the patented invention in order to verify its effectiveness.[9]

b. The Laws Applicable to the Experimental Use Exemption in the UPC

The Experimental Use exemption is codified in Article 27(b) UPCA (for its wording see section 1.b. above). There is yet no case law regarding the Experimental Use exemption from the UPC. As this exemption is not directly covered by any provision of

6. Directive 2001/82/EC of the European Parliament and of the Council of 6 November 2001 on the Community code relating to veterinary medicinal products (OJ L 311, 28.11.2001, p. 1) including any subsequent amendments.
7. Directive 2001/83/EC of the European Parliament and of the Council of 6 November 2001 on the Community code relating to medicinal products for human use (OJ L 311, 28.11.2001, p. 67) including any subsequent amendments.
8. See Article 31(b) of the Convention for the European patent for the common market (Community Patent Convention), 76/76/EEC, Official Journal L 017, 26/01/1976 P. 0001 – 0028.
9. Cornish, Experimental Use of Patented Inventions in European Community States, IIC 1998 s. 735 ff. See also account in The European Research and Bolar Exemptions – Background, Status Quo and a Look at the Agreement on a Unified Patent Court (UPCA) and the EU Commission's New Draft Directive for the Reform of Pharmaceutical Legislation, Dr Marco Stief, GRUR International, 73(9), 2024, 824–837, page 824 ff.

Union law,[10] the UPC will develop its own approach, taking into account international agreements binding on all Member States (Article 24(1)(d) UPCA). This includes the so called three-step-rule in Article 30 of the TRIPS Agreement,[11] which provides that any exceptions to the exclusive rights conferred by a patent may not unreasonably conflict with a normal exploitation of the patent and do not unreasonably prejudice the legitimate interests of the patent owner, taking account of the legitimate interests of third parties. Further, the UPC may draw from approaches under national law (as allowed by Article 24(1)(e) UPCA).

c. Procedural Aspects of Invoking the Experimental Use Exemption

The UPC has two instances, the Court of First Instance and the Court of Appeal.[12] The Court of First Instance is structured in several types of divisions that are distributed throughout the UPC Member States; Central Divisions, Local Divisions and Regional Divisions.[13] Article 33 UPCA sets out rules on which first instance division(s) are competent to hear actions regarding infringement, revocation and other types of actions which fall under the jurisdiction of the UPC.

The Experimental Use exemption can be invoked by a defendant in an infringement case before the UPC. In theory it may also be possible to lodge a declaratory action of non-infringement on this basis pursuant to Article 32(1)(b) UPCA.[14] A defendant in an infringement case is expected to raise the defence already in its first written submission to the court (the statement of defence).[15]

d. Scope of the Experimental Use Exemption in the UPC

i. Fields of Technology

There are no field-of-technology-based limitations or restrictions on the Experimental Use exemption in the UPCA. Thus, all types of technology may utilize the exemption, provided the requirements for application are met.

ii. Purpose of Experiments/Infringing Activities

To benefit from the exemption, the acts must be (i) be done for experimental purposes; and (ii) relate to the subject-matter of the patented invention.

---

10. This exemption is not addressed for instance in Directive 2004/48/EC of the European Parliament and of the Council Of 29 April 2004 on the enforcement of intellectual property rights.
11. Agreement on Trade-Related Aspects of Intellectual Property Rights.
12. Article 6(1) UPCA.
13. Article 4(2) UPCA.
14. The chance of this happening in practice is limited given, for instance, the nature of the defence and the requirement of legal standing to sue.
15. Rule 24 in the Rules of Procedure of the UPC. The UPC provides mechanisms for later submissions or new arguments under specific conditions.

A contentious issue in several UPC Member States applying their national exemptions has been whether the exemption covers experiments with a clear commercial motivation, in particular whether it covers large-scale clinical trials. The wording of the Article 27(b) UPCA does not exclude from exemption acts which are done with a commercial purpose. That the Experimental Use exemption covers acts done with a commercial purpose also aligns with how the Experimental Use exemption has been treated in several UPC Member States.[16] Acts done privately and for non-commercial purposes are subject to a separate exemption in Article 27(a) UPCA:

> The rights conferred by a patent shall not extend to any of the following:
> (a) acts done privately and for non-commercial purposes; ...

It is not clear whether clinical trials may as such be encompassed by the Experimental Use exemption. However, these acts will often be exempted through the Bolar-type exemption in Article 27(d) UPCA if they are necessary to gain market approval within the EU for a medicinal product (see section 3. below).

In certain UPC Member States, the Experimental Use exemption extended also to research performed *with* a patented invention, for instance a patented measuring tool.[17] As the wording under the UPCA requires that the use relates to the subject-matter of the patented invention, research with a patented invention concerning subject-matter other than the patented invention will likely not be allowed under the Experimental Use exemption. This interpretation also aligns with the UPC Member States' obligations under the TRIPS Agreement. As research tools are regularly only used in the context of research, extending the Experimental Use exemption to use of patented research tools may result in a de facto denial of patent protection for the research tools, which could contradict the UPC Member States' obligations under Article 30 of the TRIPS Agreement.

iii. Exempted and Prohibited Activities

As there is no case law concerning the scope of the Experimental Use exemption, no definitive list of allowed activities can be provided. However, the wording of the provision does not contain any limitation as to which 'use' is encompassed by the exemption. Thus, any use such as manufacture, storage, import would likely be allowed as long as the use relates to the subject-matter of the patented invention. In this regard, it is relevant to also mention the principle of exhaustion in Article 29 UPCA as this principle would allow for a right to purchase a patented product that has been put on the market with the consent of the patent holder and reverse engineer it to understand how it was manufactured.

16. Please see the chapters on Germany, France and Sweden in this volume.
17. For example the Belgian Experimental Use exemption, which is considered broad but is subject to amendments to align it with the Experimental Use exemption in Article 27 UPCA, see The Unitary Patent Package & Unified Patent Court. Problems, Possible Improvements and Alternatives, Desaunettes, Luc; de Visscher, Fernand ; Strowel, Alain, Chapter 22, Research and bolar exemptions from UPC, Belgian and French perspectives, Olivier Mignolet, François Jonquères, Estelle Thiebaut & Hannelore Daems, p. 502 ff.

iv. Pure Academic vs Commercially Motivated Experimental Use

The wording of Article 27(b) UPCA does not exclude from exemption acts which are done with a commercial purpose. That the Experimental Use exemption covers acts done with a commercial purpose also aligns with how the Experimental Use exemption has been treated in several UPC Member States.[18]

The UPC will through its case law have to define to what extent an act may be determined by commercial intent for it to still qualify under the exemption.

e. Beneficiary Limitations

Third party contributions do not appear to have been contemplated in Article 27(b) UPCA. Of course, this provision only aims to exempt those acts that would otherwise be an act of infringement. If acts by third persons are also done for experimental purposes related to the patented invention, they may also be exempted. It remains unresolved yet whether a commercial act by a third party made in the context of an exempted act by one of its clients would also be exempted.[19]

f. Territoriality Issues

Decisions of the UPC generally have effect throughout all UPC Member States where the patent in suit (a European patent, a Unitary Patent or a supplementary patent certificate ('SPC')) has effect.[20] Under certain circumstances, the territorial scope of the UPC's decisions may be limited.[21]

g. Burden of Proof and Onus

According to Article 54 UPCA, the burden of the proof of facts shall be on the party relying on those facts.[22] In one of its first judgments, the UPC Court of Appeal (in Preliminary Injunction proceedings) addressed the distribution of the burden of proof between the parties:

> The burden of presentation and proof for facts allegedly establishing the entitlement to initiate proceedings and the infringement or imminent infringement

18. Please see the chapters on Germany, France and Sweden in this volume.
19. In relation to the so-called Bolar-type exemption (to be addressed below), the CJEU was seized with this question in *Astellas Pharma Inc. v. Polpharma SA Pharmaceutical Works* in C-661/13. Unfortunately, the referral to the CJEU was withdrawn before the Court could issue its judgment.
20. SPCs are protected according to Article 30 UPCA.
21. The designations of a European patent may belong to different patent owners because some designations may have been transferred from the original patent owner to other persons. In such scenario, the decision of the UPC on infringement may only have the effect of Article 34 UPCA for the designation of the patent owner bringing an infringement action, see Von Falck and Dorn in: Tilmann/Plassmann. Unified Patent Protection in Europe (2018). Article 34 UPCA recital 58 et seqq.
22. See also Rules 171-172 in the Rules of Procedure of the UPC.

of the patent, as well as for all other circumstances allegedly supporting the Applicant's request, lies with the Applicant, whereas, unless the subject-mater of the decision is the ordering of measures without hearing the defendant pursuant to Article 60(5) in conjunction with Article 62(5) UPCA, the burden of presentation and proof for facts concerning the lack of validity of the patent and other circumstances allegedly supporting the Defendant's position lies with the Defendant.[23]

Although an experimental use defence is not explicitly mentioned, one may derive from this that, once the plaintiff has made its case for material infringement, it is up to the defendant to carry the burden of presentation and proof of the circumstances supporting any eligibility under the Experimental Use exemption.

In Rules of Procedures, specifically in Rule 170, the means of evidence and means of obtaining evidence in proceedings before the UPC are set out. If facts presented by one party are not specifically contested by the other party, they are held to be true between the parties.[24] To prevent this assumed truth, the other party must specifically and substantially contest the presented facts, for example by providing evidence and presenting its version of the relevant facts.

h. Applicability during Patent Term Extension or Supplementary Protection Certificate

An SPC shall confer the same rights as conferred by the patent and shall be subject to the same limitations and the same obligations (Article 30 UPCA). As a result, the exemption applies during an SPC period.

3. THE BOLAR-TYPE EXEMPTION

a. History and Rationale of Adopting the Bolar-Type Exemption

As said, the UPCA largely harmonizes the scope of rights, exceptions and limitations for European patents, as well as for Unitary Patents for which the UPC will have jurisdiction. In contrast to the Experimental Use exemption (discussed *supra*), the so-called Bolar-type exemption has already been the subject of harmonization efforts through EU law.

The EU Bolar-type exemption was introduced with the aim of addressing a structural disadvantage of medicinal products. These products require extensive clinical and non-clinical testing to obtain the required marketing authorization to put them on the market. If these activities, which may take months and in some cases years, could only be conducted after a patent has expired, the exclusivity provided by the patent could be factually extended. Thus, the Bolar-type exemption was

23. UPC Court of Appeal in *NanoString v. 10xGenomics*, UPC_CoA_335/2023, 26 February 2024, headnote 3.
24. Rule 171.2 in the Rules of Procedure of the UPC.

introduced to facilitate the timely entry of generic veterinary and human medicines into the market after patent expiration.[25]

However, being introduced into national law through EU directives, the Bolar-type exemption was interpreted differently among EU Member States. Within the UPC Member States, this should now change with the codification of the exemption in Article 27(d) UPCA.

b. The Laws Applicable to the Bolar-Type Exemption

Article 27(d) UPCA provides that the rights conferred by a patent shall not extend to:

> the acts allowed pursuant to Article 13(6) of Directive 2001/82/EC[26] [the 'Veterinary Medicinal Products Directive'] or Article 10(6) of Directive 2001/83/EC[27] [the 'Human Medicinal Products Directive'] in respect of any patent covering the product within the meaning of either of those Directives.

The Bolar-type exemption in Article 27(d) UPCA thus implements the EU Bolar-type exemption in the same scope as it was introduced by Article 10(6) of the Human Medicinal Products Directive[28] and Article 13(6) of the Veterinary Medicinal Products Directive.

Article 10(6) of the Human Medicinal Products Directive, which concerns applications for generic medicinal products within the EU, provides that 'conducting the necessary studies and trials with a view to the application of paragraphs 1, 2, 3 and 4 and the consequential practical requirements shall not be regarded as contrary to patent rights or to supplementary protection certificates for medicinal products.'

Accordingly, tests and studies that are performed to obtain data for an authorization procedure in an EU or EEA country do not constitute patent infringement if they are necessary for the authorization application. Paragraphs 1-4, to which reference is made, contain explanations and definitions of generics and biosimilars.

Article 13(6) of the Veterinary Medicinal Products Directive is largely identical to Article 10(6) Human Medicinal Products Directive.

The Veterinary Medicinal Products Directive (2001/82/EC) has been repealed and replaced by Regulation (EU) 2019/6 (the 'Veterinary Medicinal Products Regulation'),[29] which became applicable on 28 January 2022. According to Article 149 of

25. Recital 14 of the Directive 2004/27/EEG OF THE EUROPEAN PARLIAMENT AND OF THE COUNCIL of 31 March 2004 amending Directive 2001/83/EC on the Community code relating to medicinal products for human use.
26. Directive 2001/82/EC of the European Parliament and of the Council of 6 November 2001 on the Community code relating to veterinary medicinal products (OJ L 311, 28.11.2001, p. 1) including any subsequent amendments.
27. Directive 2001/83/EC of the European Parliament and of the Council of 6 November 2001 on the Community code relating to medicinal products for human use (OJ L 311, 28.11.2001, p. 67) including any subsequent amendments.
28. It was introduced by Directive 2004/27/EC amending Directive 2001/82/EC relating to medicinal products for human use.
29. Regulation (EU) 2019/6 of the European Parliament and of the Council of 11 December 2018 on veterinary medicinal products and repealing Directive 2001/82/EC (the Veterinary Medicinal Products Regulation). Article 41 of said regulation (Patent-related rights) provides

the Veterinary Medicinal Products Regulation, references to the repealed Veterinary Medicinal Products Directive shall be construed as references to the Veterinary Medicinal Products Regulation. Therefore, Article 27(d) UPCA shall instead be considered to refer to Article 41 of the Veterinary Medicinal Products Regulation. The Bolar-type exemption in said regulation is similar to the exemption in the Veterinary Medicinal Products Directive.[30]

There is also a pending proposal from the EU legislator for a new human medicinal products directive to repeal and replace the current directive (the 'Draft').[31] The Draft is part of a proposal from the EU Commission for the reform of pharmaceutical legislation in the EU, which according to the Commission is the most far-reaching reform in twenty years.[32]

The Draft seeks to, inter alia, amend and broaden the scope of the Bolar-type exemption for human medicinal products. The Draft proposal contains three significant amendments to the current Bolar-type exemption:

(i) Not only studies and trials to studies, trials and the consequential practical requirements which are necessary to obtain the marketing authorization will be exempted, but also those necessary for the obtention of health technology assessment and pricing and reimbursement.
(ii) In addition to the current exemption related to activities to obtain a generic or biosimilar drug, the proposed exemption aims to allow also the conduct of studies, trials, and other activities to obtain data for hybrid or biohybrid drugs and subsequent variants.
(iii) Further, the Draft also clarifies that third-party suppliers and service providers which supply medicinal products protected by a patent or SPC to generic

---

that 'Conducting the necessary tests, studies and trials with a view to applying for a marketing authorisation in accordance with Article 18 shall not be regarded as contrary to patent-related rights or to supplementary-protection certificates for veterinary medicinal products and medicinal products for human use'.

30. Article 13.6 of the Veterinary Medicinal Products Directive provides that '6. Conducting the necessary studies, tests and trials with a view to the application of paragraphs 1 to 5 and the consequential practical requirements shall not be regarded as contrary to patent-related rights or to supplementary-protection certificates for medicinal products.' Article 41 has a slightly different wording stipulating that 'Conducting the necessary tests, studies and trials with a view to applying for a marketing authorisation in accordance with Article 18 shall not be regarded as contrary to patent-related rights or to supplementary-protection certificates for veterinary medicinal products and medicinal products for human use.' Thus, the wording 'the consequential practical requirements' has been removed in the current provision without any motivation if this is intended to have any practical effect.
31. Article 85 of the Proposal for a Directive of the European Parliament and of the Council on the Union code relating to medicinal products for human use, and repealing Directive 2001/83/EC and Directive 2009/35/EC of 26 April 2023 (COM(2023) 192 final, 2023/0132 (COD)).
32. The proposal is available at https://health.ec.europa.eu/medicinal-products/pharmaceutical-strategy-europe/reform-eu-pharmaceutical-legislation_en. This chapter is based on the wording of the Draft dated 26 April 2023. The legislation may be subject to further amendments and revisions.

manufacturers to conduct studies to obtain marketing approval are also covered by the exemption.

Like the Veterinary Medicinal Products Regulation, the Draft contains a provision stipulating that references to the repealed Directive shall be construed as references to the replacing Directive. There is still some uncertainty as to how the Draft will evolve during the legislative process. Hower, once finalized and assuming that the Draft does not undergo any material amendments in this respect, Article 27(d) UPCA will refer to Article 81 of the Draft once it will enter into force.

c. Procedural Aspects of Invoking the Bolar-Type Exemption

Please see the account for Procedural Aspects of Invoking the Experimental Use Exemption in section 2.c. above.

d. Scope of the Bolar-Type Exemption

The exact scope of allowed measures has not yet been clarified in any case law. Until the first binding decisions have been rendered by the UPC in this regard, several uncertainties will remain regarding the exact scope of exemption offered by Article 27(d) UPCA.

i. Fields of Technology

The Bolar-type exemption is limited to medicinal products (for human and veterinary use).

ii. Purpose of Experiments/Infringing Activities

The current Bolar-type exemption in the UPCA is by its wording limited to activities in connection with the marketing authorization of generics, bioequivalents and biosimilars, for example pre-clinical and clinical trials. Thus, activities required for market approval of innovative medicinal products are most likely not exempted under the Bolar-type exemption in the UPCA.

Exempted activities are by its wording limited to authorizations within the EU/EEA which means that activities necessary for market authorizations outside the EU/EEA are likely not covered by the exemption.

As a result, the current UPC Bolar-type exemption appears to be narrower than what is applied in certain UPC Member States, for example Germany.[33]

The UPC Bolar-type exemption does not by its wording cover activities required for market approval of medical devices. Medical devices are governed by a separate EU regulation,[34] to which Article 27(d) UPCA does not refer.

---

33. Please see the chapter on Germany in this volume.
34. Regulation (EU) 2017/745 of the European Parliament and of the Council of 5 April 2017 on medical devices, amending Directive 2001/83/EC, Regulation (EC) No. 178/2002 and Regulation (EC) No. 1223/2009 and repealing Council Directives 90/385/EEC and 93/42/

Research made with the aim of improving an invention but that is not necessary to obtain a market approval does not fall under the Bolar-type exemption (but may be exempt under the Experimental Use exemption in Article 27(b) UPCA).

If the Draft proposal enters into force, the Bolar-type exemption will significantly broaden in scope (see section 3.b. above).

iii. Exempted and Prohibited Activities

The Bolar-type exemption in Article 10.6 of the Human Medicinal Products Directive, to which Article 27(d) UPCA refers, allows for conducting the necessary studies and trials to obtain a marketing authorization within the EU/EEA and any 'consequential practical requirements'. Thus, it is the regulatory authority's requirements that set the frame for allowed activities. Through the catch-all 'practical requirements' it is not only clinical studies and trials that are covered by the exemption. Also, other patent uses necessary prior to studies and trial, such as import, development work regarding manufacturing methods, and manufacturing of the reference pharmaceutical, are exempted as long as the measures are necessary to obtain a market approval.

The exact scope of allowed measures has however not yet been clarified in any case law. Until the first binding decisions have been rendered by the UPC in this regard, several uncertainties will remain regarding the exact scope of exemption offered by Article 27(d) UPCA.

e. Beneficiary Limitations

Third party contributions do not appear to have been contemplated in Article 27(d) UPCA. Thus, whether the person seeking regulatory approval can contract a third party for performance of any of the necessary measures is unresolved.[35] UPC Member States have taken different approaches to this issue in the context of applying their national exemptions.[36] If the Draft proposal enters into force, it will be clarified that third party suppliers and providers will fall under the exemption.

f. Territoriality Issues

The exemption applies by its wording to applications for regulatory approval within the EU or EEA. This means that activities necessary for market authorizations outside the EU/EEA are most likely not covered by the UPC Bolar-type exemption.

Decisions of the UPC generally have effect throughout all UPC Member States where the patent in suit (a European patent, a Unitary Patent or an SPC) has effect.

EEC (Medical Devices Regulation). The Medical Devices Regulation does not contain a provision comparable to the Bolar privilege.

35. Cf. the withdrawn CJEU referral in *Astellas Pharma Inc. v. Polpharma SA Pharmaceutical Works* (C-661/13).
36. See account in The European Research and Bolar Exemptions – Background, Status Quo and a Look at the Agreement on a Unified Patent Court (UPCA) and the EU Commission's New Draft Directive for the Reform of Pharmaceutical Legislation, Dr Marco Stief, GRUR International, 73(9), 2024, 824–837, page 832.

Under certain circumstances, the territorial scope of the UPC's decisions may be limited.[37]

g. Burden of Proof and Onus

Please see the account for Burden of Proof and Onus for the Experimental Use exemption in section 2.g. above.

h. Applicability during Patent Term Extension or Supplementary Protection Certificate

The exemption is not limited in time. As a result, the exemption applies during an SPC period.

4. DIFFERENCES BETWEEN THE TWO EXEMPTIONS IN THE UPC

The Experimental Use exemption and the Bolar-type exemptions are regulated by two distinct provisions in the UPCA and have, at least partially, different purposes. They may also overlap. For example, clinical experiments done for the purpose of researching a patented invention which are also necessary for gaining marketing approval may be covered by both exemptions. The exemptions also differ. The Experimental Use exemption is not limited to any specific technology or market sector. In contrast, the Bolar-type exemption is limited to uses necessary to obtain a marketing authorization for generic or biosimilar human or veterinary medicines. However, the Bolar-type exemption is also broader in many ways, as it includes all activities that are necessary for a market approval, while the Experimental Use exemption is limited acts done for experimental purposes relating to the subject-matter of the patented invention. Thus, the two exemptions are distinct and differ in several aspects.

37. The designations of a European patent may belong to different patent owners because some designations may have been transferred from the original patent owner to other persons. In such scenario, the decision of the UPC on infringement may only have the effect of Article 34 UPCA for the designation of the patent owner bringing an infringement action, see Von Falck and Dorn in: Tilmann/Plassmann. Unified Patent Protection in Europe (2018). Article 34 UPCA recital 58 et seqq.

Chapter 41

United Kingdom

Milly Wickson, Shohta Ueno and Trevor Cook

1. GENERAL

a. Terminology

The Experimental Use exemption is set out in Section 60(5)(b) of the Patents Act 1977 ('PA') and provides that an activity will not constitute patent infringement if it is 'done for experimental purposes relating to the subject-matter of the invention'.

The Bolar-type exemption is set out in Section 60(5)(i) PA and provides that an activity will not constitute infringement if it is done in conducting a study, test or trial which is necessary for, and conducted with a view to, securing the regulatory approval of a generic medicinal drug for human or veterinary use. This is also referred to in this chapter as the 'old Bolar-type exemption'.

In 2014, a wider Bolar-type exemption was added in Sections 60(6D) – (6G) PA to exempt from infringement activities done for the purpose of a medicinal product assessment (i.e. tests including clinical trials), whether for originator medicines or generic/biosimilar medicines. Rather than expand the original narrow Bolar provision, the UK decided to incorporate the provisions of a wider Bolar-type exemption into the Experimental Use exemption in Section 60(5). This is also referred to in this chapter as the 'medicinal product assessment exemption'.

b. Legal Basis in the UK

The Experimental Use exemption was codified in Section 60(5)(b) PA.

> (5) An act which, apart from this subsection, would constitute an infringement of a patent for an invention shall not do so if …
>
> (b) it is done for experimental purposes relating to the subject-matter of the invention;

The application of the Experimental Use exemption under Section 60(5)(b) PA has been considered in the case law and *Meter-Tech v. British Gas* [2016] EWHC 2278 (Pat) summarizes the scope of the exemption by reference to the key case law (see below).

The old Bolar-type exemption provided by Section 60(5)(i) PA was introduced into the PA in 2005 by the Medicines (Marketing Authorisations etc.) Amendment Regulations 2005 (S.I. 2005/2759), regs. 1(a), 3(a) and is narrow in scope:

> (5) An act which, apart from this subsection, would constitute an infringement of a patent for an invention shall not do so if …
>
> (i) it consists of –
>
> (i) an act done in conducting a study, test or trial which is necessary for and is conducted with a view to the application of paragraphs 1 to 5 of article 13 of Directive 2001/82/EC or paragraphs 1 to 4 of article 10 of Directive 2001/83/EC, or
>
> (ii) any other act which is required for the purpose of the application of those paragraphs.

Section 60(5)(i) applies to acts done in conducting studies, tests or trials which are necessary for, and conducted with a view to, securing the regulatory approval of a generic or biosimilar medicinal drug for human or veterinary use, or any other which is required for that purpose.

The scope of the Experimental Use exemption in the UK was extended in 2014 by Sections 60(6D) – (6G) PA to include a wider Bolar-type exemption (referred to in this chapter as the 'medicinal product assessment exemption').

> (6D) For the purposes of subsection (5)(b), anything done in or for the purposes of a medicinal product assessment which would otherwise constitute an infringement of a patent for an invention is to be regarded as done for experimental purposes relating to the subject-matter of the invention.
>
> (6E) In subsection (6D), 'medicinal product assessment' means any testing, course of testing or other activity undertaken with a view to providing data for any of the following purposes –
>
> (a) obtaining or varying an authorisation to sell or supply, or offer to sell or supply, a medicinal product (whether in the United Kingdom or elsewhere);
>
> (b) complying with any regulatory requirement imposed (whether in the United Kingdom or elsewhere) in relation to such an authorisation;
>
> (c) enabling a government or public authority (whether in the United Kingdom or elsewhere), or a person (whether in the United Kingdom or elsewhere) with functions of –
>
> (i) providing health care on behalf of such a government or public authority, or
>
> (ii) providing advice to, or on behalf of, such a government or public authority about the provision of health care,
>
> to carry out an assessment of suitability of a medicinal product for human use for the purpose of determining whether to use it, or recommend its use, in the provision of health care.
>
> (6F) In subsection (6E) and this subsection –

> 'medicinal product' means a medicinal product for human use or a veterinary medicinal product;
>
> 'medicinal product for human use' has the meaning given by article 1 of Directive 2001/83/EC;
>
> 'veterinary medicinal product' has the meaning given by article 1 of Directive 2001/82/EC.
>
> (6G) Nothing in subsections (6D) to (6F) is to be read as affecting the application of subsection (5)(b) in relation to any act of a kind not falling within subsection (6D).

2. THE EXPERIMENTAL USE EXEMPTION

a. History and Rationale of Adopting the Experimental Use Exemption

There has been a common law basis for an experimental use defence to patent infringement since the late 1870s. In *Frearson v. Loe* (1878),[1] Jessel M.R. found that potentially infringing articles made for the purpose of 'bona fide experiments', such as to improve upon the patented invention, are not necessarily liable to an action for patent infringement, providing said articles are not made and used for profit (even if to a limited extent). As the rationale for this, Jessel M.R. held that '[p]atent rights were never granted to prevent persons of ingenuity exercising their talents in a fair way'. Almost a century later the House of Lords in *Bristol v. Beecham* (1973) addressed what constitutes 'use' of an invention under the Patents Act 1949 (albeit in the context of validity).[2] It considered 'use' requires something done for gain or for industrial or commercial purposes, and for which where is some benefit other than mere knowledge. Such commercial use may be distinguished from experiments that are not commercial in nature.

The statutory exemptions to patent infringement in the Patents Act 1977 originate from Article 27 of Council Agreement 89/695/EEC,[3] and as such must be read and construed in light of the wording and purpose of the Agreement on Trade Related Aspects of Intellectual Property Rights (TRIPS), in particular Article 30, which provides:

> Members may provide limited exceptions to the exclusive rights conferred by a patent, provided that such exceptions do not unreasonably conflict with a normal exploitation of the patent and do not unreasonably prejudice the legitimate interests of the patent owner, taking account of the legitimate interests of third parties.

The Experimental Use exemption under Section 60(5)(b) PA excepts from infringement acts 'done for experimental purposes relating to the subject-matter of the invention'.

1. *Frearson v. Loe* (1878) 9 Ch. D. 48.
2. *Bristol-Myers Co. v. Beecham Group Ltd.* [1974] 2 W.L.R. 79.
3. Council Agreement 89/695/EEC of 15 December 1989 relating to Community patents.

The old Bolar-type exemption under Section 60(5)(i) PA was enacted in 2005 through European Directive 2001/83/EC[4] to exempt from infringement tests and trials for the purposes of manufacturing generic versions of medicinal products protected by patents to remove unnecessary barriers to generic entry onto the market.

Then in 2014, as a result of calls to extend the scope of the UK's research exemptions, led in part by fear that the UK would fail to compete with other European countries as a location for clinical trials, the scope of the Experimental Use exemption in the UK was extended by Sections 60(6D) – (6G) PA to include a medicinal product assessment exemption. Rather than expand the original narrow Bolar provision, the UK decided to incorporate the provisions of a much wider Bolar-type exemption into the Experimental Use exemption in order to be as competitive as possible within Europe and to achieve consistency with the nascent UPC legislation to which the UK was then a party. This brought into the scope of the Experimental Use exemption acts done for the purposes of a medicinal product assessment (i.e. clinical trials).

b. The Laws Applicable to the Experimental Use Exemption in the UK

The Experimental Use exemption is codified in Section 60(5)(b) PA and provides:

> (5) An act which, apart from this subsection, would constitute an infringement of a patent for an invention shall not do so if …
>
> (b) it is done for experimental purposes relating to the subject-matter of the invention;

The scope of the Experimental Use exemption was extended in 2014 by Sections 60(6D) – (6G) PA to include a wider medicinal product assessment exemption:

> (6D) For the purposes of subsection (5)(b), anything done in or for the purposes of a medicinal product assessment which would otherwise constitute an infringement of a patent for an invention is to be regarded as done for experimental purposes relating to the subject-matter of the invention.
>
> (6E) In subsection (6D), 'medicinal product assessment' means any testing, course of testing or other activity undertaken with a view to providing data for any of the following purposes –
>
> (a) obtaining or varying an authorisation to sell or supply, or offer to sell or supply, a medicinal product (whether in the United Kingdom or elsewhere);
>
> (b) complying with any regulatory requirement imposed (whether in the United Kingdom or elsewhere) in relation to such an authorisation;
>
> (c) enabling a government or public authority (whether in the United Kingdom or elsewhere), or a person (whether in the United Kingdom or elsewhere) with functions of –
>
> (i) providing health care on behalf of such a government or public authority, or
>
> (ii) providing advice to, or on behalf of, such a government or public authority about the provision of health care,

4. Directive (EU) 2001/83/EC of the European Parliament and of the Council of 6 November 2001 on the Community code relating to medicinal products for human use.

to carry out an assessment of suitability of a medicinal product for human use for the purpose of determining whether to use it, or recommend its use, in the provision of health care.

(6F) In subsection (6E) and this subsection –

'medicinal product' means a medicinal product for human use or a veterinary medicinal product;

'medicinal product for human use' has the meaning given by article 1 of Directive 2001/83/EC;

'veterinary medicinal product' has the meaning given by article 1 of Directive 2001/82/EC.

(6G) Nothing in subsections (6D) to (6F) is to be read as affecting the application of subsection (5)(b) in relation to any act of a kind not falling within subsection (6D).

The bounds of the Experimental Use exemption and guidance on its scope have been considered in the case law that is mentioned throughout this chapter. From this case law, the following principles emerge:

- Generally, the Experimental Use exemption will only cover experiments for the purpose of furthering the technology concerned (e.g. finding out new properties or features) and will not cover experiments with a commercial focus (e.g. customer demonstrations). However, the medicinal product assessment exemption does permit commercially focused tests for pharmaceutical products.
- A commercial end point does not negate the application of the exemption, but care must be taken to restrict the experiments to those having a real and direct connection with the subject-matter of the invention.
- A protected end point (e.g. experiments into the subject-matter of an invention) does not protect prior acts that are of a commercial nature (e.g. sale of equipment which falls within the scope of the granted patent(s) to be used in the protected experiments).
- Use of a patented invention as a research tool to investigate other subject-matter will not be protected by the exemption but experiments investigating the subject-matter of that patented invention should be protected.
- Where there is mixed use in experiments, part research and part commercial, the courts will look at the dominant or preponderant use.

c. Procedural Aspects of Invoking the Experimental Use Exemption

The Experimental Use exemption is raised as a defence in patent infringement proceedings. In the UK, such proceedings are under the jurisdiction of the Patents Court (or, in limited circumstances, the Intellectual Property Enterprise Court) and, if appealed, the Court of Appeal and the Supreme Court. Therefore, it is these courts which determine the legitimacy of the Experimental Use exemption raised as a defence in patent infringement proceedings in the UK.

d. Scope of the Experimental Use Exemption in the UK

i. Fields of Technology

The Experimental Use exemption under Section 60(5)(b) PA is not limited to particular fields of technology in the UK. The medicinal product assessment exemption which was introduced by Sections 60 (6D) – (6G) PA applies only to medicinal and veterinary products governed by European Directives 2001/83/EC and 2001/82/EC,[5] respectively. These Directives, however, do not preclude an experimenter from relying upon the medicinal product assessment exemption for the purposes of satisfying a regulatory requirement imposed outside of the EU, such as in the UK or elsewhere.

ii. Purpose of Experiments/Infringing Activities

The Experimental Use exemption under Section 60(5)(b) PA excepts from infringement activities done for experimental purposes relating to the subject-matter of the invention. It applies to all patented subject-matter and so will serve to protect work directed to improving upon rather than merely using the patented subject-matter. The distinction is an important one and turns upon the meaning of the words 'relating to the subject-matter of the invention'.

'Experimental purposes'

The meaning of 'experimental purposes' has been considered extensively in the case law and the key cases and principles have been summarized by Daniel Alexander KC, sitting as Deputy High Court Judge, in *Meter-Tech LLC v. British Gas Trading Limited* at paragraphs [231] – [236].

> 231. This requirement was considered by the Court of Appeal in *Monsanto Co. v Stauffer Chemical Co. and Another* [1985] R.P.C. 515. That case concerned a herbicide product which was required to go through four stages of testing in order to achieve regulatory approval for a full commercial launch. The defendant carried out testing in laboratories and glasshouses, on a larger scale on its farm in Essex, and on a larger scale still on third party farms. At p538, Dillon LJ (with whom the Court agreed) rejected the submission that the words 'for experimental purposes' are limited to experiments in laboratories or glasshouses. He held that the line falls between 'discovery' and 'demonstration', and in this case the experiments on the defendant's own farms were within the statutory exemption, but those on third party farms were not. At page 542 he said:
>
> > 'Trials carried out in order to discover something unknown or to test a hypothesis or even in order to find out whether something which is known to work in specific conditions, e.g. of soil or weather, will work in different conditions can fairly, in my judgment, be regarded as experiments. But trials carried out in order to demonstrate to a third party that a product works or,

5. Directive (EU) 2001/82/EC of the European Parliament and of the Council of 6 November 2001 on the Community code relating to veterinary medicinal products.

> in order to amass information to satisfy a third party, whether a customer or a body such as the PSPS or ACAS, that the product works as its maker claims are not, in my judgment, to be regarded as acts done "for experimental purposes". The purposes for which tests or trials are carried out may in some cases be mixed and may in some cases be difficult to discern…'.

Daniel Alexander KC went on to consider paragraphs [73] to [81] of the judgment of Peter Prescott KC sitting as a Deputy High Court Judge in *CoreValve Inc v. Edwards Lifesciences AG* [2009] EWHC 6 (Pat) on the issue of mixed purposes. In *CoreValve*, the Deputy Judge made reference to an earlier decision of the Federal Supreme Court of Germany which considered the equivalent provision in *Klinische Versuche (Clinical Trials) I* [1997] RPC 623 (English translation):

> An act for experimental purposes which is related to the subject-matter of the invention and therefore legitimate can exist if a patented pharmaceutically active substance is used in clinical trials with the aim of finding whether and, where appropriate, in what form the active substance is suitable for curing or alleviating certain other human diseases.

In *Klinische Versuche* the substance in question (an interferon), which was the subject-matter of the invention, was a known treatment for rheumatoid arthritis, and the defendants were conducting clinical trials to investigate whether the substance could also be used in the treatment of other diseases, including cancer, AIDS and hepatitis. The Deputy Judge opined at paragraph [74]:

> I can see that those clinical trials were squarely within the purpose of the exception, for their immediate purpose was to generate scientific information by experimenting with the substance that was the subject of the patent claim.

However, the Deputy Judge went on to explain that there must be an 'outward limit' to that principle. For instance, if the defendants were selling a pharmaceutical product that was fairly new to the market in order to gain valuable information that was not otherwise available (for example, contraindications which would be stated in the product literature), would those acts be done for 'experimental purposes'? The Deputy Judge accepted that in placing its product on the market, a defendant would necessarily gain valuable information about its product which may lead to it making modifications, and therefore the existence of a commercial endpoint does not necessarily preclude reliance on the exemption:

> 77. I acknowledge that the mere fact that the purpose of the defendant is commercial is no rebuttal of the statutory defence. After all, most pharmaceutical research organisations are commercial. They do research because they hope to make money one day. However, in the present case it cannot be denied that an immediate and present purpose of CoreValve is to generate revenue – which was not so in the German case.
>
> 78. I therefore think that a more complete statement of the principle – it did not arise in the German case – should involve the consideration whether the immediate purpose of the transaction in question is to generate revenue.
>
> 79. The relevant statutory phrase is 'acts done for experimental purposes'. The difficulty arises where the defendant has mixed purposes. I would reject

the extreme proposition that, so long as one of the defendant's purposes is to generate information of scientific or technical value, it is irrelevant that another of his purposes is to generate ready cash. There may be no help for it but to consider the defendant's preponderant purposes.

80. On the evidence in this case I would hold that CoreValve's purposes are threefold: (1) to establish confidence in their product within the relevant market; (2) to generate immediate revenue of a substantial character; and (3) to gain information about clinical indications and, possibly, future modifications to be made to the physical structure of the device in the light of experience. I do not find that purpose (3) was their preponderant purpose.

81. I have not found this point easy, but on the whole I would hold that, on the assumption that the CoreValve device falls within Claim 1 of the patent in suit, section 60(5)(b) of the Patents Act 1977 is not a valid defence on the facts of this case.

The Deputy Judge therefore applied a multi-factorial assessment to the facts of the case, which placed significant weight on whether the defendant's acts were for the predominant purpose of finding out further information about the invention.

Daniel Alexander KC in *Meter-Tech* found this approach to be consistent with that taken by the Bundesgerichtshof in *Klinische Versuche (Clinical Trials) II* (Case X ZR 68/94) [1998] RPC 423, in which it was found that there is no 'handy demarcation' on the degree of commercial intention required to allow or preclude the availability of the defence. In that case, it was impossible to establish whether the active agent worked as claimed by the patent without conducting clinical trials, and the defence was held to apply.

Daniel Alexander KC concluded at [235] that it is not appropriate to 'place a gloss on the statutory wording', and that instead the evaluation in each case involves consideration of a range of factors, including:

a. whether the acts in question are properly characterized as trials and whether those trials can be described as undertaking scientific or development research;
b. whether the trials were carried out in order to discover something technically unknown or to test a technical hypothesis or whether they were carried out to discover whether the product was commercially acceptable to the market;
c. whether the trials were intended to find out whether something which was known to work in specific conditions would work in different conditions and, in the case of a system intended to operate on a large scale, whether it was capable of operating on such a scale;
d. whether the trials were carried out mainly in order to demonstrate or collect information to demonstrate to a third-party customer or regulator that a product works – which points away from experimental purposes;
e. whether the purpose of the trial was mainly directly or indirectly to generate revenue as a result of the use of the invention in the trial itself – which points away from experimental purposes.

236. It is, in my judgment, impossible to allocate a precise ranking to the importance of these factors and the evaluation must take an overall view. Moreover, the court must take into account the extent to which the acts undertaken were

reasonably necessary to determine the facts sought to be determined. A small-scale trial of a product may be treated as involving acts done for experimental purposes whereas the supply of a product in quantities far beyond that required to find out how it worked in certain conditions may not do so.

'Relating to the subject-matter of the invention'

The second requirement, that the experiments done 'relate to the subject matter of the invention', requires there to be a 'real and direct relationship' with the subject-matter of the invention.[6] As summarized by Daniel Alexander KC in *Meter-Tech*:

> 238. This too requires the court to take an overall view. One factor which may be important is the extent to which an alleged infringer is testing a product designed by a third party designer of such products to determine whether that product is suitable for the alleged infringer's use or whether the alleged infringer is testing a product with a view to further development of the subject matter of the patent – i.e. real research to take that sort of design forward.
>
> 239. An undertaking may buy and test a range of commercially available equipment, of which some may have patent protection, to work out which was most suitable for its purposes. To that extent, they may be trialling it. However, the fact that the undertaking was testing those products to see whether (for example) the invention resulted in a better product than one without, would not inevitably mean that the defence would apply.

It will be appreciated from the foregoing judgment extracts that this is a nuanced area in which the facts and circumstances play a significant role. Although difficult to be conclusive, it is nevertheless possible to derive a number of key points:

i. To constitute 'experimental purposes', the experiments must be carried out in order to discover something unknown, test a hypothesis or find out whether something which is known to work in specific conditions will work under different test experimental conditions. In contrast, tests conducted for demonstration purposes, or in order to amass information to satisfy a third party (e.g. a regulatory body) that a product works, are not acts done for 'experimental purposes'.
ii. Where a defendant has several purposes for carrying out the experiments, they are able to rely on the Experimental Use exemption provided that the dominant or preponderant purpose of the defendant's act is to generate information of scientific or technical value, and not for commercial reasons such as to establish market confidence or to generate revenue.[7]
iii. Another relevant factor is the scale of the acts undertaken and the extent to which they are reasonably necessary to achieve the experimental purpose. Therefore, a small-scale trial of a product may constitute an act done for 'experimental purposes', whereas the supply of products in quantities which

6. *Per Aldous J in SK&F v. Evans Medical* [1989] 1 FSR 513.
7. *CoreValve Inc v. Edwards Lifesciences* [2009] EWHC 6 (Pat).

exceed that required to test how the product works may fall outside the exemption.

iv. For the experiment to 'relate to the subject-matter of the invention', there must be a real and direct relationship between the subject-matter of the claimed invention and the experiment. Therefore, a defendant seeking to investigate a chemical patent using a reagent which is itself patented, would only be able to rely on the Experimental Use exemption with respect to the chemical patent, and not the reagent patent (the latter being used as a research tool only).

v. It is the defendant who bears the burden of proof to show that (i) the acts complained of were done for experimental purposes and (ii) those purposes relate to the subject-matter of the invention.

Further, to rely on Sections 60(6D)-(6G) PA, the use of a patented product must be for the purpose of a 'medicinal product assessment' (i.e. tests including clinical trials). A medicinal product assessment includes *any testing, course of testing or other activity* undertaken with a view to providing data for the purposes of:

a. obtaining or varying a marketing authorization;
b. complying with any regulatory requirement in relation to such a marketing authorization; or
c. conducting health technology assessments.

The definition of 'medicinal product' covers medicinal products both for human use or veterinary use, and extends to innovative products, as well as generic and biosimilar medicinal products (Section 60(6F) PA).

Health Technology Assessments (HTAs) are defined in Regulation (EU) 2021/2282[8] as scientific evidence-based processes that allow competent authorities to determine the relative effectiveness of new or existing health technologies. An HTA is carried out to assess the benefits and costs of a drug or treatment and how it compares with the available alternatives. An HTA often takes place alongside the later stages of the regulatory approval process. In England, the National Health Service (NHS) is required by Regulations to fund a drug or treatment which has received a positive HTA from the National Institute for Health and Care Excellence (NICE). Although much of the data submitted for the purposes of the HTA is the same as that submitted to obtain a marketing authorization, the authorities may request further information before making a decision.

Therefore, clinical trials should be exempt from patent infringement under the medicinal product assessment exemption insofar as they constitute acts in pursuance of any marketing authorization granted by any regulatory authority in the world. The legislation is silent as to the different phases of clinical trial. Phase 4 trials take place after the drug is already approved and on the market. It is therefore anticipated that arguments would surface about whether the activities involved with, for example, pharmacovigilance studies were protected. In the UK, sales of medicine with a mixed purpose (e.g. part commercial sale, part data gathering for phase 4 trials) would be

8. Regulation (EU) 2021/2282 of the European Parliament and of the Council of 15 December 2021 on health technology assessment and amending Directive 2011/24/EU.

judged according to the dominant purpose of the activity according to the principles from *Meter-Tech LLC v. British Gas Trading Limited*. In so far as phase 4 trials were directed to matters such as complying with post-authorization requirements imposed by regulators when granting a marketing authorization, or towards extending the authorized indication, these should be within the safe harbour, although it is anticipated that it could be very difficult to persuade a court that pharmacovigilance / safety surveillance is a purpose dominant over the commercial aims of the manufacturer.

To rely on the medicinal products assessment exemption, the clinical trials must be conducted 'in or for the purposes of' a medicinal product assessment (Section 60(6D) PA) and 'medicinal product assessment' means any testing, course of testing or other activity undertaken with a view to providing data for any of the named purposes (e.g. obtaining a marketing authorization) (Section 60(6E) PA). Therefore, what appears to matter is the intention at the time at which the trials are conducted and not whether the regulatory approval application is ultimately submitted. It is common for products to fail in clinical trials with no application for a marketing authorization being submitted in such circumstances. The conduct of clinical trials in the UK does however require a clinical trial authorization.

Generally speaking, commercial negotiations on price will be seen as an impermissible step towards market and not within the safe harbour. But providing data and scientific evidence to show patient benefit so that the NHS agrees to pay for patients to access the drug should be within the safe harbour.

Whilst there has been no case law to date interpreting the phrase 'any testing, course of testing or other activity' in Section 60(6E) PA, Section 60.24.3 of the UKIPO's Manual of Patent Practice suggests that the following activities would appear to fall within the scope of the exemption:

a. Activities carried out to provide data to regulatory authorities.
b. Activities carried out to provide data to bodies carrying out health technology assessments.
c. Post-approval studies to comply with regulatory requirements.
d. Activities carried out to amend an authorization for a medicine.
e. Activities done to obtain an authorization for a new indication of an existing drug.
f. Any tests or studies required by regulatory bodies.
g. Activities carried out for the purposes of obtaining full authorization of a generic drug or biosimilar, for example where the abridged procedure exempted by the Bolar-type exemption (see Section 60.28) is not used.
h. Activities related to health technology assessment of a generic or biosimilar product.
i. Activities carried out to provide data for obtaining regulatory approval for a generic or biosimilar product in another country.

The UKIPO's guidance on the Changes to patents legislation made by the Legislative Reform (Patents) Order 2014 ('UKIPO Guidance') further suggests that the medicinal product assessment definition under Section 60(6E) PA does not extend to commercial activities, but does apply to the use of patented medicines in clinical trials as comparators, and where the patented medicine is part of a combination medicinal product.

In the pharmaceutical sector, the medicinal product assessment exemption should permit use of a patented invention as a research tool provided the use is for regulatory purposes (for a so-called 'medicinal product assessment'). The UKIPO Guidance indicates that 'Research tools may be an integral part of a drug therapy and when they are used in, or for, the purposes of a medicinal product assessment, they are within the scope of the amendment. However, their use is only exempt for the specific activities defined in the [legislation], and a licence agreement would be needed to use a research tool once the product is commercialised.'

The medicinal product assessment exemption is not limited to clinical trials conducted for the purposes of securing an authorization in the UK, and in fact extends to experiments conducted in order to obtain regulatory approval for medicinal products worldwide, under Section 60(6E) PA.

iii. Exempted and Prohibited Activities

The UKIPO Guidance suggests that the Experimental Use exemption does not extend to commercial activities, and therefore a commercial supply of the patented invention for experimental use would not be exempt from patent infringement.

Further, commercial negotiations on price, absent providing data and scientific evidence to show patient benefit so that the NHS agrees to pay for patients to access the drug, will be seen as an impermissible step towards market and not within the safe harbour of the medicinal product assessment exemption.

Further, the use of the patented subject-matter as a research tool when investigating different subject-matter is not exempt from patent infringement. To repeat the earlier-mentioned example provided by Mr Justice Aldous in *Smith, Kline & French Laboratories Ltd v Evans Medical Ltd*,[9] a defendant seeking to investigate a chemical patent using a reagent which is itself patented, would only be able to rely on the experimental use defence with respect to the chemical patent, and not the reagent patent (the latter being used as a research tool only).

iv. Pure Academic vs Commercially Motivated Experimental Use

The exemption is not limited to 'academic activities' having 'no commercial value'. Where a defendant has several purposes for carrying out the experiments, they are able to rely on the Experimental Use exemption provided that the dominant or preponderant purpose of the defendant's act is to generate information of scientific or technical value, and not for commercial reasons such as to establish market confidence or to generate revenue.[10] In *Monsanto*, the Court of Appeal held that whilst the defendant could rely on the Experimental Use exemption for conducting experiments to find out more information about the herbicide, the exemption did not extend to trials for the purpose of obtaining commercial approval of the defendant's herbicide.

---

9. [1989] F.S.R. 513.
10. *Corevalve Inc v. Edwards Lifesciences* [2009] EWHC 6 (Pat).

e. Beneficiary Limitations

The acts of patent infringement are set out in Sections 60(1)(a) – (c) and Section 60(2) PA. A third party committing any of the cited acts in the UK risks being liable for patent infringement, unless they can rely on an exemption.

The UKIPO Guidance suggests that the commercial supply by a third party of the patented invention to another party for the latter's experimental use would not be covered by the Experimental Use exemption. This also appears to be the position taken by the UK courts in jurisprudence predating the change in legislation, which indicates that where a third party's involvement is to exploit or sell the patented technology, such involvement would amount to patent infringement, and the Experimental Use exemption would not apply because such commercial purposes cannot be experimental use.[11]

The extent to which other third parties (for example, those engaged by the sponsor of a clinical trial) could benefit from the Experimental Use exemption is unclear. In principle, provided the acts of those third parties meet the criteria set out in *Meter-Tech LLC v. British Gas Trading Limited*, the exemption should be available to them. Further, it would appear to frustrate the purpose of the Experimental Use exemption if it did not extend to third parties involved in the clinical trials on behalf of pharmaceutical companies.

f. Territoriality Issues

To be liable for patent infringement under Section 60 PA, the infringing acts must take place in the UK (and indeed for infringement under Section 60(2), there is a double territoriality requirement, such that both the supply and the putting into effect of the invention must take place in the UK).

Importation into the UK is *prima facie* an infringing act. Therefore, if done commercially it is likely to be an infringement. If not done commercially, it is possible that the Experimental Use exemption would apply in respect of an act of importation done in connection with experimental use conducted in the UK.

Where the product or results generated by a protected experimental use in the UK are used in another jurisdiction much will depend on the facts as to whether the further use abroad is protected. Consideration would need to be given to whether there is local patent protection, what the law is on the experimental use defence in that country and the nature of the further use abroad. If the use abroad is for commercial purposes, it is unlikely to benefit from the exemption and it is possible that in such circumstances the defence in the UK may cease to apply, given that seeking to exploit or sell technology cannot be protected by the Experimental Use exemption in the UK.

According to Section 60.24.2 of the UKIPO Manual of Patent Practice, the medicinal product assessment exemption under Sections 60(6D)-(6G) PA applies to

11. *Hoffmann-La Roche & Co AG v. Harris Pharmaceuticals Ltd* [1977] F.S.R. 200; the principle has been said to apply under the PA 1977 by Laddie J in *Inhale Therapeutics v. Quadrant* [2002] R.P.C. 21 at [419].

acts done to obtain regulatory approval for a medicinal product outside the UK, and potentially anywhere in the world.

g. Burden of Proof and Onus

It is the defendant who bears the burden of proof to show that (i) the acts complained of were done for experimental purposes and (ii) those purposes relate to the subject-matter of the invention.

h. Applicability during Patent Term Extension or Supplementary Protection Certificate

There is nothing in the legislation, guidance or case law to suggest that the scope of protection of the Experimental Use exemption differs during the original patent term and any patent term extension, including an SPC.

3. THE BOLAR-TYPE EXEMPTION

a. History and Rationale of Adopting the Bolar-Type Exemption

The wider Bolar-type exemption embedded within the UK Experimental Use defence by Sections 60(6D) – (6G) PA, also referred to in this chapter as the 'medicinal product assessment exemption', is discussed in section 2. above.

Additionally, Section 60(5)(i) PA provides what we have called in this chapter the 'old Bolar-type exemption' to patent law infringement in the UK and was introduced by The Medicines (Marketing Authorisation etc.) Amendment Regulations 2005 (S.I. 2005/2759), which implemented Article 10(6) of Directive 2001/83/EC, and Article 13(6) of Directive 2001/82/EC. Under Article 10(6), certain activities which are performed for the regulatory approval in the EU of generic (via the abridged procedure) or biosimilar medicinal products (via the hybrid-abridged or biosimilar procedures) are exempt from patent infringement.

However, this old Bolar-type exemption is now redundant for there is nothing that fell within the old exemption that does not now fall within the medicinal product assessment exemption.

b. The Laws Applicable to the Bolar-Type Exemption in the UK

The old Bolar-type exemption is codified in Section 60(5)(i) PA:

> (5) An act which, apart from this subsection, would constitute an infringement of a patent for an invention shall not do so if …
>
> (i) it consists of –
>
> (i) an act done in conducting a study, test or trial which is necessary for and is conducted with a view to the application of paragraphs 1 to 5 of article 13 of Directive 2001/82/EC or paragraphs 1 to 4 of article 10 of Directive 2001/83/EC, or

(ii) any other act which is required for the purpose of the application of those paragraphs.

The old Bolar-type exemption is narrow in scope and expressly limited to the application of paragraphs 1 to 4 of Article 10 of Directive 2001/83/EC and thus restricted to the approval of generic medicinal products under the 'abridged' procedure and 'hybrid-abridged' procedure. As mentioned in section 2., those acts are also now covered by the wider medicinal product assessment exemption in Sections 60(6D) – (6G) PA, rendering the original, narrow old Bolar-type exemption somewhat redundant.

Whilst there has been no case law to date on the operation of the old Bolar-type exemption in the UK, Section 60.28 of the UKIPO's Manual of Patent Practice suggests it applies to any studies, tests and trials carried out to show that a generic medicine is bioequivalent to an approved, patented product, where these acts are required to obtain marketing authorization for the generic medicine under an abbreviated authorization procedure (where the generic can rely on the data for the patented product to demonstrate its safety and efficacy, provided that bioequivalence is demonstrated).

c. Procedural Aspects of Invoking the Bolar-Type Exemption

The old Bolar-type exemption is raised as a defence in litigation proceedings. In the UK, such proceedings are under the jurisdiction of the Patents Court (or, in limited circumstances, the Intellectual Property Enterprise Court) and, if appealed, the Court of Appeal and the Supreme Court. Accordingly, it is these courts which determine the legitimacy of the exemption raised as a defence in patent infringement proceedings in the UK.

d. Scope of the Bolar-Type Exemption in the UK

i. Fields of Technology

The old Bolar-type exemption under Section 60(5)(i) PA is limited to the field of testing generic or biosimilar pharmaceutical products for the purposes of regulatory approval. These tests would include clinical trials as well as pre-clinical tests.

ii. Purpose of Experiments/Infringing Activities

The old Bolar-type exemption excepts from infringement acts done in conducting a study, test or trial which are necessary for, and conducted with a view to, securing the regulatory approval of a generic or biosimilar medicinal drug for human or veterinary use.

To rely on the old Bolar-type exemption under Section 60(5)(i), the purpose of the activities must be for the regulatory approval in the EU of generic (via the abridged procedure) or biosimilar medicinal products (via the hybrid-abridged or biosimilar procedures). As described above, the exemption applies to any studies, tests and trials carried out to show that a generic medicine is bioequivalent to an approved, patented product, where these acts are required to obtain marketing authorization for the generic medicine under an abbreviated authorization procedure (where the generic can rely on the data for the patented product to demonstrate its safety and efficacy, provided that bioequivalence is demonstrated).

Clinical and field trials carried out on new, or innovative, drugs, and activities done for the purposes of an HTA, which involve the use of a patented product, for example as a comparator, are not within the scope of the old Bolar-type exemption.

iii. Exempted and Prohibited Activities

The narrow old Bolar-type exemption under Section 60(5)(i) is limited to studies, tests and trials to obtain a marketing authorization for a generic or biosimilar version of a patented product.

e. Beneficiary Limitations

The acts of patent infringement are set out in Sections 60(1)(a) – (c) and Section 60(2) PA. A third party committing any of the cited acts in the UK risks being liable for patent infringement, unless they can rely on an exemption.

As mentioned above, it is understood that the narrow old Bolar-type exemption under Section 60(5)(i) can only be relied upon by generic or biosimilar companies seeking the regulatory approval of their medicinal products in the EU. The extent to which other third parties involved in the manufacture of generic or biosimilar products could benefit from the Bolar-type exemption is unclear.

f. Territoriality Issues

To be liable for patent infringement under Section 60 PA, the infringing acts must take place in the UK (and indeed for infringement under Section 60(2), there is a double territoriality requirement, such that both the supply and the putting into effect of the invention must take place in the UK).

The reference to European Directive 2001/83/EC in Section 60(5)(i) suggests the old Bolar-type exemption applies to studies, tests or trials conducted for the purpose of obtaining regulatory approval within any EU Member State. In any event, the medicinal product assessment exemption in Sections 60(6D)-(6G) PA described above applies to obtaining regulatory approvals anywhere in the world outside the UK, and therefore provides a safe harbour.

g. Burden of Proof and Onus

It is the defendant who bears the burden of proof to show that the acts were done in conducting a study, test or trial necessary for and conducted with a view to regulatory approval.

h. Applicability during Patent Term Extension or Supplementary Protection Certificate

There is nothing in the legislation, guidance or case law to suggest that the scope of protection of the old Bolar-type exemption differs during the original patent term and any patent term extension.

4. DIFFERENCES BETWEEN THE TWO EXEMPTIONS IN THE UK

The Experimental Use exemption, old Bolar-type exemption and medicinal product assessment exemption continue to co-exist in the UK. As discussed earlier in this chapter, there are key differences between each of these exemptions.

The old Bolar-type exemption under Section 60(5)(i) PA was enacted in 2005 through European Directive 2001/83/EC and is narrow in scope, as it only applies to securing the regulatory approval in the EU of a generic or biosimilar medicinal product. The Experimental Use exemption in Section 60(5)(b) is wider since it applies to all fields of technology and requires that the activity is done for experimental purposes relating to the subject-matter of the invention. The medicinal product assessment exemption in Sections 60(6D)-(6G) PA was introduced in 2014 under the powers conferred by the UK Legislative and Regulatory Reform Act 2006 as a result of calls to extend the scope of the UK's research exemptions. This medicinal product assessment exemption is much broader in scope than the old Bolar-type exemption since it is not limited to obtaining regulatory approval of generic or biosimilar products in Europe; instead it applies more broadly to activities done for the purpose of the regulatory assessment of any medicinal product (originator products as well as generics and biosimilars) anywhere in the world.

The medicinal product assessment exemption is also wider reaching in scope than the Experimental Use exemption when it comes to the commercialization of medicinal products. For instance, whilst experiments which are commercial in focus (e.g. customer demonstrations) will not find safe harbour under the Experimental Use exemption, the medicinal product assessment exemption does permit commercially focussed tests for pharmaceutical products and covers both originator and generic or biosimilar medicines.

It should be noted, however, that since the introduction of the medicinal product assessment exemption under Sections 60(6D)-(6G) PA, the old Bolar-type exemption under Section 60(5)(i) PA is now effectively redundant for there is nothing that fell within the old exemption that does not now fall within the medicinal product assessment exemption. Therefore, in practice, it is the Experimental Use exemption extended by the medicinal product assessment exemption in Sections 60(6D)-(6G) PA that is operational in the UK.

Moreover, since the UK's withdrawal from the European Union on 31 January 2020 and the introduction of the UK Retained EU Law (Revocation and Reform) Act 2023, the EU Directive which governs the old Bolar-type exemption is now 'assimilated law' and therefore must be interpreted in a way that is compatible with UK law (rather than in accordance with the principle of EU law supremacy). Notably, this gives the old Bolar-type exemption secondary status to the medicinal product assessment exemption, which was made under the powers conferred by the UK Legislative and Regulatory Reform Act 2006.

Chapter 42

United States

Wan Chieh (Jenny) Lee and John C. Todaro

1. GENERAL

a. Terminology

The following terms will be used in this chapter:

The term 'experimental', as used in 'experimental use', is not defined in a statute or regulation of the United States.

'Infringement' is defined in 35 U.S.C. § 271(a), which provides that:

> whoever without authority makes, uses, offers to sell, or sells any patented invention, within the United States or imports into the United States any patented invention during the term of the patent therefor, infringes the patent.

The statute further defines induced infringement and contributory infringement.

'Defenses' to patent infringement are generally listed in 35 U.S.C. § 282, which provides that:

> The following shall be defenses in any action involving the validity or infringement of a patent and shall be pleaded:
>
> (1) Noninfringement, absence of liability for infringement or unenforceability,
>
> (2) Invalidity of the patent or any claim in suit on any ground specified in part II of this title as a condition for patentability,
>
> (3) Invalidity of the patent or any claim in suit for failure to comply with –
> (A) any requirement of section 112, except that the failure to disclose the best mode shall not be a basis on which any claim of a patent may be canceled or held invalid or otherwise unenforceable; or
> (B) any requirement of section 251.

b. Legal Basis in the United States

The Bolar-type exemption to infringement is codified in the United States at 35 US.C. § 271(e)(1):

> It shall not be an act of infringement to make, use, offer to sell, or sell within the United States or import into the United States a patented invention (other than a new animal drug or veterinary biological product (as those terms are used in the Federal Food, Drug, and Cosmetic Act and the Act of March 4, 1913) which is primarily manufactured using recombinant DNA, recombinant RNA, hybridoma technology, or other processes involving site specific genetic manipulation techniques) solely for uses reasonably related to the development and submission of information under a Federal law which regulates the manufacture, use, or sale of drugs or veterinary biological products.

There is no statutory basis in the United States for a broad 'Experimental Use' exemption to patent infringement. As outlined below, an Experimental Use exemption is supported by case law in the United States.

In the United States, there are at least two statutes applying to very limited situations, which recognize an exception to patent infringement for certain acts of research. There is an experimental use provision in the Atomic Energy Act. The Act, which was enacted in 1946, created the Atomic Energy Commission as an agency of the US government.[1] The Act exempts the Commission from patent infringement for 'the conduct of research and development activities' for various purposes related to nuclear research, including the use of 'fissionable and radioactive materials for medical biological health or military purposes ...'[2]

Further, the Plant Variety Act, enacted in 1994, provides that the 'use and reproduction of a protected variety for plant breeding or other bona fide research shall not constitute an infringement of the protection provided under this chapter.'[3]

We were unable to find any reported cases in which defendants successfully relied on the statutory research exemptions in either the Atomic Energy Act or the Plant Variety Act to defend against a claim of patent infringement.

---

1. Publ. Law 79-585, 60 Stat. 755 (1946), codified at 12 U.S.C. § 1801-1819. The quoted
2. Atomic Energy Act § 11(b), codified at § 1811(b). The Act was amended by the Atomic Energy Act of 1954, 68 Stat. 919, and the corresponding provisions was codified at chapter 23 of title 42 of the US Code. The particular language of § 1811(b) was not included in the new statute. The current statute sets out a procedure for the Nuclear Energy Commission to declare a patent 'affected with the public interest', if the patented invention 'is of primary importance in the production or utilization of ... atomic energy.' Any person can apply to the Commission for a nonexclusive licence to use an invention affected with the public interest. See 42 U.S.C. § 2183.
3. 7 U.S.C. § 2544.

2. THE EXPERIMENTAL USE EXEMPTION

a. History and Rationale of Adopting the Experimental Use Exemption

There is no statutory basis in the United States for a broad exception to infringement for the experimental use of a patented invention. However, an experimental use defence to patent infringement is part of the common law of the United States. Most commentators assert that the concept of an experimental use defence in the United States dates from an 1813 decision of the Circuit Court for the District in Massachusetts, in *Whittemore v. Cutter.*[4] In *Whittemore,* it appears the defendant argued that he should not be liable for patent infringement for making a patented machine, when the defendant did not use the patented machine. The Court stated that 'it could never have been the intention of the legislature to punish a man, who constructed such a machine merely for philosophical experiments, or for the purpose of ascertaining the sufficiency of the machine to produce its described effects.'[5]

Similar interpretations of an experimental use provision can be found in other decisions in the nineteenth century. For example, in *Poppenhusen v. Falke,*[6] the court denied an experimental use defence in a case involving a company's use of a patented vulcanized rubber and related process. However, in the course of its decision the court commented that it is 'well settled' 'that an experiment with a patented article for the sole purpose of gratifying a philosophical taste, or curiosity, or for mere amusement is not an infringement of the rights of the patentee.'[7]

The Patent Act of 1952 effectively modernized US patent law. The statute did not include any provision for an Experimental Use exemption to patent infringement.

In 1983, the case of *Roche Products, Inc. v. Bolar Pharmaceutical Co.* arose in the US District Court. The defendant Bolar, a generic pharmaceutical manufacturer, used a patented drug product to conduct studies that were required to obtain regulatory approval of a generic version of the drug product. The District Court found that the defendant could rely on the experimental use as an exception to infringement.[8] The Court of Appeals for the Federal Circuit reversed.[9] The Federal Circuit noted that Bolar's use of the patented drug product 'is solely for business reasons and not for amusement, to satisfy idle curiosity, or for strictly philosophical inquiry.'[10] The Federal Circuit noted that the Experimental Use exemption is 'truly narrow', and that Bolar's intended use of the patented drug 'with a view to the adaption of the patented invention to the experimentor's business is a violation of the rights of the patentee to exclude others from using his patented invention'. By denying an Experimental Use exemption to a developer of generic drugs, the decision effectively frustrated

4. 29 Fed. Case 1210.
5. Id. at 1211.
6. 19 F. Cas. 1048 (Cir. N.Y. 1861).
7. Id. at 1049. *See also* S. Bible, 'Does the Experimental-Use Defense to Patent Infringement Still Exist?', SMU Science and Technology Law Review 13:1; 17 (Jan. 2010), for an extensive discussion of cases in the nineteenth and early part of the twentieth century.
8. 572 F. Supp. 255 (E.D.N.Y. 1983).
9. *Roche Products, Inc. v. Bolar Pharmaceutical Co., Inc.*, 733 F.2d 858 (Fed. Cir. 1984).
10. Id. at 863.

the generic drug provisions of the recently enacted Federal Food Drug and Cosmetic Act of 1982. The decision led to the enactment of 35 US.C. §271 (e)(1), called the 'Bolar-type exemption', as discussed in detail later in this chapter.

The Federal Circuit's narrow interpretation of experimental use in its 1984 *Roche Products* decision was continued in *Embrex, Inc. v. Service Engineering Corp.*[11] In *Embrex*, the plaintiff sued the manufacturer Service Engineering Corporation (SEC) for infringing its patent on methods for controlling an immunizable disease in poultry, by injecting the vaccine into an egg. SEC was the manufacturer of a machine that enabled the injection of vaccines into chicken eggs. The plaintiff alleged that in the course of developing the device, SEC's researchers practised the claimed invention. At trial, the Court found that the SEC research did not constitute an exempted experimental use. The CAFC affirmed on the experimental use ruling. The court explained:

> In this case, SEC's acts of hiring Drs. Davis and Rosenberger, and the doctors' acts injecting eggs with vaccine cannot be deemed experimental use or *de minimis*. While SEC tries to cloak these tests in the guise of scientific inquiry, that alone cannot immunize its acts. The district court determined on the record before it that SEC performed the tests expressly for commercial purposes.[12]

In *Madey v. Duke University*,[13] the Court of Appeals for the Federal Circuit seemed to even further limit the Experimental Use exemption, ruling that it does not apply to a university's use of a patented invention in laboratory research. The Court noted that acts may not be entitled to the experimental use defence if they are done 'in the guise of scientific inquiry but [have] definite cognizable and not insubstantial commercial purposes.'[14] The Court explained that while the University may be conducting research, the experimental use precedent 'does not immunize any conduct that is in keeping with the alleged infringers legitimate business regardless of commercial implications.'[15] The Court noted that major research universities:

> often sanction and fund research projects with arguably no commercial application whatsoever. However, these projects unmistakably further the legitimate business objectives, including educating enlightening students and faculty participating in these projects. These projects also serve, for example, to increase the status of the institution and lure lucrative research grants, students and faculty.[16]

Thus, even a university professor conducting academic research cannot qualify for an Experimental Use exemption, and risks being sued for patent infringement for conducting an experiment in the university laboratory.

Even after *Madey*, the courts have continued to debate the purpose and proper interpretation of experimental use. In *Integra Lifesciences I, Ltd. v. Merck*

11. 216 F.3d 1343 (Fed. Cir. 2000).
12. Id. at 1349.
13. 307 F.3d 1351 (Fed. Cir. 2002).
14. *Id.* at 1362 (quoting *Embrex, Inc. v. Service Engineering Corp.*, 216 F.3d 1343, 1349 (Fed. Cir. 2000)).
15. *Id.*
16. *Id.*

KGaA,[17] for example, Judge Newman advanced a compelling argument for a broader Experimental Use exemption to patent infringement. Judge Newman referenced Judge Story's decision in *Whittemore*, noting the often cited statement that 'it could never have been the intention of the legislature to punish a man who constructed such a machine merely for philosophical experiments.'[18] Judge Newman explained in a footnote that the reference to 'philosophy' was 'the term then used for what we today call "science"'.[19] According to Judge Newman, Justice Story 'distinguished the making with an intent to use for profit, and not for the mere purpose of philosophical experiment, or to ascertain the verity and exactness of the specification.'[20]

Judge Newman made the case for expanding experimental use to include broad scientific inquiry. The Judge explained that the information contained in patents is a major source of scientific as well as technologic knowledge.

> The subject matter of patents may be studied in order to understand it, or to improve upon it, or to find a new use for it, or to modify or 'design around' it. Were such research subject to prohibition by the patentee the advancement of technology would stop, for the first patentee in the field could bar not only patent-protected competition, but all research that might lead to such competition, as well as barring improvement or challenge or avoidance of patented technology. Today's accelerated technological advance is based in large part on knowledge of the details of patented inventions and how they are made and used. Prohibition of research into such knowledge cannot be squared with the framework of the patent law.[21]

Further, in June 2024, the United States Patent and Trademark Office (PTO) issued a Notice and Request for Comments, seeking comment on whether 'the current state of the common law Experimental Use exemption and where the legislative action should be considered to enact the statutory Experimental Use exemption.'[22] The PTO acknowledges the disparity between the state of experimental use law in the United States as compared to most other jurisdictions. The PTO noticed a report from the United States Congressional Research Service, noting a dispute among commentators in the United States. The PTO noted that 'some argued that a narrow exception enhances innovation by rewarding innovators with robust patent rights while others noted that restricting researchers access to patented technologies would impede innovation.'[23]

17. 331 F.3d 860, 874-75 (Fed. Cir. 2003) (Newman, J. concurring in part and dissenting in part), vacated by *Merck KGaA v. Integra Lifesciences I, Ltd.*, 545 U.S. 193 (2005).
18. *Id.* at 875 (quoting *Whittemore v. Cutter*, 29 Fed. Cas. 1120, 1121 (C.C.D. Mass. 1813).
19. *Id.* (footnote 8).
20. *Id.* (quoting *Sawin v. Guild*, 21 Fed. Cas. 554 (C.C.D.Mass.1813)).
21. *Id.*
22. Experimental Use Exception Request for Comments, United States and Patent and Trademark Office, 89 Fed. Reg. 125, 53963 (June 28, 2024).
23. 89 Fed. Reg. 53964 (citing John R. Thomas, 'Scientific Research and the Experimental Use of Privilege in Patent Law', CRAS Report No. RL32651 (2004)).

US intellectual property law associations have also supported a broader Experimental Use exemption to patent infringement.[24]

b. The Laws Applicable to the Experimental Use Exemption in the United States

There is no statutory basis for an 'experimental use' as a defence to patent infringement in the US. In contast, the Bolar provision is codified in the U.S patent laws in 35 U.S.C. § 271(e)(1), as follows:

> It shall not be an act of infringement to make, use, offer to sell, or sell within the United States or import into the United States a patented invention (other than a new animal drug or veterinary biological product (as those terms are used in the Federal Food, Drug, and Cosmetic Act and the Act of March 4, 1913) which is primarily manufactured using recombinant DNA, recombinant RNA, hybridoma technology, or other processes involving site specific genetic manipulation techniques) solely for uses reasonably related to the development and submission of information under a Federal law which regulates the manufacture, use, or sale of drugs or veterinary biological products.

c. Procedural Aspects of Invoking the Experimental Use Exemption

In the United States, an Experimental Use exemption to patent infringement can be raised as a defence to an allegation of patent infringement. Experimental use is not among the defences to patent infringement provided by statute.[25] However, case law has recognized it as a potential defence to patent infringement.

Patent infringement is litigated in the federal courts. US law provides that federal District Courts 'shall have original jurisdiction of any civil action arising under any Act of Congress relating to patents, plant variety protection, copyrights and trademarks.'[26]

In patent litigation in the United States, the plaintiff patentee has the initial burden of proving patent infringement by the defendant.[27] Thereafter, the burden falls on the defendant to prove his or her defence to infringement, including the exception to infringement for experimental use.

---

24. *See, e.g.*, Intellectual Property Owners Organization Resolution of 24 December 2019, entitled 'Supporting Legislative Creation of a Research Defense To Patent Infringement', and American Intellectual Property Lawyers' Association Resolution No. 230-06, 'Patent Law – Experimental Use', resolved 17 March 2005, retained 15 July 2015.
25. The statutory defences include non-infringement, unenforceability and invalidity. See 35 U.S.C. § 282 (b).
26. 28 U.S.C. § 1338(a).
27. *See, e.g., Ultra-Tex Surfaces Inc. v. Hill Brothers Chemical Co.*, 204 F.3d 1360, 1364 (Fed. Cir. 2000).

d. Scope of the Experimental Use Exemption in the United States

i. Fields of Technology

There are no technology limitations on the scope of the Experimental Use exemption in the United States.

ii. Purpose of Experiments/Infringing Activities

As explained above, the Experimental Use exemption in the United States is very narrow. Despite statements by the courts that the law recognizes an Experimental Use exemption, in most of the reported cases the court found that the exemption did not apply, and that the conduct constituted patent infringement. For example:

- *Albright v Celluloid Harness-Trimming Co.*:[28] the defendant business' manufacture of a patented die in order to experiment on improvements to the die were held to be an infringement, and is not exempt as an experimental use;
- *Beedle v. Bennett*:[29] use of a patented process to build a well on defendants' property for personal use (and not for commercial gain), constitutes an infringement, and is not exempt as an experimental use;
- *Poppenhusen v. Falke*:[30] use of a patented process to manufacture rubber items constitutes a patent infringement, and is not exempt as an experimental use, though the stated purpose of the defendant business was that the use was experimental; and
- *Bonsack Machinery Co. v. Underwood*:[31] manufacture of a patented cigarette-making machine constitutes a patent infringement, and is not exempt as an experimental use though the stated purpose of defendant business was that the use was experimental.

There are also a number of cases that refused an Experimental Use exemption which the use was characterized as for a limited period of time, for the purposes of evaluating the patented technology.[32]

Under the current case law, activity having any commercial purpose will not qualify for the exemption. Under the *Madey v. Duke University*[33] decision of the Court of Appeals for the Federal Circuit, laboratory research by a university professor does not qualify, on the grounds that the research is within the business function of the

28. 1 F. Cas. 320 (D. N. J. 1877).
29. 7 S. Ct. 1090 (1887).
30. 19 F. Cas. 1048 (S.D.N.Y. 1861).
31. 73 F. 206 (E.D.N.C. 1896).
32. See S. Bible, 'Does the Experimental Use Defense to Patent Infringement Still Exist?', SMU Science and Technology Law Review 13:1; pp. 23-24 (Jan. 2010) (citing *Clerk v. Tannage Patent Co.*, 84 F. 643 (3d Cir. 1898) (nine months of use), *Cimiotti Unhairing Co. v. Derboklow*, 87 F. 997 (E.D.N.Y. 1898) (three years of use).
33. 307 F.3d 1351 (Fed. Cir. 2002).

university. The court relied on the university's 'business objectives' of educating students, attracting funding and growing the school's reputation.[34]

iii. Exempted and Prohibited Activities

As explained above, the Experimental Use exemption in the United States is very narrow. Under the current case law, activity having any commercial purpose will not qualify for the exemption.

iv. Pure Academic vs Commercially Motivated Experimental Use

As explained above, the Experimental Use exemption in the United States is very narrow. The case law generally provides that any activity having a commercial purpose or motivation does not qualify for the Experimental Use exemption. The case law suggests that a 'pure academic use' would qualify for the experimental use, and would not constitute patent infringement. However, it is difficult to envision a court so finding, as even research activity conducted by a university professor has been deemed ineligible, on the grounds that the university has a commercial motivation to conduct the research. As explained above, under the *Madey v. Duke University*[35] decision of the Court of Appeals for the Federal Circuit, laboratory research by a university professor does not qualify, on the grounds that the research is within the business function of the university. The court relied on the university's 'business objectives' of educating students, attracting funding and growing the school's reputation.[36]

e. Beneficiary Limitations

There is no precedent for whether a party that contracts with a third party to perform an activity that, if performed by the party would be considered exempt, can take advantage of the Experimental Use exemption. There are limited circumstances under which the Experimental Use exemption would apply.

f. Territoriality Issues

Actions taken outside the US would not typically constitute infringement of a US patent. As a result, the Experimental Use exemption would not apply to activities performed outside the United States.

34. *Id.*
35. 307 F.3d 1351 (Fed. Cir. 2002).
36. *Id.*

g. Burden of Proof and Onus

In the United States, the general rule in patent infringement litigation is that the patent owner (or the party asserting patent infringement) bears the burden of proof on infringement.[37]

h. Applicability during Patent Term Extension or Supplementary Protection Certificate

There is no case law on the issue of whether an experimental use provision applies during the period of patent term extension. Under US law, the scope of the patent is extended under the patent term extension statute 35 U.S.C. § 156. Section 156 (b) provides that the scope of the extended compound patent is limited to 'any use approved for the product.' The extension only applies to the approved product, which is defined in the statute as 'the active ingredient of … a new drug … including any salt or ester of the active ingredient.'[38]

In any event, the use of the subject matter of an extended patent is likely related to the use for developing data for use in an Abbreviated New Drug Application, in order to obtain approval by the Food and Drug Administration of a generic drug product. This would be covered by the US Bolar-type exemption, under 35 U.S.C. § 271(e)(1), as explained further in this chapter.

3. THE BOLAR-TYPE EXEMPTION

a. History and Rationale of Adopting the Bolar-Type Exemption

In the United States, the Bolar-type exemption was codified in 35 U.S.C. § 271(e)(1) in 1984, as part of the Hatch-Waxman Act,[39] which includes a statutory scheme that links generic drug approval to a patent listing and litigation process. The enactment of this provision by Congress was in response to the 1984 decision in *Roche Products Inc. v. Bolar Pharmaceutical Co.*, where the Court of Appeals for the Federal Circuit held that use of a patented drug in premarketing tests, during the life of the patent, to prepare data for submission to the US Food and Drug Administration (FDA) of a generic version of the patented drug was considered an infringement.[40]

Defendant Bolar sought to market a generic version of Roche's patented drug, Dalmane, after expiration of Roche's patent. However, Bolar initiated FDA required testing and obtained from a foreign manufacturer the active drug before expiration of Roche's patent. The active drug was formed into 'dosage form capsules, to obtain

37. See e.g., *Bio-Rad Laboratories, Inc. v. International Trade Commission*, 998 F.3d 1320, 1329 (Fed. Cir. 2021).
38. 35 U.S.C. § 156(f)(2)(A). *See also Biogen International GmbH v. Banner Life Sciences LLC*, 956 F.3d 1351 (Fed. Cir. 2020).
39. P.L. 98-417, the Drug Price Competition and Patent Term Restoration Act of 1984 (also known as the Hatch-Waxman Act).
40. *Roche Products Inc. v. Bolar Pharmaceutical Co.*, 733 F.2d 858 (Fed. Cir. 1984, *cert. denied*, 469 U.S. 856 (1984)).

stability data, dissolution rates, bioequivalency studies, and blood serum studies', necessary for a New Drug Application. The court held that the common law Experimental Use exemption to infringement did not apply. The Court explained that Bolar's use was intended not 'solely for business reasons and not for amusement, to satisfy idle curiosity, or for strict philosophical inquiry', but instead for adaption to Bolar's business.

Under *Roche v. Bolar*, patent owners would enjoy a *de facto* patent term extension because generic competitors are required to spend time after patent expiration to generate experimental data before they can obtain FDA approval for market entry of a generic product. Bolar argued that public policy requires a new exception to infringement for this type of activity because there is a conflict between the statutory provisions for FDA approval and patent term. However, the Court of Appeals for the Federal Circuit declined to create a new exception to infringement. Instead, the Court stated that '[i]t is the role of Congress to maximize public welfare through legislation' and that '[n]o matter how persuasive the policy arguments are for or against these proposed bills, this court is not the proper forum in which to debate them.'[41]

Congress considered preventing activities such as those of Bolar as extending the patent owner's commercial exclusivity beyond the patent expiration date. In response to the *Roche v. Bolar* decision, Congress enacted 35 U.S.C. 271(e)(1) in 1984, which stated that:

> It shall not be an act of infringement to make, use, or sell a patented invention (other than a new animal drug or veterinary biological product (as those terms are used in the Federal Food, Drug, and Cosmetic Act and the Act of March 4, 1913)) solely for uses reasonably related to the development and submission of information under a Federal law which regulates the manufacture, use, or sale of drugs.

This exception under 35 U.S.C. §271(e)(1) became commonly known as the Bolar-type exemption or §271(e)(1) safe harbour.

b. The Laws Applicable to the Bolar-Type Exemption in the United States

The Bolar-type exemption in the United States is codified by statute under 35 U.S.C. §271(e)(1), which currently states that:

> It shall not be an act of infringement to make, use, offer to sell, or sell within the United States or import into the United States a patented invention (other than a new animal drug or veterinary biological product (as those terms are used in the Federal Food, Drug, and Cosmetic Act and the Act of March 4, 1913) which is primarily manufactured using recombinant DNA, recombinant RNA, hybridoma technology, or other processes involving site specific genetic manipulation techniques) solely for uses reasonably related to the development and submission of information under a Federal law which regulates the manufacture, use, or sale of drugs or veterinary biological products.

41. *Roche Products Inc.*, 733 F.2d at 865.

Therefore, '[w]hile performing development work and seeking such approval, a generic drug manufacturer is free from liability for patent infringement based solely upon acts necessary to prepare the ANDA.'[42]

The Supreme Court has interpreted the scope of the Bolar-type exemption of 35 U.S.C. §271(e)(1) to provide 'a wide berth for the use of patented drugs in activities related to the federal regulatory process' and that the exemption applies to 'all uses of patented inventions that are reasonably related to the development and submission of any information under the [Federal Food, Drug and Cosmetics Act].'[43] This broad interpretation of the §271(e)(1) exemption includes '(1) experimentation on drugs that are not ultimately the subject of an FDA submission or (2) use of patented compounds in experiments that are not ultimately submitted to the FDA.'[44] Although the Bolar-type exemption is broadly interpreted, it does not cover all research activities. The Court noted that '[b]asic scientific research on a particular compound, performed without the intent to develop a particular drug or a reasonable belief that the compound will cause the sort of physiological effect the researcher intends to induce', would not be within the scope permitted by the Bolar-type exemption.[45]

c. Procedural Aspects of Invoking the Bolar-Type Exemption

Patent infringement in the United States is litigated in the federal courts. US law provides that federal District Courts 'shall have original jurisdiction of any civil action arising under any Act of Congress relating to patents, plant variety protection, copyrights and trademarks.'[46] In addition, the International Trade Commission (ITC) has jurisdiction to investigate:

> [t]he importation into the United States, the sale for importation, or the sale within the United States after importation by the owner, importer, or consignee, of articles that – (i) infringe a valid and enforceable United States patent or a valid and enforceable United States copyright registered under title 17; or (ii) are made, produced, processed, or mined under, or by means of, a process covered by the claims of a valid and enforceable United States patent.[47]

The §271(e)(1) exemption serves as a defence to patent infringement in a litigation before federal courts[48] or a proceeding before the ITC.[49] Therefore, federal courts and the ITC have jurisdiction to evaluate whether the §271(e)(1) exemption is applicable in response to allegations of patent infringement.

Under 35 U.S.C. §282(b)(1), non-infringement must be pleaded as a defence. Therefore, a defendant is required to affirmatively assert the §271(e)(1) exemption as a defence to patent infringement in litigation.

42. *Glaxo Inc. v. Novopharm Ltd.*, 110 F.3d 1562, 1567(Fed. Cir. 1997).
43. *Merck KGaA v Integra Lifesciences I, Ltd.*, 545 U.S. 193, 202 (2005).
44. *Merck KGaA*, 545 U.S. at 206.
45. *Id.* at 205-06.
46. 28 U.S.C. §1338(a).
47. 19 U.S.C. §1337(a)(1)(B).
48. *See e.g., Merck KGaA v Integra Lifesciences I, Ltd.*, 545 U.S. 193 (2005).
49. *See e.g., Amgen, Inc. v. Int'l Trade Comm'n*, 565 F. 3d 846 (Fed. Cir. 2009).

d. Scope of Bolar-Type Exemption in the United States

i. Fields of Technology

As discussed above, the Bolar-type exemption was codified in 35 U.S.C. § 271(e)(1) in 1984, as part of the Hatch-Waxman Act. The statute provides safe harbour to patent infringement for use of a patented invention 'solely for uses reasonably related to the development and submission of information under a Federal law which regulates the manufacture, use, or sale of drugs or veterinary biological products.'[50] Although the language of the statute refers to 'drugs or veterinary biological products', the Supreme Court in *Eli Lilly & Co. v. Medtronic, Inc.* interpreted this to extend beyond just drug products and veterinary biological products.[51]

The Court in *Eli Lilly & Co. v. Medtronic, Inc.* considered the history of the Hatch-Waxman Act and reasoned that the Bolar-type exemption codified in 35 U.S.C. § 271(e)(1) is generally complementary to 35 U.S.C § 156(a), which provides patent term extension for patents relating to products that were subject to regulatory delays and could not be marketed prior to regulatory approval.[52] The combination of these two statutory provisions represents a compromise struck in the enactment of the Hatch-Waxman Act in 1984 that gave additional patent term for products that were subject to regulatory delays and could not be marketed prior to regulatory approval, but removed the *de facto* patent term extension created by the combined effect of patent law and the requirement for premarketing regulatory approval discussed in *Roche v. Bolar*. All of the types of products that are eligible for patent term extension under § 156(a) are also eligible for the Bolar-type exemption under § 271(e)(1) and *vice versa*. Therefore, the Bolar-type exemption is applicable to medical devices, food additives, colour additives, new drugs, antibiotic drugs, human biological products, new animal drugs and veterinary biological products that require regulatory approval by the FDA.[53]

ii. Purpose of Experiments/Infringing Activities

Under 35 U.S.C. § 271(e)(1), the Bolar-type exemption is limited only to those activities that are 'solely for uses reasonably related to the development and submission of information under a Federal law which regulates the manufacture, use, or sale of drugs or veterinary biological products.' Although the Bolar-type exemption is to be broadly interpreted, this exemption does not cover all research activities. The Court in *Merck KGaA v. Integra* specified that '[b]asic scientific research on a particular compound, performed without the intent to develop a particular drug or a reasonable belief that the compound will cause the sort of physiological effect the researcher intends to induce', is not within the scope of the Bolar-type exemption.[54]

---

50. 35 U.S.C. §271(e)(1).
51. *Eli Lilly & Co. v. Medtronic, Inc.*,496 U.S. 661 (1990).
52. *Id.* at 673.
53. *Id.* at 673-74; *AbTox, Inc. v. Exitron Corp.*, 122 F.3d 1019, 1030 (Fed. Cir.1997) (holding that the §271(e)(1) exemption applies to Class II medical devices).
54. *Merck KGaA*, 545 U.S. at 205-06.

iii. *Exempted and Prohibited Activities*

One of the earliest reported decisions addressing the Bolar-type exemption took a limited view of the exemption, essentially ruling that all alleged infringing activity must be for the purposes of developing information for obtaining regulatory review. In *Scripps Clinic and Research Foundation v. Genentech, Inc.*,[55] the plaintiff Scripps and its licensee sued Genentech under patents covering a purified Factor VIII:C, and a process for obtaining Factor VIII:C from human blood. The plaintiffs alleged that Genentech infringed the patents by manufacturing and selling Factor VIII:C. Genentech raised the Bolar provision in its defence, asserting, in the words of the District Court, that 'all its uses of Factor VIII:C, though not solely for purposes related to FDA testing, bear some reasonable relationship to such purposes and hence are noninfringing' under the *Bolar* provision.[56] The District Court rejected Genentech's argument, and ruled that the Bolar-type exemption did not apply. The Court stated that the meaning of the Bolar provision is clear, 'the use of a patented invention is protected so long as that use is solely for purposes reasonably related to meeting the reporting requirements of federal drug laws.'[57] The Court went on to cite the stated purpose of the Bolar provision in Congressional reports.

Despite the District Court ruling in *Scripps*, subsequent case law has had a more expansive view of the Bolar-type exemption.

Although 35 U.S.C. §271(e)(1) states that the exemption applies to those activities that are 'solely for uses reasonably related to the development and submission of information under a Federal law which regulates the manufacture, use, or sale of drugs or veterinary biological products',[58] it is not limited only to information that is submitted to the FDA. Rather, the statute has been interpreted by the US Supreme Court to apply to preclinical studies 'as long as there is a reasonable basis for believing that the experiments will produce the type of information that are relevant to an IND or NDA.'[59] These preclinical studies may relate to a drug's safety, efficacy, mechanism of action, pharmacokinetics, and pharmacology.[60] The §271(e)(1) exemption does not require data generated from protected activities to ultimately be part of an FDA submission. Rather, this exemption is sufficiently broad to encompass '(1) experimentation on drugs that are not ultimately the subject of an FDA submission or (2) use of patented compounds in experiments that are not ultimately submitted to the FDA.'[61]

The §271(e)(1) exemption does not require the protected activities to be generated exclusively for the purpose of submitting data for FDA approval, but allows uses for more than FDA approval, as long as the use is reasonably related to FDA approval.[62] The Court of Appeal for the Federal Circuit in *AbTox, Inc. v. Exitron Corp.*

55. 666 F. Supp. 1379 (N.D. Cal. 1987).
56. *Id.* at 1396.The court asserted that Genentech practised the patented invention to develop a commercial process to manufacture Factor VIII:C.
57. *Id.*
58. 35 U.S.C. §271(e)(1).
59. *Merck KGaA*, 545 U.S. at 208 (internal citations omitted).
60. *Id.* at 203-204.
61. *Id.* at 206.
62. *AbTox, Inc.*, 122 F.3d at 1030.

explained that the statute 'does not look to the underlying purposes or attendant consequences of the activity (e.g., tests led to the sale of the patent), as long as the use is reasonably related to FDA approval.'[63] The actual intent or alternative uses for an activity, even for activity intended to be promotional, does not negate protection under §271(e)(1), as long as the activity is reasonably related to FDA approval.[64]

Recently, in *Edwards Lifesciences Corp. v. Meril Life Scis. Priv. Ltd.*, the Court of Appeals for the Federal Circuit considered whether importation of two transcatheter heart valve systems to attend a medical conference falls within the §271(e)(1) exemption.[65] In this case, Meril developed a transcatheter heart valve system that was approved in India and Europe, but required collecting clinical data for FDA pre-marketing approval in the US. Meril initiated significant steps towards FDA approval prior to the conference and submitted a premarket approval submission to the FDA for its proposed clinical trials after the conference. Meril discussed its device with several US doctors to identify potential clinicians for its premarket approval application and did not offer the device for US sale at the conference. The Court in *Edward v. Meril* reiterated the standard from *Merck KGaA v. Integra* that 'for each act of infringement the safe harbor is available only for acts or uses that bear a reasonable relation to the development and submission of information to the FDA.'[66] Therefore, 'the relevant inquiry is not why Meril imported the two transcatheter heart valve systems, or how Meril used the imported transcatheter heart valve systems, but whether the act of importation was for a use reasonably related to submitting information to the FDA.'[67] In view of this framework, the Court determined that 'Meril's importation of the transcatheter heart valves [to the medical conference] constituted another step in the right direction "on the road to regulatory approval"', and therefore, 'firmly resides in the §271(e)(1) safe harbor.'[68]

Furthermore, 'subsequent disclosure or use of information obtained from an exempt clinical study, even for purposes other than regulatory approval, does not repeal that exemption of the clinical study, provided that the subsequent disclosure or use is itself not an act of infringement of the asserted claims.'[69] In *Telectronics Pacing Sys. v. Ventritex, Inc.*, the defendant conducted clinical trials to obtain data for FDA approval, and subsequently disseminated the data for non-FDA reporting purposes, such as presenting clinical trial data at a cardiology conference, reporting clinical trial progress to investors, analysts and journalists, and describing clinical trial results in a private fund-raising memorandum.[70] The Court in *Telectronics* held that the statute 'only requires that the making, using or selling of the patented invention be solely for uses reasonably related to FDA approval' and declined to repeal the §271(e)(1)

63. *Id.*
64. *Id.*
65. *Edwards Lifesciences Corp. v. Meril Life Scis. Priv. Ltd.*, 96 F.4th 1347 (Fed. Cir. 2024).
66. *Edwards Lifesciences Corp.*, 96 F.4th at 1353 (Fed. Cir. 2024) (citing *Merck KGaA*, 545 U.S. at 205-07).
67. *Edwards Lifesciences Corp.*, 96 F.4th at 1353.
68. *Id.* at 1353-1354.
69. *Classen Immunotherapies v. Elan Pharms., Inc.*,786 F.3d 892, 898 (Fed. Cir. 2015) (citing *Telectronics Pacing Sys. v. Ventritex, Inc.*, 982 F.2d 1520, 1523-24 (Fed. Cir. 1992).
70. *Telectronics Pacing Sys. v. Ventritex, Inc.*, 982 F.2d at 1524.

exemption for subsequent disclosure of data generated from protected clinical trial studies for non-FDA related purposes.[71]

While the §271(e)(1) is to be broadly applied, there are some activities that do not fall within the scope of the exemption.

In *Proveris Sci. Corp. v. Innovasystems, Inc.*, the Court of Appeals for the Federal Circuit declined to extend the §271(e)(1) exemption to research tools used for generating data for FDA submission.[72] The defendant, Innova, produces an optical spray analyser that measures the physical parameters of aerosol sprays used in drug delivery devices subject to a required FDA approval process. However, neither plaintiff Proveris' patented product nor Innova's optical spray analyser are subject to FDA approval. The Court in *Proveris* declined to extend the §271(e)(1) exemption to Innova's sale of the optical spray analyser, because the product at issue does not require FDA approval.[73]

In *Classen v. Biogen*, the Court explained that '§271(e)(1) provides an exception to the law of infringement in order to expedite development of information for regulatory approval of generic counterparts of patented products', but 'does not apply to information that may be routinely reported to the FDA, long after marketing approval has been obtained.'[74] At issue in *Classen* were post-approval studies conducted to evaluate suggested association between childhood vaccinations and risk of developing type 1 diabetes, and to determine whether timing of vaccination influences risk.[75] Biogen and GlaxoSmithKline provided vaccines, advised on immunization schedules, and reported any adverse vaccine effects to the FDA. The Court in *Classen* found that 'the Biogen and Glaxo activities charged with infringement are not related to producing information for an IND or NDA, and are not a "phase of research" possibly leading to marketing approval.'[76] Therefore, the §271(e)(1) exemption was found not applicable to these activities.

However, not all post-approval activities fall outside of the §271(e)(1) exemption. In *Momenta Pharms. Inc. v. Amphastar Pharm., Inc.*, the Court of Appeals for the Federal Circuit declined to adopt a bright line pre-/post-approval distinction for §271(e)(1), and instead held that 'post-approval studies that are "reasonably related to the development and submission of information under a Federal law which regulates the manufacture, use, or sale of drugs" fall within the scope of the § 271(e)(1) safe harbor.'[77] In a subsequent proceeding, the Court clarified that 'routine record retention requirements associated with testing and other aspects of the commercial production process' are different from 'non-routine submissions that may occur both pre- and post-approval, such as the submission of investigational new drug applications ("INDs"), new drug applications ("NDAs"), supplemental NDAs, or other post-approval research results.'[78] Therefore, '[t]he routine quality control

71. *Id.*
72. *Proveris Sci. Corp. v. Innovasystems, Inc.*, 536 F.3d 1256 (Fed. Cir. 2008).
73. *Id. at 1265-1266*
74. *Classen Immunotherapies, Inc. v. Biogen Idec*, 659 F.3d 1057, 1070 (Fed. Cir. 2011).
75. *Id.*
76. *Id.* at 1072.
77. *Momenta Pharms. Inc. v. Amphastar Pharm., Inc.*, 686 F.3d 1348,1358-1360 (Fed. Cir. 2012).
78. *Momenta Pharms., Inc. v. Teva Pharms. USA Inc.*, 809 F. 3d 610, 620 (Fed. Cir. 2015).

testing of each batch of generic [drug] as part of the post-approval, commercial production process is... not "reasonably related to the development and submission of information" to the FDA', and not exempt from infringement under §271(e)(1).[79]

In contrast, in *Classen Immunotherapies v. Elan Pharms., Inc.*, the Court of Appeal for the Federal Circuit held that a post-approval clinical study and submission of the results from the study to the FDA to revise an approved product's label was exempt from infringement under §271(e)(1).[80] The Court explained that in the post-approval context the analysis may be less straightforward, however, the §271(e)(1) exemption 'does not categorically exclude post-approval activities from the ambit of the safe harbor.'[81] The §271(e)(1) exemption allows drug manufacturers to voluntarily conduct post-approval studies on their products for purposes of developing and submitting information to the FDA, such as supplemental new drug applications seeking the FDA's approval to revise the label of their products.[82] The Court considered these post-approval studies to 'serve similar purposes as pre-approval studies in ensuring the safety and efficacy of approved drugs' and is therefore 'an integral part of the regulatory approval process' and exempt from infringement under §271(e)(1).[83]

In *Amgen Inc. v. Hospira, Inc.*, the issue of whether the manufacture and stockpiling of batches of product would be exempt from infringement under §271(e)(1) was determined at trial by a jury and upheld by the Court of Appeals for the Federal Circuit.[84] The patented inventions in this case are related to a method of manufacturing. Amgen asserted that Hospira's manufacture of twenty-one batches of drug substance for its biosimilar drug product infringes the patented methods. The Court found that the jury instructions 'properly asked whether each act of manufacture, that is, each accused activity, was for uses reasonably related to submitting information to the FDA.'[85] Of the twenty-one accused drug substance batches, the jury found seven batches entitled to protection under the §271(e)(1) safe harbour. The protected batches include two batches used for qualifying Hospira's process to make the drug and for qualifying alternate equipment, and five batches used for a mandatory pre-approval inspection by the FDA. In affirming the jury finding, the Court explained that manufacturing to stockpile commercial inventory does not automatically remove the activity from the §271(e)(1) safe harbour, but can be probative evidence of whether the use was reasonably related to seeking FDA approval.[86] Therefore, certain stockpiling activities are permitted under the §271(e)(1) exemption, but manufacturing solely for the purpose of stockpiling without any relationship to submitting information to the FDA is not exempt from infringement under §271(e)(1).

79. *Id.*
80. *Classen Immunotherapies v. Elan Pharms., Inc.*, 786 F.3d 892, 896-897 (Fed. Cir. 2015).
81. *Id.* at 897.
82. *Id.*
83. *Id.*
84. *Amgen Inc. v. Hospira, Inc.*, 944 F.3d 1327 (Fed. Cir. 2019).
85. *Id.* at 1339.
86. *Id.*

e. Beneficiary Limitations

Although §271(e)(1) was enacted to allow generic drug manufacturers to prepare data for submission in an Abbreviated New Drug Application (ANDA) without risk of patent infringement, this provision is not limited to only generic drug manufacturers. As discussed above, the 35 U.S.C. §271(e)(1) exemption has been interpreted by the Supreme Court to apply to 'all uses of patented inventions that are reasonably related to the development and submission of any information under the [Federal Food, Drug and Cosmetics Act].'[87] Therefore, the Bolar-type exemption is available to generic drug manufacturers as well as innovative manufacturers, as long as the use is reasonably related to seeking approval before the FDA.

The exemption under §271(e)(1) may also extend to third parties, for example an active pharmaceutical ingredient (API) supplier, engaged by the party seeking FDA approval. In *Shire, LLC v. Amneal Pharms., LLC,*[88] Johnson Matthey did not seek FDA approval to sell a generic drug, but supplied the API to the ANDA defendants for use in obtaining FDA approval. The Court found that Johnson Matthey, as an API supplier, cannot be liable for API it sold to the ANDA defendants for use in obtaining FDA approval, because these sales were reasonably related to the submission of an ANDA and protected under the §271(e)(1) safe harbour.[89]

f. Territoriality Issues

Under 35 U.S.C. §271(e)(1), the Bolar-type exemption is limited only to those activities that are 'solely for uses reasonably related to the development and submission of information under a Federal law which regulates the manufacture, use, or sale of drugs or veterinary biological products.' Although the Supreme Court in *Eli Lilly & Co. v. Medtronic, Inc.* interpreted this statutory provision to encompass all products that require approval under the Food, Drug and Cosmetics Act,[90] this statutory regime appears to be limited to regulatory submissions under US law. However, under certain circumstances, the § 271(e)(1) exemption may still apply to activities performed to support regulatory filings outside of the United States. The Supreme Court in *Merck KGaA v. Integra* did not require the activities to ultimately result in data actually submitted to the FDA.[91] Instead, the activities are protected by § 271(e)(1) exemption 'as long as there is a reasonable basis for believing that the experiments will produce the types of information that are relevant to an IND or NDA.'[92] Therefore, if the data generated to support regulatory filing outside the US are the type of information that would be relevant to an IND or NDA in the US, then it is possible that the Bolar-type exemption may still apply.

The Bolar-type exemption as codified in 35 U.S.C. §271(e)(1) serves as an exemption to patent infringement for activities that 'make, use, offer to sell, or sell

87. *Merck KGaA.*, 545 U.S. at 202.
88. *Shire, LLC v. Amneal Pharms., LLC,* 802 F.3d 1301 (Fed. Cir. 2015).
89. *Id.* at 1310.
90. *Eli Lilly & Co.*, 496 U.S. at 673-74.
91. *Merck KGaA*, 545 U.S. at 206.
92. *Id.*, 545 U.S. at 208 (internal citations omitted).

within the United States or import into the United States a patented invention.' Therefore, the §271(e)(1) exemption does not apply for uses that infringe a corresponding patent outside of the United States.

g. Burden of Proof and Onus

In the United States, the party asserting patent infringement, such as the patent owner, bears the burden of proving infringement by a preponderance of the evidence in litigation.[93] The §271(e)(1) exemption serves as a defence to patent infringement in a litigation. Therefore, under 35 U.S.C. §282(b)(1), a defendant is required to affirmatively assert the §271(e)(1) exemption as a defence to patent infringement in litigation. If the patentee establishes infringement, the burden shifts to the defendant asserting the §271(e)(1) exemption to demonstrate by a preponderance of the evidence that the Bolar-type exemption is applicable.

h. Applicability during Patent Term Extension or Supplementary Protection Certificate

The Bolar-type exemption codified in 35 U.S.C. §271(e)(1) is applicable as a defence to infringement during the period of patent term extension granted under 35 U.S.C § 156(a). The statute does not distinguish between infringement during the normal patent term or during the period of patent term extension. As explained by the Supreme Court in *Eli Lilly & Co. v. Medtronic, Inc.* the Bolar-type exemption codified in 35 U.S.C. § 271(e)(1) is complementary to patent term extension under 35 U.S.C § 156(a).[94] Both of these provisions were enacted in 1984 as part of the Hatch-Waxman Act and intended to address patent term distortions caused by the requirement for premarketing regulatory approval. It is noted that during the period of patent term extension granted under 35 U.S.C § 156(a), the scope of an extended compound patent is limited to 'any use approved for the product.'[95] In view of the narrower scope during the patent term extension, in some circumstances, a defendant may not need to assert §271(e)(1) as basis for non-infringement.

4. DIFFERENCES BETWEEN THE TWO EXEMPTIONS IN UNITED STATES

Both the Experimental Use exemption to patent infringement and the Bolar-type exemption may be available to defendants as defences to allegations of patent infringement. If applicable, both defences may be asserted in litigation in response to allegations of infringement.

There is no statutory basis in the United States for an exception to infringement for the experimental use of an invention of a patented invention. Rather, an experimental use defence to patent infringement is part of the common law of the United

93. *Glaxo Inc. v. Novopharm Ltd.*, 110 F.3d 1562, 1565-1566 (Fed. Cir. 1997).
94. *Eli Lilly & Co.*, 496 U.S. at 673.
95. 35 U.S.C. § 156(f)(2)(A).

States. The experimental use defence is broadly applicable to any technological field. There are no technology limitations on the scope of the Experimental Use exemption in the United States. However, the case law has interpreted the scope of the Experimental Use exemption in the United States to be very narrow. Furthermore, under the current case law, activity having any commercial purpose will not qualify for the Experimental Use exemption.

In contrast, the Bolar-type exemption is codified in 35 U.S.C. §271(e)(1). This exemption is 'solely for uses reasonably related to the development and submission of information under a Federal law which regulates the manufacture, use, or sale of drugs or veterinary biological products', which includes medical devices, food additives, colour additives, new drugs, antibiotic drugs, human biological products, new animal drugs and veterinary biological products that require regulatory approval by the FDA.[96] Under §271(e)(1), the commercial character of the act is not relevant as long as the act is reasonably related to the development and submission of information for FDA approval. Contrary to the Experimental Use exemption, the scope of the Bolar-type exemption is broadly interpreted. However, for technologies that are not subject to FDA premarketing approval, i.e., non-pharmaceutical or non-medical technologies, the §271(e)(1) exemption is not available.

96. 35 U.S.C. §271(e)(1); *Eli Lilly & Co.*, 496 U.S. at 673-74.

Chapter 43

Uruguay

Eugenio Hoss and Martin Bensadon

1. GENERAL

a. Terminology

There is no distinction between the terms 'exemption' and 'exception' under the applicable law and case law. To maintain consistency, the term 'exemption' will be used as the general term, while the term 'exception' is restricted to issues of evidence and interpretation rules.

The Experimental Use exemption and the Bolar-type exemption both appear in Section 39 of the Patent Act. In both cases, the legislation refers to these as situations where the patent has no legal effect and should thus be considered as exemptions to infringement.

b. Legal Basis in Uruguay

The Experimental Use exemption and the Bolar-type exemption were enacted under Section 39 of the new Patent Act, which was passed in 1999 after approval of the TRIPS Agreement. The previous Patent Act had been enacted in 1941 and did not include any specific provision on Experimental Use or Bolar-type exemptions.

> 39. The right conferred by a patent shall not extend to the following acts:
> - Those performed in the private sphere and for non-industrial or commercial purposes, provided that they do not cause an economic loss to the patent holder.
>
> ...
> - Those carried out exclusively for experimental purposes, even if preparatory for a future commercial exploitation, carried out within the year prior to the expiration of the patent.

- Those carried out for teaching or research purposes, either scientific or academic.

To date, there have not been any court cases discussing the scope or particularities of these exemptions.

2. THE EXPERIMENTAL USE EXEMPTION

a. History and Rationale of Adopting the Experimental Use Exemption

The Experimental Use exemption was included in the original text of the new Patent Act, enacted in 1999 after approval of the TRIPS Agreement.

The purpose of this provision is clearly to encourage experimental research in the private sphere, as well as scientific and academic research, by exempting these activities from the scope of exclusivity rights granted by patents. The exemption intends to provide a secure research environment for private or for purely academic or scientific experimentation.

b. The Laws Applicable to the Experimental Use Exemption in Uruguay

The Experimental Use exemption was enacted in 1999 under Section 39 of the new Patent Act. The relevant part of Section 39 reads as follows:

> 39. The right conferred by a patent shall not extend to the following acts:
> - Those performed in the private sphere and for non-industrial or commercial purposes, provided that they do not cause an economic loss to the patent holder.
>
> ...
> - Those carried out for teaching or research purposes, either scientific or academic.

To date, we are not aware of any relevant case law providing further interpretation of Section 39 and there are no additional guidelines or regulations from the Patent and Trademark Office clarifying its scope.

c. Procedural Aspects of Invoking the Experimental Use Exemption

The Experimental Use exemption may be used as a defence in patent litigation proceedings. In Uruguay, such proceedings are always under the jurisdiction of the federal courts. Accordingly, the only body that can make a determination of the legitimacy of an experimental use defence is a federal court.

d. Scope of the Experimental Use Exemption in Uruguay

i. Fields of Technology

The Patent Act does not include any field limitations on the Experimental Use exemption. The exemption is thus applicable in all fields of technology.

ii. Purpose of Experiments/Infringing Activities

The language of Section 39 of the Patent Act clearly indicates that it is the purpose of the experimental acts which determines whether those acts fall within the exemption or not, i.e.:

- *non-industrial or non-economical purposes*: applicable to acts performed in the private sphere only and if there is no economic loss for the patent holder; or
- *teaching or research purpose*: applicable to acts performed in the private sphere or not and not necessarily limited to academic research.

In other words, the exemption does not apply in cases where the research activities have a commercial purpose.

For acts performed for research purposes, the provision does not require that the purpose of the research is to improve an invention. Also, it does not make any distinction between cases where the exemption is invoked for researching on a patented technology ('research on') and cases where the exemption is invoked for using a patented technology ('research with').

iii. Exempted and Prohibited Activities

Section 39 of the Patent Act provides for a relatively broad defence and does not indicate which specific activities are exempted.

iv. Pure Academic vs Commercially Motivated Experimental Use

As mentioned in section 2.d.ii., the scope of the exempted acts excludes any commercial acts or acts that could result in an economic loss to the patent holder. However, acts can be performed in the private sphere or if they are done for research purposes, the research can be either academic or scientific. Therefore, the intention is not to limit research to purely academic research.

e. Beneficiary Limitations

The Patent Act does not contemplate third party contributions, and we are not aware of any case law on this issue either. However, if a party contracts a third party to perform an activity that, if performed by that party, would be considered exempt, it is likely that that third party would also be protected by the Experimental Use exemption.

f. Territoriality Issues

As a rule, Uruguayan courts only enforce and decide on Uruguayan patents. Therefore, Uruguayan courts would probably not address any infringement issue taking place in a territory subject to foreign patents.

g. Burden of Proof and Onus

We are not aware of any case law on the burden of proof for experimental uses. However, applying general procedural principles under Uruguayan Law, the onus would be on the defendant to prove that the exemption applies.

h. Applicability during Patent Term Extension or Supplementary Protection Certificate

This is not applicable since there is no SPC available in Uruguay.

3. THE BOLAR-TYPE EXEMPTION

a. History and Rationale of Adopting the Bolar-Type Exemption

The Bolar-type exemption was also enacted in 1999 in the new Patent Act as an additional exemption, with the peculiarity that such an exemption only applies from a certain point in time: one year before the expiration of the patent.

The rationale for this exemption was clearly to allow companies to make the necessary experimental acts, allowing them to prepare and be ready for commercial launch as soon as possible after the expiration of the relevant patent.

b. The Laws Applicable to the Bolar-Type Exemption in Uruguay

The Bolar-type exemption was enacted in 1999 under Section 39 of the new Patent Act. In its relevant part, Section 39 provides as follows:

> 39. The right conferred by a patent shall not extend to the following acts:
>
> ...
>
> - Those carried out exclusively for experimental purposes, even if preparatory for a future commercial exploitation, carried out within the year prior to the expiration of the patent.

The exemption is limited to 'acts' whose purpose is experimental and would not allow preparatory acts of manufacture or stockpiling. It does not clarify whether the acts must be intended to gather information in view of a regulatory approval, but it does state that they can be preparatory for a future commercial exploitation which would naturally encompass such acts. Moreover, the exemption is limited to experimental acts carried out within one year prior to the expiration of the patent.

c. Procedural Aspects of Invoking the Bolar-Type Exemption

The Bolar-type exemption may be used as a defence in patent litigation proceedings. In Uruguay, such proceedings are always under the jurisdiction of the federal courts. Accordingly, the only body that can decides the legitimacy of a Bolar-type exemption defence is a judicial federal court.

d. Scope of the Bolar-Type Exemption in Uruguay

i. Fields of Technology

Whilst the Bolar-type exemption provision was enacted to address concerns from the pharmaceutical industry, the language of the provision is not limited to pharmaceutical products. The exemption is applicable to any field of technology in which it is necessary to carry out preparatory experimental acts and for which a market approval is necessary.

ii. Purpose of Experiments/Infringing Activities

As indicated above, the Bolar-type exemption is limited to acts with an experimental purpose. They may be preparatory for a future commercial exploitation.

iii. Exempted and Prohibited Activities

The Bolar-type exemption is limited to uses for experimental activities, even if preparatory for a future commercial exploitation. Therefore, importation, purchase, manufacture, storage or use will only be exempted if the activities are limited to the referred purpose.

Uruguayan law does not include any specific provision on stockpiling, and we are not aware of any relevant case law either. However, courts would likely interpret that stockpiling does not fall within the scope of the Bolar-type exemption, which is limited to acts with experimental purposes. This interpretation would also be supported by the decision issued by the WTO Panel Report in Case DS114.[1]

e. Beneficiary Limitations

There are no limitations with respect to beneficiaries. Therefore, in the field of pharmaceuticals, the exemption would apply both to generic companies applying for regulatory approval and to innovative companies. The exemption would also seem to apply to third parties contracted to perform studies on behalf of the party seeking regulatory approval, though we are not aware of any relevant case law on this issue.

f. Territoriality Issues

The exemption would likely apply for experimental activities performed in Uruguay, even if the purpose is a regulatory submission or launch in a country other than Uruguay, although we are not aware of any relevant case law yet.

If the experimental acts are carried out by a party that infringes a corresponding patent in another jurisdiction, it should be noted that, as a rule, Uruguayan courts

1. Panel Report, Canada — Patent Protection of Pharmaceutical Products, WTO Doc. WT/DS114/R (adopted April 7, 2000, available at, https://www.wto.org/english/tratop_e/dispu_e/cases_e/ds114_e.htm).

only enforce and decide on Uruguayan patents. Therefore, Uruguayan courts would probably not address any infringement issue relating to foreign patents in another jurisdiction.

g. Burden of Proof and Onus

We are not aware of any case law on the burden of proof for the Bolar-type exemption. However, applying general procedural principles under Uruguayan Law, the onus would be on the defendant to prove that the exemption applies.

4. DIFFERENCES BETWEEN THE TWO EXCEPTIONS IN URUGUAY

The Experimental Use exemption in Uruguay is limited by its purpose which is either non-commercial or non-industrial, either teaching, or scientific or academic research.

The Bolar-type exemption is limited in time (one year before the expiry of the patent) but is rather broad as it encompasses all experimental acts including those with a view to commercialize. However, the rationale for this exemption was intended for the pharmaceutical industry and aimed at preventing a regulatory lag between expiry of a patent and generic market entry.

AIPPI LAW SERIES

1. Sanna Wolk, Kacper Szkalej (eds), *Employees' Intellectual Property Rights*, Second Edition, 2018 (ISBN 978-90-411-9230-1).
2. Jochen Bühling (ed.), *Patent Protection for Second Medical Uses*, Second Edition, 2020 (ISBN 978-94-035-0935-8).
3. Christopher V. Carani (ed.), *Design Rights: Functionality and Scope of Protection*, Second Edition, 2022 (ISBN 978-94-035-3210-3).
4. Eléonore Gaspar (ed.), *Genuine Use of Trademarks*, Second Edition, 2021 (ISBN 978-94-035-2833-5).
5. Jürgen Meier, Oswin Ridderbusch (eds), *Antibody Patenting: A Practitioner's Guide to Drafting, Prosecution and Enforcement*, Second Edition, 2023 (ISBN 978-94-035-3626-2).
6. Christian Czychowski, Jan Bernd Nordemann (eds), *Law of Raw Data*, 2021 (ISBN 978-94-035-3280-6).
7. John C. Todaro, Martin Bensadon, Brigitte Carion-Taravella (eds), *Pharmaceutical Test Data Exclusivity: A Multi-Jurisdictional Survey*, 2022 (ISBN 978-94-035-0106-2).
8. Jonathan P. Osha (ed.), *Artificial Intelligence and Patents: An International Perspective on Patenting AI-Related Inventions*, 2023 (ISBN 978-94-035-2215-9).
9. Christof Augenstein, Johanna Flythström (eds), *Enforcement of Decisions of the Unified Patent Court: A Survey of Participating Member States*, 2023 (ISBN 978-94-035-4846-3).
10. Guillaume Henry, Sanna Wolk (eds), *Artificial Intelligence and Copyright*, 2025 (ISBN 978-94-035-4278-2).
11. David Gilat, Charles A. Boulakia, Daphné Derouane, Ralph Nack (eds), *Experimental Use and Bolar Exemptions*, 2025 (ISBN 978-94-035-1869-5).

www.ingramcontent.com/pod-product-compliance
Lightning Source LLC
LaVergne TN
LVHW020647300926
849161LV00004B/849